W9-BZG-744

See the Difference with LearningCurve!

LearningCurve
macmillan learning

learningcurveworks.com

LearningCurve is a winning solution for everyone: students come to class better prepared and instructors have more flexibility to go beyond the basic facts and concepts in class. LearningCurve's game-like quizzes are book-specific and link back to the textbook in LaunchPad so that students can brush up on the reading when they get stumped by a question. The reporting features help instructors track overall class trends and spot topics that are giving students trouble so that they can adjust lectures and class activities.

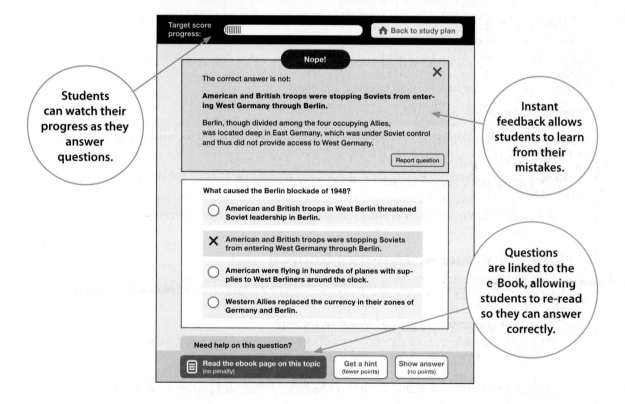

Students can watch their progress as they answer questions.

Instant feedback allows students to learn from their mistakes.

Questions are linked to the e Book, allowing students to re-read so they can answer correctly.

LearningCurve is easy to assign, easy to customize, and easy to complete.
See the difference LearningCurve makes in teaching and learning history.

Guide to Analyzing Primary Sources

In their search for an improved understanding of the past, historians look for a variety of evidence — written documents, visual sources, and material artifacts. When they encounter any of these primary sources, historians ask certain key questions. You should ask these questions too. Sometimes historians cannot be certain about the answers, but they always ask the questions. Indeed, asking questions is the first step in writing history. Moreover, facts do not speak for themselves. It is the task of the historian to organize and interpret the facts in a reasoned and verifiable manner.

Analyzing a Written Document

- What kind of document is this? For example, is it a diary, letter, speech, sermon, court opinion, newspaper article, witness testimony, poem, memoir, or advertisement?

- Who wrote the document? How can you identify the author? Was the source translated by someone other than the author or speaker (for example, American Indian speeches translated by whites)?

- When and where was it written?

- Why was the document written? Is there a clear purpose?

- Who was, or who might have been, its intended audience?

- What point of view does it reflect?

- What can the document tell us about the individual(s) who produced it and the society from which he, she, or they came?

- How might individuals' race, ethnicity, class, gender, and region have affected the viewpoints in the documents?

- In what ways does the larger historical context help you evaluate individual sources?

Analyzing a Visual or Material Source

- What kind of visual or material source is this? For example, is it a map, drawing or engraving, physical object, painting, photograph, or political cartoon?

- Who made the image or artifact, and how was it made?

- When and where was the image or artifact made?

- Can you determine if someone paid for or commissioned it? If so, how can you tell that it was paid for or commissioned?

- Who might have been the intended audience or user? Where might it have originally been displayed or used?

- What message or messages is it trying to convey?

- How might it be interpreted differently depending on who viewed or used it?

- What can the visual or material source tell us about the individual who produced it and the society from which he or she came?

- In what ways does the larger historical context help you evaluate individual sources?

Comparing Multiple Sources

- In what ways are the sources similar in purpose and content? In what ways are they different?

- How much weight should one give to who wrote or produced the source?

- Were the sources written or produced at the same time or at different times? If they were produced at different times, does this account for any of the differences between or among the sources?

- What difference does it make that some sources (such as diaries and letters) were intended to be private and some sources (such as political cartoons and court opinions) were meant to be public?

- How do you account for different perspectives and conclusions? How might these be affected by the author's relative socioeconomic position or political power in the larger society?

- Is it possible to separate fact from personal opinion in the sources?

- Can the information in the sources under review be corroborated by other evidence? What other sources would you want to consult to confirm your conclusions?

Cautionary Advice for Interpreting Primary Sources

- A single source does not tell the whole story, and even multiple sources may not provide a complete account. Historians realize that not all evidence is recoverable.

- Sources have biases, whether they appear in personal or official documents. Think of biases as particular points of view, and try to figure out how they influence the historical event and the accounts of that event.

- Sources reflect the period in which they were written or produced and must be evaluated within the historical time frame from which they came. Explain how people understood the world in which they lived, and be careful to avoid imposing contemporary standards on the past. Nevertheless, remember that even in any particular time period people disagreed over significant principles and practices such as slavery, imperialism, and immigration.

- Sources often conflict or contradict each other. Take into account all sides. Do not dismiss an account that does not fit into your interpretation; rather, explain why you are giving it less weight or how you are modifying your interpretation to conform to all the evidence.

Seattle

Olympia
WASHINGTON
★
Mt. Rainier
(14,411 ft.; 4,392 m)
▲
Mt. St. Helens
(8,366 ft.; 2,550 m)
▲
Portland
●
★ Salem
Eugene ●
OREGON

Columbia River

CASCADE MTS.

COAST RANGES

Helena
●

MONTANA

Billings
●

Missouri River

Yellowstone River

NORTH
DAKOTA
Bismarck
★

BADLANDS

SOUTH
DAKOTA
Pierre
★

Sioux
Falls

★ Boise
IDAHO

Snake River

ROCKY

WYOMING

BLACK
HILLS

Cheyenne
★

GREAT
DIVIDE
BASIN

GREAT

PLAINS

NEBRASKA

Platte River

40°N

SIERRA

Carson
City ●

Great
Salt
Lake

GREAT
BASIN

★ Salt Lake
City

COLORADO

Denver
★

Cheyenne
★

San
Francisco ●
Oakland ●
San Jose ●

★ Sacramento

NEVADA

NEVADA

UTAH

Mt. Elbert
(14,433 ft.; 4,399 m)

Colorado
Springs ●

KANSAS

Wichita
●

San Joaquin
River

Sacramento River

Fresno ●
▲
Mt. Whitney
(14,494 ft.; 4,418 m)

Las
Vegas ●

Colorado River

Pikes Peak
(14,110 ft.; 4,301 m)
▲

Arkansas River

CALIFORNIA

MOJAVE
DESERT

ARIZONA

NEW
MEXICO

Santa Fe
★

MOUNTAINS

OKLAHOMA

Oklahoma
City ●

Los Angeles ●

San Diego ●

Phoenix
★

Albuquerque
●

Lubbock
●

PACIFIC
OCEAN

Tucson
●

Pecos River

LLANO
ESTACADO

Fort Worth
●

Red River

TEXAS

Colorado River

El Paso
●

EDWARDS
PLATEAU

Austin
★

Rio Grande

San Antonio
●

MEXICO

ARCTIC OCEAN

RUSSIA

170°W

130°W

BROOKS RANGE

70°N

ALASKA

Arctic Circle

Mt. McKinley
(20,320 ft.; 6,194 m)
▲

Yukon River

ALASKA RANGE

CANADA

30°N

60°N

Anchorage
●

Bering
Sea

Gulf of Alaska

Juneau
★

ALEUTIAN
ISLANDS

0   250   500 miles
0   250   500 kilometers

160°W   150°W   140°W

Kauai

Niihau

Oahu

Honolulu
★

Molokai

HAWAII

22°N

PACIFIC
OCEAN

Lanai
Kahoolawe

Maui

20°N

Hawaii

0   50   100 miles
0   50   100 kilometers

160°W   158°W   156°W

Greenland
(Den.)

ICELAND

Alaska

CANADA

UNITED
KINGDOM

IRELAND

FRANCE

SPAIN

PORTUGAL

MOROCCO

Azores
(Port.)

Canary Is.
(Sp.)

MAURITANIA

UNITED STATES

ATLANTIC
OCEAN

Western Sahara
(Mor.)

Hawaii

MEXICO

BAHAMAS
DOMINICAN
REPUBLIC

HAITI

CUBA

JAMAICA

BELIZE

GUATEMALA

HONDURAS

EL SALVADOR

NICARAGUA

COSTA RICA

PANAMA

COLOMBIA

ECUADOR

Galápagos Is.
(Ec.)

Puerto Rico (U.S.)

ST. KITTS AND NEVIS

Guadeloupe (Fr.)

Martinique (Fr.)

ST. LUCIA

ANTIGUA AND BARBUDA

DOMINICA

ST. VINCENT AND THE GRENADINES

BARBADOS

GRENADA

TRINIDAD AND TOBAGO

GUYANA

SURINAME

French Guiana (Fr.)

VENEZUELA

CAPE
VERDE

SENEGAL

GAMBIA

GUINEA-BISSAU

MALI

GUINEA

SIERRA LEONE

LIBERIA

CÔTE D'IVOIRE

BURKINA FASO

GHANA

PACIFIC OCEAN

PERU

BRAZIL

BOLIVIA

SAMOA

TONGA

PARAGUAY

Easter I.
(Chile)

CHILE

URUGUAY

ATLANTIC
OCEAN

ARGENTINA

	1,500		3,000 miles
0			
0	1,500	3,000 kilometers	

Falkland Is.
(U.K.)

Abbreviations

ALB.	ALBANIA
AUS.	AUSTRIA
BEL.	BELGIUM
B.H.	BOSNIA AND HERZEGOVINA
CR.	CROATIA
CZ. REP.	CZECH REPUBLIC
DEN.	DENMARK
F.Y.R.O.M.	FORMER YUGOSLAV REPUBLIC OF MACEDONIA
HUNG.	HUNGARY
K.	KOSOVO
LUX.	LUXEMBOURG
M.	MONTENEGRO
NETH.	NETHERLANDS
SLK.	SLOVAKIA
SLN.	SLOVENIA
S.M.	SERBIA AND MONTENEGRO
SWITZ.	SWITZERLAND

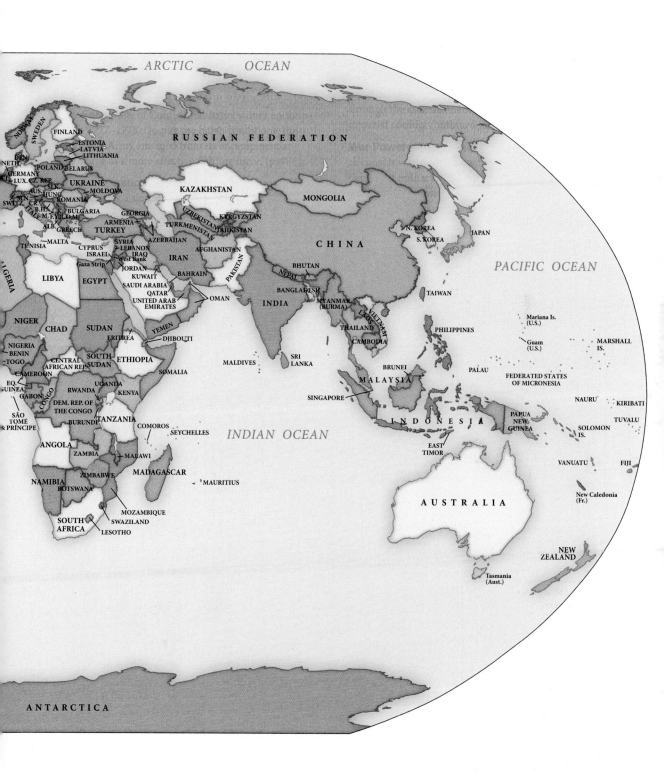

Volume 1 To 1877

Exploring American Histories

A SURVEY WITH SOURCES

SECOND EDITION

Nancy A. Hewitt

Rutgers University

Steven F. Lawson

Rutgers University

bedford/st.martin's
Macmillan Learning
Boston | New York

To Mary and Charles Takacs, Florence and Hiram Hewitt,

Sarah and Abraham Parker, Lena and Ben Lawson,

who made our American Histories possible.

For Bedford/St. Martin's
Vice President, Editorial, Macmillan Learning Humanities: Edwin Hill
Publisher for History: Michael Rosenberg
Senior Executive Editor for History: William J. Lombardo
Director of Development for History: Jane Knetzger
Senior Developmental Editor: Heidi L. Hood
Senior Production Editor: Kerri A. Cardone
Editorial Assistant: Mary Posman
Media Producer: Sarah O'Connor
Senior Production Supervisor: Jennifer L. Wetzel
Executive Marketing Manager: Sandra McGuire

Copy Editor: Lisa Wehrle
Cartography: Mapping Specialists, Ltd.
Photo Researchers: Naomi Kornhauser, Christine Buese
Permissions Editor: Kalina Ingham
Senior Art Director: Anna Palchik
Text Design: Jerilyn Bockorick, Cenveo Publisher Services
Cover Design: William Boardman
Cover Art/Cover Photo: View of Baltimore, c. 1859 (oil on canvas), Lane, Fitz Henry (1804–1865)/Private Collection/Bridgeman Images
Composition: Cenveo Publisher Services
Printing and Binding: LSC Communications

Copyright © 2017, 2013 by Bedford/St. Martin's.

All rights reserved. No part of this book may be reproduced, stored in a retrieval system, or transmitted in any form or by any means, electronic, mechanical, photocopying, recording, or otherwise, except as may be expressly permitted by the applicable copyright statutes or in writing by the Publisher.

Manufactured in the United States of America.

11   10   9   8
f   e   d   c

For information, write: Bedford/St. Martin's, 75 Arlington Street, Boston, MA 02116   (617-399-4000)

ISBN 978-1-4576-9462-2 (Combined Edition)
ISBN 978-1-4576-9470-7 (Volume 1)
ISBN 978-1-4576-9471-4 (Volume 2)

Acknowledgments
Text: **Chapter 1:** Document 1.3: *The Voyage of Magellan, the Journal of Antonio Pigafetta,* translated by Paula Spurlin Paige (Prentice-Hall, 1969), pp. 76–78. Copyright © 1969 Paula Spurgin Paige. Used with permission.   Document 1.6: Camilla Townsend, ed. and trans, *American Indian History: A Documentary Reader* (Malden, MAWiley-Blackwell, 2009), 29–30. Used with permission from the author.   **Chapter 2:** Document 2.1: Marie de L'Incarnation, Correspondance, ed. Dom Guy Oury (Abbave de Saint-Pierre, 1971), trans. Natalie Zemon Davis, *Women on the Margins Three Seventeenth-Century Lives* (Harvard University Press, 1995), pp. 111–112. Used with permission from the author.   **Chapter 4:** Table 4.2: From *Rape and Sexual Power in Early America* by Sharon Block. Copyright © 2006 by the University of North Carolina Press. Published for the Omohundro Institute of Early American History and Culture. Used by permission of the publisher. www.uncpress.unc.edu.   **Chapter 8:** Document 8.6: W. Raymond Wood and Thomas D. Thiessen, eds., *Early Fur Trade on the Northern Plains Canadian Traders among the Mandan and Hidatsa Indians, 1738–1818.* Copyright © 1985 University of Oklahoma Press. Used with permission.   **Chapter 13:** Document 13.5: Spooner, Fred. "Letter to Henry Joshua Spooner, 30 April 1861," Henry Joshua Spooner Paper, MSS 732, Box 1, Folder 6, the Rhode Island Historical Society. Used by permission.   Document 13.6: "Letter to His Parents," April 22, 1862, by John Hines. Hines Family Collection, MSS 91, Library Special Collections, Western Kentucky University, Bowling Green. Courtesy of Kentucky Library & Museum, Western Kentucky University.

Art acknowledgments and copyrights appear on the same page as the art selections they cover.

Why This Book This Way?

We are delighted to publish the second edition of *Exploring American Histories*. Users of the first edition have told us our book gives them and their students opportunities to actively engage with both the narrative of American history and primary sources from that history in a way previously not possible. Our book offers a new kind of U.S. history survey text, one that makes a broad and diverse American history accessible to a new generation of students and instructors interested in a more engaged learning and teaching style. To accomplish this, we carefully weave an unprecedented number of written and visual primary sources, representing a rich assortment of American perspectives, into each chapter. We measure our success as teachers and authors by how well students demonstrate that they understand this rich complexity.

We know that students in the introductory survey course often need help in developing the ability to think critically about sources. Accordingly, in this second edition we have done even more to ensure students can move easily and systematically from working with single and paired sources to tackling a set of documents from multiple perspectives. We have also strengthened our digital tools and instructor resources so faculty have more options for engaging students in active learning and assessing their progress, whether it be with traditional lecture classes, smaller discussion-oriented classes, "flipped" classrooms, or online courses.

A Unique Format That Places Sources at the Heart of the Story

Students learn history most effectively when they read historical narrative in conjunction with primary sources. Sources bring the past to life in ways that narrative alone cannot, while the narrative offers the necessary framework, context, and chronology that documents by themselves do not typically provide.

We believe that the most appealing entry to the past starts with individuals and how people in their daily lives connect to larger political, economic, cultural, and international developments. This approach makes history relevant and memorable.

Throughout our teaching experience, the available textbooks left us unsatisfied, compelling us to assign additional books, readers, and documents we found on the Web. However, these supplementary texts raised costs for our students, and too often students had difficulty seeing how the different readings related to one another. Simply remembering what materials to bring to class became unwieldy. So we decided to write our own book that would provide everything we would want to use in class, in one place. Many texts include some documents, but the balance between narrative (too much) and primary sources (too few) was off-kilter, so we carefully crafted the narrative to make room for us to include more documents and integrate them in creative ways that help students make the necessary connections and that spur them to think critically. *Exploring American Histories* is comprehensive in the essentials of American history, but with a carefully selected amount of detail that is more in tune with what instructors can realistically expect their students to comprehend. Thus, the most innovative aspect of *Exploring American Histories*, is its format, which provides just the right balance between narrative and primary sources.

Abundant Sources Woven Throughout the Narrative. In *Exploring American Histories*, we have selected an extensive and varied array of written and visual primary source material—more than 250 sources in all—and we have integrated them at key points as teaching moments within the text. In this second edition we are underscoring the importance of documents by opening each chapter with a facsimile of some portion of a primary source that appears subsequently within the chapter. These "Windows to the Past" are designed to pique students' curiosity for working with sources.

To help students move seamlessly between narrative and sources, we embed **Explore** prompts at key junctures in the narrative, which describe what the sources illuminate. Such integration is designed to help students make a firm connection between the narrative of history and the evidence upon which it is built. These documents connect directly with discussions in the narrative and give a real sense of multiple viewpoints that make history come alive. By integrating sources and narrative, we help students engage divergent experiences from the past and give them the skills to think critically about sources and their interpretation. Because of our integrated design, every source flows from the narrative, and each source is clearly cross-referenced within the text so that students can easily incorporate them into their reading as well as reflect on our interpretation.

Progression in Source Work. We are excited to offer a new building-blocks approach to the primary sources. Each chapter contains 8–9 substantial, featured sources—both written and visual—with a distinctive pedagogy aimed at helping students make connections between the documents and the text's major themes. In every chapter we offer a progression of primary sources that moves from a single source with guiding annotations to paired sources that lead students to understand each source better through comparison, and then to an individual source for students to use to hone their skills. Finally, each chapter culminates with what we call a "Document Project"—a set of interrelated documents that address an important topic or theme related to the chapter. Instructors across the country confirm that with *Exploring American Histories* we have made teaching the breadth of American history and working with primary sources easier and more rewarding than ever.

Variety of Sources and Perspectives. Because the heart of *Exploring American Histories* is its primary sources, we carefully selected documents from which students can evaluate the text's interpretations and construct their own versions of history. These firsthand accounts include maps, engravings, paintings, illustrations, sermons, speeches, translations, letters, diaries, journals, memoirs, newspaper articles, political cartoons, laws, wills, court cases, petitions, advertisements, photographs, and blogs. In selecting documents, we have provided manifold perspectives on critical issues, including both well-known sources and those that are less familiar. In all time periods, some groups of Americans are far better represented in primary sources than others. Those who were wealthy, well educated, and politically powerful produced and preserved many sources about their lives, and their voices are well represented in this textbook. But we have also provided documents by American Indians, enslaved Africans, colonial women, rural residents, immigrants, working people, and young people. Moreover, the lives of those who left few sources of their own can often be illuminated by reading documents written by elites to see what information they yield, intentionally or unintentionally, about less well-documented groups. The questions that we ask about these sources are intended to help students read between the lines or see beyond the main image to uncover new meanings.

In weaving a wide variety of documents into the narrative, we challenge students to consider diverse viewpoints. For example, in chapter 5, students read contradictory testimony and examine an engraving to analyze the events that became known as the Boston Massacre. In chapter 10, they compare the views on Texas independence of an abolitionist and a defender of the Alamo. In chapter 18, students have to reconcile two very different views by a Chinese immigrant and a Supreme Court justice concerning the status of Chinese Americans in the late nineteenth century. In chapter 26, we ask readers to contrast the depiction of the 1960s as a radical time period with a statement proclaiming the creation of a young conservative movement.

Flexibility for Assignments. We recognize from the generous feedback reviewers have offered us that instructors want flexibility in assigning primary sources. Our book easily allows faculty to assign all the documents in a chapter or a subset depending on the activities they have planned. With this range of choices, instructors are free to teach their courses just as they like and to tailor them to their students. Even if not featured on specific course assignments, these sources expose students to the multitude of voices from the past and hammer home the idea that history is not just a story passed on from one person to another but a story rooted in historical evidence. For instructors who value even more options, we make available with the second edition a **new companion primary source reader** that provides an additional document project for each chapter. This reader, *Document Projects for Exploring American Histories,* can be packaged with the book at no additional cost to students.

Narrative Approach: Diverse Stories

Recent historical scholarship has transformed our vision of the past, most notably by dramatically increasing the range of people historians study, and thus deepening and complicating traditional understandings of change over time. The new research has focused particularly on gender, race, ethnicity, and class, and historians have produced landmark work in women's history, African American history, American Indian history, and labor history.

Throughout the narrative we acknowledge recent scholarship by highlighting the theme of diversity and recognizing the American past as a series of interwoven stories made by a great variety of historical actors. We do this within a strong national framework that allows our readers to see how the numerous stories fit together and to understand why they matter. Our approach to diversity also allows us to foreground the role of individual agency as we push readers to consider the many forces that create historical change. Each chapter opens with a pair of **American Histories**, biographies that showcase individuals who experienced and influenced events in a particular period, and then returns to them throughout the chapter to strengthen the connections and highlight their place in the larger picture. These biographies cover both well-known Americans—such as Daniel Shays, Frederick Douglass, Andrew Carnegie, and Eleanor Roosevelt—and those who never gained fame or fortune—such as the activist Amy Kirby Post, labor organizer Luisa Moreno, and World War II internee Fred Korematsu. Introducing such a broad range of biographical subjects illuminates the many ways that individuals shaped and were shaped by historical events. This strategy also makes visible throughout the text the intersections where history from the top down meets history from the bottom up, and the relationships between social and political histories and economic, cultural, and diplomatic developments.

Helping Students Work with Primary Sources

New to the second edition, we have placed the chapter documents in the following regular progression so that students can increase their confidence and skills in analyzing primary sources through a building-blocks approach:

- Each chapter begins with **Guided Analysis** of a textual or visual source, with a headnote offering historical context and questions in the margins to help students consider a specific phrase or feature and analyze the source as a whole. These targeted questions are intended to guide students in reading and understanding a primary source. A **Put It in Context** question prompts students to consider the source in terms of the broad themes of the chapter.

- Next, each chapter contains **Comparative Analysis**, a paired set of documents that show contrasting or complementary perspectives on a particular issue. This task marks a step up in difficulty from the previous Guided Analysis by asking students to analyze sources through their similarities and differences. These documents are introduced by a single headnote and are followed by **Interpret the Evidence** and **Put It in Context** questions that prompt students to analyze and compare the items and place them in a larger historical framework.

- Toward the end of each chapter a **Solo Analysis** appears, a single document that encourages students to further practice working with sources. In addition to furnishing another perspective to engage with the narrative, it requires students to analyze a source without the guidance of annotations or specific comparisons. This document is accompanied by an informative headnote and concludes with **Interpret the Evidence** and **Put It in Context** questions.

- Finally, a **Document Project** at the end of every chapter provides the capstone of our integrated primary-sources approach. Each Document Project brings together four or five documents focused on a critical issue central to that chapter. It is introduced by a brief overview and ends with **Interpret the Evidence** and **Put It in Context** questions that ask students to draw conclusions based on what they have learned in the chapter and read or seen in the sources.

We understand that the instructor's role is crucial in teaching students how to analyze primary-source materials and develop interpretations. Instructors can use the primary sources in many different ways—as in-class discussion prompts, for take-home writing assignments, and even as the basis for exam questions—and also in different combinations with documents throughout or across chapters being compared and contrasted with one another. The instructor's manual for *Exploring American Histories* provides a wealth of creative suggestions for using the documents program effectively. As authors of the textbook, we have written a new section, entitled **"Teaching American Histories with Documents,"** which provides ideas and resources for both new and experienced faculty. It offers basic guidelines for teaching students how to analyze sources critically and suggests ways to integrate selected primary sources into lectures, discussions, small group projects, and writing assignments. We also suggest ideas for linking in-text documents with the opening biographies, maps, and illustrations in a particular chapter and for using the **Document Projects** to help students understand the entangled histories of the diverse groups that comprise North America and the United States. (See the Versions and Supplements description on pages 000–000 for more information on all the available instructor resources.)

In the second edition, we have also increased support for teaching with documents by providing an expanded **Guide to Analyzing Primary Sources**. This 2-page checklist at the front of the book gives students a quick and efficient lesson on how to read and analyze sources and what kinds of questions to ask in understanding them. We know that many students find primary sources intimidating. Eighteenth and nineteenth century sources contain spellings and language often difficult for modern students to comprehend. Yet, students also have difficulty with contemporary primary sources because in the digital age of Facebook and Twitter they are exposed to information in tiny fragments and without proper verification. Thus, the expanded checklist will guide students in how to approach documents from any era and what to look for in exploring them.

Helping Students Understand the Narrative

We also know that students need help making sense of their reading. As instructors, all of us have had students complain that they cannot figure out what's important in the textbooks we assign. For many of our students, especially those just out of high school, their college history survey textbook is likely the most difficult book they have ever encountered. Also, students come to the U.S. history survey with different levels of preparation. We understand the challenges our students face, so in addition to the extensive document program, we have included the following pedagogical features designed to help students get the most from the narrative:

- New **Learning Objectives** in the chapter openers prepare students to read the chapter with clear goals in mind.
- Clear **chapter overviews** and **conclusions** preview and summarize the chapters to help students identify central developments.
- **Review and Relate** questions help students focus on main themes and concepts presented in each major section of the chapter.
- **Key terms** in boldface highlight important content. All terms are explained in the narrative as well as defined in a glossary at the end of the book.
- A full-page **Chapter Review** lets students review key terms, important concepts, and notable events.

In addition, whenever an instructor assigns the LaunchPad e-book (which is free when bundled with the print book), students get full access to **Learning-Curve,** an online adaptive learning tool that promotes mastery of the book's content and diagnoses students' trouble spots. With this adaptive quizzing students accumulate points toward a target score as they go, giving the interaction a game-like feel. Feedback for incorrect responses explains why the answer is incorrect and directs students back to the text to review before they attempt to answer the question again. The end result is a better understanding of the key elements of the text. Instructors who actively assign LearningCurve report their students come to class prepared for discussion and their students enjoy using it. In addition, LearningCurve's reporting feature allows instructors to quickly diagnose which concepts students in their classes are struggling with so they can adjust lectures and activities accordingly. The LaunchPad ebook with LearningCurve is thus an invaluable asset for instructors who need to support students in all settings, from traditional lectures to hybrid, online, and newer "flipped" classrooms. See "Versions and Supplements" following this preface for more details.

Helping Instructors Teach with Digital Resources for the Classroom

The second edition of *Exploring American Histories* also offers flexibility in formats, including easy-to-use digital resources that can make an immediate impact in their classrooms. *Exploring American Histories* is offered in Macmillan's premier learning platform, **LaunchPad**, an intuitive, interactive e-book and course space. Ready to assign as is with key assessment resources built into each chapter, instructors can also edit and customize LaunchPad as their imaginations and innovations dictate. Free when packaged with the print text, LaunchPad grants students and teachers access to a wealth of online tools and resources built specifically for our text to enhance reading comprehension and promote in-depth study.

Developed with extensive feedback from history instructors and students, LaunchPad for *Exploring American Histories* includes the complete narrative of the print book, the companion reader *Document Projects for Exploring American Histories*, and **Learning-Curve**, an adaptive learning tool that is designed to get

students to read before they come to class. With **new source-based questions in the test bank and in the LearningCurve** and the ability to **sort test bank questions by chapter learning objectives**, instructors now have more ways to test students on their understanding of sources and narrative in the book.

For the second edition we include other features to enhance active learning, including **new Thinking through Sources** activities inLaunchPad, which extend and enhance the additional document projects in the companion source reader. Designed to prompt students to build arguments and to practice historical reasoning, these sophisticated auto-graded exercises guide students to assess their understanding of the sources, organize those sources for use in an essay, and draw useful conclusions from them. This unique pedagogy does for skill development what LearningCurve does for content mastery and reading comprehension. This edition also includes **Guided Reading Exercises** that prompt students to be active readers of the chapter narrative and auto-graded **primary source quizzes** to test comprehension of written and visual sources. These features, plus **additional primary source documents, video sources and tools for making video assignments, map activities, flashcards, and customizable test banks**, make LaunchPad a great asset for any instructor who wants to enliven American history for students.

New Coverage and Updates to the Narrative

As a consequence of the constructive feedback we have received from many reviewers, in this second edition we present an even more rounded view of the history of the United States.

Enriched Diversity and Increased Focus on the West. We continue to pay significant attention to African Americans and women throughout the text and provide greater coverage on the histories of American Indians, Hispanic and Latino Americans, and Asian Americans. Also, we have incorporated more about the West, in both primary sources and visuals and in the narrative. As important, we have not confined our discussion of these subjects to a few chapters, but we have placed them throughout the book and integrated them into the narrative and sources. For example, while American Indians were already featured in Volume 1, there is additional attention to Indian-Spanish encounters in chapter 1; more about alliances among Indian nations and with Europeans in chapter 3; additional coverage of Mandan Indians leading up to and in chapter 8, which concludes with a Documents Project on interactions between Indians and the Lewis and Clark expedition; more in-depth coverage of Indian Removal in chapters 9 and 10; and more about Indians in the Civil War era. Furthermore, the coverage of Aztecs, Incas, Mexicans and Mexican-Americans has been updated in Volume 1, especially in chapters 1, 2, 10, and 12. In Volume 2 we have updated the struggles of American Indians in chapter 15, which covers Westward expansion and in chapter 22 on the Great Depression and New Deal. We have also added considerable new material on Native Americans in relationship to Progressivism (chapter 19); World War I (chapter 20); World War II (chapter 23); and the 1950s and 1960s (chapters 25 and 26). Hispanic and Latino Americans and Asian Americans are also featured in these and other chapters in Volume 2 both in additions to the narrative and the presentation of new documentary sources relating to immigration, labor, and politics. For example, Chicana feminism is compared with that of African American women in chapter 27. With the added attention to these groups, the American West now appears prominently in nearly every chapter.

New Written and Visual Sources. The second edition contains more than 250 primary sources for exploration—more than 100 of them new. We are pleased to add new visual sources, including an early world map (chapter 1), the sketch of a slave ship (chapter 3), a seventeenth-century family portrait (chapter 4), engravings of African Americans during the Patriot and British occupations of New York City (chapter 6), a 1792 painting that incorporates women and blacks into the new nation (chapter 8), an 1848 painting of Americans eagerly awaiting news from the war with Mexico (chapter 10), a banner from the 1860 presidential election (chapter 12), contrasting Civil War photographs (chapter 13), a photo of two young women flaunting conventional gender roles

(chapter 16), and a anti-imperialist political cartoon (chapter 20).

We have also added important and engaging new print documents. These include, in Volume 1, reports of early Spanish encounters with native people (chapter 1); petitions from indentured servants (chapter 2); Olaudah Equiano on the Middle Passage (chapter 3); a letter from a pioneering female plantation owner (chapter 4); Mary Jemison's account of Continental soldiers' attacks on Seneca Indians (chapter 6); women and free blacks petitioning for rights in the new United States (chapter 7); Thomas Jefferson's response to the Haitian revolution (chapter 8), debates over Texas independence in the 1830s (Chapter 10); Frederick Douglass' 5th of July speech (Chapter 11); and contentious responses to the Fugitive Slave Law (chapter 12). The new Volume 2 documents include an essay by Ida B. Wells criticizing policies advocated by Booker T. Washington for African-American advancement (chapter 19); a Mexican-American labor union petition to the government to protect exploited workers in the 1930s (chapter 22); a letter from the Roosevelt administration explaining why it would not approve bombing rail lines leading to concentration camps in Germany and an entry from the diary of a Japanese-American interned in the United States (chapter 23); the announcement of the blacklist of Hollywood movie personnel suspected of membership in communist organizations (chapter 24); and the manifesto of the American Indians who took over Alcatraz Island in protest of government policies (Chapter 26).

Other primary sources that are new to the second edition appear in the 7 new Document Projects. New Document Projects in Volume 1 cover encounters between Spanish explorers and native peoples (chapter 1); the development of slavery and the rise of tobacco (chapter 3); arguments for and against the adoption of the national Constitution (chapter 7); and relations between the Lewis and Clark expedition and the Indian nations it encountered (chapter 8). In Volume 2, new Document Projects explore the Supreme Court case of *Muller v. Oregon* (1908) (chapter19); the cultural significance of the Harlem Renaissance (Chapter 22); and the conflicts between the New Right and its critics beginning in the 1970s (chapter 27).

Updated and Expanded Coverage. We have also absorbed the most recent scholarship to ensure that the most useful and accurate textbook is placed in the hands of students. In addition to the new material on American Indians, Hispanic/Latino Americans, and Asian Americans, we revised our approach to a number of other historical developments. Chapter 1 incorporates recent research on the settlement of the Americas and illustrates the ways that new technologies can help trace American Indian settlements while chapter 2 includes new archaeological research on the Jamestown settlement and expands attention to indentured servants. Chapter 4 addresses the complex relationship between Enlightenment thought and religious revivals. More coverage of naval and maritime developments appears in chapters 7, 9, and 13; Indian Removal is discussed in more depth in chapters 9 and 10, and slave resistance and rebellion is more richly detailed in chapter 10 as well. The coverage of military campaigns in chapter 13 is now framed around the concept of "hard war." Chapter 22 on the New Deal, shows how corporate leaders harnessed Christian ministers to promote their pro-capitalism, anti-New Deal message, and how the United States Chamber of Commerce and the National Association of Manufacturers allied with clergymen to challenge so-called "creeping socialism." Likewise, chapter 27 on the development of political conservatism, contains a larger discussion of Reaganomics and the influence of people such as Phyllis Schlafly on the construction of the New Right agenda that went beyond politics to shape such social and cultural issues as reproductive rights for women, religious freedom, and family values.

Adjustments to Chapter Organization and Focus. Based on reviewers' comments, we also reframed and re-organized several chapters. Chapter 7 is more clearly focused around the ways that competing ideas and interests required compromises to ensure the stability of the new nation. Chapter 8 focuses on the development of "American" identities among diverse groups living in or on the margins of the United States in the late eighteenth and early nineteenth centuries. Chapters 24 and 25 have been extensively reorganized: the former now traces the Cold War from 1945–1960 and the latter contains the origins of the civil rights movement and its development from 1945–1960, as well as the politics of the Truman and Eisenhower administrations.

The final chapter of a history textbook is necessarily and continuously evolving, and for this edition we have added material on President Obama's second term; the legalization of same-sex marriage; the formation of the Black Lives Matter movement; the revelations of Edward Snowden concerning the government's domestic spy apparatus; the clash over restricting immigration from Mexico and Central America as well as refugees from Syria; renewed conflict between the United States and Russia; and the creation of the terroristic organization Islam in Iraq and Syria (ISIS) and the threat it poses to democratic nations in the West and to moderate Muslims in the Middle East.

Strengthened Attention to Global Affairs. Much of the material we have added both in primary sources and the narrative, underscore the steadily evolving relationship between the United States and the rest of the world. This coverage begins with the early chapters of Volume 1, as the Americas were incorporated into and then became a driving force in major developments in Europe, Africa, and Asia. Once the United States gained its independence, its relations with Britain, France, Haiti, Mexico, China, and especially Africa and the West Indies transformed the nation in dramatic ways. Throughout U.S. history, immigrants from diverse cultures have reshaped the country in vital ways. Increasingly in the twentieth and twenty-first centuries, the role of the United States in global affairs has transformed the nation and the world economically, culturally, and militarily. Indeed, new technologies, new terrorist threats, environmental disasters, and international trade make it more difficult than ever to understand U.S. history without attention to the wider world. Here, too, we have incorporated multiple perspectives and diverse voices from Hernán Cortés and Gottlieb Mittelberger to Saum Song Bo and Mikhail Gorbachev.

Acknowledgments

We wish to thank the talented scholars and teachers who were kind enough to give their time and knowledge to help us with our revision, as well as those who provided advice in preparation for the first edition. Historians who provided special insight for the second edition include the following:

Daniel Allen, *Trinity Valley Community College*
Leann Almquist, *Middle Georgia State University*
Rebecca Arnfeld, *California State University, Sacramento*
David Arnold, *Columbia Basin College*
Brian Alnutt, *Northampton Community College*
John Belohlavek, *University of South Florida*
Jeff Bloodworth, *Gannon University*
Carl Bon Tempo, *University at Albany - SUNY*
Martha Jane Brazy, *University of South Alabama*
Richard Buckelew, *Bethune-Cookman University*
Timothy Buckner, *Troy University*
Monica Butler, *Seminole State College of Florida*
Jacqueline Campbell, *Francis Marion University*
Amy Canfield, *Lewis-Clark State College*
Michael Cangemi, *Binghamton University*
Roger Carpenter, *University of Louisiana, Monroe*
Keith Chu, *Bergen Community College*
Remalian Cocar, *Georgia Gwinnett College*
Lori Coleman, *Tunxis Community College*
Wilbert E. Corprew, *SUNY Broome*
Vanessa Crispin-Peralta, *Moorpark College*
David Cullen, *Collin College*
Gregory K. Culver, *Austin Peay State University*
Robert Chris Davis, *Lone Star College - Kingwood*
Thomas Devine *California State University, Northridge*
Tom Dicke, *Missouri State University*
Andy Digh, *Mercer University*
Gary Donato, *Massachusetts Bay Community College*
David Dzurec, *University of Scranton*
Susan Eckelmann, *University of Tennessee, Chattanooga*
George Edgar, *Modesto Junior College*
Taulby Edmondson, *Virginia Tech*
Ashton Ellett, *University of Georgia*
Keona K. Ervin, *University of Missouri*
Gabrielle Everett, *Jefferson College*
Robert Glen Findley, *Odessa College*
Tiffany Fink, *Hardin-Simmons University*
Roger Flynn, *TriCounty Technical College*
Jonathan Foster, *Great Basin College*
Sarah Franklin, *University of North Alabama*
Michael Frawley, *University of Texas of the Permian Basin*
Robert Genter, *Nassau Community College*

Dana Goodrich, *Northwest Vista College*
Audrey Grounds, *University of South Florida*
Abbie Grubb, *San Jacinto College - South*
Kenneth Grubb, *Wharton County Junior College*
Ashley Haines, *Mt. San Antonio College*
Dennis Halpin, *Virginia Tech*
Hunter Hampton, *University of Missouri*
Tona Hangen, *Worcester State University*
Stephen Henderson, *William Penn University*
Kimberly Hernandez, *University of Wisconsin-Milwaukee*
Lacey A. Holley-McCann, *Columbia State Community College*
Creed Hyatt, *Lehigh Carbon Community College*
Joe Jaynes, *Collin College*
Stephen Katz, *Community College of Philadelphia*
Lesley Kauffman, *San Jacinto College-Central*
Tina M. Kibbe, *Lamar University*
Melanie Kiechle, *Virginia Tech*
Stephanie Lamphere, *Sierra College*
Todd Laugen, *Metropolitan State University of Denver*
Carolyn J. Lawes, *Old Dominion University*
John Leazer, *Carthage College*
Marianne Leeper, *Trinity Valley Community College*
Alan Lehmann, *Blinn College - Brenham*
Carole N. Lester, *University of Texas at Dallas*
Amanda Littauer, *Northern Illinois University*
Carmen Lopez, *Miami Dade College*
Robert Lyle, *University of North Georgia*
Amani Marshall, *Georgia State University*
Phil Martin, *San Jacinto College - South*
David Mason, *Georgia Gwinnett College*
Jason Mead, *Johnson University*
Robert Miller, *California State University, San Marcos*
Ricky Moser, *Kilgore College*
Alison Parker, *College at Brockport, SUNY*
Craig Pascoe, *Georgia College*
Linda Pelon, *McLennan Community College*
Jamie Pietruska, *Rutgers University*
Sandra Piseno, *Clayton State University*
Ray Rast, *Gonzaga University*
Jason Ripper, *Everett Community College*
Gregory L. Schneider, *Emporia State University*
Debra Schultz, *Kingsborough Community College, CUNY*
Scott Seagle, *University of Tennessee at Chattanooga*
Donald Seals, *Kilgore College*
Gregory Shealy, *Saint John's River State College*

Cathy Hoult Shewring, *Montgomery County Community College*

Jill Silos-Rooney, *Massachusetts Bay Community College*

Beth Slutsky, *California State University, Sacramento*

Karen Smith, *Emporia State University*

Suzie Smith, *Trinity Valley Community College*

Troy Smith, *Tennessee Tech University*

David Soll, *University of Wisconsin - Eau Claire*

Gary Sprayberry, *Columbus State University*

Bethany Stollar, *Tennessee State University*

Jason Stratton, *Bakersfield College*

Kristen Streater, *Collin College*

Joseph Stromberg, *San Jacinto College - Central*

Sarah Swedberg, *Colorado Mesa University*

Christopher Thrasher, *Calhoun Community College*

Jeffrey Trask, *Georgia State University*

Linda Upham-Bornstein, *Plymouth State University*

Mark VanDriel, *University of South Carolina*

Kevin Vanzant, *Tennessee State University*

Ramon C. Veloso, *Palomar College*

Morgan Veraluz, *Tennessee State University*

Melissa Walker, *Converse College*

William Wantland, *Mount Vernon Nazarene University*

David Weiland, *Collin College*

Eddie Weller, *San Jacinto College-South*

Shane West, *Lone Star College-Greenspoint Center*

Geoffrey West, *San Diego Mesa College*

Kenneth B. White, *Modesto Junior College*

Matt White, *Paris Junior College*

Anne Will, *Skagit Valley College*

John P. Williams, *Collin College*

Zachery R. Williams, *University of Akron*

Kurt Windisch, *University of Georgia*

Jonathan Wlasiuk, *The Ohio State University*

Timothy Wright *Shoreline Community College*

Timothy L. Wood, *Southwest Baptist University*

Nancy Beck Young, *University of Houston*

We are also grateful for those who contributed to the creation of the first edition, upon which this revised edition is built:

Benjamin Allen, *South Texas College*

Christine Anderson, *Xavier University*

Uzoamaka Melissa C. Anyiwo, *Curry College*

Anthony A. Ball, *Housatonic Community College*

Terry A. Barnhart, *Eastern Illinois University*

Edwin Benson, *North Harford High School*

Paul Berk, *Christian Brothers University*

Deborah L. Blackwell, *Texas A&M International University*

Thomas Born, *Blinn College*

Margaret Bramlett, *St. Andrews Episcopal High School*

Lauren K. Bristow, *Collin College*

Tsekani Browne, *Duquesne University*

Jon L. Brudvig, *Dickinson State University*

Dave Bush, *Shasta College*

Barbara Calluori, *Montclair State University*

Julia Schiavone Camacho, *The University of Texas at El Paso*

Jacqueline Glass Campbell, *Francis Marion University*

Amy E. Canfield, *Lewis-Clark State College*

Dominic Carrillo, *Grossmont College*

Mark R. Cheathem, *Cumberland University*

Laurel A. Clark, *University of Hartford*

Myles L. Clowers, *San Diego City College*

Hamilton Cravens, *Iowa State University*

Audrey Crawford, *Houston Community College*

John Crum, *University of Delaware*

Alex G. Cummins, *St. Johns River State College*

Susanne Deberry-Cole, *Morgan State University*

Julian J. DelGaudio, *Long Beach City College*

Patricia Norred Derr, *Kutztown University*

John Donoghue, *Loyola University Chicago*

Timothy Draper, *Waubonsee Community College*

David Dzurec, *University of Scranton*

Keith Edgerton, *Montana State University Billings*

Blake Ellis, *Lone Star College*

Christine Erickson, *Indiana University–Purdue University Fort Wayne*

Todd Estes, *Oakland University*

Gabrielle Everett, *Jefferson College*

Julie Fairchild, *Sinclair Community College*

Randy Finley, *Georgia Perimeter College*

Kirsten Fischer, *University of Minnesota*

Michelle Fishman-Cross, *College of Staten Island*

Jeffrey Forret, *Lamar University*

Kristen Foster, *Marquette University*

Susan Freeman, *Western Michigan University*

Nancy Gabin, *Purdue University*

Kevin Gannon, *Grand View University*

Benton Gates, *Indiana University–Purdue University Fort Wayne*

Bruce Geelhoed, *Ball State University*

Mark Gelfand, *Boston College*

Jason George, *The Bryn Mawr School*

Judith A. Giesberg, *Villanova University*

Sherry Ann Gray, *Mid-South Community College*

Patrick Griffin, *University of Notre Dame*

Aaron Gulyas, *Mott Community College*

Scott Gurman, *Northern Illinois University*

Melanie Gustafson, *University of Vermont*

Brian Hart, *Del Mar College*

Paul Hart, *Texas State University*

Paul Harvey, *University of Colorado Colorado Springs*

Woody Holton, *University of Richmond*

Vilja Hulden, *University of Arizona*

Colette A. Hyman, *Winona State University*

Brenda Jackson-Abernathy, *Belmont University*

Troy R. Johnson, *California State University, Long Beach*

Shelli Jordan-Zirkle, *Shoreline Community College*

Jennifer Kelly, *The University of Texas at Austin*

Kelly Kennington, *Auburn University*

Andrew E. Kersten, *University of Wisconsin–Green Bay*

Janilyn M. Kocher, *Richland Community College*

Max Krochmal, *Duke University*

Peggy Lambert, *Lone Star College*

Jennifer R. Lang, *Delgado Community College*

John S. Leiby, *Paradise Valley Community College*

Mitchell Lerner, *The Ohio State University*

Matthew Loayza, *Minnesota State University, Mankato*

Gabriel J. Loiacono, *University of Wisconsin Oshkosh*

John F. Lyons, *Joliet Junior College*

Lorie Maltby, *Henderson Community College*

Christopher Manning, *Loyola University Chicago*

Marty D. Matthews, *North Carolina State University*

Eric Mayer, *Victor Valley College*

Suzanne K. McCormack, *Community College of Rhode Island*

David McDaniel, *Marquette University*

J. Kent McGaughy, *Houston Community College, Northwest*

Alan McPherson, *Howard University*

Sarah Hand Meacham, *Virginia Commonwealth University*

Brian Craig Miller, *Emporia State University*

Brett Mizelle, *California State University, Long Beach*

Mark Moser, *The University of North Carolina at Greensboro*

Jennifer Murray, *Coastal Carolina University*

Peter C. Murray, *Methodist University*

Steven E. Nash, *East Tennessee State University*

Chris Newman, *Elgin Community College*

David Noon, *University of Alaska Southeast*

Richard H. Owens, *West Liberty University*

David J. Peavler, *Towson University*

Laura A. Perry, *University of Memphis*

Wesley Phelps, *University of St. Thomas*

Merline Pitre, *Texas Southern University*

Eunice G. Pollack, *University of North Texas*

Kimberly Porter, *University of North Dakota*

Cynthia Prescott, *University of North Dakota*

Gene Preuss, *University of Houston*

Sandra Pryor, *Old Dominion University*

Rhonda Ragsdale, *Lone Star College*

Michaela Reaves, *California Lutheran University*

Peggy Renner, *Glendale Community College*

Steven D. Reschly, *Truman State University*

Barney J. Rickman, *Valdosta State University*

Pamela Riney-Kehrberg, *Iowa State University*

Paul Ringel, *High Point University*

Timothy Roberts, *Western Illinois University*

Glenn Robins, *Georgia Southwestern State University*

Alicia E. Rodriquez, *California State University, Bakersfield*

Mark Roehrs, *Lincoln Land Community College*

Patricia Roessner, *Marple Newtown High School*

John G. Roush, *St. Petersburg College*

James Russell, *St. Thomas Aquinas College*

Eric Schlereth, *The University of Texas at Dallas*

Ronald Schultz, *University of Wyoming*

Stanley K. Schultz, *University of Wisconsin–Madison*

Sharon Shackelford, *Erie Community College*

Donald R. Shaffer, *American Public University System*

David J. Silverman, *The George Washington University*

Andrea Smalley, *Northern Illinois University*

Molly Smith, *Friends School of Baltimore*

David L. Snead, *Liberty University*

David Snyder, *Delaware Valley College*

Jodie Steeley, *Merced College*

Bryan E. Stone, *Del Mar College*

Emily Straus, *SUNY Fredonia*

Jean Stuntz, *West Texas A&M University*

Nikki M. Taylor, *University of Cincinnati*

Heather Ann Thompson, *Temple University*

Timothy Thurber, *Virginia Commonwealth University*

T. J. Tomlin, *University of Northern Colorado*

Laura Trauth, *Community College of Baltimore County–Essex*

Russell M. Tremayne, *College of Southern Idaho*

Laura Tuennerman-Kaplan, *California University of Pennsylvania*

Vincent Vinikas, *The University of Arkansas at Little Rock*

David Voelker, *University of Wisconsin–Green Bay*

Ed Wehrle, *Eastern Illinois University*

Gregory Wilson, *University of Akron*

Maria Cristina Zaccarini, *Adelphi University*

Nancy Zens, *Central Oregon Community College*

Jean Hansen Zuckweiler, *University of Northern Colorado*

We also appreciate the help the following scholars, archivists, and students gave us in providing the information we needed at critical points in the writing of this text: Lori Birrell, Leslie Brown, Andrew Buchanan, Gillian Carroll, Susan J. Carroll, Jacqueline Castledine, Paul Clemens, Dorothy Sue Cobble, Kayo Denda, Jane Coleman-Harbison, Alison Cronk, Elisabeth Eittreim, Phyllis Hunter, Tera Hunter, Molly Inabinett, Kenneth Kvamme, William Link, James Livingston, Julia Livingston, Justin Lorts, Melissa Mead, Gilda Morales, Vicki L. Ruiz, Julia Sandy-Bailey, Susan Schrepfer, Bonnie Smith, Melissa Stein, Margaret Sumner, Camilla Townsend, Jessica Unger, Anne Valk, and Melinda Wallington.

We want to thank Rob Heinrich and Julia Sandy for compiling the document projects for the new companion source reader. They have paid careful attention to locating interesting and varied sources that aptly fit with the themes of the second edition of *Exploring American Histories* and give instructors and students compelling documents to explore. Jen Jovin at Bedford/St. Martin's deftly orchestrated the development of the reader and we owe her our thanks as well.

We would particularly like to applaud the many hardworking and creative people at Bedford/St. Martin's who guided us through the labyrinthine process of writing this second edition. No one was more important to us than the indefatigable and unflappable Heidi Hood, our senior editor. We could not have had a better team than Edwin Hill, Michael Rosenberg, William Lombardo, Jane Knetzger, Mary Posman, Jennifer Jovin, Kerri Cardone, Jennifer Wetzel, Sarah O'Connor, Stephanie Ellis, Sandi McGuire, Alex Kaufman, Christine Buese, and Kalina Ingham. The team at Bedford/St. Martin's also enlisted help from Naomi Kornhauser, Lisa Wehrle, Janet Renard, and John Reisbord, for which we are grateful. We will always remain thankful to Sara Wise and Patricia Rossi for their advice about and enthusiasm for a document-based American History textbook and to Joan Feinberg, who had the vision that has guided us through every page of this book. Finally, we would like to express our gratitude to our friends and family who have encouraged us through two editions and have even read the book without it being assigned.

Nancy A. Hewitt and Steven F. Lawson

VERSIONS AND SUPPLEMENTS

Adopters of *Exploring American Histories* and their students have access to abundant print and digital resources and tools, the acclaimed Bedford Series in History and Culture volumes, and much more. The LaunchPad course space for *Exploring American Histories* provides access to the narrative as well as a wealth of primary sources and other features, along with assignment and assessment opportunities at the ready. Available in both LaunchPad and in print, the new companion reader, *Thinking through Sources for Exploring American Histories,* Second Edition, provides additional options for working with written and visual sources. See below for more information, visit the book's catalog site at **macmillanlearning .com**, or contact your local Bedford/St. Martin's sales representative.

Get the Right Version for Your Class

To accommodate different course lengths and course budgets, *Exploring American Histories* is available in several different formats, including a Value Edition (narrative only in 2 colors with select maps and images), loose-leaf versions and low-priced PDF e-books. And for the best value of all, package a new print book with LaunchPad at no additional charge to get the best each format offers—a print version for easy portability with a LaunchPad interactive e-book and course space with LearningCurve and loads of additional assignment and assessment options.

- **Combined Volume** (Chapters 1–29): available in paperback, Value Edition, loose-leaf, and e-book formats and in LaunchPad.
- **Volume 1: To 1877** (Chapters 1–14): available in paperback, Value Edition, loose-leaf, and e-book formats and in LaunchPad
- **Volume 2: Since 1865** (Chapters 14–29): available in paperback, Value Edition, loose-leaf, and e-book formats and in LaunchPad

As noted below, any of these volumes can be packaged with additional titles for a discount. To get ISBNs for discount packages, visit **macmillanlearning .com** for the comprehensive version or Value Edition or contact your Bedford/St. Martin's representative.

LaunchPad Assign LaunchPad— an Assessment-Ready Interactive e-book and Course Space

Available for discount purchase on its own or for packaging with new books at no additional charge, LaunchPad is a breakthrough solution for history courses. Intuitive and easy-to-use for students and instructors alike, LaunchPad is ready to use as is, and can be edited, customized with your own material, and assigned quickly. *LaunchPad for Exploring American Histories* includes Bedford/St. Martin's high-quality content all in one place, including the full interactive e-book and the new companion reader *Thinking through Sources for Exploring American Histories*, plus LearningCurve formative quizzing, guided reading activities designed to help students read actively for key concepts, autograded quizzes for each primary source, Thinking through Sources activities that use the document projects in the companion source reader to prompt students to build arguments and practice historical reasoning, and chapter summative quizzes. Through a wealth of formative and summative assessments, including the adaptive learning program of LearningCurve (see the full description ahead), students gain confidence and get into their reading before class. These features, plus additional primary source documents, video sources and tools for making video assignments, map activities, flashcards, and customizable test banks, make LaunchPad an invaluable asset for any instructor.

LaunchPad easily integrates with course management systems, and with fast ways to build assignments, rearrange chapters, and add new pages, sections, or links, it lets teachers build the courses they want to teach and hold students accountable. For more information, visit **launchpadworks.com** or to arrange a demo, contact us at **history@macmillan.com**.

LearningCurve macmillan learning **Assign LearningCurve So Your Students Come to Class Prepared**

Students using LaunchPad receive access to Learning-Curve for *Exploring American Histories*. Assigning Learn-ingCurve in place of reading quizzes is easy for instruc-tors, and the reporting features help instructors track overall class trends and spot topics that are giving stu-dents trouble so they can adjust their lectures and class activities. This online learning tool is popular with stu-dents because it was designed to help them rehearse con-tent at their own pace in a nonthreatening, game-like environment. The feedback for wrong answers provides instructional coaching and sends students back to the book for review. Students answer as many questions as necessary to reach a target score, with repeated chances to revisit material they haven't mastered. When Learning-Curve is assigned, students come to class better prepared.

Take Advantage of Instructor Resources

Bedford/St. Martin's has developed a rich array of teach-ing resources for this book and for this course. They range from lecture and presentation materials and assess-ment tools to course management options. Most can be found in LaunchPad or can be downloaded or ordered from the Instructor's Resources tab of the book's catalog site at macmillanlearning.com.

Bedford Coursepack for Blackboard, Canvas, Brightspace by D2L, or Moodle. We can help you integrate our rich content into your course man-agement system. Registered instructors can download coursepacks that include our popular free resources and book-specific content for *Exploring American Histories*. Visit macmillanlearning.com to find your version or download your coursepack.

Instructor's Resource Manual. The instructor's manual offers both experienced and first-time instruc-tors tools for presenting textbook material in engaging ways. It includes content learning objectives, annotated

chapter outlines, and strategies for teaching with the textbook, plus suggestions on how to get the most out of LearningCurve, and a survival guide for first-time teaching assistants. In addition, a new guide for teach-ing with documents, written by the textbook authors, provides detailed advice for getting the most out of the book's sources in the classroom.

Guide to Changing Editions. Designed to facili-tate an instructor's transition from the previous edition of *Exploring American Histories* to this new edition, this guide presents an overview of major changes as well as of changes in each chapter.

Online Test Bank. The test bank includes a mix of fresh, carefully crafted multiple-choice, matching, short-answer, and essay questions for each chapter. Many of the multiple-choice questions feature a map, an image, or a primary-source excerpt as the prompt. All questions appear in easy-to-use test bank software that allows instructors to add, edit, re-sequence, filter by question type or learning objective, and print ques-tions and answers. Instructors can also export ques-tions into a variety of course management systems.

***The Bedford Lecture Kit:* Lecture Outlines, Maps, and Images.** Look good and save time with *The Bedford Lecture Kit*. These presentation materials include fully customizable multimedia presentations built around chapter outlines that are embedded with maps, figures, and images from the textbook and are supplemented by more detailed instructor notes on key points and concepts.

America in Motion: Video Clips for U.S. History. Set history in motion with *America in Motion*, an instructor DVD containing dozens of short digital movie files of events in twentieth-century American his-tory. From the wreckage of the battleship *Maine* to FDR's fireside chats, to Ronald Reagan speaking before the Brandenburg Gate, *America in Motion* engages students with dynamic scenes from key events and challenges them to think critically. All files are classroom-ready, edited for brevity, and easily integrated with presentation slides or other software for electronic lectures or assign-ments. An accompanying guide provides each clip's historical context, ideas for use, and suggested questions.

Print, Digital, and Custom Options for More Choice and Value

For information on free packages and discounts up to 50%, visit macmillanlearning.com, or contact your local Bedford/St. Martin's sales representative.

NEW *Thinking through Sources for Exploring American Histories,* **Second Edition.** This new companion reader provides an additional document project with 4-5 written and visual sources focused on a central topic to accompany each chapter of *Exploring American Histories.* To aid students in approaching and interpreting the sources, the project for each chapter contains an introduction, document headnotes, and questions for discussion. Available free when packaged with the print book and included in the LaunchPad e-book. Also available on its own as a downloadable PDF e-book.

NEW Bedford Custom Tutorials for History. Designed to customize textbooks with resources relevant to individual courses, this collection of brief units, each 16 pages long and loaded with examples, guides students through basic skills such as using historical evidence effectively, working with primary sources, taking effective notes, avoiding plagiarism and citing sources, and more. Up to two tutorials can be added to a Bedford/St. Martin's history survey title at no additional charge, freeing you to spend your class time focusing on content and interpretation. For more information, visit macmillanlearning.com/historytutorials.

NEW Bedford Digital Collections for U.S. History. This source collection provides a flexible and affordable online repository of discovery-oriented primary-source projects ready to assign. Each curated project—written by a historian about a favorite topic—poses a historical question and guides students step by step through analysis of primary sources. Examples include What Caused the Civil War?; The California Gold Rush: A Trans-Pacific Phenomenon; and, War Stories: Black Soldiers and the Long Civil Rights Movement. For more information, visit macmillanlearning.com/bdc /ushistory/catalog. Available free when packaged.

NEW Bedford Digital Collections Custom Print Modules. Choose one or two document projects from the collection (see above) and add them in print to a Bedford/St. Martin's title, or select several to be bound together in a custom reader created specifically for your course. Either way, the modules are affordably priced. For more information, visit macmillanlearning .com/custombdc/ushistory or contact your Bedford/St. Martin's representative.

The Bedford Series in History and Culture. More than 100 titles in this highly praised series combine first-rate scholarship, historical narrative, and important primary documents for undergraduate courses. Each book is brief, inexpensive, and focused on a specific topic or period. Revisions of several best-selling titles, such as *The Cherokee Removal: A Brief History with Documents* by Theda Perdue; *Narrative of the Life of Frederick Douglass,* edited by David Blight; and *The Triangle Fire: A Brief History with Documents* by Jo Ann Argersinger, are now available. For a complete list of titles, visit macmillanlearning.com. Package discounts are available.

Rand McNally Atlas of American History. This collection of more than eighty full-color maps illustrates key events and eras from early exploration, settlement, expansion, and immigration to U.S. involvement in wars abroad and on U.S. soil. Introductory pages for each section include a brief overview, timelines, graphs, and photos to quickly establish a historical context. Free when packaged.

The Bedford Glossary for U.S. History. This handy supplement for the survey course gives students historically contextualized definitions for hundreds of terms— from *abolitionsim* to *zoot suit*—that they will encounter in lectures, reading, and exams. Free when packaged.

Trade Books. Titles published by sister companies Hill and Wang; Farrar, Straus and Giroux; Henry Holt and Company; St. Martin's Press; Picador; and Palgrave Macmillan are available at a 50% discount when packaged with Bedford/St. Martin's textbooks. For more information, visit macmillanlearning.com.

A Pocket Guide to Writing in History. This portable and affordable reference tool by Mary Lynn Rampolla provides reading, writing, and research advice useful to students in all history courses.

Concise yet comprehensive advice on approaching typical history assignments, developing critical reading skills, writing effective history papers, conducting research, using and documenting sources, and avoiding plagiarism—enhanced with practical tips and examples throughout—have made this slim reference a best-seller. Package discounts are available.

A Student's Guide to History. This complete guide to success in any history course provides the practical help students need to be successful. In addition to introducing students to the nature of the discipline, author Jules Benjamin teaches a wide range of skills from preparing for exams to approaching common writing assignments, and explains the research and documentation process with plentiful examples. Package discounts are available.

Going to the Source: The Bedford Reader in American History. Developed by Victoria Bissell Brown and Timothy J. Shannon, this reader combines a rich diversity of primary and secondary sources with in-depth instructions for how to use each type of source. Mirroring the chronology of the U.S. history survey, each of the main chapters familiarizes students with a single type of source—from personal letters to political cartoons—while focusing on an intriguing historical episode such as the Cherokee Removal or the 1894 Pullman Strike. The reader's wide variety of chapter topics and sources provoke students' interest as it teaches them the skills they need to successfully interrogate historical sources. Package discounts are available.

America Firsthand. With its distinctive focus on first person accounts from ordinary people, this primary documents reader by Anthony Marcus, John M. Giggie, and David Burner, offers a remarkable range of perspectives on America's history from those who lived it. Popular Points of View sections expose students to different perspectives on a specific event or topic. Package discounts are available.

BRIEF CONTENTS

CONTENTS

8 The Early Republic

1790–1820 *241*

9 Defending and Redefining the Nation

1809–1832 *275*

13 Civil War
1861–1865   *413*

14 Emancipation and Reconstruction

1863–1877   *447*

MAPS, FIGURES, AND TABLES

Maps

Figures and Tables

Volume 1 To 1877

Exploring American Histories

A
SURVEY
WITH
SOURCES

SECOND EDITION

How to Use This Book

Use the chapter tools to focus on what's important as you read.

Learning Objectives preview what is important to take away from each section of the chapter.

A pair of **American Histories biographies** at the start of each chapter personalizes the history of the period, and the chapter touches on these stories throughout to bring history to life.

At the end of each major section and repeated in the chapter review, the **Review & Relate questions** review key concepts.

LEARNING OBJECTIVES

After reading this chapter you should be able to:

- Analyze the ways that social and cultural leaders worked to craft an American identity and how that was complicated by racial, ethnic, and class differences.
- Interpret how the Democratic-Republican ideal of limiting federal power was transformed by international events, westward expansion, and Supreme Court rulings between 1800 and 1808.
- Explain the ways that technology reshaped the American economy and the lives of distinct groups of Americans.

AMERICAN HISTORIES

When Parker Cleaveland graduated from Harvard University in 1799, his parents expected him to pursue a career in medicine, law, or the ministry. Instead, he turned to teaching. In 1805 Cleaveland secured a position in Brunswick, Maine, as professor of mathematics and natural philosophy at Bowdoin College. A year later, he married Martha Bush. Over the next twenty years, the Cleavelands raised eight children on the Maine frontier, entertained visiting scholars, corresponded with families at other colleges, and boarded dozens of students. While Parker taught those students math and science, Martha trained them in manners and morals. The Cleavelands also

(*left*) **Parker Cleaveland.** Courtesy the Bowdoin College Library, Brunswick, Maine, USA

(*right*) **Shoshone woman.** (No image of Sacagawea exists.) Joslyn Museum, Omaha, Nebraska, USA/Alecto Historical Editions/Bridgeman Images

242

served as a model of new ideals of companionate marriage, in which husbands and wives shared interests and affection.

Professor Cleaveland believed in using scientific research to benefit society. When Brunswick workers asked him to identify local rocks, Parker began studying geology and chemistry. In 1816 he published his *Elementary Treatise on Mineralogy and Geology*, providing a basic text for students and interested adults. He also lectured throughout New England, displaying mineral samples and performing chemical experiments.

The Cleavelands viewed the Bowdoin College community as a laboratory in which distinctly American values and ideas could be developed and sustained. So, too, did the residents of other college towns. Although less than 1 percent of men in the United States attended universities at the time, frontier colleges were considered important vehicles for bringing virtue—especially the desire to act for the public good—to the far reaches of the early republic. Yet several of these colleges were constructed with the aid of slave labor, and all were built on land bought or confiscated from Indians.

The purchase of the Louisiana Territory by President Thomas Jefferson in 1803 marked a new American frontier and ensured further encroachments on native lands. The territory covered 828,000 square miles and stretched from the Mississippi River to the Rocky Mountains and from New Orleans to present-day Montana. The area was home to tens of thousands of Indian inhabitants.

In the late 1780s, a daughter, later named Sacagawea, was born to a family of Shoshone Indians who lived in an area that became part of the Louisiana Purchase. In 1800 she was taken captive by a Hidatsa raiding party. Sacagawea and her fellow captives were marched hundreds of miles to a Hidatsa-Mandan village on the Missouri River. Eventually Sacagawea was sold to a French trader, Toussaint Charbonneau, along with another young Shoshone woman, and both became his wives.

In November 1804, an expedition led by Meriwether Lewis and William Clark set up winter camp near the Hidatsa village where Sacagawea lived. The U.S. government sent Lewis and Clark to document

from the dangers embedded in the nation's oppressive racial history.

REVIEW & RELATE

How did new inventions and infrastructure improvements contribute to the development of the American economy?

Why did slavery expand and become more deeply entrenched in southern society in the early nineteenth century? What fears did this reinforce?

Use the integrated, stepped approach to primary sources to strengthen your interpretive skills while bringing history to life.

Step 1: Guided Analysis

Near the start of each chapter, a **Guided Analysis** of a textual or visual source with annotated questions in the margins models how to analyze a specific phrase or detail of the source as well as the source as a whole.

Red Explore callouts highlight connections between the narrative and specific sources and help you move easily to the sources and back.

GUIDED ANALYSIS

Plea from the Scottsboro Prisoners, 1932

In 1931, nine black youths were arrested in Scottsboro, Alabama, and charged with raping two white women. They were quickly convicted, and eight were sentenced to death. (One of the nine, Roy Wright, was twelve years old, and the prosecution did not seek the death penalty.) In this letter to the editor of the *Negro Worker*, a Communist magazine, the Scottsboro Nine plead their innocence and ask for help. A year had passed since their arrest and trial, which would account for their ages in the following statement recorded as between thirteen to twenty. Only those sentenced to death signed the letter.

Document 22.1

> Why do you think they mention their ages?

> What tactics did Alabama officials use on the prisoners? What was their purpose?

> Why do the Scottsboro prisoners repeatedly emphasize that they were workers?

We have been sentenced to die for something we ain't never done. Us poor boys have been sentenced to burn up on the electric chair for the reason that we is workers—and the color of our skin is black. We like any one of you workers is none of us older than 20. Two of us is 14 and one is 13 years old.

What we guilty of? Nothing but being out of a job. Nothing but looking for work. Our kinfolk was starving for food. We wanted to help them out. So we hopped a freight—just like any one of you workers might a done—to go down to Mobile to hunt work. We was taken off the train by a mob and framed up on rape charges.

At the trial they gave us in Scottsboro we could hear the crowd yelling, "Lynch the Niggers." We could see them toting those big shotguns. Call 'at a fair trial? And while we lay here in jail, the boss-man make us watch 'em burning up other Negroes on the electric chair. "This is what you'll get," they say to us.

Working class boys, we asks you to save us from being burnt on the electric chair. We's only poor working class boys whose skin is black. . . . Help us boys. We ain't done nothing wrong.

[Signed] Andy Wright, Olen Montgomery, Ozie Powell, Charlie Weems, Clarence Norris, Haywood Patterson, Eugene Williams, Willie Robertson

Source: "Scottsboro Boys Appeal from Death Cells to the 'Toilers of the World,'" *The Negro Worker* 2, no. 5 (May 1932): 8–9.

Put It in Context

Why was it unlikely that black men in Alabama could receive a fair trial on the charge of raping a white woman?

Explore ▸

See Document 22.1 for a letter from the Scottsboro prisoners.

legal representation and the jury pool. Although dence of r time the d ing the cha of whom this racist

See also the **Guide to Analyzing Primary Sources** at the front of the book for additional help with sources.

Step 2: Comparative Analysis

Next, each chapter progresses to the more complex **Comparative Analysis**, a paired set of documents that reveal contrasting or complementary perspectives on a particular issue or event.

COMPARATIVE ANALYSIS

Letters to Eleanor Roosevelt

During the 1930s Americans wrote to President Roosevelt and the First Lady in unprecedented numbers, revealing their personal desperation and their belief that the Roosevelts would respond to their individual pleas. Though most requested government assistance, not all letter writers favored the New Deal. In the following letters written to Eleanor Roosevelt, a high school girl from Albertville, Alabama, asks the First Lady for personal help, while Minnie Hardin of Columbus, Indiana, expresses her frustration with direct relief programs.

Document 22.2

Mildred Isbell to Mrs. Roosevelt, January 1, 1936

Dear Mrs. Roosevelt,

My life has been a story to me and most of the time a miserable one. When I was 7 years old my father left for a law school and never returned. This leaving my mother and 4 children. He left us a small farm, but it could not keep us up. For when we went back to mother's people the renters would not give us part, and we were still dependent. I have been shoved to pillar to post that I feel very

I am now 15 ye[...] have always been s[...] as all of us is so poo[...] education, but I will[...] there is no clothes [...] that we are on the r[...] faithful servent for [...] see how she has ma[...]

Mrs Roosevelt, don't think I am just begging, but that is all you can call it I guess. There is no harm in asking I guess eather. Do you have any old clothes you have throwed back. You don't realize how honored I would feel to be wearing your clothes. I don't have a coat at all to wear. The clothes may be too large but I can cut them down so I can wear them. Not only clothes but old shoes, hats, hose, and under wear would be

Document 22.3

Minnie Hardin to Mrs. Roosevelt, December 14, 1937

Mrs. Roosevelt:

I suppose from your point of view the work relief, old age pensions, slum clearance, and all the rest seems like a perfect remedy for all the ills of this country, but I would like for you to see the results, as the other half see them.

We have always had a shiftless, never-do-well class of people whose one and only aim in life is to live without work. I have been rubbing elbows with this class for nearly sixty years and have tried to help some of the most promising and have seen others try to help them, but it can't be done. We cannot help those who will not try to help themselves and if they do try, a square deal is all they need, and by the way that is all this country needs or ever has needed: a square deal

for all and then, let each paddle their own canoe, or sink.

There has never been any necessity for any one who is able to work, being on relief in this locality, but there have been many eating the bread of charity and they have lived better than ever before. I have had taxpayers tell me that their children came from school and asked why they couldn't have nice lunches like the children on relief. The women and children around here have had to work at the fields to help save the crops and several women fainted while at work and at the same time we couldn't go up or down the road without stumbling over some of the reliefers, moping around carrying dirt from one side of the road to the other and back again, or else asleep.

Sources: Mildred Isbell, letter to [...]
Eleanor Roosevelt Papers, Serie[...]

Interpret the Evidence

1. How does each writer explain the source of poverty and the attitudes of poor people?
2. If Minnie Hardin were answering Mildred Isbell's letter, what would she say to her?

Put It in Context

How did the New Deal tackle poverty?

Step 3: Solo Analysis

Near the end of each chapter you will encounter a **Solo Analysis**, a single document that encourages further practice working with sources without the aid of annotations or a comparative source to focus interpretation.

Interpret the Evidence questions help you analyze the sources.

A **Put It in Context** question at the end of each source feature helps you connect primary sources to the larger historical narrative.

SOLO ANALYSIS

Retire or Move Over, 1937

In his first term, President Roosevelt secured legislation to implement his New Deal; however, by 1937 the Supreme Court had overturned several key pieces of New Deal legislation, arguing that Congress had exceeded its constitutional authority. As the Social Security Act and the National Labor Relations Act came up for review before the Court, Roosevelt tried to dilute the influence of the Court's conservative majority. Following his landslide reelection in 1936, he asked Congress to enlarge the Court so that he could appoint justices more favorable to his liberal agenda. This cartoon reacts to Roosevelt's court-packing plan.

Document 22.4

Granger, NYC

Interpret the Evidence

1. How does the cartoonist portray Roosevelt? How does it portray the Supreme Court?
2. How does this cartoon appeal to the fears of the American public during the late 1930s?

Put It in Context

How important was the Supreme Court in shaping the outcome of the New Deal?

Step 4: Document Project

Finally, for the opportunity to draw deeper conclusions, a **Document Project** of 4-5 sources focused on a central topic concludes each chapter.

DOCUMENT PROJECT 8

The Corps of Discovery: Paeans to Peace and Instruments of War

From 1804 to 1806, the Corps of Discovery mapped vast regions of the West, documented plants and animals, and initiated trade relations with Indian nations. When the Corps built its winter camp at Fort Mandan in October 1804, its members hoped to develop commercial relations with local Mandan, Hidatsa, and Arikara villages. Most of these tribes had been ravaged by smallpox in the early 1780s and were now subject to raids by more powerful nations in the region. Meriwether Lewis and William Clark hoped to persuade all of these nations that peaceful relations would benefit them politically and economically. To aid negotiations, the Corps offered gifts to the Indian leaders they encountered (Document 8.5). The Mandan, however, expected more gifts than the expedition could offer. Although Lewis and Clark assured Mandan leaders they would benefit from future trade with and protection from the United States, the Indians had heard such promises before and were wary of giving away vital food as winter descended (Document 8.6).

Worried about surviving the winter, Lewis and Clark finally found an unexpected item to trade with the Mandan. When their men finished building a smithy in December 1804, they discovered that Indians would exchange almost any item for metal hatchets, especially those desi[red] [Doc]uments 8.7 and 8.8).

In April the Corps moved [to present-]day Idaho and traded with S[hoshone for] horses. The Shoshone were e[ngaged in a] lucrative trade in horses with [Indians who] had split from the Shoshones [and had] developed ties with the Spanis[h ...]

had a harder time getting guns, a concern [they] expressed to Lewis (Document 8.9). While Lewis [and] Clark advocated peace among Indian nations, o[ne of] their most desired trade items was weaponry. [And as] their explorations inspired white settlement in [the] vast western territory, that weaponry would bec[ome] more important than ever.

270

Document 8.5

William Clark, Journal | October 12, 1804

As the Corps of Discovery traveled up the Missou[ri] River from St. Louis, they stopped at Indian villag[es] along the way to advocate peace; offer presents [from] President Jefferson; and learn about local plants, animals, and potential trade items. In his journal [e] entry for October 12, William Clark describes a [visit] to a Ricara (Arikara) village near where the Corps planned to stay for the winter.

After breakfast, we went on shore to the house of the chief of the second village named Lassel, where we found his chief[s] and warriors. They made us a present of about se[veral] bushels of corn, a pair of leggings, a twist of their tobacco, and the seeds of two different species of tobacco. The chief then delivered a speech expressive of his gratitude for the presents and the good [... give]ven him; his intention of [... visiting t]he president of the United [... the] Sioux; and requested us to [... chi]efs up to the Mandans and [... betwee]n the two nations. . . . A[fter we ex]plained the magnitude a[nd ...]s, the three chiefs came [... gave th]em some sugar, a little [... th]em left us, and the chie[f ...]

Document 8.6

Charles McKenzie | Narrative of a Fur Trader, November 1804

Charles McKenzie was a Scotsman working as a clerk for the Hudson Bay Company. He arrived with six traders at a Hidatsa village in November 1804. Over time, McKenzie adopted Indian dress, married an Indian woman, and became an advocate for Indian concerns. Here he recounts Lewis's frustration in his efforts to gain favor with local Indian leaders as well as Mandan concerns about the Corps' lack of generosity.

Here we also found a party of forty Americans under the command of Captains Lewis and Clark exploring a passage by the Mississouri [Missouri] to the Pacific Ocean—they came up the River in a Boat of twenty oars accompanied by two

Document 8.8

William Clark | Journal, January 28, 1805, and Meriwether Lewis, Journal, February 1, 1805

By early 1805 it was clear to Lewis and Clark that metal goods, especially axes or hatchets, were the most valuable means of obtaining the corn and other items they needed from the Mandans and neighboring Indians. These two short entries, by Clark and then Lewis, describe the value of the trade in hatchets to the Corps and their continued commitment to peace among Indian nations.

Document 8.7

William Clark | Journal, November 18, 1804

By November 1804, the Corps had built and settled into Fort Mandan, at the convergence of the Missouri and Knife Rivers, for the winter. Lewis and Clark became increasingly aware that their trade with particular groups, like the Mandans, might shift the balance of power in the region. But given the extended journey ahead, they were limited in what goods they could give or trade with local Indians even as they sought to reassure them of U.S. support.

Use the Chapter Review to identify significant historical developments and how they fit together over time.

Review the **Timeline of Events**, which shows the relationship among chapter events.

Study the **Key Terms** list to see if you can define each term and describe its significance.

Answer the **Review & Relate** questions, which prompt you to recall major concepts in each section.

CHAPTER 22 REVIEW

TIMELINE OF EVENTS

1931	Scottsboro Nine tried for rape
1932–1939	Dust Bowl storms
1932	Reconstruction Finance Corporation created
	River Rouge autoworkers' strike
	Farm Holiday Association formed
	Bonus Army marches
1933	Roosevelt moves to stabilize banking and financial systems
	Agricultural Adjustment Act passed
	Federal Emergency Relief Administration created
	Tennessee Valley Authority created
	National Recovery Administration created
	Civilian Conservation Corps created
1934	Indian Reorganization Act passed
	Francis Townsend forms Old-Age Revolving Pensions Corporation
	Huey Long establishes Share Our Wealth movement
	Securities and Exchange Commission created
1935	Charles E. Coughlin organizes National Union for Social Justice
	Works Progress Administration created
	Social Security Act passed
	National Labor Relations Act passed
	Congress of Industrial Organizations founded
1937	Sit-down strike against General Motors
	Roosevelt proposes to increase the size of the Supreme Court
1938	Fair Labor Standards Act passed

KEY TERMS

Scottsboro Nine, *723*
Bonus Army, *728*
New Deal, *730*
Federal Deposit Insurance Corporation (FDIC), *730*
Agricultural Adjustment Act, *730*
Tennessee Valley Authority (TVA), *731*
National Recovery Administration (NRA), *731*
Civilian Conservation Corps (CCC), *733*
Works Progress Administration (WPA), *737*
Social Security Act, *738*
National Labor Relations Act, *739*
sit-down strike, *741*
Fair Labor Standards Act, *741*
Indian Reorganization Act (IRA), *742*
court-packing plan, *743*
conservative coalition, *743*

REVIEW & RELATE

1. How did President Hoover respond to the problems and challenges created by the Great Depression?
2. How did different segments of the American population experience the depression?
3. What steps did Roosevelt take to stimulate economic recovery and provide relief to impoverished Americans during his first term in office?
4. What criticisms did Roosevelt's opponents level against the New Deal?
5. Why and how did the New Deal shift to the left in 1934 and 1935?
6. Despite the president's landslide victory in 1936, why did the New Deal stall during Roosevelt's second term in office?

Mapping Global Frontiers

to 1585

WINDOW TO THE PAST

Universalis Cosmographia, 1507

This image of the Americas was engraved on one of the first world maps of the sixteenth century. The elongated shape was based on information supplied by early European explorers. ▶ To discover more about what this primary source can show us, see Document 1.1 on page 13.

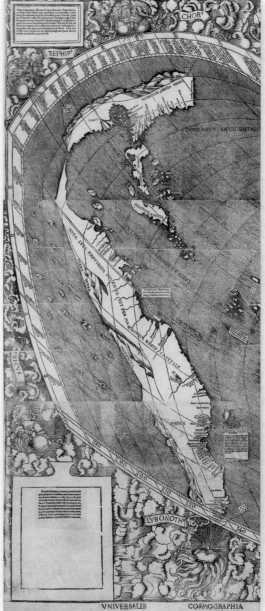

Geography and Maps Division, Library of Congress

After reading this chapter you should be able to:

- Identify the diverse societies that populated the Americas prior to European exploration.

- Explain the reasons for European exploration and expansion, and describe the impact of this expansion on Europe and Africa.

- Evaluate the reasons for Europeans' success in reaching the Americas and the impact of the Columbian Exchange on American Indians, Africans, and Europeans.

- Analyze how the Spanish created an empire in the Americas, and describe the impact of Spain's empire building on Indian empires and European nations.

AMERICAN HISTORIES

In 1519 a young Indian woman named Malintzin was thrust into the center of dramatic events that transformed not only her world but also the world at large. As a young girl, Malintzin, whose birth name is lost to history, lived in the rural area of Coatzacoalcos on the frontier between the expanding kingdom of the Mexica and the declining Mayan states of the Yucatán peninsula. Raised in a noble household, Malintzin was fluent in Nahuatl, the language of the Mexica.

In 1515 or 1516, when she was between the ages of eight and twelve, Malintzin was taken by or given

(left) **Portrait of Malintzin.** Gianni Dagli Orti/The Art Archive at Art Resource, NY

(right) ***Universalis Cosmographia*, 1507 (detail).** Geography and Maps Division, Library of Congress

to Mexica merchants, perhaps as a peace offering to stave off military attacks. She then entered a well-established trade in slaves, consisting mostly of women and girls, who were sent eastward to work in the expanding cotton fields or the households of their owners. She may also have been forced into a sexual relationship with a landowner. Whatever her situation, Malintzin learned the Mayan language during her captivity.

In 1517 Mayan villagers sighted Spanish adventurers along local rivers and drove them off. But in 1519 the Spaniards returned. The Maya's lightweight armor made of dense layers of cotton, cloth, and leather and their wooden arrows were no match for the invaders' steel swords, guns, and horses. Forced to surrender, the Maya offered the Spaniards food, gold, and twenty enslaved women, including Malintzin. The Spanish leader, Hernán Cortés, baptized the enslaved women and assigned each of them Christian names, although the women did not consent to this ritual. Cortés then divided the women among his senior officers, giving Malintzin to the highest-ranking noble.

Already fluent in Nahuatl and Mayan, Malintzin soon learned Spanish. Within a matter of months, she became the Spaniards' chief translator. As Cortés moved into territories ruled by the Mexica (whom the Spaniards called Aztecs), his success depended on his ability to understand Aztec ways of thinking and to convince subjugated groups to fight against their despotic rulers. Malintzin thus accompanied Cortés at every step, including his triumphant conquest of the Aztec capital in the fall of 1521.

At the same time that Malintzin played a key role in the conquest of the Aztecs, Martin Waldseemüller sought to map the frontiers along which these conflicts erupted. Born in present-day Germany in the early 1470s, Waldseemüller enrolled at the University of Fribourg in 1490, where he probably studied theology. He would gain fame, however, as a cartographer, or mapmaker.

In 1507 Waldseemüller and Mathias Ringmann, working at a scholarly religious institute in St. Dié in northern France, produced a map of the world, a small globe, and a Latin translation of the four voyages of the Italian explorer Amerigo Vespucci. The map and the globe, entitled *Universalis*

Cosmographia, depict the "known" world as well as the "new" worlds recently discovered by European explorers. The latter include an elongated territory labeled *America*, in honor of Amerigo, who first recognized that the lands Columbus reached were part of a separate continent. It was set between the continents of Africa and Asia. The map, covering some 36 square feet, offered a view of the world never before attempted.

In 1516 Waldseemüller produced an updated map of the world, the *Carta Marina*. Apparently in response to challenges regarding Vespucci's role in discovering new territories, he substituted the term *Terra Incognita* ("unknown land") for the region he had earlier labeled America. But the 1507 map had already circulated widely, and *America* became part of the European lexicon. ■

T he personal histories of Malintzin and Martin Waldseemüller were shaped by the profound consequences of contact between the peoples of Europe and those of the Americas. The Mexica, or Aztec, and the Spanish were affected most significantly in this period, but France and England also sought footholds in the Americas. For centuries, travel and communication between their worlds had been limited. In the sixteenth century, despite significant obstacles, animals, plants, goods, ideas, and people began circulating between Europe and what became known as America. Malintzin and Waldseemüller, in their very different ways, helped map the frontiers of this global society and contributed to the dramatic transformations that followed.

Native Peoples in the **Americas**

It is almost certain that the Americas were peopled by migrations from northeast Asia, but the timing of such migrations remains uncertain. They likely began at least 25,000 years ago. It is also difficult to estimate the population of the Americas before contact with Europeans. Estimates range from 37 million to 100 million. It is clear, however, that the vast majority of people lived within a few hundred miles of the equator, and the smallest number—perhaps 4 to 7 million—lived in present-day North America. By the fifteenth century, like other regions of the world, the Americas were home to diverse societies, ranging from coastal fishing villages to nomadic hunter-gatherers to settled horticulturalists to large city-centered empires.

Native Peoples Develop Diverse Cultures. The settlement of the Americas was encouraged by the growth of glaciers on the North American continent between about 38,000 and 14,000 B.C.E. This development led to a dramatic drop in sea levels and created a land bridge in the Bering Strait, between present-day Siberia and Alaska. The first migrations may have occurred about 25,000 years ago, during a warming trend when melting glaciers retreated from large areas of land. During the warming trend, some settlers probably traveled from northeast Asia to present-day Alaska over a land bridge, called **Beringia**, following herds of mammoths, musk oxen, and woolly rhinoceroses inland. But some 13,000 years ago immense expanses of ice returned to many regions, shifting the routes that migrants could follow. In both periods, some people likely journeyed along the coastline,

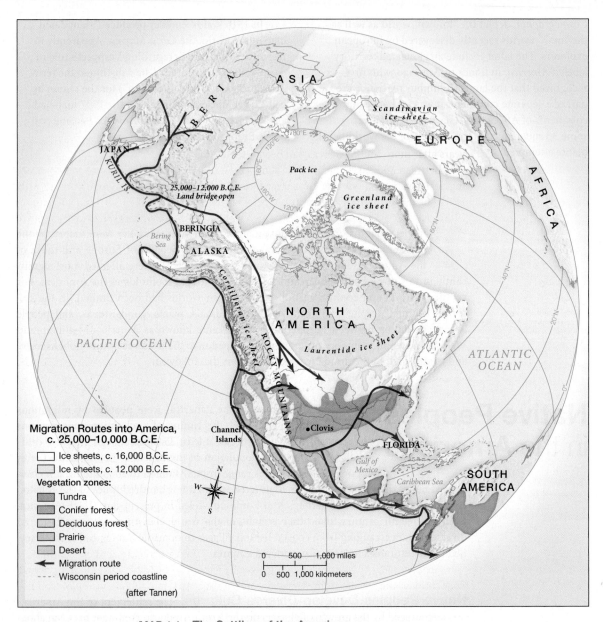

MAP 1.1   The Settling of the Americas

Beginning about 25,000 B.C.E., Asian peoples likely migrated to America across a land bridge after expanding glaciers lowered sea levels. Others probably followed the coastline in boats. As glaciers retreated over several centuries, they opened corridors along which people migrated, leaving traces in archaeological sites in present-day Wisconsin, New Mexico, Florida, Central America, and Chile.

taking advantage of rich maritime resources. These coastal journeys may help explain how Asiatic migrants peopled vast areas of South America in just a few thousand years.

Whether over land or sea, most early groups traveled southward. Those moving inland had to skirt melting glaciers to find better hunting grounds and more abundant plant life. When the mammoths and other large game disappeared from large areas about 10,000 years ago, people became more dependent on smaller game, fish, roots, berries, and other plant foods to survive. At the same time, new migrations likely continued across the Bering Strait, with Inuit and Aleut peoples arriving in present-day Alaska thousands of years after more southern areas had been settled (Map 1.1).

Between 8000 and 2000 B.C.E., some communities in the Americas began establishing agricultural systems that encouraged more stable settlements and population growth. **Horticulture**—a form of agriculture in which people work small plots of land with simple tools—became highly developed in the area of present-day Mexico. There men and women developed improved strains of maize (or Indian corn). They also cultivated protein-rich beans, squash, tomatoes, potatoes, and manioc (a root vegetable). The combination of beans, squash, and corn offered an especially nutritious diet while maintaining the fertility of the soil. Moreover, high yields produced surplus food that could be stored or traded to neighboring communities.

By 500 C.E., complex societies, rooted in intensive agriculture, began to thrive in the equatorial region. Between 500 and 1500 C.E., thousands of separate societies and cultures were established in the Americas. Small bands of hunters and gatherers continued to thrive in deserts and forests while impressive civilizations arose on swamplands and in the mountains.

The Aztecs, the Maya, and the Incas. Three significant civilizations had emerged by the early sixteenth century: Aztec and Mayan societies in the equatorial region and the Inca society along the Pacific coast in present-day Peru. Technologically advanced and with knowledge of mathematics and astronomy, these societies were characterized by vast mineral wealth, large urban centers, highly ritualized religions, and complex political systems. Unlike their counterparts in Europe, Asia, and Africa, they did not develop the wheel to aid in transportation, nor did they have steel tools and weapons. Since most of their commerce was carried out over land or along rivers and coastlines, they did not build large boats. They also lacked horses, which had disappeared from the region thousands of years earlier. Still, the Aztecs, Maya, and Incas established grand cities and civilizations.

Around 1325 C.E., the **Aztecs**, who called themselves Mexica, built their capital, Tenochtitlán, on the site of present-day Mexico City. As seminomadic warriors who had invaded and then settled in the region, the Aztecs drew on local residents' knowledge of irrigation and cultivation and adopted their written language. Aztec commoners, who tilled communally owned lands, were ruled over by priests and nobles. The nobles formed a warrior class and owned vast estates on which they employed both serfs and slaves captured from non-Aztec communities in the region. Priests promised fertility—for the land and its people—but demanded human sacrifices, including thousands of men and women from captured tribes. To sustain their society, Aztecs extended their trade networks, offering pottery, cloth, and leather goods in exchange for textiles and obsidian to make sharp-edged tools and weapons. As Malintzin's story illustrates, slaves made up an important component of this trade.

Female Figurine, Peru, c. 1430–1532 This figurine made of gold depicts a Mamacona, who was similar to a nun in Incan society. Daughters of the nobility or young women of exceptional beauty lived in temple sanctuaries and dedicated themselves to the sun god, Inti. They served the Inca people and priests. The multicolored woolen robe and gold pin indicate this woman's special status. Werner Forman/Universal Images Group/Getty Images

When Malintzin was sold to a Mayan village by Aztec merchants, she was being traded from one grand civilization to another. The **Maya** had slowly settled the Yucatán peninsula and the rain forests of present-day Guatemala between roughly 900 B.C.E. and 300 C.E. They established large cities that were home to skilled artisans and developed elaborate systems for irrigation and water storage. Farmers worked the fields and labored to build huge stone temples and palaces for rulers who claimed to be descended from the gods. Learned men developed mathematical calculations, astronomical systems, hieroglyphic writing, and a calendar.

Yet the Mayan civilization began to decline around 800 C.E. An economic crisis, likely the result of drought and exacerbated by heavy taxation, probably drove peasant families into the interior. Many towns and religious sites were abandoned. Yet some communities survived the crisis and reemerged as thriving city-states. By the early sixteenth century, they were trading with the Aztecs.

The **Incas** developed an equally impressive civilization in the Andes Mountains along the Pacific coast. The Inca empire, like the Aztec empire, was built on the accomplishments of earlier societies. At the height of their power, in the fifteenth century, the Incas controlled some sixteen million people spread over 350,000 square miles. They constructed an expansive system of roads and garrisons to ensure the flow of food, trade goods, and soldiers from their capital at Cuzco through the surrounding mountains and valleys.

The key to Inca success was the cultivation of fertile mountain valleys. Cuzco, some eleven thousand feet above sea level, lay in the center of the Inca empire, with the Huaylas and Titicaca valleys on either side. Here residents cultivated potatoes and other crops on terraces watered by an elaborate irrigation system. Miners dug gold and silver from the mountains, and artisans crafted the metals into jewelry and decorative items. Thousands of laborers constructed elaborate palaces and temples. And like the Aztec priests, Inca priests sacrificed humans to the gods to stave off natural disasters and military defeat.

Native Cultures to the North. To the north of these grand civilizations, smaller societies with less elaborate cultures thrived. In present-day Arizona and New Mexico, the Mogollon and Hohokam established communities around 500 C.E. The Mogollon were expert potters, while the Hohokam developed extensive irrigation systems. Farther north, in present-day Utah and Colorado, the ancient Pueblo people built adobe and masonry homes cut into cliffs around 750 C.E. After migrating south and constructing large buildings that included administrative offices, religious centers, and craft shops, the Pueblo returned to their cliff dwellings in the 1100s for protection from invaders. There, drought eventually caused them to disperse into smaller groups.

Farther north on the plains that stretched from present-day Colorado into Canada, hunting societies developed around herds of bison. A weighted spear-throwing device, called an *atlatl*, allowed hunters to capture smaller game, while nets, hooks, and snares allowed them to catch birds, fish, and small animals. These Plains societies generally remained small and widely scattered since they needed a large expanse of territory to ensure their survival as they followed migrating animals or seasonal plant sources. But other native societies, like the Mandan, settled along rivers in the heart of the continent (present-day North and South Dakota). The rich soil along the banks fostered farming, while forests and plains attracted diverse animals for hunting. Around 1250 C.E., however, an extended drought forced these settlements to contract, and competition for resources increased among Mandan villages and with other native groups in the region.

Hunting-gathering societies also emerged along the Pacific coast, where the abundance of fish, small game, and plant life provided the resources to develop permanent settlements. The Chumash Indians, near present-day Santa Barbara, California, harvested resources from the land and the ocean. Women gathered acorns and pine nuts, while men fished and hunted. The Chumash, whose villages sometimes held a thousand inhabitants, participated in regional exchange networks up and down the coast.

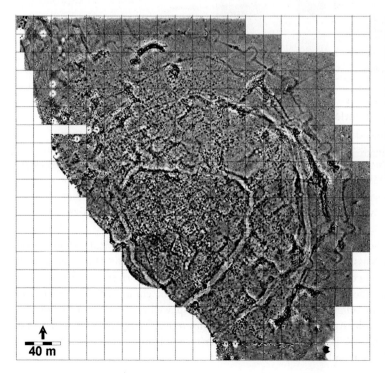

40 m

Double Ditch State Historic Site
Magnetic gradiometry can reveal changes in landscapes invisible to the human eye. This image shows Mandan villagers retreating into smaller settlements as they rebuilt their fortified walls between the early 1500s and 1600. Drought, shortages of resources, conflict with rival groups, or disease likely contributed to a decline in population and the gradual retrenchment of the area of settlement. Courtesy of Professor Kenneth L. Kvamme, University of Arkansas

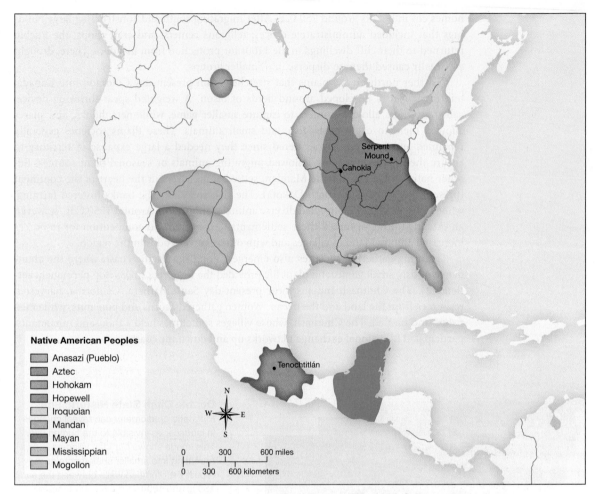

MAP 1.2   Native American Peoples, c. 500–1500 C.E.

Many distinct cultures developed in the Americas in the ten centuries before 1500. Some societies, like the Mississippians, developed extensive trade networks over land or along rivers and coastlines. Societies in the same region often learned from those who preceded them, such as the Aztec from the Maya, but other groups battled over scarce resources.

Even larger societies with more elaborate social, religious, and political systems developed near the Mississippi River. A group that came to be called the **Hopewell people** established a thriving culture there in the early centuries C.E. The river and its surrounding lands provided fertile fields and easy access to distant communities. Centered in present-day southern Ohio and western Illinois, the Hopewell constructed towns of four to six thousand people. Artifacts from their burial sites reflect extensive trading networks that stretched from the Missouri River to Lake Superior, and from the Rocky Mountains to the Appalachian region and Florida.

Beginning around 500 C.E., the Hopewell culture gave birth to larger and more complex societies that flourished in the Mississippi River valley and to the south and east. As bows and arrows spread into the region, people hunted more game in the thick forests. But Mississippian groups also learned to cultivate corn. The development of corn as a staple crop allowed the population to expand dramatically, and more complex political and religious systems developed in which elite rulers gained greater control over the labor of farmers and hunters. Mississippian peoples created massive earthworks sculpted in the shape of serpents, birds, and other creatures. Some earthen sculptures stood higher than 70 feet and stretched longer than 1,300 feet. Mississippians also constructed huge temple mounds that could cover nearly 16 acres.

By about 1100 C.E., the Cahokia people established the largest Mississippian settlement, which may have housed ten to thirty thousand inhabitants (Map 1.2). Powerful chieftains extended their trade networks from the Great Lakes to the Gulf of Mexico, conquered smaller villages, and created a centralized government. But in the 1200s environmental factors affected the Cahokian people, too. Deforestation, drought, and perhaps disease as well as overhunting diminished their strength, and many settlements dispersed. After 1400, increased warfare and political turmoil joined with environmental changes to cause Mississippian culture as a whole to decline.

REVIEW & RELATE

- Compare and contrast the Aztecs, Incas, and Maya. What similarities and differences do you note?

- How did the societies of North America differ from those of the equatorial zone and the Andes?

Europe Expands Its **Reach**

The complex societies that emerged in the Americas were made possible by an agricultural revolution that included the establishment of crop systems, the domestication of animals, and the development of tools. These developments had occurred between 4000 and 3000 B.C.E. in the Fertile Crescent (see Map 1.3) in southwest Asia and in China. The increased productivity in these areas ensured population growth and allowed attention to science, trade, politics, religion, and the arts. Over millennia, knowledge from these civilizations made its way into Europe. At the height of the Roman empire in the early centuries C.E., dense global trade networks connected the peoples of Europe, Africa, and Asia. With the decline of Roman power in western Europe, those connections broke down, but commercial ties continued to thrive among diverse peoples surrounding the Mediterranean Sea. Because Portugal was denied access to that rich Mediterranean world, explorers there sought trade routes along the coast of Africa. Increased trade with African kingdoms by Portugal and other European societies included the purchase of slaves. This lucrative and devastating form of commerce would expand dramatically as European nations colonized the Americas.

The Mediterranean World. Beginning in the seventh century Islam proved one of the most dynamic cultural, political, and military forces in the world. By the ninth century, Islamic (also known as Muslim) regimes created an Arab empire that controlled most of

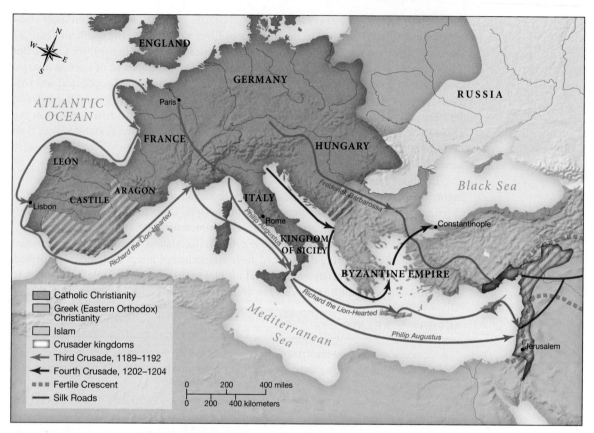

MAP 1.3   The Mediterranean World, c. 1150–1300

The Mediterranean Sea sat at the center of dynamic religious, political, and commercial networks. Crusaders traveled from Europe to Turkey, Arabia, and Persia, hoping to spread Christianity among Islamic peoples. In the thirteenth century, Marco Polo and other adventurers followed the Silk Road deeper into Asia, returning with goods, technologies, and diseases from the eastern Mediterranean, India, and China.

southwest Asia and North Africa and conquered parts of the Iberian peninsula in Europe (Map 1.3). In the eleventh and twelfth centuries, Catholic leaders launched several military and religious campaigns to reclaim Jerusalem and other sites associated with Jesus for the church. Later known as the **Crusades**, these campaigns largely failed, but they enhanced the roles of Italian merchants, who profited from both outfitting Crusaders and opening new trade routes to the East. Moreover, these campaigns inspired explorers and adventurers throughout Europe.

Europeans also learned of successful civilizations in the Middle East, where inhabitants had managed to survive droughts and other ecological crises, largely because of their productive economic systems. In the Mediterranean world, this productivity depended on technological advances in irrigation and navigation and a vast network of slave-trading centers and enslaved laborers. It was the productivity of agriculture—developed centuries

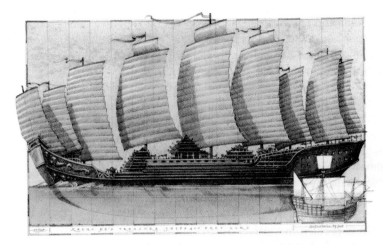

Comparing Chinese and European Sailing Ships   The lateen sail used by the Chinese in the early fifteenth century marked a considerable improvement over the square sails used by Europeans such as Columbus, illustrated in the lower right corner by a contemporary artist. The lateen sail was developed as early as the sixth century C.E. by Byzantine shipbuilders in the Mediterranean region. © Dugald Stermer

earlier than in Europe or America—that allowed societies along the southern Mediterranean, in northern Africa, and in southwest Asia to excel in astronomy, mathematics, architecture, and the arts.

Medieval European states proved far less adept at staving off human and environmental disasters than their counterparts to the south. Besieged by drought and disease as well as wars and peasant rebellions, rulers across the continent expended most of their resources on trying to sustain their population and protect their borders. In the 1340s, as Europeans began to trade with various regions of Asia, fleas on rats carried the bubonic plague and similar epidemic diseases on board ships and into European seaports. From the 1340s to the early fifteenth century, the plague—later called the **Black Death**—periodically ravaged European cities and towns. During the initial outbreak between 1346 and 1350, about 36 million people—half of Europe's population—perished. At the same time, France and England engaged in a century-long war that added to the death and destruction.

By the early fifteenth century, the plague had retreated from much of Europe, and the climate had improved. Only then were European peoples able to benefit significantly from the riches of the East. Smaller populations led to an improved standard of living. Then rising birthrates and increased productivity, beginning in Italian city-states, fueled a resurgence of trade with other parts of the world. The profits from agriculture and commerce allowed the wealthy and powerful to begin investing in the arts and luxury goods. Indeed, a cultural **Renaissance** (from the French word for "rebirth") flourished in the Italian city-states and then spread to France, Spain, the Low Countries, and central Europe.

The cultural rebirth went hand in hand with political unification as more powerful rulers extended their control over smaller city-states and principalities. A vibrant and religiously tolerant culture had existed in Muslim Spain from the eighth to the tenth century, but that was followed by a long period of persecution of Christians. When Christians began reconquering Spain after 1200, Muslims and Jews alike became targets. Then in 1469, the marriage of Isabella of Castile and Ferdinand II of Aragon sealed the unification of Christian Spain. By 1492 their combined forces expelled the last Muslim conquerors from the Iberian peninsula. Promoting Catholicism to create a more unified national identity, Isabella and Ferdinand launched an Inquisition against supposed heretics and executed or expelled some 200,000 Jews as well. Despite the brutality of the reconquest and the Inquisition, Catholic Spain had the wealth and military power to forge its own trade networks with North Africa, India, and other Asian lands.

Explore ▸

For one cartographer's vision of the world during this period, see Document 1.1.

Yet Italy controlled the most important routes through the Mediterranean, so leaders in Spain and neighboring Portugal sought alternate paths to riches. Their efforts were aided by explorers, missionaries, and merchants who traveled to Morocco, Turkey, India, and other distant lands. They brought back trade goods and knowledge of astronomy, shipbuilding, map-making, and navigation that allowed Iberians to venture farther south along the Atlantic coast of Africa and, eventually, west into the uncharted Atlantic Ocean.

Portugal Pursues Long-Distance Trade. Cut off from the Mediterranean by Italian city-states and Muslim rulers in North Africa, Portugal looked toward the Atlantic. Although a tiny nation, Portugal benefited from the leadership of its young prince, Henry, who launched explorations of the African coast in the 1420s, hoping to find a passage to India via the Atlantic Ocean. Prince Henry—known as Henry the Navigator—gathered information from astronomers, geographers, mapmakers, and craftsmen in the Arab world and recruited Italian cartographers and navigators along with Portuguese scholars, sailors, and captains. He then launched a systematic campaign of exploration, observation, shipbuilding, and long-distance trade that revolutionized Europe and shaped developments in Africa and the Americas.

Prince Henry and his colleagues developed ships known as caravels—vessels with narrow hulls and triangular sails that were especially effective for navigating the coast of West Africa. His staff also created state-of-the-art maritime charts, maps, and astronomical tables; perfected navigational instruments; and mastered the complex wind and sea currents along the African coast. Soon Portugal was trading in gold, ivory, and slaves from West Africa.

In 1482 Portugal built Elmina Castle, a trading post and fort on the Gold Coast (present-day Ghana). Further expeditions were launched from the castle; and five years later, a fleet led by Bartolomeu Dias rounded the Cape of Good Hope, on the southernmost tip of Africa. This feat demonstrated the possibility of sailing directly from the Atlantic to the Indian Ocean. Vasco da Gama followed this route to India in 1497, returning to Portugal in 1499, his ships laden with valuable cinnamon and pepper.

By the early sixteenth century, Portuguese traders had wrested control of the India trade from Arab fleets. They established fortified trading posts at key locations on the Indian Ocean and extended their expeditions to Indonesia, China, and Japan. Within a decade, the Portuguese had become the leaders in international trade. Spain, England, France, and the Netherlands competed for a share of this newfound wealth by developing long-distance markets that brought spices, ivory, silks, cotton cloth, and other luxury goods to Europe.

With expanding populations and greater agricultural productivity, European nations developed more efficient systems of taxation, built larger military forces, and adapted gunpowder to new kinds of weapons. The surge in population provided the men to labor on merchant vessels, staff forts, and protect trade routes. More people began to settle in cities, which grew into important commercial centers. Slowly, a form of capitalism based on market exchange, private ownership, and capital accumulation and reinvestment developed across much of Europe.

GUIDED ANALYSIS

Martin Waldseemüller and Mathias Ringmann │ *Universalis Cosmographia*, 1507

In 1507 German cartographers Waldseemüller and Ringmann produced a map of the "known" world, which included those areas in the Western Hemisphere recently discovered by European explorers. They were the first to use the term *America*, and their *Universalis Cosmographia* was also the first map to show the Americas as separate from Asia. The map was printed from wood engravings and produced in twelve sections covering 36 square feet.

Document 1.1

Geography and Maps Division, Library of Congress

What does the shape of the Americas suggest about European understandings of these two continents?

Why are Africa and Europe centered in this depiction of the world?

What does the size and shape of the Indian Ocean indicate about European knowledge of and interest in the surrounding countries?

Put It in Context

How does this new map of the world both reflect and reinforce European nations' growing interest in trade with Africa and Asia?

African slaves were among the most lucrative goods traded by European merchants. Slavery had been practiced in Europe, America, Africa, and other parts of the world for centuries. But in most times and places, slaves were captives of war or individuals sold in payment for deaths or injuries to conquering enemies. Under such circumstances, slaves

Elmina Castle, 1603 This engraving by Johann Theodor de Bry depicts the fortress of São Jorge da Mina, known as Elmina Castle, on the African Gold Coast. Built in 1482 at the order of King John II of Portugal, the fort served as a supply base for Portuguese navigators and later housed thousands of Africans bound for slavery in the Americas. Granger, NYC

generally retained some legal rights, and bondage was rarely permanent and almost never inheritable. With the advent of large-scale European participation in the African slave trade, however, the system of bondage began to change, transforming Europe and Africa and eventually the Americas.

European Encounters with West Africa.

In the fifteenth century, Europeans were most familiar with North Africa, a region deeply influenced by Islam and characterized by large kingdoms, well-developed cities, and an extensive network of trading centers. In northeast Africa, including Egypt, city-states flourished, with ties to India, the Middle East, and China. In northwest Africa, Timbuktu linked North Africa to empires south of the Great Desert as well as to Europe. Here African slaves labored for wealthier Africans in a system of bound labor long familiar to Europeans.

As trade with western Africa increased, however, Europeans learned more about communities that lived by hunting and subsistence agriculture. By the mid-sixteenth century, European nations established competing forts along the African coast from the Gold Coast and Senegambia in the north to the Bight of Biafra and West Central Africa farther south. The men and women shipped from these forts to Europe generally came from communities that had been raided or conquered by more powerful groups. They arrived at the coast exhausted, hungry, dirty, and with few clothes. They worshipped gods unfamiliar to Europeans, and their cultural customs and social practices seemed strange and primitive. Over time, it was the image of the West African slave that came to dominate European visions of the entire continent.

As traders from Portugal, Spain, Holland, and England brought back more stories and more African slaves, these negative portraits took deeper hold. Woodcuts and prints circulated in Europe showing half-naked Africans who were portrayed more like apes than humans. Biblical stories also reinforced notions of Africans as naturally inferior to

Europeans. In the Bible, Ham had sinned against his father, Noah. Noah then cursed Ham's son Canaan to a life of slavery. Increasingly, European Christians considered Africans the "sons of Ham," infidels rightly assigned by God to a life of bondage. This self-serving idea was used to justify the enslavement of black men, women, and children.

Of course, these images of West Africa failed to reflect the diverse peoples who lived in and the diverse societies that developed in the area's tropical rain forests, plains, and savannas. As the slave trade expanded in the sixteenth and seventeenth centuries, it destabilized large areas of western and central Africa, with smaller societies decimated by raids and even larger kingdoms damaged by the extensive commerce in human beings.

Still, rulers of the most powerful African societies helped shape the slave trade. For instance, because women were more highly valued by Muslim traders in North Africa and Asia, African traders steered women to these profitable markets. At the same time, African societies organized along matrilineal lines—where goods and political power passed through the mother's line—often tried to protect women against enslavement. Other groups sought to limit the sale of men.

Ultimately, men, women, and children were captured by African as well as Portuguese, Spanish, Dutch, and English traders. Still, Europeans did not institute a system of perpetual slavery, in which enslavement was inherited from one generation to the next. Instead, Africans formed another class of bound labor, alongside peasants, indentured servants, criminals, and apprentices. Crucially, distinctions among bound laborers on the basis of race did not exist. Wealthy Englishmen, for instance, viewed both African and Irish laborers as ignorant and unruly heathens. However, as Europeans began to conquer and colonize the Americas and demands for labor increased dramatically, ideas about race and slavery would change significantly.

REVIEW & RELATE

How and why did Europeans expand their connections with Africa and the Middle East in the fifteenth century?

How did early European encounters with West Africans influence Europeans' ideas about African peoples and reshape existing systems of slavery?

Worlds Collide

In the 1520s and 1530s, Spain and Portugal chartered traders to ship enslaved Africans to the Caribbean, Brazil, Mexico, and Peru. The success of this trade relied heavily on the efforts of European cartographers, who used information from explorers and adventurers to map these areas. The maps illustrate the growing connections among Europe, Africa, and the Americas even as they also reflect the continued dominance of the Mediterranean region, the Middle East, India, and China in European visions of the world. Yet that world was changing rapidly as Europeans introduced guns, horses, and new diseases to the Americas and came in contact with previously unknown flora and fauna. The resulting exchange of plants, animals, and germs transformed the two continents as well as the wider world.

Europeans Cross the Atlantic. The first Europeans to discover lands in the western Atlantic were Norsemen. In the late tenth century, Scandinavian seafarers led by Erik the Red reached Greenland. Sailing still farther west, Erik's son Leif led a party that discovered an area in North America that they called Vinland, near the Gulf of St. Lawrence. The Norse established a small settlement there around 1000 C.E., and people from Greenland continued to visit Vinland for centuries. By 1450, however, the Greenland settlements had disappeared.

Nearly a half century after Norse settlers abandoned Greenland, a Genoese navigator named Christopher Columbus visited the Spanish court of Ferdinand and Isabella and proposed an **Enterprise of the Indies**. Portuguese explorers used this name for the region that included present-day South Asia and Southeast Asia and surrounding islands. Because Italian city-states controlled the Mediterranean and Portugal dominated the routes around Africa, Spain sought a third path to the rich Eastern trade. Columbus claimed he could find it by sailing west across the Atlantic to Japan, China, or the Indies themselves.

Columbus's 1492 proposal was timely. Having just expelled the last Muslims and Jews from Granada and imposed Catholic orthodoxy on a now-unified nation, the Spanish monarchs sought to expand their empire. After winning Queen Isabella's support, the Genoese captain headed off in three small ships with ninety men. They stopped briefly at the Canary Islands and then headed due west on September 6, 1492.

Columbus had calculated the distance to Japan, which he judged the nearest island, based on Ptolemy's division of the world into 360 degrees of north-south lines of longitude. But in making his calculations, Columbus made a number of errors that led him to believe that it was possible to sail from Spain to Asia in about a month. The miscalculations nearly led to mutiny, but disaster was averted when a lookout finally spotted a small island on October 12. Columbus named the island San Salvador and made contact with local residents, whom he named Indians in the belief that he had found East Indies islands near Japan or China. Columbus was impressed with their warm welcome and considered the gold jewelry Indians wore as a sign of great riches in the region.

Although native inhabitants and Columbus's men did not speak a common language, the Indians aided the Spanish in exploring the area, likely in hopes of encouraging trade. The crew then sailed on to an island they named Hispaniola. Nothing they saw resembled contemporary descriptions of China or the East Indies, but Columbus was convinced he had reached his destination. Leaving a small number of men behind, he sailed for Spain with samples of gold jewelry and tales of more wonders to come.

Explore ▶

Read two accounts by early explorers of their encounters with native peoples in Documents 1.2 and 1.3.

Columbus and his crew were welcomed as heroes when they returned to Spain in March 1493. Their discovery of islands seemingly unclaimed by any known power led the pope to confer Spanish sovereignty over all lands already claimed or to be claimed 100 leagues west of the Cape Verde Islands. A protest by Portugal soon led to a treaty that moved the line 270 leagues farther west, granting Portugal control of territory that became Brazil and Spain control of the rest of what became known as South America.

Europeans Explore the Americas. Columbus made two more voyages to the Caribbean to claim land for Spain and sought to convince those who accompanied him to build houses, plant crops, and cut logs for forts. But the men had come for gold, and when the Indians stopped trading willingly, the Spaniards used force to claim their riches. Columbus sought to impose a more rigid discipline but failed. On his final voyage, he was forced to introduce a system of *encomienda*, by which leading men received land and the

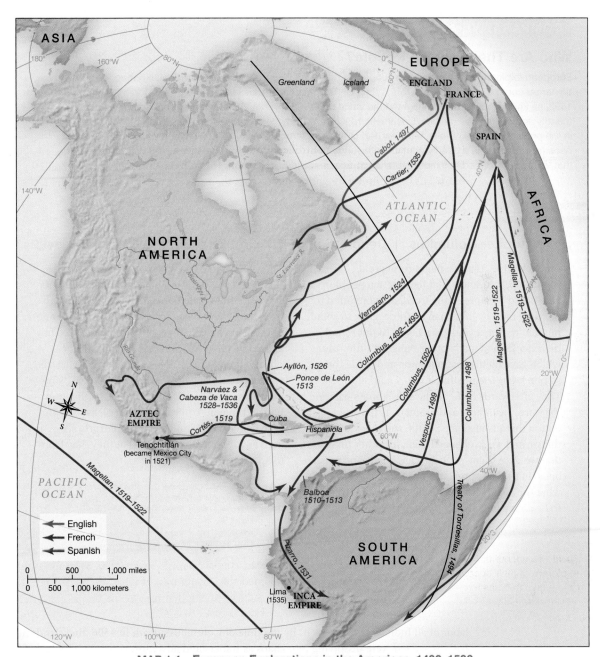

MAP 1.4   European Explorations in the Americas, 1492–1536

Early explorers, funded by Spain, sought trade routes to Asia or gold, silver, and other riches in the Americas. The success of these voyages encouraged adventurous Spaniards to travel throughout the West Indies, South America, and regions immediately to the north. It also inspired the first expeditions by the French and the English in North America.

Who Are These Native People?

European explorers portrayed native peoples in disparate ways, shaped by individual experiences and the larger context in which they wrote. When Christopher Columbus landed in the West Indies in October 1492, he kept a journal that highlighted the value of his discoveries to his Spanish sponsors, including friendly and submissive natives (Document 1.2). Nearly thirty years later, when Ferdinand Magellan landed in the present-day Philippines, his crew had already suffered disease, starvation, and desertion and soon became embroiled in a deadly conflict between native groups. Antonio Pigafetta, a paying passenger on that voyage, described this more brutal encounter in his journal for April 1521 (Document 1.3).

Document 1.2

Christopher Columbus | Description of His First Encounter with Indians, 1492

I [believed] . . . that we might form great friendship, for I knew that they were a people who could be more easily freed and converted to our holy faith by love than by force, gave to some of them red caps, and glass beads to put round their necks, and many other things of little value, which gave them great pleasure, and made them so much our friends that it was a marvel to see. They afterwards came to the ship's boats where we were, swimming and bringing us parrots, cotton threads in skeins, darts, and many other things; and we exchanged them for other things that we gave them, such as glass beads and small bells. In fine [In short], they took all, and gave what they had with good will. It appeared to me to be a race of people very poor in everything.

They go as naked as when their mothers bore them, and so do the women, although I did not see more than one young girl. . . . They have no iron, their darts being wands without iron, some of them having a fish's tooth at the end. . . . They should be good servants and intelligent, for I observed that they quickly took in what was said to them, and I believe that they would easily be made Christians, as it appeared to me that they had no religion. I, our Lord being pleased, will take hence, at the time of my departure, six natives for your Highnesses, that they may learn to speak.

Source: *The Journal of Christopher Columbus (during His First Voyage, 1492–93) and Documents Relating to the Voyages of John Cabot and Gaspar Corte Real* (London: Hakluyt Society, 1893), 37–38.

labor of all Indians residing on it. By the time of Columbus's death in 1506, the islands he had discovered were dissolving into chaos as traders and adventurers fought with Indians and one another over the spoils of conquest. By then, no one believed that Columbus had discovered a route to China, but few people understood the revolutionary importance of the lands he had found.

Nonetheless, Columbus's voyages inspired others to head across the Atlantic (Map 1.4). In 1497 another Genoese navigator, John Cabot (or Caboto), sailing under the English flag, reached an island off Cape Breton in the North Atlantic, where he discovered

Document 1.3

Antonio Pigafetta | Journal, 1521

When day came, our men leaped into the water up to our thighs, forty-nine of them. . . . The boats could not come in closer because of certain rocks in the water. . . . [When the natives saw that we were firing muskets without any result] . . . they cried out determined to stand firm . . . shooting so many arrows and hurling bamboo lances, charred pointed stakes, stones and mud at the Captain [Magellan] that he could scarce defend himself. When the Captain saw this he sent some men to burn their houses to frighten them. And when they saw their houses burning they were all the more fierce. . . . And so great a number came upon us that they pierced the right leg of the Captain with a poisoned arrow, wherefore he ordered that they gradually retreat. . . . [But] they had so many spears, darts and stones that they [the soldiers] could not withstand them, and the artillery of the fleet was so far away that it could not help them.

And our men withdrew to the shore, fighting all the while. . . . They [the natives] recognized the Captain and so many assailed him that twice they knocked his sallet [helmet] from his head. And he, like a good knight, continued to stand firm with a few others, and they fought thus for more than an hour. . . . An Indian threw his bamboo spear into his [the Captain's] face and he immediately killed him [the native] with his own spear. . . . And the Captain tried to draw his sword and was able to draw it only half way, because he had been wounded in the arm with a spear. . . . The Christian king [a rival chief who converted to Christianity] would have helped us but . . . the Captain bade him not to leave the ship. . . . When the king learned that the Captain was dead he grieved much, and not without cause.

Source: *The Voyage of Magellan, the Journal of Antonio Pigafetta*, trans. Paula Spurlin Paige (Englewood Cliffs, NJ: Prentice-Hall, 1969), 76–78.

Interpret the Evidence

1. How might Columbus's journal entry, which was circulated among clerics and officials in Spain, have shaped Spanish views about native peoples in the 1490s?
2. What does Pigafetta's description of the battle between Magellan's forces and native warriors suggest about how Spanish explorers viewed the native peoples they encountered in the Philippines? How does the response of the Christianized chief complicate our understanding of Spanish-native encounters?

Put It in Context

How might changing expectations and perceptions of native peoples between the 1490s and the 1520s have affected the actions of explorers as they encountered groups in newly discovered locations?

good cod fishing but met no local inhabitants. Over the next several years, Cabot and his son Sebastian made more trips to North America, but England failed to follow up on their discoveries.

More important at the time, Portuguese and Spanish mariners continued to explore the western edges of the Caribbean. Amerigo Vespucci, a Florentine merchant, joined one such voyage in 1499. It was Vespucci's account of his journey that led Martin Waldseemüller to identify the new continent he charted on his 1507 *Universalis Cosmographia* as "America." Meanwhile, Spanish explorers subdued tribes like the Arawak and Taino in the

Caribbean and headed toward the mainland. In 1513 Vasco Nuñez de Balboa traveled across the Isthmus of Darien (now Panama) and became the first known European to see the Pacific Ocean. That same year, the Spanish explorer Juan Ponce de León launched a search for gold and slaves along a peninsula he named Florida and claimed for Spain.

Ferdinand Magellan launched an even more impressive expedition in August 1519 when he, with the support of Charles V of Spain, sought a passageway through South America to Asia. In October 1520, after fifteen months of struggle and travail, his crew discovered a strait at the southernmost tip of South America that connected the Atlantic and Pacific Oceans. Ill with scurvy and near starvation, the crew reached Guam and then the Philippines in March 1521. Magellan died there a month later, but one of his five ships and eighteen of the original crew finally made it back to Seville in September 1522, having successfully circumnavigated the globe. Despite the enormous loss of life and equipment, Magellan's lone ship was loaded with valuable spices and detailed information for cartographers, and his venture allowed Spain to claim the Philippine Islands.

Mapmaking and Printing. Waldseemüller's 1507 map reflected the expanding contacts among Europe, Africa, and the Americas. Over the following decades, cartographers charted newly discovered islands, traced coastlines and bays, and situated each new piece of data in relation to lands already known.

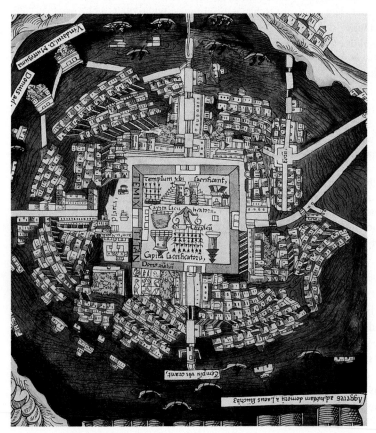

The Aztec City of Tenochtitlán
German geographers drew this map of Tenochtitlán in 1524 based on Aztec sources. At its peak, the city contained some 100,000 people. Temples, a marketplace, schools, the palace of the Aztec chief Montezuma, and a ball-game court stood at its center. The Aztecs viewed Tenochtitlán as the intersection of the secular and divine worlds. Bildarchiv Preussischer Kulturbesitz/Dietmar Katz/Art Resource, NY

The dissemination of geographical knowledge was greatly facilitated by advances in information technology. The Chinese had developed a form of printing with wood blocks in the tenth century, and woodcut pictures appeared in Europe in the fifteenth century. In the 1440s, German craftsmen invented a form of movable metal type in which each letter was created in a separate mold. This allowed printers to rearrange the type for each page and create multiple copies of a single manuscript more quickly and more cheaply than ever before. Between 1452 and 1455, Johannes Gutenberg, a German goldsmith, printed some 180 copies of the Bible with movable type. Although this was not the first book printed using the new system, Gutenberg's Bible marked a revolutionary change in the production and circulation of written texts.

Innovations in printing helped publicize Portuguese and Spanish explorations, the travels of European adventurers, and the atlases created by Waldseemüller and other cartographers. Italian craftsmen contributed by manufacturing paper that was thinner and cheaper than traditional vellum and parchment. Books were still expensive, and they could be read only by the small minority of Europeans who were literate. Still, mechanical printing rapidly increased the speed with which knowledge was circulated. The enhanced ability to exchange ideas encouraged their expression and ensured the flow of information among scholars and rulers across Europe.

The peoples of the Americas had their own ways of charting land, waterways, and boundary lines and of circulating information. The Maya, for instance, developed a system of glyphs—images that represented prefixes, suffixes, numbers, people, or words. Scribes carved glyphs into large flat stones, or *stela*, providing local residents with histories of important events. In settled farming villages, this system communicated information to a large portion of the population. But it could not serve, as printed pages did, to disseminate ideas more widely. Similarly, the extant maps created by the Maya, Aztecs, and other native groups tended to focus on specific locales. Still, we know that these groups traded across long distances, so they must have had some means of tracing rivers, mountains, and villages beyond their own communities.

The Columbian Exchange.

The Spaniards were aided in their conquest of the Americas as much by germs as by maps, guns, or horses. Because native peoples in the Western Hemisphere had had almost no contact with the rest of the world for millennia, they lacked immunity to most germs carried by Europeans. Disease along with warfare first eradicated the Arawak and Taino on Hispaniola, wiping out some 300,000 people. In the Inca empire, the population plummeted from about 9 million in 1530 to less than half a million by 1630. Among the Aztecs, the Maya, and their neighbors, the population collapsed from some 40 million people around 1500 to about 3 million a century and a half later. The germs spread northward as well, leading to catastrophic epidemics among the Pueblo peoples of the Southwest and the Mississippian cultures of the Southeast.

These demographic disasters—far more devastating even than the bubonic plague in Europe—were part of what historians call the **Columbian exchange**. But this exchange also involved animals, plants, and seeds and affected Africa and Asia as well as Europe and the Americas. The transfer of flora and fauna and the spread of diseases transformed the economies and environments of all four continents. Initially, it was the catastrophic decline in Indian populations that ensured the victory of Spain and other European powers over American populations. Africans' partial immunity to malaria and yellow fever then made

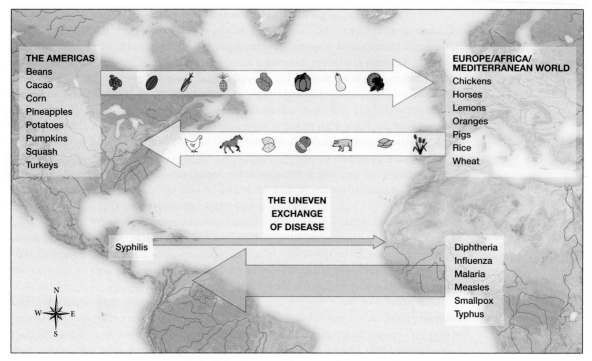

MAP 1.5   The Columbian Exchange, Sixteenth Century

When Europeans made contact with Africa and the Americas, they initiated an exchange of plants, animals, and germs that transformed all three continents. The contact among these previously isolated ecosystems caused dramatic transformations in food, labor, and mortality. American crops changed eating habits across Europe, while diseases devastated native populations even as foreign grains and domesticated animals thrived in the Americas.

them attractive to Europeans seeking laborers for Caribbean islands after the native population was decimated. At the same time, African coconuts and bananas were traded to Europe, while European traders provided their African counterparts with iron and pigs. Asia also participated in the exchange, introducing both Europe and Africa not only to the bubonic plague but also to sugar, rice, tea, and highly coveted spices.

America provided Europeans with high-yielding, nutrient-rich foods like maize and potatoes, as well as new indulgences like tobacco and cacao. The conquered Inca and Aztec empires also provided vast quantities of gold and silver, making Spain the treasure-house of Europe and ensuring its dominance on the continent for several decades. Sugar was first developed in the East Indies, but it also became a source of enormous profits once it took root on Caribbean islands, which became known as the West Indies. Moreover, when mixed with cacao, sugar created an addictive drink known as chocolate.

In exchange for products that America offered to Europe and Africa, these continents sent rice, wheat, rye, lemons, and oranges as well as horses, cattle, pigs, chickens, and honeybees to the Western Hemisphere (Map 1.5). The grain crops transformed the American landscape, particularly in North America, where wheat became a major food source. Cattle and pigs, meanwhile, changed native diets, while horses inspired new methods of farming, transportation, and warfare throughout the Americas.

The Columbian exchange benefited Europe far more than the Americas. Initially, it also benefited Africa, providing new crops with high yields and rich nutrients. Ultimately, however, the spread of sugar and rice to the West Indies and European cravings for tobacco and cacao increased the demand for labor, which could not be met by the declining population of Indians. This situation ensured the expansion of the African slave trade. The consequences of the Columbian exchange were thus monumental for the peoples of all three continents.

REVIEW & RELATE

What were the short-term consequences in both Europe and the Americas of Columbus's voyages?

How did the Columbian exchange transform both the Americas and Europe?

Europeans Make Claims to **North America**

With the help of native translators, warriors, and laborers, Spanish soldiers called **conquistadors** conquered some of the richest and most populous lands in South America in the early sixteenth century. Others then headed north, hoping to find gold in the southern regions of North America or develop new routes to Asia. At the same time, rulers of other European nations began to fund expeditions to North America. France and England both launched efforts to claim colonies in the Americas, though they failed to find the riches Spain had acquired. By the late sixteenth century, Spanish supremacy in the Americas and the wealth acquired there transformed the European economy. But conquest also raised critical questions about Spanish responsibilities to God and humanity.

Spaniards Conquer Indian Empires. Although rulers in Spain supposedly set the agenda for American ventures, it was difficult to control the campaigns of their emissaries at such a distance. The Spanish crown held the power to grant successful leaders vast amounts of land and Indian labor via the encomienda system. But the leaders themselves then divided up their prizes to reward those who served under them, giving them in effect an authority that they sometimes lacked in law. This dynamic helped make Cortés's conquest of the Aztecs possible.

Diego de Velásquez, the Spanish governor of Cuba, granted Cortés the right to explore and trade along the coast of South America. He gave him no authority, however, to attack native peoples in the region or claim land for himself. But seeing the possibility for gaining great riches, Cortés forged alliances with local rulers willing to join the attack against the Aztec chief, Montezuma. From the perspective of local Indian communities, Cortés's presence offered an opportunity to strike back against the brutal Aztec regime.

Despite their assumption of cultural superiority, many Spaniards who accompanied Cortés were astonished by Aztec cities, canals, and temples, which rivaled those in Europe. Seeing these architectural wonders may have given some soldiers pause about trying to conquer the Indian kingdom. But when Montezuma presented Cortés with large quantities of precious objects, including gold-encrusted jewelry, as a peace offering, he alerted Spaniards to the vast wealth awaiting them in the Aztec capital.

Hernán Cortés Meeting Montezuma   This engraving from the Durán Codex depicts
Montezuma giving Cortés a gift in 1519. The Codex was compiled decades later by Diego Durán
(c. 1537–1588), a Dominican friar who was fluent in Nahuatl, the Aztec language. By consulting
Indians and Aztec codices as well as work done by earlier friars, Durán offered a relatively positive image of the Aztecs. Biblioteca Nacional, Madrid, Spain/Bridgeman Images

When Cortés and his men marched to Tenochtitlán in 1519, Montezuma was indeci-
sive in his response. After an early effort to ambush the Spaniards failed, the Aztec leader
allowed Cortés to march his men into the capital city, where they took Montezuma hostage.
In response, Aztec warriors attacked the Spaniards, but Cortés and his men managed to
fight their way out of Tenochtitlán. They suffered heavy losses and might have been crushed
by their Aztec foes but for the alliances forged with native groups in the surrounding area.
Given time to regroup, the remaining Spanish soldiers and their allies attacked the Aztecs
with superior steel weapons, horses, and trained dogs and gained a final victory.

The Spanish victory was also aided by the germs that soldiers carried with them.
Smallpox swept through Tenochtitlán in 1521, killing thousands and leaving Montezuma's
army dramatically weakened. This human catastrophe as much as military resources and
strategies allowed Cortés to conquer the capital that year. He then claimed the entire
region as New Spain, assigned soldiers to construct the new capital of Mexico City, and
asserted Spanish authority over the native groups that had allied with him.

As news of Cortés's victory spread, other Spanish conquistadors sought gold and
glory in the Americas. Most important, in 1524 Francisco Pizarro conquered the vast Inca
empire in present-day Peru. Once again, the Spaniards were aided by the spread of European diseases and conflicts among peoples subjected to Inca rule. This victory ensured
Spanish access to vast supplies of silver in Potosí (in present-day Bolivia) and the
surrounding mountains. Spain was now in control of the most densely populated regions
of South America, which also contained the greatest mineral wealth. In one decade, life for
Aztecs and other Indians as well as the Spanish changed dramatically. **See Document
Project 1: Indian and Spanish Encounters in the Americas, 1520–1530, page 32.**

An Aztec with Smallpox Smallpox followed the Spanish conquest, killing thousands of native peoples. In the sixteenth century, Bernardino de Sahagún, a missionary and educator, learned Nahuatl and wrote an illustrated history of New Spain with the aid of indigenous students. This illustration shows a woman with smallpox aided by a native healer. But the incurable disease ultimately led to death or disfigurement. Granger, NYC

Spanish Adventurers Head North. In 1526, a company of Spanish women and men traveled from the West Indies as far north as the Santee River in present-day South Carolina. They planned to settle in the region and then search for gold and other valuables. The effort failed, but two years later Pánfilo de Narváez—one of the survivors—led four hundred soldiers from Cuba to Florida's Tampa Bay. Seeking precious metals, the party instead confronted hunger, disease, and hostile Indians. The ragtag group continued to journey along the Gulf coast, until only four men, led by Álvar Núñez Cabeza de Vaca, made their way from Galveston Bay back to Mexico City.

A decade later, in 1539, a survivor of Narváez's ill-fated venture—a North African named Esteban—led a party of Spaniards from Mexico back north. Lured by tales of Seven Golden Cities, the party instead encountered Zuñi Indians, who attacked the Spaniards and killed Esteban. Still, the men who returned to Mexico passed on stories of large and wealthy cities. Hoping to find fame and fortune, Francisco Vásquez de Coronado launched a grand expedition northward in 1540. Angered when they failed to discover fabulous wealth, Coronado and his men terrorized the region, burning towns, killing residents, and stealing goods before returning to Mexico.

Hernando de Soto headed a fourth effort to find wealth in North America. An experienced conquistador, de Soto received royal authority in 1539 to explore Florida. That spring he established a village near Tampa Bay with more than six hundred Spanish, Indian, and African men, and a few women. A few months later, de Soto and the bulk of his company traveled up the west Florida coast with Juan Ortiz, a member of the Narváez expedition and an especially useful guide and interpreter. That winter, the expedition traveled into present-day Georgia and the Carolinas in an unsuccessful search for riches (Map 1.6).

On their return trip, de Soto's men engaged in a brutal battle with local Indians led by Chief Tuskaloosa. Although the Spaniards claimed victory, they lost a significant number of men and horses and most of their equipment. Fearing that word of the disaster would reach Spain, de Soto steered his men away from supply ships in the Gulf of Mexico and headed back north. The group continued through parts of present-day Tennessee, Arkansas, Oklahoma, and Texas, and in May 1541 they became the first Europeans to report seeing the vast Mississippi River. By the winter of 1542, the expedition had lost more men and supplies to Indians, and de Soto had died. The remaining members finally returned to Spanish territory in the summer of 1543.

The lengthy journey of de Soto and his men brought European diseases into new areas, leading to epidemics and the depopulation of once-substantial native communities. At the same time, the Spaniards left horses and pigs behind, creating new sources of transportation and food for native peoples. Although most Spaniards considered de Soto's journey a failure, the Spanish crown claimed vast new territories. Two decades later, in 1565, Pedro Menéndez de Avilés established a mission settlement on the northeast coast of Florida, named St. Augustine. It became the first permanent European settlement in North America.

Europeans Compete in North America. Spain's early ventures in North America helped inspire French and English explorers to establish their own footholds on the continent. The French entered the race for empire in 1524, when an Italian navigator named Giovanni da Verrazano led a French company along the coast of North America.

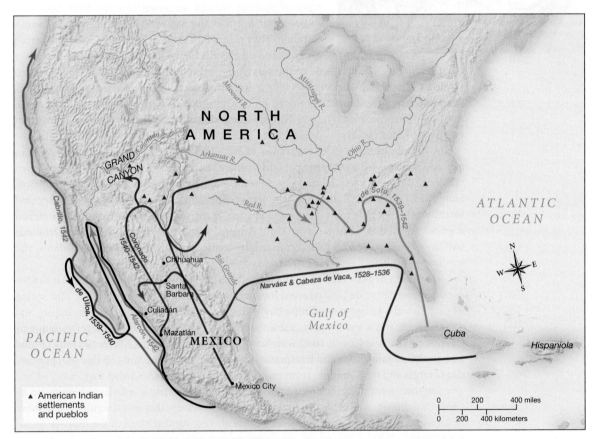

MAP 1.6 Spanish Explorations in North America, 1528–1542

Spanish explorers in North America hoped to find gold and other treasures. Instead, they encountered difficult terrain and native peoples hostile to Spanish intruders. Many Spaniards died on these expeditions, and they failed to discover new sources of wealth. But they laid the foundations for Spanish settlements in Florida, northern Mexico, and California while devastating local Indian populations.

Landing initially near Cape Fear on the Carolina coast, the expedition headed north, sailing into what would become New York harbor. Verrazano then continued north, claiming lands all along the coast for France.

A decade later, in 1534, the Frenchman Jacques Cartier sailed to the Gulf of St. Lawrence. In two subsequent expeditions, Cartier pushed deeper into the territory known as Canada. Although he failed to discover precious metals or the elusive passage to the Pacific Ocean, he did trade for furs with local Indians. Cartier also inspired a French nobleman, the Sieur de Roberval, and several hundred followers to attempt a permanent settlement at Quebec in 1542. But the project was abandoned within a year because of harsh weather, disease, and high mortality.

English interest in North America was ignited by Spanish and French challenges to claims Cabot had made along the North Atlantic coast in the 1490s. To secure these rights, the English needed to colonize the disputed lands. Since the English crown did not have funds to support settlement, the earliest ventures were financed by minor noblemen who hoped to gain both wealth and the crown's favor. The earliest of these, in Newfoundland and Maine, failed.

The most promising effort to secure an English foothold was organized by Sir Walter Raleigh. Claiming all the land north of Florida for England, Raleigh called the vast territory Virginia (after Elizabeth I, "the Virgin Queen"). In 1585 Raleigh sent a group of soldiers to found a colony on Roanoke Island, off the coast of present-day North Carolina. The colony would establish England's claims and allow English sailors stationed there to seize Spanish ships laden with valuables. This venture lasted less than a year. But in 1587 Raleigh tried again, sending a group of 117 men, women, and children to Roanoke. However, when supply ships came to fortify the settlement in 1590, no trace of the English settlers remained.

By 1590, then, nearly a century after Columbus's initial voyage, only Spain had established permanent colonies in the Americas, mostly in the West Indies, Mexico, and South America. The French and the English, despite numerous efforts, had not sustained a single ongoing settlement by the end of the sixteenth century. Yet neither nation gave up hope of benefiting from the wealth of the Americas.

Spain Seeks Dominion in Europe and the Americas. The continued desire of European nations to gain colonies in the Americas resulted from the enormous wealth garnered by Spanish conquests. That wealth transformed economies throughout Europe. Between 1500 and 1650, Spanish ships carried home more than 180 tons of gold and 16,000 tons of silver from Mexico and Potosí. About one-fifth of this amount was taken by the Spanish crown for taxes; the rest was dispersed among supporters of the expeditions; family and friends of those who conquered lands, gained encomiendas, or participated in trade; and soldiers and sailors who returned from America. The money was spent mainly on luxury goods imported from the Americas, Asia, or other European nations. Very little of this wealth was invested in improving conditions at home. Indeed, the rapid infusion of gold and silver fueled inflation, making it harder for ordinary people to afford the necessities of life.

In one area, however, employment for the poor expanded rapidly. Spain's King Philip II (r. 1556–1598) used American gold and silver to fund a variety of military campaigns, ensuring an endless demand for soldiers and sailors. The king, a devout

Catholic, claimed to be doing God's work as Spain conquered Italy and Portugal, including the latter's colonies in Africa, and tightened its grip on the Netherlands, which had been acquired by Spain through marriage in the early sixteenth century.

Despite the obvious material benefits, the Spaniards were not blind to the enormous human costs of colonization, and the conquest of the Americas inspired heated debates within Spain. Catholic leaders believed that the conversion of native peoples to Christianity was critical to Spanish success in the Americas. However, most royal officials and colonial agents viewed the extraction of precious metals as far more important. They argued that cheap labor was essential to creating wealth. Yet brutal conditions led to the death of huge numbers of Indians, which made it nearly impossible to convert others to Catholicism.

By 1550, tales of the widespread torture and enslavement of Indians convinced the Spanish king Carlos V (r. 1519–1556) to gather a group of theologians, jurists, and philosophers at Valladolid to discuss the moral and legal implications of conquest. Bartolomé de Las Casas took a leading role in defending the rights of Indians. A former conquistador and Dominican friar, Las Casas had spent many years preaching to Indians in America. He asked, "And so what man of sound mind will approve a war against men who are harmless, ignorant, gentle, temperate, unarmed, and destitute of every human defense?" Las Casas reasoned that even if Spain defeated the Indians, the souls of those killed would be lost to God, while among the survivors "hatred and loathing of the Christian religion" would prevail. He even suggested replacing Indian labor with African labor, apparently less concerned with the souls of black people.

> **Explore ▶**
>
> To examine a European depiction of interactions between Spanish and native peoples, see Document 1.4.

Juan Ginés de Sepúlveda, the royal historian, attacked Las Casas's arguments. Although he had never set foot in America, he read reports of cannibalism and other violations of "natural law" among native peoples. Since the Indians were savages, the civilized Spaniards were obligated to "destroy barbarism and educate these people to a more humane and virtuous life." If they refused such help, Spanish rule "can be imposed upon them by force of arms." Although Ginés de Sepúlveda spoke for the majority at Valladolid, Las Casas and his supporters continued to press their case as Spain expanded its reach into North America.

At the same time, American riches increasingly flowed beyond Spain's borders. The Netherlands was a key beneficiary of this wealth, becoming a center for Spanish shipbuilding and trade. Still, the Dutch were never completely under Spanish control, and they traded gold, silver, and other items to France, England, and other European nations. Goods also followed older routes across the Mediterranean to the Ottoman empire, where traders could make huge profits on exotic items from the Americas. Thus, while some Europeans suffered under Spanish power, others benefited from the riches brought to the continent. By the late sixteenth century, the desire for a greater share of those riches revitalized imperial dreams among the French and English as well as the Dutch.

REVIEW & RELATE

What motivated the Spanish to conquer and colonize the Americas?

What were the consequences in Europe of Spain's acquisition of an American empire?

SOLO ANALYSIS

Theodor de Bry | Engraving of the Black Legend, 1598

In the late 1500s, the engraver Theodor de Bry and his sons created a series of copperplate illustrations depicting the Americas. By the 1590s, critics labeled the Spanish conquest of America "the Black Legend" because of the brutal treatment of Indians. The de Brys depended on reports from explorers and missionaries for their illustrations. While not necessarily accurate, the detailed and graphic scenes they created became enormously popular and thus shaped debates about the legitimacy of Spanish actions in the Americas. Although the de Brys did depict Indians torturing Spanish explorers, this illustration highlights Spanish cruelty against Indians.

Document 1.4

Beinecke Rare Book and Manuscript Library, Yale University

Interpret the Evidence

1. How do the de Brys depict Indians and Spaniards differently?
2. How might this image shape public perceptions of Spanish encounters with Indians?

Put It in Context

How did these popular illustrations contribute to the fierce debates among Spanish royalty, the Catholic Church, and ordinary people over what was at stake in conquering territory in the Americas?

Conclusion:
A **New America**

For centuries, Asian peoples migrated to the Americas by land and sea. They developed an astonishing array of cultures and societies, from small hunting-and-gathering bands to complex empires. In the fourteenth and fifteenth centuries, extensive commercial and political networks existed among the Mississippians, the Aztecs, and the Incas, although only the latter two continued to thrive by the late 1400s. In southern Europe, too, during the fifteenth century, economic, cultural, and political advances fueled interest in long-distance trade and exploration. Italy and Portugal led these efforts, but their monopoly of trade routes across the Mediterranean and around Africa to Asia forced Spain to look west in hopes of gaining access to China and the Indies. In doing so, the Spanish unexpectedly came into contact with the Americas.

When Spanish explorers happened upon Caribbean islands and the nearby mainland, they created contacts between populations that would be dramatically transformed in a matter of decades. While native residents of the Americas were sometimes eager to trade with the newcomers and to form alliances against their traditional enemies, they fought against those they considered invaders. Yet some of the most significant invaders—plants, pigs, and especially germs—were impossible to defend against. Even Europeans seeking peaceful relations with native inhabitants or bent on conversion rather than conquest brought diseases that devastated local populations and plants and animals that transformed their landscape, diet, and traditional ways of life.

Waldseemüller died in 1521 or 1522, so he did not see the most dramatic changes that his remarkably accurate maps inspired. Malintzin, however, experienced those changes firsthand. She watched as disease ravaged not only rural villages but even the capital city of Tenochtitlán. She encountered horses, pigs, attack dogs, and other European animals. She ate the foods and wore the clothes that her Spanish captors provided. In 1522, Malintzin gave birth to Cortés's son; two years later, she served as interpreter when he ventured north to conquer more territory. In 1526 or 1527, however, she married a Spanish soldier, Juan Jaramillo, settled in Mexico City, and bore two more children. As more and more Spaniards, including the first women, settled in New Spain, Malintzin realized that her children would grow up in a world very different from the one in which she was raised.

From the 1490s to the 1580s, the most dramatic and devastating changes for native peoples occurred in Mexico, the West Indies, Central America, and South America. But events there also presaged what would happen throughout the Americas. As Spanish conquistadors ventured into Florida and the Gulf Coast and French and English explorers sought to gain footholds along the Atlantic seaboard, they carried sufficient germs, seeds, and animals to transform native societies even before Europeans established permanent settlements in North America.

In the century to come, contacts and conflicts between native peoples and Europeans escalated as France, England, and the Netherlands joined Spain in colonizing North America. Conflicts among European nations also multiplied as they struggled to control land, labor, and trade. Moreover, as Indian populations died out in some regions and fended off conquest in others, Europeans turned increasingly to the trade in Africans to provide the labor to produce enormously profitable items like sugar, coffee, and tobacco.

CHAPTER 1 REVIEW

TIMELINE OF EVENTS

25,000–13,000 B.C.E.	First northeast Asians migrate to the Americas
900 B.C.E.–300 C.E.	Maya settle Yucatán peninsula
500 C.E.	Mogollon and Hohokam settle in southwestern North America
500–1400	Mississippian peoples establish complex cultures
800	Mayan civilization begins to decline
1000	Norse settle in North America
1325	Aztecs build Tenochtitlán
1340s	Bubonic plague in Europe
1400–1500	Inca empire reaches its height
1440s	Portuguese begin to trade along the coast of West Africa
1452–1455	Johannes Gutenberg prints Bibles using movable type
1469	Unification of Spain
1487	Bartolomeu Dias rounds the Cape of Good Hope
1492	Spain expels Muslim conquerors and Jews
	Christopher Columbus launches Enterprise of the Indies
1497	Vasco da Gama sails to India
1507	Martin Waldseemüller and Mathias Ringmann publish *Universalis Cosmographia*
1519	Malintzin captured by Spaniards
1519–1521	Hernán Cortés conquers the Aztecs
1519–1522	Ferdinand Magellan's fleet circumnavigates the globe
1524	Francisco Pizarro conquers the Incas
1587	English settle Roanoke Island

KEY TERMS

Beringia, *3*

horticulture, *5*

Aztecs, *5*

Maya, *6*

Incas, *6*

Hopewell people, *8*

Crusades, *10*

Black Death, *11*

Renaissance, *11*

Enterprise of the Indies, *16*

encomienda, *16*

Columbian exchange, *21*

conquistadors, *23*

REVIEW & RELATE

1. Compare and contrast the Aztecs, Incas, and Maya. What similarities and differences do you note?

2. How did the societies of North America differ from those of the equatorial zone and the Andes?

3. How and why did Europeans expand their connections with Africa and the Middle East in the fifteenth century?

4. How did early European encounters with West Africans influence Europeans' ideas about African peoples and reshape existing systems of slavery?

5. What were the short-term consequences in both Europe and the Americas of Columbus's voyages?

6. How did the Columbian exchange transform both the Americas and Europe?

7. What motivated the Spanish to conquer and colonize the Americas?

8. What were the consequences in Europe of Spain's acquisition of an American empire?

Indian and Spanish Encounters in the Americas, 1520–1530

The arrival of Europeans in the Americas in the fifteenth century reshaped the society, culture, and economy of the entire world. For the Indians who had inhabited the region for thousands of years, these encounters began a story of devastation. Europeans came in search of wealth and glory. They brought with them superior firepower and, more significantly, deadly diseases. The Indian population declined rapidly and dramatically, a demographic catastrophe that allowed the Europeans to achieve their imperial aims. After the Spanish explorer Hernán Cortés conquered the Aztec city of Tenochtitlán in 1521, Spain emerged as the world's preeminent empire.

On the local level, the Columbian exchange of plants, animals, diseases, and ideas between Europe, Africa, and the Americas meant a clash of distinct cultures (see Documents 1.6 and 1.8). Confident in their superiority, the Spanish questioned the Indians' religions, social norms, and work habits. They sought to impose Catholicism and control the Indians' labor, and they used extreme violence to reach these ends (see Documents 1.5). The Indians tried to resist the imposition of Spanish culture, but the military and biological advantages of the Europeans, along with divisions within the Indians' own ranks, undermined their efforts (see Documents 1.6 and 1.7). Although the Indians achieved some victories against the European intruders, their way of life was permanently altered (see Document 1.8).

The following documents explore early contact between Europeans, specifically the Spanish, and Indians, primarily the Aztecs. As you read, consider the many levels of cultural misunderstanding and misinterpretation that occurred when these worlds collided.

Document 1.5

Hernán Cortés | Letter to King Charles I, 1520

Hernán Cortés wrote a series of letters to the Spanish king Charles I detailing his experiences and progress in Mexico. In the following excerpt from his second letter, Cortés explains how the Indians refused to accept Catholicism and the rule of the Spanish king. He then describes military actions that he carried out against the Indians.

When I undertook to [read] my requirements in due form, through the interpreters whom I had brought with me, and . . . the more diligent I was to admonish and require them to keep the peace, just so much the more diligent were they in committing hostilities upon us, and, seeing that neither requirements nor protests were of any avail, we began to defend ourselves as best we could, and thus they kept us fighting, until we found ourselves in the midst of an hundred thousand warriors, who surrounded us on all sides. This went on all day long, until about an hour before sunset, when they retired. In this fight I did them a good deal of harm with about half a dozen cannon, and five or six muskets, forty archers, and thirteen horsemen . . . without our receiving any hurt from them. . . . And it truly appeared that it was God who battled for us, because amongst such a multitude of people, so courageous and skilled in fighting, and with so many kinds of offensive arms, we came out unhurt.

That night I fortified myself in a small tower of their idols, which stood on a small hill, and afterwards, at daybreak, I left two hundred men and all the artillery in the camp. As I was the attacking party I went out towards evening with the horsemen, and a hundred foot soldiers, and four hundred Indians whom I had brought from Cempoal, and three hundred from Yztacmastitan. Before the enemy had time to assemble, I set fire to five or six small places of about a hundred houses each, and brought away about four hundred prisoners, both men and women, fighting my way back to my camp without their doing me any harm. At daybreak the following morning, more than a hundred and forty-nine thousand men, covering all the country, attacked our camp so determinedly that some of them penetrated into it, rushing about, and thrusting with their swords at the Spaniards. We mustered against them, and Our Lord was pleased so to aid us, that, in about four hours, we managed that they should no more molest us in our camp. . . .

The next day I again went out before daybreak, in another direction, without having been observed by the enemy, taking with me the horsemen, a hundred foot-soldiers, and the friendly Indians. I burned more than a hundred villages, one of which had more than three thousand houses, where the villagers fought with me, though there were no other people there. As we carried the banner of the Holy Cross, and were fighting for our Faith, and in the service of Your Sacred Majesty, to Your Royal good fortune God gave us such a victory that we slew many people without our own sustaining any injury. . . .

Messengers came from the chiefs the next day, saying that they wished to become vassals of Your Highness and my friends, beseeching me to pardon their past fault; and they brought me provisions, and certain feather-work which they use, and esteem and prize. I answered that they had behaved badly, but that I was satisfied to be their friend, and pardon them for all they had done. . . .

When we had somewhat rested, I made a sally [foray] one night . . . taking a hundred foot[men], the friendly Indians, and the horsemen; and about a league from our camp five horses and mares fell, unable to go on, so I sent them back. Although those who accompanied me, said that I ought to return, as this was an evil omen, I still pushed ahead, confiding in God's supremacy above everything. Before daybreak I fell upon two towns, in which I slaughtered many people, but I did not want to burn the houses, so as to avoid attracting the attention of other people who were very near. When day dawned I fell upon another large town, . . . and, as I had surprised them, I found them unarmed, and the women and children, running naked through the streets; and we did them some harm. Seeing they could offer no resistance, a certain number of the inhabitants came to beseech me not to do them further injury, for they desired to become vassals of Your Highness, and my friends.

Source: Francis Augustus MacNutt, ed. and trans., *Fernando Cortés: His Five Letters of Relation to the Emperor Charles V* (Cleveland: Arthur H. Clark, 1908), 201–3, 205–6.

Source: Francis Augustus MacNutt, ed. and trans., *Fernando Cortés: His Five Letters of Relation to the Emperor Charles V* (Cleveland: Arthur H. Clark, 1908), 201–3, 205–6.

Document 1.6

Aztec Priests | Respond to the Spanish, 1524

As Indian resistance to the *requerimiento*—the requirement for obedience to the Catholic Church—indicated, most Aztecs did not want to renounce their own religion in favor of Catholicism. In 1524 twelve Franciscan friars organized a series of meetings with Aztec political and religious leaders, who defended the legitimacy of their own customs. In the 1560s another friar published the notes from these meetings, providing insight into how Aztec leaders viewed the differences between their own beliefs and those of the Spanish.

You say that we [the Aztecs] do not recognize the being that is everywhere, lord of heaven and earth. You say our gods are not true gods. The new words that you utter are what confuse us; due to them we feel foreboding. Our makers [our ancestors] who came to live on earth never uttered such words. They gave us their *laws*, their ways of doing things. They believed in the gods, served them and honored them. They are the ones who taught us everything, the gods' being served and respected. Before them we eat earth [kiss the ground]; we bleed; we pay our debts to the gods, offer incense, make sacrifice. . . . Indeed, we live by the grace of those gods. They rightly made us out of the time, the place where it was still dark. . . . They give us what we go to sleep with, what we get up with [our daily sustenance], all that is drunk, all that is eaten, the produce, corn, beans, green maize, chia. We beg from them the water, the rain, so that things grow upon the earth.

The gods are happy in their prosperity, in what they have, always and forever. Everything sprouts and turns green in their home. What kind of place is the land of Tlaloc [the god of rain]? Never is there any famine there, nor any illness, nor suffering. And they [the gods] give people virility, bravery, success in the hunt, [bejeweled] lip rings, blankets, breeches, cloaks, flowers, tobacco, jade, feathers and gold.

Since time immemorial they have been addressed, prayed to, taken as gods. It has been a very long time that they have been revered. . . . These gods are the ones who established the mats and thrones [that is, the inherited chieftainships], who gave people nobility, and kingship, renown and respect.

Will we be the ones to destroy the ancient traditions of the Chichimeca, the Tolteca, the Colhuaca? [No!] It is our opinion that there is life, that people are born, people are nurtured, people grow up, [only] by the gods' being called upon, prayed to. Alas, o our lords, beware lest you make the common people do something bad. How will the poor old men, the poor old women, forget or erase their upbringing, their education? May the gods not be angry with us. Let us not move towards their anger. And let us not agitate the commoners, raise a riot, lest they rebel for this reason, because of our saying to them: address the gods no longer, pray to them no longer.

Source: Camilla Townsend, ed. and trans., *American Indian History: A Documentary Reader* (Malden, MA: Wiley-Blackwell, 2009), 29–30.

Hernán Cortés and Malintzin Meet Montezuma at Tenochtitlán, 1519

This image, depicting Cortés and Malintzin meeting Montezuma in November 1519, is one of eighty illustrations from a sixteenth-century mural cycle detailing the conquest of Mexico and its aftermath. The originals were painted by Tlaxcalan artists and represent an Indian perspective on these events. Malintzin is standing between Cortés (seated) and Montezuma (in gold robe). The Spanish and Aztec leaders are accompanied by leading warriors.

Gianni Dagli Orti/The Art Archive at Art Resource, NY

Álvar Núñez Cabeza de Vaca | *La Relación*, c. 1528

In 1528 a group of Spaniards sailed from Cuba to Tampa Bay in present-day Florida. After failing to find great riches, the survivors tried to return to Cuba but were washed ashore at Galveston Bay. Álvar Núñez Cabeza de Vaca and three other men survived the expedition, but only after enduring a nine-year, six-hundred-mile trek across Texas and Mexico and enslavement by Indians. In an account of his journey, Cabeza de Vaca described his experiences on the Isla de Malhado (Island of Misfortune) off the coast of Texas.

All the people of this country go naked; only the women cover part of their bodies with a kind of wool that grows on trees. The girls go about in deer skins. They are very liberal towards each other with what they have. There is no ruler among them. All who are of the same descendancy [ancestry] cluster together. There are two distinct languages spoken on the island; those of one language are called Capoques, those of the other Han. They have the custom, when they know each other and meet from time to time, before they speak, to weep for half an hour. After they have wept the one who receives the visit rises and gives the other all he has. The other takes it, and in a little while goes away with everything. Even sometimes, after having given and obtained all, they part without having uttered a word. There are other very queer customs, but having told the principal ones and the most striking, I must now proceed to relate what further happened to us. . . .

I had to remain with those same Indians of the island for more than one year, and as they made me work so much and treated me so badly I determined to flee and go to those who live in the woods on the mainland, and who are called those from Charruco. . . .

Among many other troubles I had to pull the eatable roots out of the water and from among the canes where they were buried in the ground, and from this my fingers had become so tender that the mere touch of a straw caused them to bleed. . . . This is why I went to work and joined the other Indians. Among these I improved my condition a little by becoming a trader, doing the best in it I could, and they gave me food and treated me well.

They entreated me to go about from one part to another to get the things they needed, as on account of constant warfare there is neither travel nor barter in the land.

So, trading along with my wares I penetrated inland as far as I cared to go and along the coast as much as forty or fifty leagues. My stock consisted mainly of pieces of seashells and cockles, and shells with which they cut a fruit which is like a bean, used by them for healing and in their dances and feasts. This is of greatest value among them, besides shell-beads and other objects. These things I carried inland, and in exchange brought back hides and red ochre with which they rub and dye their faces and hair; flint for arrow points, glue and hard canes wherewith to make them, and tassels made of the hair of deer, which they dye red. This trade suited me well because it gave me liberty to go wherever I pleased; I was not bound to do anything and no longer a slave. Wherever I went they treated me well, and gave me to eat for the sake of my wares. My principal object in doing it, however, was to find out in what manner I might get further away. . . .

My sufferings, while trading thus, it would take long to tell; danger, hunger, storms and frost overtaking me often in the open field and alone, and from which through the mercy of God, Our Lord, I escaped. For this reason I did not go out trading in winter, it being the time when the Indians themselves remain in their huts and abodes, unable to go out or assist each other.

Nearly six years I spent thus in the country, alone among them and naked, as they all were themselves.

Source: Adolph F. Bandelier, ed., *The Journey of Álvar Núñez Cabeza de Vaca and His Companions from Florida to the Pacific, 1528–1536* (New York: A. S. Barnes, 1905), 71–76.

Interpret the Evidence

1. How does Hernán Cortés treat his Indian adversaries (Document 1.5)? How does he justify this treatment? How does Cortés's description of these events reveal conflicts among the Indians themselves?

2. How do the Aztec priests respond to Spanish criticisms of their religion? Why do they refuse to abandon their gods (Document 1.6)?

3. What does the mural image, created by Tlaxcalan Indians, suggest about the relative power of Montezuma and Cortés at this meeting (Document 1.7)? What images of cooperation or conflict does it depict? Given the information in Documents 1.5 and 1.6, what concerns might Malintzin, as the translator, have about conveying information to each leader?

4. What does Álvar Núñez Cabeza de Vaca find surprising about Indian culture, and how might that reflect differences between the Spanish and Indians (Document 1.8)? How does his story differ from the information provided in Documents 1.5, 1.6, and 1.7?

Put It in Context

How would you describe the various encounters between Spaniards and Indians in the early years of contact? How did these encounters shape Spanish debates over the conquest in the 1550s?

What roles did religion, military power, and economic interests play in the differing perspectives among the Indians, among Spaniards, and between the Indians and the Spanish?

Colonization and Conflicts

1550–1680

WINDOW TO THE PAST

William Nahaton, Petition to Free an Indian Slave, 1675

William Nahaton, a Christianized Indian in Massachusetts Bay, sent this petition to gain the release of a relative whom he feared would be sold into slavery by the English. While hundreds of native people were sold into slavery, petitions for their release were rare. This petition offers important insights into the views of an Indian who had chosen to adopt many English ways. ▶ To discover more about what this primary source can show us, see Document 2.5 on page 64.

Massachusetts Archives Collection. 30:176. Petition from William Nahaton, 1675. SC1/series 45X. Courtesy of the Massachusetts Archives, Boston, Massachusetts.

After reading this chapter you should be able to:

■ Understand the impact of the Reformation and Counter-Reformation on European nations and their imperial goals in the American colonies.

■ Identify the ways that England's hopes for its North American colonies were transformed by relations with Indians, upheavals among indentured servants, the development of tobacco, and the emergence of slavery.

■ Discuss the influence of Puritanism on New England's development and how religious and political upheavals in England fueled Puritan expansion and conflicts with Indians in the colonies.

AMERICAN HISTORIES

Born in 1580 to a yeoman farm family in Lincoln-shire, John Smith left England as a young man "to learne the life of a Souldier." After fighting and traveling in Europe, the Mediterranean, and North Africa for several years, Captain Smith returned to England around 1605. There he joined the Virginia Company, whose wealthy investors planned to establish a private settlement on mainland North America. In April 1607, Captain Smith and 104 men arrived in Chesapeake Bay, where they founded Jamestown, named in honor of King James I, and claimed the land for themselves and their country. However, the area was already controlled by a powerful Indian leader, Chief Powhatan.

(*left*) **John Smith** Beinecke Rare Book and Manuscript Library, Yale University
(*right*) **Anne Hutchinson** Schlesinger Library, Radcliffe Institute, Harvard University/Bridgeman Images

In December 1607, when Powhatan's younger brother discovered Smith and two of his Jamestown comrades in the chief's territory, the Indians executed the two comrades but eventually released Smith. It is likely that before sending him back to Jamestown, Powhatan performed an adoption ceremony in an effort to bring Smith and the English under his authority. A typical ceremony would have involved Powhatan sending out one of his daughters—in this case, Pocahontas, who was about twelve years old—to indicate that the captive was spared. Refusing to accept his new status, if he understood it, Smith returned to Jamestown and urged residents to build fortifications for security.

The following fall, the colonists elected Smith president of the Jamestown council. Smith insisted that intimidating the Indians was the way to win Powhatan's respect. He also demanded that the English labor on farms and fortifications six hours a day. Many colonists resisted. Those who claimed the status of gentlemen considered manual labor beneath them, and the many who were adventurers sought wealth and glory, not hard work. The Virginia Company soon replaced Smith with a new set of leaders. In October 1609, angry and bitter, he returned to England.

Captain Smith published his criticisms of Virginia Company policies in 1612, which brought him widespread attention. He then set out to map the Atlantic coast farther north. In 1616 Smith published a tract that emphasized the similarity of the area's climate and terrain to the British Isles, calling it New England. He argued that colonies there could be made commercially viable but that success depended on recruiting settlers with the necessary skills and offering them land and a say in the colony's management.

English men and women settled New England in the 1620s, but they sought religious sanctuary, not commercial success or military dominance. Yet they, too, suffered schisms in their ranks. Anne Hutchinson, a forty-five-year-old wife and mother, was at the center of one such division. Born in Lincolnshire in 1591, Anne was well educated when she married William Hutchinson, a merchant, in 1612. The Hutchinsons and their children began attending Puritan sermons and by 1630 embraced the new faith. Four years later, they followed the Reverend John Cotton to Massachusetts Bay.

The Reverend Cotton soon urged Anne Hutchinson to use her exceptional knowledge of the Bible to hold prayer meetings in her home on Sundays for pregnant and nursing women who could not attend regular services. Hutchinson, like Cotton, preached that individuals must rely solely on God's grace rather than a saintly life or good works to ensure salvation.

Hutchinson began challenging Puritan ministers who opposed this position, charging that they posed a threat to their congregations. She soon attracted a loyal and growing following that included men as well as women. Puritan leaders met in August 1637 to denounce Hutchinson's views and condemn her meetings. In November 1637, after she refused to recant, she was put on trial. Hutchinson mounted a vigorous defense. Unmoved, the Puritan judges convicted her of heresy and banished her from Massachusetts Bay. Hutchinson and her family, along with dozens of followers, then settled in the recently established colony of Rhode Island. ∎

The American histories of John Smith and Anne Hutchinson illustrate the diversity of motives that drew English men and women to North America in the seventeenth century. Smith led a group of artisans, gentlemen, and adventurers whose efforts to colonize Virginia were in many ways an extension of a larger competition between European states. Hutchinson's journey to North America was rooted in the Protestant Reformation, which divided Europe into rival factions. Yet as different as these two people were, both furthered English settlement in North America even as they generated conflict within their own communities. Communities like theirs also confronted the expectations of diverse native peoples and the colonial aspirations of other Europeans while reshaping North America between 1550 and 1680.

Religious and Imperial Transformations

The Puritans were part of a relatively new religious movement known as **Protestantism** that had emerged around 1520. Protestants challenged Catholic policies and practices but did not form a single church of their own. Instead, a number of theologians formed distinct denominations in various regions of Europe. Catholics sought to counter their claims by revitalizing their faith and reasserting control. These religious conflicts shaped developments in North America as the Spanish, French, Dutch, and English competed for lands and sometimes souls.

The Protestant Reformation. Critiques of the Catholic Church multiplied in the early sixteenth century, driven by papal involvement in conflicts among monarchs and corruption among church officials. But the most vocal critics focused on immorality, ignorance, and absenteeism among clergy. These anticlerical views appeared in popular songs and printed images as well as in learned texts by theologians such as Martin Luther.

Luther, a professor of theology in Germany, believed that faith alone led to salvation, which could be granted only by God. He challenged the Catholic Church's claim that individuals could achieve salvation by buying indulgences, which were documents that absolved the buyer of sin. The church profited enormously from these sales, but they suggested that God's grace could be purchased. In 1517 Luther wrote an extended argument against indulgences and sent it to the local bishop. Although intended for learned clerics and academics, his writings soon gained a wider audience.

Luther's followers, who protested Catholic practices, became known as Protestants. His teachings circulated widely through sermons and printed texts, and his claim that ordinary people should read and reflect on the Scriptures appealed to the literate middle classes. Meanwhile his attacks on indulgences and corruption attracted those who resented the church's wealth and priests' lack of attention to their flocks. In Switzerland, John Calvin developed a version of Protestantism in which civil magistrates and reformed ministers ruled over a Christian society. Calvin argued that God had decided at the beginning of time who was saved and who was damned. Calvin's idea, known as predestination, energized Protestants who understood salvation as a gift from an all-knowing God in which the "works" of sinful humans played no part.

The Protestant Reformation quickly spread through central and northern Europe. England, too, came under the influence of Protestantism in the 1530s, although for different reasons. When the pope refused to annul the marriage of King Henry VIII (r. 1509–1547) and Catherine of Aragon, Henry denounced papal authority and established the **Church of England**, or Anglicanism, with himself as "defender of the faith." Despite the king's conversion to Protestantism, the Church of England retained many Catholic practices.

In countries like Spain and France with strong central governments and powerful ties to the Catholic Church, a strong Catholic Counter-Reformation largely quashed Protestantism. At the same time, Catholic leaders initiated reforms to counter their critics. In 1545 Pope Paul II called together a commission of cardinals, known as the Council of Trent (1545–1563), which initiated a number of reforms, such as the founding of seminaries to train priests and the return of monastic orders to their spiritual foundations.

Religious upheavals in Europe contributed significantly to empire building in North America. Protestant and Catholic leaders urged followers to spread their faith across the Atlantic, while religious minorities sought a safe haven in North America. Just as important, political struggles erupted between Catholic and Protestant rulers in Europe following the Reformation. The resulting economic and military crises pushed (or forced) people to seek new opportunities in the Americas. Thus in a variety of ways, religious transformations in Europe fueled the construction of empires in America.

Spain's Global Empire Declines.

As religious conflicts escalated in Europe, the Spaniards in America continued to push north from Florida and Mexico in hopes of expanding their empire. The nature of Spanish expansion, however, changed. As a result of the Council of Trent and the Catholic Counter-Reformation, Spain increasingly emphasized its religious mission. Thus Spanish authorities decided in 1573 that missionaries rather than soldiers should direct all new settlements. Franciscan priests began founding missions on the margins of Pueblo villages north of Mexico. They named the area Nuevo México (New Mexico), and many learned Indian languages. Over the following decades, as many as twenty thousand Pueblos officially converted to Catholicism, although many still retained traditional beliefs and practices. Missionaries made a considerable effort to eradicate such beliefs and practices, including flogging ceremonial leaders, but to no avail.

At the same time, the Franciscans tried to force the Pueblo people to adopt European ways. They insisted that men rather than women farm the land and that the Pueblos speak,

San Esteban del Rey Mission
Opened in 1644 after fourteen years of construction, this Spanish mission in present-day New Mexico provided instruction in Christianity and Hispanic customs for the Acoma (Pueblo) people. To this end, Spanish missionaries prohibited traditional Pueblo practices such as performing dances and wearing masks. The mission was one of the few to survive Pueblo revolts in the late seventeenth century. © age fotostock/SuperStock

cook, and dress like the Spaniards. Yet the missionaries largely ignored Spanish laws intended to protect Indians from coerced labor, demanding that the Pueblos build churches, provide the missions with food, and carry their goods to market. Wealthy landowners who followed the missionaries into New Mexico also demanded tribute in the form of goods and labor.

Then in 1598 Juan de Oñate, a member of a wealthy mining family, established a trading post and fort in the upper Rio Grande valley. The 500 soldiers who accompanied him seized corn and clothing from Pueblo villages and murdered or raped those who resisted. When the Spanish force was confronted by Indians at the Acoma pueblo, 11 soldiers were killed. The Spanish retaliated, slaughtering 500 men and 300 women and children. Fearing reprisals from outraged Indians, most Spanish settlers withdrew from the region.

In 1610 the Spanish returned, founded Santa Fe, and established a network of missions and estates owned by *encomenderos*, Spanish elites granted land and the right to exploit local Indian labor. The Pueblo people largely accepted the new situation. In part, they feared military reprisals if they challenged Spanish authorities. But they were also faced with drought and disease and with raids by hostile Apache and Navajo tribes. The Pueblos hoped to gain protection from Spanish soldiers and priests. Yet their faith in the Franciscans' spiritual power soon began to fade when conditions did not improve. Although Spain maintained a firm hold on Florida and its colonies in the West Indies, it began focusing most of its efforts on staving off growing resistance among the Pueblo people. Thus as other European powers expanded their reach into North America, the Spaniards were left with few resources to protect their eastern frontier.

France Enters the Race for Empire. In the late sixteenth century, French, Dutch, and English investors became increasingly interested in gaining a foothold in North America. But until Catholic Spain's grip on the Atlantic world was broken, other nations could not hope to compete for an American empire. It was the Protestant Reformation that helped shape the alliances that shattered Spain's American monopoly. As head of the Church of England, Queen Elizabeth I (King Henry VIII's daughter, r. 1558–1603) sought closer political and commercial ties with Protestant nations like the Netherlands. The queen also assented to, and benefited from, Francis Drake's raids on Spanish ships. In 1588 King Philip II of Spain (r. 1556–1598) decided to punish England for its attacks against Spanish shipping and intervention in the Netherlands and sent a massive armada to spearhead the invasion of England. Instead, the English, aided by Dutch ships, defeated the armada and ensured that other nations could compete for riches and colonies in North America.

Although French rulers shared Spain's Catholic faith, the two nations were rivals, and the defeat of the armada provided them as well as the Dutch and English with greater access to North American colonies. Moreover, once in North America, the French adopted attitudes and policies that were significantly different from those of Spain. This was due in part to their greater interest in trade than in conquest. The French had fished the North Atlantic since the mid-sixteenth century, but in the 1580s they built stations along the Newfoundland coast for drying codfish. French traders then established relations with local Indians, exchanging iron kettles and other European goods for valuable beaver skins.

By the early seventeenth century, France's King Henry IV (r. 1589–1610) sought to profit more directly from the resources in North America. With the Edict of Nantes (1598), the king ended decades of religious wars by granting political rights and limited toleration to French Protestants, known as Huguenots, many of whom had earlier sought refuge in North America. Now he could focus on developing the increasingly lucrative trade in American fish and furs. Samuel de Champlain founded the first permanent French settlement in North America in 1608 at Quebec. Accompanied by several dozen men, Champlain joined a Huron raid on the Iroquois, who resided south of the Great Lakes. By using guns, the French helped ensure a Huron victory and a powerful ally for the French. But the battle also fueled lasting bitterness among the Iroquois.

Trade relations flourished between the French and their Indian allies, but relatively few French men and even fewer French women settled in North America in the seventeenth century. Government policies discouraged mass migration, and peasants were also concerned by reports of short growing seasons and severe winters in Canada. Cardinal Richelieu, the king's chief minister, urged priests and nuns to migrate to New France, but he barred continued emigration by Huguenots, which further limited colonization. Thus into the 1630s, French settlements in North America consisted largely of fishermen, fur traders, and Catholic missionaries.

Fur traders were critical to sustaining the French presence and warding off encroachment by the English. They journeyed throughout eastern Canada, aided by the Huron tribe. Some Frenchmen took Indian wives, who provided them with both domestic labor and kinship ties to powerful trading partners. Despite Catholic criticism of these marriages, they enhanced French traders' success and fostered alliances among the Ojibwe and Dakota nations to the west. These alliances, in turn, created a middle ground in which economic and cultural exchanges led to a remarkable degree of mutual adaptation. French traders benefited from Indian women's skills in preparing beaver skins for market as well as from Indian canoes, while natives adopted iron cooking pots and European cloth.

Explore ▶

In Document 2.1, read a Catholic nun's report of a Huron woman's complaints about the Jesuits.

GUIDED ANALYSIS

A French Nun Reports a Huron Woman's Views of the Jesuits, 1640

Jesuit missionaries and Ursuline nuns brought the Catholic faith to Indians in New France along with germs and guns. In this letter, the nun Marie de L'Incarnation writes to her superiors about the views expressed by an elderly and respected Huron woman. She conveys a report she heard about this woman, who told her village that the Jesuits, known as Black Robes, were destroying their communities. L'Incarnation summarizes and then analyzes the Huron woman's speech.

Document 2.1

What is the Huron woman's evidence of the Jesuits' danger to her people?

What are the sources, in her experience, of the Jesuits' power to do harm?

It's the Black Robes who are making us die by their spells. Listen to me, I will prove it by reasons that you will recognize as true. They set themselves up in a village where everyone is feeling fine; no sooner are they there, but everyone dies except for three or four people. They move to another place, and the same thing happens. They visit cabins in other villages, and only those where they have not entered are exempt from death and illness. Don't you see that when they move their lips in what they call prayer, spells are coming out of their mouths? It's the same when they read their books. They have big pieces of wood [guns] in their cabins by which they make noise and send their magic everywhere. If they are not promptly put to death, they will end up ruining the country, and no one will be left, young or old. . . .

When she stopped speaking, everyone agreed that this was true, . . . [and] it seemed true . . . , for wherever the [Jesuit] Fathers went, God permitted death to accompany them so as to render more pure the faith of those who converted.

How does Marie de L'Incarnation interpret the message of this Huron woman?

Source: Marie de L'Incarnation, *Correspondance*, ed. Dom Guy Oury (Abbaye de Saint-Pierre, 1971), trans. Natalie Zemon Davis, *Women on the Margins: Three Seventeenth-Century Lives* (Cambridge, MA: Harvard University Press, 1995), 111–12.

Put It in Context

How might this account of a Huron woman's perspective have been transformed in its retelling and translation? Despite these changes, what can it tell us about Huron interactions with Catholic priests and nuns in the early 1600s?

In their ongoing search for new sources of furs, the French established a fortified trading post at Montreal in 1643, and over the next three decades they continued to push farther west. However, as they extended the fur trade beyond the St. Lawrence River valley, the French left their Huron allies behind. The Iroquois wanted to keep the Huron tribe from trading their high-quality furs to the Dutch. With guns supplied by Dutch merchants, the Iroquois could fend off economic competition and secure captives to restore their population, which was decimated by disease. The result was a series of devastating assaults on Huron villages.

The ongoing wars among native rivals limited the ability of France to capitalize on its North American colonies. Indeed, the only hope of maintaining profits from the fur trade was to continue to move westward. But in doing so, the French carried European diseases into new areas, ignited warfare among more native groups, and stretched their always small population of settlers ever thinner. Still, French explorers, traders, and priests extended their reach across Canada and by 1681 had moved southward along the Mississippi to a territory they named Louisiana in honor of King Louis XIV (r. 1643–1715).

The conflicts between commerce and conversion so evident in Spanish America were far less severe in New France. French traders relied on Indian allies, and some French Jesuit priests also sought to build on native beliefs and to learn the Indians' language and customs. Although Catholics assumed that their own religious beliefs and cultural values were superior to those of the Indians, many sought to engage Indians on their own terms. Thus one French Jesuit employed the Huron belief that "our souls have desires which are inborn and concealed" to explain Christian doctrines of sin and salvation to potential converts. Still, French traders and missionaries carried deadly germs, and Catholics sought conversion, not mutual adaptation. Thus while Indians clearly benefited from their alliances with the French in the short term, the long-term costs were devastating.

The Dutch Expand into North America.

The Protestant Dutch made no pretense of bringing religion to Indians in America. From the beginning, their goals were primarily economic. As Spain's shipbuilding center, the Netherlands benefited from the wealth pouring in from South America, and an affluent merchant class emerged. But the Dutch also embraced Calvinism and sought to separate themselves from Catholic Spain. In 1581 the Netherlands declared its independence from King Philip II (r. 1556–1598), although Spain refused to recognize the new status for several decades. Still, by 1600 the Netherlands was both a Protestant haven and the trading hub of Europe. Indeed, the Dutch East India Company controlled trade routes to much of Asia and parts of Africa.

With the technology and skills developed under Spanish control, the Dutch decided to acquire their own American colonies. In 1609 the Dutch established a fur-trading center on the Hudson River in present-day New York. The small number of Dutch traders developed especially friendly relations with the powerful Mohawk nation, and in 1614 the trading post was relocated to Fort Orange, near present-day Albany.

In 1624, to fend off French and English raids on ships sent downriver from Fort Orange, the Dutch established New Amsterdam on Manhattan Island, which they purchased from the Lenape Indians. The new settlement was organized by the Dutch West India Company, which had been chartered three years earlier. New Amsterdam was the centerpiece of the larger New Netherland colony and attracted a diverse community of traders, fishermen, and farmers. It was noted for its representative government and religious toleration.

The European settlers of New Netherland may have gotten along with one another, but the same could not be said for settlers and local Indians. Tensions increased as Dutch colonists carved out farms north of New Amsterdam where large communities of Algonquian Indians lived. In 1639 conflict escalated when Governor William Kieft demanded an annual tribute in wampum or grain. Local Algonquians resisted, raiding Dutch farms on the frontier and killing at least two colonists. Then in 1643 Kieft launched a surprise attack on an Indian encampment on Manhattan Island, murdering eighty people, mostly women and children. Outraged Algonquians burned and looted homes north of the city, killed

New Amsterdam   This engraving on copper offers one of the oldest extant images of New Amsterdam. It captures the thriving commercial center of New Netherland at the tip of Manhattan. It also illustrates the importance of enslaved Africans to the colony's success and the significant role played by Dutch women as well as men in its economic development.
New York Public Library, USA/Bridgeman Images

livestock, and murdered settlers. For two decades, sporadic warfare continued, but eventually the Algonquians were defeated.

At the same time, the Dutch eagerly traded for furs with Mohawk Indians along the upper Hudson River. The Mohawks were a powerful tribe that had the backing of the even more powerful Iroquois Confederacy. Their ties to Indian nations farther west allowed them to provide beaver skins to Dutch traders long after beavers had died out in the Hudson valley. Still, the Mohawk people did not deceive themselves. As one chief proclaimed in 1659, "The Dutch say we are brothers and that we are joined together with chains, but that lasts only so long as we have beavers."

Meanwhile reports of atrocities by both Indians and the Dutch circulated in the Netherlands. These damaged New Amsterdam's reputation and slowed migration dramatically. Exhausted by the unrelenting conflicts, the Dutch surrendered New Amsterdam to the English without a fight when the latter sent a convoy to oust their former allies in 1664.

REVIEW & RELATE

- How did the Protestant Reformation shape the course of European expansion in the Americas?

- How did the French and Dutch colonies in North America differ from the Spanish empire to the south?

The **English** **Seek** an **Empire**

The English, like the French and the Dutch, entered the race for an American empire well after the Spanish. The English did not have a permanent settlement in the Americas until the founding of **Jamestown** on the Chesapeake River in 1607. In the 1620s, the English also established settlements in the West Indies, which quickly became the economic engine of English colonization. Expansion into these areas demanded new modes of labor to ensure a return on investment. Beginning in the mid-sixteenth century, large numbers of European indentured servants crossed the Atlantic while growing numbers of Africans were forced onto ships for sale in the Americas. This rapid expansion of English settlement not only fostered conflicts with Indian nations but also fueled tensions among settlers themselves.

The English Establish Jamestown. England's success in colonizing North America depended in part on a new economic model in which investors sold shares in joint-stock companies and sought royal support for their venture. In 1606 a group of London merchants formed the Virginia Company, and King James I granted them the right to settle a vast area of North America, from present-day New York to North Carolina.

Some of the men that the Virginia Company recruited as colonists were gentlemen who hoped to get rich through the discovery of precious metals. Even more skilled artisans and laborers were recruited to launch the settlement, though many of them also hoped to become wealthy. Arriving on the coast of North America in April 1607, the colonists established Jamestown on a site they chose mainly for its easy defense. Although bothered by the settlement's mosquito-infested environment, the colonists variously focused their energies on constructing buildings, producing food, and searching for gold and silver.

The Englishmen quickly made contact with the Indian chief Powhatan. He presided over a confederation of some 14,000 Algonquian-speaking Indians from twenty-five to thirty tribes, which surrounded the small Jamestown

Village of Pomeiooc, Virginia   This engraving is based on a 1585 painting by John White, an early Virginia colonist. He captured the everyday lives of Indians along the Atlantic coast. His bird's-eye image was altered slightly by Theodore De Bry and republished by William Strachey in 1618. In this Indian village, houses and sheds are grouped around an open space and surrounded by a palisade. © British Library Board/ Robana/Art Resource, NY

settlement. The **Powhatan Confederacy** was far more powerful than the English settlers, and, indeed, for the first two years the settlers depended on the Indians to survive. A shortage of food, caused by a severe drought between 1606 and 1612, affected both Indians and the English. It was exacerbated in Jamestown by some colonists' refusal to engage in manual labor. Moreover, the nearby water was tainted by salt from the ocean, and diseases that festered in the low-lying area killed more than half of the original settlers.

Despite the Englishmen's aggressive posture, Powhatan assisted the new settlers in hopes they could provide him with English cloth, iron hatchets, and even guns. His capture and subsequent release of John Smith in 1607 suggests his interest in developing trade relations with the newcomers even as he sought to subordinate them. But leaders like Captain Smith considered Powhatan and his warriors a threat rather than an asset. When unable to feed themselves that first year, Jamestown residents raided Indian villages for corn and other food, making Powhatan increasingly wary. The settlers' decision to construct a fort under Smith's direction only increased the Indians' concern.

Meanwhile the Virginia Company devised a new plan to stave off the collapse of its colony. It started selling seven-year joint-stock options to raise funds and recruited new settlers to produce staple crops, glassware, or other items for export. Interested individuals who could not afford to invest cash could sign on for service in Virginia. After seven years, these colonists would receive a hundred acres of land. In June 1609, a new contingent of colonists attracted by this plan—five hundred men and a hundred women—sailed for Jamestown.

The new arrivals, however, had not brought enough supplies to sustain the colony through the winter. Powhatan did offer some aid, but Indians, too, suffered from shortages in the winter of 1609–1610. A "starving time" settled on Jamestown. By the spring of 1610, seven of every eight settlers who had arrived in Jamestown since 1607 were dead.

That June, the sixty survivors decided to abandon Jamestown and sail for home. But they changed their minds when they met three English ships in the harbor loaded with supplies and three hundred more settlers. Emboldened by fresh supplies and an enlarged population, Jamestown's new leaders adopted an aggressive military posture, attacking native villages, burning crops, killing many Indians, and taking others captive. They believed that such brutality would convince neighboring tribes to obey English demands for food and labor.

Tobacco Fuels Growth in Virginia.

It was not military aggression, however, but the discovery of a viable cash crop that saved the colony. Orinoco tobacco, grown in the West Indies and South America, sold well in England and Europe. Virginia colonist John Rolfe began to experiment with its growth in 1612, just as the drought lifted. Production of the leaf soared as eager investors poured seeds, supplies, and labor into Jamestown. Exports multiplied rapidly, from 2,000 pounds in 1615 to 40,000 pounds five years later and an incredible 1.5 million pounds by 1629.

Tobacco cultivation exacerbated tensions between the English and the Indians. As production increased and prices declined, farmers could increase their profits only by obtaining more land and more laborers. The Virginia Company sought to expand the region under cultivation by offering those who could pay their own way land for themselves and their families. Those who could not afford passage could sign an indenture, agreeing to labor for landowners for seven years. They would then gain their independence

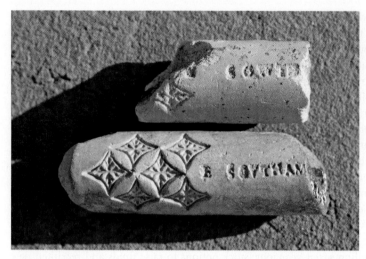

Clay Tobacco Pipe, James Fort, Virginia   Robert Cotton, a pipe maker from England, arrived in Jamestown in 1608. He copied Indian designs in crafting pipes from Virginia clay. Cotton added decorations and the names of leading men before the clay was fired. These fragments, discovered at an archaeological dig, suggest the importance of local artisans in Jamestown and the interplay of Indian and English styles.
Courtesy Jamestown Rediscovery (Historic Jamestowne)

and perhaps land of their own. Yet in most cases, the land the Virginia Company offered would-be colonists was already settled by members of the Powhatan Confederacy. Thus the rapid increase in tobacco cultivation intensified competition between colonists and Indians.

Nonetheless, Powhatan tried one last time to create an alliance between his confederacy and the English settlers. Perhaps he was encouraged by the return of rain, assuming that increased productivity would ensure better trade relations with the English. In 1614 he agreed to allow his daughter Pocahontas to marry John Rolfe. Pocahontas converted to Christianity and two years later traveled to England with Rolfe and their infant son. While there, she fell ill and died in 1617. Rolfe returned to Virginia just as relations with the Powhatan Confederacy began to change. In 1618 Powhatan died, and his younger brother Opechancanough took over as chief.

A year later, in 1619, the English crown granted Virginia the right to establish a local governing body, the **House of Burgesses**. Its members could make laws and levy taxes, although the English governor or the company council in London held veto power. The Virginia Company also resolved to recruit more female settlers as a way to increase the colony's population. More young women and men arrived as **indentured servants**, working in the fields and homes of more affluent Englishmen for a set period of time in exchange for passage to America. A Dutch ship carried the first boatload of twenty Africans to Jamestown that same year, and they were bound as indentured servants to farmers desperate for labor.

Although the English colony still hugged the Atlantic coast, its expansion increased conflict with native inhabitants. In March 1622, after repeated English incursions on land cleared and farmed by Indians, Chief Opechancanough and his allies launched a surprise attack that killed nearly a third of the colonists. In retaliation, Englishmen assaulted native villages, killed inhabitants, burned cornfields, and sold captives into slavery.

The English proclaimed victory in 1623, but hostilities continued for nearly a decade. In 1624, in the midst of the crisis, King James annulled the Virginia Company charter and took control of the colony. He appointed the governor and a small advisory council,

Engraving of Pocahontas, 1616
Simon van de Passe created this portrait of Pocahontas during her visit to England in 1616. The engraving was commissioned by the Virginia Company to promote settlement in Jamestown. It was the only portrait of Pocahontas made before her death in London. While van de Passe clothes her in English aristocratic style, he retains her dark complexion and direct gaze. Library of Congress, 3a10723

required that legislation passed by the House of Burgesses be ratified by the Privy Council, and demanded that property owners pay taxes to support the Church of England. These regulations became the model for royal colonies throughout North America.

Still, royal proclamations could not halt Indian opposition. In 1644 Opechancanough launched a second uprising against the English, killing hundreds of colonists. After two years of bitter warfare, Chief Opechancanough was finally captured and then killed. With the English population now too large to eradicate, the Chesapeake Indians finally submitted to English authority in 1646.

Expansion, Rebellion, and the Emergence of Slavery. By the 1630s, despite continued conflicts with Indians, Virginia was well on its way to commercial success. The most successful tobacco planters used indentured servants, including some Africans as well as thousands of English and Irish immigrants. Between 1640 and 1670, some 40,000 to 50,000 of these migrants settled in Virginia and neighboring Maryland (Map 2.1). Maryland was founded in 1632 when King Charles I, the successor to James I, granted most of the territory north of Chesapeake Bay to Cecilius Calvert and appointed him Lord Baltimore. Calvert was among the minority of English who remained a Catholic, and he planned to create Maryland as a refuge for his persecuted co-worshippers. Appointing his brother Leonard Calvert as governor, he carefully prepared for the first settlement.

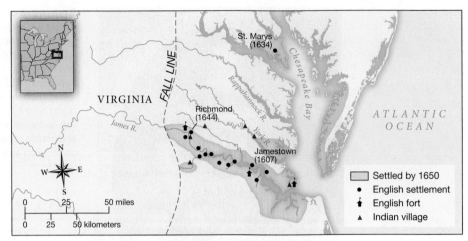

MAP 2.1   The Growth of English Settlement in the Chesapeake, c. 1650

With the success of tobacco, English plantations and forts spread along the James River and north to St. Mary's. By 1650 most Chesapeake Indian tribes had been vanquished or forced to move north and west. The fall line, which marked the limit of navigable waterways, kept English settlements close to the Atlantic coast but also ensured easy shipment of goods.

The Calverts recruited artisans and farmers (mainly Protestant) as well as wealthy merchants and aristocrats (mostly Catholic) to settle the colony. Although conflict continued to fester between the Catholic elite and the Protestant majority, Governor Calvert convinced the Maryland assembly to pass the Act of Religious Toleration in 1649, granting religious freedom to all Christians.

Taken together, Maryland and Virginia formed the Chesapeake region of the English empire. Both colonies relied on tobacco to produce the wealth that fueled their growth, and both introduced African labor to complement the supply of white indentured servants. Still, neither colony had yet developed a legal code of slavery. From 1650 on, however, improved economic conditions in England meant fewer English men and women were willing to gamble on a better life in North America. Thus even though the number of African laborers remained small until late in the century, colonial leaders considered measures to increase their control over the African population. Thus in 1660 the House of Burgesses passed an act that allowed black laborers to be enslaved and in 1662 defined slavery as an inherited status passed on from mothers to children. In 1664 Maryland followed suit. The slow march toward full-blown racial slavery had begun. In legalizing human bondage, Virginia legislators followed a model established in Barbados, where the booming sugar industry spurred the development of plantation slavery. By 1660 Barbados had become the first English colony with a black majority population. Twenty years later, there were seventeen slaves for every white indentured servant on Barbados. The growth of slavery on the island depended almost wholly on imports from Africa since slaves there died faster than they could reproduce themselves. In the context of high death rates, brutal working conditions, and massive imports, Barbados systematized its slave code, defining enslaved Africans as chattel—that is, as mere property more akin to livestock than to human beings.

Explore ▶

In Documents 2.2 and 2.3, analyze the experiences of indentured servants in Maryland.

While African slaves would become, in time, a crucial component of the Chesapeake labor force, indentured servants made up the majority of bound workers in Virginia and Maryland for most of the seventeenth century. They labored under harsh conditions, and punishment for even minor infractions could be severe. They were beaten, whipped, and branded for a variety of behaviors. Some white servants made common cause with black laborers who worked side by side with them on tobacco plantations. They ran away together, stole goods from their masters, and planned uprisings and rebellions.

By the 1660s and 1670s, the population of former servants who had become free formed a growing and increasingly unhappy class. Most were struggling economically, working as common laborers or tenants on large estates. Those who managed to move west and claim land on the frontier were confronted by hostile Indians like the Susquehannock. Virginia governor Sir William Berkeley, who levied taxes to support nine forts on the frontier, had little patience with the complaints of these colonists. The labor demands of wealthy tobacco planters needed to be met, and frontier settlers' call for an aggressive Indian policy would hurt the profitable deerskin trade with the Algonquian Indians.

In late 1675, conflict erupted when frontier settlers attacked Indians in the region. Unlike colonial leaders back east, men on the frontier generally considered all Indians hostile. Rather than attacking only the Susquehannock nation, they also assaulted Indian communities allied with the English. When a large force of local Virginia militiamen did surround a Susquehannock village, they ignored pleas for peace and murdered five chiefs. Susquehannock warriors retaliated with raids on frontier farms. Despite the outbreak of open warfare, Governor Berkeley still refused to send troops, so disgruntled farmers turned to Nathaniel Bacon. Bacon came from a wealthy family and was related to Berkeley by marriage. But he defied the governor's authority and called up an army to attack Indians across the colony. **Bacon's Rebellion** had begun. Frontier farmers formed an important part of Bacon's coalition. But affluent planters who had been left out of Berkeley's inner circle also joined Bacon in hopes of gaining access to power and profits. And bound laborers, black and white, assumed that anyone who opposed the governor was on their side.

In the summer of 1676, Governor Berkeley declared Bacon guilty of treason. Rather than waiting to be captured, Bacon led his army toward Jamestown. Berkeley then arranged a hastily called election to undercut the rebellion. Even though Berkeley had rescinded the right of men without property to vote, Bacon's supporters won control of the House of Burgesses, and Bacon won new adherents. These included "news wives," lower-class women who spread information (and rumors) about oppressive conditions to aid the rebels. As Bacon and his followers marched across Virginia, his men plundered the plantations of Berkeley and his supporters. In September they reached Jamestown after the governor and his administration fled across Chesapeake Bay. The rebels burned the capital to the ground, victory seemingly theirs.

Only a month later, however, Bacon died of dysentery, and the movement he formed unraveled. Governor Berkeley quickly reclaimed power. He hanged twenty-three rebel leaders and incited his followers to plunder the estates of planters who had supported Bacon. But he could not undo the damage to Indian relations on the Virginia frontier. Bacon's army had killed or enslaved hundreds of once-friendly Indians and left behind a tragic and bitter legacy.

COMPARATIVE ANALYSIS

Indentured Servants In Maryland

Indentured servants, who generally worked for tobacco farmers in seventeenth-century Maryland, had little control over their lives. They could ask local courts or county councils, however, to intervene if they were severely abused. In Document 2.2 Sarah Tailer accuses her master and mistress of physical abuse. Although she did not win this case, evidence of repeated abuse led the court to free her two years later. In Document 2.3 several male servants charge their master with providing them insufficient food. Many of the witnesses in such cases were other servants, while those hearing the cases were property-owning white men.

Document 2.2

Sarah Tailer Charges Captain and Mrs. Thomas Bradnox with Abuse, 1659

A Court holden on Kent the first day of October 1659

Sarah Tailer Complaineth to the Majestrate mr Joseph [W]ickes of divers wronges & abuses given her by her Master and Mrs, Capt Thomas Bradnox & Mary his wife. . . .

John Jenkins sworne in Court Examined saith That he never saw Capt Bradnox or his wife strike his Servant Sarah Tailer with either Bulls pisle [whip] or Rope but he saw the said Sarah have a blacke place crosse one of her shoulders & this Deponent heard her Mrs give her som bad words. . . .

Tobias [W]ells on oath saith that he saw Sarah Tailer Stript & on her backe he saw severall blacke spotts and on her Arme a great black spott about as broad as his hand. . . .

Mr Joseph [W]ickes doth Informe the Court that Mrs Mary Bradnox broake the peace in strikeinge her Sarvant before him beinge a Majestrate, And on the time when the said Sarvant was there to make her Complaint which the said [M]r [W]ickes could not in Justice passe by or suffer, which was one blow or stroke with a Ropes ende.

Source: J. Hall Pleasants, ed., *Archives of Maryland*, vol. 54, *Proceedings of the County Courts of Kent, 1648–1676* (Baltimore: Maryland Historical Society, 1937), 167–69.

An even more important consequence of the rebellion was that wealthy planters and investors realized the depth of frustration among poor whites who were willing to make common cause with their black counterparts. Having regained power, the planter elite worked to crush any such interracial alliance. Virginia legislators began to improve the conditions and rights of poor white settlers while imposing new restrictions on blacks. At nearly the same time, in an effort to meet the growing demand for labor in the West Indies and the Chesapeake, King Charles II chartered the Royal African Company in 1672 to carry enslaved Africans to North America.

Document 2.3

John Smith et al. Petition the Governor and Council for Redress, 1663

To the hon[ora]ble the Go[v]ernor & Councell

The humble Pet[itio]n of John Smith, Richard Gibbs, Samuel Coplen,

Samuel Styles &c: Ser[v]ents to W Rich: Preston Senior Sheweth

That Mr Preston doth not allow yor Pet[itione]rs sufficient Pro[v]isions for the [e]nablemt to our worke, but streightens us soe far that wee are brought soe weake, wee are not able to performe the [e]mploymts hee putts us uppon. Wee desyre but soe much as is sufficient, but hee will allow us nothing but Beanes & Bread. These premises seriously considered yor Pet[itione]rs humbly addresse themsel[v]es unto yor honors to relei[v]e our wants, & provide tht Our Master may afford us such sustenance as may enable us to goe through wth our labors for the future, & yor Pet[itione]rs shall as in duty bownd E[v]er pray &c:

[U]ppon these Pet[itio]ns of Mr Richard Preston [who complained of his servants' refusal to work] & his ser[v]ants, & uppon Examina[tio]n of the s[ai]d ser[v]ants prsent in Court: The Court

taking the same into serious Considera[ti]on, Ordered tht these ser[v]ants now Petitioning (Viz) John Smith, Richard Gibbs, Samuel Coeplen, Samuel Styles, Henry Gorslett, & Thomas Broxam bee forthwth whipped wth 30 Lashes each. Then the Court further ordered tht Two of the mildest (not soe refractory as the other) should be pardoned & tht those two soe pardoned should inflict the censure or punishm[en]t on their other Companions. And thereupon the s[ai]d Ser[v]ants kneeling on their knees, asking & Cra[v]ing forgi[v]enes of their Master and the Court for their former misdemeanor & promising all complyance & obedience hereafter, Their Penalty is remitted or suspended att prsent. But they are to bee of the good beha[v]ior towards their s[ai]d Master e[v]er hereafter (uppon their promise of amendmt as aforesd).

Source: J. Hall Pleasant, ed., *Archives of Maryland*, vol. 49, *Proceedings of the Provincial Court* (Baltimore: Maryland Historical Society, 1932), 9–10, http://msa.maryland.gov/megafile/msa/speccol/sc2900/sc2908/000001/000049/html/am49--9.html.

Interpret the Evidence

1. How would you compare the complaints of Sarah Tailer and those of John Smith and his fellow servants?
2. What do the rulings in these two cases suggest about the power of indentured servants to defend themselves against abuse by masters and mistresses?

Put It in Context

Why was indentured servitude so important to Maryland in the 1650s and 1660s, and why was it gradually replaced by African slavery by the end of the century?

The English Compete for West Indies Possessions.

While tobacco held great promise in Virginia, investors were eager to find other lucrative exports. Some turned their sights on the West Indies. In the 1620s, the English developed more permanent settlements on St. Christopher, Barbados, and Nevis. Barbados quickly became the most attractive of these West Indies colonies. English migrants settled Barbados in growing numbers, bringing in white indentured servants, many Irish and Scotch, to cultivate tobacco and cotton and raise livestock.

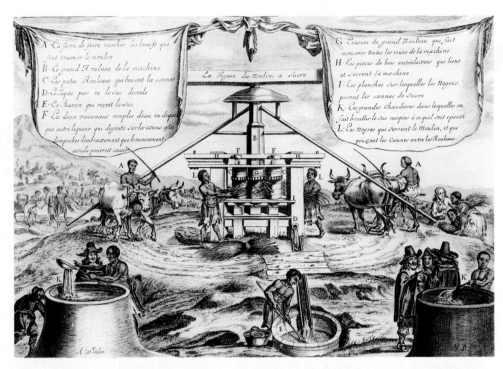

Sugar Manufacturing in the West Indies This 1665 engraving depicts the use of slave labor in the production of sugar in the Antilles (West Indies). As shown in the illustration, the Dutch and English used slaves to plant sugarcane and then cut, press, and boil it to produce molasses. The molasses was turned into rum and refined sugar, which were among America's most profitable exports. Private Collection/ Bridgeman Images

In the 1630s, falling tobacco prices resulted in economic stagnation on Barbados. By that time, however, a few forward-looking planters were already considering another avenue to wealth: sugarcane. English and European consumers absorbed as much sugar as the market could provide, but producing sugar was difficult, expensive, and labor-intensive. In addition, the sugar that was sent from America needed further refinement in Europe before being sold to consumers. The Dutch had built the best refineries in Europe, but their small West Indies colonies could not supply sufficient raw material. By 1640 they formed a partnership with English planters, offering them the knowledge and financing to cultivate sugar on Barbados, which then would be refined in the Netherlands. That decision reshaped the economic and political landscape of North America and intensified competition for both land and labor.

REVIEW & RELATE

How did the Virginia colony change and evolve between 1607 and the 1670s?

How did the growth of the English colonies on the mainland and in the West Indies shape conflicts in Virginia and demands for labor throughout North America?

Pilgrims and Puritans Settle New England

Along with merchants, planters, and indentured servants, religious dissenters also traveled to North America. Critics of the Church of England formed a number of congregations in the early seventeenth century, and some sought refuge in New England. One such group, the **Pilgrims** (also known as Separatists), landed on the Massachusetts coast in 1620 and established a permanent settlement at Plymouth. Their goal was to establish a religious community wholly separate from the Anglican Church. The Puritans, who hoped to purify rather than separate from the Church of England, arrived a decade later with plans to develop their own colony. Over the next two decades, New England colonists prospered, but they also confronted internal dissent and conflicts with local Indians.

Pilgrims Arrive in Massachusetts. In the 1610s, to raise capital, the Virginia Company began offering legal charters to groups of private investors, who were promised their own tract of land in the Virginia colony with minimal company oversight. One such charter was purchased by a group of English Pilgrims who wanted to form a separate church and community in a land untainted by Catholicism, Anglicanism, or European cosmopolitanism. Thirty-five Pilgrims from Leiden in the Dutch Republic and several dozen from England set sail on the *Mayflower* from Plymouth, England, in September 1620.

Battered by storms, the ship veered off course, landing at Cape Cod in present-day Massachusetts in early December. Before leaving the ship, the settlers, led by William Bradford, signed a pact to form a "civill body politick," which they considered necessary because they were settling in a region where they had no legal authority. The pact, known as the **Mayflower Compact**, was the first written constitution adopted in North America. It followed the Separatist model of a self-governing religious congregation.

After several forays along the coast, the Pilgrims located an uninhabited village surrounded by cornfields where they established their new home, Plymouth. Uncertain of native intentions, the Pilgrims were unsettled by sightings of Indians. They did not realize that a smallpox epidemic in the area only two years earlier had killed nearly 90 percent of the local Wampanoag population. Indeed, fevers and other diseases proved far more deadly to the settlers than did Indians. By the spring of 1621, only half of the 102 Pilgrims remained alive.

Desperate to find food, the survivors were stunned when two English-speaking Indians—Samoset and Squanto—appeared at Plymouth that March. Both had been captured as young boys by English explorers, and they now negotiated a fragile peace between the Pilgrims and Massasoit, chief of the Wampanoag tribe. Although concerned by the power of English guns, Massasoit hoped to create an alliance that would assist him against his traditional native enemies. With Wampanoag assistance, the surviving Pilgrims soon regained their health.

In the summer of 1621, reinforcements arrived from England, and the next year the Pilgrims received a charter granting them rights to Plymouth Plantation and a degree of self-government. Although some Pilgrims hoped to convert the Indians, other leaders favored a more aggressive stance toward hostile Indians. One Indian nation, the Massachusetts, posed an especially serious threat. So in 1623 Captain Miles Standish led an attack on a Massachusetts tribal village after kidnapping and killing the chief and his younger brother. Standish's strategy, though controversial, ensured that Massasoit, the colonists' Wampanoag ally, was now the most powerful chief in the region.

The Puritan Migration. As the Pilgrims gradually expanded their colony during the 1620s, a new group of English dissenters, the **Puritans**, made plans to develop their own settlement. As religious dissenters, Puritans faced persecution in England, but they also believed that their country's church and government had grown corrupt and was being chastened by an all-powerful God. During the early seventeenth century, the English population boomed but harvests failed, leading to famine, crime, unemployment, and inflation. The enclosure movement, in which landlords fenced in fields and hired a few laborers and tenants to replace a large number of peasant farmers, increased the number of landless vagrants. At the same time, the English cloth industry nearly collapsed under the weight of competition from abroad. In the Puritans' view, all of these problems were divine punishments for the nation's sins.

The Puritans envisioned New England as a safe haven from God's wrath. Under Puritan lawyer John Winthrop's leadership, a group of affluent Puritans obtained a royal charter for the Massachusetts Bay Company. To the Puritans, however, New England was more than just a place of safety. Unlike the Pilgrims, they believed that England and the Anglican Church could be redeemed. By prospering spiritually and materially in America, they could establish a model "City upon a Hill" that would then inspire reform among residents of the mother country.

About one-third of English Puritans chose to leave their homeland for North America. They were better supplied, more prosperous, and more numerous than either their Pilgrim or Jamestown predecessors. Following John Smith's recommendations, the settlers, arriving on seventeen ships, included ministers, merchants, craftsmen, and farmers. Many Puritans sailed with entire families. The community benefited from being well supplied, including women who traditionally nursed their families, and settling in a cold climate that reduced the spread of disease. These factors ensured the rapid growth of the colony.

The first Puritan settlers arrived on the coast north of Plymouth in 1630 and named their community Boston, after the port city in England from which they had departed. Once established, they relocated the Massachusetts Bay Company's capital and records to New England, thereby converting their commercial charter into the founding document of a self-governing colony. They instituted a new kind of polity in which adult male church members participated in the election of a governor, deputy governor, and legislature. Although the Puritans suffered a difficult first winter, they quickly recovered and soon cultivated sufficient crops to feed themselves and a steady stream of new migrants. During the 1630s, some eighteen thousand Puritans migrated to New England. Even without a cash crop like tobacco or sugar, the Puritan colony flourished.

Eager to take advantage of the abundant land, the close-knit community spread quickly beyond its original boundaries. The legislature was thus forced early on to develop policies for establishing townships with governing bodies that supported a local church and school. By the time the migration of Puritans slowed around 1640, the settlers had turned their colony into a thriving commercial center. They shipped codfish, lumber, grain, pork, and cheese to England in exchange for manufactured goods and to the West Indies for rum and molasses. This trade, along with the healthy climate, relatively egalitarian distribution of property, and more equal ratio of women to men, ensured a stable and prosperous colony.

Puritans also sought friendly relations with some local natives, particularly the neighboring Massachusetts tribe, who were longtime enemies of the Pilgrims' allies, the

Wampanoags. Many Puritans hoped that their Indian neighbors might be converted to Christianity. Puritan missionaries taught their pupils how to read the Bible, and a few students attended Harvard College, founded in 1636. In an effort to wean converts from their traditional customs and beliefs, missionary John Eliot created "praying towns." There Christian Indians could live among others who shared their faith while being protected from English settlers seeking to exploit them. Yet most "praying Indians" continued to embrace traditional rituals and beliefs alongside Christian practices.

The Puritan Worldview.

Opposed to the lavish rituals and hierarchy of the Church of England and believing that few Anglicans truly felt the grace of God, Puritans set out to establish a simpler form of worship. They focused on their inner lives and on the purity of their church and community. Puritans followed Calvin, believing in an all-knowing God whose true Word was presented in the Bible. The biblically sanctioned church was a congregation formed by a group of believers who made a covenant with God. Only a small minority of people, known as Saints, were granted God's grace.

Whether one was a Saint and thereby saved was predetermined by and known only to God. Still, some Puritans believed that the chosen were likely to lead a saintly life. Visible signs included individuals' passionate response to the preaching of God's Word, their sense of doubt and despair over their own soul, and that wonderful sense of reassurance that came with God's "saving grace." God's hand in the world appeared in nature as well. Comets and eclipses were considered "remarkable providences." But so, too, was a smallpox

Mrs. Elizabeth Freake and Baby Mary
This anonymous 1674 portrait shows Elizabeth Freake, the wife of merchant John Freake, and their eighth child, Mary. Large families helped ensure Puritan expansion and financial success. Here Elizabeth and her daughter capture Puritan simplicity in their white head coverings and aprons. But they display their family's wealth and John Freake's commercial ties through their silk gowns and embroidered cloth. Worcester Art Museum, Massachusetts, USA/Bridgeman Images

epidemic that killed several thousand Massachusetts Indians in 1633–1634 and thereby opened up land for Puritan settlers.

Shared religious beliefs helped forge a unified community where faith guided civil as well as spiritual decisions. While ministers were discouraged from holding political office, political leaders were devout Puritans who were expected to promote a godly society. Such leaders determined who got land, how much, and where; they also served as judge and jury for those accused of crimes or sins. Their leadership was largely successful. Even if colonists differed over who should get the most fertile strip of land, they agreed on basic principles. Still, almost from the beginning, certain Puritans challenged some of the community's fundamental beliefs and, in the process, the community itself.

Dissenters Challenge Puritan Authority.

In the early 1630s, Roger Williams, a Salem minister, criticized Puritan leaders for not being sufficiently pure in their rejection of the Church of England and the English monarchy. He preached that not all the Puritan leaders were Saints and that some were bound for damnation. By 1635 Williams was forced out of Salem and moved south with his followers to found Providence in the area that became Rhode Island. Believing that there were very few Saints in the world, Williams and his followers accepted that one must live among those who were not saved. Thus unlike Massachusetts Bay, Providence welcomed Quakers, Baptists, and Jews to the community, and Williams's followers insisted on a strict separation of church and state. Williams also forged alliances with the Narragansetts, the most powerful Indian nation in the region.

A year after Williams's departure, Anne Hutchinson was accused of sedition, or trying to overthrow the government by challenging colonial leaders. She was put on trial in November 1637. An eloquent orator, Hutchinson ultimately claimed that her authority to challenge the Puritan leadership came from "an immediate revelation" from God, "the voice of his own spirit to my soul." Since Puritans believed that God spoke only through the intermediary of properly appointed male ministers, her claim was condemned as heretical.

Hutchinson was seen as a threat not only because of her religious beliefs but also because she was a woman. The Reverend Hugh Peter, for example, reprimanded her at trial: "You have stept out of your place, you have rather bine a Husband than a Wife and a preacher than a Hearer; and a Magistrate than a Subject." Many considered her challenge to Puritan authority especially serious because she also challenged traditional gender hierarchies. After being banished from Massachusetts Bay, Hutchinson and her followers joined Williams's Rhode Island colony.

Wars in Old and New England.

As Anne Hutchinson and Roger Williams confronted religious leaders, Puritans and Pilgrims faced serious threats from their Indian neighbors as well. The Pequot nation, which was among the most powerful tribes in New England, had been allies of the English for several years. Yet some Puritans feared that the Pequots, who opposed the colonists' continued expansion, "would cause all the Indians in the country to join to root out all the English." Using the death of two Englishmen in 1636 to justify a military expedition against the Pequots, the colonists went on the attack. The Narragansetts, whom Roger Williams had befriended, allied with the English in the **Pequot War**. After months of bloody conflict, the English and their Indian allies launched a brutal attack on a Pequot fort in May 1637 that left some four hundred men, women, and children dead.

Explore ▶

To understand how the English captain who led the final assault on the Pequot depicted the event, see Document 2.4.

Captain John Underhill | Attack at Mystic, Connecticut, 1638

The Pequot War culminated when the English and their Narragansett allies brutally attacked a Pequot fort at Mystic, Connecticut, in 1637. John Underhill, an English captain who helped lead the raid, claimed that 400 Pequots were killed during the short but bloody battle. By the end of the war, most Pequots had either died, been sold into slavery, or fled the region. The following image, an engraving created by Underhill himself, gives the English perspective on the attack.

Document 2.4

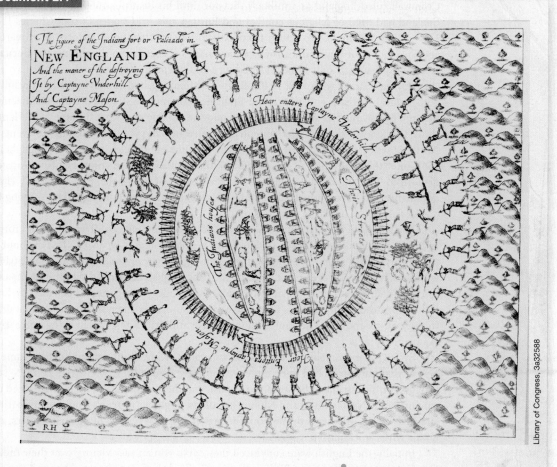

Library of Congress, 3a32588

Interpret the Evidence

1. According to this image, how did the English defeat the Pequots, and what role did their Narragansett allies play?
2. How had the Pequots attempted to defend themselves and their community?

Put It in Context

How might this image affect relations between the English and the Narragansett and other Indian allies?

Puritans in England were soon engaged in armed conflict as well, but this time against other Englishmen. Differences over issues of religion, taxation, and royal authority had strained relations between Parliament and the crown for decades, as James I (r. 1603–1625) and his son Charles I (r. 1625–1649) sought to consolidate their own power at Parliament's expense. In 1642 the relationship between Parliament and King Charles I broke down completely, and the country descended into civil war. Oliver Cromwell, a Puritan, emerged as the leader of the Protestant parliamentary forces, and after several years of fighting, he claimed victory. Charles I was executed, Parliament established a republican common-wealth, and bishops and elaborate rituals were banished from the Church of England. Cromwell ruled England as a military dictator until his death in 1658. By then, much of England had tired of religious conflict and Puritan rule, so Charles I's son, Charles II (r. 1660–1685), was invited to return from exile on the continent and restore the monarchy and the Church of England. In 1660, when Charles II acceded to the throne, the Puritans recognized that their only hope for building a godly republic lay in North America.

During the civil war of the 1640s, English settlements had quickly spread as a result of both natural increase and migration. English communities stretched from Connecticut through Massachusetts and Rhode Island and into Maine and what became New Hamp-shire. The English king and Parliament, embroiled in war, paid little attention to events in North America, allowing these New England colonies to develop with little oversight. In 1664, after the restoration of the monarchy, the English wrested control of New Amster-dam from the Dutch and renamed it New York. By 1674 the English could claim dominance—in population, trade, and politics—over the other European powers vying for empires along the northern Atlantic coast.

The spread of English control was still contested, however, by diverse Indian groups. In New England, only 15,000 to 16,000 native people remained by 1670, a loss of about 80 percent over fifty years. Meanwhile the English population reached more than 50,000, with settlers claiming ever more land. In 1671 the English demanded that the Wampano-ags, who had been their allies since the 1620s, surrender their guns and be ruled by Eng-lish law. Instead, many Indians hid their weapons and, over the next several years, raided frontier farms and killed several settlers. English authorities responded by hanging three Wampanoag men.

By 1675 the Wampanoag chief Metacom, called King Philip by the English, came to believe that Europeans had to be forced out of New England if Indians were going to sur-vive. As conflict escalated between the English and the Wampanoags, Metacom gained the support of the Narragansett and Nipmuck Indians. Together warriors from the three tribes attacked white settlements throughout the region, burning fields, killing male settlers, and taking wives and children captive.

Initially, the English were convinced they could win an easy victory over their Indian foes, but the war, called **King Philip's War** by the English, dragged on and became increas-ingly brutal on both sides. Some 1,000 English settlers were killed and dozens were taken captive during the war. Metacom's forces attacked Plymouth and Providence and marched within twenty miles of Boston. The English meanwhile made an alliance with Mohawks, Pequots, Mohegans, and praying Indians (mostly Christian Wampanoags) in the region, who ambushed Narragansett forces. The English attacked enemy villages, killing hundreds of Indians and selling hundreds more into slavery in the West Indies, including Metacom's wife and son. Indian losses were catastrophic on both sides of the conflict, as food short-ages and disease combined with military deaths to kill as many as 4,500 men, women, and children. About a quarter of the remaining Indian population of New England died in 1675–1676.

The war finally ended when Wampanoag, Narragansett, and Nipmuck forces ran short of guns and powder and the Mohawks ambushed and killed Metacom. **See Document Project 2: King Philip's War, page 64.** The remaining Algonquian-speaking Indians moved north and gradually intermarried with tribes allied with the French. As the carnage of the war spilled into New York, Iroquois leaders and colonists met at Albany in 1677 in hopes of salvaging their lucrative fur trade. There they formed an alliance, the Covenant Chain, to forestall future conflict. In the following decades, furs and land would continue to define the complex relations between Indians and Europeans across the north-ern regions of North America.

REVIEW & RELATE

- How did Puritan religious views shape New England's development?

- Why did conflict between New England settlers and the region's Indians escalate over the course of the seventeenth century?

Conclusion: European Empires in **North America**

When John Smith died in 1631, the English were just begin-ning to establish colonies in North America. Smith realized early on that a successful empire in Virginia required a differ-ent approach than the Spanish had taken in Mexico and Peru. North American colonies demanded permanent settlement, long-term investment, and hard work. Liberal land policies, self-government, and trade formed the touchstones of colo-nies along the north Atlantic coast. Colonies in New England, established by Pilgrims and Puritans, were especially successful. These religious dissenters benefited from liberal land policies, self-government, and trade. In addition, their large families, diverse skills, and settlement in relatively healthy northern climes aided their success.

European colonists found ways to prosper in Virginia, Quebec, and New Amsterdam as well as Massachusetts Bay, but they still faced daunting choices. Most important, should they create alliances with local Indians for sustenance and trade, or should they seek to dominate them and take what they needed? Smith, Miles Standish, and many others sup-ported an aggressive policy, much like that of Spain. In Virginia this policy ended the most serious threats from the Powhatan Confederacy by the 1640s. But many Europeans, especially in New England, New Amsterdam, and Canada, advocated a less violent approach. A few French Jesuit priests and Puritans like Roger Williams focused on the spiritual and material benefits of conversion. Far more argued that building alliances was the most effective means of advancing trade and gaining land, furs, and other goods val-ued by Europeans.

Throughout the early and mid-seventeenth century, English, Dutch, and French colonists profited from trade relations and military alliances with Indian nations. Nonetheless, European demands for land fueled repeated conflicts with tribes like the Pequot in the 1630s and the Wampanoag and Narragansett in the 1670s. The exhaustion of furs along the Atlantic coast only increased the vulnerability of those Indians who could no longer provide this valuable trade item. Already devastated by European-borne diseases, their very survival was at stake. Indians in New Amsterdam as well as New England resisted the loss of their land and livelihood, often with violence. It was such violence that led to the death of Anne Hutchinson. In 1642 she and her six youngest children moved to the outskirts of New Netherland after the death of her husband. A year later, Anne and all but one of her children were massacred by Indians outraged by Dutch governor William Kieft's 1643 slaughter of peaceful Indians on Manhattan Island.

Still, as European settlements reached deeper into North America in the late seventeenth century and early eighteenth century, their prosperity continued to depend on trade goods and land that were often in Indian hands. At the same time, a growing demand for labor led wealthier settlers to seek an increased supply of indentured servants from Europe and enslaved workers from Africa. Over the next half century, relations between wealthy and poor settlers, between whites and blacks, between settlers and Indians, and among the European nations that vied for empire would grow only more complicated.

TIMELINE OF EVENTS

1517	Protestant Reformation begins
1530s	England breaks with the Roman Catholic Church
1545–1563	Council of Trent
1598	Acoma pueblo uprising
	Edict of Nantes
1607	Jamestown founded
1608	French settle in Quebec
1609	Dutch settle on the Hudson River
1612–1614	Tobacco cultivation begins in Virginia
1619	First Africans arrive in Virginia
1620	Pilgrims found Plymouth settlement
1624	Dutch establish New Amsterdam
1630	Puritans found Massachusetts Bay colony
1632	Maryland founded
1635	Roger Williams moves to Rhode Island
1636–1637	Pequot War
1637	Anne Hutchinson banished from Massachusetts Bay colony
1642–1649	English civil war
1660	Monarchy restored in England
1660–1664	Virginia and Maryland establish lifelong, inherited slavery
1664	Dutch surrender New Amsterdam to the English
1675–1676	King Philip's War
1676	Bacon's Rebellion

KEY TERMS

Protestantism, *39*
Church of England, *40*
Jamestown, *46*
Powhatan Confederacy, *47*
House of Burgesses, *48*
indentured servants, *48*
Bacon's Rebellion, *51*
Pilgrims, *55*
Mayflower Compact, *55*
Puritans, *56*
Pequot War, *58*
King Philip's War, *60*

REVIEW & RELATE

1. How did the Protestant Reformation shape the course of European expansion in the Americas?

2. How did the French and Dutch colonies in North America differ from the Spanish empire to the south?

3. How did the Virginia colony change and evolve between 1607 and the 1670s?

4. How did the growth of the English colonies on the mainland and in the West Indies shape conflicts in Virginia and demands for labor throughout North America?

5. How did Puritan religious views shape New England's development?

6. Why did conflict between New England settlers and the region's Indians escalate over the course of the seventeenth century?

King Philip's War

Despite decades of relative peace between Indians and colonists, tensions escalated during the 1660s. Metacom, whom colonists called King Philip, became grand sachem (primary chief) of the Wampanoag Confederacy in 1662, when New England Indians had lost both land and population. Especially troubled by English encroachments on native lands, King Philip forged an alliance that brought together two-thirds of the region's Indian population, including the Narragansett. This New England Confederation coordinated attacks on white settlements, burning fields, taking captives, and killing male colonists.

In 1675 Indian attacks on New England towns escalated. The English, in turn, sold Indians into slavery (Document 2.5). As relations between settlers and Indians deteriorated, the Rhode Island colony sent representatives to meet with King Philip in June. Some colonists and Indian leaders also met independently to discuss the growing conflict (Documents 2.6 and 2.7). However, these diplomatic efforts failed, and Indian attacks increased throughout the summer. In September, the New England Confederation declared war. Fighting continued for a year, leading to the deaths of 1,000 colonists and more than 4,000 Indians. Edward Randolph, a customs agent, criticized both colonists and Indians for their parts in the conflict (Document 2.8). The English, who had forged alliances with the surviving Pequot and powerful Mohawk nations, finally gained the upper hand in August 1676. Then soldiers led by Captain Benjamin Church ambushed King Philip near Bristol, Rhode Island. Philip was shot and killed by John Alderman, an Indian ally of the colonists, which signaled the end of the war. Six years later, Mary Rowlandson, who had been captured in 1675, published an account of her captivity, which was widely read by New Englanders (Document 2.9).

Because there are fewer Indian sources, historians have struggled to develop a balanced picture of the war. William Nahaton (Document 2.5) learned firsthand that the English would go to great lengths to devastate Indian communities, Christian or otherwise. Some other documents also provide information about Indian perceptions of the war even though written by the English.

Document 2.5

William Nahaton | Petition to Free an Indian Slave, 1675

The English sold a number of Indians into slavery before and during King Philip's War. Many English colonists petitioned the government of Massachusetts Bay to stop this practice. As the following document indicates, Indians also tried to find recourse through petitions. William Nahaton, an Indian who had embraced Christianity, sent this petition to convince colonial leaders to release a relative who was about to be sold into slavery in the West Indies.

To the honored counsel now siting at boston to the humble petition of william [n]ahaton hee humbly sheweth.

I have seing a woman taken by the mohegins and now brought to boston which woman although she did belong to [King] phillip his Company yet shee is a kinn to me and all so to john huntar as severall of the indians of punkapoag do know[.] my humble and right request there fore to the Renowned Counsel is that if it may stand with there plesure and with out futur inconvenience her Life may be spared and her Liberty granted under such conditions as the honored Counsel see most fit: shee being a woman whatever her mind hath been it is very probable she hath not dun much mischefe and if the honored counsel shall plese so grant me that favor I shall understand to leve her at punkapoag[.] . . . I shall obtaine so much favor from the honored counsel which will further oblige him who is your honored to command william [n]ahaton.

Source: Massachusetts State Archives, Massachusetts Archives, Series 45X, Vol. 176.

Source: Massachusetts State Archives, Massachusetts Archives, Series 45X, Vol. 176.

Document 2.6

Benjamin Church | A Visit with Awashonks, Sachem of the Sakonnet, 1716

Benjamin Church was an aide to Plymouth governor Josiah Winslow. But Church was also viewed as a fair man by local Indian leaders. Thus in June 1675, before the outbreak of war, Awashonks, the sachem of the Sakonnet Indians, invited Church to meet with her. He offered his advice on how best to secure the protection of her people. Although the Sakonnets initially allied with King Philip, they later switched to the English side. Meanwhile, as captain in the Plymouth militia, Church adopted Indian fighting tactics, and his unit conducted many successful raids, eventually ambushing King Philip. In 1716 Church's son, Thomas, published an account of the war from his father's notes.

The next Spring advancing, while Mr. Church was diligently settling his new Farm, stocking, leasing, and disposing of his Affairs, and had a fine prospect of doing no small things; and hoping that his good success would be inviting unto other good Men to become his Neighbours; Behold! the rumor of a War between the English and the Natives gave check to his projects. People began to be very jealous of the Indians, and indeed they had no small reason to suspect that they had form'd a design of War upon the English. Mr. Church had it daily suggested to him that the Indians were plotting a bloody design. That Philip the great Mount-hope Sachem was leader therein: and so it prov'd, he was sending his Messengers to all the Neighbouring Sachems, to ingage them in a Confederacy with him in the War.

Among the rest he sent Six Men to Awashonks Squaw-Sachem of the Sogkonate [Sakonnet] Indians, to engage her in his Interests: Awashonks so far listened unto them as to call her Subjects together, to make a great Dance, which is the custom of that Nation when they advise about Momentous Affairs. But what does Awashonks do, but sends away two of her Men that well understood the English Language . . . to invite Mr. Church to the Dance. Mr. Church upon the Invitation, immediately takes with him Charles Hazelton his Tennants Son, who well understood the Indian Language, and rid [rode] down to the Place appointed: Where they found hundreds of Indians gathered together from all Parts of her Dominion. Awashonks her self in a foaming Sweat was leading the Dance. But she was no sooner sensible of Mr. Churches arrival, but she broke off, sat down, calls her Nobles round her, orders Mr. Church to be invited into her presence. Complements being past, and each one taking Seats. She told him, King Philip had sent Six Men of his with two of her People that had been over at Mount-hope, to draw her into a confederacy with him in a War with the English. . . .

Then Mr. Church turn'd to Awashonks, and told her, if Philip were resolv'd to make War, her best way would be to knock those Six Mount-hopes on the head, and shelter her self under the Protection of the English: upon which the Mount-hopes were for the present Dumb. . . .

Then he told Awashonks he thought it might be most advisable for her to send to the Governour of Plymouth, and shelter her self, and People under his Protection. She lik'd his advice, and desired him to go on her behalf to the Plymouth Government, which he consented to: And at parting advised her what ever she did, not to desert the English Interest, to joyn with her Neighbours in a Rebellion which would certainly prove fatal to her. He mov'd none of his Goods from his House that there might not be the least umbrage from such an Action. She thank'd him for his advice, and sent two of her Men to guard him to his House; which when they came there, urged him to take care to secure his Goods, which he refused for the reasons before mentioned. But desired the Indians that if what they feared should happen, they would take care of what he left, and directed them to a Place in the woods where they should dispose them; which they faithfully observed.

Source: Benjamin Church, *The History of King Philip's War* (Boston: John Kimball Wiggin, 1865), 5–11.

Document 2.7

John Easton | A Relation of the Indian War, 1675

As relations between English settlers and Indians grew more tense, a meeting was arranged for June 1675 between King Philip and John Easton, attorney general of the Rhode Island colony. At this meeting, Philip related the Indians' many complaints, which included the sale of liquor to Indians, the destruction of their crops, and their mistreatment under the colonial justice system. This meeting was unsuccessful in preventing further violence, however, and by the end of the month King Philip's War began.

Another Grievance was, when their King sold Land, the English would say, it was more than they agreed to, and a Writing must be prove against all them, and some of their Kings had dun Rong [done wrong] to sell so much. He left his Peopell [people] none, and some being given to Drunknes the English made them drunk and then cheated them in Bargains, but now their Kings were forewarned not for to part with Land, for nothing in Comparison to the Value thereof. Now home [some] the English had owned for King or Queen, they would disinherit, and make another King that would give or sell them these Lands; that now they had no Hopes left to keep any Land. Another Grievance, the English Catell [cattle] and Horses still increased; that when they removed 30 Miles from where English had any thing to do, they could not keep their Corn from being spoiled, they never being used to fence, and thought when the English bought Land of them they would have kept their Catell upon their owne Land. Another Grievance, the English were so eager to sell the Indians Lickers [liquor], that most of the Indians spent all in Drunknes, and then ravened upon the sober Indians, and they did believe often did hurt the English Cattel, and their King could not prevent it.

Source: John Easton, "A Relation of the Indian War," in *A Narrative of the Causes Which Led to Philip's Indian War, of 1675 and 1676* (Albany: J. Munsell, 1858), 13–15.

Document 2.8

Edward Randolph | Report on the War, 1676

Edward Randolph was an English customs official sent to the colonies to investigate colonial compliance with English laws. He criticized the Puritan colonies for pursuing political autonomy, like coining money and administering their own oath of allegiance, and called for greater control by Parliament. Randolph's reports to his superiors in London also described the outbreak of violence. He reported on what he saw as the causes of the war, criticizing the actions of both colonists and Indians.

Various are the reports and conjectures of the causes of the late Indian wars. Some impute it to an imprudent zeal in the magistrates of Boston to Christianize those heathens, before they were civilized, and enjoining them to the strict observation of their laws, which, to people so rude and licentious hath proved even intolerable; and that the more, for while the magistrates, for their profit, severely put the laws in execution against the Indians, the people on the other side, for lucre [money] and gain, intice and provoke the Indians to the breach thereof, especially to drunkenness, to which these people are so generally addicted, that they will strip themselves to the skin to have their fill of rum and brandy.

The Massachusetts government having made a law that every Indian being drunk should pay ten shillings or be whipped, according to the discretion of the magistrate, many of these poor people willingly offered their backs to the lash, to save their money. Upon the magistrate finding much trouble and no profit to arise to the government by whipping, did change that punishment of the whip into ten days' work, for such as would not or could not pay the fine of ten shillings; which did highly incense the Indians. . . .

Others impute the cause to arise from some injuries offered to the Sachem Philip; for he being possessed of a tract of land called Mount Hope, a very fertile, pleasant and rich soil, some English had a mind to dispossess him thereof, who, never wanting some pretence or other to attain their ends, complained of injuries done by Philip and his Indians to their stock and cattle. Whereupon the Sachem [King] Philip was often summoned to appear before the magistrates, sometimes imprisoned, and never released but upon parting with a considerable part of his lands.

But the government of the Massachusetts . . . do declare [the following acts] are the great and provoking evils which God hath given the barbarous heathen commission to rise against them: . . .

For men wearing long hair and perriwigs made of women's hair.

For women wearing borders of hair and cutting, curling and laying out their hair and disguising themselves by following strange fashions in their apparel.

For profaneness of the people in not frequenting their [church] meetings, and others going away before the blessing is pronounced.

For suffering the Quakers to dwell among them, and to set up their thresholds by God's thresholds, contrary to their old laws and resolutions, with many such reasons.

But whatever was the cause, the English have contributed very much to their misfortunes, for they first taught the Indians the use of arms and admitted them to be present at all their musters and trainings, and showed them how to handle, mend and fix their muskets, and have been constantly furnished with all sorts of arms by permission of the government, so that the Indians are become excellent fire-men.

Source: John Norris McClintock, *History of New Hampshire* (Boston: B. B. Russell, 1888), 79–80.

Mary Rowlandson | Narrative of Captivity, 1682

In February 1675, the Wampanoags and their allies attacked Lancaster, Massachusetts, setting fire to the town and killing many residents. Mary Rowlandson and her three children were captured and forced to flee with the Indians as they tried to outrun colonial forces. Mary's six-year-old daughter, Sarah, died, but she and her other children survived and were sold for ransom after eleven weeks and reunited with her husband, Joseph. After the war, she published an account of her captivity that highlighted the ways in which her Puritan faith helped her survive the ordeal. The book became one of the most popular publications of its era.

Upon a *Friday*, a little after noon we came to this River. When all the company was come up, and were gathered together, I thought to count the number of them, but they were so many, and being somewhat in motion, it was beyond my skil. In this travel, because of my wound, I was somewhat favored in my load; I carried only my knitting work and two quarts of parched meal: Being very faint I asked my mistriss to give me one spoonfull of the meal, but she would not give me a taste. They quickly fell to cutting dry trees, to make Rafts to carry them over the river: and soon my turn came to go over: By the advantage of some brush which they had laid upon the Raft to sit upon, I did not wet my foot (which many of themselves at the other end were mid-leg deep) which cannot but be acknowledged as a favour of God to my weakened body, it being a very cold time. I was not before acquainted with such kind of doings or dangers. *When thou passeth through the waters I will be with thee, and through the rivers they shall not overflow thee*, Isai. 43.2. A certain number of us got over the River that night, but it was the night after the Sabbath before all the company was got over. On the *Saturday* they boyled [boiled] an old Horses leg which they had got, and so we drank of the broth, as soon as they thought it was ready, and when it was almost all gone, they filled it up again.

The first week of my being among them, I hardly ate any thing; the second week, I found my stomach grow very faint for want of something; and yet it was very hard to get down their filthy trash: but the third week, though I could think how formerly my stomach would turn against this or that, and I could starve or die before I could eat such things, yet they were sweet and savory to my taste. I was at this time knitting a pair of white cotton stockins for my mistriss: and had not yet wrought upon a Sabbath day; when the Sabbath came they bade me go to work; I told them it was the Sabbath-day, and desired them to let me rest, and told them I would do as much more tomorrow; to which they answered me, they would break my face. And here I cannot but take notice of the strange providence of God in preserving the heathen: They were many hundreds, old and young, some sick, and some lame, many had *Papooses* [infants] at their backs, the greatest number at this time with us, were *Squaws*, and they travelled with all they had, bag and baggage, and yet they got over this River aforesaid; and on *Munday* they set their *Wigwams* on fire, and away they went: On that very day came the English Army after them to this River, and saw the smoak of their *Wigwams*, and yet this River put a stop to them. God did not give them courage or activity to go over after us; we were not ready for so great a mercy as victory and deliverance; if we had been, God would have found out a way for the *English* to have passed this River, as well as for the *Indians* with their *Squaws* and *Children*, and all their Luggage. . . .

   On Munday *(as I said) they set their* Wigwams *on fire, and went away.* It was a cold morning, and before us there was a great Brook with ice on it; some waded through it, up to the knees & higher, but others went till they came to a Beaver dam, and I amongst them, where through the good providence of God, I did not wet my foot. I went along that day mourning and lamenting, leaving farther my own Country, and travelling into the vast and howling *Wilderness*, and I understood something of *Lot's* Wife's Temptation, *when she looked back.* We came that day to a great Swamp, by the side of which we took up our lodging that night. When I came to the brow of the hill, that looked toward the Swamp, I thought we had been come to a great *Indian* Town (though there were none but our own Company). The *Indians* were as thick as the trees: it seemed as if there had been a thousand Hatchets going at once: if one looked before one, there was nothing but *Indians*, and behind one, nothing but *Indians*, and so on either hand, I my self in the midst, and no Christian soul near me, *and yet how hath the Lord preserved me in safety! Oh the experience that I have had of the goodness of God, to me and mine!*

Source: Henry S. Nourse, ed., *The Narrative of the Captivity and the Restoration of Mrs. Mary Rowlandson* (Lancaster, MA, 1903), 17–20.

Interpret the Evidence

1. What does William Nahaton's petition (Document 2.5) reveal about English leaders' main goal when dealing with the Indians, Christian and non-Christian?

2. What types of complaints did the Wampanoag have against the English, and which seem the most grievous (Documents 2.6, 2.7, and 2.8)? What do these complaints reveal about how the colonists viewed the Wampanoag?

3. What does Benjamin Church's meeting with Awashonks (Document 2.6) suggest about the difficult choices faced by some Indians and some colonists as war approached?

4. What does Edward Randolph's description of the causes of the war (Document 2.8) reveal about how the conflict might be viewed by Englishmen who were not colonists? How do his perceptions compare with those of Benjamin Church and John Easton (Documents 2.6 and 2.7)?

5. How does Mary Rowlandson employ religion to explain the events that happen to her during her captivity (Document 2.9)? What does the enormous popularity of her book indicate about the place of religion and of Indians in New England in the 1680s?

Put It in Context

King Philip's War was one of the bloodiest in American history. From these documents, what do you think accounts for its ferociousness?

What does the war and its outcome suggest about the trajectory of Indian-English relations from 1620 to 1680?

Colonial America amid Global Change

1680–1750

WINDOW TO THE PAST

Plan of a Slave Ship, 1794

By the mid-eighteenth century, slave traders were designing ships specifically for the purpose of transporting captured Africans to the Americas for sale.

This image of the English slave ship *Brooks*, based on a ship maker's diagram, was initially created as a broadside in 1789 by English opponents of the slave trade to highlight the trade's brutality. A few years later, a shipboard insurrection by enslaved Africans was added to the original diagram, suggesting one likely response to such brutality. ▸ To discover more about what this primary source can show us, see Document 3.2 on page 86.

REPRESENTATION of an INSURRECTION on board A SLAVE-SHIP.

Shewing how the crew fire upon the unhappy Slaves from behind the BARRICADO, erected on board all Slave ships, as a security whenever such commotions may happen.

See the privy councils report part I. Art: SLAVES.
Minutes of evidence before the House of Commons.
Wadstrom's Essay on Colonization § 472.

The Art Archive at Art Resource, NY

After reading this chapter you should be able to:

- Compare the development of Spanish, French, and English colonies from the late sixteenth to the mid-seventeenth century.

- Analyze the effects of European wars on relations among different groups of European colonists and between colonists and diverse Indian nations in North America.

- Examine how the American colonies became part of a global trading network.

- Describe the changing character of labor in the English colonies and the rise of slavery.

AMERICAN HISTORIES

In 1729, at age thirty, William Moraley Jr. signed an indenture to serve a five-year term as a "bound servant" in the "American Plantations." This was not what his parents had imagined for him. The son of a journeyman watchmaker, Moraley received a good education and was offered a clerkship with a London lawyer. But Moraley preferred London's pleasures to legal training. At age nineteen, out of money, he was forced to return home and become an apprentice watchmaker for his father. Moraley made a poor apprentice, and in 1725, fed up with his son's lack of enterprise, Moraley's father rewrote his will, leaving him just 20 shillings. When Moraley's father died

unexpectedly, his wife gave her son 20 pounds, and in 1728 Moraley headed back to London.

But times were hard in London, and Moraley failed to find work. After being imprisoned for debt, he sold his labor for five years in return for passage to America. Arriving in the colonies in December 1729, Moraley was indentured to Isaac Pearson, a Quaker clockmaker and goldsmith in Burlington, New Jersey. Preferring to live in a large city like Philadelphia, Moraley ran away but was soon captured. Most runaway servants had their contracts extended, but Moraley did not. For the next three years, he worked for Pearson alongside another indentured servant and an enslaved boy. Pearson allowed Moraley to travel the countryside fixing clocks and watches, and the servant observed the far worse conditions of enslaved workers. Perhaps having recouped his investment, Pearson released Moraley from his contract two years early.

Moraley spent the next twenty months traveling the northern colonies, but found no steady employment. Hounded by creditors, he returned to England, penniless and unemployed. In 1743, hoping to cash in on popular interest in adventure tales, he published an account of his travels. In the book, entitled *The Infortunate, the Voyage and Adventures of William Moraley, an Indentured Servant*, he offered a poor man's view of eighteenth-century North America. Like so much else in Moraley's life, the book was not a success.

In 1738, while Moraley was back in England trying to carve out a career as a writer, sixteen-year-old Eliza Lucas, the eldest daughter of Colonel George Lucas, arrived at Wappoo, her father's estate near Charleston, South Carolina. Eliza had been born on Antigua, where her father served with the British army and owned a sugar plantation. The move north, made necessary by her mother's ill health, created an unusual opportunity for Eliza, who was left in charge of the estate when Colonel Lucas was called back to Antigua in May 1739.

For the next five years, Eliza Lucas managed Wappoo and two other Carolina plantations owned by her father. Rising each day at 5 a.m., she checked on the fields and the enslaved laborers who worked them, balanced the books, nursed her mother, taught her younger sister to read, and wrote to her younger brothers at school in England. She also befriended

(*left*) **Indentured Servant** (No image of William Moraley exists) Granger, NYC
(*right*) **Fabric dyed with indigo** (No image of Eliza Lucas Pinkney exists) Cooper Hewitt, Smithsonian Deisgn Museum/Art Resource, NY (detail)

neighboring planters, including Charles Pinckney, whom she would later marry, adding her landholdings to his.

While still single, Eliza improved the value of her family's estates by experimenting with new crops. With her father's enthusiastic support, she cultivated indigo, a plant used for making textile dyes. When her experiments proved successful, Eliza Lucas encouraged other planters to follow her lead, and with financial aid from the colonial legislature and Parliament, indigo became a profitable export from South Carolina, second only to rice. ■

The American histories of William Moraley and Eliza Lucas were shaped by a profound shift in global trading patterns that resulted in the circulation of labor and goods among Asia, Africa, Europe, and the Americas. Between 1680 and 1750, indentured servants, enslaved Africans, planters, soldiers, merchants, and artisans traveled along these new trade networks. So, too, did sugar, rum, tobacco, indigo, cloth, and a host of other items. As England, France, and Spain expanded their empires, colonists developed new crops for export and increased the demand for manufactured goods from home. Yet the vibrant, increasingly global economy was fraught with peril. Economic crises, the uncertainties of maritime navigation, and outbreaks of war caused constant disruptions. For some, the opportunities offered by colonization outweighed the dangers; for others, fortune was less kind, and the results were disappointing, even disastrous.

Europeans Expand Their **Claims**

Beginning with the restoration of the monarchy in 1660, English kings began granting North American land and commercial rights to men who were loyal to the crown. France and Spain also expanded their empires in North America, frequently coming into conflict with each other in the late seventeenth and early eighteenth centuries. At the same time, American Indians challenged various European efforts to displace them from their homelands.

English Colonies Grow and Multiply. Shortly after Charles II (r. 1660–1685) was restored to the English throne, Connecticut and Rhode Island requested and received royal charters that granted them some local authority. Because the charters could be changed only with the agreement of both parties, Connecticut and Rhode Island maintained this local autonomy throughout the colonial period. In other colonies, however, Charles II asserted his authority by rewarding loyal supporters with land grants and commercial rights, which could more easily be changed or revoked than royal charters could. He also appointed his supporters to the newly formed Councils for Trade and Plantations, and provided them other privileges. He gave his brother James, the Duke of York, control over all the lands between the Delaware and Connecticut Rivers, once known as New Netherland, but now known as New York. He then conveyed the adjacent lands to investors who established the colonies of East and West Jersey. Finally, Charles II repaid debts to Admiral Sir William Penn by granting his son huge tracts of land in the Middle Atlantic region. Six years later, William Penn Jr. left the Church of England and joined the Society of Friends, or Quakers. This radical Protestant sect was severely persecuted in England, so the twenty-two-year-old Penn turned his holdings into a Quaker refuge named Pennsylvania.

Between 1660 and 1685, York, Penn, and other English gentlemen were established as the proprietors of a string of **proprietary colonies** from Carolina to New York. Although Charles II could have intruded into the government of these colonies, he rarely did. Instead, local conditions largely dictated what was possible. Most proprietors envisioned the creation of a manorial system in their colony, one in which they and other gentry presided over workers producing goods for export. In practice, however, a range of relationships emerged between property owners and workers. For instance, small farmers and laborers in northern Carolina rose up and forced proprietors there to offer land at reasonable prices and a semblance of self-government. In the southern part of Carolina, however, English planters with West Indies connections dominated. They created a mainland version of Barbados by introducing enslaved Africans as laborers, carving out plantations, and trading with the West Indies.

William Penn provided a more progressive model of colonial rule. He established friendly relations with the local Lenni-Lenape Indians and drew up a Frame of Government in 1681 that recognized religious freedom for all Christians. It also allowed all property-owning men to vote and hold office. Under Penn's leadership, Pennsylvania attracted thousands of middling farm families, most of them Quakers, as well as artisans and merchants.

Charles's death in 1685 marked an abrupt shift in crown-colony relations. Charles's successor, James II (r. 1685–1688), instituted a more authoritarian regime both at home and abroad. He consolidated the colonies in the Northeast and established tighter controls. His royal officials banned town meetings, challenged land titles granted under the original colonial charters, and imposed new taxes. Fortunately for the colonists, the Catholic James II alienated his subjects in England as well as in the colonies, inspiring a bloodless coup in 1688, the so-called **Glorious Revolution**. His Protestant daughter Mary and her husband, William of Orange (r. 1689–1702), then ascended the throne, introducing more democratic systems of governance in England and the colonies. Two years later, John Locke, a physician and philosopher, wrote a widely circulated treatise supporting the initiatives of William and Mary by insisting that government depended on the consent of the governed.

Eager to restore political order and create a commercially profitable empire, William and Mary established the new colony of Massachusetts (which included Plymouth, Massachusetts Bay, and Maine) and restored town meetings and an elected assembly. But the 1692 charter also granted the English crown the right to appoint a royal governor and officials to enforce customs regulations. It ensured religious freedom to members of the Church of England and allowed all male property owners (not just Puritans) to be elected to the assembly. In Maryland, too, the crown imposed a royal governor and replaced the Catholic Church with the Church of England as the established religion. And in New York, wealthy English merchants won the backing of the newly appointed royal governor, who instituted a representative assembly and supported a merchant-dominated Board of Aldermen. Thus, taken as a whole, William and Mary's policies instituted a partnership between England and colonial elites by allowing colonists to retain long-standing local governmental institutions but also asserting royal authority to appoint governors and ensure the influence of the Church of England (Table 3.1).

In the early eighteenth century, England's North American colonies took the form that they would retain until the revolution in 1776. In 1702 East and West Jersey united

TABLE 3.1   English Colonies Established in North America, 1607–1750

Colony	Date	Original Colony Type	Religion	Status in 1750
Virginia	1624	Proprietary	Church of England	Royal
Massachusetts	1630	Charter	Congregationalist	Royal with charter
Maryland	1632	Royal	Catholic	Royal
Connecticut	1662	Charter	Congregationalist	Charter
Rhode Island	1663	Charter	No Established Church	Charter
Carolina	1663	Proprietary	Church of England	
North	1691			Royal
South	1691			Royal
New Jersey	1664	Proprietary	Church of England	Royal
New York	1664	Proprietary	Church of England	Royal
Pennsylvania	1681	Proprietary	Quaker	Proprietary
Delaware	1704	Proprietary	Lutheran/Quaker	Proprietary
Georgia	1732	Charter	Church of England	(Royal 1752)
New Hampshire (separated from Massachusetts)	1741	Royal	Congregationalist	Royal

into the colony of New Jersey. Delaware separated from Pennsylvania in 1704. By 1710 North Carolina became fully independent of South Carolina. Finally, in 1732, the colony of Georgia was chartered as a buffer between Spanish Florida and the plantations of South Carolina. At the same time, settlers pushed back the frontier in all directions.

France Seeks Land and Control. When James II became king of England, he modeled his style of governance after Louis XIV of France (r. 1643–1715), who claimed absolute power derived from what he believed was his divine right to rule. However, the French king was far more successful than James II in establishing and sustaining his authority. During his long reign, France extended the boundaries of its North American colonies more through exploration and trade than through settlement. In 1682 French adventurers and their Indian allies journeyed down the lower Mississippi River. Led by René-Robert Cavelier, Sieur de La Salle, the party traveled to the Gulf of Mexico and claimed all the land drained by the river's tributaries for France. The new territory of Louisiana promised great wealth, but its development stalled when La Salle failed in his attempt to establish a colony.

Still eager for a southern outlet for furs, the French did not give up. After several more attempts at colonization in the early eighteenth century, French settlers maintained a toehold along Louisiana's Gulf coast. Most important, Pierre LeMoyne d'Iberville and his brother established forts at Biloxi and Mobile bays, where they traded with local Choctaw Indians. They recruited settlers from Canada and France, and the small outpost survived despite conflicts among settlers, pressure from the English, a wave of epidemics, and a lack of supplies from France. Still, Louisiana counted only three hundred French settlers by 1715.

Continuing to promote commercial relations with diverse Indian nations, the French built a string of missions and forts along the upper Mississippi and Illinois Rivers. The most important of these, Kaskaskia (just south of Cahokia), became a multicultural community of diverse Indian groups, French fur traders, and Jesuit missionaries. These outposts in the continent's interior allowed France to challenge both English and Spanish claims to North America. In addition, extensive trade with a range of Indian nations ensured that French power was far greater than the small number of French settlers suggested.

The Pueblo Revolt and Spain's Fragile Empire.

As New France pushed westward and southward, Spain continued to oversee an empire that was spread dangerously thin on its northern reaches. In New Mexico, tensions between Spanish missionaries

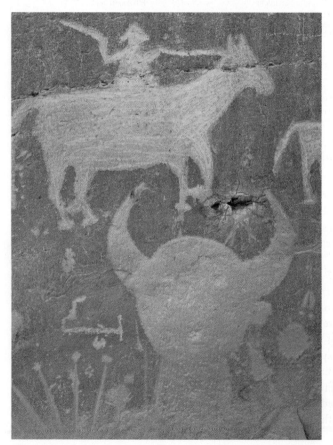

and *encomenderos* and the Pueblo nation had simmered for decades (see "Spain's Global Empire Declines" in chapter 2). Relations worsened in the 1670s when a drought led to famine among many area Indians and brought a revival of Indian rituals that the Spaniards considered threatening. In addition, Spanish forces failed to protect the Pueblos against devastating raids by Apache and Navajo warriors. Finally, Catholic prayers proved unable to stop Pueblo deaths in a 1671 epidemic. When some of the Pueblos returned to their traditional priests, Spanish officials hanged three Indian leaders for idolatry and whipped and incarcerated forty-three others. Among those punished was Popé, a militant Pueblo who upon his release began planning a broad-based revolt.

Battling the Spaniards After the Pueblo revolt in 1680 drove out the Spaniards, the Pueblos established close contact with the Navajo people. In 1692 Spain reconquered the region, and skirmishes continued. This Navajo petroglyph (rock engraving) in Largo Canyon, New Mexico, records one such battle, with Spanish soldiers on horseback wielding swords. Suzi McGregor/Getty Images

On August 10, 1680, seventeen thousand Pueblo Indians initiated a coordinated assault on numerous Spanish missions and forts. They destroyed buildings and farms, burned crops and houses, and smeared excrement on Christian altars. The Spaniards retreated to Mexico without launching any significant counterattack.

Yet the Spaniards returned in the 1690s and reconquered parts of New Mexico, aided by growing internal conflict among the Pueblos and raids by the Apache. The governor general of New Spain worked hard to subdue the province and in 1696 crushed the rebels and opened new lands for settlement. Meanwhile Franciscan missionaries improved relations with the Pueblos by allowing them to retain more indigenous practices.

Yet despite the Spanish reconquest, in the long run the **Pueblo revolt** limited Spanish expansion by strengthening other indigenous peoples in the region. In the aftermath of the revolt, some Pueblo refugees moved north and taught the Navajo how to grow corn, raise sheep, and ride horses. Through the Navajo, the Ute, Shoshone, and Comanche peoples also gained access to horses. By the 1730s, the Comanches launched mounted bison hunts as well as raids on other Indian nations. At Taos, they traded Indian captives into slavery for more horses and guns. Thus the Pueblos provided other Indian nations with the means to support larger populations, wider commercial networks, and more warriors, allowing them to continue to contest Spanish rule.

At the same time, Spain sought to reinforce its claims to Texas (named after the Tejas Indians) in response to French settlements in the lower Mississippi valley. In the early eighteenth century, Spanish missions and forts appeared along the route from San Juan Batista to the border of present-day Louisiana. Although small and scattered, these outposts were meant to ensure Spain's claim to Texas. But the presence of large and powerful Indian nations, including the Caddo and the Apache, forced Spanish residents to accept many native customs in order to maintain their presence in the region.

Spain also faced challenges to its authority in Florida, where Indians resisted the spread of cattle ranching in the 1670s. Meanwhile the English wooed Florida natives by exchanging European goods for deerskins. Some Indians then moved their settlements north to the Carolina border. The growing tensions along this Anglo-Spanish border would turn violent when Europe itself erupted into war.

REVIEW & RELATE

What role did the crown play in the expansion of the English North American colonies in the second half of the seventeenth century?	How did the development of the Spanish and French colonies in the late seventeenth century differ from that of the English colonies?

European Wars and American Consequences

Developments in North America in the late seventeenth and early eighteenth centuries were driven as much by events in Europe as by those in the colonies. From 1689 until 1713, Europe was in an almost constant state of war, with continental conflicts spilling over into colonial possessions in North America. The result was increased tensions between colonists of different nationalities, Indians and colonists, and colonists and their home countries.

Colonial Conflicts and Indian Alliances. France was at the center of much of the European warfare of the period. Louis XIV hoped to expand France's borders and gain supremacy in Europe. To this end, he built a powerful professional army under state authority. Having gained victories in the Spanish Netherlands, Flanders, Strasbourg, and Lorraine, the French army seemed invincible.

Between 1689 and 1697, France and England fought their first sustained war in North America, **King William's War**. The war began over conflicting French and English interests on the European continent, but it soon spread to the American frontier when English and Iroquois forces attacked French and Huron settlements around Montreal and northern New York.

Although neither side had gained significant territory when peace was declared in 1697, the war had important consequences. Many colonists serving in the English army died of battle wounds, smallpox, and inadequate rations. Those who survived resented their treatment and the unnecessary deaths of so many comrades. The Iroquois fared even worse. Their fur trade was devastated, and hundreds of Mohawks and Oneidas were forced to flee from France's Indian allies along the eastern Great Lakes. "French Indians" and Iroquois continued to attack each other after the peace settlement, but in 1701 the Iroquois agreed to end the raids and remain neutral in all future European conflicts. Wary of further European entanglements, Iroquois leaders focused on rebuilding their tattered confederacy.

A second protracted conflict, known as the **War of the Spanish Succession** (1702–1713) or Queen Anne's War, had even more devastating effects on North America. The conflict erupted in Europe when Charles II of Spain (r. 1665–1700) died without an heir, launching a contest for the Spanish kingdom and its colonies. France and Spain squared off against England, the Netherlands, Austria, and Prussia. In North America, however, it was England alone that faced France and Spain, with each nation hoping to gain additional territory. Both sides recruited Indian allies.

After more than a decade of savage fighting, Queen Anne's War ended in 1713 with the Treaty of Utrecht, which sought to secure a prolonged peace by balancing the interests of the great powers in Europe and their colonial possessions. Yet England benefited the most in North America. At the same time, it consolidated power at home by incorporating Scotland into Great Britain through the 1707 Act of Union. Just six years later, France surrendered Newfoundland, Nova Scotia, and the Hudson Bay Territory to England, while Spain granted England control of St. Kitts in the West Indies, Gibraltar, and Minorca as well as the right to sell African slaves in its American colonies. Yet neither the treaty nor Britain's consolidation forestalled further conflict. Indeed, Spain, France, and Britain all strengthened fortifications along their North American borders (Map 3.1).

Indians Resist European Encroachment. The European conflicts in North America put incredible pressure on Indian peoples to choose sides. It was increasingly difficult for native peoples in colonized areas to remain autonomous, yet Indian nations were not simply pawns of European powers. Some actively sought European allies against their native enemies, and nearly all desired European trade goods like cloth, guns, and horses. As colonial expansion and trade led to war, however, the power of young male warriors increased in many tribes. In societies like the Cherokee and Iroquois, in which older women had long held significant economic and political authority, this change threatened

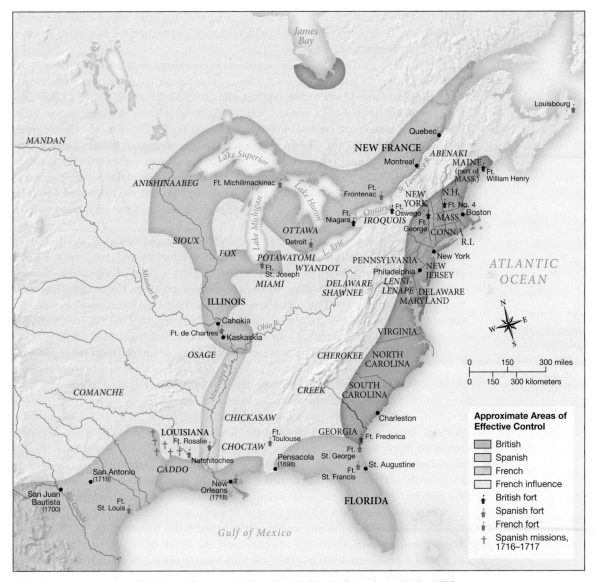

MAP 3.1   European Empires in North America, 1715 –1750

European nations competed with one another and with numerous Indian nations for control of vast areas of North America. Although wars continually reshaped areas under European and Indian control, this map shows the general outlines of the empires claimed by each European nation, the key forts established to maintain those claims, and the major Indian nations in each area.

traditional gender and generational relations. Moreover, struggles among English, French, and Spanish forces both reinforced conflicts among Indian peoples that existed before European settlement and created new ones.

The trade in guns was especially significant in escalating conflicts among tribes in the Southeast during the late seventeenth century. By that period, the most precious commodity Indians had to trade was Indian captives sold as slaves. Indians had always taken captives in war, but some of those captives had been adopted into the victorious nation. Now, however, war was almost constant in some areas, and captives were more valuable when sold as slaves to Europeans. The English in Carolina encouraged the Westo and later the Savannah nation to raid tribes in Spanish Florida, exchanging the captives for guns. As slave raiding spread across the Anglo-Spanish borders, more peaceful tribes were forced to acquire guns for self-protection. In addition, many Indian nations were forced off traditional lands by slave-raiding Indian foes. Some of these displaced groups merged to form new tribes, like the Yamasee in the Southeast.

By the 1710s, the vicious cycle of guns and slaves convinced some southern Indians to develop a pan-Indian alliance similar to that forged by New England Indians in the 1670s (see "Wars in Old and New England" in chapter 2). First, a group of Tuscarora warriors, hoping to gain support from other tribes, launched an attack on North Carolina settlements in September 1711. In the **Tuscarora War** that followed, South Carolina colonists came to the aid of their North Carolina countrymen and persuaded the Yamasee, Catawba, and Cherokee nations to join forces against the Tuscarora. Meanwhile political leaders in North Carolina convinced a competing group of Tuscarora to ally with the colonists. By 1713 the war was largely over, and in 1715 the Tuscarora signed a peace treaty and forfeited their lands. Many then migrated north and were accepted as the sixth nation of the Iroquois Confederacy.

Explore ▶

For a Tuscarora appeal to avoid war, see Document 3.1.

The end of the Tuscarora War did not mean peace, however. For the next two years, a Yamasee-led coalition attacked the South Carolina militia. The Yamasee people remained deeply in debt to British merchants as the trade in deerskins and slaves moved west. They thus secured allies among the Creeks and in 1715 launched an all-out effort to force the British out. The British gained victory in the **Yamasee War** only after the Cherokee switched their allegiance to the colonists in early 1716. The final Indian nations withdrew from the conflict in 1717, and a fragile peace followed.

The Yamasee War did not oust the British, but it did transform the political landscape of native North America. In its aftermath, the Creek and Catawba tribes emerged as powerful new confederations, the Cherokee became the major trading partner of the British, and the Yamasee nation was seriously weakened. Moreover, as the Cherokees allied with the British, the Creek and the Caddo tribes strengthened their alliance with the French.

Despite the British victory, colonists on the Carolina frontier faced raids on their settlements for decades to come. In the 1720s and 1730s, settlers in the Middle Atlantic colonies also experienced fierce resistance to their westward expansion. And attacks on New Englanders along the Canadian frontier periodically disrupted settlement there. Still, many Indian tribes were pushed out of their homelands. As they resettled in new regions, they alternately allied and fought with native peoples already living there. At the same time, the trade in Indian slaves expanded in the west as the French and the Spanish competed for economic partners and military allies.

GUIDED ANALYSIS

The Tuscarora Appeal to the Pennsylvania Government, 1710

Shortly before the outbreak of a pan-Indian war led by the Tuscarora, a delegation from that nation traveled to Pennsylvania to negotiate with British colonial officials and representatives of the Iroquois Confederacy. The views of Tuscarora representatives Iwaagenst Terrutawanaren and Teonnottein are summarized below by two white officials, John French and Henry Worley, who sought to present the arguments of the Indians. The Pennsylvania government subsequently denied their requests. The Iroquois were apparently more sympathetic since, when the war ended in 1715, the Tuscarora became the sixth nation of the Iroquois Confederacy.

Document 3.1

At Conestogo, June 8th, 1710.

The Indians were told that according to their request we were come from the Govr. and Govmt. to hear what proposals they had to make anent [about] a peace, according to the purport of their Embassy from their own People.

What groups did the Tuscarora representatives speak for, and what does this suggest about political dynamics within the Tuscarora nation?

They signified to us by a Belt of Wampum, which was sent from their old Women, that those Implored their friendship of the Christians & Indians of this Govmt., that without danger or trouble they might fetch wood & Water.

The second Belt was sent from their Children born, & those yet in the womb, Requesting that Room to sport & Play without danger of Slavery, might be allowed them.

The third Belt was sent from their young men fitt to Hunt, that privilege to leave their Towns, & seek provision for their aged, might be granted to them without fear of Death or Slavery.

What are the most important demands of the Tuscarora?

The fourth was sent from the men of age, Requesting that the Wood, by a happy peace, might be as safe for them as their forts.

The fifth was sent from the whole nation, requesting peace, that thereby they might have Liberty to visit their Neighbours.

The sixth was sent from their Kings and Chiefs, Desiring a lasting peace with the Christians & Indians of this Govmt., that thereby they might be secured against those fearful apprehensions they have for these several years felt. . . .

What is the most immediate concern of the Tuscarora?

These Belts (they say) are only sent as an Introduction, & in order to break off hostilities till next Spring, for then their Kings will come and sue for the peace they so much Desire.

Source: Sherman Day, *Historical Collections of the State of Pennsylvania* (Philadelphia: George W. Gorton, 1853), 391–92.

Put It in Context

To what extent does the Tuscarora appeal illuminate important concerns of other Indian tribes in the early 1700s?

Conflicts on the Southern Frontier. Indians were not the only people to have their world shaken by war. By 1720 years of warfare and upheaval had transformed the mind-set of many colonists. Although most considered themselves loyal British subjects, many believed that British proprietors remained largely unconcerned with the colonies' welfare. Others resented the British army's treatment of colonial militia and Parliament's unwillingness to aid settlers against Indian attacks. Moreover, the growing numbers of settlers who arrived from other parts of Europe had little investment in British authority.

The impact of Britain's ongoing conflicts with Spain during the 1730s and 1740s illustrates this development. Following the Yamasee War, South Carolina became a royal colony, and its profitable rice and indigo plantations spread southward. Then, in 1732, Parliament established Georgia (named after King George II, r. 1727–1760) on lands north of Florida as a buffer between Carolina colonists and their longtime Spanish foes.

Spanish authorities were furious at this expansion of British territorial claims. Thus in August 1739, a Spanish naval ship captured an English ship captain who was trading illegally in the Spanish West Indies and severed his ear. In response, Great Britain attacked St. Augustine and Cartagena (in present-day Colombia), but its troops were repulsed. In 1742 Spain sent troops into Georgia, but the colonial militia pushed back the attack. By then, the American war had become part of a more general European conflict. Once again France and Spain joined forces while Great Britain supported Germany in Europe. When the war ended in 1748, Britain had ensured the future of Georgia and reaffirmed its military superiority. Once again, however, victory cost the lives of many colonial settlers and soldiers, and some colonists began to wonder whether their interests and those of the British government were truly the same.

Southern Indians were also caught up in ongoing disputes among Europeans. While both French and Spanish forces attacked the British along the Atlantic coast, they sought to outflank each other in the lower Mississippi River valley and Texas. With the French relying on Caddo, Choctaw, and other Indian allies for trade goods and defense, the Spaniards needed to expand their alliances beyond those with the Tejas. In 1749, when Spaniards agreed to stop kidnapping and enslaving Apache women and children, they were able to negotiate peace with that powerful Indian nation.

The British meanwhile became increasingly dependent on a variety of European immigrants to defend colonial frontiers against the French, Spaniards, and Indians. Certainly many Anglo-Americans moved westward as coastal areas became overcrowded, but frontier regions also attracted immigrants from Scotland and Germany who sought refuge and economic opportunity in the colonies. Many headed to the western regions of Virginia and Carolina and to Georgia in the 1730s and 1740s. Meanwhile, South Carolina officials recruited Swiss, German, and French Huguenot as well as Scots-Irish immigrants in the 1740s. Small communities of Jews settled in Charleston as well. Gradually many of these immigrants moved south into Georgia, seeking more and cheaper land. Thus when Spanish, French, or Indian forces attacked the British colonial frontier, they were as likely to face Scots-Irish and German immigrants as Englishmen.

REVIEW & RELATE

• How did the European wars of the late seventeenth and early eighteenth centuries impact relations between colonists and England?	• How were Indian alliances, with other Indians and with European nations, shaped by the trade in slaves and guns and by wars between European powers?

The **Benefits** and **Costs** of **Empire**

The combined forces of global trade and international warfare altered the political and economic calculations of imperial powers. This was especially true for British North America, where colonists settled as families and created towns that provided key markets for Britain's commercial expansion. Over the course of the eighteenth century, British colonists became increasingly avid consumers of products from around the world. Meanwhile the king and Parliament sought greater control over these far-flung commercial networks.

Colonial Traders Join Global Networks.
In the late seventeenth and early eighteenth centuries, trade became truly global. Not only did goods from China, India, the Middle East, Africa, and North America gain currency in England and the rest of Europe, but the tastes of European consumers also helped shape goods produced in other parts of the world. For instance, by the early eighteenth century the Chinese were making porcelain teapots and bowls specifically for the English market. The trade in cloth, tea, tobacco, and sugar was similarly influenced by European tastes. The exploitation of African laborers contributed significantly to this global commerce. They were a crucial item of trade in their own right, and their labor in the Americas ensured steady supplies of sugar, rice, tobacco, and indigo for the world market.

By the early eighteenth century, both the volume and the diversity of goods multiplied. Silk, calico, porcelain, olive oil, wine, and other items were carried from the East to Europe and the American colonies, while cod, mackerel, shingles, pine boards, barrel staves, rum, sugar, rice, and tobacco filled ships returning west. A healthy trade also grew up within North America as New England fishermen, New York and Charleston merchants, and Caribbean planters met one another's needs. Salted cod and mackerel flowed to the Caribbean, and rum, molasses, and slaves flowed back to the mainland. This commerce required ships, barrels, docks, warehouses, and wharves, all of which ensured a lively trade in lumber, tar, pitch, and rosin (Map 3.2).

The flow of information was critical to the flow of goods and credit. By the early eighteenth century, coffeehouses flourished in port cities around the Atlantic, providing access to the latest news. Merchants, ship captains, and traders met in person to discuss new ventures and to keep apprised of recent developments. British and American periodicals reported on parliamentary legislation, commodity prices in India and Great Britain, the state of trading houses in China, the outbreak of disease in foreign ports, and stock ventures in London. Still, these markets were volatile. In 1720 shares in the British South Seas Company, which had risen to astronomical heights, collapsed. Thousands of investors, including William Moraley's father, lost a great deal of money.

Imperial Policies Focus on Profits.
European sovereigns worked to ensure that this international trade and their colonial possessions benefited their own European treasuries. In the late seventeenth century, both Louis XIV and his English rivals embraced a system known as **mercantilism**, which centered on the maintenance of a favorable balance of trade, with more gold and silver flowing into the home country than flowed out. In France, finance minister Jean-Baptiste Colbert honed the system. Beginning in the 1660s, he taxed foreign imports while removing all barriers to trade within French territories. Colonies provided valuable raw materials that could be used to produce manufactured items for sale to foreign nations and to colonists.

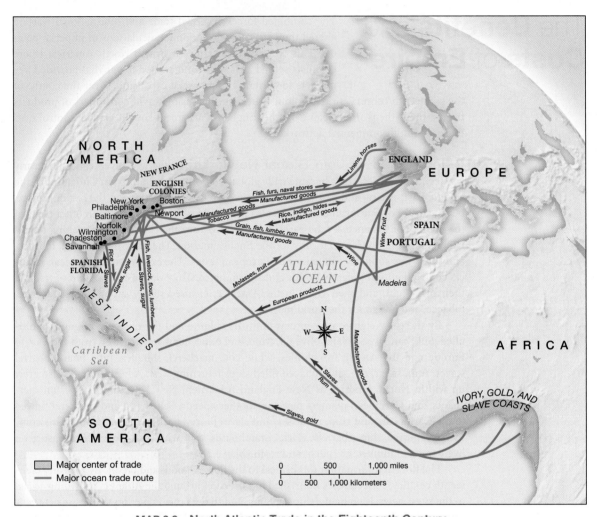

MAP 3.2 North Atlantic Trade in the Eighteenth Century

North Atlantic trade provided various parts of the British empire with raw materials, manufactured goods, and labor. Many ships traveled between only two regions because they were equipped to carry particular kinds of goods—slaves, grains, or manufactured goods. Ultimately, however, people and goods were exchanged among four key points: the West Indies, mainland North America, West Africa, and Great Britain.

While France's mercantile system was limited by the size of its empire, England benefited more fully from such policies. The English crown had access to a far wider array of natural resources from which to manufacture goods and a larger market for these products. Beginning in 1660, Parliament passed a series of **Navigation Acts** that required merchants to conduct trade with the colonies only in English-owned ships. In addition, certain items imported from foreign ports had to be carried in English ships or in ships with predominantly English crews. Finally, a list of "enumerated articles"—including tobacco,

Industrious Americans in Boston 1770   This English engraving appeared as a broadsheet in London. It depicts American colonists engaged in agricultural and artisanal labors on the outskirts of Boston. The anonymous artist titled his image "Political electricity," and intended it as a warning to the British government that industrious Americans might one day rebel against parliamentary policies that sought to limit colonial productivity and profits. © Pictorial Press Ltd./Alamy

cotton, sugar, and indigo—had to be shipped from the colonies to England before being reexported to foreign ports. Thus the crown benefited directly or indirectly from nearly all commerce conducted by its colonies. But colonies, too, often benefited, as when Parliament helped subsidize the development of indigo in South Carolina.

In 1663 Parliament expanded its imperial reach through additional Navigation Acts, which required that goods sent from Europe to English colonies also pass through British ports. And a decade later, ship captains had to pay a duty or post bond before carrying enumerated articles between colonial ports. These acts ensured not only greater British control over shipping but also additional revenue for the crown as captains paid duties in West Indies, mainland North American, and British ports. Beginning in 1673, England sent customs officials to the colonies to enforce the various parliamentary acts. By 1680, London, Bristol, and Liverpool all thrived as barrels of sugar and tobacco and stacks of deer and beaver skins were unloaded and bolts of dyed cloth and cases of metal tools and guns were put on board for the return voyage. As mechanization and manufacturing expanded in England, Parliament sought to keep the profits at home by quashing nascent industries in the colonies. It thus prohibited the sale of products such as American-made textiles (1699), hats (1732), and iron goods (1750). In addition, Parliament worked to restrict trade among the North American colonies, especially between those on the mainland and in the West Indies.

Despite the increasing regulation, American colonists could own British ships and transport goods produced in the colonies. Indeed, by the mid-eighteenth century, North

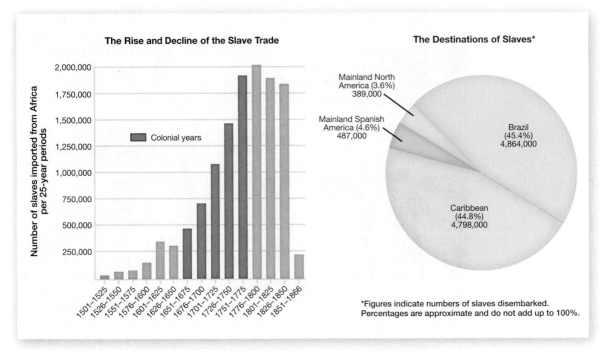

FIGURE 3.1   The Slave Trade in Numbers, 1501–1866

Extraordinary numbers of Africans were shipped as slaves to other parts of the world from the sixteenth to the nineteenth century. These shipments increased dramatically during North America's colonial era (1601–1775). Although the slave trade transformed mainland North America, the vast majority of Africans were sent to Brazil and the West Indies.

Source: Estimates Database. 2009. Voyages: Trans-Atlantic Slave Trade Database, http://www.slavevoyages.org/tast/assessment /estimates.faces. Accessed June 15, 2010.

American merchants oversaw 75 percent of the trade in manufactures sent from Bristol and London to the colonies and 95 percent of the trade with the West Indies. Ironically, then, a system established to benefit Great Britain ended up creating a mercantile elite in British North America. Most of those merchants traded in goods, but some traded in human cargo.

The Atlantic Slave Trade. Parliament chartered the Royal African Company in 1672 as it expanded its role in the Atlantic slave trade. Between 1700 and 1808, some 3 million captive Africans were carried on British and Anglo-American ships, about 40 percent of the total of those sold in the Americas in this period (Figure 3.1). Half a million Africans died on the voyage across the Atlantic. Huge numbers also died in Africa, while being marched to the coast or held in forts waiting to be forced aboard ships. Yet despite this astounding death rate, the slave trade yielded enormous profits and had far-reaching consequences: The Africans whom British traders bought and sold transformed labor systems in the colonies, fueled international trade, and enriched merchants, planters, and their families and communities.

European traders worked closely with African merchants to gain their human cargo, trading muskets, metalware, and linen for men, women, and children. Originally many of those sold into slavery were war captives. But by the time British and Anglo-American merchants became central to this notorious trade, their contacts in Africa were procuring labor in any way they could. Over time, African traders moved farther inland to fill the demand, devastating large areas of West Africa, particularly the Congo-Angola region, which supplied some 40 percent of all Atlantic slaves.

The trip across the Atlantic, known as the **Middle Passage**, was a brutal and often deadly experience for Africans. Exhausted and undernourished by the time they boarded the large oceangoing vessels, the captives were placed in dark and crowded holds. Most had been poked and prodded by slave traders, and some had been branded to ensure that a trader received the exact individuals he had purchased. Once in the hold, they might wait for weeks before the ship finally set sail. By that time, the foul-smelling and crowded hold became a nightmare of disease and despair. There was never sufficient food or fresh water for the captives, and women especially were subject to sexual abuse by crew members. Many captives could not communicate with each other since they spoke different languages, and none of them knew exactly where they were going or what would happen when they arrived.

Explore ▶

Examine two sources that reveal the horrors of the Middle Passage in Documents 3.2 and 3.3.

Those who survived the voyage were likely to find themselves in the slave markets of Barbados or Jamaica, where they were put on display for potential buyers. Once purchased, the slaves went through a period of seasoning as they regained their strength, became accustomed to their new environment, and learned commands in a new language. Some did not survive seasoning, falling prey to malnutrition and disease or committing suicide. Others adapted to the new circumstances and adopted enough European or British ways to carry on even as they sought means to resist the shocking and oppressive conditions.

Seaport Cities and Consumer Cultures.

The same trade in human cargo that brought misery to millions of Africans provided traders, investors, and plantation owners with huge profits that helped turn America's seaport cities into centers of culture and consumption. Charleston was one of the main ports receiving African slaves in the early 1700s, and Eliza Lucas was impressed with its prosperous character. Arriving in 1738, she noted that "the Metropolis is a neat pretty place. The inhabitants [are] polite and live in a very gentile [genteel] manner." North American seaports, with their elegant homes, fine shops, and lively social seasons, did capture the most dynamic aspects of colonial life. Although cities like New York, Boston, Philadelphia, Baltimore, and Charleston contained less than 10 percent of the colonial population, they served as focal points of economic, political, social, and cultural activity.

Affluent urban families created a consumer revolution in North America. Changing patterns of consumption challenged traditional definitions of status. Less tied to birth and family pedigree, status in the colonies became more closely linked to financial success and a genteel lifestyle. Successful men of humble origins and even those of Dutch, Scottish, French, and Jewish heritage might join the British-dominated colonial gentry.

Of those who made this leap in the early eighteenth century, Benjamin Franklin was the most notable. Franklin was apprenticed to his brother, a printer, an occupation that matched his interest in books, reading, and politics. At age sixteen, Benjamin published

COMPARATIVE ANALYSIS

The Middle Passage

To increase their profits, slave traders built ships specifically to transport Africans. They were designed to hold as many people as possible at the least expense. The image of the slave ship *Brooks* vividly portrays the profit motive in transporting human cargo while *The Interesting Narrative of the Life of Olaudah Equiano* captures the horrific personal experience. Unusually for a slave, Equiano learned to read and write and purchased his freedom in 1766. His narrative likely combines his own experience with that of other slaves. Both documents were widely used by British abolitionists in late eighteenth-century campaigns against the slave trade.

Document 3.2

Plan of a Slave Ship, 1794

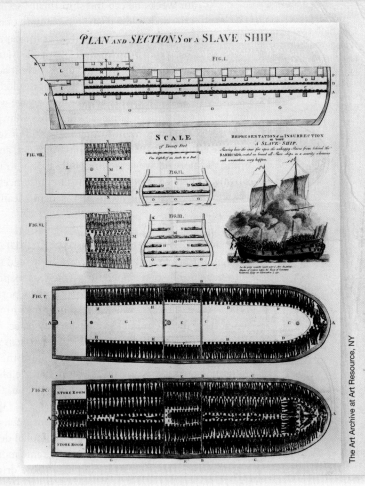

The Art Archive at Art Resource, NY

Document 3.3

The Interesting Narrative of the Life of Olaudah Equiano, 1789

At last, when the ship we were in had got in all her cargo, they made ready with many fearful noises, and we were all put under deck, so that we could not see how they managed the vessel. . . . [N]ow that the whole ship's cargo were confined together, it became absolutely pestilential. The closeness of the place, and the heat of the climate, added to the number in the ship, which was so crowded that each had scarcely room to turn himself, almost suffocated us. This produced copious perspirations, so that the air soon became unfit for respiration, from a variety of loathsome smells, and brought on a sickness among the slaves, of which many died, thus falling victims to the improvident avarice, as I may call it, of their purchasers. This wretched situation was again aggravated by the galling of the chains, now become insupportable; and the filth of the necessary tubs, into which the children often fell, and were almost suffocated. The shrieks of the women, and the groans of the dying, rendered the whole a scene of horror almost inconceivable.

Happily perhaps for myself I was soon reduced so low here that it was thought necessary to keep me almost always on deck; and from my extreme youth I was not put in fetters. . . . One day, when we had a smooth sea and moderate wind, two of my wearied countrymen who were chained together (I was near them at the time), preferring death to such a life of misery, somehow made through the nettings and jumped into the sea: immediately another quite dejected fellow, who, on account of his illness, was suffered to be out of irons, also followed their example. . . . Those of us that were the most active were in a moment put down under the deck, and there was such a noise and confusion amongst the people of the ship as I never heard before, to stop her, and get the boat out to go after the slaves. However two of the wretches were drowned, but they got the other, and afterwards flogged him unmercifully for thus attempting to prefer death to slavery.

Source: *The Interesting Narrative of the Life of Olaudah Equiano, or Gustavas Vassa, The African, Written by Himself* (London, 1789), 78–82.

Interpret the Evidence

1. What aspects and challenges of the slave trade does the plan of a slave ship emphasize?
2. How does the narrative of Olaudah Equiano complement and deepen our understanding of the image of the ship?

Put It in Context

What do these sources reveal about the role of the Middle Passage in transforming African captives into slaves?

A View of Charleston, South Carolina, c. 1760s This eighteenth-century oil painting by English artist Thomas Mellish offers a view of Charleston harbor c. 1760s. A ship flying an English flag looms in the foreground. The other ships and small boats along with the substantial buildings surrounding the harbor reflect Charleston's stature as one of the main commercial centers of the North American colonies. Ferens Art Gallery, Hull Museums, UK/Bridgeman Images

(anonymously) his first essays in his brother's paper, the *New England Courant*. Two years later, a family dispute led Benjamin to try his luck in New York and then Philadelphia. His fortunes were fragile, but unlike William Moraley Jr., he combined hard work with a quick wit, good luck, and political connections, which together led to success. In 1729 Franklin purchased the *Pennsylvania Gazette* and became the colony's official printer.

While Franklin worried about the concentration of wealth in too few hands, most colonial elites in the early eighteenth century happily displayed their profits. Leading merchants in Boston, Salem, New York, and Philadelphia emulated British styles and built fine homes that had separate rooms for sleeping, eating, and entertaining guests. Mercantile elites also redesigned the urban landscape, donating money for brick churches and stately town halls. They constructed new roads, wharves, and warehouses to facilitate trade, and they invested in bowling greens and public gardens.

The spread of international commerce created a lively cultural life and great affluence in colonial cities. The colonial elite replicated British fashions, including elaborate tea rituals. In Boston, the wives of merchants served fine teas imported from East Asia in cups and saucers from China while decorated bowls held sugar from the West Indies. However, the emergence of a colonial aristocracy also revealed growing inequality. Wealthy urban merchants and professionals lived alongside a middling group of artisans and shopkeepers and a growing class of unskilled laborers, widows, orphans, the elderly, the disabled, and the unemployed. In seaport cities, enslaved laborers might live in their owners' homes or be relegated to separate and impoverished communities. In New York City, which boasted the second largest slave market in the mainland colonies in the 1710s, blacks were regularly buried outside the city limits. The frequent wars of the late seventeenth and early eighteenth centuries contributed to these economic and social divisions by boosting the profits of merchants, shipbuilders, and artisans. They temporarily improved the wages of seamen as well. But in their aftermath, rising prices, falling wages, and a lack of jobs led to the concentration of wealth in fewer hands.

REVIEW & RELATE

- What place did North American colonists occupy in the eighteenth-century global trade network?

- How and with what success did the British government maintain control over the colonial economy and ensure that it served Britain's economic and political interests?

Labor in North America

What brought the poor and the wealthy together was the demand for labor. Labor was sorely needed in the colonies, but this did not mean that it was easy to find steady, high-paying employment. Many would-be laborers had few skills and faced fierce competition from other workers for limited, seasonal manual labor. Moreover, a majority of European immigrants and nearly all Africans arrived in America with significant limits on their freedom.

Finding Work in the Colonies. The demand for labor did not necessarily help free laborers find work. Many employers preferred indentured servants, apprentices, or others who came cheap and were bound by contract. Others employed criminals or purchased slaves, who would provide years of service for a set price. Free laborers who sought a decent wage and steady employment needed to match their desire to work with skills that were in demand.

When William Moraley ended his indenture and sought work, he discovered that far fewer colonists than Englishmen owned timepieces, leaving him without a useful trade. So he tramped the countryside, selling his labor when he could, but found no consistent employment. Thousands of other men and women, most without Moraley's education or skills, also found themselves at the mercy of unrelenting economic forces.

Many poor men and women found jobs building homes, loading ships, or spinning yarn. But they were usually employed for only a few months a year. The rest of the time they scrounged for bread and beer, begged in the streets, or stole what they needed. Most lived in ramshackle buildings filled with cramped and unsanitary rooms. Children born into such squalid circumstances were lucky to survive their first year. Those raised in seaport cities might earn a few pence running errands for captains or sailors, but they would never have access to the bounteous goods unloaded at the docks.

By the mid-eighteenth century, older systems of labor, like indentured servitude, began to decline in many areas. In some parts of the North and across the South, white servants were gradually replaced by African slaves (Figure 3.2). At the same time, farm families who could not usefully employ all their children began to bind out sons and daughters to more prosperous neighbors. Apprentices, too, competed for positions. Unlike most servants, apprentices contracted to learn a trade. They trained under the supervision of a craftsman, who gained cheap labor by promising to teach a young man (and most apprentices were men) his trade. But master craftsmen limited the number of apprentices they accepted to maintain the value of their skills.

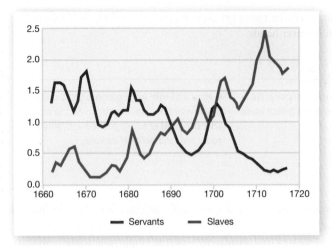

FIGURE 3.2 Indentured Servants and Slaves in Six Maryland Counties, 1662–1717

This chart illustrates a dramatic shift in the Chesapeake labor force between 1662 and 1717. Although based on a study of estate inventories from six Maryland counties, the trend shown here represents a larger transition in Chesapeake households and farms from the use of white indentured servants to black slaves.

Based on Gloria L. Main, *Tobacco Colony: Life in Early Maryland, 1650–1720* (Princeton: Princeton University Press, 1982), p. 26.

Another category of laborers emerged in the 1720s. A population explosion in Europe and the rising price of wheat and other items convinced many people to seek passage to America. Shipping agents offered them loans for their passage that were repaid when the immigrants found a colonial employer who would redeem (that is, repay) the agents. In turn, these **redemptioners**, who often traveled with families, labored for the employer for a set number of years. The redemption system was popular in the Middle Atlantic colonies, especially among German immigrants who hoped to establish farms on the Pennsylvania frontier. While many succeeded, their circumstances could be extremely difficult.

Explore ▸

Read Document 3.4 for an immigrant's description of indentured servitude in Pennsylvania.

Large numbers of convicts, too, entered the British colonies in the eighteenth century. Jailers in charge of Britain's overcrowded prisons offered inmates the option of transportation to the colonies. Hundreds were thus bound out each year to American employers. The combination of indentured servants, redemptioners, apprentices, and convicts ensured that as late as 1750 the majority of white workers—men and women—in the British colonies were bound to some sort of contract.

Sometimes white urban workers also competed with slaves, especially in the northern colonies. Africans and African Americans formed only a small percentage of the northern population, just 5 percent from Pennsylvania to New Hampshire in 1750. In the colony of New York, however, blacks formed about 14 percent of inhabitants. While some enslaved blacks worked on agricultural estates in the Hudson River valley and New Jersey, even more labored as household servants, dockworkers, seamen, and blacksmiths in New York City alongside British colonists and European immigrants.

Coping with Economic Distress. Some white workers who were bound by contracts felt common cause with their black counterparts. But whites had a far greater chance of gaining their freedom even before slavery was fully entrenched in colonial law. Still, several challenges confronted white servants, apprentices, redemptioners, and convicts looking to purchase land, open a shop, or earn a decent wage. First, white women and men who gained their freedom from indentures or other contracts had to compete for jobs with

SOLO ANALYSIS

Gottlieb Mittelberger | Laboring in Pennsylvania, 1756

German colonists began moving to Pennsylvania in the late seventeenth century, encouraged by reports of rich land and religious freedom. In 1750 Gottlieb Mittelberger, a professional organist, left his home in Württemberg, Germany, and headed to Pennsylvania. He returned home in 1754 and two years later published a book warning others against settling in the American colonies. Although Mittelberger was not an indentured servant or a redemptioner, he focused on the hardships experienced by these bound laborers.

Document 3.4

Our Europeans, who are purchased [indentured servants and redemptioners], must always work hard, for new fields are constantly laid out; and so they learn that stumps of oak-trees are in America certainly as hard as in Germany. In this hot land they fully experience in their own persons what God has imposed on man for his sin and disobedience; for in Genesis we read the words: In the sweat of thy brow shalt thou eat bread. Who therefore wishes to earn his bread in a Christian and honest way, and cannot earn it in his fatherland otherwise than by the work of his hands, let him do so in his own country, and not in America; for he will not fare better in America. However hard he may be compelled to work in his fatherland, he will surely find it quite as hard, if not harder, in the new country. Besides, there is not only the long and arduous journey lasting half a year, during which he has to suffer, more than with the hardest work; he has also spent about 200 florins which no one will refund to him. If he has so much money, it will slip out of his hands; if he has it not, he must work his debt off as a slave and poor serf. Therefore let every one stay in his own country and support himself and his family honestly. Besides I say that those who suffer themselves to be persuaded and enticed away by the man-thieves, are very foolish if they believe that roasted pigeons will fly into their mouths in America or Pennsylvania without their working for them.

Source: Gottlieb Mittelberger, *Gottlieb Mittelberger's Journey to Pennsylvania in the Year 1750 and Return to Germany in the Year 1754*, trans. Carl Theo. Eben (Philadelphia: John Jos. McVey, 1898), 30–31.

Interpret the Evidence

1. What myths about America does Mittelberger try to dispel?
2. How does Mittelberger perceive the situation of indentured servants and redemptioners in colonial Pennsylvania?

Put It in Context

How might this account affect German individuals or families considering migration to North America?

a steady supply of redemptioners, convicts, and apprentices as well as other free laborers. Second, by the early eighteenth century, many areas along the Atlantic coast faced a land shortage that threatened the fortunes even of long-settled families. Finally, a population boom in Britain's North American colonies produced growing numbers of young people seeking land and employment. Thus many free laborers migrated from town to town and from country to city seeking work. They hoped to find farmers who needed extra hands for planting and harvesting, ship captains and contractors who would hire them to load or unload cargo or assist in the construction of homes and churches, or wealthy families who needed cooks, laundresses, or nursemaids.

Seasonal and temporary demands for labor created a corps of transient workers. Many New England towns developed systems to "warn out" those who were not official residents. Modeled after the British system, warning-out was meant to ensure that strangers did not become public dependents. Still, being warned did not mean immediate removal. Sometimes transients were simply warned that they were not eligible for poor relief. At other times, constables returned them to an earlier place of residence. In many ways, warning-out served as an early registration system, allowing authorities to encourage the flow of labor, keep residents under surveillance, and protect the town's coffers. But it rarely aided those in need of work.

Residents who were eligible for public assistance might be given food and clothing or boarded with a local family. Many towns began appointing Overseers of the Poor to deal with the growing problem of poverty. By 1750 every seaport city had constructed an almshouse that sheltered residents without other means of support. In 1723 the Bridewell prison was added to Boston Almshouse, built in 1696. Then in 1739 a workhouse was opened on the same site to employ the "able-bodied" poor in hopes that profits from it would help fund the almshouse and prison. Still, these efforts at relief fell far short of the need, especially in hard economic times.

Rural Americans Face Changing Conditions. While seaport cities and larger towns fostered a growing cohort of individuals who lived outside traditional households, families remained the central unit of economic organization in rural areas, where the vast majority of Americans lived. Yet even farms were affected by the transatlantic circulation of goods and people.

In areas along the Atlantic coast, rural families were drawn into commercial networks in a variety of ways. Towns and cities needed large supplies of vegetables, meat, butter, barley, wheat, and yarn. Farm families sold these goods to residents and bought sugar, tea, and other imported items that diversified their diet. Few rural families purchased ornamental or luxury items, but cloth or cheese bought in town saved hours of labor at home. Just as important, coastal communities like Salem, Massachusetts, and Wilmington, Delaware, that were once largely rural became thriving commercial centers in the late seventeenth century.

In New England, the land available for farming shrank as the population soared. In the original Puritan colonies, the population rose from 100,000 in 1700 to 400,000 in 1750, and many parents were unable to provide their children with sufficient land for profitable farms. The result was increased migration to the frontier, where families were more dependent on their own labor and a small circle of neighbors. And even this option was not accessible to all. Before 1700, servants who survived their indenture had a good chance of securing land, but by the mid-eighteenth century only two of every ten were likely to become landowners.

In the Middle Atlantic region, the population surged from 50,000 in 1700 to 250,000 in 1750. The increase was due in part to the rapid rise in wheat prices, which leaped by more than 50 percent in Europe. Hoping to take advantage of this boon, Anglo-Americans, Germans, Scots-Irish, and other non-English groups flooded into western Pennsylvania, New York's Mohawk River valley, and the Shenandoah Valley of Virginia in the early eighteenth century. By the 1740s, German families had created self-contained communities in these areas. They worshipped in German churches, read German newspapers, and preserved

German traditions. Meanwhile Scots-Irish immigrants established churches and communities in New Jersey, central Pennsylvania, and western Maryland and Virginia (Map 3.3).

In the South, immigrants could acquire land more easily, but their chances for economic autonomy were increasingly influenced by the spread of slavery. As hundreds and then thousands of Africans were imported into the Carolinas in the 1720s and 1730s, economic and political power became more entrenched in the hands of planters and merchants. Increasingly, they controlled the markets, wrote the laws, and set the terms by which white as well as black families lived. Farms along inland waterways and on the frontier were crucial in providing food and other items for urban residents and for planters with large labor forces. But farm families depended on commercial and planter elites to market their goods and help defend their communities against hostile Indians or Spaniards.

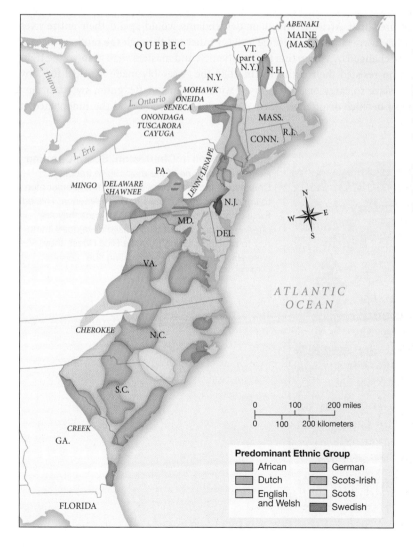

MAP 3.3   Ethnic and Racial Diversity in British North America, 1750

By 1750 British North America was a far more diverse region than it had been fifty years earlier. In 1700 the English dominated most regions, while the Dutch controlled towns and estates in the Hudson River valley. By 1750, however, growing numbers of African Americans, German and Scots-Irish immigrants, and smaller communities of other ethnic groups predominated in various regions.

Slavery Takes Hold in the South. The rise of slavery reshaped the South in numerous ways. A major shift from white indentured servants to black slaves began in Virginia after 1676 and soon spread across the Chesapeake (see Figure 3.2). The Carolinas, meanwhile, developed as a slave society from the start. Slavery in turn allowed for the expanded cultivation of cash crops like tobacco, rice, and indigo, which promised high profits for planters as well as merchants. But these developments also made southern elites more dependent on the global market and limited opportunities for poorer whites and all blacks. They also ensured that Indians and many whites were pushed farther west as planters sought more land for their ventures.

In the 1660s, as tobacco cultivation spread across the Chesapeake, the Virginia Assembly passed a series of laws that defined slavery as a distinct status based on racial identity and passed on through future generations. The enactment of these **slave laws** was driven largely by the growing need for labor, which neither enslaved Indians nor indentured servants could fill. Modeling their laws on statutes passed earlier in Barbados, political leaders ensured that Africans and their descendants would spend their entire lives laboring for white owners. Slavery became a status inherited through the mother; the status could not be changed by converting to Christianity; and masters were granted the right to kill slaves who resisted their authority. In 1680 the Assembly made it illegal for "any negro or other slave to carry or arme himself with any club, staffe, gunn, sword, or any other weapon of defence or offence." (See "Expansion, Rebellion, and the Emergence of

Sale of Slaves in Charleston, South Carolina
Henry Laurens, one of the major slave traders in Charleston, formed a partnership with two other men to import enslaved Africans to North America. This ad focuses on the health of the 250 Africans they are offering for sale, half of whom have developed immunity to smallpox. Being from the Rice Coast, they were also likely skilled in cultivating rice. Library of Congress, 3a52072

Slavery" in chapter 2.) Nor could slaves leave their master's premises without a certificate of permission. Increasingly harsh laws in Virginia and Maryland coincided with a rise in the number of slaves imported to the colony. The statutes also ensured the decline of the free black population in the Chesapeake. In 1668 one-third of all Africans and African Americans in Virginia and Maryland were still free, but the numbers dwindled year by year. Once the Royal African Company started supplying the Chesapeake with slaves directly from Africa in the 1680s, the pace of change quickened. By 1750, 150,000 blacks resided in the Chesapeake, and only about 5 percent remained free. **See Document Project 3: Tobacco and Slaves, page 99.**

Direct importation from Africa had other negative consequences on slave life. Far more men than women were imported, skewing the sex ratio in a population that was just beginning to form families and communities. Women, like men, performed heavy field work, and few bore more than one or two children. When these conditions, along with brutal work regimens, sparked resistance by the enslaved, fearful whites imposed even stricter regulations, further distinguishing between white indentured servants and enslaved blacks.

While slavery in the Carolinas was influenced by developments in the Chesapeake, it was shaped even more directly by practices in the British West Indies. Many wealthy families from Barbados, Antigua, and other sugar islands—including that of Colonel Lucas—established plantations in the Carolinas. At first, they brought slaves from the West Indies to oversee cattle and pigs and assist in the slaughter of livestock and curing of meat for shipment back to the West Indies. Some of the slaves grew rice, using techniques learned in West Africa, to supplement their diet. Owners soon realized that rice might prove very profitable. Although not widely eaten in Europe, rice could provide cheap and nutritious food for sailors, orphans, convicts, and peasants. Relying initially on Africans' knowledge, planters began cultivating rice for export.

The need for African rice-growing skills and the fear of attacks by Spaniards and Indians led Carolina owners to grant slaves rights unheard of in the Chesapeake or the West Indies. Initially slaves were allowed to carry guns and serve in the militia. For those who nonetheless ran for freedom, Spanish and Indian territories offered refuge. Still, most stayed, depending for support on bonds they had developed in the West Indies. The frequent absence of owners also offered Carolina slaves greater autonomy.

As rice cultivation expanded, however, slavery in the Carolinas turned more brutal. The Assembly enacted harsher and harsher slave codes to ensure control of the growing labor force. No longer could slaves carry guns, join militias, meet in groups, or travel without a pass. As planters began to import more slaves directly from Africa, sex ratios, already male dominated, became even more heavily skewed, and older community networks were disrupted. Military patrols by whites were initiated to enforce laws and labor practices. Some plantations along the Carolina coast turned into virtual labor camps, where thousands of slaves worked under harsh conditions with no hope of improvement.

By 1720 blacks outnumbered whites in the Carolinas, and fears of slave rebellions inspired South Carolina officials to impose even harsher laws and more brutal enforcement measures. When indigo joined rice as a cash crop in the 1740s, the demand for slave labor increased further. Although far fewer slaves—about 40,000 by 1750—resided in South Carolina than in the Chesapeake, they constituted more than 60 percent of the colony's total population.

Africans Resist Their Enslavement. Enslaved laborers in British North America resisted their subjugation in a variety of ways. They sought to retain customs, foods, belief systems, and languages from their homelands. They tried to incorporate work patterns passed down from one generation to the next into new environments. They challenged masters and overseers by refusing to work, breaking tools, feigning illness, and other means of disputing whites' authority. Some ran for freedom, others fought back in the face of punishment, and still others used arson, poison, or other means to defy owners. A few planned revolts.

The consequences for resisting were severe, from whipping, mutilation, and branding to summary execution. Because whites were so fearful of rebellion, they often punished people falsely accused of planning revolts. Yet some slaves did plot ways to rise up against their owners or whites in general. Southern whites, living amid large numbers of blacks, were most deeply concerned about resistance and rebellion. But even in the North, whites did not doubt slaves' desire for freedom. As more slaves were imported directly from Africa, both the fear and the reality of rebellion increased.

In New York City in 1712, several dozen enslaved Africans and Indians set fire to a building. When whites rushed to the scene, the insurgents attacked them with clubs, pistols, axes, and staves, killing 8 and injuring many more. The rebels were soon defeated by the militia, however. Authorities executed 18 insurgents, burning several at the stake as a warning to others, while 6 of those imprisoned committed suicide. In 1741 a series of suspicious fires in the city led to accusations against a white couple who owned an alehouse where blacks gathered to drink. To protect herself from prosecution, an Irish indentured servant testified that she had overheard discussions of an elaborate plot involving black and white conspirators. Frightened of any hint that poor whites and blacks might make common cause, authorities immediately arrested suspects and eventually executed 34 people, including 4 whites. They also banished 72 blacks from the city. Among those executed was Cuffee, a slave who claimed that "a great many people have too much, and others too little."

The most serious slave revolt, however, erupted in South Carolina, just a few miles from Wappoo, the Lucas plantation. A group of recently imported Africans led the **Stono rebellion** in 1739. On Sunday, September 9, a group of enslaved men stole weapons from a country store and killed the owners. They then marched south, along the Stono River, beating drums and recruiting others to join them. Torching plantations and killing whites along the route, they had gathered more than fifty insurgents when armed whites overtook them. In the ensuing battle, dozens of rebels died. The militia, along with Indians hired to assist them, killed another twenty over the next two days and then captured a group of forty, who were executed without trial.

This revolt reverberated widely in a colony where blacks outnumbered whites nearly two to one, direct importation from Africa was at an all-time high, and Spanish authorities in Florida promised freedom to runaway slaves. In 1738 the Spanish governor formed a black militia company, and he allowed thirty-eight fugitive families to settle north of St. Augustine and build Fort Mose for their protection. When warfare erupted between Spain and Britain over commercial rivalries in 1739, Carolina slaves may have seen their chance to gain freedom en masse. But as with other rebellions, this one failed, and the price of failure was death.

REVIEW & RELATE

What were the sources of economic inequality in North America in the early eighteenth century?

How did the laws and conditions under which poor black and white workers lived during the late seventeenth and early eighteenth centuries differ?

Conclusion: Changing Fortunes in British North America

Global commerce, international wars, and immigration reshaped the economy and geography of North America between 1680 and 1750. Many colonists and some Indians thrived as international trade boomed. In seaport cites, a consumer revolution transformed daily life, fueling the emergence of a colonial elite and the demand for skilled artisans. Others found greater opportunities by pushing inland and establishing farms and communities along new frontiers. But many people failed to benefit from these changes. Indians were often dispossessed of their land as white settlers pushed west. Many indentured servants found it impossible to obtain land or decent wages after they gained their independence. Still, even if white servants and unskilled workers struggled amid periodic economic upheavals, they had the benefit of freedom. Black workers were increasingly forced into slavery, with the shrinking percentage of free blacks suffering from intensifying discrimination against the race as a whole. The consequences of international trade and imperial conflicts only widened the gap between economically successful and impoverished or enslaved Americans.

Increased mechanization and the growth of manufacturing in England shaped the lives of working people on both sides of the Atlantic Ocean. William Moraley Jr., for example, lived out his life in Newcastle-upon-Tyne, making and repairing watches at a time when cheap watches were being turned out in large numbers. Yet these economic changes had far more positive effects for some colonists. The mechanization of cloth production in England demanded vast amounts of raw material from the English countryside and the colonies. It ensured, for example, the profitability of indigo. This crop benefited South Carolina planters like Eliza Lucas and—after her marriage in 1744—her husband, Charles Pinckney, a successful planter himself. Still, profits from indigo could be gained only through the labor of hundreds of slaves.

Eliza Pinckney's sons became important leaders in South Carolina, and despite their English education and the benefits they gained through British trade, both developed a strong belief in the rights of the colonies to control their own destinies. Like many American colonists, they were spurred by the consumer revolution, geographical expansion, growing ethnic diversity, and conflicts with Indian and European enemies to develop a mind-set that differed significantly from their counterparts in England. Yet at the very same time, some colonists reimagined their relationships to the religious and political beliefs that had sustained them for generations.

CHAPTER 3 REVIEW

TIMELINE OF EVENTS

1660	Monarchy restored in England
1660–1673	Navigation Acts
1660–1685	Charles II grants North American proprietorships
1672	Royal African Company chartered
1680	Pueblo revolt
1688	Glorious Revolution
1689–1697	King William's War
1691–1710	North Carolina separates from South Carolina
1692	Colony of Massachusetts established
1700–1750	New England colonial population quadruples
	Middle Atlantic colonial population quintuples
1700–1808	British ships 3 million African slaves to the Americas
1702	East and West Jersey unite into New Jersey
1702–1713	War of the Spanish Succession
1704	Delaware separates from Pennsylvania
1711–1713	Tuscarora War
1715–1717	Yamasee War
1732	Colony of Georgia established
1739	Stono rebellion
1749	Spanish settlers in Texas make peace with the Apache

KEY TERMS

proprietary colonies, *72*
Glorious Revolution, *72*
Pueblo revolt, *75*
King William's War, *76*
War of the Spanish Succession, *76*
Tuscarora War, *78*
Yamasee War, *78*
mercantilism, *81*
Navigation Acts, *82*
Middle Passage, *85*
redemptioners, *90*
slave laws, *94*
Stono rebellion, *96*

REVIEW & RELATE

1. What role did the crown play in the expansion of the English North American colonies in the second half of the seventeenth century?

2. How did the development of the Spanish and French colonies in the late seventeenth century differ from that of the English colonies?

3. How did the European wars of the late seventeenth and early eighteenth centuries impact relations between colonists and England?

4. How were Indian alliances, with other Indians and with European nations, shaped by the trade in slaves and guns and by wars between European powers?

5. What place did North American colonists occupy in the eighteenth-century global trade network?

6. How and with what success did the British government maintain control over the colonial economy and ensure that it served Britain's economic and political interests?

7. What were the sources of economic inequality in North America in the early eighteenth century?

8. How did the laws and conditions under which poor black and white workers lived during the late seventeenth and early eighteenth centuries differ?

Tobacco and Slaves

Tobacco was a popular commodity among Europeans, and they relied on colonies like Virginia and Maryland to provide it. Consumption and production expanded dramatically between the 1670s and the 1750s. The 17.5 million pounds of tobacco exported from the Chesapeake in 1672 leapt to nearly 51 million pounds by 1750. While many small farmers cultivated tobacco with only the aid of family members or indentured servants, increased demand drove others to seek new sources of labor. Laws that codified the status of slaves encouraged more planters to invest in Africans (Document 3.5).

Many planters worried about how to balance proper care of slaves, in whom they had invested significant capital, with the need for discipline (Documents 3.6 and 3.8). At the same time, tobacco planters sought to promote a positive image that would appeal to consumers and English authorities (Document 3.7). While large slave owners could find themselves deeply in debt when prices fell, they were still likely to gain the greatest profits from the tobacco trade.

As tobacco production increased in Virginia, so did the importation of enslaved Africans. While 4,000 Africans were imported in the 1690s, more than 15,000 arrived in the 1730s. By 1740, natural reproduction added to the steady rise in Virginia's African American population. The vast majority of black Virginians were enslaved, and the greatest number worked in tobacco. While much of the work of clearing fields, weeding, and hoeing was considered unskilled, the cutting, stemming, and packing of tobacco leaf required considerable skill (Documents 3.7 and 3.8). In response to the arduous labor and harsh discipline, some slaves ran away and others organized collective escapes (Document 3.9). However, most of Virginia's enslaved workers remained locked into the tobacco cycle, along with their children and grandchildren.

The following documents highlight the roles that legislators, planters, and enslaved workers played in the production of tobacco and the challenges they faced. Although no slaves left us direct descriptions of their lives, consider what these documents tell us about their experiences.

Document 3.5

Virginia Slave Laws, 1662 and 1667

As the demand for labor on tobacco farms increased in the mid-seventeenth century and the flow of white indentured servants to Virginia slowed, tobacco planters imported more Africans to fill their labor needs. In the 1660s Virginia legislators passed a series of laws to clarify the status of this new category of worker. Several were based on laws in effect in the West Indies, including the 1662 law that defined slavery as an inherited position.

[1662]

WHEREAS some doubts have arisen whether children got by any Englishman upon a negro woman should be slave or free, *Be it therefore enacted and declared by this present grand assembly,* that all children borne in this country shall be held bond or free only according to the condition of the mother, *And* that if any christian shall commit fornication with a negro man or woman, he or she so offending shall pay double the fines imposed by the former act.

[1667]

WHEREAS some doubts have risen whether children that are slaves by birth, and by the charity and piety of their owners made pertakers of the blessed sacrament of baptisme, should by vertue of their baptisme be made free; *It is enacted and declared by this grand assembly, and the authority thereof*, that the conferring of baptisme doth not alter the condition of the person as to his bondage or freedome; that diverse masters, freed from this doubt, may more carefully endeavour the propagation of christianity by permitting children, though slaves, or those of greater growth if capable to be admitted to that sacrament.

Source: William W. Hening, ed., *The Statutes at Large; Being a Collection of All Laws of Virginia, from the First Session of the Legislature in the Year 1619* (Samuel Pleasants, 1810), 2:170, 260.

Document 3.6

Joseph Ball Instructs His Nephew on Managing Enslaved Workers, 1743

Joseph Ball of Stratford, England, owned a tobacco plantation named Morattico in Lancaster County, Virginia. He lived in England, where he practiced law, so he employed his nephew Joseph Chinn to manage his estate. Ball sent Chinn detailed instructions about handling crops, livestock, the overseer, and the slaves. He also visited Morattico regularly. This letter from February 1743 focuses on Chinn's care of the slaves.

will have what Goods I send to Virginia to the use of my Plantation there, kept in my House at Morattico.

If I should not send Goods enough, you must Supply the rest out of the stores there with my Tobacco.

The Coarse Cotton . . . was assign'd for blankets for my Negroes: there must be four yards a half to each Blanket. They that have [now] two blankets already; that is one tolerable one, and one pretty good one, must have what is wanting to make it up, 4½ yards in a blanket. And Everyone of the workers

must have a Good Suite of the Welsh Plain [wool] made as it should be. Not to[o] Scanty, nor bobtail'd. And Each of the Children must have a Coat of Worser Cotton . . . and two shirts or shifts of ozenbrig [coarse linen] and the Workers must Each of them have Summer Shirtfs of the brown Rolls. And All the workers must have Good strong Shoes, & stockings; and they that go after the Creatures [livestock], or Much in the Wet, must have two pair of Shoes . . . and all must be done in Good time; and not for Winter to be half over before they get their summer Clothes; as the Common Virginia fashion is.

If any of the Negroes should be sick, let them ly by a Good fire; and have fresh Meat & brot[h]; and blood, and vomit [purge] them, as you shall think proper. . . . I would have no Doctor unless in very violent Cases: they Generally do more harm than Good. . . .

Let not the overseers abuse my People. Nor let them abuse their overseer.

Let the Breeding Wenches have Baby Clothes, for wh[ic]h you may tear up old sheets, or any other old Linen . . . (I shall Send things proper hereafter) and let them have Good Midwives; and what is necessary. Register all the Negro Children that shall be born and after keep an account of their ages among my Papers.

Source: Joseph Ball Letterbook, 1743–1759, in *Correspondence of Joseph Ball, 1743–1780*, Library of Congress.

Document 3.7

Enslaved Blacks Working on a Tobacco Plantation, c. 1750

This wood engraving, created by nineteenth-century English author and engraver Frederich W. Fairholt, was based on a mid-eighteenth-century drawing. Fairholt published it in his 1859 book, *Tobacco, Its History and Associations*. Fairholt depicts bare-chested slaves packing tobacco leaves in hogsheads and rolling them to waiting ships while well-dressed whites oversee their work. The overhead banner reminds readers that Indians introduced tobacco to the English.

A TOBACCO PLANTATION

Peter Newark American Pictures/Bridgeman Images

Richard Corbin Describes How to Become a Successful Planter, 1759

Richard Corbin (c. 1708–1790) owned tobacco plantations in King and Queen County, Virginia, and served as a burgess and receiver general of Virginia. Here he writes to his new manager, James Semple, describing his duties as well as the work of overseers and slaves. Corbin describes the crucial processes in preparing cut leaves for market—"striking" them down from the rafters where they are hung to cure; "stripping" the leaves from the stalk; and "stemming," or rolling, individual leaves, which are then "prized" or packed in a hogshead.

As it will be Necessary to . . . Suggest to you my Thoughts upon the business you have undertaken, I shall endeavor to be particular and Circumstanial. . . .

Observe a prudent and a Watchful Conduct over the Overseers that they attend their business with diligence; keep the Negroes in good order and enforce obedience by the Example of their own Industry, wch [which] is a more effectual method in every respect . . . than Hurry and Severity; the ways of Industry are constant and regular, not to be in a hurry at one time and do nothing at another, but to be always Usefully and Steadily employed. . . .

Take an Exact account of all the Negroes & Stocks [animals] at each Plantation and send to me; & tho[ugh] once a year may be sufficient to take this acct, yet it will be advisable to see them once a Month at least, as such an Inspection will fix more closely the overseers attention to these points.

As complaints have been made by the Negroes in respect to their provision of corn, I must desire you to put that matter under such a Regulation, as your own Prudence will dictate. . . . The allowance to be sure is Plentiful and they ought to have their Belly full but care must be taken with this Plenty that no Waiste [waste] is Committed. . . .

Tob[acc]o h[ogs]h[ea]ds [large casks] should always be provided the 1st Week in Sept; every morning of that month is fit for Striking & Stripping; every morning therefore of this month, they should Strike as much Tob[acc]o as they can strip whilst the Dew is upon the Ground and what they Strip in the morning must be Stem'd in the Evening; this method constantly practiced, the Tobacco will be prised before Christmas, Weigh well, and at least one hhd in Ten gained by finishing the Tob[acc]o thus early.

Source: Richard Corbin to Mr. James Semple, January 1, 1759, Richard Corbin Letterbook, Manuscript DMS 1971.5, John D. Rockefeller, Jr. Library, Colonial Williamsburg Foundation.

Document 3.9

Lieutenant Governor William Gooch to the Board of Trade, London, 1729

William Gooch served as lieutenant governor and governor of the Virginia colony from 1727 to 1749. His success depended in large part on his support for Virginia's tobacco planters, who comprised the colony's ruling elite. His frequent letters to the Board of Trade in London addressed planters' and the board's concerns regarding trade relations, debt collection, the quality of tobacco, and, in the letter below, resistance among some enslaved workers.

Some time after my last [letter] a number of negroes, about fifteen, belonging to a new plantation, . . . formed a design to withdraw from their master and to fix themselves in the fastnesses of the neighbouring mountains: they had found means to get into their possession some arms and ammunition, and they took along with them some provisions, their cloaths, bedding and working tools; but the Gentleman to whom they belonged with a party of men made such diligent pursuit after them, that he soon found them out in their settlement, a very obscure place among the mountains, where they had already begun to clear the ground, and obliged them after exchanging a shot or two by which one of the slaves was wounded, to surrender and return back, and so prevented for this time a design which might have proved as dangerous to this country, as is that of the negroes in the mountains of Jamaica to the inhabitants of that island. Tho' this attempt has happily been defeated, it ought nevertheless to awaken us into some effectual measures for preventing the like hereafter, it being certain that a very small number of negroes once settled in those parts, would very soon be encreas'd by the accession of other runaways and prove dangerous neighbours to our frontier inhabitants.

Source: Lt. Gov. William Gooch to Board of Trade, June 29, 1729, *Calendar of State Papers, Colonial Series, America and the West Indies, 1728–1729* (London, 1937), 414–15, in Paul G. E. Clemens, ed., *The Colonial Era: A Documentary Reader* (Malden, MA: Blackwell, 2008), 135–36.

Interpret the Evidence

1. Why did Virginia lawmakers decide that slave status should pass through the mother's (rather than father's) line and would be unaffected by baptism (Document 3.5)?

2. What do the descriptions of slave life and labor by Joseph Ball and Richard Corbin reveal about the attitudes of Virginia planters toward enslaved workers (Documents 3.6 and 3.8)?

3. How does the engraving (Document 3.7) portray the roles of planters, managers, and enslaved workers? What are the most notable differences between the black and white figures in this image?

4. What issues about slave life on a tobacco plantation are raised by Lieutenant Governor William Gooch (Document 3.9), and how do they compare with the image presented in the engraving (Document 3.7) and the writings by planters (Documents 3.6 and 3.8)?

Put It in Context

What were the relationships among the growing demand for tobacco, the actions of Virginia politicians and planters, and the lives of enslaved laborers?

What were the greatest challenges faced by white colonists (slave owners and non-slave owners) and by black laborers as the Atlantic slave trade expanded between 1680 and 1750?

Religious Strife and Social Upheavals

1680–1750

WINDOW TO THE PAST

Abigail Faulkner Appeals Her Conviction for Witchcraft, 1692

Abigail Faulkner, the daughter of a minister and wife of a large landowner, was convicted of witchcraft in Salem, Massachusetts, but maintained her innocence. Any woman sentenced to death had her execution postponed if she was pregnant. Faulkner used the delay in carrying out her death penalty to petition the Massachusetts governor for her release based on what she considered insufficient evidence. ▶ To discover more about what this primary source can show us, see Document 4.1 on page 108.

Source: The Salem Witchcraft Papers, Case Files, Petition of Abigail Faulkner.

After reading this chapter you should be able to:

- Explain the relationships among religious, economic, and political tensions and accusations of witchcraft.

- Describe family dynamics, particularly between husbands and wives, and how they changed over time and differed by class and region.

- Understand the ways that economic developments and increasing diversity fueled conflicts in early eighteenth-century colonial society.

- Explain the emergence of the Great Awakening and identify its critics and legacies.

- Describe how the Great Awakening shaped political developments in the 1730s and 1740s.

AMERICAN HISTORIES

The son of a Scots-Irish clergyman, Gilbert Tennent was born in Vinecash, Ireland, in 1703 and at age fifteen moved with his family to Philadelphia. After receiving an M.A. from Yale College in 1725, Gilbert was ordained a Presbyterian minister in New Brunswick, New Jersey, with little indication of the role he would play in a major denominational schism.

Tennent entered the ministry at a critical moment, when leaders of a number of denominations had become convinced that the colonies were descending into spiritual apathy. Tennent dedicated himself to sparking a rebirth of Christian commitment, and by

the mid-1730s the pastor had gained fame as a revival preacher. At the end of the decade, he journeyed through the middle colonies with Englishman George Whitefield, an Anglican preacher known for igniting powerful revivals. Then in the fall of 1740, following the death of his wife, Tennent launched his own evangelical "awakenings."

Revivals inspired thousands of religious conversions across denominations, but they also fueled conflicts within established churches. Presbyterians in Britain and America disagreed about whether only those who had had a powerful, personal conversion experience were qualified to be ministers. Tennent made his opinion clear by denouncing unconverted ministers in his sermons, a position that led to his expulsion from the Presbyterian Church in 1741. But many local churches sought converted preachers, and four years later a group of ejected pastors formed a rival synod that trained its own evangelical ministers.

While ministers debated the proper means of saving sinners, ordinary women and men searched their souls. In Pomfret, Connecticut, Sarah Grosvenor certainly feared for hers in the summer of 1742 when the unmarried nineteen-year-old realized she was pregnant. Her situation was complicated by her status in the community. She was the daughter of Leicester Grosvenor, an important landowner, town official, and member of the Congregational Church.

The pew next to Sarah and her family was occupied by Nathaniel Sessions and his sons, including the twenty-six-year-old Amasa, who had impregnated Sarah. Many other young women became pregnant out of wedlock in the 1740s, but families accepted the fact as long as the couple married before the child was born. In Sarah's case, however, Amasa refused to marry her and suggested instead that she have an abortion.

Although Sarah was reluctant to follow this path, Amasa insisted. When herbs traditionally used to induce a miscarriage failed, Amasa introduced Sarah to John Hallowell, a doctor who claimed he could remove the fetus with forceps. After admitting her agonizing situation to her older sister Zerviah and her cousin Hannah, Sarah allowed Hallowell to proceed. He finally induced a miscarriage, but Sarah soon grew feverish, suffered convulsions, and died ten days later.

(*left*) **Gilbert Tennent**. Granger, NYC

(*right*) **Gravestone of Sarah Grosvenor**. Jessica C. Linker

Apparently Sarah's and Amasa's parents were unaware of the events leading to her demise. Then in 1745, a powerful religious revival swept through the region, and Zerviah and Hannah suffered great spiritual anguish. It is likely they finally confessed their part in the affair since that year officials brought charges against Amasa Sessions and John Hallowell for Sarah's death. At the men's trial, Zerviah and Hannah testified about their roles and those of Sessions and Hallowell. Still, their spiritual anguish did not lead to earthly justice. Hallowell was found guilty but escaped punishment by fleeing to Rhode Island. Sessions was acquitted and remained in Pomfret, where he married and became a prosperous farmer. ◾

The American histories of Gilbert Tennent and Sarah Grosvenor were shaped by powerful religious forces—later called the Great Awakening—that swept through the colonies in the early eighteenth century. Those forces are best understood in the context of larger social, economic, and political changes. Many young people became more independent of their parents and developed tighter bonds with siblings, cousins, and neighbors their own age. Towns and cities developed clearer hierarchies by class and status, which could protect wealthier individuals from being punished for their misdeeds. A double standard of sexual behavior became more entrenched as well, with women subject to greater scrutiny than men for their sexual behavior. Of course, most young women did not meet the fate of Sarah Grosvenor. Still, pastors like Gilbert Tennent feared precisely such consequences if the colonies—growing ever larger and more diverse—did not reclaim their religious foundations.

An **Ungodly Society?**

As American colonists became more engaged in international and domestic commerce, spiritual commitments appeared to wane. In New England, Congregational ministers condemned the apparent triumph of worldly ambition over religiosity. Nonetheless, some ministers saw economic success as a reward for godly behavior even as they worried that wealth and power opened the door to sin. In the late seventeenth century, these anxieties deepened when accusations of witchcraft erupted across southern New England.

The Rise of Religious Anxieties. In 1686 the Puritan minister Samuel Sewell railed against the behavior of Boston mercantile elites. Citing examples of their depravity in his diary, including drunkenness and cursing, he claimed that such "high-handed wickedness has hardly been heard of before." Sewell was outraged as well by popular practices such as donning powdered wigs in place of God-given hair, wearing scarlet and gold jackets rather than simple black cloth, and offering toasts rather than prayers.

While Sewell spoke for many Puritans concerned with the consequences of commercial success, other religious leaders tried to meld old and new. The Reverend Cotton Mather complained that many colonists showed greater interest in the latest fashions than in the state of their souls. Yet he was attracted by the luxuries available to colonists and hoped to make his own son "a more finished Gentleman." Mather was also fascinated by new scientific endeavors and supported inoculations for smallpox, which others viewed as challenging God's power.

Certainly news of the Glorious Revolution in England (1688) offered Puritans hope of regaining their customary authority (see "English Colonies Grow and Multiply" in chapter 3). But the outbreak of King William's War in 1689 quickly ended any notion of an easy return to peace and prosperity. Instead, continued conflicts and renewed fears of Indian attacks on rural settlements heightened the sense that Satan was at work in the region. Soon, accusations of witchcraft joined outcries against other forms of ungodly behavior.

Cries of Witchcraft. Belief in witchcraft had been widespread in Europe and England for centuries. It was part of a general belief in supernatural causes for events that could not otherwise be explained—severe storms, a suspicious fire, a rash of deaths among livestock. When a community began to suspect witchcraft, they often pointed to individuals who challenged cultural norms. Women who were quarrelsome, eccentric, poor, or simply too independent were easy to imagine as cavorting with evil spirits and invisible demons.

Witchcraft accusations tended to be most common in times of change and uncertainty. Over the course of the seventeenth century, colonists had begun to spread into new areas seeking more land and greater economic opportunities. But expansion brought with it confrontations with Indians, exposure to new dangers, and greater vulnerability to a harsh environment. As the stress of expansion mounted, witchcraft accusations emerged. Some 160 individuals, mostly women, were accused of witchcraft in Massachusetts and Connecticut between 1647 and 1692, although only 15 were put to death. Many of the accused were poor, childless, or disgruntled women, but widows who inherited property also came under suspicion, especially if they fought for control against male relatives and neighbors.

The social and economic complexities of witchcraft accusations are well illustrated by the most famous American witch-hunt, the Salem witch trials of the early 1690s. In 1692 residents of Salem, Massachusetts, confronted conflicts between long-settled farmers and newer mercantile families, political uncertainties following the Glorious Revolution, ongoing threats from Indians, and quarrels over the choice of a new minister. These tensions were brought to a head when the Reverend Samuel Parris's daughter and niece learned voodoo lore and exotic dances from the household's West Indian slave, Tituba. The daughters and servants of neighboring families also became entranced by Tituba's tales and began to tell fortunes, speak in gibberish, and contort their bodies into painful positions. When the girls were questioned about their strange behavior, they pointed not only to Tituba but also to other people in the community. They first accused an elderly female pauper and a homeless widow of bewitching them, but later singled out respectable churchwomen as well as a minister, a wealthy merchant, and a four-year-old child.

Within weeks, more than one hundred individuals, 80 percent of them women, stood accused of witchcraft. Governor William Phips established a special court to handle the cases, over which the Reverend Samuel Sewell presided. Twenty-seven of the accused came to trial, and twenty were found guilty based on testimony from the girls and on **spectral evidence**, that is, evidence that came to the girls in dreams or visions. In court, the young accusers were seen writhing, shaking, and crying out in pain as spirits of the accused, invisible to everyone else, came to them in visions and pinched, choked, and bit them. Based on such evidence, nineteen people were hanged, and one was pressed to death with stones.

Explore ▶

Read the appeal of a woman accused of witchcraft in Document 4.1.

But when accusations reached into prominent Salem and Boston families, Governor Phips ended the proceedings and released the remaining suspects. In the following months, leading ministers and colonial officials condemned the use of spectral evidence, and some of the young accusers recanted their testimony.

The Salem trials illuminate far more than beliefs in witchcraft. The trials pitted the daughters and servants of prosperous farmers against the wives and widows of recently arrived merchants. The accusers included young women like nineteen-year-old Mercy Lewis, who was bound out as a servant when her parents were killed by Indians. Fear of attack from hostile Indians, hostile officials in England, or hostile neighbors fostered anxieties in Salem, as it did in many colonial communities. Other anxieties also haunted the accusers. A shortage of land led many New England men to seek their fortune farther west, leaving young women with few eligible bachelors to choose from. Marriage prospects were affected as well by battles over inheritance. Thomas Putnam Jr., who housed three of the accusers, was in the midst of one such battle, which left his three sisters—the accusers' aunts—in limbo as they awaited legacies that could enhance their marriage prospects. As young women in Salem forged tight bonds in the face of such uncertainties, they turned their anger not against men, but instead against older women, including respectable "goodwives" like Abigail Faulkner.

REVIEW & RELATE

- What factors led to a rise in tensions within colonial communities in the early 1700s?
- How did social, economic, and political tensions contribute to an increase in accusations of witchcraft?

Family and Household Dynamics

Concerns about marriage, property, and inheritance were not limited to Salem or to New England. As the American colonies became more populous and the numbers of women and men more balanced, husbands gained greater control over the behavior of household members, and the legal and economic rewards available to most women declined. Yet some women improved their situation by wielding their skills as midwives, brewers, or even plantation managers to benefit their families.

Women's Changing Status. In most early American colonies, the scarcity of women and workers ensured that many white women gained economic and legal leverage. In the first decades of settlement in the Chesapeake, where women were in especially short supply and mortality was high, young women who arrived as indentured servants and completed their term might marry older men of property. If the husbands died first, widows often took control of the estate and passed on the property to their children. Even in New England, where the numbers of men and women were more balanced from the beginning, the crucial labor of wives in the early years of settlement was sometimes recognized by their control of family property after a husband's death.

By the late seventeenth century, however, as the sex ratio in the Chesapeake evened out, women lost the opportunity to marry "above their class" (see Table 4.1). And across the colonies, widows lost control of family estates. Even though women still performed vital labor, the spread of indentured servitude and slavery lessened the recognition of their

Abigail Faulkner Appeals Her Conviction for Witchcraft, 1692

While most women accused of witchcraft in Salem were marginal to society, Abigail Faulkner was the daughter of a minister and the wife of a large landowner. Nonetheless, she was declared guilty on the basis of spectral evidence and the charges made by "bewitched" girls. When Faulkner's execution was postponed, she petitioned Governor Phips to release her. Faulkner was released, but only after Massachusetts officials stepped in and ended the trials.

Document 4.1

What evidence does Faulkner provide of her innocence?

What saved Faulkner from being executed initially?

How does Faulkner try to persuade Governor Phips of the need for immediate action?

The humblee Petition of Abigall: Falkner unto his Excellencye S'r W'm Phipps knight and Govern'r of their Majestyes Dominions in America: humbly sheweth

That your poor and humble Petitioner having been this four monthes in Salem Prison and condemned to die having had no other evidences against me but the Spectre Evidences and the Confessors w'ch Confessors have lately since I was condemned owned to my selfe and others and doe still own that they wronged me and what they had said against me was false: and that they would not that I should have been put to death for a thousand worldes for they never should have enjoyed themselves againe in this world; w'ch undoubtedly I shouled have been put to death had it not pleased the Lord I had been with child. Thankes be to the Lord I know my selfe altogether Innocent & Ignorant of the crime of witchcraft w'ch is layd to my charge: as will appeare at the great day of Judgment (May it please yo'r Excellencye) my husband about five yeares a goe was taken w'th fitts w'ch did very much impaire his memory and understanding but w'th the blessing of the Lord upon my Endeavors did recover of them againe but now through greife and sorrow they are returned to him againe as bad as Ever they were: I having six children and having little or nothing to subsist on being in a manner without a head [husband] to doe any thinge for my selfe or them and being closely confined can see no otherwayes but we shall all perish Therfore may it please your Excellencye your poor and humble petition'r doe humbly begge and Implore of yo'r Excellencye to take it into yo'r pious and Judicious consideration that some speedy Course may be taken w'th me for my releasement.

Source: Paul Boyer and Stephen Nissenbaum, eds., *The Salem Witchcraft Papers, Verbatim Transcripts of the Legal Documents of the Salem Witchcraft Outbreak of 1692* (New York: Da Capo Press, 1977), 1:333–34.

Put It in Context

How might the conviction of a woman like Abigail Faulkner have helped bring an end to the Salem witch trials?

TABLE 4.1   Sex Ratios in the White Population for Selected Colonies, 1624–1755

Date	Colony	White Male Population	White Female Population	Females per 100 Males
1624–1625	Virginia	873	222	25
1660	Maryland	c. 600	c. 190	32
1704	Maryland	11,026	7,136	65
1698	New York	5,066	4,677	92
1726	New Jersey	15,737	14,124	90
1755	Rhode Island	17,860	17,979	101

contributions, while in urban areas the rise of commerce highlighted their role as consumers rather than as producers. As a result, most wives and daughters of white settlers were assigned primarily domestic roles. They also found their legal and economic rights restricted to those accorded their female counterparts in Great Britain.

According to English common law, a wife's status was defined as *feme covert*, which meant that she was legally covered over by (or hidden behind) her husband. The husband controlled his wife's labor, the house in which she lived, the property she brought into the marriage, and any wages she earned. He was also the legal guardian of their children, and through the instrument of a will he could continue to control the household after his death.

> **Explore ▶**
>
> Compare the images of elite women conveyed in a family portrait and a personal letter in Documents 4.2 and 4.3.

With the growth and diversity of colonial towns and cities, the **patriarchal family**—a model in which fathers held absolute authority over wives, children, and servants—came to be seen as a crucial bulwark against disorder. Families with wealth were especially eager to control the behavior of their sons and daughters as the parents sought to build social, commercial, and political alliances. The refusal of Amasa Sessions to marry Sarah Grosvenor, for instance, may have resulted from his father's expectation of a better match.

Working Families. Still, for most colonial women and men, daily rounds of labor shaped their lives more powerfully than legal statutes or inheritance rights. Husbands and wives depended on each other to support the family. By the early eighteenth century, many colonial writers promoted the idea of marriage as a partnership, even if the wife remained the junior partner.

This concept of marriage as a partnership took practical form in communities across the colonies. In towns, the wives of artisans often learned aspects of their husband's craft and assisted their husbands in a variety of ways. Given the overlap between homes and workplaces in the eighteenth century, women often cared for apprentices, journeymen, and laborers as well as their own children. Husbands meanwhile labored alongside their subordinates and represented their families' interests to the larger community. Both spouses were expected to provide models of godliness and to encourage prayer and regular church attendance among household members.

On farms, where the vast majority of colonists lived, women and men played crucial if distinct roles. In general, wives and daughters labored inside the home as well as in the

Elite Women's Lives in the North American Colonies

By the 1740s, elite women were viewed as paragons of piety and domesticity. Yet many contributed wealth and management skills to family enterprises. The painting by Robert Feke (Document 4.2) portrays Isaac Royall of Medford, Massachusetts, with his wife, Elizabeth, and his daughter, sister, and sister-in-law. Isaac's estate was built on his deceased father's trade in rum, sugar, and slaves from Antigua. Elizabeth cared for the family and its staff, including several slaves. In Document 4.3, twenty-year-old Eliza Lucas, born on Antigua, describes her typical routine. Although young and single, she managed her father's South Carolina plantations, adding substantially to the family's wealth.

Document 4.2

Isaac Royall and His Family, 1741

Historical & Special Collections, Harvard Law School Library

Document 4.3

Eliza Lucas | Letter to Miss Bartlett, London, c. 1742

Why, my dear Miss B, will you so often repeat your desire to know how I triffle away my time. . . . [H]ere it is.

In general then I rise at five o'Clock in the morning, read till Seven, then take a walk in the garden or field, see that the Servants [slaves] are at their respective business, then to breakfast. The first hour after breakfast is spent at my musick, the next is constantly employed in recolecting something I have learned least . . . , such as French and short hand. . . . I devote the rest of the time till I dress for dinner to our little Polly and two black girls who I teach to read, and if I have my papa's approbation (my Mamas I have got) I intend [them] for school mistres's for the rest of the Negroe children. . . . [After dinner, musick and then] the rest of the afternoon in Needle work till candle light, and from that time to bed read or write. . . . I have particular matter for particular days. . . . Mondays my musick Master is here. Tuesday my friend Mrs. Chardon (about 3 miles distant) and I are constantly engaged to each other, she at our house one Tuesday—I at hers the next, and this is one of the happiest days I spend at Woppoe. Thursday the whole day . . . is spent in writing, either on the business of the plantation, or letters to my friends. Every other Fryday . . . we go a vizeting so that I go abroad once a week and no oftener. . . .

O! I had like to forgot the last thing I have done a great while. I have planted a large figg orchard with design to dry and export them. . . . [W]as I to tell you how great an Estate I am to make this way . . . you would think me far gone in romance.

Source: Eliza Lucas Pinckney Letterbook, 1739–1762, South Carolina Historical Society.

Interpret the Evidence

1. What do the positions of the Royall family members, their clothing, and the furnishings indicate about the family's and the women's status?
2. How does Eliza Lucas's description of her activities compare with those you imagine the Royall women perform? In what ways do these sources reflect or challenge patriarchal ideals?

Put It in Context

How did the profits of slavery and the slave trade shape the lives of elite women in northern and southern colonies?

surrounding yard with its kitchen garden, milk house, chicken coop, dairy, or washhouse. Husbands and sons worked the fields, kept the livestock, and managed the orchards. Many families supplemented their own labor with that of servants, slaves, or hired field hands. And surplus crops and manufactured goods such as cloth or sausage were exchanged with neighbors or sold at market, creating an economic network of small producers.

Indeed, in the late seventeenth and early eighteenth centuries, many farm families in long-settled areas participated in a household mode of production. Men lent each other tools and draft animals and shared grazing land, while women gathered to spin, sew, and quilt. Individuals with special skills like midwifery or blacksmithing assisted neighbors, adding farm produce or credit to the family ledger. One woman's cheese might be bartered for another woman's jam. A family that owned the necessary equipment might brew barley and malt into beer, while a neighbor with a loom would turn yarn into cloth. The system of exchange, managed largely through barter, allowed individual households to function even as they became more specialized in what they produced. Whatever cash was obtained could be used to buy sugar, tea, and other imported goods.

Farm Life This colorful piece of needlework embroidered by Mehitable Starkey of Boston around 1760 portrays three farmers harvesting grain. A woman at the center holds up a sickle, while a man at her right cuts the wheat and a man at her left bundles it. The frontier environment is suggested by the wild game running across the field at the bottom. Image copyright © The Metropolitan Museum of Art. Image source: Art Resource, NY

Reproduction and Women's Roles. Maintaining a farm required the work of both women and men, which made marriage an economic as well as a social and religious institution. In the early eighteenth century, more than 90 percent of white women married. By 1700 a New England wife who married at age twenty and survived to forty-five bore an average of eight children, most of whom lived to adulthood. In the Chesapeake, mortality rates remained higher and the sex ratio still favored men. It took another generation for southern white women to come close to the reproductive rates of their northern counterparts.

Fertility rates among enslaved Africans and African Americans were much lower than those among whites in the early eighteenth century, and fewer infants survived to adulthood. It was not until the 1740s that the majority of slaves were born in the colonies rather than imported as some southern slave owners began to realize that encouraging reproduction made good economic sense. Still, enslaved women, most of whom worked in the fields, gained only minimal relief from their labors during pregnancy.

Colonial mothers combined childbearing and child rearing with a great deal of other work. While some affluent families could afford wet nurses and nannies, most women fended for themselves or hired temporary help for particular tasks. In rural areas, mothers with babies on hip and children under foot hauled water, fed chickens, collected eggs, picked vegetables, prepared meals, spun thread, and manufactured soap and candles. Children were at constant risk of disease and injury, but were spared the overcrowding, the raw sewage, and the foul water that marked most cities in this period.

Infants were the most vulnerable to disease, and parents were relieved when their children passed their first birthdays. Colonists feared the deaths of mothers as well. In 1700 roughly one out of thirty births ended in the mother's death. Women who bore six to eight children thus faced death on a regular basis. One minister urged pregnant women to prepare their souls, "For ought you know your Death has entered into you."

When a mother died while her children were still young, her husband was likely to remarry soon afterward in order to maintain the family and his farm or business. Even though fathers held legal guardianship over their children, there was little doubt that child rearing, especially for young children, was women's work. Many husbands acknowledged this role, prayed for their wife while in labor, and sought to ease her domestic burdens near the end of a pregnancy. But some women drew little help or protection from their husbands.

The Limits of Patriarchal Order. While most families accepted the idea of female subordination in return for patriarchal protection, there were signs of change in the early eighteenth century. Sermons against fornication; ads for runaway spouses, servants, and slaves; reports of domestic violence; poems about domineering wives; petitions for divorce; and legal suits charging rape, seduction, or breach of contract make clear that ideals of patriarchal authority did not always match the reality. It is impossible to quantify the frequency with which women contested their subordination, but a variety of evidence points to increasing tensions around issues of control—by husbands over wives, fathers over children, and men over women.

Women's claims about men's misbehavior were often demeaned as gossip, but gossip could be an important weapon for those who had little chance of legal redress. In colonial communities, credit and trust were central to networks of exchange, so damaging a man's reputation could be a serious matter. Still, gossip was not as powerful as legal sanctions.

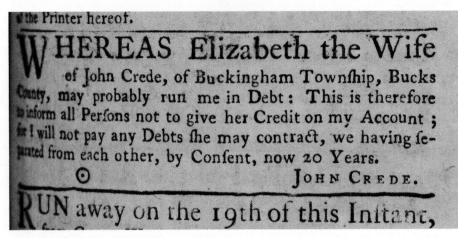

Advertising a Married Couple's Separation   Although it was difficult to obtain a legal divorce, husbands and wives sometimes abandoned each other or agreed to separate. In this June 1743 notice in the *Pennsylvania Gazette*, John Crede notified merchants and other creditors that he would not pay debts contracted by his wife, Elizabeth, from whom he claimed to have been separated for twenty years. Library of Congress

Thus some women who bore illegitimate children, suffered physical and sexual abuse, or were left penniless by a husband who drank might seek assistance from the courts.

Divorce was as rare in the colonies as it was in England. In New England, colonial law allowed for divorce, but few were granted and almost none to women before 1750. In other colonies, divorce could be obtained only by an act of the colonial assembly and was therefore confined to the wealthy and powerful. If a divorce was granted, the wife usually received an allowance for food and clothing. Yet without independent financial resources, she nearly always had to live with relatives. Custody of any children was awarded to fathers who had the economic means to support them, although infants or young girls might be assigned to live with the mother. A quicker and cheaper means of ending an unsatisfactory marriage was to abandon one's spouse. Again wives were at a disadvantage since they had few means to support themselves or their children. Colonial divorce petitions citing desertion and newspaper ads for runaway spouses suggest that husbands fled in at least two-thirds of such cases.

In the rare instances when women did obtain a divorce, they had to bring multiple charges against their husbands. Domestic violence, adultery, or abandonment alone was insufficient to gain redress. Indeed, ministers and relatives were likely to counsel abused wives to change their behavior or suffer in silence. Even evidence of brutal assaults on a wife rarely led to legal redress because husbands had the legal right to "correct" their wives and children and because physical punishment was widely accepted.

Single women also faced barriers in seeking legal redress. By the late seventeenth century, church and civil courts in New England gave up on coercing sexually active couples to marry. Judges, however, continued to hear complaints of seduction or breach of contract brought by the fathers of single women who were pregnant but unmarried. Had Sarah Grosvenor survived the abortion, her family could have sued Amasa Sessions on the grounds that he gained "carnal knowledge" of her through "promises of marriage." If the

TABLE 4.2   Sexual Coercion Cases Downgraded in Chester County, Pennsylvania, 1731–1739

Date	Defendant/Victim	Charge on Indictment in Testimony	Charge in Docket
1731	Lawrence MacGinnis/Alice Yarnal	Assault with attempt to rape	None
1731	Thomas Culling/Martha Claypool	Assault with attempt to rape	Assault
1734	Abraham Richardson/Mary Smith	Attempted rape	Assault
1734	Thomas Beckett/Mindwell Fulfourd	Theft (testimony of attempted rape)	Theft
1734	Unknown/Christeen Pauper	(Fornication charge against Christeen)	None
1735	Daniel Patterson/Hannah Tanner	Violent assault to ravish	Assault
1736	James White/Hannah McCradle	Attempted rape/adultery	Assault
1737	Robert Mills/Catherine Parry	Rape	None
1738	John West/Isabella Gibson	Attempt to ravish/assault	Fornication
1739	Thomas Halladay/Mary Mouks	Assault with intent to ravish	None

Source: Sharon Block, *Rape and Sexual Power in Early America* (Chapel Hill: University of North Carolina Press). Data from Chester County Quarter Sessions Docket Books and File Papers, 1730–1739.

plaintiffs won, the result was no longer marriage, however, but financial support for the child. In 1730 in Concord, Massachusetts, Susanna Holding sued a farmer, Joseph Bright, whom she accused of fathering her illegitimate child. When Bright protested his innocence, Holding found townsmen to testify that the farmer, "in his courting of her . . . had designed to make her his Wife." In this case, the abandoned mother mobilized members of the community, including men, to uphold popular understandings of patriarchal responsibilities. Without such support, women were less likely to win their cases.

Women who were raped faced even greater legal obstacles than those who were seduced and abandoned. In most colonies, rape was a capital crime, punishable by death, and all-male juries were reluctant to find men guilty. Unlikely to win and fearing humiliation in court, few women charged men with rape. Yet more did so than the records might show since judges and justices of the peace sometimes downgraded rape charges to simple assault or fornication, that is, sex outside of marriage (Table 4.2).

Young white women had the best chance of gaining support and redress for seduction or rape if they confided in their parents or other elders. But by the mid-eighteenth century, young people were seeking more control over their sexual behavior and marriage prospects, and certain behaviors—for example, sons settling in towns distant from the parental home, younger daughters marrying before their older sisters, and single women finding themselves pregnant—increased noticeably. In part, these trends were natural consequences of colonial growth and mobility. The bonds that once held families and communities together began to loosen. But in the process, young women's chances of protecting themselves against errant and abusive men diminished. Just as important, even when they faced desperate situations, young women like Sarah Grosvenor increasingly turned to sisters and friends rather than fathers or ministers.

Poor women, especially those who labored as servants, had even fewer options. Servants faced tremendous obstacles in obtaining legal independence from masters or mistresses who beat or sexually assaulted them. Colonial judges and juries generally refused to declare a man who was wealthy enough to support servants guilty of criminal acts against them. Moreover, poor women generally and servants in particular were regularly depicted as lusty and immoral, making it unlikely that they would gain the sympathy of white judges or juries. Slaves faced many of the same obstacles and had even less hope of prevailing against brutal owners. Thus for most servants and slaves, running away was their sole hope for escaping abuse; however, if they were caught, their situation would likely worsen. Even poor whites who lived independently had little chance of addressing issues of domestic violence, seduction, or rape through the courts.

REVIEW & RELATE

Why and how did the legal and economic status of colonial women decline between 1650 and 1750?

How did patriarchal ideals of family and community shape life and work in colonial America? What happened when men failed to live up to those ideals?

Diversity and Competition in Colonial Society

As the English colonies in North America expanded, divisions increased between established families living in long-settled regions—whether on rural farmsteads or in urban homesteads—and the growing population of women and men with few resources. Although most colonists still hoped to own their own land and establish themselves as farmers, artisans, or shopkeepers, fewer were likely to succeed than in the past. By 1760 half of all white men in North America were propertyless. This growing class cleavage was accompanied by increasing racial, national, and religious diversity, which also fostered economic competition and conflict.

Population Growth and Economic Competition. After 1700, the population grew rapidly across the colonies. In 1700 about 250,000 people lived in England's North American colonies. By 1725 that number had doubled, and fifty years later it had reached 2.5 million. Much of the increase was due to natural reproduction, but in addition nearly 250,000 immigrants and Africans arrived in the colonies between 1700 and 1750.

Because more women and children arrived than in earlier decades, higher birthrates and a more youthful population resulted. At the same time, most North American colonists enjoyed a better diet than their counterparts in Europe and had access to more abundant natural resources. Thus colonists in the eighteenth century began living longer, with more adults surviving to watch their children and grandchildren grow up.

However, as the population soared, the chance for individuals to obtain land or start a business of their own diminished. Those who had established businesses early generally expanded to meet new needs, making it more difficult for others to compete. Those bent on making their living from the land often found the soil exhausted in long-settled regions. On the frontier, settlers might have to carve out farms amid forests, swamps, or areas already claimed by Indian, French, or Spanish residents. While owning land did not

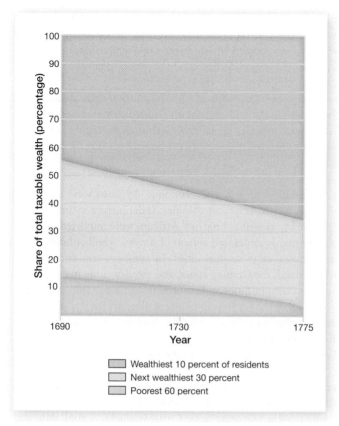

FIGURE 4.1 Wealth Inequality in Northern Cities, 1690–1775

During the eighteenth century, the wealth of merchants rose much faster than that of artisans and laborers. By 1750 the wealthiest 10 percent of the taxable residents of major northern cities owned 60 percent of the taxable wealth, while the poorest 60 percent owned less than 10 percent. This gap between rich and poor only increased over the next quarter century.

Data from Gary B. Nash, *The Urban Crucible: Social Change, Political Consciousness, and the Origins of the American Revolution* (Cambridge, MA: Harvard University Press, 1979).

Legend:
- Wealthiest 10 percent of residents
- Next wealthiest 30 percent
- Poorest 60 percent

automatically lead to prosperity, those who were landless had to find work as tenant farmers, laborers, or in other unskilled occupations. In the South Carolina backcountry, a visitor in the mid-eighteenth century noted that many residents "have nought but a Gourd to drink out of, nor a Plate, Knive or Spoon, a Glass, Cup, or anything."

In prosperous parts of the Middle Atlantic colonies like Pennsylvania, many landless laborers abandoned rural life and searched for urban opportunities. They moved to Philadelphia or other towns and cities in the region, seeking jobs as dockworkers, street vendors, or servants, or as apprentices in one of the skilled trades. But newcomers found the job market flooded and the chances for advancement growing slim (Figure 4.1).

In the South, too, divisions between rich and poor became more pronounced in the early decades of the eighteenth century. Tobacco was the most valuable product in the Chesapeake, and the largest tobacco planters lived in relative luxury. They developed mercantile contacts in seaport cities on the Atlantic coast and in the Caribbean and imported luxury goods from Europe. They also began training some of their slaves as domestic workers to relieve wives and daughters of the strain of household labor.

Small farmers could also purchase and maintain a farm based on the profits from tobacco. In 1750 two-thirds of white families farmed their own land in Virginia, a larger percentage than in northern colonies. An even higher percentage did so in the Carolinas.

Yet small farmers became increasingly dependent on large landowners, who controlled markets, political authority, and the courts. Many artisans, too, depended on wealthy planters for their livelihood, either working for them directly or for the shipping companies and merchants that relied on plantation orders. And the growing number of tenant farmers relied completely on large landowners for their sustenance.

Some southerners fared far worse. One-fifth of all white southerners owned little more than the clothes on their backs in the mid-eighteenth century. At the same time, free blacks in the South found their opportunities for landownership and economic independence increasingly curtailed, while enslaved blacks had little hope of gaining their freedom and held no property of their own.

Increasing Diversity. Population growth and economic divisions were accompanied by increased diversity in the North American colonies. Indentured servants arrived from Ireland, Scotland, and Germany as well as England. Africans were imported in growing numbers and entered a more highly structured system of slavery, whether laboring on southern farms, on northern estates, or in seaport cities. In addition, free families and redemptioners from Ireland, Scotland, the German states, and Sweden came in ever-larger numbers and developed their own communities and cultural institutions. There were also more colonists who had spent time in the Caribbean before settling on the mainland, and the frontiers of British North America were filled with American Indians and French and Spanish settlers as well as European immigrants.

As the booming population demanded more land, colonists pushed westward to find territory that either was not claimed by others or could be purchased. At the beginning of the eighteenth century, German and Scots-Irish immigrants joined Anglo-American settlers in rural areas of New Jersey, Pennsylvania, and Delaware. Many immigrants to Pennsylvania settled in areas like Shamokin that were dotted with Iroquois, Algonquian, and Siouan towns and negotiated with Indians to obtain farmland. At the same time, Delaware and Shawnee groups, who were pushed out of New Jersey and the Ohio Valley by pressure from settlers, also moved into Pennsylvania. They negotiated with colonists, the colonial government, and other Indian groups to establish communities for themselves. All along the Pennsylvania frontier, the lines between Indian and immigrant settlements blurred. Still, many communities prospered in the region, with white settlers exchanging European and colonial trade goods for access to Indian-controlled orchards, waterways, and lands (Map 4.1).

In the 1720s and 1730s, however, Scots-Irish settlers flooded into Pennsylvania when bad harvests and high rents caused them to flee oppressive conditions back home. The new immigrants overwhelmed native communities that had welcomed earlier settlers. The death of William Penn in 1718 exacerbated the situation as his sons and closest advisers struggled to gain control over the colony. Indians were increasingly pushed to the margins as growing numbers of European settlers moved into frontier territories.

Expansion and Conflict. As more and more colonists sought economic opportunities on the frontier, conflicts erupted regularly between earlier British and newer immigrant settlers as well as among immigrant groups. In Pennsylvania, Dutch, Scots-Irish, and German colonists took each other to court, sued land surveyors, and even burned down cabins built by their immigrant foes. For longtime British settlers, such acts only

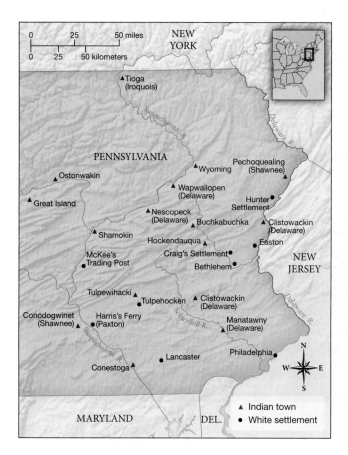

0   25   50 miles
0   25   50 kilometers

MAP 4.1   Frontier Settlements and Indian Towns in Pennsylvania, 1700–1740

German and Scots-Irish immigrants to Pennsylvania mingled with Indian settlements in the early eighteenth century as Delaware and Shawnee groups were pushed west from New Jersey. In the 1720s and 1730s, however, European migration escalated dramatically in the fertile river valleys. In response, once-independent Indian tribes joined the Delaware and Shawnee nations to strengthen their position against the influx of colonists.

From *At the Crossroads: Indians & Empires on a Mid-Atlantic Frontier, 1700–1763* by Jane T. Merritt, Published for the Omohundro Institute of Early American History and Culture. Copyright © 2003 by the University of North Carolina Press. Used by permission of the publisher. www.uncpress.unc.edu.

reinforced their sense that recent immigrants were a threat to their society. In 1728 James Logan, William Penn's longtime secretary, complained that the "Palatines [Germans] crowd in upon us and the Irish yet faster." For Logan, these difficulties were exacerbated by what he considered the "idle," "worthless," and "indigent" habits of Scots-Irish and other recent arrivals.

Anglo-Americans hardly set high standards themselves, especially when negotiating with Indians. Even in Pennsylvania, where William Penn had established a reputation for (relatively) fair dealing, the desire for Indian land led to dishonesty and trickery. Conflicts among Indian nations aided colonial leaders in prying territory from the Indians. Hoping to assert their authority over the independent-minded Delaware Indians, Iroquois chiefs insisted that they held rights to much of the Pennsylvania territory and therefore must be the ones to negotiate with colonial officials. Those colonial authorities, however, produced a questionable treaty supposedly drafted by Penn in 1686 that allowed them to claim large portions of the contested territory. James Logan "discovered" a copy of this treaty, which allowed the English to control an area that could be walked off in a day and a half. Seeking to maintain control of at least some territory, the Iroquois finally agreed to this **Walking Purchase**. The Delaware tribe, far smaller, was then pressured into letting Pennsylvania

Bethlehem, Pennsylvania, 1757 This painting by Nicholas Garrison shows Bethlehem sixteen years after its settlement by German Moravians. The Moravians fled religious persecution in Germany in the early 1700s and established communal societies in Pennsylvania and New Jersey. Moravians pooled their labor and resources so they could sustain farms and shops, establish separate schools for their children, and missionize among local Indians. Art Resource, NY

officials walk off the boundaries. By the time the Delaware acquiesced in the fall of 1737, Pennsylvania surveyors had already marked off the "shortest and best course," which allowed them to extend the boundaries by at least thirty miles beyond those set in the original, and questionable, treaty.

The rapid expansion of the colonial population ensured that conflicts between Indian and colonial leaders over land rights would continue to erupt. Meanwhile migrants and immigrants on the Anglo-American frontier claimed land simply by taking control of it, building houses, and planting crops. This led to conflicts with Indian communities that considered the territory their own, with English officials who demanded legal contracts and deeds, and among immigrants who settled in the same area.

Yet some religiously minded immigrants improved relations with Indians in Pennsylvania, at least temporarily. The tone had been set by William Penn's Quakers, who generally accepted Indian land claims and tried to pursue honest and fair negotiations. German Moravians who settled in eastern Pennsylvania in the 1740s also developed good relations with area tribes. On Pennsylvania's western frontier, Scots-Irish Presbyterians established alliances with Delaware and Shawnee groups. These alliances, however, were rooted less in religious principles than in the hope of profiting from the fur trade as Indians sought new commercial partners when their French allies became too demanding.

Still, as tensions escalated between English and French officials in the region, conflicts intensified among the various immigrant and religious communities and with Indians. The distinct religious traditions and the dramatically different visions of Indian-settler relations drawn from these traditions also sharpened boundaries within and between colonial communities. German Moravians and Scots-Irish Presbyterians in Pennsylvania established churches and schools separate from their Quaker neighbors, while Puritan New Englanders remained suspicious of Quakers as well as other Protestant sects. Moravians and other German sects also flourished in Georgia and the Carolinas, and nearly all sought to isolate themselves from the influences of other religious and ethnic groups.

Some religious groups were isolated as much by force as by choice. While most early Irish immigrants were Protestant, by the early eighteenth century more Irish Catholics began to arrive. Then in 1745 some forty thousand Scots who had supported the Catholic monarchs in England prior to the Glorious Revolution were shipped to the Carolinas after a failed rebellion. Even long-settled Catholics, like those in Maryland, were looked on with suspicion by many Protestants. Although only a few hundred Jewish families resided in the colonies by 1750, they formed small but enduring communities in a number of seaport cities, where they established synagogues and developed a variety of mercantile ventures.

Africans, too, brought new ideas and practices to North America. Transported by force to an unknown land, they may have found religious faith particularly important. Enslaved blacks included some Catholics from regions long held by the Portuguese and a few thousand Muslims, but many Africans embraced religions that were largely unknown to their Anglo-American masters.

As religious affiliations in the colonies multiplied, they reinforced existing concerns about spiritual decline. Moreover, spiritual differences often exacerbated cleavages rooted in nationality and class. And they heightened concerns among many well-established families over the future of British culture and institutions in North America.

REVIEW & RELATE

- How and why did economic inequality in the colonies increase in the first half of the eighteenth century?

- How did population growth and increasing diversity contribute to conflict among and anxieties about the various groups inhabiting British North America?

Religious Awakenings

Whether rooted in fears that worldly concerns were overshadowing spiritual devotion or that growing religious diversity was undermining the power of the church, many Protestant ministers lamented the state of faith in eighteenth-century America. Church leaders in Britain and the rest of Europe shared their fears. Ministers eager to address this crisis of faith—identified in the colonies as **New Light clergy**—worked together to reenergize the faithful and were initially welcomed, or at least tolerated, by more traditional **Old Light clergy**. But by the 1740s, fears that the passionate New Light clergy had gone too far led to a backlash.

The Roots of the Great Awakening. By the eighteenth century, the **Enlightenment**, a European cultural movement that emphasized rational and scientific thinking over traditional religion and superstition, had taken root in the colonies, particularly among elites. Enlightenment thinkers like the English philosopher John Locke, the German intellectual Immanuel Kant, and the French writer Voltaire argued that through reason humans could discover the laws that governed the universe and thereby improve society. Philadelphia printer Benjamin Franklin was one of the foremost advocates of Enlightenment ideas in the colonies. His experiments with electricity reflected his faith in rational thought.

North American colonies attracted settlers from new denominations and as more and more colonists were influenced by Enlightenment thought, the colonists as a whole became more accepting of religious diversity. Enlightenment ideas also undermined the religious vitality of the colonies. While many Enlightenment thinkers believed in a Christian God, they rejected the revelations and rituals that defined traditional church practices and challenged the claims of many ministers that God was directly engaged in the daily workings of the world.

There were, however, countervailing forces. The German **Pietists** in particular challenged Enlightenment ideas that had influenced many Congregational and Anglican leaders in Europe. Pietists decried the power of established churches and urged individuals to follow their hearts rather than their heads in spiritual matters. Persecuted in Germany, Pietists migrated to Great Britain and North America, where their ideas influenced Scots-Irish Presbyterians and members of the Church of England. John Wesley, the founder of Methodism and a professor of theology at Oxford University, taught Pietist ideas to his students, including George Whitefield. Like the German Pietists, Whitefield considered the North American colonies a perfect venue for restoring intensity and emotion to religious worship.

Some colonists had begun rethinking their religious commitments before Whitefield or the Pietists arrived. By 1700 both laymen and ministers voiced growing concern with the state of colonial religion. Preachers educated in England or at colonial colleges like Harvard and William and Mary often emphasized learned discourse over passion. At the same time, there were too few clergy to meet the demands of the rapidly growing population in North America. In many rural areas, residents grew discouraged at the lack of ministerial attention. Meanwhile urban churches increasingly reflected the class divisions of the larger society with wealthier members paying substantial rents to seat their families in the front pews. Farmers and shopkeepers rented the cheaper pews in the middle of the church, while the poorest congregants sat on free benches at the very back or in the gallery. Educated clergy might impress the richest parishioners with their learned sermons, but they did little to move the spirits of the congregation at large.

In 1719 the Reverend Theodorus Freylinghuysen, a Dutch Reformed minister in New Jersey, began emphasizing parishioners' emotional investment in Christ. The Reverend William Tennent arrived in neighboring Pennsylvania with his family about the same time. He despaired that Presbyterian ministers were too few in number to reach the growing population and, like Freylinghuysen, feared that their approach was too didactic. Tennent soon established his own one-room academy to train his sons and other young men for the ministry. Though disparaged by Presbyterian authorities, the school attracted devout students.

Jonathan Edwards, a Congregational minister in Northampton, Massachusetts, joined Enlightenment ideas with religious fervor. A brilliant scholar who studied natural philosophy and science as well as theology, Edwards viewed the natural world as powerful evidence of God's design. He came to view the idea that God elected some individuals for salvation and others for damnation as a source of mystical joy. Although Edwards wrote erudite books and essays, he proclaimed that "our people do not so much need to have their heads stored [with knowledge] as to have their hearts touched." In 1733 to 1735, his sermons on God's absolute sovereignty over man initiated a revival in Northampton that reached hundreds of parishioners.

A few years earlier, Gilbert Tennent had begun urging his flock in New Brunswick, New Jersey, to embrace "a true living faith in Jesus Christ." He took his lead from Freylinghuysen, who viewed conversion as a three-step process: Individuals must be convinced of their sinful nature, experience a spiritual rebirth, and then behave piously as evidence of their conversion. Tennent embraced these measures, believing they could lance the "boil" of an unsaved heart and apply the "balsam" of grace and righteousness. Then in 1739 Tennent met Whitefield, who launched a wave of revivals that revitalized and transformed religion across the colonies.

An Outburst of Revivals.

Whitefield was perfectly situated to extend the series of revivals that scholars later called the **Great Awakening**. Gifted with a powerful voice, he understood that the expanding networks of communication and travel—developed to promote commerce—could also be used to promote religion. Advertising in newspapers and broadsides and traveling by ship, coach, and horseback, Whitefield made seven trips to the North American colonies beginning in 1738. He reached audiences from Georgia to New England to the Pennsylvania backcountry and inspired ministers in the colonies to expand upon his efforts.

In 1739 Whitefield launched a fifteen-month preaching tour that reached tens of thousands of colonists. Like Edwards, Freylinghuysen, and Tennent, he asked individuals to invest less in material goods and more in spiritual devotion. If they admitted their depraved and sinful state and truly repented, God would hear their prayers. Whitefield danced across the platform, shouted and raged, and gestured dramatically, drawing huge crowds everywhere he went. He attracted 20,000 people to individual events, at a time when the entire city of Boston counted just 17,000 residents.

New Light ministers carried on Whitefield's work throughout the 1740s, honing their methods and appeal. Less concerned with denominational affiliation than with core beliefs, they denounced urbane and educated clergy, used extemporaneous oratorical styles and outdoor venues to attract crowds, and invited colonists from all walks of life to build a common Christian community. Some became itinerant preachers, preferring to carry their message throughout the colonies than be constrained by a single church.

New Light clergy brought young people to religion by the thousands. In addition, thousands of colonists who were already church members were "born again," recommitting themselves to their faith. Poor women and men who felt little connection to preaching when they sat on the back benches eagerly joined the crowds at outdoor revivals, where they could stand as close to the pulpit as a rich merchant.

Religious Dissension.

Initially, the Great Awakening drew support from large numbers of ministers because it increased religious enthusiasm and church attendance throughout the colonies. After decades of decline, religion once again took center stage.

But the early embrace by Old Light clergy diminished as revivals spread farther afield, as critiques of educated clergy became more pointed, and as worshippers left established congregations for new churches. A growing number of ministers and other colonial leaders began to fear that revivalists were providing lower-class whites, free blacks, women, and even slaves with compelling critiques of those in power. As the Great Awakening peaked in 1742, a backlash developed among more settled ministers and their congregations. **See Document Project 4: Awakening Religious Tensions, page 132.**

Itinerant preachers traveling across the South seemed especially threatening as they invited blacks and whites to attend revivals together and proclaimed their equality before God. Although it was rare that New Light clergy directly attacked slavery, they implicitly challenged racial hierarchies. Revivalists also attracted African Americans and Indians by emphasizing communal singing and emotional expressions of the spirit, which echoed traditional African and Indian practices.

In the North, too, Old Light ministers and local officials began to question New Light techniques and influences. One of the most radical New Light preachers, James Davenport, attracted huge crowds when he preached in Boston in the early 1740s. Drawing thousands of colonists to Boston Common day after day, Davenport declared that the people "should drink rat poison rather than listen to corrupt, unconverted clergy." Boston officials finally called a grand jury into session to silence him "on the charge of having said that Boston's ministers were leading the people blindfold to hell."

Even some New Light ministers, including Tennent, considered Davenport extreme. Yet revivals continued throughout the 1740s, as the awakening in Pomfret, Connecticut, indicates. Still, over time they lessened in intensity as churches and parishioners settled back into a more ordered religious life. Moreover, the central tenets of revivalist preaching—criticisms of educated clergy, itinerancy, and extemporaneous preaching—worked against the movement's institutionalization. The Great Awakening echoed across the colonies for at least another generation, but its influence was felt more often in attitudes and practices than in institutions.

For example, when, in 1750, King George II (r. 1727–1760) threatened to appoint an Anglican bishop for the North American colonies, many North American ministers, both Old Light and New, resisted the appointment. Most colonists had become used to religious diversity and toleration, at least for Protestants, and had little desire to add church officials to the existing hierarchies of colonial authorities. In various ways, revivalists also highlighted the democratic tendencies in the Bible, particularly in the New Testament. Even as they proclaimed God's wrath against sinners, they also preached that a lack of wealth and power did not diminish a person in God's eyes. And revivalists honed a style of passionate and popular preaching that would shape American religion as well as politics for centuries to come. This mode of communication had immediate application as colonists mobilized to resist what they saw as tyrannical actions by colonial officials and others in authority.

REVIEW & RELATE

What was the relationship between the Enlightenment and the religious revivals of the early eighteenth century?

What was the immediate impact of the Great Awakening, and what were its legacies for American religious and social life?

Political Awakenings

The effects of eighteenth-century religious awakenings rippled out from churches and revivals to influence social and political relations. In various areas, colonists began to question the right of those in power to impose their will on the community as a whole. Similar issues had surfaced before the revivals, but New Light clergy gave greater weight to political and social challenges, allowing colonists to view their resistance to traditional authorities as part of their larger effort to create a better and more just world.

Changing Political Relations. The settlements of the seventeenth century could be regulated with a small number of officials, and in most colonies male settlers agreed on who should rule. However, with geographical expansion, population growth, and commercial development, colonial officials—whether appointed by the crown or selected by local residents—found themselves confronted with a more complex, and more contentious, situation. Most officials were educated men who held property and had family ties to other colonial elites. Although ultimate political authority—or sovereignty—rested with the king and Parliament, many decisions were made by local officials because the king and Parliament were too distant to have a hand in daily colonial life. Another factor that weakened the power of royal officials was the tradition of town meetings and representative bodies, like the Virginia House of Burgesses, that gave colonists a stake in their own governance. Officials in England and the colonies assumed that most people would defer to those in authority, and they minimized resistance by holding public elections in which freemen cast ballots by voice vote. Not surprisingly, those with wealth and power continued to win office.

Still, evidence from throughout the colonial period indicates that deference to authority was not always sufficient to maintain order. Roger Williams and Anne Hutchinson, Bacon's Rebellion, the Stono rebellion, the Salem witchcraft trials, and the radical preaching of James Davenport make clear that not everyone willingly supported their supposed superiors. These episodes of dissent and protest were widely scattered across time and place. But as the ideas disseminated by New Light clergy converged with changing political relations, resistance to established authority became more frequent and more collective.

Dissent and Protest. Protests against colonial elites multiplied from the 1730s on. The issues and methods varied, but they indicate a growing sense of political and economic autonomy among North American colonists. Some protests focused on royal officials like governors and Royal Navy captains; others focused on local authorities, merchants, or large landowners. Whatever the target of resistance, protests demonstrated colonists' belief that they had rights that were worth protecting, even against those who held legitimate authority. Just as importantly, dissenters included the poor, women, and African Americans as well as property-owning white men.

Access to reasonably priced food, especially bread, inspired regular protests in the eighteenth century. During the 1730s, the price of bread—a critical staple in colonial diets—rose despite falling wheat prices and a recession in seaport cities. Bread rioters attacked grain warehouses, bakeries, and shops, demanding more bread at lower prices. Such uprisings were often led by women, who were responsible for putting bread on the table; thus when grievances involved domestic or consumer issues, women felt they had the right to make their voices heard.

Boston Town Hall   Boston's Town Hall and the broad avenue on which it sat was engraved by the German artist Franz Xavier Habermann, who specialized in scenes of urban North America. The buildings reflect a European view of the city's affluence in the mid-eighteenth century, as do the clothes worn by the two gentlemen talking over their walking sticks.
Bibliotheque Nationale, Paris, France/Bridgeman Images

Public markets were another site where struggles over food led to collective protests. In 1737, for instance, Boston officials decided to construct a public market and charge fees to farmers who sold their goods there. Small farmers, who were used to selling produce from the roadside for free, clashed with officials and with larger merchants over the venture. Many Boston residents supported the protesters because the market fees would lessen competition and raise prices for consumers. When petitions to city officials had no effect, opponents demolished the market building and stalls in the middle of the night. Local authorities could find no witnesses to the crime.

Access to land was also a critical issue in the colonies. Beginning in the 1740s, protests erupted on estates in New Jersey and along the Hudson River in New York over the leasing policies of landlords as well as the amount of land controlled by speculators. When tenants and squatters petitioned colonial officials and received no response, they took collective action. They formed associations, targeted specific landlords, and then burned barns, attacked livestock, and emptied houses and farm buildings of furniture and tools. Eventually, they established regional committees to hear grievances and formed "popular" militia companies and courts to mete out justice to recalcitrant land owners. When landlords and colonial officials called out local militia to arrest the perpetrators, they failed to consider that militia members were often the same poor men whose protests they ignored.

In seaport cities, a frequent source of conflict was the **impressment** of colonial men who were seized and forcibly drafted into service in the Royal Navy. Not only sailors but also dockworkers and men drinking at taverns along the shore might find themselves suddenly pressed into military service. Facing the navy's high mortality rates, bad food, rampant disease, and harsh discipline, these men were unwilling to wait while colonial officials, worried about labor shortages, petitioned the British government to stop the impressment. Instead, they fought back. In 1747 in Boston, a general impressment led to three days of rioting. An observer noted that "Negros, servants, and hundreds of seamen seized a naval lieutenant, assaulted a sheriff, and put his deputy in stocks, surrounded the governor's house, and stormed the Town House (city hall)." Such riots did not end the system of impressment, but they showed that colonists would battle those who sought to deprive them of their liberty.

The religious upheavals and economic uncertainties of the 1730s and 1740s led colonists to challenge colonial and British officials with greater frequency than in earlier decades. But most protests also accentuated class lines as the poor, small farmers, and craftsmen fought against merchants, landowners, and local officials. Still, the resistance to impressment proved that colonists could mobilize across economic differences when British policies affected diverse groups of colonial subjects.

Transforming Urban Politics. The development of cross-class alliances in the 1730s and 1740s was also visible in the more formal arena of colonial politics. Beginning in the 1730s, some affluent political leaders in cities like New York and Philadelphia began to seek support from a wider constituency. In most cases, it was conflicts among the elite that led to these appeals to the "popular" will. In 1731, for instance, a new royal charter confirmed New York City's existence as a "corporation" and stipulated the rights of freemen (residents who could vote in local elections after paying a small fee) and freeholders (individuals, whether residents or not, who held property worth £40 and could vote on that basis). A large number of artisans, shopkeepers, and laborers acquired the necessary means to vote, and shopkeepers and master craftsmen now sat alongside wealthier men on the Common Council. Yet most laboring men did not participate actively in elections until 1733, when local elites led by Lewis Morris sought to mobilize the mass of voters against royal officials, like Governor William Cosby, appointed in London.

Morris, a wealthy man and a judge, joined other colonial elites in believing that the royal officials recently appointed to govern New York were tied to ministerial corruption in England. Morris, as chief justice of the provincial court, ruled against Governor Cosby in a suit the new governor brought against his predecessor. Cosby then suspended Morris from office. In the aftermath, Morris and his supporters—the Morrisites—took his case to the people, who were suffering from a serious economic depression. Morrisites launched an opposition newspaper, published by apprentice printer John Peter Zenger, to mobilize artisans, shopkeepers, and laborers around an agenda to stimulate the economy and elect men supportive of workers to the city's common council

Explore ▶

See part of Hamilton's defense of Zenger in Document 4.4.

In his *New-York Weekly Journal*, Zenger leaped into the political fray, accusing Governor Cosby and his cronies of corruption, incompetence, election fraud, and tyranny. The vitriolic attacks led to Zenger's indictment for seditious libel and his imprisonment in November 1734. At the time, libel related only to whether published material undermined government authority, not whether it was true or false.

SOLO ANALYSIS

Andrew Hamilton's Defense of John Peter Zenger, 1736

In 1734 John Peter Zenger, the publisher of the *New-York Weekly Journal*, was arrested for printing articles accusing New York's colonial governor of corruption and fraud. Colonists widely protested Zenger's arrest and followed his trial closely. Zenger's attorney, Andrew Hamilton, argued that his client's accusations against the governor were true and therefore not libel. Since English common law defined libel as a statement undermining government authority, regardless of whether it was truthful, Hamilton's successful defense of Zenger signaled an important moment in the history of free speech and the press.

Document 4.4

Mr. Hamilton. May it please Your Honour; I agree with Mr. Attorney, that Government is a sacred Thing, but I differ very widely from him when he would insinuate, that the just Complaints of a Number of Men, who suffer under a bad Administration, is libelling that Administration. Had I believed that to be Law, I should not have given the Court the Trouble of hearing any Thing that I could say in this cause. . . . What strange Doctrine is it, to press every Thing for Law here which is so in England? I believe we should not think it a Favour, at present at least, to establish this Practice. In England so great a Regard and Reverence is had to the Judges, that if any man strike another in Westminster Hall, while the Judges are sitting, he shall lose his Right Hand, and forfeit his Land and Goods, for so doing. And tho' the Judges here claim all the Powers and

Authorities within this Government, that a Court of King's Bench has in England, yet I believe Mr. Attorney will scarcely say, that such a Punishment could be legally inflicted on a Man for committing such an Offence, in the Presence of the Judges sitting in any Court within the Province of New-York. The Reason is obvious; a Quarrel or Riot in New-York cannot possibly be attended with those dangerous Consequences that it might in Westminster Hall; nor (I hope) will it be alledged, that any Misbehaviour to a Governor in the Plantations will, or ought to be, judged of or punished, as a like Undutifulness would be to Our Sovereign.

Source: Livingston Rutherfurd, ed., *John Peter Zenger, His Press, His Trial, and a Bibliography of Zenger Imprints* (New York: Dodd, Mead, 1904), 74, 77.

Interpret the Evidence

1. What do Hamilton's arguments tell us about colonial perceptions of government?
2. What argument is Hamilton making about the relationship between the colonies and Britain?

Put It in Context

Why were jurors willing to ignore English common law in finding Zenger innocent and to thereby set a novel legal precedent?

But Zenger's lead attorney, Andrew Hamilton of Philadelphia, argued that truth must be recognized as a defense against charges of libel. Appealing to a jury of Zenger's peers, Hamilton proclaimed, "It is not the cause of a poor printer, nor of New York alone, which you are now trying. . . . It is the best cause. It is the cause of liberty." In response, jurors ignored the law as written and acquitted Zenger.

Although the decision in the Zenger case did not lead to a change in British libel laws, it did signal the willingness of colonial juries to side with fellow colonists against king and Parliament in at least some situations. Building on their success, Morris and his followers continued to gain popular support. In 1737 his son, Lewis Morris Jr., was appointed speaker of the new Assembly, and the Assembly appointed Zenger as its official printer. But soon the group fell into disarray when royal officials offered political prizes to a few of their leaders. Indeed, the elder Morris accepted appointment as royal governor of New Jersey, after which he switched allegiances and became an advocate of executive authority. Nonetheless, the political movement he led had aroused ordinary freemen to participate in elections, and newspapers and pamphlets now readily attacked corrupt officials and threats to the rightful liberties of British colonists.

Even as freemen gained a greater voice in urban politics, they could challenge the power of economic and political leaders only when the elite were divided. Moreover, the rewards they gained sometimes served to reinforce class divisions. Thus many city work-ers had benefited when the elder Morris used his influence to ensure the building of the city's first permanent almshouse in 1736. The two-year project employed large numbers of artisans and laborers in a period of economic contraction. Once built, however, the alms-house became a symbol of the growing gap between rich and poor. Its existence was also used by future city councils as a justification to eliminate other forms of relief, leaving the poor in worse shape than before.

REVIEW & RELATE

- How did ordinary colonists, both men and women, black and white, express their political opinions and preferences in the first half of the eighteenth century?

- How did politics bring colonists together across economic lines in the first half of the eighteenth century? How did politics highlight and reinforce class divisions?

Conclusion: A Divided Society

By 1750 religious and political awakenings had transformed colonists' sense of their relation to spiritual and secular authorities. Both Gilbert Tennent and Sarah Grosvenor were caught up in these transitions. As a man and a minister, how-ever, Tennent had far more power to control his destiny than did Grosvenor. While wives and daughters in elite families benefited from their wealth and position, they were also constrained by the strictures of the patriarchal family. Women who were poor, indentured, or enslaved were forced into the greatest dependency on male employers and civic officials. But even women in farm and artisanal families depended on loving husbands and fathers to offset the strictures of patriarchal authority. While few col-onists conceived of themselves as part of a united body politic, women probably identified most deeply with their family, town, or church. Yet men, too, thought of themselves as English, or Scots-Irish, or German, rather than more broadly American. At best, they claimed identity as residents of Massachusetts, New Jersey, or South Carolina rather than British North America.

Between 1680 and 1750, the diversity and divisions among colonists increased as class, racial, religious, and regional differences multiplied across the colonies. Immigrants from Germany, Ireland, and Scotland created their own communities; religious awakenings led to cleavages among Protestants and between them and other religious groups; and economic inequality deepened in seacoast cities. At the same time, conflicts between Indians and settlers intensified along the frontier as growing numbers of enslaved Africans reshaped economic and social relations in the urban North and the rural South.

Still, by midcentury, the colonies as a whole had been transformed in significant ways. Religious leaders had gained renewed respect, colonial assemblies had wrested more autonomy from royal hands, freemen participated more avidly in political contests and debates, printers and lawyers insisted on the rights and liberties of colonists, and local communities defended those rights in a variety of ways. When military conflicts brought British officials into more direct contact with their colonial subjects in the following decade, they sought to check these trends, with dramatic consequences.

TIMELINE OF EVENTS

1636	Harvard College established
1688	Glorious Revolution
1692	Salem witch trials
1700–1750	250,000 immigrants and Africans arrive in the colonies
1700–1775	Population of British North America grows from 250,000 to 2.5 million
1720–1740	Influx of Scots-Irish to Pennsylvania
1734	John Peter Zenger acquitted of libel
1737	Iroquois and Delaware acquiesce to Walking Purchase
	Protest against public market in Boston
1739	George Whitefield launches preaching tour of the colonies
1745	40,000 Scottish Catholics shipped to the Carolinas after failed rebellion
1747	Rioting in Boston against impressment
1750	Colonists resist appointment of an Anglican bishop for North America

KEY TERMS

spectral evidence, *106*
patriarchal family, *109*
Walking Purchase, *119*
New Light clergy, *121*
Old Light clergy, *121*

Enlightenment, *122*
Pietists, *122*
Great Awakening, *123*
impressment, *127*

REVIEW & RELATE

1. What factors led to a rise in tensions within colonial communities in the early 1700s?

2. How did social, economic, and political tensions contribute to an increase in accusations of witchcraft?

3. Why and how did the legal and economic status of colonial women decline between 1650 and 1750?

4. How did patriarchal ideals of family and community shape life and work in colonial America? What happened when men failed to live up to those ideals?

5. How and why did economic inequality in the colonies increase in the first half of the eighteenth century?

6. How did population growth and increasing diversity contribute to conflict among and anxieties about the various groups inhabiting British North America?

7. What was the relationship between the Enlightenment and the religious revivals of the early eighteenth century?

8. What was the immediate impact of the Great Awakening, and what were its legacies for American religious and social life?

9. How did ordinary colonists, both men and women, black and white, express their political opinions and preferences in the first half of the eighteenth century?

10. How did politics bring colonists together across economic lines in the first half of the eighteenth century? How did politics highlight and reinforce class divisions?

Awakening Religious Tensions

The Great Awakening and the Enlightenment were two of the most influential developments in the early eighteenth-century colonies. Although often considered as oppositional, some New Light ministers embraced Enlightenment ideas, and some advocates of the Enlightenment respected popular New Light preachers (Document 4.6). Ultimately, conflicts over the Great Awakening came mainly from Old Light preachers who feared the disruption of traditional church structures and discipline and from civic leaders who feared the social disruption fostered by New Light revivals.

Certainly there were significant differences between the rational approach of scientific observers like Benjamin Franklin and the passion of preachers like George Whitefield. Moreover, many colonists favored the emotional connections they found in religious revivals over the Enlightenment's intellectual approach to social ills. Still, the two were not always in direct competition. Differences were at least as great between New Light and Old Light ministers. Old Light ministers initially embraced the Awakening as a way to revive religiosity in the colonies. The powerful preaching of George Whitefield and Jonathan Edwards attracted thousands of people who were deeply moved by their sermons (Documents 4.5, 4.6, and 4.7). But as revivalist preachers grew more popular, Old Lights became increasingly uneasy. By 1742 the controversial actions of itinerant preachers like James Davenport led Old Light ministers as well as newspaper editors and civic leaders to critique the movement as a whole (Document 4.8). One concern of many critics was the challenge the Awakening posed to established relations of class and status. At mass revivals, women and men, old and young, upper and lower classes, and even blacks and whites mingled. And sermons often included pointed critiques of colonial elites (Documents 4.8 and 4.9). Thus New Light preachers revitalized but also challenged established churches and the established order.

The following selections reflect the views of the New Lights, advocates of the Enlightenment, and critics of the revivals. As you read, consider the religious, social, and political issues at stake in the Great Awakening.

Document 4.5

Nathan Cole | On George Whitefield Coming to Connecticut, 1740

As the Great Awakening swept through British North America in the 1730s and 1740s, thousands flocked to revivals led by traveling ministers. George Whitefield, an English evangelical preacher, launched an extensive speaking tour of the colonies in 1739 to 1740. In the following passage, Nathan Cole, a Connecticut farmer, describes his own reaction and that of the crowd assembled at Wethersfield to hear Whitefield preach.

We went down in the Stream; I heard no man speak a word all the way three mile but every one pressing forward in great haste and when we got down to the old meeting house there was a great multitude; it was said to be 3 or 4000 of people assembled together. We got off from our horses and shook off the dust and the ministers were then coming to the meeting house. I turned and looked toward the great river and saw the ferry boats running swift forward and backward bringing over loads of people; the oars rowed nimble and quick. Every thing men horses and boats all seemed to be struggling for life; the land and the banks over the river looked black with people and horses all along the 12 miles. I see no man at work in his field but all seemed to be gone—when I saw Mr. Whitefield come upon the Scaffold [platform] he looked almost angelical, a young slim slender youth before some thousands of people and with a bold undaunted countenance, and my hearing how God was with him every where as he came along it solemnized my mind and put me in a trembling fear before he began to preach; for he looked as if he was clothed with authority from the great God, and a sweet solemn solemnity sat upon his brow. And my hearing him preach gave me a heart wound; by God's blessing my old foundation was broken up and I saw that my righteousness would not save me; then I was convinced of the doctrine of Election and went right to quarreling with God about it because all that I could do would not save me; and he had decreed from Eternity who should be saved and who not.

Source: George Leon Walker, *Some Aspects of the Religious Life of New England* (New York: Silver, Burnett, 1897), 91–92.

Document 4.6

Benjamin Franklin | On George Whitefield, the Great Revivalist, 1739

Benjamin Franklin, the Philadelphia printer, inventor, and politician, was an ardent advocate of the Enlightenment. But he was also interested in popular causes and thus attended one of Whitefield's sermons in Philadelphia in 1739, and several thereafter. While Franklin remained a religious skeptic, he and Whitefield became friends. In his *Autobiography* Franklin printed several of Whitefield's sermons and described the preacher's power.

In 1739 arriv'd among us from England the Rev. Mr. Whitefield, who had made himself remarkable there as an itinerant Preacher. . . . The Multitudes of all Sects and Denominations that attended his Sermons were enormous and it was [a] matter of Speculation to me who was one of the Number, to observe the extraordinary Influence of his Oratory on his Hearers, and how much they admir'd and respected him, notwithstanding his common Abuse of them, by assuring them they were naturally *half Beasts and half Devils*. It was wonderful to see the Change soon made in the Manners of our Inhabitants; from being thoughtless or indifferent about Religion, it seem'd as if all the World were growing Religious. . . .

He us'd indeed sometimes to pray for my Conversion, but never had the Satisfaction of believing that his Prayers were heard. . . .

He had a loud and clear Voice, and articulated his Words and Sentences so perfectly that he might be heard and understood at a great Distance, especially as his Auditors [audience], however numerous, observ'd the most exact Silence. He preach'd one Evening from the Top of the Court House Steps, which are in the middle of Market Street, and on the West Side of Second Street which crosses it at right angles. Both Streets were fill'd with his Hearers to a considerable distance. Being among the hindmost in Market Street, I had the Curiosity to learn how far he could be heard, by retiring backwards down the Street towards the River; and I found his Voice distinct till I came near Front Street. . . . Imagining then a Semicircle, of which my Distance should be the Radius, and that it were fill'd with Auditors, . . . I computed that he might well be heard by more than Thirty Thousand. . . .

His delivery . . . was so improv'd by frequent Repetitions that every Accent, every Emphasis, every Modulation of Voice, was so perfectly well turn'd and well plac'd, that without being interested in the Subject, one could not help being pleas'd with the Discourse, a Pleasure of much the same kind with that receiv'd from an excellent Piece of Music. This is an Advantage itinerant Preachers have over those who are stationary: as the latter cannot well improve their Delivery of a Sermon by so many Rehearsals.

Source: *The Autobiography of Benjamin Franklin, The Unmutilated and Correct Version*, comp. and ed. John Bigelow (New York: G. P. Putnam's Sons, 1912), 220–25.

Jonathan Edwards | Sinners in the Hands of an Angry God, 1741

Before enrolling at Yale College at age twelve, Jonathan Edwards studied natural history and wrote an essay titled "The Flying Spider." However, his adult fame came from his theological works; his ministry at Christ Church in Northampton, Massachusetts; and his sermons, which he delivered in a quiet yet emotive voice. He first delivered "Sinners in the Hands of an Angry God" at a revival in Enfield, Connecticut, in 1741. Religious opposition to the revivals eventually forced Edwards from his Northampton pulpit, but he continued to publish and to preach, including to New England Indians.

There is nothing that keeps wicked Men at any one Moment, out of Hell, but the meer Pleasure of GOD.

By the meer Pleasure of God, I mean his sovereign Pleasure, his arbitrary Will, restrained by no Obligation, hinder'd by no manner of Difficulty, any more than if nothing else but God's meer Will had in the least Degree, or in any Respect whatsoever, any Hand in the Preservation of wicked Men. . . .

He is not only able to cast wicked Men into Hell, but he can most easily do it. . . .

We find it easy to tread on and crush a Worm that we see crawling on the Earth; so 'tis easy for us to cut or singe a slender Thread that any Thing hangs by; thus easy is it for God when he pleases to cast his Enemies down to Hell. . . .

[What] Use may be of [an] *Awakening* to unconverted Persons in this Congregation[?] . . . That World of Misery, that Lake of burning Brimstone is extended abroad under you. . . .

You probably are not sensible of this. . . . [But] if God should let you go, you would immediately sink and swiftly descend & plunge into the bottomless Gulf, and your healthy Constitution, and your own Care and Prudence, and best Contrivance, and all your Righteousness, would have no more Influence to uphold you and keep you out of Hell, than a Spider's Web would have to stop a falling Rock. . . .

The God that holds you over the Pit of Hell, much as one holds a Spider, or some loathsome Insect, over the Fire, abhors you, and is dreadfully provoked. . . .

[But] now you have an extraordinary Opportunity, a Day wherein CHRIST has flung the Door of Mercy wide open, and stands in the Door calling and crying with a loud Voice to poor Sinners. . . .

And you that are *young* Men, and *young* Women, will you neglect this precious Season that you now enjoy, when so many others of your Age are renouncing all youthful Vanities, and flocking to CHRIST? You especially have now an extraordinary Opportunity; but if you neglect it, it will soon be with you as it is with those Persons that spent away all the precious Days of Youth in Sin, and are now come to such a dreadful pass in blindness and hardness. . . .

Therefore let every one that is out of CHRIST, now awake and fly from the Wrath to come. The Wrath of almighty GOD is now undoubtedly hanging over great Part of this Congregation: Let every one fly out of *Sodom: Haste and escape for your Lives, look not behind you, escape to the Mountain, least you be consumed.*

Source: Jonathan Edwards, *"Sinners in the Hands of an Angry God," A Sermon Preached at Enfield, July 8, 1741* (Boston: S. Kneeland and T. Grant, 1741), 5, 12–13, 15, 23–24, 25.

Document 4.8

Newspaper Report on James Davenport, 1743

James Davenport, whose popular sermons denounced Old Light clergy as corrupt and worldly, was a controversial New Light minister. During the early 1740s, his behavior became increasingly erratic, culminating in a public burning of "immoral" books in New London, Connecticut, in 1743. Davenport also urged his audience to throw luxury items and clothing into the fire. Davenport even took off his own pants and threw them into the fire. His actions, and the ensuing controversy, caused some New Light ministers to turn against Davenport, and by 1744 he issued a public apology for his behavior. The following selection from a Boston newspaper describes the incident in New London.

Multitudes hasten'd toward the Place of Rendezvous, directing themselves by the Clamor and Shouting, which together, with the ascending Smoak [smoke] bro't them to one of the most public Places in the Town, and there found these good People encompassing a Fire which they had built up in the Street, into which they were casting Numbers of Books, principally on Divinity, and those that were well-approved by Protestant Divines, viz. . . . Mr. Russel's Seven Sermons, one of Dr. Colman's, and one of Dr. Chauncy's Books, and many others. Nothing can be more astonishing than their insolent Behaviour was during the Time of their Sacrifice, as 'tis said they call'd it; whilst the Books were in the Flames they cry'd out, *Thus the Souls of the Authors of those Books, those of them that are dad [dead], are roasting in the Flames of Hell; and that the Fate of those surviving, would be the same, unless speedy Repentance prevented:* On the next Day they had at the same Place a second Bonfire of the like Materials, and manag'd in the same manner. Having given this fatal Stroke to Heresy, they made ready to attack Idolatry, and sought for Direction, as in the Case before; and then Mr. [Davenport] told them to look at Home first, and that they themselves were guilty of idolizing their Apparel, and should therefore divest themselves of those Things especially which were for Ornament, and let them be burnt: Some of them in the heighth of their Zeal, conferred not with Flesh and Blood, but fell to stripping and cast their Cloaths [clothes] down at their Apostle's Feet; one or two hesitated about the Matter, and were so bold as to tell him they had nothing on which they idoliz'd: He reply'd, that such and such a Thing was an Offence to him; and they must down with them. . . . Next Mr. [Davenport] pray'd himself; and now the Oracle spake clear to the Point, without Ambiguity, and utter'd that *the Things must be burnt*; and to confirm the Truth of the Revelation, took his wearing Breeches, and hove them with Violence into the Pile, saying, *Go you with the Rest.*

Source: "Religious Excess at New London," *Boston Weekly Post-Boy*, March 28, 1743, in *The Great Awakening: Documents on the Revival of Religion, 1740–1745*, ed. Richard L. Bushman (New York: Institute of Early American History and Culture, 1970), 51–52.

George Whitefield Preaching, c. 1760

Paintings and engravings of the Great Awakening highlighted the most famous preachers and the diverse women and men who attended revivals. This painting by English artist John Collet captures an outdoor revival and shows Whitefield's appeal to a mixed audience of women and men. Collet was known for his satirical images of English life, so it is not clear whether the inclusion of working people and dogs is meant to illustrate or demean Whitefield's broad appeal.

Private Collection/Bridgeman Images

Interpret the Evidence

1. How does Benjamin Franklin's description of George Whitefield compare to Nathan Cole's, and how might the Enlightenment have influenced Franklin's view (Documents 4.5 and 4.6)?

2. What aspects of God's will and human sin does Jonathan Edwards emphasize in his sermon? How is Edwards's interest in science revealed in Document 4.7?

3. Why does James Davenport (Document 4.8) encourage his followers to burn religious books by Old Light ministers as well as items considered idolatrous, and how does the Boston newspaper respond to the resulting bonfires?

4. How does the image in Document 4.9 compare to the descriptions by Cole, Franklin, and the Boston newspaper (Documents 4.5, 4.6, and 4.8)? What aspects of these descriptions and of Edwards's sermon (Document 4.7) do Old Light ministers and civic leaders find threatening?

Put It in Context

How do these documents help explain the appeal of the Great Awakening, particularly to women, workers and other non-elites? What legacies—ideas or practices—remained after the revivals ended?

What was the relationship between the Enlightenment and the Great Awakening in the American colonies?

War and Empire

1750–1774

WINDOW TO THE PAST

The Stamp Act Repealed, 1766

In 1765 the British Parliament passed the Stamp Act, which imposed a tax on a variety of paper items and documents in the American colonies to help pay debts from the French and Indian War. But the Stamp Act aroused widespread protests in the colonies, forcing its repeal in 1766. This political cartoon depicts a funeral service for the American stamps held by its British supporters. ▶ To discover more about what this primary source can show us, see Document 5.3 on page 157.

Library of Congress, 3g02568

After reading this chapter you should be able to:

- Understand the causes and consequences of the French and Indian War.

- Explain how British policies following the French and Indian War fostered colonial grievances.

- Analyze the major British policies from 1764 to 1774 and how colonial responses to them became more unified.

AMERICAN HISTORIES

Praised as the father of the United States, George Washington remained a loyal British subject for forty-three years. He was born in 1732 to a prosperous farm family in eastern Virginia. When his father died in 1743, George became the ward of his half-brother Lawrence, who took control of the family's Mount Vernon estate. Lawrence's father-in-law, William Fairfax, was an agent for Lord Fairfax, one of the chief proprietors of the colony. When George was sixteen, William hired him to help survey Lord Fairfax's land on Virginia's western frontier.

As a surveyor, George journeyed west, coming into contact with Indians, both friendly and hostile, as well as other colonists seeking land. George began investing in western properties, but when Lawrence Washington died in 1752, George suddenly became head of a large estate. He gradually expanded Mount

Vernon's boundaries and its enslaved workforce, increasing its profitability.

George was soon appointed Lieutenant Colonel in the Virginia militia, and in the fall of 1753 Virginia's governor sent him to warn the French against encroaching on British territory in the Ohio River valley. The French commander rebuffed Washington and, within six months, gained control of a British post near present-day Pittsburgh, Pennsylvania, and named it Fort Duquesne. With help from Indians hostile to the French, Washington's surprise attack on Fort Duquesne in May 1754 led the governors of Virginia and North Carolina to provide the newly promoted Colonel Washington with more troops. The French then responded with a much larger force that compelled Washington to surrender.

Washington's fortunes and his family increased when he married the wealthy widow Martha Dandridge Custis in 1759. With more land to defend, Washington supported efforts to extend Britain's North American empire westward to create a protective buffer against European and Indian foes.

Like Washington, Hermon Husband hoped to improve his lot through hard work and new opportunities on the frontier. Born to a modest farm family in Maryland in 1724, he was swept up by George Whitefield's preaching in 1739, but eventually joined the Society of Friends, or Quakers. Although his farm in Maryland was thriving, Husband explored prospects on the North Carolina frontier. In 1784 he settled with his family at Sandy Creek.

Husband once again proved a successful farmer, but he denounced wealthy landowners and speculators who made it difficult for small farmers to obtain sufficient land. He also challenged established leaders in the Quaker meeting and was among a number of worshippers disowned from the Cane Creek Friends Meeting in 1764. Disputes within radical Protestant congregations were not unusual in this period as members with deep religious convictions chose the liberty of their individual conscience over church authority.

In 1766 local farmers joined Husband in organizing the Sandy Creek Association, through which they sought to increase their political clout in order to combat corruption among local officials. The

(*left*) **George Washington.** Granger, NYC

(*right*) **Hermon Husband's Deed.** Courtesy of the State Archives of North Carolina

association disbanded after two years, but its ideas lived on in a group called the Regulation, which brought together frontier farmers to "regulate" government abuse. The Regulators petitioned the North Carolina Assembly and Royal Governor William Tryon, demanding legislative reforms and suing local officials for extorting labor, land, and money from poorer residents.

Husband quickly emerged as one of the organization's chief pamphleteers, articulating the demands of

the Regulators and echoing other colonial protesters of the period. Governor Tryon viewed the Regulators as threatening the colony's peace and order and, in 1768 and 1771, had Husband and other Regulators arrested. This confirmed the group's belief that they could not receive fair treatment at the hands of colonial officials. They then turned to extralegal methods to assert their rights, such as taking over courthouses so that legal proceedings against debt-ridden farmers could not proceed. ■

The American histories of Washington and Husband were shaped by both opportunities and conflicts. Mid-eighteenth-century colonial America offered greater opportunities for social advancement and personal expression than anywhere in Europe, but collective efforts to take advantage of these opportunities often led to tension and discord. Frontier conflicts foreshadowed a broader struggle for land and power within the American colonies. Religious and economic as well as political discord intensified in the mid-eighteenth century as upheavals among colonists increasingly occurred alongside challenges to British authority. Whatever their grievances, most colonists worked hard to reform systems they considered unfair or abusive before resorting to more radical means of instituting change.

Imperial Conflicts and Indian Wars, 1754–1763

The war that erupted in the Ohio valley in 1754 sparked an enormous shift in political and economic relations in colonial North America. What began as a small-scale, regional conflict expanded into a series of brutal and lengthy wars around the world. The French and Indian War in North America, known as the Seven Years' War in Great Britain and Europe, had the greatest impact. It led to a dramatic expansion of British territory in North America and to increasing demands from American colonists for more control over their own lives.

The Opening Battles. Even before Washington and his troops were defeated in July 1754, the British sought to protect the colonies against threats from the French and the Indians. To limit such threats, the British were especially interested in cementing an alliance with the powerful Iroquois Confederacy, composed of six northeastern tribes. Thus the British invited an official delegation from the Iroquois to a meeting in June 1754 in Albany, New York, with representatives from several colonies. Benjamin Franklin of Philadelphia had drawn up a Plan of Union that would establish a council of representatives from the various colonial assemblies to debate issues of frontier defense, trade, and territorial expansion and to recommend terms mutually agreeable to colonists and Indians. Their deliberations were to be overseen by a president-general appointed and supported by the British crown.

Join or Die Benjamin Franklin created the first political cartoon in American history to accompany an editorial he wrote in the *Pennsylvania Gazette* in 1754. Franklin's cartoon urged the mainland British colonies to unite politically during the French and Indian War. Legend had it that a snake could come back to life if its severed sections were attached before dusk. Library of Congress, 3g05315

The **Albany Congress** created new bonds among a small circle of colonial leaders, but it failed to establish a firmer alliance with the Iroquois or resolve problems of colonial governance. The British government worried that the proposed council would undermine the authority of the royal government. At the same time, the individual colonies were unwilling to give up any of their autonomy in military, trade, and political matters to some centralized body. Moreover, excluded from Franklin's Plan of Union, the Iroquois delegates at the Albany Congress broke off talks with the British in early July.

Yet if war was going to erupt between the British and the French, the Iroquois and other Indian tribes could not afford to have the outcome decided by imperial powers alone. For most Indians, contests among European nations for land and power offered them the best chance of survival in the eighteenth century. They gained leverage as long as various imperial powers needed their trade items, military support, and political alliances. This leverage would be far more limited if one European nation controlled most of North America.

Still, Indian tribes adopted different strategies. The Delaware, Huron, Miami, and Shawnee nations, for example, allied themselves with the French, hoping that a French victory would stop the far more numerous British colonists from invading their settlements in the Ohio River valley. Members of the Iroquois Confederacy, on the other hand, tried to play one power against the other, hoping to win concessions from the British in return for their military support. The Creek, Choctaw, and Cherokee nations also sought to perpetuate the existing stalemate among European powers by bargaining alternately with the British in Georgia and the Carolinas, the French in Louisiana, and the Spaniards in Florida. Faced with incursions into their lands, some Indian tribes, like the Abenaki in northern New England, launched preemptive attacks on colonial settlements.

The British government soon decided it had to send additional troops to defend its American colonies against attacks from Indians and intrusions from the French. General

Edward Braddock and two regiments arrived in 1755 to expel the French from Fort Duquesne. At the same time, colonial militia units were sent to battle the French and their Indian allies along the New York and New England frontiers. Colonel Washington joined Braddock as his personal aide-de-camp. Within months, however, Braddock's forces were ambushed, bludgeoned by French and Indian forces, and Braddock was killed.

Other British forces fared little better during the next three years. Despite having far fewer colonists in North America than the British, the French had established extensive trade networks that helped them sustain a protracted war with support from numerous Indian nations. Alternating guerrilla tactics with conventional warfare, the French captured several important forts, built a new one on Lake Champlain, and moved troops deep into British territory. The ineffectiveness of the British and colonial armies also encouraged Indian tribes along the New England and Appalachian frontiers to reclaim land from colonists. Bloody raids devastated many outlying settlements, leading to the death and capture of hundreds of Britain's colonial subjects.

A Shift to Global War. As the British faced defeat after defeat in North America, European nations began to contest imperial claims elsewhere in the world. In 1756 France and Great Britain officially declared war against each other. Eventually Austria, Russia, Sweden, most of the German states, and Spain allied with France, while Portugal and Prussia sided with Great Britain. Naval warfare erupted in the Mediterranean Sea and the Atlantic and Indian Oceans. Battles were also fought in Europe, the West Indies, India, and the Philippines. By the end of 1757, Britain and its allies had been defeated in nearly every part of the globe. The war appeared to be nearing its end, with France in control.

Then in the summer of 1757, William Pitt took charge of the British war effort. He transformed the political and military landscape in the American colonies, while Prussian forces held the line in Europe. Pouring more soldiers and arms into the North American campaign along with young and ambitious officers like Colonel Henry Bouquet, Pitt energized colonial and British troops.

By the summer of 1758, the tide began to turn. In July, British generals recaptured the fort at Louisburg on Cape Breton Island, a key to France's defense of Canada. Then British troops with Bouquet and Washington's aid seized Fort Duquesne, which was renamed Fort Pitt. Other British forces captured Fort Frontenac

Colonel George Washington This 1772 oil painting by Charles Willson Peale portrays George Washington as a colonel in the Virginia militia. Washington commanded this militia during the French and Indian War following the death of General Braddock. After the war, Washington prospered as a planter and land speculator. Granger, NYC

along the St. Lawrence River, while Prussia defeated France and its allies in Europe and Britain gained key victories in India (Map 5.1). In 1759 General Jeffrey Amherst captured Forts Ticonderoga and Crown Point on Lake Champlain while General James Wolfe attacked a much larger French force in Quebec. Despite heavy casualties, including Wolfe himself, the British won Quebec and control of Canada.

The Costs of Victory.   Despite Wolfe's dramatic victory, the war dragged on in North America, Europe, India, and the West Indies for three more years. By then, however, King George III had tired of Pitt's grand, and expensive, strategy and dismissed him. He then opened peace negotiations with France and agreed to give up a number of conquered

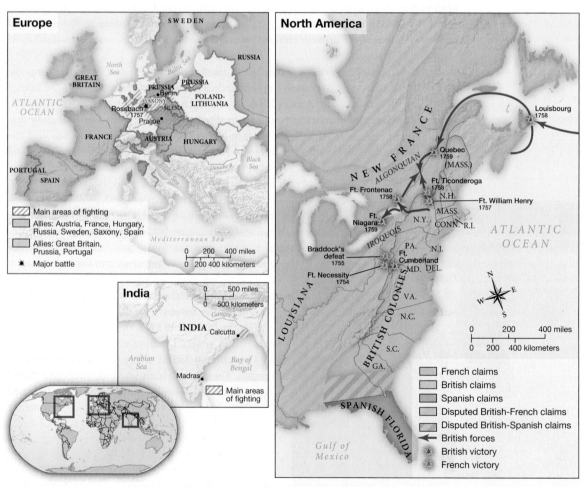

MAP 5.1   The French and Indian War, 1754–1763

Clashes between colonial militia units and French and Indian forces erupted in North America in 1754. The conflict helped launch a wider war that engulfed Europe as well as the West Indies and India. In the aftermath of this first global war, Britain gained control of present-day Canada and India, but France retained its West Indies colonies.

territories in order to finalize the **Peace of Paris** in 1763. Other countries were ready to negotiate as well. To regain control of Cuba and the Philippines, Spain ceded Florida to Great Britain. While France was expelled from North America, it rewarded Spanish support by granting Spain Louisiana and all French lands west of the Mississippi River. Despite these concessions, the British empire reigned supreme, regaining control of India as well as North America east of the Mississippi, all of Canada, and a number of Caribbean islands.

The wars that erupted between 1754 and 1763 reshaped European empires, transformed patterns of global trade, and initially seemed to tighten bonds between North American residents and the mother country. Yet the Peace of Paris did not resolve many of the problems that had plagued the colonies before the war, and it created new ones as well.

The incredible cost of the war raised particularly difficult problems. Over the course of the war, the national debt of Great Britain had more than doubled. At the same time, as the North American colonies grew and conflicts erupted along their frontiers, the costs of administering these colonies increased fivefold. With an empire that stretched around the globe, the British crown and Parliament were forced to consider how to pay off war debts, raise funds to administer their far-flung territories, and keep sufficient currency in circulation for expanding international trade. Just as important, the Peace of Paris ignored the claims of Indian tribes to the territories that France and Spain turned over to Great Britain. Nor did the treaty settle contested claims among the colonies themselves over lands in the Ohio River valley and elsewhere along British North America's new frontiers.

Battles and Boundaries on the Frontier. The sweeping character of the British victory encouraged thousands of colonists to move farther west, into lands once controlled by France. This exacerbated tensions that were already rising on the southern and western frontiers of British North America.

In late 1759, for example, the Cherokee nation, reacting to repeated incursions on its hunting grounds, dissolved its long-term trade agreement with South Carolina. Cherokee warriors attacked backcountry farms and homes, leading to counterattacks by British troops. The fighting continued into 1761, when Cherokees on the Virginia frontier launched raids on colonists there. General Jeffrey Amherst then sent 2,800 troops to invade Cherokee territory and end the conflict. The soldiers sacked fifteen villages; killed men, women, and children; and burned acres of fields.

Although British raids diminished the Cherokees' ability to mount a substantial attack, sporadic assaults on frontier settlements continued for years. These conflicts fueled resentments among backcountry settlers not only against Indians but also against political leaders in eastern parts of the colonies who rarely provided sufficient resources for frontier defense.

A more serious conflict erupted in the Ohio River valley when Indians realized the consequences of British victories. When the British captured French forts along the Great Lakes and in the Ohio valley in 1760, they immediately antagonized local Indian groups by hunting and fishing on tribal lands and depriving villages of much-needed food. British traders also defrauded Indians on numerous occasions and ignored traditional obligations of gift giving.

The harsh realities of the British regime led some Indians to seek a return to ways of life that preceded the arrival of white men. An Indian visionary named Neolin preached that Indians had been corrupted by contact with Europeans and urged them to purify themselves by returning to their ancient traditions, abandoning white ways, and reclaiming their lands. Neolin was a prophet, not a warrior, but his message inspired others, including an Ottawa leader named Pontiac.

When news arrived in early 1763 that France was about to cede all of its North American lands to Britain and Spain, Pontiac convened a council of more than four hundred

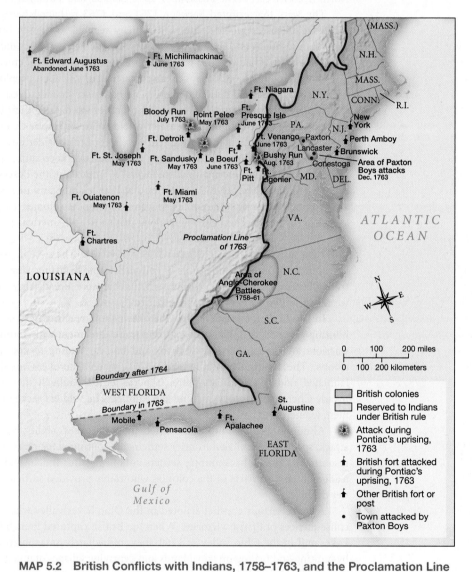

MAP 5.2 British Conflicts with Indians, 1758–1763, and the Proclamation Line

The entrance of British troops into former French territory in the Ohio River valley following the French and Indian War fueled conflicts with Indian nations. Colonists in Pennsylvania and the Carolinas also battled with Indians, including tribes who were allies or remained neutral during the war. Parliament established the Proclamation Line to limit westward expansion and thereby diminish such hostilities.

Ottawa, Potawatomi, and Huron leaders near Fort Detroit. Drawing on Neolin's vision, he proclaimed, "It is important my brothers, that we should exterminate from our land this nation [Britain], whose only object is our death. You must all be sensible," he continued, "that we can no longer supply our wants the way we were accustomed to do with our Fathers the French." Pontiac then mobilized support to drive out the British. In May 1763, Pontiac's forces laid siege to Detroit and soon gained the support of eighteen Indian nations. They then attacked Fort Pitt and other British frontier outposts as well as white settlements along the Virginia and Pennsylvania frontier (Map 5.2).

Accounts of violent encounters with Indians on the frontier circulated throughout the colonies and sparked resentment among settlers as well as British troops. Many colonists did not distinguish between friendly and hostile Indians. In December 1763, a group of men from Paxton Creek, Pennsylvania, raided families of peaceful, Christian Conestoga Indians near Lancaster, killing thirty. Protests from eastern colonists infuriated the Paxton Boys, who then marched on Philadelphia demanding protection from "savages" on the frontier.

Although violence on the frontier slowly subsided, neither side had achieved victory. Without French support, Pontiac and his followers had to retreat. Meanwhile, Benjamin Franklin negotiated a truce between the Paxton Boys and the Pennsylvania authorities, but it did not settle the fundamental issues over protection of western settlers. Convinced that it could not endure further costly frontier clashes, the British crown issued a proclamation in October 1763 forbidding colonial settlement west of a line running down the Appalachian Mountains to create a buffer between Indians and colonists. But Parliament also ordered Colonel Bouquet to subdue hostile Indians in the Ohio region.

The **Proclamation Line of 1763** denied colonists the right to settle west of the Appalachian Mountains. Instituted just months after the Peace of Paris was signed, the Proclamation Line frustrated colonists who sought the economic benefits won by a long and bloody war. Small farmers, backcountry settlers, and squatters who had hoped to improve

The Indians Delivering Up English Captives to Colonel Bouquet, 1764 Conflicts continued in the Ohio territory well after the Peace of Paris. Colonel Henry Bouquet led an army of 1,500 men into the region, forcing the Shawnee and Delaware to accept peace terms. These included the return of all English captives. Artist Benjamin West makes clear that some women and children did not want to leave their Indian families. Yale Center for British Art, Paul Mellon Collection, USA / Bridgeman Images

their lot by acquiring rich farmlands were told to stay put. Meanwhile Washington and other wealthy speculators managed to acquire additional western lands, certain that the Proclamation was merely "a temporary expedient to quiet the Minds of the Indians."

Conflicts over Land and Labor Escalate.

Conflicts among colonists and with Britain were not confined to frontier regions. Land riots directed against the leasing policies of landlords and the greed of speculators had plagued New York's Hudson valley and New Jersey before the war, and these struggles continued into the 1760s. New clashes also occurred in the Carolinas as settlers like Hermon Husband stood up to landlords and government officials.

Even before the French and Indian War ended, the owners of large estates along the Hudson River in New York State raised rents and reduced the rights of tenants. In the early eighteenth century, the titles to some of these estates were challenged by small land-owners and tenants, but even where legitimate titles existed, tenants declared a moral right to own the land they had long farmed. The manors and estates of the Hudson valley, they claimed, were more appropriate to a feudal government than to an enlightened empire.

Farmers in neighboring New Hampshire were drawn into battles over land when the king's Privy Council in London decided in 1764 that the Green Mountains belonged to New York rather than New Hampshire. Landlords along the Hudson River hoped to expand eastward into this region, but the farmers already living there claimed they had bought the land in good faith and deserved to keep it. These farmers launched guerrilla warfare against New York authorities and large landowners as well as against New York farmers who claimed land that New Hampshire families had cleared and settled. These Green Mountain Boys, led by Ethan Allen, refused to recognize New York authorities as legitimate and established their own local governments and popular courts.

Inspired by the Green Mountain Boys and uprisings in New Jersey, tenants in the Hudson valley banded together in 1765 and 1766. Under the leadership of Irish immigrant William Prendergast, a group of tenants calling themselves Levellers refused to pay rent and instead claimed freehold title to the land they farmed. New York tenants petitioned the colonial assembly and sought redress in a variety of ways. But landowners refused to negotiate, and Prendergast concluded that "there was no law for poor men."

In many ways, the beliefs of Allen, Prendergast, and their followers echoed those of Hermon Husband and the North Carolina **Regulators**. All of these groups developed visible, well-organized networks of supporters, targeted specific landlords, sought redress first through colonial courts and assemblies, and then established popular militias and other institutions to govern themselves and to challenge those in authority.

Explore ▶

Read part of Hermon Husband's account of the Regulators' grievances in Document 5.1.

REVIEW & RELATE

● How did the French and Indian War and the subsequent peace treaty affect relations among Britain, American Indian nations, and American colonies?

● How did the French and Indian War and the increasing power of large landowners contribute to conflict between average colonists and colonial elites?

GUIDED ANALYSIS

Hermon Husband | Causes of Armed Resistance in North Carolina, 1770

Frontier settler Hermon Husband owned substantial land, but most of his neighbors were poor families who had cleared vacant lands in the southern backwoods. They planned to gain legal title when agents for Earl Granville, Lord Proprietor of a large tract in North Carolina, arrived, but the agents failed to appear. Having paid taxes and fees on their land, many farmers joined the Regulators to resist what they saw as abusive practices. In a 1770 pamphlet, *An Impartial Relation*, Husband summarized his understanding of the causes of the Regulator uprising.

Document 5.1

What justifies the right of people to clear and cultivate vacant land before gaining legal title to it?

What actions by the Earl of Granville, his agents, and North Carolina officials does Husband consider abusive?

How does Husband explain the actions of poor families who organized to oppose British authorities?

[I]t has been the Opinion of all the several Legislative Bodies, both of Great-Britain and her Colonies, that peaceable Possession, especially of back waste vacant Lands, is a Kind of Right, always looked upon quite sufficient to entitle them to the Preference or Refusal of a farther [legal] Title. . . . This method has been used from New-England to Georgia, some Hundreds of Years Past. . . .

Now the Earl of Granville's Office, shut in such a manner, that no one in the Province knew but it would open again every year. . . . [B]ut four or five years being now elapsed, there is so much of the Lands seated under these Circumstances [cleared and cultivated], that Individuals in Power, and who has Money, are Marking them out for a Prey. . . .

It is to be feared too many of our Rulers have an eye to make a Prey of these poor People, because an Opinion seems to be propagated, that it is Criminal to cut a Tree down off the vacant Lands. Whether this Notion took its Rise from the great Men's making Tar and Turpentine on vacant Lands . . . or from the Motive's above mentioned [powerful men seeking improved lands], I would advise no honest Man to suffer such an Opinion to take Place with him; for the Thing is so inhuman and base, that you will not find a man but he will deny and clear himself, or hide such a Design as long as he can. . . .

Who can justify the Conduct of any Government who have countenanced and encouraged so many Thousands of poor Families to bestow their All, and the Labour of many Years, to improve a Piece of waste Land, with full Expectation of a Title, to deny them Protection from being rob[b]ed of it all by a few roguish Individuals, who never bestowed a Farthing thereon?

Source: Hermon Husband, *Impartial Relation of the First Rise and Cause of the Recent Differences in Publick Affairs, in the Province of North Carolina; and of the Past Tumults and Riots that Lately Happened in that Province* (North Carolina, 1770), 74, 77–78.

Put It in Context

How do Husband's complaints against colonial officials and elites compare with those of Hudson River tenants and the Green Mountain Boys?

Postwar British Policies and Colonial Unity

Throughout the 1750s and 1760s, ordinary colonists challenged the authority of economic and political elites to impose their will on local communities and individual residents. Before and during the French and Indian War, most of these challenges involved conflicts among colonists themselves. Yet in the decade following the war, from 1764 to 1774, common grievances against Britain united colonists across regional and economic differences. British policies, like the Proclamation Line of 1763, inspired widespread dissent as poor farmers, large landowners, and speculators sought to expand westward. A second policy, impressment, by which the Royal Navy forced young colonial men into military service, also aroused anger across regions and classes. At the same time, the Great Awakening provided colonists with shared ideas about moral principles and new techniques for mass communication. Finally, Britain's efforts to repay its war debts by taxing colonists and its plan to continue quartering troops in North America led colonists to forge intercolonial protest movements.

Common Grievances. Like the Proclamation Line, which denied all colonists the right to settle beyond the Appalachian Mountains, the policy of impressment affected port city residents of all classes. Impressment had been employed by the British during the extended wars of the eighteenth century to procure seamen. While plucking poor men from ports throughout the British empire, the Royal Navy faced growing resistance to this practice in the American colonies from merchants and common folk alike.

Seamen and dockworkers had good reason to fight off impressment agents. Men in the Royal Navy faced low wages, bad food, harsh punishment, rampant disease, and high mortality. As the practice escalated with each new war, the efforts of British naval officers and impressment agents to capture new "recruits" met violent resistance, especially in the

Impressment by the British
This eighteenth-century engraving depicts the harsh impressment of men into the British navy. Set in England, this illustration shows that impressment was widely practiced at home. Thus the British government did not single out colonists for special mistreatment. © Mary Evans/The Image Works

North American colonies where several hundred men might be impressed at one time. In such circumstances, whole communities joined in the battle.

In the aftermath of the French and Indian War, serious impressment riots erupted in Boston, New York City, and Newport, Rhode Island. Increasingly, poor colonial seamen and dockworkers made common cause with owners of merchant ships and mercantile houses in protesting British policy. Colonial officials—mayors, governors, and custom agents—were caught in the middle. Some insisted on upholding the Royal Navy's right of impressment; others tried to placate both naval officers and local residents; and still others resisted what they saw as an oppressive imposition on the rights of colonists. Both those who resisted British authority and those who sought a compromise had to gain the support of the lower and middling classes to succeed.

Employers and politicians who opposed impressment gained an important advantage if they could direct the anger of colonists away from themselves and toward British policies. The decision of British officials to continue quartering troops in the colonies gave local leaders another opportunity to join forces with ordinary colonists. Colonial towns and cities were required to quarter (that is, house and support) British troops even after the Peace of Paris was signed. While the troops were intended to protect the colonies, they also provided reinforcements for impressment agents and surveillance over other illegal activities like smuggling and domestic manufacturing. Thus a range of issues and policies began to bind colonists together through common grievances against the British Parliament.

Forging Ties across the Colonies.

The ties forged between poorer and wealthier colonists over issues of westward expansion, impressment, and quartering grew stronger in the 1760s, but they tended to be localized in seaport cities or in specific areas of the frontier. Creating bonds across the colonies required considerably more effort in a period when communication and transportation beyond local areas were limited. Means had to be found to disseminate information and create a sense of common purpose if the colonists were going to persuade Parliament to take their complaints seriously. One important model for such intercolonial communication was the Great Awakening.

By the 1750s, the Great Awakening seemed to be marked more by dissension than by unity as new denominations continued to split from traditional churches. For example, in the Sandy Creek region of North Carolina, home to Hermon Husband, radical Protestants formed the Separate Baptists, who proclaimed a message of absolute spiritual equality. From the late 1750s through the 1770s, Separate Baptists converted thousands of small farmers, poor whites, and enslaved women and men and established churches throughout Virginia, Georgia, and the Carolinas.

Like Separate Baptists, Methodists, Dunkards, Moravians, and Quakers also offered southern residents religious experiences that highlighted spiritual equality. Some dissenting preachers invited slaves and free blacks to attend their services alongside local white farmers, farmwives, and laborers. Slaveholders and other elite southerners considered such practices outrageous and a challenge to the political as well as the social order.

Most women and men who converted to Separate Baptism, Methodism, or other forms of radical Protestantism did not link their religious conversion directly to politics. But as more and more ordinary colonists and colonial leaders voiced their anger at offensive British policies, evangelical techniques used to rouse the masses to salvation became important for mobilizing colonists to protest.

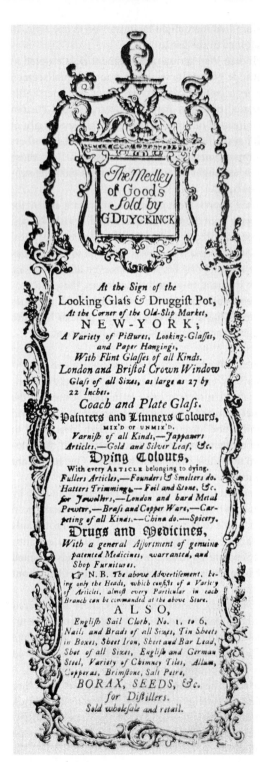

Thus even though the Great Awakening had spent its religious passion in most parts of North America by the 1760s, the techniques of mass communication and critiques of opulence and corruption it initiated provided emotional and practical ways of forging ties among widely dispersed colonists. Many evangelical preachers had condemned the lavish lifestyles of colonial elites and the spiritual corruption of local officials. Now in the context of conflicts with Great Britain, colonial leaders used such rhetoric to paint Parliament and British officials as aristocrats with little faith and less compassion.

The public sermons and mass gatherings used during the Great Awakening to inspire loyalty to a greater moral cause could now be translated into forms applicable to political protest. The efforts of Great Britain to assert greater control over its North American colonies provided colonial dissidents an opportunity to test out these new ways to forge intercolonial ties.

Great Britain Seeks Greater Control. Until the French and Indian War, British officials and their colonial subjects coexisted in relative harmony. Economic growth led Britain to ignore much of the smuggling and domestic manufacturing that took place in the colonies, since such activities did not significantly disrupt Britain's mercantile policies (see "Imperial Policies Focus on Profits" in chapter 3). Similarly, although the king and Parliament held ultimate political sovereignty, or final authority, over the American colonies, it was easier to allow some local control over political decisions, given the communication challenges created by distance.

This pattern of **benign** (or "salutary") **neglect** led some American colonists to view themselves as more independent of British control than they really were. Many colonists came to see smuggling, domestic manufacturing, and local self-governance as rights rather than privileges. Thus when British officials decided to assert greater control, many colonists protested.

The Medley of Goods Sold by G. Duyckinck, 1769   This ornate advertising lithograph was intended to attract customers. The variety of goods listed here by one New York City merchant includes items, like glass and cloth, that were taxed under various parliamentary acts in the 1760s. As these taxes aroused protests, merchants had to decide which items to remove from their stock and consumers which items to boycott. Private Collection/Peter Newark American Pictures/Bridgeman Images

To King George III and to Parliament, asserting control over the colonies was both right and necessary. In 1763 King George appointed George Grenville to lead the British government. As Prime Minister and Chancellor of the Exchequer, Grenville faced an economic depression in England, rebellious farmers opposed to a new tax on domestic cider, and growing numbers of unemployed soldiers returning from the war. He believed that regaining political and economic control in the colonies could help resolve these crises at home.

Eighteenth-century wars, especially the French and Indian War, cost a fortune. British subjects in England paid taxes to help offset the nation's debts, even though few of them benefited as directly from the British victory as did their counterparts in the American colonies. The colonies would cost the British treasury more if the crown could not control colonists' movement into Indian territories, limit smuggling and domestic manufacturing, and house British troops in the colonies cheaply.

To reassert control, Parliament launched a three-prong program. First, it sought stricter enforcement of existing laws and established a Board of Trade to centralize policies and ensure their implementation. The **Navigation Acts**, which prohibited smuggling, established guidelines for legal commerce, and set duties on trade items, were the most important laws to be enforced. Second, Parliament extended wartime policies into peacetime. For example, the Quartering Act of 1765 ensured that British troops would remain in the colonies to enforce imperial policy. Colonial governments were expected to support them by allowing them to use vacant buildings and providing them with food and supplies.

The third part of Grenville's colonial program was the most important. It called for the passage of new laws to raise funds and reestablish the sovereignty of British rule. The first revenue act passed by Parliament was the American Duties Act of 1764, known as the **Sugar Act**. It imposed an **import duty**, or tax, on sugar, coffee, wines, and other luxury items. The act actually reduced the import tax on foreign molasses, which was regularly smuggled into the colonies from the West Indies, but insisted that the duty be collected. The crackdown on smuggling increased the power of customs officers and established the first vice-admiralty courts in North America to ensure that the Sugar Act raised money for the crown. That same year, Parliament passed the Currency Act, which prohibited colonial assemblies from printing paper money or bills of credit. Taken together, these provisions meant that colonists would pay more money into the British treasury even as the supply of money (and illegal goods) diminished in the colonies.

Some colonial leaders protested the Sugar Act through speeches, pamphlets, and petitions, and Massachusetts established a **committee of correspondence** to circulate concerns to leaders in other colonies. However, dissent remained disorganized and ineffective. Nonetheless, the passage of the Sugar and Currency Acts caused anxiety among many colonists, which was heightened by passage of the Quartering Act the next year. Colonial responses to these developments marked the first steps in an escalating conflict between British officials and their colonial subjects.

REVIEW & RELATE

How did Britain's postwar policies lead to the emergence of unified colonial protests?

Why did British policymakers believe they were justified in seeking to gain greater control over Britain's North American colonies?

Resistance to Britain Intensifies

Over the next decade, between 1764 and 1774, the British Parliament sought to extend its political and economic control over the American colonies, and the colonists periodically resisted. With each instance of resistance, Parliament demanded further submission to royal authority. With each demand for submission, colonists responded with greater assertions of their rights and autonomy. Still, no one imagined that a revolution was in the making.

The Stamp Act Inspires Coordinated Resistance. Grenville decided next to impose a stamp tax on the colonies similar to that long used in England. The stamp tax required that a revenue stamp be affixed to all transactions involving paper items, from newspapers and contracts to playing cards and diplomas. Grenville announced his plans in 1764, a full year before Parliament enacted the **Stamp Act** in the spring of 1765. The tax was to be collected by colonists appointed for the purpose, and the money was to be spent within the colonies at the direction of Parliament for "defending, protecting and securing the colonies." To the British government, the Stamp Act seemed completely fair. After all, Englishmen paid on average 26 shillings in tax annually, while Bostonians averaged just 1 shilling. Moreover, the act was purposely written to benefit the American colonies.

The colonists viewed it in a more threatening light. The Stamp Act differed from earlier parliamentary laws in three important ways. First, by the time of its passage, the colonies were experiencing rising unemployment, falling wages, and a downturn in trade. All of these developments were exacerbated by the Sugar, Currency, and Quartering Acts passed by Parliament the previous year. Second, critics viewed the Stamp Act as an attempt to control the *internal* affairs of the colonies. It was not an indirect tax on trade, paid by importers and exporters, but a direct tax on daily business. Third, such a direct intervention in the economic affairs of the colonies unleashed the concerns of both local officials and ordinary residents that Parliament was taxing colonists who had no representation in its debates and decisions.

By announcing the Stamp Act a year before its passage, Grenville allowed colonists plenty of time to organize their opposition. In New York City, Boston, and other cities, merchants, traders, and artisans formed groups dedicated to the repeal of the Stamp Act. Soon Sons of Liberty, Daughters of Liberty, Sons of Neptune, Vox Populi, and similar organizations emerged to challenge the imposition of the Stamp Act. Even before the act was implemented, angry mobs throughout the colonies attacked stamp distributors. Some were beaten, others tarred and feathered, and all were forced to take an oath never to sell stamps again.

Colonists lodged more formal protests with the British government as well. The Virginia House of Burgesses, led by Patrick Henry, acted first. It passed five resolutions, which it sent to Parliament, denouncing taxation without representation. The Virginia Resolves were reprinted in many colonial newspapers and repeated by orators to eager audiences in Massachusetts and elsewhere. At the same time, the Massachusetts House adopted a circular letter—a written protest circulated to the other colonial assemblies—calling for a congress to be held in New York City in October 1765 to consider the threat posed by the Stamp Act.

In the meantime, popular protests multiplied. The protests turned violent in Boston, where **Sons of Liberty** leaders like Samuel Adams, a Harvard graduate and town official, organized mass demonstrations. Adams modeled his oratory on that of itinerant preach-ers, but with a political twist. Other activists used more visual means of inspiring their audiences. At dawn on August 14, 1765, the Boston Sons of Liberty hung an effigy of stamp distributor Andrew Oliver on a tree and called for his resignation. A mock funeral procession, joined by farmers, artisans, apprentices, and the poor, marched to Boston Common. The crowd, led by shoemaker and French and Indian War veteran Ebenezer Mackintosh, carried the fake corpse to the Boston stamp office and destroyed the building. Demonstrators saved pieces of lumber, "stamped" them, and set them on fire outside Oli-ver's house. Oliver, wisely, had already left town.

Oliver's brother-in-law, Lieutenant Governor Thomas Hutchinson, arrived at the scene and tried to quiet the crowd, but he only angered them further. They soon destroyed Oliver's stable house, coach, and carriage, which the crowd saw as signs of aristocratic opulence.

The battle against the Stamp Act unfolded across the colonies with riots, beatings, and resignations reported from Newport, Rhode Island, to New Brunswick, New Jersey, to Charles Town (later Charleston), South Carolina. On November 1, 1765, when the Stamp Act officially took effect, not a single stamp agent remained in his post in the colonies.

Protesters carefully chose their targets: stamp agents, sheriffs, judges, and colonial officials. Even when violence erupted, it remained focused, with most crowds destroying stamps and stamp offices first and then turning to the private property of Stamp Act sup-porters. These protests made a mockery of notions of deference toward British rule. But they also revealed growing autonomy on the part of middling- and working-class colonists who attacked men of wealth and power, sometimes choosing artisans rather than wealth-ier men as their leaders. However, this was not primarily a class conflict because many wealthier colonists made common cause with artisans, small farmers, and the poor. Indeed, colonial elites considered themselves the leaders, inspiring popular uprisings through the power of their political arguments and oratorical skills. Still, they refused to support actions they considered too radical.

It was these more affluent protesters who dominated the Stamp Act Congress that met in New York City in October 1765. It brought together twenty-seven delegates from nine colonies. The delegates petitioned Parliament to repeal the Stamp Act, arguing that taxa-tion without representation was tyranny. Delegates then urged colonists to boycott British goods and refuse to pay the stamp tax. Yet they still proclaimed their loyalty to king and country.

The question of representation became a mainstay of colonial protests. Whereas the British accepted the notion of "virtual representation," by which members of Parliament gave voice to the views of particular classes and interests, the North American colonies had developed a system of representation based on locality. According to colonial leaders, only members of Parliament elected by colonists could represent their interests.

Even as delegates at the Stamp Act Congress declared themselves loyal, if disaffected, British subjects, they participated in the process of developing a common identity in the American colonies. Christopher Gadsden of South Carolina expressed the feeling most directly. "We should stand upon the broad common ground of natural rights," he argued. "There should be no New England man, no New-Yorker, known on the continent, but all of us Americans."

Eventually the British Parliament was forced to respond to colonial protests and even more to rising complaints from English merchants and traders whose business had been damaged by the colonists' boycott. Parliament repealed the Stamp Act in March 1766, and King George III granted his approval a month later. Victorious colonists looked forward to a new and better relationship between themselves and the British government.

From the colonists' perspective, the crisis triggered by the Stamp Act demonstrated the limits of parliamentary control. Colonists had organized effectively and forced Parliament to repeal the hated legislation. Protests had raged across the colonies and attracted support from a wide range of colonists. Individual leaders, like Patrick Henry of Virginia and Samuel Adams of Massachusetts, became more widely known through their fiery oratory and their success in appealing to the masses. The Stamp Act agitation also demonstrated the growing influence of ordinary citizens who led parades and demonstrations and joined in attacks on stamp agents and the homes of British officials. And the protests revealed the growing power of the written word and printed images in disseminating ideas among colonists. Broadsides, political cartoons, handbills, newspapers, and pamphlets circulated widely, reinforcing discussions and proclamations at taverns, rallies, demonstrations, and more formal political assemblies.

> **Explore ▶**
>
> See Documents 5.2 and 5.3 for two different types of dissent.

For all the success of the Stamp Act protests, American colonists still could not imagine in 1765 that protest would ever lead to open revolt against British sovereignty. More well-to-do colonists were concerned that a revolution against British authority might fuel a dual revolution in which small farmers, tenants, servants, slaves, and laborers would rise up against their political and economic superiors in the colonies. Even most middling- and working-class protesters believed that the best solution to the colonies' problems was to gain greater economic and political rights within the British empire, not to break from it.

The Townshend Act and the Boston Massacre. The repeal of the Stamp Act in March 1766 led directly to Parliament's passage of the Declaratory Act. That act declared that Parliament had the authority to pass any law "to bind the colonies and peoples of North America" closer to Britain. No new tax or policy was established; Parliament simply wanted to proclaim Great Britain's political supremacy in the aftermath of the successful stamp tax protests.

Following this direct assertion of British sovereignty, relative harmony prevailed in the colonies for more than a year. Then in June 1767, a new chancellor of the Exchequer, Charles Townshend, rose to power in England. He persuaded Parliament to return to the model offered by the earlier Sugar Act. The **Townshend Act**, like the Sugar Act, instituted an import tax on a range of items sent to the colonies, including glass, lead, paint, paper, and tea.

Now, however, even an indirect tax led to immediate protests and calls for a boycott of taxed items. In February 1768, Samuel Adams wrote a circular letter reminding colonists of the importance of the boycott, and the Massachusetts Assembly disseminated it to other

> **Explore ▶**
>
> See Document 5.4 for one colonist's objection to the Townshend Act.

colonial assemblies. In response, Parliament posted two more British army regiments in Boston and New York City to enforce the law. Angry colonists did not retreat when confronted by this show of military force. Instead, a group of outspoken colonial leaders demanded that colonists refuse to import goods of any kind from Britain.

This boycott depended especially on the support of women, who were often in charge of the day-to-day purchase of household items that appeared on the boycott list. Wives and mothers were expected to boycott a wide array of British goods, and even single women and widows who supported themselves as shopkeepers were expected not to sell British goods. To make up for the boycotted goods, women produced homespun shirts and dresses and brewed herbal teas to replace British products.

Despite the hardships, many colonial women embraced the boycott. Twenty-two-year-old Charity Clarke voiced the feelings of many colonists when she wrote to a friend in England, "If you English folks won't give us the liberty we ask . . . I will try to gather a number of ladies armed with spinning wheels [along with men] who shall learn to weave & keep sheep, and will retire beyond the reach of arbitrary power." Women organized spinning bees in which dozens of participants produced yards of homespun cloth, the wearing of which symbolized female commitment to the cause.

Refusing to drink tea offered another way for women to protest parliamentary taxation. In February 1770, more than "300 Mistresses of Families, in which number the Ladies of the Highest Rank and Influence," signed a petition in Boston and pledged to abstain from drinking tea. Dozens of women from less prosperous families signed their own boycott agreement.

Boston women's refusal to drink tea and their participation in spinning bees were part of a highly publicized effort to make their city the center of opposition to the Townshend Act. Printed propaganda, demonstrations, rallies, and broadsides announced to the world that Bostonians rejected Parliament's right to impose its will, or at least its taxes, on the American colonies. Angry over Parliament's taxation policies, Boston men also considered the soldiers, who moonlighted for extra pay, as economic competitors. Throughout the winter of 1769–1770, boys and young men reacted by harassing the growing number of British soldiers stationed in the city.

On the evening of March 5, 1770, young men began throwing snowballs at the lone soldier guarding the Boston Customs House. An angry crowd began milling about, now joined by a group of sailors led by Crispus Attucks, an ex-slave of mixed African and Indian ancestry. The guard called for help, and Captain Thomas Preston arrived at the scene with seven British soldiers. He appealed to the "gentlemen" present to disperse the crowd. Instead, the harangues of the crowd continued, and snowballs, stones, and other projectiles flew in greater numbers. Then a gun fired, and soon more shooting erupted. Eleven men in the crowd were hit, and four were "killed on the Spot," including Attucks.

Despite confusion about who, if anyone, gave the order to fire, colonists expressed outrage at the shooting of ordinary men on the streets of Boston. Samuel Adams and other Sons of Liberty recognized the incredible potential for anti-British propaganda. Adams organized a mass funeral for those killed, and thousands watched the caskets being paraded through the city. Newspaper editors and broadsides printed by the Sons of Liberty labeled the shooting a "massacre." But when the accused soldiers were tried in Boston for the so-called **Boston Massacre**, the jury acquitted six of the eight of any crime. Still, ordinary colonists as well as colonial leaders were growing more convinced that British rule had become tyrannical and that such tyranny must be opposed. **See Document Project 5: The Boston Massacre, page 165.**

Protesting the Stamp Act

The announcement of the Stamp Act in 1764 ignited widespread protests throughout the colonies. Colonial governments petitioned Parliament for its repeal, crowds attacked stamp agents and distributors, broadsides and newspapers denounced "taxation without representation," and boycotts and mass demonstrations were organized in major cities. As the first document shows, London merchants also protested, arguing that they were losing revenue because of colonial boycotts of British goods. The second document celebrates the repeal of the Stamp Act by depicting a funeral for the act led by its supporters. Dr. William Scott, who published letters supporting the Stamp Act in a London newspaper, leads the procession.

Document 5.2

London Merchants Petition to Repeal the Stamp Act, 1766

And that, in consequence of the trade between the colonies and the mother country, as established and permitted for many years, and of the experience which the petitioners have had of the readiness of the Americans to make their just remittances to the utmost of their real ability, they have been induced to make and venture such large exportations of British manufactures, as to leave the colonies indebted to the merchants of Great Britain in the sum of several millions sterling; at that at this time the colonists, when pressed for payment, appeal to past experience, in proof of their willingness; but declare it is not in their power, at present, to make good their engagements, alleging, that the taxes and restrictions laid upon them, and the extension of the jurisdiction of vice admiralty courts established by some late acts of parliament, particularly . . . by an act passed in the fifth year of his present Majesty, for granting and applying certain stamp duties, and other duties, in the British colonies and plantations in America, with several regulations and restraints, which, if founded in acts of parliament for defined purposes, are represented to have been extended in such a manner as to disturb legal commerce and harass the fair trader, have so far interrupted the usual and former most fruitful branches of their commerce, restrained the sale of their produce, thrown the state of the several provinces into confusion, and brought on so great a number of actual bankruptcies, that the former opportunities and means of remittances and payments are utterly lost and taken from them; and that the petitioners are, by these unhappy events, reduced to the necessity of applying to the House, in order to secure themselves and their families from impending ruin; to prevent a multitude of manufacturers from becoming a burthen to the community, or else seeking their bread in other countries, to the irretrievable loss of this kingdom; and to preserve the strength of this nation entire.

Source: Guy Steven Callender, *Selections from the Economic History of the United States, 1765–1860* (Boston: Ginn, 1909), 146–47.

Document 5.3

The Repeal, 1766

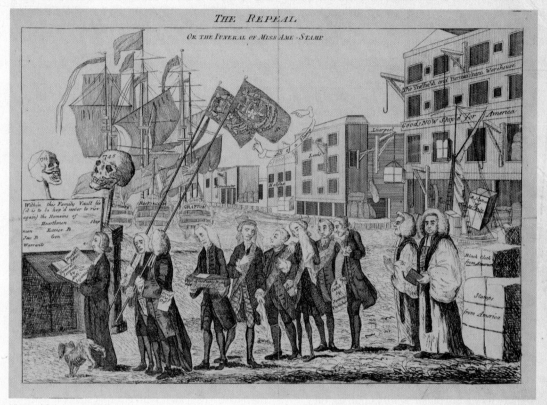

Library of Congress, 3g02568

Interpret the Evidence

1. How do both the petition and the cartoon emphasize the economic arguments against the Stamp Act? What role, if any, do arguments about political representation play in these documents?

2. Who do you think was the intended audience for each of these documents? What evidence can you find in each document to support your answer?

Put It in Context

What do these documents suggest about the more general relations among the colonies, British merchants, and Parliament in 1766?

John Dickinson | Letter from a Farmer, 1768

In 1767 the British Parliament passed a series of taxes on the American colonies to raise revenue and gain greater control of colonial government and trade. These Townshend duties outraged many colonists. John Dickinson, a prominent Pennsylvania attorney, wrote the most famous attacks on the Townshend Act using the pseudomyn "A Farmer." Dickinson's letters criticized British taxation policies, comparing them in Letter VII with enslavement, but he called for peaceful resistance to these policies.

Document 5.4

I hope to demonstrate before these letters are concluded, yet even in such a supposed case, these colonies ought to regard the act with abhorrence. For who are a free people? Not those over whom government is reasonably and equitably exercised but those who live under a government, so *constitutionally checked* and *controuled*, that proper provision is made against its being otherwise exercised. The late act is founded on the destruction of this constitutional security.

If the parliament have a right to lay a duty of four shillings and eight pence on a hundred weight of glass, or a ream of paper, they have a right to lay a duty of any other sum on either. They may raise the duty, as the author before quoted says has been done in some countries, till it "exceeds seventeen or eighteen times the value of the commodity." In short, if they have a right to levy a tax of *one penny* upon us, they have a right to levy a *million* upon us: For where does their right stop? At any given number of pence, shillings, or pounds? To attempt to limit their right, after granting it to exist at all, is as contrary to reason, as granting it to exist at all is contrary to justice. If they have any right to tax us, then, whether our own money shall continue in our own pockets, or not, depends no longer on *us*, but on *them*. "There is nothing which we can call our own," or to use the words of Mr. Locke, "What property have we in that, which another may, by right, take, when he pleases, to himself?"

These duties, which will inevitably be levied upon us, and which are now levying upon us, are expressly laid for the sole purpose of taking money. This is the true definition of taxes. They are therefore taxes. This money is to be taken from us. We are therefore taxed. Those who are taxed without their own consent, given by themselves, or their representatives, are slaves. We are taxed without our own consent given by ourselves, or our representatives. We are therefore—I speak it with grief—I speak it with indignation—we are slaves.

Source: John Dickinson, *Letters from a Farmer in Pennsylvania to the Inhabitants of the British Colonies* (New York: Outlook, 1903), 75–78.

Interpret the Evidence

1. What are Dickinson's economic and political criticisms of the Townshend duties?
2. Why does Dickinson use the pseudonym "A Farmer," and how does he define a just government?

Put It in Context

What does Dickinson's complaint about colonists being treated as slaves suggest about the limits of his political vision?

To ensure that colonists throughout North America learned about the Boston Massacre, committees of correspondence formed once again to spread the news. These committees became important pipelines for sending information about plans and protests across the colonies. They also circulated an engraving by Bostonian Paul Revere that suggested the soldiers purposely shot at a peaceful crowd.

Parliament was already considering the repeal of the Townshend duties, and in the aftermath of the shootings, public pressure increased to do so. Merchants in England and North America insisted that parliamentary policies had resulted in economic losses on both sides of the Atlantic. In response, Parliament repealed all of the Townshend duties except the import tax on tea, which it retained to demonstrate its political authority to tax the colonies.

Continuing Conflicts at Home. As colonists in Boston and other seaport cities rallied to protest British taxation, other residents of the thirteen colonies continued to challenge authorities closer to home. In the same years as the Stamp Act and Townshend Act protests, tenants in New Jersey and the Hudson valley continued their campaign for economic justice. So, too, did Hermon Husband and the Regulators. Conflicts escalated when the North Carolina Assembly, dominated by the eastern slaveholding elite, approved a measure in 1768 to build a stately mansion for Governor Tryon with public funds. Outraged frontier farmers withheld their taxes, took over courthouses, and harassed corrupt local officials. While Governor Tryon claimed that Parliament abused its power in taxing the colonies, he did not recognize such abuses in his own colony. Instead, he increasingly viewed the Regulators as traitors. In spring 1771, he recruited a thousand militiamen to quell what he considered open rebellion on the Carolina frontier. The Regulators amassed two thousand farmers to defend themselves, although Husband, a pacifist, was not among them. But when twenty Regulators were killed and more than a hundred wounded at the Battle of Alamance Creek in May 1771, he surely knew many of the fallen. Six of the defeated Regulators were hanged a month later. Many local residents harbored deep resentments against colonial officials for what they viewed as the slaughter of honest, hardworking men. Hermon Husband fled the Carolina frontier and headed north.

Resentments against colonial leaders were not confined to North Carolina. An independent Regulator movement had emerged in South Carolina in 1767. Far more effective than their North Carolina counterparts, South Carolina Regulators seized control of the western regions of the colony, took up arms, and established their own system of frontier justice. In 1769 the South Carolina Assembly negotiated a settlement with the Regulators, establishing new parishes in the colony's interior that ensured greater representation for frontier areas and extending colonial political institutions, such as courts and sheriffs, to the region.

Tea and Widening Resistance. For a brief period after the Boston Massacre, conflicts within the colonies generally overshadowed protests against British policies. During this period, the tea tax was collected, the increased funds ensured that British officials in the colonies were less dependent on local assemblies to carry out their duties, and general prosperity seemed to lessen the antagonism between colonists and royal authorities. In May 1773, however, all that changed. That month Parliament passed a new act that granted the revered but financially struggling East India Company a monopoly on shipping and selling tea in the colonies. Although this did not add any new tax or raise the price of tea, it did fuel a new round of protests.

Samuel Adams, Patrick Henry, Christopher Gadsden, and other radicals had continued to view the tea tax as an illegal imposition on colonists and refused to pay it as a matter of principle. They had established committees of correspondence to keep up the pressure for a colony-wide boycott, and Adams published and circulated "Rights of the Colonies," a pamphlet that listed a range of grievances against British policies. Their concerns became the basis for a new round of protests when Parliament, many of whose members invested in the East India Company, granted its monopoly. By eliminating colonial merchants from the profits to be made on tea and implementing a monopoly for a single favored company, Parliament pushed merchants into joining with radicals to demand redress.

Committees of correspondence quickly organized another colony-wide boycott. In some cities, like Charleston, South Carolina, tea was unloaded from East India Company ships but never sold. In others, like New York, the ships were turned back at the port. Only in Boston, however, did violence erupt as ships loaded with tea sat anchored in the harbor. On the night of December 16, 1773, the Sons of Liberty organized a "tea party." After a massive rally against British policy, a group of about fifty men disguised as Indians boarded the British ships and dumped forty-five tons of tea into the sea.

Although hundreds of spectators knew who had boarded the ship, witnesses refused to provide names or other information to British investigators. The Boston Tea Party was a direct challenge to British authority and resulted in large-scale destruction of valuable property.

The Edenton Proclamation, 1774 In Edenton, North Carolina, a group of women published a proclamation in 1774 stating their allegiance to the cause of liberty by refusing to serve or drink British tea. Their public statement received much attention in the American and the British press. This political cartoon, which satirizes the women who signed the declaration, appeared in several London newspapers. Library of Congress, LC-DIG-ppmsca-19468

Parliament responded immediately with a show of force. The **Coercive Acts**, passed in 1774, closed the port of Boston until residents paid for the tea, moved Massachusetts court cases against royal officials back to England, and revoked the colony's charter in order to strengthen the authority of royal officials and weaken that of the colonial assembly. The British government also approved a new Quartering Act, which forced Boston residents to accommodate more soldiers in their own homes or build more barracks.

The royal government passed the Coercive Acts to punish Massachusetts and to discourage similar protests in other colonies. Instead, the legislation, which colonists called the **Intolerable Acts**, spurred a militant reaction. Committees of correspondence spread news of the fate of Boston and of Massachusetts. Colonial leaders, who increasingly identified themselves as patriots, soon formed committees of safety—armed groups of colonists who gathered weapons and munitions and vowed to protect themselves against British encroachments on their rights and institutions. Other colonies sent support, both political and material, to Massachusetts and instituted a boycott of British goods. All ranks of people throughout the colonies joined the boycott.

At the same time, a group of patriots meeting in Williamsburg, Virginia, in the spring of 1774 called for colonies to send representatives to a **Continental Congress** to meet in Philadelphia the following September to discuss relations between the North American colonies and Great Britain.

By passing the Coercive Acts, Parliament had hoped to dampen the long-smoldering conflict with the colonies. Instead, it flared even brighter, with radical leaders committing themselves to the use of violence, moderate merchants and shopkeepers making common cause with radicals, and ordinary women and men embracing a boycott of all British goods.

The Continental Congress and Colonial Unity.

When the Continental Congress convened in Philadelphia in September 1774, fifty-six delegates represented every colony but Georgia. Many of these men—and they were all men—had met before. Some had worked together in the Stamp Act Congress in 1765; others had joined forces in the intervening years on committees of correspondence or in petitions to Parliament. Still, the representatives disagreed on many fronts. Some were radicals like Samuel Adams, Patrick Henry, and Christopher Gadsden. Others held moderate views, including George Washington and John Dickinson of Pennsylvania. And a few, like John Jay of New York, voiced more conservative positions.

Despite their differences, all the delegates agreed that the colonies must resist further parliamentary encroachments on their liberties. They talked not of independence but rather of reestablishing the freedoms that colonists had enjoyed in an earlier period. Washington voiced the sentiments of many. Although opposed to the idea of independence, he echoed John Locke by refusing to submit "to the loss of those valuable rights and privileges, which are essential to the happiness of every free State, and without which life, liberty, and property are rendered totally insecure."

To demonstrate their unified resistance to the Coercive Acts, delegates called on colonists to continue the boycott of British goods and to end all colonial exports to Great Britain. Committees were established in all of the colonies to coordinate and enforce these actions. Delegates also insisted that Americans were "entitled to a free and exclusive power of legislation in their several provincial legislatures." By 1774 a growing number of colonists supported these measures and the ideas on which they were based.

The delegates at the Continental Congress could not address all the colonists' grievances, and most had no interest in challenging race and class relations within the colonies themselves. Nonetheless, it was a significant event because the congress drew power away from individual colonies and local organizations and placed the emphasis instead on colony-wide plans and actions. To some extent, the delegates also shifted leadership of the protests away from more radical artisans, like Ebenezer Mackintosh, and put planning back in the hands of men of wealth and standing. Moreover, even as they denounced Parliament, many representatives felt a special loyalty to the king and sought his intervention to rectify relations between the mother country and the colonies.

REVIEW & RELATE

- How and why did colonial resistance to British policies escalate in the decade following the conclusion of the French and Indian War?

- How did internal social and economic divisions shape the colonial response to British policies?

Conclusion: Liberty within Empire

From the Sugar Act in 1764 to the Continental Congress in 1774, colonists reacted strongly to parliamentary efforts to impose greater control over the colonies. Their protests grew increasingly effective as colonists developed organizations, systems of communication, and arguments to buttress their position. Residents of seacoast cities like Boston and New York City developed especially visible and effective challenges, in large part because they generally had the most to lose if Britain implemented new economic, military, and legislative policies.

In frontier areas, such as the southern backcountry, the Hudson valley, and northern New England, complaints against British tyranny vied with those against colonial land speculators and officials throughout the 1760s and 1770s. Still, few of these agitators questioned the right of white colonists to claim Indian lands or enslave African labor. In this sense, at least, most frontier settlers made common cause with more elite colonists, including the many planters and large landowners who attended the Continental Congress.

One other tie bound the colonists together in 1774. No matter how radical the rhetoric, the aim continued to be resistance to particular policies, not independence from the British empire. Colonists sought greater liberty within the empire. Only on rare occasions did a colonist question the fundamental framework of imperial governance. And despite some colonists' opposition to certain parliamentary acts, many others supported British policies. Indeed, the majority of colonists did not participate in protest activities. Most small farmers and backcountry settlers were far removed from centers of protest activity, while poor families in seaport cities who purchased few items to begin with had little interest in boycotts of British goods. Finally, some colonists hesitated to consider open revolt against British rule for fear of a revolution from below. The activities of land rioters, Regulators, evangelical preachers, female petitioners, and African American converts to Christianity reminded more well-established settlers that the colonies harbored their own tensions and conflicts.

The fates of George Washington and Hermon Husband suggest the uncertainties that plagued the colonies and individual colonists in 1774. As Washington returned to his Virginia estate from the Continental Congress, he began to devote more time to military affairs. He took command of the volunteer militia companies in the colonies and chaired the committee on safety in his home county. Although still opposed to rebellion, he was nonetheless preparing for it. Hermon Husband, on the other hand, had watched his rebellion against oppressive government fail at the Battle of Alamance Creek. When the Continental Congress met in Philadelphia, he was working to reestablish his farm and family on the Pennsylvania frontier. Whether ruled by Great Britain or eastern colonial elites, Husband was most concerned with the rights of poor farmers and working people. Yet he and Washington would have agreed with the great British parliamentarian Edmund Burke, who, on hearing of events in the American colonies in 1774, lamented, "Clouds, indeed, and darkness, rest upon the future."

CHAPTER 5 REVIEW

TIMELINE OF EVENTS

1754–1763	French and Indian War
1754	George Washington attacks Fort Duquesne
	Albany Congress convenes
1757	William Pitt takes charge of British war effort
May 1763	Pontiac launches pan-Indian revolt
June 1763	Peace of Paris
October 1763	Proclamation Line of 1763 established
December 1763	Paxton Boys attack Conestoga Indians
1764	Green Mountain Boys resist New York authorities
	Sugar Act passed
1765	Stamp Act passed
	Stamp Act Congress convenes
1766	Sandy Creek Association formed
	Stamp Act repealed and Declaratory Act passed
1767	Townshend Act passed
1770	Boston Massacre
1771	Battle of Alamance Creek, North Carolina
1773	Boston Tea Party
1774	Coercive Acts passed
	Continental Congress convenes

KEY TERMS

REVIEW & RELATE

1. How did the French and Indian War and the subsequent peace treaty affect relations among Britain, American Indian nations, and American colonies?

2. How did the French and Indian War and the increasing power of large landowners contribute to conflict between average colonists and colonial elites?

3. How did Britain's postwar policies lead to the emergence of unified colonial protests?

4. Why did British policymakers believe they were justified in seeking to gain greater control over Britain's North American colonies?

5. How and why did colonial resistance to British policies escalate in the decade following the conclusion of the French and Indian War?

6. How did internal social and economic divisions shape the colonial response to British policies?

The Boston Massacre

The Boston Massacre was a critical episode in the American independence movement. The origins of this skirmish between Bostonians and British troops lay in the passage of the Townshend Act in 1767, three years before the so-called massacre.

There was widespread resistance to the Townshend duties, including public demonstrations, petitions, and boycotts against British goods. The situation in Boston became so tense that four thousand British troops were brought in to enforce the Townshend Act. In late February 1770, a British sympathizer tore down an anti-British poster, and an angry mob then threw stones at his house and hit his wife. The homeowner fired into the crowd and killed an eleven-year-old boy. A mass funeral for the boy set the stage for the events of March 5.

On that chilly evening, an exchange between young men and a British officer outside the Customs House escalated with supporters joining both sides. Church bells were rung, bringing more colonial sailors and soldiers to the scene (Document 5.5). Captain Thomas Preston, the officer in charge, called in reinforcements to regain control (Document 5.8). As Bostonians overwhelmed the British regulars, someone fired his gun. A number of British soldiers then followed suit, killing three men immediately, including Crispus Attucks, and fatally injuring two others (Documents 5.5 and 5.8).

Within the month, Preston and eight British soldiers were indicted for murder; they were tried in October 1770. Unable to find attorneys, Preston appealed directly to patriot John Adams, who agreed to take the case to ensure a fair trial. Adams provided a strong defense (Document 5.9), resulting in the acquittal of Preston, who was tried

separately, and of six of the other eight soldiers. Two soldiers were found guilty of murder, a charge later reduced to manslaughter.

The following documents reveal the chaos of that night from the differing perspectives of Bostonians and British soldiers. They also illustrate the ways that some colonial leaders used the event to promote the patriot cause (Documents 5.6 and 5.7).

Document 5.5

Deposition of William Wyatt, March 7, 1770

Just two days after the Boston Massacre, city officials began deposing dozens of witnesses to the event. They later published their descriptions as part of a pamphlet that criticized the event as a "Horrid Massacre." The following selection is from the testimony of William Wyatt and describes his version of the scene just as British soldiers were loading their weapons.

That last Monday evening, being the fifth day of March current, I was in Boston, down on Treat's wharf, where my vessel was lying, and hearing the bells ring, supposed there was a fire in the town, whereupon I hastened up to the Townhouse, on the south side of it, where I saw an officer of the army lead out of the guard-house there seven or eight soldiers of the army, and lead them down in seeming haste, to the Custom-house on the north side of King street, where I followed them, and when the officer had got there with the men, he bid them face about. I stood just below them on the left wing, and the said officer ordered his men to load, which they did accordingly, with the utmost dispatch, then they remained about six minutes, with their firelocks rested and bayonets fixed, but not standing in exact order. I observed a considerable number of young lads, and here and there a man amongst them, about the middle of the street, facing the soldiers, but not within ten or twelve feet distance from them; I observed some of them, viz., the lads, etc., had sticks in their hands, laughing, shouting, huzzaing, and crying fire; but could not observe that any of them threw anything at the soldiers, or threatened any of them. Then the said officer retired from before the soldiers and stepping behind them, towards the right wing, bid the soldiers fire; they not firing, he presently again bid 'em fire, they not yet firing, he stamped and said, "Damn your bloods, fire, be the consequence what it will"; then the second man on the left wing fired off his gun, then, after a very short pause, they fired one after another as quick as possible, beginning on the right wing; the last man's gun on the left wing flashed in the pan, then he primed again, and the people being withdrawn from before the soldiers, most of them further down the street, he turned his gun toward them and fired upon them. Immediately after the principal firing, I saw three of the people fall down in the street; presently after the last gun was fired off, the said officer, who had commanded the soldiers (as above) to fire, sprung before them, waving his sword or stick, said, "Damn ye, rascals, what did ye fire for?" and struck up the gun of one of the soldiers who was loading again, whereupon they seemed confounded and fired no more.

Source: *A Short Narrative of the Horrid Massacre in Boston Perpetrated in the Evening of the Fifth Day of March, 1770, by the Soldiers of the 29th Regiment* (Boston, 1770), republished with additional material by John Doggett Jr. (New York, 1849), 72.

Account of Boston Massacre Funeral Procession, March 12, 1770

One week after the Boston Massacre, a massive public funeral was held for the four victims who had already died: Samuel Gray, Samuel Maverick, James Caldwell, and Crispus Attucks. Shops were closed, church bells marked the event in Boston and nearby Charlestown and Roxbury, and Bostonians of all ranks attended the funeral.

Last Thursday, agreeable to a general request of the inhabitants, and by the consent of parents and friends, were carried to their grave in succession, the bodies of Samuel Gray, Samuel Maverick, James Caldwell, and Crispus Attucks, the unhappy victims who fell in the bloody massacre of the Monday evening preceding!

On this occasion most of the shops in town were shut, all the bells were ordered to toll a solemn peal, as were also those in the neighboring towns of Charlestown, Roxbury, etc. The procession began to move between the hours of 4 and 5 in the afternoon; two of the unfortunate sufferers, Messrs. James Caldwell and Crispus Attucks, who were strangers [not residents of Boston], borne from Faneuil Hall, attended by a numerous train of persons of all ranks; and the other two, Mr. Samuel Gray, from the house of Mr. Benjamin Gray (his brother), on the north side of the Exchange, and Mr. Maverick, from the house of his distressed mother, Mrs. Mary Maverick, in Union Street, each followed by their respective relations and friends: The several hearses forming a junction in King Street, the theatre of the inhuman tragedy! proceeded from thence through the Main Street, lengthened by an immense concourse of people, so numerous as to be obliged to follow in ranks of six, and brought up by a long train of carriages belonging to the principal gentry of the town. The bodies were deposited in one vault in the middle burying ground. The aggravated circumstances of their death, the distress and sorrow visible in every countenance, together with the peculiar solemnity with which the whole funeral was conducted, surpass description.

Source: *Boston Gazette and Country Journal*, March 12, 1770.

Paul Revere | Etching of the Boston Massacre, 1770

Published three weeks after the Boston Massacre, Paul Revere's famous etching of the event stirred anti-British sentiment among the colonists. Revere had produced an earlier sketch that showed the position of Attucks, Caldwell, and the other men killed near the Customs House. The etching that circulated widely, however, was based on an engraving by another artist, Henry Pelham, which depicted an organized line of British soldiers firing into a crowd of unarmed colonists. At the time of the Boston Massacre, Revere was a prominent silversmith and a member of the Sons of Liberty.

Library of Congress, LC-DIG-ppmsca-01657

Account of Captain Thomas Preston, June 25, 1770

Captain Thomas Preston, the officer in charge on March 5, was tried separately from the other soldiers. His trial centered on whether he had ordered his men to fire on the crowd. Assuming that defendants in criminal trials would perjure themselves to gain an acquittal, English legal custom prohibited them from testifying. But Preston presented his version of events to British authorities just a week after the event, strenuously denying the charges against him. That account was published in the *Boston Gazette* on March 12, 1770; later appeared in London papers; and was republished in the *Boston Evening-Post* on June 25, 1770.

On Monday night about Eight o' Clock two Soldiers were attacked and beat. But the Party of the Towns-People, in order to carry Matters to the utmost Length, broke into two Meeting-Houses, and rang the Alarm Bells, which I supposed was for Fire as usual, but was soon undeceived. About Nine some of the Guard came to and informed me, the Town-Inhabitants were assembling to attack the Troops, and that the Bells were ringing as the Signal for that Purpose, and not for Fire, and the Beacon intended to be fired to bring in the distant People of the Country. This, as I was Captain of the Day, occasioned my repairing immediately to the Main-Guard. In my Way there I saw the People in great Commotion, and heard them use the most cruel and horrid Threats against the Troops. In a few Minutes after I reached the Guard, about an hundred People passed it, and went towards the Custom-House, where the King's Money is lodged. They immediately surrounded the Sentinel posted there, and with Clubs and other Weapons threatened to execute their Vengeance on him. I was soon informed by a Townsman, their Intention was to carry off the Soldier from his Post, and probably murder him. On which I desired him to return for further Intelligence; and he soon came back and assured me he heard the Mob declare they would murder him. This I feared might be a Prelude to their plundering the King's Chest. I immediately sent a non-commissioned Officer and twelve Men to protect both the Sentinel and the King's-Money, and very soon followed myself, to prevent (if possible) all Disorder; fearing lest the Officer and Soldiery by the Insults and Provocations of the Rioters, should be thrown off their Guard and commit some rash Act. They soon rushed through the People, and, by charging their Bayonets in half Circle, kept them at a little Distance. Nay, so far was I from intending the Death of any Person, that I suffered the Troops to go to the Spot where the unhappy Affair took Place, without any Loading in their Pieces, nor did I ever give Orders for loading them. This remiss Conduct in me perhaps merits Censure; yet it is Evidence, resulting from the Nature of Things, which is the best and surest that can be offered, that my Intention was not to act offensively, but the contrary Part, and that not without Compulsion. The mob still increased, and were more outrageous, striking their clubs or bludgeons one against another, and calling out, "Come on you rascals, you bloody backs, you lobster scoundrels, fire if you dare, G–d damn you, fire and be damned; we know you dare not"; and much more such language was used. At this time I was between the soldiers and the mob, parleying with and endeavouring all in my power to persuade them to retire peaceably; but to no purpose. They advanced to the points of the bayonets, struck some of them, and even the muzzles of the pieces, and seemed to be endeavouring to close with the soldiers. On which some well-behaved persons asked me if the guns were charged. I replied, yes. They then asked me if I intended to order the men to fire. I answered no, by no means; observing to them that I was advanced before the muzzles of the men's pieces, and must fall a sacrifice if they fired; that the soldiers were upon the half-cock and charged bayonets, and my giving the word fire under those circumstances would prove me no officer. While I was thus speaking, one of the soldiers, having received a severe blow with a stick, stepped a little on one side and instantly fired, on which turning to and asking him why he fired without orders, I was struck with a club on my arm, which for some time deprived me of the use of it, which blow, had it been placed on my head, most probably would have destroyed me. On this a general attack was made on the men by a great number of heavy clubs, and snowballs being thrown at them, by which all our lives were in imminent danger; some persons at the same time from behind calling out, "Damn your bloods, why don't you fire?" Instantly three or four of the soldiers fired, one after another, and directly after three more in the same confusion and hurry.

The mob then ran away, except three unhappy men who instantly expired, in which number was Mr. Gray, at whose rope-walk the prior quarrel took place; one more is since dead, three others are dangerously, and four slightly wounded. The whole of this melancholy affair was transacted in almost 20 minutes. On my asking the soldiers why they fired without orders, they said they heard the word "Fire" and supposed it came from me. This might be the case, as many of the mob called out "Fire, fire," but I assured the men that I gave no such order, that my words were, "Don't fire, stop your firing."

Source: *Supplement to the Boston Evening-Post*, June 25, 1770.

John Adams | Defense of the British Soldiers at Trial, October 1770

A descendant of Puritans, John Adams was a Harvard graduate, Enlightenment thinker, and lawyer. He wrote some of the most important legal defenses of colonial rights in response to Parliament's passage of the Stamp Act. A staunch patriot, Adams agreed to defend the British soldiers because he believed that everyone deserved a fair trial. This decision did not injure Adams's reputation. Indeed, he was elected to the Massachusetts General Court (legislature) while preparing for the trial.

I shall endeavour to make some few observations on the testimonies of the witnesses, such as will place the facts in a true point of light. . . .

The next witness is Dodge, he says, there were fifty people near the soldiers pushing at them; now the witness before says, there were twelve sailors with clubs, but now here are fifty more aiding and abetting of them, ready to relieve them in case of need; now what could the people expect? It was their business to have taken themselves out of the way; some prudent people by the Town-house told them not to meddle with the guard, but you hear nothing of this from these fifty people; no, instead of that, they were huzzaing and whistling, crying damn you, fire! why don't you fire? So that they were actually assisting these twelve sailors that made the attack; he says the soldiers were pushing at the people to keep them off, ice and snow balls were thrown, and I heard ice rattle on their guns, there were some clubs thrown from a considerable distance across the street. . . .

. . . When the multitude was shouting and huzzaing, and threatening life, the bells ringing, the mob whistling, screaming, and rending like an Indian yell, the people from all quarters throwing every species of rubbish they could pick up in the street, and some who were quite on the other side of the street throwing clubs at the whole party, Montgomery in particular smote with a club and knocked down, and as soon as he could rise and take up his firelock, another club from afar struck his breast or shoulder, what could he do? Do you expect he should behave like a stoic philosopher lost in apathy? . . . It is impossible you should find him guilty of murder. You must suppose him divested of all human passions, if you don't think him at the least provoked, thrown off his guard, and into the furor brevis [brief madness], by such treatment as this. . . .

. . . Facts are stubborn things; and whatever may be our wishes, our inclinations, or the dictates of our passions, they cannot alter the state of facts and evidence: nor is the law less stable than the fact; if an assault was made to endanger their lives, the law is clear, they had a right to kill in their own defence; if it was not so severe as to endanger their lives, yet if they were assaulted at all, struck and abused by blows of any sort, . . . this was a provocation, for which the law reduces the offence of killing, down to manslaughter, in consideration of those passions in our nature, which cannot be eradicated. To your candor and justice I submit the prisoners and their cause.

Source: Frederick Kidder, *History of the Boston Massacre, March 5, 1770* (Albany, NY: J. Munsell, 1870), 249, 252, 257–58.

Interpret the Evidence

1. What are the major similarities and differences between the testimonies of William Wyatt and Captain Preston (Documents 5.5 and 5.8)?

2. How does Revere's portrayal (Document 5.7) compare with the testimonies of Wyatt (Document 5.5) and Preston (Document 5.8)? Why does he show only white men being shot?

3. How might the funeral procession (described in Document 5.6) have incited popular sentiment against the British before March 5?

4. Why does John Adams challenge the eyewitness accounts of the event (Document 5.9)?

5. What explains the Boston jury's decision to acquit most of the British soldiers?

Put It in Context

How might the deaths of the five colonists and the outcome of the trial have changed the way patriots and ordinary colonists viewed the British authorities?

What events occurred between March 1770 and March 1774 that heightened the meaning of the Boston Massacre for colonial patriots?

The American Revolution

6

1775–1783

WINDOW TO THE PAST

The War's Impact on the Seneca Nation, 1823

General John Sullivan, with 4,000 patriot troops, sought to end the support that the Seneca and other Iroquois Indians in New York State gave to British troops by destroying their villages in 1779. Mary Jemison, a white woman captured by Indians in 1758, had married a Seneca man and lived with him and their children through the American Revolution. Jemison provided this account of her life to minister James Seaver in 1823. ▸ To discover more about what this primary source can show us, see Document 6.4 on page 193.

In one or two days after the skirmish at Connessius lake, Sullivan and his army arrived at Genesee river, where they destroyed every article of the food kind that they could lay their hands on. A part of our corn they burnt, and threw the remainder into the river. They burnt our houses, killed what few cattle and horses they could find, destroyed our fruit trees, and left nothing but the bare soil and timber. But the Indians had eloped and were not to be found.

After reading this chapter you should be able to:

- Explain the relationship between the beginning of armed conflict and patriots' decision to declare independence.

- Understand the choices of colonists, American Indians, and African Americans to support or oppose independence.

- Analyze the military strategies of the British and the Americans in 1776–1777, the roles that various allies played, and the importance of women and other groups on the home front.

- Explain the major accomplishments of and conflicts within the new state and federal governments during the Revolution.

- Analyze the shift of warfare to the South and West from 1778 to 1781; the importance of American Indians, foreign allies, and colonial soldiers in patriot victories there; and the challenges Americans faced once they defeated the British.

AMERICAN HISTORIES

One of the foremost pamphleteers of the patriot cause, Thomas Paine was born in 1737 in England, where his parents trained him as a corset maker. Eventually he left home and found work as a seaman, a teacher, and a tax collector. He drank heavily and beat both his wives. Yet he also taught working-class children to read and pushed the British government

to improve the working conditions and pay of tax collectors. In 1772 Paine was fired from his government job, but a pamphlet he wrote had caught the eye of Benjamin Franklin, who persuaded him to try his luck in the colonies.

Arriving in Philadelphia in November 1774 at age thirty-seven, Paine secured a job on the *Pennsylvania Magazine*. The newcomer quickly gained in-depth political knowledge of the intensifying conflicts between the colonies and Great Britain. He also gained patrons for his political tracts among Philadelphia's economic and political elite. When armed conflict with British troops erupted in April 1775, colonial debates over whether to declare independence intensified. Pamphlets were a popular means of influencing these debates, and Paine wrote one entitled *Common Sense* to tip the balance in favor of independence.

Published in January 1776, *Common Sense* proved an instant success. It provided a rationale for independence and an emotional plea for creating a new democratic republic. Paine urged colonists to separate from England and establish a political structure that would ensure liberty and equality for all Americans. "A government of our own is our natural right," he concluded. "'Tis time to part."

When *Common Sense* was published, sixteen-year-old Deborah Sampson was working as an indentured servant to Jeremiah and Susanna Thomas in Marlborough, Massachusetts. Jeremiah Thomas thought education was above the lot of servant girls, but Sampson insisted on reading whatever books she could find. However, her commitment to American independence likely developed less from reading and more from the fighting that raged in Massachusetts and drew male servants and the Thomases' five sons into the Continental Army.

When Deborah Sampson's term of service ended in 1778, she sought work as a weaver and then a teacher. In March 1782 she disguised herself as a man and enlisted in the Continental Army. Her height and muscular frame allowed her to fool local recruiters, and she accepted the bounty paid to those who enlisted. But Deborah never reported for duty, and when her charade was discovered, she was forced to return the money.

(*left*) **Thomas Paine**. Library of Congress, 3g02542

(*right*) **Deborah Sampson**. Granger, NYC

In May 1782 Sampson enlisted a second time under the name Robert Shurtliff. For the next year, Sampson, disguised as Shurtliff, marched, fought, and lived with her Massachusetts regiment. Her ability to carry off the deception was helped by lax standards of hygiene: Soldiers rarely undressed fully to bathe, and most slept in their uniforms.

Even after the formal end of the war in March 1783, Sampson/Shurtliff continued to serve in the Continental Army. That fall, she was sent to Philadelphia to help quash a mutiny by Continental soldiers angered over the army's failure to provide back pay. While there, Sampson/Shurtliff fell ill with a raging fever, and a doctor at the army hospital discovered that "he" was a woman. The doctor reported the news to General John Paterson, and Sampson was honorably discharged, having served the army faithfully for more than a year. ■

The American histories of Thomas Paine and Deborah Sampson demonstrate how the American Revolution transformed individual lives as well as the life of the nation. Paine had failed financially and personally in England but gained fame in the colonies through his skills as a patriot pamphleteer. Sampson, who was forced into an early independence by her impoverished family, excelled as a soldier. Still, while the American Revolution offered opportunities for some colonists, it promised hardship for others. Most Americans had to choose sides long before it was clear whether the colonists could defeat Great Britain, and the long years of conflict (1775–1783) took a toll on families and communities across the thirteen colonies. Moreover, even with English converts like Paine and homegrown supporters like Sampson, the patriots would need foreign allies to achieve victory. And even battlefield victory could not ensure political stability in the new nation.

The **Question** of **Independence**

The Continental Congress that met to protest the Coercive Acts adjourned in October 1774, but delegates reconvened in May 1775. During the intervening months, patriot leaders honed their arguments for resisting British tyranny, and committees of correspondence circulated the latest news. While some patriots began advocating resistance in the strongest terms, the eruption of armed clashes between British soldiers and local farmers created the greatest push for independence. It also led the Continental Congress to establish the Continental Army in June 1775. A year later, in July 1776, the congress declared independence.

Armed Conflict Erupts. As debates over independence intensified, patriots along the Atlantic coast expanded their efforts. The Sons of Liberty and other patriot groups spread propaganda against the British, gathered and stored weapons, and organized and trained local militia companies. In addition to boycotting British goods, female patriots manufactured bandages and bullets. Some northern colonists freed enslaved African Americans who agreed to enlist in the militia. Others kept close watch on the movements of British troops.

On April 18, 1775, Boston patriots observed British movement in the harbor. British soldiers were headed to Lexington, intending to confiscate guns and ammunition hidden there and in neighboring Concord and perhaps arrest patriot leaders. To warn his fellow patriots, Paul Revere raced to Lexington on horseback but was stopped on the road to Concord by the British. By that time, however, a network of riders was spreading the alarm and alerted Concord residents of the impending danger.

Early in the morning of April 19, the first shots rang out on the village green of Lexington. After a brief exchange between British soldiers and local militiamen—known as minutemen for the speed with which they assembled—eight colonists lay dead. The British troops then marched on Concord, where they burned colonial supplies. However, patriots in nearby towns had now been alerted. Borrowing guerrilla tactics from American Indians, colonists hid behind trees, walls, and barns and battered the British soldiers as they marched back to Boston, killing 73 and wounding 200.

Word of the conflict traveled quickly. Outraged Bostonians attacked British troops and forced them to retreat to ships in the harbor. The victory was short-lived, however, and the British soon regained control of Boston. But colonial forces entrenched themselves on hills just north of the city. Then in May, Ethan Allen and his Green Mountain Boys

The Battle of Bunker Hill   On June 16, 1775, 2,500 British infantry sought to dislodge 1,500 patriot volunteers from Breeds Hill, 600 yards below Charlestown's strategic Bunker Hill. Although the British managed to dislodge the patriots during a third assault, more than a thousand British soldiers were wounded or killed. British General Thomas Gage lost his command, and the Royal Army no longer seemed invincible. akg-images

joined militias from Connecticut and Massachusetts to capture the British garrison at Fort Ticonderoga, New York. The battle for North America had begun.

When the **Second Continental Congress** convened in Philadelphia on May 10, 1775, the most critical question for delegates like Pennsylvania patriot John Dickinson was how to ensure time for discussion and negotiation. Armed conflict had erupted, but should, or must, revolution follow? Other delegates, including Patrick Henry, insisted that independence was the only appropriate response to armed attacks on colonial residents.

Just over a month later, on June 16, British forces under General Sir William Howe attacked patriot fortifications on Breed's Hill and Bunker Hill, north of Boston. The British won the **Battle of Bunker Hill** when patriots ran out of ammunition. But the redcoats—so called because of their bright red uniforms—suffered twice as many casualties as the patriots. The victory allowed the British to maintain control of Boston for nine more months, but the heavy losses emboldened patriot militiamen.

Building a Continental Army.
The Battle of Bunker Hill convinced the Continental Congress to establish an army for the defense of the colonies. They appointed forty-three-year-old George Washington as commander in chief, and he headed to Massachusetts to take command of militia companies already engaged in battle. Since the congress had not yet proclaimed itself a national government, Washington depended largely on the willingness of local militias to accept his command and of individual colonies to supply soldiers, arms, and ammunition. Throughout the summer of 1775, Washington wrote numerous letters to patriot political leaders detailing the army's urgent need for men and supplies. He also sought to remove incompetent officers and improve order among the troops, who spent too much time carousing.

As he worked to forge a disciplined army, Washington and his officers developed a twofold military strategy. They sought to drive the British out of Boston and to secure the colonies from attack by British forces and their Indian allies in New York and Canada. In November 1775, American troops under General Richard Montgomery captured Montreal. However, the difficult trek in cold weather and the spread of smallpox decimated the patriot reinforcements led by General Benedict Arnold, and American troops failed to dislodge the British from Quebec.

Despite the disastrous outcome of the Canadian invasion, the Continental Army secured important victories in the winter of 1775–1776. To improve Washington's position in Massachusetts, General Henry Knox retrieved weapons captured at Fort Ticonderoga. In March, Washington positioned the forty-three cannons on Dorchester Heights and surprised the British with a bombardment that drove them from Boston and forced them to retreat to Nova Scotia.

Reasons for Caution and for Action.
When the British retreated from Boston, the war had already spread into Virginia. In spring 1775, local militias forced Lord Dunmore, Virginia's royal governor, to take refuge on British ships in Norfolk harbor. Dunmore encouraged white servants and black slaves to join him there, and hundreds of black men fought with British troops when the governor led his army back into Virginia in November 1775. After the Battle of Great Bridge, Dunmore reclaimed the governor's mansion and issued an official proclamation that declared "all indent[ur]ed Servants, Negroes

or others (appertaining to Rebels)" to be free if they were "able and willing to bear Arms" for the British.

Dunmore's Proclamation, offering freedom to slaves who fought for the crown, heightened concerns among patriot leaders about the consequences of declaring independence. Although they wanted liberty for themselves, most did not want to disrupt the plantation economy or the existing social hierarchy. Given these concerns, many delegates at the Continental Congress, which included large planters, successful merchants, and professional men, hesitated to act.

Moreover, some still hoped for a negotiated settlement. But the king and Parliament refused to compromise in any way with colonies they considered in rebellion. Instead, in December 1775, the king prohibited any negotiation or trade with the colonies, increasing the leverage of radicals who argued independence was a necessity. The January 1776 publication of Thomas Paine's **Common Sense** bolstered their case. Wielding both biblical references and Enlightenment ideas, Paine's best-selling pamphlet impressed patriot leaders as well as ordinary farmers and artisans, who debated his ideas at taverns and coffeehouses.

Explore ▶

Read some of Paine's arguments in Document 6.1.

By the spring of 1776, a growing number of patriots believed that independence was necessary. Colonies began to take control of their legislatures and instruct their delegates to the Continental Congress to support independence. Meanwhile, the congress requested economic and military assistance from France. And in May, the congress advised colonies that had not yet done so to establish independent governments.

Still, many colonists opposed the idea of breaking free from Britain. Charles Inglis, the rector at Trinity Church in New York City, insisted that "limited monarchy is the form of government which is most favorable to liberty."

Declaring Independence.

As colonists argued back and forth, Richard Henry Lee of Virginia introduced a motion to the Continental Congress in early June 1776 resolving that "these United Colonies are, and of right ought to be, Free and Independent States." A heated debate followed in which Lee and John Adams argued passionately for independence. Eventually, even more cautious delegates, like Robert Livingston of New York, were convinced. Livingston concluded that "they should yield to the torrent if they hoped to direct it." He then joined Adams, Thomas Jefferson, Benjamin Franklin, and Roger Sherman on a committee to draft a formal statement justifying independence.

The thirty-three-year-old Jefferson took the lead in preparing the declaration, building on ideas expressed by Paine, Adams, and Lee. He also drew on language used in dozens of "declarations" written by town meetings, county officials, and colonial assemblies, particularly the Virginia Declaration of Rights drafted by George Mason in May 1776. Central to many of these documents was the contract theory of government proposed by the seventeenth-century British philosopher John Locke. Locke argued that sovereignty resided in the people, who submitted voluntarily to laws and authorities in exchange for protection of their life, liberty, and property. The people could therefore reconstitute or overthrow a government that abused its powers. Jefferson summarized this argument and then listed the abuses and crimes perpetrated by King George III against the colonies, which justified patriots' decision to break their contract with British authorities.

GUIDED ANALYSIS

Thomas Paine | *Common Sense*, January 1776

Thomas Paine's *Common Sense* was the most widely read pamphlet supporting American independence. Paine's plain style and use of biblical allusions appealed to ordinary people and ignited the Revolutionary movement. As a government employee in England, Paine had been hired, transferred, dismissed, rehired, and dismissed again, which likely influenced his critique of the monarchy. But he offered a broader vision as well, providing colonists with a new understanding of the relationship between a government and its citizens.

Document 6.1

How does Paine characterize the role of the King in England?

In England a King hath little more to do than to make war and give away places; which, in plain terms, is to impoverish the nation, and set it together by the ears. A pretty business, indeed, for a man to be allowed eight hundred thousand sterling a year for, and worshipped into the bargain! Of more worth is one honest man to society, and in the sight of God, than all the crowned ruffians that ever lived. . . .

But where, say some, is the King of America? I will tell you, friend, he reigns above, and does not make havock of mankind like the royal brute of Great Britain. Yet that we may not appear to be defective even in earthly honors, let a day be solemnly set apart for proclaiming the charter; let it be brought forth, placed on the divine law, the word of God: let a crown be placed thereon, by which the world may know that so far we approve of monarchy, that in America, THE LAW IS KING.

What does Paine consider the proper relationship between the law and political authority?

For as in absolute governments the King is law, so in free countries the Law *ought* to be King; and there ought to be no other. But lest any ill use should afterwards arise, let the crown, at the conclusion of the ceremony, be demolished, and scattered among the people whose right it is.

A government of our own is our natural right; and when a man seriously reflects on the precariousness of his human affairs, he will become convinced, that it is infinitely wiser and safer, to form a constitution of our own in a cool deliberate manner, while we have it in our power, than to trust such an interesting event to time and chance.

What system of government does Paine advocate for the American colonies?

Source: Thomas Paine, *Common Sense; Addressed to the Inhabitants of America* (London: H. D. Symonds, 1792), 11, 20.

Put It in Context

What was the influence of this 1776 pamphlet on colonial support for independence from Britain?

Once prepared, the **Declaration of Independence** was debated and revised. In the final version, all references to slavery were removed. But delegates agreed to list among the abuses suffered by the colonies the fact that the king "excited domestic insurrections amongst us," referring to the threat posed by Dunmore's Proclamation. On July 2, 1776, delegates from twelve colonies approved the Declaration, with only New York abstaining. Independence was publicly proclaimed on July 4 when the Declaration was published as a broadside to be circulated throughout the colonies.

REVIEW & RELATE

What challenges did Washington face when he was given command of the Continental Army?

How and why did proponents of independence prevail in the debates that led to the Declaration of Independence?

Choosing Sides

Probably no more than half of American colonists actively supported the patriots. Perhaps a fifth actively supported the British. The rest tried to stay neutral or were largely indifferent unless the war came to their doorstep. Both patriots and loyalists included men and women from all classes and races and from both rural and urban areas.

Colonel Guy Johnson and Karonghyontye (Captain David Hill), 1776 Benjamin West painted this portrait of Colonel Johnson, British superintendent of Indian affairs, with the Mohawk chief Karonghyontye. Johnson directed joint Mohawk and British attacks against patriots during the Revolution. His red coat and musket are combined with moccasins, a wampum belt, and an Indian blanket while Karonghyontye holds a peace pipe, representing the Mohawk-British alliance before and during the war. National Gallery of Art, Washington DC, USA/Bridgeman Images

Recruiting Supporters. Men who took up arms against the British before independence was declared and the women who supported them clearly demonstrated their commitment to the patriot cause. In some colonies, patriots organized local committees, courts, and assemblies to assume governance should British officials lose their authority. At the same time, white servants and enslaved blacks in Virginia who fled to British ships or marched with Lord Dunmore made their loyalties known as well. Some Indians, too, declared their allegiance early in the conflict. In May 1775, Colonel Guy Johnson, the British superintendent for Indian affairs, left Albany, New York, and sought refuge in Canada. He was accompanied by 120 British loyalists and 90 Mohawk warriors led by their mission-educated chief, Joseph Brant (Thayendanegea).

The Continental Congress, like Johnson, recognized the importance of Indians to the outcome of any colonial war. It appointed commissioners from the "United Colonies" to meet with representatives of the Iroquois Confederacy in August 1775. While Brant's group of Mohawk warriors were already committed to the British, some Oneida Indians, influenced by missionaries and patriot sympathizers, wanted to support the colonies. Others, however, urged neutrality, at least for the moment.

Once independence was declared, there was far more pressure to choose sides. The stance of political and military leaders and soldiers was clear. But to win against Great Britain required the support of a large portion of the civilian population as well. As battle lines shifted back and forth across New England, the Middle Atlantic region, and the South, civilians caught up in the fighting were faced with difficult decisions.

Many colonists who remained loyal to the king found safe haven in cities like New York, Newport, and Charleston, which remained under British control throughout much of the war. **Loyalist** men were welcomed by the British army. Still, those who made their loyalist sympathies clear risked a good deal. When British troops were forced out of cities or towns they had temporarily occupied, many loyalists faced harsh reprisals. Patriots had no qualms about invading the homes of loyalists, punishing women and children, and destroying or confiscating property.

Many loyalists were members of the economic and political elite. Others came from ordinary backgrounds. Tenants, small farmers, and slaves joined the loyalist cause in defiance of their landlords, large property owners, and wealthy planters. Many poorer loyalists lived in the Hudson valley, their sympathy for the British heightened by the patriot commitments of the powerful men who controlled the region. When the fighting moved south, many former Regulators also supported the British, who challenged the domination of patriot leaders among North Carolina's eastern elite.

> **Explore ▶**
>
> For images of African Americans' varied responses to the war, see Documents 6.2 and 6.3.

Perhaps most important, the majority of Indian nations ultimately sided with the British. The Mohawk, Seneca, and Cayuga nations in the North and the Cherokee and Creek nations in the South were among Great Britain's leading allies. Although British efforts to limit colonial migration, such as the Proclamation Line of 1763, had failed, most Indian nations still believed that a British victory offered the only hope of ending further encroachments on their territory.

Choosing Neutrality. Early in the war, many Indian nations proclaimed their neutrality. This included the Delaware and Shawnee in the Ohio River valley and the Oneida in Connecticut. The Oneida's chief warriors declared that the English and patriots were "*two brothers of one blood. We are unwilling to join on either side in such a contest.*" But patriots often refused to accept Indian neutrality. Indeed, colonial troops killed the Shawnee chief Cornstalk under a flag of truce in 1777, leading that nation to ally, finally, with the British.

Colonists who sought to remain neutral during the war also faced hostility. Some 80,000 Quakers, Mennonites, Amish, Shakers, and Moravians considered war immoral and embraced neutrality. These men refused to bear arms, hire substitutes, or pay taxes to new state governments. The largest number of religious pacifists lived in Pennsylvania. Despite Quakerism's deep roots there, pacifists were treated as suspect by both patriots and loyalists.

COMPARATIVE ANALYSIS

African Americans in New York City Amid the Upheavals of 1776

On July 9, the day New York's Provincial Congress approved the Declaration of Independence, a rowdy crowd of soldiers and civilians toppled a statue of King George III. However, an etching of the event presents it as the work of African Americans, with most whites simply observing (Document 6.2). In a second etching, by François Xavier Haberman (Document 6.3), Manhattan burns only days after British troops occupied the city. The fire, which may have been purposely set, burnt a mile-long swath. Here, redcoats beat suspected patriots while white and black residents carry items from burning buildings.

Document 6.2

Slaves Destroy Statue of King George III in New York City, July 1776

Library of Congress, LC-DIG-ppmsca-17521

Document 6.3

A Fire Burns British-Occupied New York City, September 1776

Library of Congress, 3b48304

Interpret the Evidence

1. Why might an American artist depict the destruction of the statue of King George III as the work mainly of blacks? What roles are whites playing in this portrayal?
2. What meanings might be attached to black and white residents carrying items out of burning buildings after the British occupation of Manhattan? Why are the blacks here and in Document 6.2 shown as barely clothed?

Put It in Context

Given the limited choices available to most African Americans during the American Revolution, what advantages (or disadvantages) were created by the patriots or the British gaining control of areas where they lived?

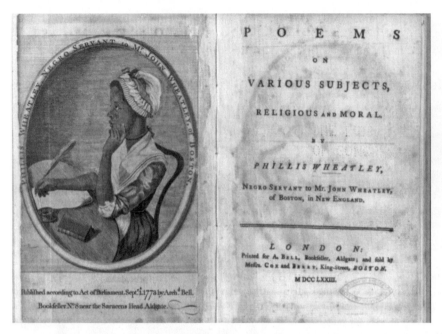

Phillis Wheatley This portrait of Phillis Wheatley appears facing the title page of her book of poems, printed in London in 1773. It was painted by another Boston slave, Scipio Moorhead. Phillis Wheatley converted to Christianity and sided with the patriots in the Revolution. She won her freedom but never gained sufficient support to publish another book of poems. Library of Congress, 3b04682

In June 1778, Pennsylvania authorities jailed nine Mennonite farmers who refused to take an oath of allegiance to the revolutionary government. Their worldly goods were sold by the state, leaving their wives and children destitute. Quakers were routinely fined and imprisoned for refusing to support the patriot cause and harassed by British authorities in the areas they controlled. At the same time, Quaker meetings regularly disciplined members who offered aid to either side. Betsy Ross was among those disowned Quakers. Her husband joined the patriot forces, and she sewed flags for the Continental Army and Navy.

Committing to Independence. After July 4, 1776, the decision to support independence took on new meaning. If the United States failed to win the war, all those who actively supported the cause could be considered traitors. The families of Continental soldiers faced especially difficult decisions as the conflict spread and soldiers moved farther and farther from home. Men too old or too young to fight proved their patriotism by gathering arms and ammunition and patrolling local communities.

Some female patriots accompanied their husbands or fiancés as camp followers, cooking, washing clothes, nursing, and providing other services for soldiers. Most patriot women remained at home, however, and demonstrated their commitment by raising funds, gathering information, and sending clothes, bedding, and other goods to soldiers at the front. The Continental Army was desperately short of supplies from the beginning of the war. Northern women were urged to increase cloth production, while southern women were asked to harvest crops for hungry troops. The response was overwhelming. Women in Hartford, Connecticut, produced 1,000 coats and vests and 1,600 shirts in 1776 alone. Across the colonies, women collected clothing door-to-door and opened their homes to sick and wounded soldiers.

Some African American women also became ardent patriots. Phillis Wheatley of Boston, whose owners taught her to read and write, published a collection of poems in 1776 and sent a copy to General Washington. She urged readers to recognize Africans as children of God. Rewarded with freedom by her master, Wheatley was among a small number of blacks who actively supported the patriot cause. Still, the vast majority of blacks labored as slaves. While some escaped and joined the British in hopes of gaining their freedom, most were not free to choose sides.

REVIEW & RELATE

- How did colonists choose sides during the Revolutionary War? What factors influenced their decisions?

- Why would some Indian tribes try to stay neutral during the conflict? Why did most of those who chose sides support the British?

Fighting for Independence, 1776–1777

After July 4, 1776, battles between British and colonial troops intensified, but it was not until December that the patriots celebrated a major military victory. In 1777, however, the tide turned for the Continental Army even as British forces remained formidable. As it became increasingly clear that the war could continue for several years, each side sought support from women on the home front as well as men on the battlefront.

British Troops Gain Early Victories. In the summer of 1776, when General Washington tried to lead his army out of Boston to confront British troops set to invade New York City, many soldiers deserted and returned home. They believed that New York men should defend New York. Among the soldiers who remained with Washington, many were landless laborers whose wives and sisters followed the troops as their only means of support. Although Washington considered these camp followers undesirable, the few hundred women provided critical services to ordinary soldiers. Ultimately, Washington arrived in New York with 19,000 men, many of whom were poorly armed and poorly trained and some of whom were coerced into service by local committees of safety.

The ragtag Continental force faced a formidable foe. Throughout the summer, British ships sailed into New York harbor or anchored off the coast of Long Island. General Howe, hoping to overwhelm the colonists, ordered 10,000 troops to march into the city in the weeks immediately after the Declaration of Independence was signed. Still, the Continental Congress rejected Howe's offer of peace and a royal pardon.

So Howe prepared to take control of New York City by force and then march up the Hudson valley, isolating New York and New England from the rest of the rebellious colonies. He was aided by some 8,000 Hessian mercenaries (Germans being paid to fight for the British). On August 27, 1776, British forces clashed with a far smaller contingent of Continentals on Long Island. More than 1,500 patriots were killed or wounded in the fierce fighting.

By November, the British had captured Fort Lee in New Jersey and attacked the Continental Army at Fort Washington, north of New York City. Meanwhile Washington led his weary troops and camp followers into Pennsylvania, while the Continental Congress, fearing a British attack on Philadelphia, fled to Baltimore.

Although General Howe might have ended the patriot threat right then by an aggressive campaign, he wanted to wear down the Continental Army and force the colonies to sue for peace. Washington did not have the troops or arms to launch a major assault, and he hoped that the British would accept American independence once they saw the enormous effort it would take to defeat the colonies. So the war continued.

Patriots Prevail in New Jersey. The Continental Army did not gain a single military victory between July and December 1776. Fortunately for Washington, Howe followed the European tradition of waiting out the winter months and returning to combat after the spring thaw. This gave the patriots the opportunity to regroup, repair weapons and wagons, and recruit soldiers. Yet Washington was reluctant to face the cold and discomfort of winter with troops discouraged by repeated defeats and retreats.

Camped in eastern Pennsylvania, Washington learned that Hessian troops had been sent to occupy the city of Trenton, New Jersey, just across the Delaware River. On Christmas Eve, Washington attacked Trenton in an icy rain, and the Continentals quickly routed the surprised Hessians. They then marched on Princeton and defeated regular British troops on January 3, 1777. The British army soon retreated from New Jersey, settling back into New York City, and the Continental Congress returned to Philadelphia. By mid-January 1777, it seemed clear to both sides that the conflict would be harder, more costly, and more deadly than anyone had imagined.

A Critical Year of Warfare. The British army emerged from winter camp in spring 1777. Its regular army units, American loyalists, Indian allies, Hessians, and naval men-of-war were concentrated largely in New York City and Canada. The Continental forces, numbering fewer than 5,000 men, were then entrenched near Morristown, New Jersey. With his troops ravaged by smallpox over the winter, Washington feared that an aggressive British assault might succeed.

Meanwhile, the Continental Congress had returned to Philadelphia, but members feared that the British would seek to capture the city and split the United States in two. General Howe did indeed plan on capturing Philadelphia, hoping to force a patriot surrender. Although Washington's force was too small to defeat Howe's army, it delayed his advance by guerrilla attacks and skirmishes. En route, Howe learned that he was expected to reinforce General John Burgoyne's soldiers, who were advancing south from Canada. Instead he continued to Philadelphia and captured it in September 1777. Meanwhile Burgoyne and his 7,200 troops regained control of Fort Ticonderoga on July 7. He continued south, but by late July his forces had to stop until supplies from Canada and reinforcements from Howe and General Barry St. Leger reached them.

St. Leger was marching his troops east through New York State, and Joseph Brant and his sister Molly Brant were gathering a force of Mohawk, Seneca, and Cayuga warriors to support them. But on August 6, they suffered a stunning defeat. In the **Battle of Oriskany** in New York, a band of German American farmers led by General Nicholas Herkimer held off the British advance, allowing General Arnold to reach nearby Fort Stanwix with reinforcements. On August 23, the British and Indian troops retreated to Canada (Map 6.1).

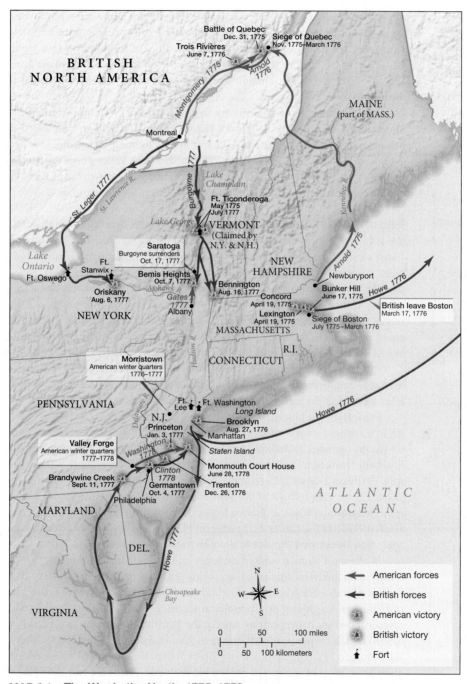

MAP 6.1 The War in the North, 1775–1778

After early battles in Massachusetts, patriots invaded Canada but failed to capture Quebec. The British army captured New York City in 1776 and Philadelphia in 1777, but New Jersey remained a battle zone through 1778. Meanwhile General Burgoyne secured Canada for Britain and then headed south, but his forces were defeated by patriots at the crucial Battle of Saratoga.

When General Howe's reinforcements also did not materialize, Burgoyne faced a brutal onslaught from patriot forces. In September patriots defeated the British at Freeman's
Farm, with the British suffering twice the casualties of the Continentals. Fighting intensified in early October, when Burgoyne lost a second battle at Freeman's Farm. Ten days
later, he surrendered his remaining army of 5,800 men to General Gates at nearby Saratoga, New York.

The Continental Army's victory in the **Battle of Saratoga** stunned the British. It
undercut the significance of Howe's victory at Philadelphia and indicated the general's
misunderstanding of the nature of the war he was fighting. Meanwhile, the patriot victory
energized Washington and his troops as they dug in at Valley Forge for another long winter. It also gave Benjamin Franklin, the Continental Congress envoy to Paris, greater leverage for convincing French officials to support American independence.

Patriots Gain Critical Assistance. Despite significant Continental victories in
the fall of 1777, the following winter proved especially difficult. The quarters at **Valley
Forge** were again marked by bitter cold, poor food, inadequate clothing, and scarce supplies. A French volunteer arrived to see "a few militia men, poorly clad, and for the most
part without shoes; many of them badly armed." Many recent recruits were also poorly
trained. Critical assistance arrived with Baron Friedrich von Steuben, a Prussian officer
recruited by Benjamin Franklin, who took charge of drilling soldiers. Other officers experienced in European warfare also joined the patriot cause that winter: the Marquis de Lafayette of France, Johann Baron de Kalb of Bavaria, and Thaddeus Kosciusko and Casimir
Count Pulaski, both of Poland. The Continental Army continued to be plagued by problems of recruitment, discipline, wages, and supplies. But the contributions of foreign volunteers, along with the leadership of Washington and his officers, sustained the military effort.

Patriots on the home front were also plagued by problems in 1777–1778. Families living in battlefield areas were especially vulnerable to the shifting fortunes of war. When British troops captured Philadelphia in fall 1777, a British officer commandeered the home of
Elizabeth Drinker, a Quaker matron. An angry Drinker reported that the officer moved in
with "3 Horses 2 Cows 2 Sheep and 3 Turkeys." Women who lived far from the conflict were
isolated from such intrusions but were forced to fend for themselves with husbands at the
front. Meanwhile, wives of patriot leaders, anxious to end the conflict, formed voluntary
associations, like the Ladies Association of Philadelphia, to provide critical resources for the
army. **See Document Project 6: Women in the Revolution, page 200.**

While most women worked tirelessly on the home front, some cast their fate with the
army. Camp followers continued to provide critical services to the military and suffered, as
the troops did, from scarce supplies and harsh weather. Some women also served as spies
and couriers for British or Continental forces. Lydia Darragh, a wealthy Philadelphian,
eavesdropped on conversations among the British officers who occupied her house and
carried detailed reports to Washington hidden in the folds of her dress. Others, like Nancy
Hart Morgan of Georgia, took more direct action. Morgan lulled half a dozen British soldiers into a sense of security at dinner, hid their guns, and shot two before neighbors came
to hang the rest.

Some patriot women took up arms on the battlefield. A few, such as Margaret Corbin,
accompanied their husbands to the front lines. When her husband was killed at Fort
Washington in November 1776, Corbin took his place loading and firing cannons. In

addition, a small number of women, like Deborah Sampson, disguised themselves as men and enlisted as soldiers.

Surviving on the Home Front. Whether black or white, enslaved or free, women and children faced hardship, uncertainty, loneliness, and fear as a result of the war. Even those who did not directly engage enemy troops took on enormous burdens during the conflict. Farm wives plowed and planted and carried on their domestic duties as well. In cities, women worked ceaselessly to find sufficient food, wood, candles, and cloth to maintain themselves and their children.

As the war intensified, Continental and British forces slaughtered cattle and hogs for food, stole corn and other crops or burned them to keep the enemy from obtaining supplies, looted houses and shops, and kidnapped or liberated slaves and servants. Some home invasions turned savage. Both patriot and loyalist papers in New York, Philadelphia, and Charleston reported cases of rape.

In these desperate circumstances, many women asserted themselves in order to survive. When merchants hoarded goods in order to make greater profits when prices rose, housewives raided stores and warehouses and took the supplies they needed. Others learned as much as they could about family finances and submitted reports to local officials when their houses, farms, or businesses were damaged or looted. Growing numbers of women banded together to assist one another, help more impoverished families, and supply troops with badly needed clothes, food, bandages, and bullets.

REVIEW & RELATE

How did the patriot forces fare in 1776? How and why did the tide of war turn in 1777?	What role did colonial women and foreign men play in the conflict in the early years of the war?

Governing in Revolutionary Times

Amid the constant upheavals of war, patriot leaders established new governments. At the national level, responsibilities ranged from coordinating and funding military operations to developing diplomatic relations with foreign countries and Indian nations. At the state level, constitutions had to be drafted and approved, laws enforced, and military needs assessed and met. Whether state or national, new governments had to assure their followers that they were not simply replacing old forms of oppression with new ones. Yet few states moved to eliminate the most oppressive institution in the nation, slavery.

Colonies Become States. For most of the war, the Continental Congress acted in lieu of a national government while the delegates worked to devise a more permanent structure. But the congress had depended mainly on states for funds and manpower. Delegates did draft the **Articles of Confederation** in 1777 and submitted them to the states for approval. Eight of the thirteen states ratified the plan for a national government by mid-1778. But nearly three more years passed before the last state, Maryland, approved the Articles.

Without a formal central government, state governments played crucial roles throughout the war. Even before the Continental Congress declared American independence, some colonies had forced royal officials to flee and established new state governments. Some states abided by the regulations in their colonial charters or by English common law. Others created new governments based on a written constitution.

These constitutions reflected the opposition to centralized power fueled by the struggle against British tyranny. In Pennsylvania, patriots developed one of the most democratic constitutions. The governor was replaced by an executive council. The legislature consisted of a single house elected by popular vote. Legislators could only serve for four in any seven years to discourage the formation of a political aristocracy. Although Pennsylvania's constitution was among the most radical, all states limited centralized power in some way.

Most states, adopting Virginia's model, included in their constitutions a bill of rights that ensured citizens freedom of the press, freedom of elections, speedy trials by one's peers, humane punishments, and the right to form militias. Some states also insisted on people's freedom of speech and assembly, the right to petition and to bear arms, and equal protection of the laws. The New Jersey constitution of 1776 enfranchised all free inhabitants who met the property qualifications, thereby allowing some single and widowed women and free blacks to vote.

Patriots Divide over Slavery.
Although state constitutions were revolutionary in many respects, few of them addressed the issue of slavery. Only Vermont abolished slavery in its 1777 constitution. Legislators in Pennsylvania approved a gradual abolition law by which slaves born after 1780 could claim their freedom at age twenty-eight. In Massachusetts, two slaves sued for their freedom in county courts in 1780–1781. Quock Walker, who had been promised his emancipation by a former master, sued his current master to gain his freedom. About the same time, an enslaved woman, Mum Bett, who was the widow of a Revolutionary soldier, initiated a similar case. Mum Bett won her case and changed her name to Elizabeth Freeman. When Walker's owner appealed the local court's decision to free his slave, the Massachusetts Supreme Court cited Mum Bett's case and ruled that slavery conflicted with the state constitution.

In southern states like Virginia, the Carolinas, and Georgia, however, life for slaves grew increasingly harsh during the war. Because British forces promised freedom to blacks who fought with them, slave owners and patriot armies in the South did everything possible to ensure that African Americans did not make it behind British lines. When the British retreated, some generals, like Lord Dunmore and Sir Henry Clinton, took black volunteers with them. But thousands more were left behind to fend for themselves.

Nonetheless, the American Revolution dealt a blow to human bondage. For many blacks, Revolutionary ideals required the end of slavery. Northern free black communities grew rapidly during the war, especially in seaport cities. In the South, too, thousands of slaves gained freedom, either by joining the British army or by fleeing in the midst of battlefield chaos. As many as one-quarter of South Carolina's slaves had emancipated themselves by the end of the Revolution. Yet as the Continental Congress worked toward developing a framework for a national government, few delegates considered the abolition of slavery a significant issue.

The Marquis de La Fayette with an Aide-de-Camp   This eighteenth-century portrait of the Marquis de Lafayette was painted by a Frenchman during the Revolution. It shows him with his aide-de-camp, probably from the French West Indies. Lafayette joined the Continental Army in September 1777, led patriot forces in numerous battles, camped at Valley Forge, and trapped British forces under General Cornwallis at the decisive Siege of Yorktown.   Musée de la Ville de Paris, Musée Carnavalet, Paris, France/Archives Charmet/Bridgeman Images

France Allies with the Patriots. The Continental Congress considered an alliance with France far more critical to patriot success than the issue of slavery. France's long rivalry with Britain made it a likely ally, and the French government had secretly provided funds to the patriots early in the war. In December 1776, the Continental Congress sent Benjamin Franklin to Paris to serve as its unofficial liaison. Franklin was enormously successful, securing supplies and becoming a favorite among the French aristocracy and ordinary citizens alike.

But the French were initially unwilling to forge a formal compact with the upstart patriots. Only after the patriot victory at Saratoga in October 1777 did King Louis XVI agree to an alliance. In February 1778, Franklin secured an agreement that approved trading rights between the United States and all French possessions. France then recognized the United States as an independent nation, relinquished French territorial claims on mainland North America, and sent troops to reinforce the Continental Army. In return, the United States promised to defend French holdings in the Caribbean. A year later, Spain allied itself with France to protect its own North American holdings.

British leaders responded by declaring war on France. Yet doing so ensured that military conflicts would spread well beyond North America and military expenditures would skyrocket. French forces attacked British outposts in Gibraltar, the Bay of Bengal, Senegal in West Africa, and Grenada in the West Indies. At the same time, the French supplied the United States with military officers, weapons, funds, and critical naval support.

Faced with this new alliance, Britain's prime minister, Lord North (1771–1782), decided to concentrate British forces in New York City. This tactic forced the British army to abandon Philadelphia in summer 1778. For the remainder of the war, New York City provided the sole British stronghold in the North, serving as a supply center and prisoner-of-war camp.

Raising Armies and Funds. The French alliance did create one unintended problem for the Continental Army. When Americans heard that France was sending troops, fewer men volunteered for military service. Local officials had the authority to draft men into the army or to accept substitutes for draftees. In the late 1770s, some draftees forced enslaved men to take their place; others hired landless laborers, the handicapped, or the mentally unfit as substitutes.

As the war spread south and west in 1778–1779, Continental forces were stretched thin, and enlistments faltered further. Soldiers faced injuries, disease, and shortages of food and ammunition. They also risked capture by the British, one of the worst fates to befall a Continental. Considered traitors by the British, most captives were held on ships in New York harbor. They faced filthy accommodations, a horrid stench, inadequate water, and widespread disease and abuse. Altogether, between 8,000 and 11,500 patriots died in British prisons in New York—more than died in battle.

Even if the British had allowed the Continental Congress to aid prisoners, it could do little, given the financial problems it faced. With no authority to impose taxes on American citizens, the congress had to borrow money from wealthy patriots, accept loans from France and the Netherlands, and print money of its own—some $200 million by 1780. However, money printed by the states was used far more widely than were Continental dollars. "Continentals" depreciated so quickly that by late 1780 it took one hundred continentals to buy one silver dollar's worth of goods. In 1779, with the cost of goods skyrocketing, housewives, sailors, and artisans in Philadelphia and other cities attacked merchants who were hoarding goods, forcing officials to distribute food to the poor.

The congress finally improved its financial standing slightly by using a $6 million loan from France to back certificates issued to wealthy patriots. Meanwhile states raised money through taxes to provide funds for government operations, backing for its paper money, and other expenses. Most residents found such taxes incredibly burdensome given wartime inflation, and even the most patriotic began to protest increased taxation. Thus the financial status of the new nation remained precarious.

Indian Affairs and Land Claims. The congress also sought to settle land claims in the western regions of the nation and build alliances with additional Indian nations. The two issues were intertwined, and both were difficult to resolve. Most Indian nations had long-standing complaints against colonists who intruded on their lands, and many patriot leaders made it clear that independence would mean further expansion.

In the late 1770s, British forces and their Indian allies fought bitter battles against patriot militias and Continental forces all along the frontier. Each side destroyed property, ruined crops, and killed civilians. In the summer and fall of 1778, Indian and American civilians suffered through a series of brutal attacks in Wyoming, Pennsylvania; Onoquaga, New York; and Cherry Valley, New York. Patriots and Indians also battled along the Virginia frontier after pioneer and militia leader Daniel Boone established a fort there in 1775. In the South, 6,000 patriot troops laid waste to Cherokee villages in the Appalachian Mountains in retaliation for the killing of white intruders along the Watauga River by a renegade Cherokee warrior, Dragging Canoe.

Regardless of Indian rights, much western land had already been claimed by individual states like Connecticut, Georgia, New York, Massachusetts, and Virginia. These states hoped to use western lands to reward soldiers and expand their settlements. However, states without such claims, like Maryland, argued that if such lands were "wrested from the common enemy by the blood and treasure of the thirteen States," they should be considered "common property, subject to be parcelled out by Congress into free and independent governments." In 1780 New York State finally ceded its western claims to the Continental Congress, and Connecticut and Massachusetts followed suit.

With land disputes settled, Maryland ratified the Articles of Confederation in March 1781, and a new national government was finally formed. But the congress's guarantee that western lands would be "disposed of for the common benefit of the United States" ensured continued conflicts with Indians.

REVIEW & RELATE

- What values and concerns shaped state governments during the Revolutionary War?

- What issues and challenges did the Continental Congress face even after the French joined the patriot side?

Winning the War and the Peace, 1778-1781

From 1778 to 1781, the battlefront in the Revolution moved south and west. The king, who believed that southern colonists' sympathies were more loyalist than patriot, insisted on pursuing a southern strategy. At the same time, patriot conflicts with Britain and its Indian allies intensified along the western frontier. The patriots' eventual victory rested on a combination of superb strategy, their French and Spanish allies, and the continued support of affluent men and women. Still, even after Britain's surrender in October 1781, the war dragged on while peace terms were negotiated. The celebrations following the signing of a peace treaty were themselves tempered by protests among Continental soldiers demanding back pay and by the realization of the new nation's looming problems.

Fighting in the West. While the congress debated the fate of western land claims, battles continued in the Ohio and Mississippi River valleys. The British commander at Fort Michilimackinac on Lake Huron recruited Sioux, Chippewa, and Sauk warriors to attack Spanish forces along the Mississippi, while soldiers at Fort Detroit armed Ottawa, Fox, and Miami warriors to assault American settlers flooding into the Ohio River valley. British forces also moved deeper into this region, establishing a post at Vincennes on the Wabash River.

The response to these British forays was effective, if not well coordinated. In 1778 a patriot surveyor, George Rogers Clark of Virginia, organized an expedition to counter Indian raids in the West and to reinforce Spanish and French allies in the upper Mississippi valley. He fought successfully against British and Indian forces at Kaskaskia and Cahokia on the Mississippi River. Then Clark launched a surprise attack on British forces at Vincennes. Although Detroit remained in British hands, Spanish troops defeated British-allied Indian forces at St. Louis, giving the patriots greater control in the Ohio River valley (Map 6.2).

In the summer of 1779, colonial General John Sullivan led a campaign to wipe out Mohawk, Seneca, Cayuga, and Onondaga villages in central and western New York. He succeeded in ending most attacks by Britain's Iroquois allies and disrupting the supplies being sent by British forces at Fort Niagara. Patriot attacks in Ohio also continued. In one of the worst atrocities fomented by patriots, Pennsylvania militiamen massacred more than one hundred Delaware men, women, and children near present-day Canton, Ohio.

Explore ▶

See Document 6.4 for an account of General Sullivan's attack on the Seneca.

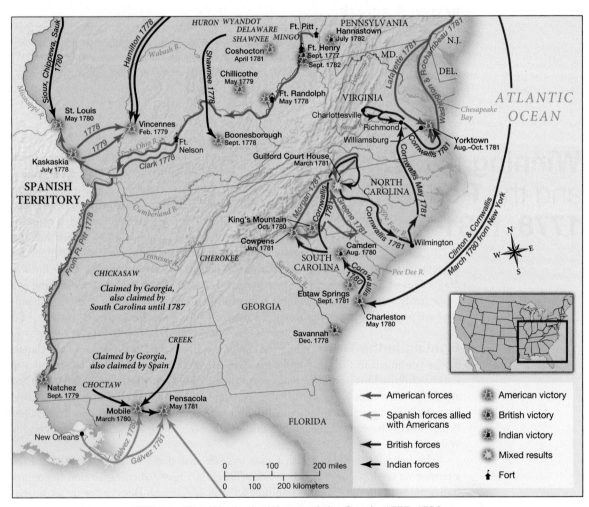

MAP 6.2   The War in the West and the South, 1777–1782

Between 1780 and 1781, major battles between Continental and British troops took place in Virginia and the Carolinas, and the British general Cornwallis finally surrendered at Yorktown, Virginia, in October 1781. But patriot forces also battled British troops and their Indian allies from 1777 to 1782 in the Ohio River valley, the lower Mississippi River, and the Gulf coast.

Battles between Indian nations and American settlers did not end with the American Revolution. For the moment, however, the patriots and their allies had defeated British and Indian efforts to control the Mississippi and Ohio River valleys.

SOLO ANALYSIS

Mary Jemison | The War's Impact on the Seneca Nation, 1823

When the Seneca nation in western New York State was forced to choose sides in the American Revolution, it—like other Iroquois groups—supported the British. Mary Jemison, an Irish immigrant, had been captured by Shawnee Indians in 1755 at the age of about twelve. She was then traded to the Seneca nation, married a Seneca man, and had six children. In 1823 she recounted her experiences in *A Narrative of the Life of Mrs. Mary Jemison*, which became a best-selling book. In the following passage, Jemison describes the 1779 attack by Continental forces and the Seneca response.

Document 6.4

[General John] Sullivan and his army arrived at Genesee river, where they destroyed every article of the food kind that they could lay their hands on. A part of our corn they burnt, and threw the remainder into the river. They burnt our houses, killed what few cattle and horses they could find, destroyed our fruit trees, and left nothing but the bare soil and timber. But the Indians had eloped and were not to be found. Having . . . finished the work of destruction, the army marched off to the east. . . . [Once] Sullivan had gone so far that there would be no danger of his returning to molest us . . . we all returned; but what were our feelings when we found that there was not a mouthful of any kind of sustenance left, not even enough to keep a child one day from perishing with hunger.

The weather by this time had become cold and stormy; and as we were destitute of houses and food too, I immediately resolved to take my children and look out for myself, without delay.

With this intention, I took two of my little ones on my back, bade the other three follow, and on the same night arrived on the Gardow Flats. . . .

The next summer after Sullivan's campaign, our Indians, highly incensed at the whites for the treatment they had received, and the sufferings which they had consequently endured, determined to obtain some redress by destroying their frontier settlements. Corn Planter . . . led the Indians and an officer by the name of Johnston [Colonel Guy Johnson] commanded the British in the expedition. . . . [T]hey burnt a number of places; destroyed all the cattle and other property that fell in their way; killed a number of white people, and brought home a few prisoners.

Source: James E. Seaver, *A Narrative of the Life of Mrs. Mary Jemison, Who Was Taken by the Indians, in the Year 1755* (Howden ed., 1826), 69–70, 72.

Interpret the Evidence

1. What effect did the attack by the Continental Army have on the Seneca village in which Jemison lived?
2. After returning to their village, how did Jemison respond to the situation the Seneca faced? How did the Seneca warriors and their British allies respond?

Put It in Context

What does the experience of the Seneca reveal about the specific dangers that Indian communities whose men fought with the British faced from the patriots?

War Rages in the South. Meanwhile British troops sought to regain control of southern states from Georgia to Virginia. British troops captured Savannah, Georgia, in 1778 and soon extended their control over the entire state. When General Clinton was called north later that year, he left the southern campaign in the hands of Lord Charles Cornwallis.

In May 1780, General Cornwallis reclaimed Charleston, South Carolina. He then evicted patriots from the city, purged them from the state government, gained military control of the state, and imposed loyalty oaths on all Carolinians able to fight. To aid his efforts, local loyalists organized militias to battle patriots in the interior. Banastre Tarleton led one especially vicious company of loyalists who slaughtered civilians and murdered many who surrendered. In retaliation, patriot planter Thomas Sumter organized 800 men who showed a similar disregard for regular army procedures, raiding largely defenseless loyalist settlements near Hanging Rock, South Carolina, in August 1780.

As retaliatory violence erupted in the interior of South Carolina, General Gates marched his Continental troops south to join 2,000 militiamen from Virginia and North Carolina. But his troops were exhausted and short of food, and on August 16 Cornwallis won a smashing victory against the combined patriot forces at Camden, South Carolina (see Map 6.2). Soon after news of Gates's defeat reached General Washington, he heard that Benedict Arnold, commander at West Point, had defected to the British.

Suddenly, British chances for victory seemed more hopeful. Cornwallis was in control of Georgia and South Carolina, and local loyalists were eager to gain control of the southern countryside. Meanwhile Continental soldiers in the North mutinied in early 1780 over enlistment terms and pay. Patriot morale was low, funds were scarce, and civilians were growing weary of the war.

Yet somehow the patriots prevailed. A combination of luck, strong leadership, and French support turned the tide. In October 1780, when Continental hopes looked especially bleak, a group of 800 frontier sharpshooters routed loyalist troops at King's Mountain in South Carolina. The victory kept Cornwallis from advancing into North Carolina and gave the Continentals a chance to regroup.

Shortly after the battle at King's Mountain, Washington sent General Nathanael Greene to replace Gates as head of southern operations. Taking advice from local militia leaders like Daniel Morgan and Francis Marion, Greene divided his limited force into even smaller units. Marion and Morgan each led 300 Continental soldiers into the South Carolina backcountry, picking up hundreds of local militiamen along the way. At the village of Cowpens, Morgan inflicted a devastating defeat on Tarleton's much larger force.

Cornwallis, enraged at the patriot victory, pursued Continental forces as they retreated. But Cornwallis's troops had outrun their cannons, and Greene circled back and attacked them at Guilford Court House. Although Cornwallis eventually forced the Continentals to withdraw from the battlefield, British troops suffered enormous losses. In August 1781, frustrated at the ease with which patriot forces still found local support in the South, he hunkered down in Yorktown on the Virginia coast and waited for reinforcements from New York.

Washington now coordinated strategy with his French allies. Comte de Rochambeau marched 5,000 troops south from Rhode Island to Virginia as General Lafayette led his troops south along Virginia's eastern shore. At the same time, French naval ships headed

Francis Marion   Francis Marion, known as "the Swamp Fox," and his militia waged guerrilla warfare against the British in South Carolina. Marion wreaked havoc by conducting quick surprise attacks. This print from an 1836 painting by John Blake White shows Marion in striking headgear inviting a British officer to share a meal, while Marion's slave Oscar kneels by the table. Brown University Library, Providence, Rhode Island, USA/Bridgeman Images

north from the West Indies. One unit cut off a British fleet trying to resupply Cornwallis by sea. Another joined up with American privateers to bombard Cornwallis's forces. By mid-October, British supplies had run out, and it was clear that reinforcements would not be forthcoming. On October 19, 1781, the British army admitted defeat.

An Uncertain Peace.   The Continental Army had managed the impossible. It had defeated the British army and won the colonies' independence. Yet even with the surrender after the **Battle of Yorktown**, the war continued in fits and starts. Peace negotiations in Paris dragged on as French, Spanish, British, and American representatives sought to settle a host of issues. Meanwhile, British forces challenged Continental troops in and around New York City.

Some Continental soldiers continued to fight, but others focused on the long-festering issue of overdue wages. When the congress decided in June 1783 to discharge the remaining troops without providing back pay, a near mutiny erupted in Pennsylvania. Nearly three hundred soldiers marched on the congress in Philadelphia. Washington sent troops, including Deborah Sampson/Robert Shurtliff, to put down the mutiny. Bloodshed was avoided when the Pennsylvania soldiers agreed to accept half pay and certificates for the remainder. Despite this compromise, the issue of back pay would continue to plague the nation.

Meanwhile patriot representatives in Paris—Benjamin Franklin, John Adams, and John Jay—continued to negotiate peace terms. Rising antiwar sentiment on the British home front forced the government's hand. But the Comte de Vergennes, the French foreign minister, opposed the Americans' republican principles and refused to consider the American delegates as his political equals. Given the importance of the French to the American victory, the congress had instructed its delegates to defer to French wishes. This blocked the American representatives from signing a separate peace with the British.

Eventually, however, U.S. delegates finalized a treaty that secured substantial benefits for the young nation. The United States gained control of all lands south of Canada and north of Louisiana and Florida stretching to the Mississippi River. In addition, the treaty recognized the United States to be "free Sovereign and independent states." Spain signed a separate treaty with Great Britain in which it regained control of Florida. Despite their role in the war, none of the Indian nations that occupied the lands under negotiation were consulted.

When the **Treaty (Peace) of Paris** was finally signed on September 2, 1783, thousands of British troops and their supporters left the colonies for Canada, the West Indies, or England. British soldiers on the western frontier were supposed to be withdrawn at the same time, but they remained for many years and continued to foment hostilities between Indians in the region and U.S. settlers along the frontier.

The evacuation of the British also entailed the exodus of thousands of African Americans who had fought against the patriots. At the end of the war, British officials granted certificates of manumission (freedom) to more than 1,300 men, 900 women, and 700 children. Most of these freed blacks settled in Nova Scotia, where they received small allotments of land from the British, but they generally lacked the resources to make such homesteads profitable. Despite these obstacles, some created a small Afro-Canadian community in Nova Scotia, while others migrated to areas considered more hospitable to black residents, such as Sierra Leone.

A Surprising Victory.

A Surprising Victory. Americans had managed to defeat one of the most powerful military forces in the world. That victory resulted from the convergence of many circumstances. Certainly Americans benefited from fighting on their own soil. Their knowledge of the land and its resources as well as earlier experiences fighting against Indians and the French helped prepare them for battles against the British.

Just as important, British troops and officers were far removed from centers of decision making and supplies. Even supplies housed in Canada could not be easily transported the relatively short distance into New York. British commanders were often hesitant to make decisions independently, but awaiting instructions from England proved costly on several occasions, especially since strategists in London often had little sense of conditions in America.

Both sides depended on outsiders for assistance, but here, too, Americans gained the advantage. The British army relied heavily on German mercenaries, Indian allies, and freed blacks to bolster its regular troops. In victory, such "foreign" forces were relatively reliable, but in defeat, many of them chose to look out for their own interests. The patriots meanwhile marched with French and Spanish armies well prepared to challenge British troops and motivated to gain advantages for France and Spain if Britain was defeated.

Perhaps most important, a British victory was nearly impossible without conquering the American colonies one by one. Because a large percentage of colonists supported the patriot cause, British troops had to contend not only with Continental soldiers but also with an aroused citizenry fighting for its independence.

REVIEW & RELATE

How and why did the Americans win the Revolutionary War?

What uncertainties and challenges did the new nation face in the immediate aftermath of victory?

Conclusion: Legacies of the **Revolution**

After the approval of the Declaration of Independence, Thomas Hutchinson, the British official who had gained fame during the Stamp Act upheavals in Boston, charged that patriot leaders had "sought independence from the beginning." But the gradual and almost reluctant move from resistance to revolution in the American colonies suggests otherwise. When faced with threats from British troops, a sufficient number of colonists took up arms to create the reality of war, and this surge of hostilities finally gave the advantage to those political leaders urging independence.

The victory over Great Britain won that independence but left the United States confronting difficult problems. Most soldiers simply wanted to return home and reestablish their former lives. But the government's inability to pay back wages and the huge debt the nation owed to private citizens and state and foreign governments hinted at difficult economic times ahead. And these problems affected American Indians and African Americans as well as whites. Using western lands to reward officers and soldiers who had not received full pay intensified conflicts along the new nation's western frontier. Warfare between settlers and Indians west of the Appalachian Mountains, from the Ohio River valley to Georgia, continued for decades. At the same time, slaveowners seeking more fertile fields also expanded into the trans-Appalachian region. By 1800 they had carried tens of thousands of enslaved blacks into Kentucky, Tennessee, and the Mississippi Territory. Separated from families back east, slaves on the frontier engaged in backbreaking labor without the support or camaraderie of the communities left behind.

Although faced with far better opportunities than enslaved laborers, many white soldiers still found the adjustment to postwar life difficult. Like many other soldiers, Deborah Sampson embraced a conventional life after the war. She married a farmer, Benjamin Gannett, and had three children. But times were hard. A decade after she was discharged, Massachusetts finally granted her a small pension for her wartime service. Deborah Gannett earned some money by lecturing on her wartime adventures and received a small federal pension in 1804. Many men waited at least as long to receive any compensation for their wartime service while they struggled to reestablish farms and businesses and pay off debts accrued while fighting for independence.

Political leaders tried to address the concerns of former soldiers and ordinary citizens while they developed a new government. Within a few years of achieving independence, financial distress among small farmers and tensions with Indians on the western frontier intensified concerns about the ability of the confederation government to secure order and prosperity. While some patriots demanded a new political compact to strengthen the national government, others feared replicating British tyranny.

In the decade following the Revolution, leading patriots engaged in heated disagreements over the best means to unify and stabilize the United States. However, key leaders like Thomas Jefferson, Benjamin Franklin, and John Adams were living abroad as ambassadors, strengthening U.S. ties to Britain and France. In 1787 Thomas Paine, too, left for England, where he wrote pamphlets supporting the French Revolution. He eventually moved to France, but his radical political ideas led to his imprisonment there, and he returned to the United States upon his release. Even here, however, Paine was maligned for his attacks on organized religion and private property. Thus he played no part in the intense debates about how to secure the political future of the United States while holding on to the republican impulses that drove Americans to revolution.

TIMELINE OF EVENTS

April 19, 1775	Battles of Lexington and Concord
June 1775	Continental Congress establishes Continental Army
June 16, 1775	Battle of Bunker Hill
August 1775	Representatives of Continental Congress and Iroquois Confederacy meet
November 1775	Lord Dunmore issues his proclamation
January 1776	Thomas Paine publishes *Common Sense*
July 4, 1776	Continental Congress publicly declares independence
July to mid-December 1776	British forces defeat Continental Army
December 1776–January 1777	Patriot victories at Trenton and Princeton
October 1777	Patriot victory at Saratoga
Winter 1777–1778	Continental Army encamps at Valley Forge
1778	Articles of Confederation ratified by eight states
February 1778	France declares alliance with the United States
Summer 1779	Patriot forces destroy Iroquois villages
1780	Elizabeth "Mum Bett" Freeman sues for freedom
March 1781	Articles of Confederation ratified
October 19, 1781	British surrender at Yorktown, Virginia
September 2, 1783	Treaty (Peace) of Paris

KEY TERMS

Second Continental Congress, *175*
Battle of Bunker Hill, *175*
Dunmore's Proclamation, *176*
Common Sense, *176*
Declaration of Independence, *178*
loyalist, *179*
Battle of Oriskany, *184*
Battle of Saratoga, *186*
Valley Forge, *186*
Articles of Confederation, *187*
Battle of Yorktown, *195*
Treaty (Peace) of Paris, *196*

REVIEW & RELATE

1. What challenges did Washington face when he was given command of the Continental Army?

2. How and why did proponents of independence prevail in the debates that led to the Declaration of Independence?

3. How did colonists choose sides during the Revolutionary War? What factors influenced their decisions?

4. Why would some Indian tribes try to stay neutral during the conflict? Why did most of those who chose sides support the British?

5. How did the patriot forces fare in 1776? How and why did the tide of war turn in 1777?

6. What role did colonial women and foreign men play in the conflict in the early years of the war?

7. What values and concerns shaped state governments during the Revolutionary War?

8. What issues and challenges did the Continental Congress face even after the French joined the patriot side?

9. How and why did the Americans win the Revolutionary War?

10. What uncertainties and challenges did the new nation face in the immediate aftermath of victory?

Women in the Revolution

The Revolutionary War had a tremendous impact on the lives of women, just as women helped shape the course of that conflict. As in all wars, women faced the fear and hardships brought on by absent men, inadequate supplies, roaming enemy soldiers, and nearby battles. But the war also expanded opportunities for women in the public sphere. They ran family farms and shops, raised money, and produced homespun goods for the Continental Army while defending themselves and their homes. Women also spied on enemy encampments, provided medical care for soldiers, and even fought alongside men on the battlefield. Women gained new skills, felt pride in their independence and abilities, and, like their male counterparts, gained satisfaction and sometimes fame in supporting the cause in which they believed. Although many cast their efforts in a political light, patriot leaders failed to treat them as equal partners in the revolution.

The following documents reflect a wide variety of women's Revolutionary-era experiences. Some women, like Christian Barnes (Document 6.5), remained loyal to Great Britain and suffered attacks by patriot neighbors and soldiers. Bett, however, an enslaved African, turned revolutionary rhetoric to her advantage and sued for her own independence (Document 6.9). Abigail Adams, wife of the patriot leader John Adams, sought greater rights for all women, though she could only plead with her husband to take action (Document 6.7). Other women with connections to patriot political and military leaders carried messages behind British lines and raised funds for Continental troops (Documents 6.6 and 6.8). Almost all women faced new challenges, but some were also offered new opportunities or created their own.

Document 6.5

Christian Barnes | Letter to Elizabeth Inman, April 29, 1775

As the conflict intensified between Great Britain and America, colonists were forced to choose sides. Whether patriots or loyalists, women were often terrorized by enemy soldiers. One such woman was Christian Barnes, the wife of a well-known loyalist who fled to Marlborough, Massachusetts, to avoid capture by the colonial government. The following selection is from a letter written by Barnes in the spring of 1775, in which she describes a frightening visit by a colonial soldier.

It is now a week since I had a line from my dear Mrs. Inman, in which time I have had some severe trials, but the greatest terror I was ever thrown into was on Sunday last. A man came up to the gate and loaded his musket, and before I could determine which way to run he entered the house and demanded a dinner. I sent him the best I had upon the table. He was not contented, but insisted upon bringing in his gun and dining with me; this terrified the young folks, and they ran out of the house. I went in and endeavored to pacify him by every method in my power, but I found it was to no purpose. He still continued to abuse me, and said that when he had eat his dinner he should want a horse and if I did not let him have one he would blow my brains out. He pretended to have an order from the General for one of my horses, but did not produce it. His language was so dreadful and his looks so frightful that I could not remain in the house, but fled to the store and locked myself in. He followed me and declared he would break the door open. Some people very luckily passing to meeting prevented his doing any mischief and staid by me until he was out of sight, but I did not recover from my fright for several days. The sound of drum or the sight of a gun put me into such a tremor that I could not command myself. I have met with but little molestation since this affair, which I attribute to the protection sent me by Col. Putnam and Col. Whitcomb. I returned them a card of thanks for their goodness tho' I knew it was thro' your interest I obtained this favor. . . . The people here are weary at his [Mr. Barnes's] absence, but at the same time give it as their opinion that he could not pass the guards. . . . I do not doubt but upon a proper remonstrance I might procure a pass for him through the Camp from our two good Colonels. . . . I know he must be very unhappy in Boston. It was never his intention to quit the family.

Source: Nina M. Tiffany, ed., *Letters of James Murray, Loyalist* (Boston, 1901), 187–88.

Document 6.6

Deborah Champion | Letter to Patience, October 2, 1775

Deborah Champion was the daughter of Henry Champion, a high-ranking officer in the Continental Army. In the fall of 1775, she traveled from Connecticut to Boston to deliver secret messages from her father to George Washington. Accompanied by a family slave named Aristarchus, she was stopped by British troops several times during her journey. Several days after her return home, she described the adventure in a letter to a friend, excerpted here.

Father laid his hand on my shoulder, (a most unusual caress with him) and said almost solemnly, "Deborah I have need of thee. Hast thee the courage to go out and ride, it may be even in the dark and as fast as may be, till thou comest to Boston town?" He continued, "I do not believe Deborah, that there will be actual danger to threaten thee, else I would not ask it of thee, but the way is long, and in part lonely. I shall send Aristarchus with thee and shall explain to him the urgency of the business. Though he is a slave, he understands the mighty matters at stake, and I shall instruct him yet further. There are reasons why it is better for you a woman to take the despatches I would send than for me to entrust them to a man; else I should send your brother Henry. Dare you go? . . ."

Everywhere we heard the same thing, love for the Mother Country, but stronger than that, that she *must* must give us our rights, that we were fighting not for independence, though that might come and would be the war-cry if the oppression of unjust taxation was not removed. Nowhere was a cup of imported tea offered us. It was a glass of milk, or a cup of "hyperion" the name they gave to a tea made of raspberry leaves. We heard that it would be almost impossible to avoid the British, unless by going so far out of the way that too much time would be lost, so plucked up what courage I could as darkness began to come on at the close of the second day. I secreted the papers in a small pocket in a saddle bag under some eatables that mother had put up. We decided to ride all night. Providentially the moon just past full, rose about 8 o'clock and it was not unpleasant, for the roads were better. I confess that I began to be weary. It was late at night or rather very early in the morning, that I heard a sentry call and knew that if at all the danger point was reached. I pulled my calash [a large hood] as far over my face as I could, thanking my wise mother's forethought, and went on with what boldness I could muster. I really believed I heard Aristarchus' teeth chatter as he rode to my side and whispered "De British missus for sure." Suddenly I was ordered to halt. As I could not help myself I did so. A soldier in a red coat appeared and suggested that I go to headquarters for examination. I told him "It was early to wake his Captain and to please let me pass for I had been sent in urgent haste to see a friend in need," which was true, if a little ambiguous. To my joy he let me go saying "Well, you are only an old woman any way." Evidently as glad to be rid of me as I of him.

Source: Deborah Champion to Patience, 2 October 1775, in *Women's Letters: America from the Revolutionary War to the Present*, ed. Lisa Grunwald and Stephen J. Adler (New York: Dial Press, 2005), 25–28.

Abigail Adams | Letter to John Adams, March 31, 1776

Abigail Adams wrote detailed letters to John Adams while he was serving as a delegate to the Continental Congress in Philadelphia. She moved to Braintree, Massachusetts, during the British occupation of Boston but described conditions in the city and surrounding area. She often highlighted the difficulties that the civilian population faced and their responses to them. But Abigail Adams also discussed specifically political matters, as here where she calls on her husband to grant women more legal rights under the new government.

D o not you want to see Boston; I am fearfull of the small pox, or I should have been in before this time. I got Mr. Crane to go to our House and see what state it was in. I find it has been occupied by one of the Doctors of a Regiment, very dirty, but no other damage has been done to it . . . am determined to get it cleand as soon as possible. . . .

I feel very differently at the approach of spring to what I did a month ago. We knew not then whether we could plant or sow with safety, . . . but now we feel as if we might sit under our own vine and eat the good of the land. . . .

I long to hear that you have declared an independency—and by the way in the new Code of Laws which I suppose it will be necessary for you to make I desire you would Remember the Ladies, and be more generous and favourable to them than your ancestors. Do not put such unlimited power into the hands of the Husbands. Remember all Men would be tyrants if they could. If perticuliar care and attention is not paid to the Laidies we are determined to foment a Rebelion, and will not hold ourselves bound by any Laws in which we have no voice, or Representation.

That your Sex are Naturally Tyrannical is a Truth so thoroughly established as to admit of no dispute, but such of you as wish to be happy willingly give up the harsh title of Master for the more tender and endearing one of Friend. Why then, not put it out

of the power of the vicious and the Lawless to use us with cruelty and indignity with impunity.

Source: Abigail Adams to John Adams, March 31–April 5, 1776, Adams Family Papers, Massachusetts Historical Society, Digital Adams Project, http://www.masshist.org/digitaladams/archive/doc?id=L17760331aa&bc=%2Fdigitaladams%2Farchive%2Fbrowse%2Fletters_1774_1777.php.

Esther De Berdt Reed | The Sentiments of an American Woman, 1780

Esther De Berdt Reed lived in England until her marriage to merchant Joseph Reed in 1770. Joseph was a leading Philadelphia patriot and was elected president (governor) of Pennsylvania during the war. In June 1780, Esther Reed, the mother of five young children and recently recovered from smallpox, called on women to aid the Continental Army. Her broadside "The Sentiments of an American Woman" was the foundation of the Ladies Association of Philadelphia, whose members raised large sums by soliciting contributions from women door-to-door.

W ho knows if persons disposed to censure, and sometimes too severely with regard to us, may not disapprove our appearing acquainted even with the actions of which our sex boasts? We are at least certain, that he cannot be a good citizen who will not applaud our efforts for the relief of the armies which defend our lives, our possessions, our liberty? . . .

We know that at a distance from the theatre of war, if we enjoy any tranquility, it is the fruit of your watchings, your labours, your dangers. If I live happy in the midst of my family; if my husband cultivates his field, and reaps his harvest in peace; if, surrounded with my children, I myself nourish the youngest, and press it to my bosom, without being affraid of seeing myself separated from it, by a ferocious enemy; if the house in which we dwell; if our barns, our orchards are safe at the present time from the hands of those incendiaries, it is to you that we owe it. And shall we hesitate to evidence to you our gratitude? Shall we hesitate to wear a cloathing more simple; hair dressed less elegant, while at the price of this small privation, we shall deserve your benedictions. Who, amongst us, will not renounce with the highest pleasure, those vain ornaments, when she shall consider that the valiant defenders of America will be able to draw some advantage from the money which she may have laid out in these; that they will be better defended from the rigours of the seasons, that after their painful toils, they will receive some extraordinary and unexpected relief; that these presents will perhaps be valued by them at a greater price, when they will have it in their power to say: *This is the offering of the Ladies.* The time is arrived to display the same sentiments which animated us at the beginning of the Revolution, when we renounced the use of teas, however agreeable to our taste, rather than receive them from our persecutors; when we made it appear to them that we placed former necessaries in the rank of superfluities, when our liberty was interested; when our republican and laborious hands spun the flax, prepared the linen intended for the use of our soldiers; when exiles and fugitives we supported with courage all the evils which are the concomitants of war. Let us not lose a moment; let us be engaged to offer the homage of our gratitude at the altar of military valour, and you, our brave deliverers, while mercenary slaves combat to cause you to share with them, the irons with which they are loaded, receive with a free hand our offering, the purest which can be presented to your virtue,

BY AN AMERICAN WOMAN

Source: Esther De Berdt Reed, "The Sentiments of an American Woman" (Philadelphia: John Dunlop, 1780).

Elizabeth "Mum Bett" Freeman, 1811

Bett, a slave, sued her owner John Ashley, Esq., for her freedom with the aid of lawyer Theodore Sedgwick. She may have been inspired to act by her mistress's beating of her sister Lizzie or by overhearing conversations about the new Massachusetts state constitution, which declared "all men . . . free and equal." A jury at the Berkshire County Court of Common Pleas set her free in 1781, after which she worked for the Sedgwick family for three decades. This portrait was painted by Susan Anne Ridley Sedgwick, Theodore's daughter-in-law, when Freeman, then known as Mum Bett, was sixty-nine years old.

© Massachusetts Historical Society, Boston, MA, USA/Bridgeman Images

Interpret the Evidence

1. What types of activities did female patriots undertake in the service of American independence (Documents 6.6, 6.7, 6.8, and 6.9)? What challenges did female loyalists face (Document 6.5)?

2. How did assumptions about the proper roles of elite white women prior to the war shape their experiences during the Revolution (Documents 6.5, 6.6, 6.7, and 6.8)?

3. How did Deborah Champion, Abigail Adams, Esther De Berdt Reed, and Bett (Elizabeth Freeman) create new opportunities for themselves during the Revolution, and how did they demonstrate their new roles in words or images (Documents 6.6, 6.7, 6.8, and 6.9)? How were these roles shaped by their race and class?

4. What dangers or limits did women face during the war (Documents 6.5, 6.7, and 6.9)?

5. How did women justify their public and political actions (Documents 6.6, 6.7, and 6.8)?

Put It in Context

How would you compare white women's experiences of the American Revolution to those of African American and American Indian women and to the experiences of white men?

How did the efforts of patriot women shape the outcome of the war?

Forging a New Nation

1783–1800

7

WINDOW TO THE PAST

The Burial of the Federal Administration

Following the Revolution, Americans had to develop political structures, economic policies, and diplomatic relations with Indians and Europeans. For the first twelve years, George Washington and the Federalists led this effort. In 1798 an opposition party emerged. When its leader, Thomas Jefferson, was inaugurated president of the United States on March 4, 1801, the *Columbia Centinel* published a broadside lamenting the death of Federalist leadership. ▶ To discover more about what this primary source can show us, see Document 7.4 on page 232.

> **Y**ESTERDAY EXPIRED,
> Deeply regretted by MILLIONS of grateful Americans,
> And by *all* GOOD MEN,
> The FEDERAL ADMINISTRATION
> Of the
> GOVERNMENT of the *United States* :
> Animated by
> A WASHINGTON, an ADAMS ;—a
> HAMILTON, KNOX, PICKERING, WOL-
> COTT, M'HENRY, MARSHALL,
> STODDERT and DEXTER.
> Æt. 12 years.

Granger, NYC

After reading this chapter you should be able to:

- Identify the major threats to the new nation after the Revolution.

- Explain how different groups of Americans were marginalized in this period and how they responded.

- Describe the chief debates over the Constitution and its ratification.

- Evaluate the ways that the young nation's economic policies affected its relations with European nations abroad and on the U.S. frontier and fostered competing political views.

- Describe how the presidency of John Adams exacerbated differences between Federalists and Democratic-Republicans and led to Thomas Jefferson's election in 1800.

AMERICAN HISTORIES

One of six children born to Irish parents in Hopkinton, Massachusetts, Daniel Shays received little formal education. In 1772, age twenty-five, he married, had a child, and settled into farming. But in April 1775, he, his father, and his brother raced toward Concord to meet the British forces. By June, he was among the patriots defending Bunker Hill.

After distinguished service in the Continental Army, Shays purchased a farm in Pelham, Massachusetts, in 1780 and hoped to return to a normal life.

(*left*) **Daniel Shays**. Granger, NYC

(*right*) **Alexander Hamilton**. Library of Congress, 3g06423

Instead, economic turmoil roiled the region and the nation. Many farmers had fallen into debt while fighting for independence. They returned to an economic recession and increased taxes as state governments labored to repay wealthy creditors and fund their portion of the federal budget. In western Massachusetts, many farmers faced eviction. Shays kept his farm and represented his town at county conventions that petitioned the state government for economic relief. However, the legislature largely ignored the farmers' concerns.

In 1786, angered by the state's failure to act, armed groups of farmers attacked courthouses throughout western Massachusetts. Although a reluctant leader, Shays headed the largest band of more than a thousand farmer-soldiers. In January 1787, this group headed to the federal arsenal at Springfield, Massachusetts, to seize guns and ammunition. The farmers were routed by state militia and pursued by governor James Bowdoin's army. Many rebel leaders were captured; others, including Shays, escaped to Vermont and New York. Four were convicted and two were hanged before Bowdoin granted amnesty to the others in hopes of avoiding further conflict.

This uprising, known as Shays's Rebellion, alarmed many state and national leaders who feared such insurgencies might emerge elsewhere. Among those outraged by the rebels was Alexander Hamilton, a young New York politician. Hamilton was born illegitimate and impoverished in the British West Indies. Orphaned at eleven, he was apprenticed to a firm of merchants that sent him to the American colonies. There Hamilton was drawn into the activities of radical patriots and joined the Continental Army in 1776.

During the war, Hamilton fell in love with Elizabeth Schuyler, who came from a wealthy New York family. They married in December 1780. After the war, Hamilton used military and marital contacts to establish himself as a lawyer and financier in New York City. In 1786, Hamilton was elected to the New York State legislature, where he focused on improving the state's finances, and served as a delegate to a convention on interstate commerce held in Annapolis, Maryland. Hamilton and several other delegates advocated a stronger central government. They pushed through a resolution calling for a second convention "to render the constitution of the Federal Government adequate to the exigencies of the Union."

Although the initial response to the call was lukewarm, the eruption of Shays's Rebellion and the government's financial problems soon convinced many political leaders that change was necessary. Although Hamilton played only a small role in the 1787 convention in Philadelphia, he worked tirelessly for ratification of the Constitution drafted there. When the new federal government was established in 1789, Hamilton became the nation's first secretary of the treasury. ◼

T he American histories of Daniel Shays and Alexander Hamilton demonstrate that the patriots may have come together to win the Revolutionary War but that they did not share a common vision of the new nation. Despite the suppression of Shays's Rebellion, the grievances that fueled the uprising persisted and Americans differed significantly over how best to resolve them. By 1787, demand for a stronger central government led to the ratification of a new U.S. Constitution. Hamilton played a leading role in advocating and establishing the new government, particularly by seeking to stabilize and strengthen the national economy. While many political and economic elites applauded his efforts, other national leaders and many ordinary citizens opposed them. These differences, exacerbated by foreign and frontier crises, eventually led to the development of competing political parties and the first contested presidential election in American history.

Financial, Frontier, and **Foreign Problems**

The United States faced serious financial instability in its formative years. The situation was so desperate that Continental Army officers threatened to march on the confederation congress if they did not receive their pay. Other issues also threatened the emerging nation. Conflicts between settlers and Indians in western areas forced the confederation government to attend more closely to its frontier territories. Meanwhile Spain closed the port of New Orleans to U.S. trade as individual states struggled to regulate domestic and foreign commerce. Off the coast of North Africa, Barbary pirates attacked U.S. merchant ships. Clearly, diplomatic relations with European powers were crucial but difficult, given America's outstanding war debts and the relative weakness of the confederation government.

Continental Officers Threaten Confederation. As the American Revolution ground to an end, issues of military pay sparked conflict. Uprisings by ordinary soldiers were common but successfully put down. Complaints from Continental officers, however, posed a greater problem. In 1780 they had extracted a promise from the Continental Congress for half pay for life but had received no compensation since. Officers encamped at Newburgh, New York, awaiting a peace treaty, petitioned the confederation government in December 1782 for back pay for themselves and their soldiers, again with no success. By March 1783, most soldiers had returned home without pay, but some five hundred officers remained at Newburgh. Many confederation leaders were sympathetic to the officers' plight and hoped to use pressure from this formidable group to enhance the powers of the congress.

Alexander Hamilton had been pressing state governments to grant the confederation congress a new duty of 5 percent on imported goods, thereby providing the federal government with an independent source of revenue. Perhaps threats of an uprising by officers could convince states like New York to agree to the collection of this import duty. Quietly encouraged by political supporters, dissident officers circulated veiled threats of a military takeover. However, on March 15, the officers were confronted by General George Washington. In an emotional speech, he urged them to respect civilian control of the government. Most officers quickly retreated from their "infamous propositions." At the same time, congressional leaders promised the officers full pay for five years. However, lacking sufficient funds, they could provide only "commutation certificates," promising future payment.

Indians, Land, and the Northwest Ordinance. One anonymous petitioner at Newburgh suggested that the officers move as a group to "some unsettled country" and let the confederation fend for itself. In reality, no such unsettled country existed beyond the thirteen states. Numerous Indian nations and growing numbers of American settlers claimed control of western lands. In 1784 some two hundred Indian leaders from the Iroquois, Shawnee, Creek, Cherokee, and other nations gathered in St. Louis, where they complained to the Spanish governor that the Americans were "extending themselves like a plague of locusts."

Cornplanter, Seneca Chief Cornplanter, son of a white father and Seneca mother, fought with the British during the Revolution. Afterward, however, he argued that Indians must adapt to American control. He helped negotiate three treaties that ceded large tracts of Indian land to the U.S. government, arousing opposition from more militant leaders. This 1796 portrait by an Italian artist suggests his mixed heritage. New York Historical Society/Getty Images

Despite the continued presence of British and Spanish troops in the Ohio River valley, the United States hoped to convince Indian nations that it controlled the territory. In October 1784, U.S. commissioners met with Iroquois delegates at Fort Stanwix, New York, and demanded land cessions in western New York and the Ohio valley. When the Seneca chief Cornplanter and other leaders refused, the commissioners insisted that "you are a subdued people" and must submit. An exchange of gifts and captives taken during the Revolution finally ensured the deal. Indian leaders not at the meeting disavowed the **Treaty of Fort Stanwix**. But the confederation government insisted it was legal, and New York State began surveying and selling the land. With a similar mix of negotiation and coercion, U.S. commissioners signed treaties at Fort McIntosh, Pennsylvania (1785), and Fort Finney, Ohio (1786), claiming lands held by the Wyandots, Delawares, Shawnees, and others.

Explore ▶

See Document 7.1 for a pan-Indian perspective on relations with the U.S. government.

As eastern Indians were increasingly pushed into the Ohio River valley, they crowded onto lands already claimed by other nations. Initially, these migrations increased conflict among Indians, but eventually some leaders used this forced intimacy to launch pan-Indian movements against further American encroachment on their land.

Indians and U.S. political leaders did share one concern: the vast numbers of squatters, mainly white men and women, living on land to which they had no legal claim. In fall 1784 George Washington traveled west to survey nearly thirty thousand acres of territory he had been granted as a reward for military service. He found much of it occupied by squatters who refused to acknowledge his ownership. Such flaunting of property rights deepened his concerns about the weaknesses of the confederation government.

The confederation congress was less concerned about individual property rights and more with the refusal of some states to cede the western lands they claimed to federal control. Slowly, between 1783 and 1785, the congress finally persuaded the two remaining states with the largest claims, Virginia and Massachusetts, to relinquish all territory north of the Ohio River (Map 7.1).

To regulate this vast territory, Thomas Jefferson drafted the **Northwest Ordinance** in 1785. It provided that the territory be surveyed and divided into adjoining townships. He hoped to carve nine small states out of the region to enhance the representation of western farmers and to ensure the continued dominance of agrarian views in the national government. The congress revised his proposal, however, stipulating that only three to five states be created from the vast territory and thereby limiting the future clout of western settlers in the federal government.

The population of the territory grew rapidly, with speculators buying up huge tracts of land and selling smaller parcels to eager settlers. In response, congressional leaders modified the Northwest Ordinance in 1787, clarifying the process by which territories could become states. The congress appointed territorial officials and guaranteed residents the basic rights of U.S. citizens. After a territory's population reached 5,000, residents could choose an assembly, but the territorial governor retained the power to veto legislation. When a prospective state reached a population of 60,000, it could apply for admission to the United States. Thus the congress established an orderly system by which territories became states in the Union.

The 1787 ordinance also tried to address concerns about race relations in the region. It encouraged fair treatment of Indian nations but did not include any means of enforcing

GUIDED ANALYSIS

United Indian Nations Council | Message to Congress, 1786

Following the Revolutionary War, one of the most pressing issues that the confederation government faced was the disposition of western lands. Although the U.S. government negotiated with a number of Indian tribes to gain clear title to western lands, it often negotiated in secret with only a few leaders and backed negotiations with the threat of force. A pan-Indian council meeting was called in 1786 at which various leaders stated their concerns about the confederation government's actions. The speech was addressed to the U.S. Congress and expressed the Indians' united stance and their hopes for fair and open dealings with the United States.

Document 7.1

To the Congress of the United States of America:

Brethren of the United States of America: It is now more than three years since peace was made between the King of Great Britain and you, but we, the Indians, were disappointed, finding ourselves not included in that peace, according to our expectations: for we thought that its conclusion would have promoted a friendship between the United States and Indians, and that we might enjoy that happiness that formerly subsisted between us and our elder brethren. . . . In the course of our councils, we imagined we hit upon an expedient that would promote a lasting peace between us.

> How did the Indians respond to their exclusion from the Treaty of Paris in 1783?

Brothers: We are still of the same opinion as to the means which may tend to reconcile us to each other; and we are sorry to find, although we had the best thoughts in our minds, during the beforementioned period, mischief has, nevertheless, happened between you and us. We are still anxious of putting our plan of accommodation into execution, and we shall briefly inform you of the means that seem most probable to us of effecting a firm and lasting peace and reconciliation: the first step towards which should, in our opinion, be, that all treaties carried on with the United States, on our parts, should be with the general voice of the whole confederacy, and carried on in the most open manner, without any restraint on either side; and especially as landed matters are often the subject of our councils with you, a matter of the greatest importance and of general concern to us, in this case we hold it indispensably necessary that any cession of our lands should be made in the most public manner, and by the united voice of the confederacy; holding all partial treaties as void and of no effect.

> What kinds of "mischief" do you think the Indians are referring to here?

> What do the Indians consider the most important ways to ensure fair treaty negotiations?

Source: *American State Papers, Class II: Indian Affairs* (Washington, 1832), 1:8.

Put It in Context

Why have Indians chosen to send this message to Congress from the United Indian Nations Council rather than from their individual nations?

MAP 7.1   Cessions of Western Land, 1782–1802

Beginning under the Articles of Confederation, political leaders sought to resolve competing state claims to western territory based on colonial charters. The confederation congress and, after ratification of the Constitution, the U.S. Congress gradually persuaded states to cede their claims and create a "national domain," part of which was then organized as the Northwest Territory.

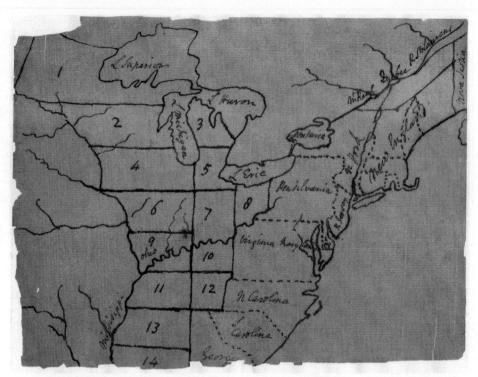

Thomas Jefferson's Map of Western Territories   Jefferson drew this 1784 map of the western territories, showing nine states in the region north of the Ohio River. He proposed giving land to settlers to encourage rapid settlement and discourage speculation and suggested prohibiting slavery in the region. Land taxes would provide funds to the federal government. Congress revised his plan significantly before adopting the Northwest Ordinance in 1785. Clements Library, University of Michigan

such treatment and failed to resolve Indian land claims. It also abolished slavery throughout the Northwest Territory but mandated the return of fugitive slaves to their owners to forestall a flood of fugitives.

The 1787 legislation did not address territory south of the Ohio River. As American settlers streamed into areas that became Kentucky and Tennessee, they confronted Creek, Choctaw, and Chickasaw tribes, well supplied with weapons by Spanish traders, as well as Cherokee who had sided with the British during the Revolution. Conflicts there were largely ignored by the national government for the next quarter century.

Depression and Debt. Disputes over western lands were deeply intertwined with the economic difficulties that plagued the new nation. Victory in the Revolution was followed by years of economic depression and mushrooming debt. While the war fueled the demand for domestic goods and ensured high employment, both the demand and the jobs declined in peacetime. International trade was also slow to recover from a decade of disruption. Meanwhile the nation was saddled with a huge war debt. Individuals, the states, and the federal government all viewed western lands as a solution to their problems. Farm families could start over on "unclaimed" land; states could distribute land in lieu of cash to veterans or creditors; and congress could sell land to fund its debts. Yet there was never enough land to meet these conflicting needs, nor did the United States hold secure title to the territory.

Some national leaders, including Hamilton, focused on other ways of repaying the war debt. Fearing that wealthy creditors would lose faith in a nation that could not repay its debts, they urged states to grant the federal government a percentage of import duties as a way to increase its revenue. But states had their own problems. Legislators in Massachusetts and other states passed hard-money laws that required debts to be repaid in gold or silver rather than in paper currency. Affluent creditors favored these measures to ensure repayment in full. But small farmers, including veterans, who had borrowed paper money during the war, now had to repay those loans in hard currency as the money supply shrank. Taxes, too, were rising as states sought to cover the interest on wartime bonds held by wealthy investors.

Failures of American diplomacy weakened the nation's economy further. In 1783 the British Parliament denied the United States the right to trade with the British West Indies. The following year, Spain, seeking leverage over disputed western territories, prohibited U.S. ships from accessing the port of New Orleans. Spain and Great Britain also threatened U.S. sovereignty by conspiring with American citizens on the frontier and promising them protection from Indians. At the same time, British troops remained in forts on America's western frontier and urged Indians to harass settlers there.

REVIEW & RELATE

What challenges did the new nation face in the immediate aftermath of the Revolutionary War?

How did farmers, financial leaders, foreign nations, and Indians react to government efforts to address challenges after the Revolution?

On the **Political Margins**

A young nation, the United States was forced to the political margins in international affairs. At the same time, some groups within the nation were marginalized as well. Small farmers suffered in the postwar period, but they were not alone. Church leaders who had enjoyed government support in the colonial period now had to compete for members and funds. African Americans, whose hopes for freedom had been raised by the Revolution, continued to fight for full-fledged citizenship and an end to slavery. Women, too, faced challenges as they sought to enhance their role in the nation.

Separating Church and State. Government support of churches ended in most states with the establishment of the United States. Anglican churches had long benefited from British support and taxed residents to support their ministry during the Revolution. But in 1786, the Virginia Assembly approved the Statute of Religious Freedom, which made church attendance and support voluntary. Many other states followed Virginia's lead and removed government support for established churches.

Churches that had dominated the various colonies now faced greater competition. Especially in frontier areas, Baptists and Methodists, the latter of which broke off from the

Anglican Church in 1784, gained thousands of converts. The Society of Friends, or Quakers, and the Presbyterians also gained new adherents, while Catholics and Jews experienced greater tolerance than in the colonial era. This diversity ensured that no single religious voice or perspective dominated the new nation. Instead, all denominations competed for members, money, and political influence.

Some Protestant churches were also challenged from within by free blacks who sought a greater role in church governance. In 1794 Richard Allen, who had been born a slave, led a small group of Philadelphia blacks in founding the first African American church in the United States. Initially, this African Methodist Episcopal Church remained within the larger Methodist fold. By the early 1800s, however, Allen's church served as the basis for the first independent black denomination.

African Americans Struggle for Rights.
It was no accident that the first independent black church was founded in Philadelphia, which attracted large numbers of free blacks after Pennsylvania adopted a gradual emancipation law in 1780. Although the northern states with the largest enslaved populations—New York and New Jersey—did not pass such laws until 1799 and 1804, the free black population increased throughout the region.

Many free blacks were migrants from the South, where tens of thousands of enslaved women and men gained their freedom during or immediately following the Revolution. A few slave owners took Revolutionary ideals to heart and emancipated their slaves following the war. Many others emancipated slaves in their wills. In addition, several states prohibited the importation of slaves from Africa during or immediately following the Revolution. At the same time, however, the enslaved population continued to grow rapidly, and southern legislators soon made it difficult for owners to free their slaves and for free blacks to remain in the region.

The limits on emancipation in the South only nurtured the growth of free black communities in the North, especially in seaport cities like Philadelphia, New York, and New Bedford. Most African Americans focused on finding jobs, supporting families, and securing the freedom of enslaved relatives. Others, like Richard Allen, sought to establish churches, schools, and voluntary societies and claim a political voice. Some northern states, such as New Jersey, granted property-owning blacks the right to vote. Others, such as Pennsylvania, did not specifically exclude them.

> **Explore ▶**
>
> Compare the claims for rights made by a northern woman and southern free blacks in Documents 7.2 and 7.3.

Some whites aided blacks in their struggles. The Society of Friends, the only religious denomination to oppose slavery in the colonial period, became more outspoken. By the 1790s, nearly all Quakers had freed their slaves and withdrawn from the slave trade. Anthony Benezet, a writer and educator, advocated tirelessly for the abolition of slavery and directed one of several schools for blacks founded by Quakers.

Women Seek Wider Roles.
Quaker women as well as men testified against slavery in the 1780s, writing statements on the topic in separate women's meetings. Although few other women experienced such spiritual autonomy, many gained a greater sense of economic and political independence during the Revolution.

Abigail Adams had written her husband John in 1776, "[I]f perticuliar care and attention is not paid to the Laidies we are determined to foment a Rebelion" (see Document 6.7 in chapter 6). While she and other elite women sought a more public voice, only New Jersey granted women—widowed or single and property-owning—the right to vote. The vast majority of women could shape political decisions only by influencing their male relatives and friends. Fortunately, many leaders of the early Republic viewed wives and mothers as necessary to the development of a strong nation. In 1787 Benjamin Rush, in his *Essay on Female Education*, claimed that women could best shape political ideas and relations by "instructing their sons in principles of liberty and government." To prepare young women for this enhanced role, Rush suggested educating them in literature, music, composition, geography, history, and bookkeeping.

Judith Sargent Murray offered a more radical approach to women's education, arguing that "girls should be enabled to procure for themselves the necessaries of life; independence should be placed within their grasp" (see Document 7.2). A few American women in the late eighteenth century did receive broad educations, and some ran successful businesses; wrote plays, poems, and histories; and established urban salons where women and men discussed the issues of the day. In 1789 Massachusetts became the first state to institute free elementary education for all children, and female academies also multiplied in this period. While schooling for affluent girls was often focused on preparing them for domesticity, the daughters of artisans and farmers learned practical skills so they could assist in the family enterprise.

While women's influence was praised in the post-Revolutionary era, state laws rarely expanded women's rights. All states limited women's economic autonomy, although a few allowed married women to enter into business. Divorce was also legalized in many states but was still available only to the wealthy and well connected. Meanwhile women were excluded from juries, legal training, and, with rare exceptions, voting rights.

African American and Indian women lived under even more severe constraints than white women. Most black women were enslaved, and those who were free could usually find jobs only as domestic servants or agricultural workers. Among Indian nations, years of warfare enhanced men's role as warriors and diplomats while restricting women's political influence. U.S. government officials and Protestant missionaries encouraged Indians to embrace gender roles that mirrored those of Anglo-American culture, further diminishing women's roles. Indian women forced to move west also lost authority tied to their traditional control of land, crops, and households.

Indebted Farmers Fuel Political Crises.

Unlike blacks, Indians, and women, many farmers and workingmen hoped to expand their political role in the new nation. Under constitutions written during the Revolution, most state governments broadened the electorate, allowing men with less property (or in some cases no property) to vote and hold office. They also increased representation from western areas.

Still, the economic interests of small farmers and workers diverged sharply from those of wealthy merchants and large landowners. As conflicts between debtors and creditors escalated between 1783 and 1787, state governments came down firmly on the side of the wealthy. But indebted farmers did not give up. They voted, petitioned, and protested to gain more favorable policies. When that failed, debt-ridden farmers in New Hampshire marched on the state capital in September 1786, demanding reform. But they were confronted by cavalry units, who quickly seized and imprisoned their leaders.

Assaults on national authority worried many political leaders far more than farmers' uprisings. The continued efforts of Great Britain and Spain to undercut U.S. sovereignty and ongoing struggles with Indian nations posed especially serious threats. When James

COMPARATIVE ANALYSIS

Women and Free Blacks Claim Rights in the Nation

Limited in their civil and political rights and educational and economic opportunities, some women and African Americans demanded change. Northern white women focused especially on gaining access to a more rigorous education. In the first selection, Judith Sargent Murray insists that women are rational creatures who could make important contributions to society. Blacks had far fewer opportunities since the vast majority were enslaved and illiterate. Even free blacks faced numerous restrictions on their activities. In the second selection, three free black men in Charleston, South Carolina, petition the state legislature for increased judicial rights.

Document 7.2

Judith Sargent Murray | On the Equality of the Sexes, 1790

Are we [women] deficient in reason? . . . [I]f an opportunity of acquiring knowledge hath been denied us, the inferiority of our sex cannot fairly be deduced from thence. . . . May we not trace its source in the difference of education, and continued advantages? Will it be said that the judgment of a male of two years old, is more sage than that of a female's of the same age? . . . But from that period what partiality! . . . As their years increase, the sister must be wholly domesticated, while the brother is led by the hand through all the flowery paths of science. . . . Now, was she permitted the same instructors as her brother, . . . for the employment of a rational mind an ample field would be opened. In astronomy she might catch a glimpse of the immensity of the Deity, and thence she would form amazing conceptions of the august and supreme Intelligence. In geography she would admire Jehovah in the midst of his benevolence; thus adapting this globe to the various wants and amusements of its inhabitants. In natural philosophy she would adore the infinite majesty of heaven, clothed in condescension; and as she traversed the reptile world, she would hail the goodness of a creating God. . . . Will it be urged that those acquirements would supersede our domestick duties. I answer that every requisite in female economy is easily attained; and, with truth I can add, that when once attained, they require no further mental attention. Nay, while we are pursuing the needle, or the superintendency of the family, I repeat, that our minds are at full liberty for reflection; that imagination may exert itself in full vigor; and that if a just foundation is early laid, our ideas will then be worthy of rational beings. . . . [I]s it reasonable, that a candidate for immortality . . . be allowed no other ideas, than those which are suggested by the mechanism of a pudding, or the sewing the seams of a garment?

Source: *Massachusetts Magazine*, March 1790, 132–35.

Madison and Alexander Hamilton attended the 1785 convention in Annapolis to address problems related to interstate commerce, they discovered that their concerns about the weakness of the confederation were shared by many large landowners, planters, and merchants. Despite these concerns, state legislatures were reluctant to give up the powers conferred on them under the Articles of Confederation.

Document 7.3

Petition from Free Blacks of Charleston, 1791

That in the enumeration of free citizens by the Constitution of the United States for the purpose of representation of the Southern states in Congress your memorialists [petitioners] have been considered under that description as part of the citizens of this state.

Although by the fourteenth and twenty-ninth clauses in an Act of Assembly made in the year 1740 . . . commonly called the Negro Act, now in force, your memorialists are deprived of the rights and privileges of citizens by not having it in their power to give testimony on oath in prosecutions on behalf of the state; from which cause many culprits have escaped the punishment due to their atrocious crimes, nor can they give their testimony in recovering debts due to them, or in establishing agreements made by them within the meaning of the Statutes of Frauds and Perjuries in force in this state except in cases where persons of color are concerned, whereby they are subject to great losses and repeated injuries without any means of redress.

That by the said clauses in the said Act, they are debarred of the rights of free citizens by being subject to a trial without the benefit of a jury and subject to prosecution by testimony of slaves without oath by which they are placed on the same footing.

Your memorialists show that they have at all times since the independence of the United States contributed and do now contribute to the support of the government by cheerfully paying their taxes proportionable to their property with others who have been during such period, and now are, in full enjoyment of the rights and immunities of citizens, inhabitants of a free independent state.

Source: Petition of Thomas Cole, Peter Bassnett Matthewes, and Matthew Webb to the South Carolina Senate, January 1, 1791, Records of the General Assembly, no. 181.

Interpret the Evidence

1. What kind of rights do Judith Sargent Murray and the free blacks in Charleston claim for women and free African Americans, respectively?
2. What explains the differences in the rights demanded by Murray and the black petitioners and the ways they justify those claims?

Put It in Context

What do these documents reveal about the positions of white women and free black men during the formation of the United States?

Still, it was **Shays's Rebellion**, the armed uprising of indebted farmers in western Massachusetts in 1786 to 1787, that crystallized fears among prominent patriots about the limits of the confederation model. On December 26, 1786, Washington wrote Henry Knox to express his concerns about the rebellion and upheavals along the frontier: "If the powers [of the central government] are inadequate, amend or alter them; but do not let us sink

Daniel Shays This sketch is the only eighteenth-century illustration in existence of Daniel Shays (on the left in this detail). He stands with Jacob Shattuck, another antigovernment leader. The picture appeared in a pro-Constitution Boston almanac, which ridiculed the two rebels by showing them in fancy uniforms and holding swords, in contrast to what would have been their usual homespun appearance. National Portrait Gallery, Smithsonian Institution/Art Resource, NY

into the lowest states of humiliation and contempt." Hamilton agreed, claiming that Shays's Rebellion "marked almost the last stage of national humiliation."

REVIEW & RELATE

○ How did America's experience of the Revolutionary War change the lives of African Americans and women?

○ What do uprisings by farmers and debtors tell us about social and economic divisions in the early Republic?

Reframing the American Government

The delegates who met in Philadelphia in May 1787 did not agree on the best way to reform the government. Some delegates, like James Monroe of Virginia, hoped to strengthen the existing government by amending the Articles of Confederation. Others joined with Madison and Hamilton, who argued for a new governmental structure. Once representatives agreed to draft a new constitution, they still disagreed over questions of representation, the powers of state and national governments, and the limits of popular democracy. Significant compromises had to be reached on these issues to frame a new Constitution.

Other issues arose once the Constitution was ratified and George Washington was inaugurated as president. The government needed to be organized and staffed. A system for levying, collecting, and distributing funds had to be put in place. Diplomatic relations with foreign powers and Indian nations needed to be reestablished. A bill of rights, demanded by many state ratifying conventions, had to be drafted and approved. Finally, both proponents and opponents of the Constitution had to be convinced that this new government could respond to the varied needs of its citizens.

The Constitutional Convention of 1787.

The fifty-five delegates who attended the Philadelphia convention were composed of white, educated men of property, mainly lawyers, merchants, and planters. Only eight had signed the Declaration of Independence eleven years earlier. The elite status of the delegates and the absence of many leading patriots raised concern among those who saw the convention as a threat to the rights of states and of citizens. Not wanting to alarm the public, delegates agreed to meet in secret until they had hammered out a new framework of government.

On May 25, the convention opened, and delegates quickly turned to the key question: Revise the Articles of Confederation or draft an entirely new document? The majority of men came to Philadelphia with the intention of amending the Articles. However, a core group who sought a more powerful central government had met before the convention and drafted a plan to replace the Articles. This **Virginia Plan** proposed a strong centralized state, including a bicameral (two-house) legislature in which representation was to be based on population. Members of the two houses would select the national executive and the national judiciary, and would settle disputes between states. Although most delegates opposed the Virginia Plan, it launched discussions in which strengthening the central government was assumed to be the goal.

Discussions of the Virginia Plan raised another issue that nearly paralyzed the convention: the question of representation. Heated debates pitted large states against small states, even though political interests were not necessarily determined by size. Yet delegates held on to size as the critical issue in determining representation. In mid-June, William Patterson introduced the **New Jersey Plan**, which highlighted the needs of smaller states. In this plan, Congress would consist of only one house, with each state having equal representation.

With few signs of compromise, the convention finally appointed a special committee to hammer out the problem of representation. Their report broke the logjam. Members of the House of Representatives were to be elected by voters in each state; members of the Senate would be appointed by state legislatures. Representation in the House would be determined by population—counted every ten years in a national census—while in the Senate, each state, regardless of size, would have equal representation. While the Senate had more authority than the House in many areas, only the House could introduce funding bills.

James Madison   James Madison of Virginia was one of the framers of the Constitution and one of the authors of *The Federalist Papers*, which supported its ratification. This striking portrait of Madison was painted around 1792 by the artist Charles Willson Peale, who had served during the Revolutionary War in the Pennsylvania militia and attained the rank of captain. Courtesy of Independence National Historical Park

Included within this compromise was one of the few direct considerations of slavery at the Philadelphia convention. With little apparent debate, the committee decided that representation in the House of Representatives was to be based on an enumeration of the entire free population and three-fifths of "all other persons," that is, slaves. If delegates had moral scruples about this **three-fifths compromise**, most found them outweighed by the urgency of settling the troublesome question of representation.

Still, slavery was on the minds of delegates. In the same week that the Philadelphia convention tacitly accepted the institution of slavery, the confederation congress in New York City outlawed slavery in the Northwest Territory. News of that decision likely inspired representatives from Georgia and South Carolina to insist that the Constitution protect the slave trade. Delegates in Philadelphia agreed that the importation of slaves would not be interfered with for twenty years. Another provision guaranteed the return of fugitive slaves to their owners. At the same time, northern delegates insisted that the three-fifths formula be used in assessing taxation as well as representation, ensuring that the South paid for the increased size of its congressional delegation with increased taxes.

Two other issues provoked considerable debate in the following weeks. All delegates supported federalism, a system in which states and the central government shared power, but they disagreed over the balance of power between them. They also disagreed over the degree of popular participation in selecting national leaders. The new Constitution increased the powers of the central government significantly. For instance, Congress would now have the right to raise revenue by levying and collecting taxes and tariffs and coining money; raise armies; regulate interstate commerce; settle disputes between the states; establish uniform rules for the naturalization of immigrants; and make treaties with foreign nations and Indians. But Congress could veto state laws only when those laws challenged "the supreme law of the land," and states retained all rights that were not specifically granted to the federal government.

One of the important powers retained by the states was the right to determine who was eligible to vote, but the Constitution regulated the influence eligible voters would have in national elections. Members of the House of Representatives were to be elected directly by popular vote for two-year terms. Senators—two from each state—were to be selected by state legislatures for a term of six years. Selection of the president was even further removed from voters. The president would be selected by an electoral college, and state legislatures would decide how to choose its members. Finally, the federal judicial system was to be wholly removed from popular influence. Justices on the Supreme Court were to be appointed by the president and approved by the Senate. Once approved, they served for life to protect their judgments from the pressure of popular opinion.

With the final debates concluded, delegates agreed that approval by nine states, rather than all thirteen, would make the Constitution the law of the land. Some delegates sought formal reassurance that the powers granted the federal government would not be abused and urged inclusion of a bill of rights, like the Virginia Declaration of Rights. But weary men eager to finish their business voted down the proposal. On September 17, 1787, the Constitution was approved and sent to the states for ratification.

Americans Battle over Ratification.

Americans Battle over Ratification. The confederation congress sent the document to state legislatures and asked them to call conventions to consider ratification. These conventions could not modify the document, but only accept or reject it. Thousands of copies of the Constitution also circulated in newspapers and as broadsides. Pamphleteers, civic leaders, and ministers proclaimed their opinions publicly while ordinary citizens in homes, shops, and taverns debated the wisdom of establishing a stronger central government.

Fairly quickly, two sides emerged. The **Federalists**, who supported ratification, came mainly from urban and commercial backgrounds and lived in towns and cities along the Atlantic coast. They viewed a stronger central government as essential to the economic and political stability of the nation. Their opponents were generally more rural, less wealthy, and more likely to live in interior or frontier regions. Labeled **Antifederalists**, they opposed increasing the powers of the central government.

The pro-Constitution position was presented in a series of editorials that appeared in New York newspapers in 1787 to 1788 and published collectively as *The Federalist Papers*. The authors James Madison, John Jay, and Alexander Hamilton articulated broad principles embraced by most supporters of the Constitution. Most notably, in *Federalist* No. 10, Madison countered the common wisdom that small units of government were most effective in representing the interests of their citizens and avoiding factionalism. He argued that in large units groups with competing interests had to collaborate and compromise, providing the surest check on the "tyranny of the majority." **See Document Project 7, Debating the Constitution in New York State, page 235.**

Still, Antifederalists worried that a large and powerful central government could lead to tyranny. Small farmers claimed that a strong congress filled with merchants, lawyers, and planters was likely to place the interests of creditors above those of ordinary (and indebted) Americans. Even some wealthy patriots, like Mercy Otis Warren of Boston, feared that the Constitution would empower a few individuals who cared little for the "true interests of the people." And the absence of a bill of rights concerned many Americans.

Federalists worked in each state to soften their critics by persuasive arguments, flattering hospitality, and the promise of a bill of rights once the Constitution was ratified. They gained strength from the quick ratification of the Constitution by Delaware, Pennsylvania, New Jersey, Georgia, and Connecticut by January 1788. Federalists also gained the support of influential newspapers based in eastern cities and tied to commercial interests.

Still, the contest in many states was heated. In Massachusetts, Antifederalists, including leaders of Shays's Rebellion, gained the majority among convention delegates. Federalists worked hard to overcome the objections of their opponents, even drafting a preliminary bill of rights. On February 6, Massachusetts delegates voted 187 to 168 in favor of ratification. Maryland and South Carolina followed in April and May. A month later, New Hampshire Federalists won a close vote, making it the ninth state to ratify the Constitution.

However, two of the most populous and powerful states—New York and Virginia—had not yet ratified. Passionate debates erupted in both ratifying conventions, and Federalists decided it was prudent to wait until these states acted before declaring victory. After promising that a bill of rights would be added quickly, Virginia Federalists finally won the day by a few votes. A month later, New York approved the Constitution by a narrow margin. The divided nature of the votes, and the fact that two states (North Carolina and Rhode Island) had still not ratified, meant that the new government would have to prove itself quickly (Table 7.1).

**TABLE 7.1
Votes of
State-Ratifying
Conventions**

State	Date	For	Against
Delaware	December 1787	30	0
Pennsylvania	December 1787	46	23
New Jersey	December 1787	38	0
Georgia	January 1788	26	0
Connecticut	January 1788	128	40
Massachusetts	February 1788	187	168
Maryland	April 1788	63	11
South Carolina	May 1788	149	73
New Hampshire	June 1788	57	47
Virginia	June 1788	89	79
New York	July 1788	30	27
North Carolina	November 1788	194	77
Rhode Island	May 1790	34	32

Organizing the Federal Government. Most political leaders hoped that the partisanship of the ratification battle would fade away with the Constitution approved. The electoral college's unanimous decision to name George Washington the first president and John Adams as vice president helped calm the political turmoil. The two took office in April 1789, launching the new government.

To bring order to his administration, Washington quickly established four departments—State, War, Treasury, and Justice—and appointed respected leaders to fill the posts. Thomas Jefferson was named secretary of state; Henry Knox, secretary of war; Alexander Hamilton, secretary of the treasury; and Edmund Randolph, attorney general, head of the Department of Justice.

Congress, meanwhile, worked to establish a judicial system. The Constitution called for a Supreme Court but provided no specific guidelines. The Judiciary Act of 1789 established a Supreme Court composed of six justices along with thirteen district courts and three circuit courts to hear cases appealed from the states. Congress also quickly produced a bill of rights. Representative James Madison gathered more than two hundred resolutions passed by state ratifying conventions and honed them down to twelve amendments, which Congress approved and submitted to the states for ratification. In 1791 ten of the amendments were ratified, and these became the **Bill of Rights**. It guaranteed the rights of individuals and states in the face of a powerful central government, including freedom of speech, the press, religion, and the right to petition.

Hamilton Forges an Economic Agenda. The new government's leaders recognized that without a stable economy, the best political structure could falter. Thus Hamilton's appointment as secretary of the treasury was especially significant. In formulating

Federal Hall   This drawing shows Federal Hall, located on Wall Street in New York City. The building housed the Stamp Act Congress in 1765 and the confederation congress from 1785 to 1788. In 1789 it became the seat of Congress under the new Constitution until the capital was moved to Philadelphia in December 1790, and the site of President Washington's first inauguration.   The New York Public Library/Art Resource, NY

his economic policy, Hamilton's main goal was to establish the nation's credit. Paying down the debt and establishing a national bank would strengthen the United States in the eyes of the world and tie wealthy Americans more firmly to the federal government.

Hamilton advocated funding the national debt at face value and assuming the remaining state debts as part of the national debt. To pay for this policy, he planned to raise revenue through government bonds and new taxes. Hamilton also called for the establishment of a central bank to carry out the financial operations of the United States. In three major reports to Congress—on public credit and a national bank in 1790 and on manufactures in 1791—he laid out a system of state-assisted economic development.

Hamilton's proposal to repay at face value the millions of dollars in securities issued by the confederation was particularly controversial. Thousands of soldiers, farmers, and shopkeepers had been paid with these securities during the war; but needing money in its aftermath, most sold them to speculators for a fraction of their value. These speculators would make enormous profits if the securities were paid off at face value. One of the policy's most ardent critics, Patrick Henry, claimed that Hamilton's policy was intended "to erect, and concentrate, and perpetuate a large monied interest" that would prove "fatal to the existence of American liberty." Despite such passionate opponents, Hamilton gained the support of Washington and other key Federalists.

The federal government's assumption of the remaining state war debts also faced fierce opposition, especially from southern states like Virginia that had already paid off their debt. Hamilton again won his case, though this time only by agreeing to "redeem" (that is, reimburse) states that had repaid their debts. In addition, Hamilton and his supporters had to agree to move the nation's capital from Philadelphia to a more central location along the Potomac River.

Funding the national debt, assuming the remaining state debts, and redeeming state debts already paid would cost $75.6 million (about $1.5 billion today). But Hamilton believed maintaining some debt was useful. He thus proposed establishing a Bank of the United States, funded by $10 million in stock to be sold to private stockholders and the national government. The bank would serve as a repository for federal revenues and grant loans and sell bills of credit to merchants and investors, thereby creating a permanent national debt. This, he argued, would bind investors to the United States, turning the national debt into a "national blessing."

Not everyone agreed. Jefferson and Madison argued vehemently against the Bank of the United States, noting that there was no constitutional sanction for a federal bank. Hamilton fought back, arguing that Congress had the right to make "all Laws which shall be necessary and proper" for carrying out the provisions of the Constitution. Once again, he prevailed. Congress chartered the bank for a period of twenty years, and Washington signed the legislation into law.

The final piece of Hamilton's plan focused on raising revenue. Congress quickly agreed to pass tariffs on a range of imported goods, which generated some $4 million to $5 million annually. Some congressmen viewed these tariffs as a way to protect new industries in the United States, from furniture to shoes. Excise taxes placed on a variety of consumer goods, most notably whiskey, generated another $1 million each year.

Hamilton's financial policies proved enormously successful in stabilizing the American economy, repaying outstanding debts, and tying men of wealth to the new government. The federal bank effectively collected and distributed the nation's resources. Commerce flourished, revenues rose, and confidence revived among foreign and domestic investors. And while the United States remained an agricultural nation, Hamilton's 1791 "Report on the Subject of Manufactures" foreshadowed the growing significance of industry, which gradually lessened U.S. dependence on European nations.

REVIEW & RELATE

What issues attracted the most intense debate during the drafting and ratification of the Constitution? Why?

How did Hamilton's policies stabilize the national economy, and why did they nonetheless arouse opposition?

Years of Crisis, 1792–1796

By 1792 Hamilton had succeeded in implementing his plan for U.S. economic development. Yet as Washington began his second term in the spring of 1793, signs of strain appeared throughout the nation. The French Revolution posed challenges to foreign trade and diplomacy. Migration to the frontier increased, which intensified conflicts between Indians and white settlers and increased hostilities between the United States and Great Britain. Yellow fever swept through Philadelphia and other cities, causing fear and disrupting political and economic life. Finally, the excise tax on whiskey fueled armed protests among frontier farmers. This cluster of crises split the Federalists into warring factions during Washington's second term.

Foreign Trade and Foreign Wars. Jefferson and Madison led the opposition to Hamilton's policies. Their supporters were mainly southern Federalists who envisioned the country's future rooted in agriculture, not the commerce and industry supported by Hamilton and his allies. Jefferson agreed with the Scottish economist Adam Smith that an international division of labor could best provide for the world's people. Americans could supply Europe with food and raw materials in exchange for manufactured goods. When wars in Europe, including a revolution in France, disrupted European agriculture in the 1790s, Jefferson's views were reinforced.

Although trade with Europe remained the most important source of goods and wealth for the United States, some merchants expanded into other parts of the globe. In the mid-1780s, the first American ships reached China, where they traded ginseng root and sea otter pelts for silk, tea, and chinaware. Still, events in Europe had a far greater impact on the United States at the time than those in the Pacific world.

Americans Trade with China   This painting by a Chinese artist c. 1800 shows the Hongs at Canton, where ships from foreign countries arrived to unload and load goods. The foreign ships were limited to this small area outside Canton's city walls. There each nation established a trading post identified by its national flag and overseen by a Chinese merchant. © Sotheby's/akg-images

The French Revolution (1789–1799) was especially significant for U.S. politics. The Revolution disrupted French agriculture, increasing demand for American wheat, while the efforts of French revolutionaries to institute an egalitarian republic gained support from many Americans. The followers of Jefferson and Madison formed Republican societies, and members adopted the French term *citizen* when addressing each other. Moreover, the strong presence of workers and farmers among France's revolutionary forces sparked further critiques of the "monied power" that drove Federalist policies.

In late 1792, as French revolutionary leaders began executing thousands of their opponents in the Reign of Terror, wealthy Federalists grew more anxious. The beheading of King Louis XVI horrified them, as did the revolution's condemnation of Christianity. When France declared war against Prussia, Austria, and finally Great Britain, merchants worried about the impact on trade. In response, President Washington proclaimed U.S. neutrality in April 1793, prohibiting Americans from providing support or war materials to any belligerent nations—including France or Great Britain.

While the Neutrality Proclamation limited the shipment of certain items to Europe, Americans simultaneously increased trade with colonies in the British and French West Indies. Indeed, U.S. ships captured much of the lucrative sugar trade. At the same time, farmers in the Chesapeake and Middle Atlantic regions filled the growing demand for wheat in Europe, causing their profits to climb.

Yet these benefits did not bring about a political reconciliation. Although Jefferson condemned the French Reign of Terror, he protested the Neutrality Proclamation by resigning his cabinet post. Tensions escalated when the French envoy to the United States, Edmond Genêt, sought to enlist Americans in the European war. Republican clubs poured out to hear him speak and donated generously to the French cause. But the British also ignored U.S. neutrality. The Royal Navy stopped U.S. ships carrying French sugar and seized more than 250 vessels. The British also supplied Indians in the Ohio River valley with guns and encouraged them to raid U.S. settlements.

More concerned with addressing issues with Britain, President Washington sent John Jay to England to resolve concerns over trade with the British West Indies, compensation for seized American ships, the continued British occupation of frontier forts, and southerners' ongoing demands for reimbursement of slaves evacuated by the British during the Revolution. Jay returned from England in 1794 with a treaty, but it was widely criticized in Congress and the popular press. While securing limited U.S. trading rights in the West Indies, it failed to address British reimbursement for captured cargoes or slaves and granted Britain eighteen months to leave frontier forts. It also demanded that U.S. planters repay British firms for debts accrued during the Revolution. While the **Jay Treaty** was eventually ratified, it remained a source of contention among Federalists.

The Whiskey Rebellion.

The Whiskey Rebellion. Despite these foreign crises, it was the effect of Federalist policies on the American frontier that crystallized opposing factions. In the early 1790s, Republican societies from Maine to Georgia demanded the removal of British and Spanish troops from frontier areas, while frontier farmers lashed out at enforcement of the so-called whiskey tax. Many farmers on the frontier grew corn and turned it into whiskey to make it easier to transport and more profitable to sell. The whiskey tax hurt these farmers, hundreds of whom petitioned the federal government for relief.

Western Pennsylvania farmers were particularly incensed and rallied in 1792 and 1793 to protest the tax and those who enforced it. Former North Carolina Regulator Hermon Husband was one of the most outspoken critics of the new excise tax (see American Histories in chapter 5). Adopting tactics from Stamp Act protests and Shays's Rebellion, farmers blocked roads, burned sheriffs in effigy, marched on courthouses, and assaulted tax collectors. Government operations in Philadelphia were largely paralyzed by a yellow fever epidemic from August to November 1793, but the lack of response only fueled the rebels' anger. By 1794 all-out rebellion had erupted.

Washington, Hamilton, and their supporters worried that the rebellion could spread and that it might encourage Indians to rise up as well. Since Spanish and British soldiers were eager to foment trouble along the frontier, the **Whiskey Rebellion** might spark their intervention as well. These Federalists also suspected that pro-French immigrants from Scotland and Ireland helped fuel the insurgency.

Unlike 1786, however, when the federal government had no power to intervene in Shays's Rebellion, Washington now federalized militias from four states, calling up nearly thirteen thousand soldiers to quash the uprising. The army that marched into western Pennsylvania in September 1794 vastly outnumbered the "whiskey rebels" and easily suppressed the uprising. Having gained victory, the federal government prosecuted only two of the leaders, who although convicted were later pardoned by Washington.

Washington proved that the Constitution provided the necessary powers to put down internal threats. Yet in doing so, the administration horrified many Americans who viewed the force used against the farmers as excessive. Jefferson and Madison voiced this outrage from within the Federalist government. The Revolutionary generation had managed to compromise on many issues, from representation and slavery to the balance between federal and state authority. But now Hamilton's economic policies had led to a frontier uprising, and Washington had used a federal army to destroy popular dissent. The Federalists were on the verge of open warfare themselves.

Further Conflicts on the Frontier. In one area, Federalists shared a common concern: the continued threats to U.S. sovereignty by Indian, British, and Spanish forces. In 1790 Congress had passed the Indian Trade and Intercourse Act to regulate Indian-white relations on the frontier and to ensure fair and equitable dealings. However, the act was widely ignored.

The government's failure to stem the flood of settlers into the Ohio and Mississippi River valleys proved costly. In 1790 Little Turtle, a war chief of the Miami nation, gathered a large force of Shawnee, Delaware, Ottawa, Chippewa, Sauk, Fox, and other Indians. This pan-Indian alliance successfully attacked federal troops in the Ohio valley that fall. A year later, the allied Indian warriors defeated a large force under General Arthur St. Clair (Map 7.2). The stunning defeat shocked Americans. In the meantime, Spanish authorities negotiated with Creeks and Cherokees to attack U.S. settlements on the southern frontier.

Washington decided to deal with problems in the Northwest Territory first, sending 2,000 men under the command of General Anthony Wayne into the Ohio frontier. In August 1794, Wayne's forces attacked 1,500 to 2,000 Indians gathered at a British fort. In the Battle of Fallen Timbers, the pan-Indian warriors, led by Little Turtle, suffered a bitter defeat. A year later, the warring Indians in the Northwest Territory signed the **Treaty of Greenville**, granting the United States vast tracks of land.

Amid this turmoil, in November 1794, John Jay signed his controversial treaty with Great Britain. With Britain agreeing to withdraw its forces from the U.S. frontier by 1796, the treaty may have helped persuade Indian nations to accept U.S. peace terms at Greenville. Nonetheless, the Jay Treaty's requirement that Americans make "full and complete compensation" to British firms for Revolutionary War debts without the British compensating U.S. merchants or slave owners for their losses nearly led Congress to reject it. In June 1795, however, the Senate finally approved the treaty without a vote to spare. Before Jay's controversial treaty took effect, Spain agreed to negotiate an end to hostilities on the southern frontier of the United States. Envoy Thomas Pinckney negotiated that treaty,

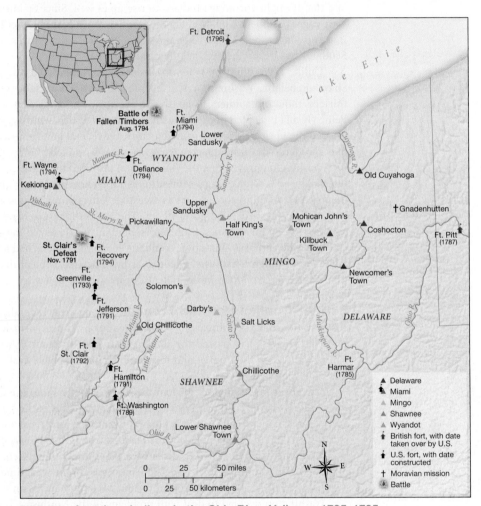

MAP 7.2   American Indians in the Ohio River Valley, c. 1785–1795

Until the mid-eighteenth century, despite conflicts, Indian tribes in the Ohio River valley forged trade and diplomatic relations with various colonial powers. But once the United States established the Northwest Territory in 1785, conflicts between Indians and U.S. settlers and soldiers escalated dramatically. As tribes created pan-Indian alliances, the United States constructed numerous forts in the region.

which recognized the thirty-first parallel as the boundary between U.S. and Spanish territory in the South and opened the Mississippi River and the port of New Orleans to U.S. shipping. Many Federalists, especially from the West and South, who opposed the Jay Treaty supported the **Pinckney Treaty**, which was ratified in 1796.

REVIEW & RELATE

- How did events overseas shape domestic American politics and frontier policy in the 1790s?

- What common concerns underlay the Whiskey Rebellion and Shays's Rebellion? How did the U.S. government deal differently with each?

The **First Party System**

By 1796 Jefferson, Madison, and other opponents of Hamilton's economic policies, Washington's assault on the whiskey rebels, and Jay's Treaty had formed a distinct party. They called themselves **Democratic-Republicans** and supported Jefferson for president. The electoral college, hoping to bring the warring sides together, chose Federalist John Adams as president and Thomas Jefferson as vice president. The two disagreed fundamentally on a wide range of issues, and events soon heightened these divisions. Foreign crises once again fueled political antagonisms as fear of war with Britain or France intensified. In this charged atmosphere, Federalists in Congress passed two acts in 1798 relating to aliens (immigrants) and to sedition (activities that promote civil disorder). Instead of resolving tensions, however, these laws exacerbated opposition to Federalist rule. By 1800, partisan differences had crystallized, and the Democratic-Republicans threatened to oust the Federalists from power.

The Adams Presidency. The election of 1796 was the first to be contested by candidates identified with opposing parties. Federalists supported John Adams for president and Thomas Pinckney for vice president. The Democratic-Republicans chose Thomas Jefferson and Aaron Burr of New York to represent their interests. When the electoral college was established, political parties did not exist and, in fact, were seen as promoting conflict. Thus electors were asked to choose the best individuals to serve, regardless of their views. In 1796 they picked Adams for president and Jefferson for vice president, perhaps hoping to lessen partisan divisions by forcing men of different views to compromise. Instead, the effects of an administration divided against itself were nearly disastrous, and opposing interests became more thoroughly entrenched.

Adams and Jefferson had disagreed on almost every major policy issue during Washington's administration. Not surprisingly, the new president rarely took advice from his vice president. At the same time, Adams retained most of Washington's appointees, who often sought advice from Hamilton, undercutting Adams's authority. Worse still, the new president had poor political instincts and faced numerous challenges.

At first, foreign disputes enhanced the authority of the Adams administration. The Federalists remained pro-British, and French seizures of U.S. ships threatened to provoke war. In 1798 Adams tried to negotiate compensation for the losses suffered by merchants. When an American delegation arrived in Paris, however, three French agents demanded a bribe to initiate talks.

Adams made public secret correspondence from the French agents, whose names were listed only as X, Y, and Z. Americans, including Democratic-Republicans, expressed outrage at this French insult to U.S. integrity, which became known as the **XYZ affair.** Congress quickly approved an embargo act that prohibited trade with France and permitted privateering against French ships. For the next two years, the United States fought an undeclared war with France.

Despite praise for his handling of the XYZ affair, Adams feared dissent from opponents at home and abroad. Consequently, the Federalist majority in Congress passed a series of security acts in 1798. The Alien Act allowed the president to order the imprisonment or deportation of noncitizens and was directed primarily at Irish and Scottish dissenters who criticized the government's pro-British policies. Congress also approved the Naturalization Act, which raised the residency requirement for citizenship from five to fourteen years. Finally, Federalists pushed through the Sedition Act, which outlawed "false, scandalous, or malicious statements against President or Congress." In the following months, nearly two dozen Democratic-Republican editors and legislators were arrested for sedition, and some were fined and imprisoned.

Democratic-Republicans were understandably infuriated by the **Alien and Sedition Acts**. They considered the attack on immigrants an attempt to limit the votes of farmers, artisans, and frontiersmen, who formed the core of their supporters. The Sedition Act threatened Democratic-Republican critics of Federalist policies and the First Amendment's guarantee of free speech. Jefferson and Madison encouraged states to pass resolutions that would counter this violation of the Bill of Rights. Using language drafted by the two Democratic-Republican leaders, legislators passed the **Virginia and Kentucky**

Matthew Lyon and Roger Griswold This political cartoon depicts a fight on the floor of the House of Representatives in February 1798 between Representatives Matthew Lyon of Vermont, a Democratic-Republican brandishing tongs, and Roger Griswold of Connecticut, a Federalist waving a cane. A newspaper editor and a critic of the Alien and Sedition Acts, Lyon was later convicted of sedition but won reelection while in jail. Library of Congress, LC-DIG-ppmsca-19356

Resolutions, which declared the Alien and Sedition Acts "void and of no force." They protested against the "alarming infractions of the Constitution," particularly the freedom of speech that "has been justly deemed, the only effectual guardian of every other right." Virginia even claimed that states had a right to nullify any powers exercised by the federal government that were not explicitly granted to it.

Although the Alien and Sedition Acts curbed dissent in the short run, they reinforced popular concerns about the power wielded by the Federalists. Combined with the ongoing war with France, continuing disputes over taxes, and relentless partisan denunciations in the press, these acts set the stage for the presidential election of 1800.

The Election of 1800.

By 1800 Adams had negotiated a peaceful settlement of U.S. conflicts with France, considering it one of the greatest achievements of his administration. However, other Federalists, including Hamilton, disagreed and continued to seek open warfare and an all-out victory. Thus the Federalists faced the election of 1800 deeply divided. Democratic-Republicans meanwhile united behind Jefferson and portrayed the Federalists as the "new British" tyrants.

Explore ▶

See Document 7.4 for a Federalist response to the election of 1800.

For the first time, congressional caucuses selected candidates for each party. The Federalists agreed on Adams and Charles Cotesworth Pinckney of South Carolina. The Democratic-Republicans again chose Jefferson and Burr as their candidates. The campaign was marked by bitter accusations and denunciations.

In the first highly contested presidential election, the different methods states used to record voters' preferences gained more attention. Only five states determined members of the electoral college by popular vote. In the rest, state legislatures appointed electors. Created at a time when political parties were considered injurious to good government, the electoral college was not prepared for the situation it faced in January 1801. Federalist and Democratic-Republican caucuses nominated one candidate for president and one for vice president on party tickets. As a result, Jefferson and Burr received exactly the same number of electoral college votes, and the House of Representatives then had to break the tie. There Burr sought to gain the presidency with the help of Federalist representatives ardently opposed to Jefferson. But Alexander Hamilton stepped in and warned against Burr's leadership. This helped Jefferson emerge victorious, but it also inflamed animosity between Burr and Hamilton that eventually led Burr to kill Hamilton in a duel in 1804.

President Jefferson labeled his election a revolution achieved not "by the sword" but by "the suffrage of the people." The election of 1800 was hardly a popular revolution, given the restrictions on suffrage and the methods of selecting the electoral college. Still, between 1796 and 1800, partisan factions had been transformed into opposing parties, and the United States had managed a peaceful transition from one party to another.

REVIEW & RELATE

• What were the main issues dividing the Federalists and the Democratic-Republicans?

• What do the Alien and Sedition Acts and the election of 1800 tell us about political partisanship in late-eighteenth-century America?

SOLO ANALYSIS

The Election of 1800

The election of 1800 marked the first transfer of political power in the United States from one party to another. The Democratic-Republican candidate for president, Thomas Jefferson, defeated the Federalist Party incumbent, John Adams. On March 4, 1801, the date of President Jefferson's inauguration, the *Columbian Centinel*, a Federalist newspaper in Boston, printed this broadside. The editors feared that Jefferson's administration would negate all of the gains achieved by the Federalists.

Document 7.4

Monumental Inscription.

" *That life is long which answers Life's great end.*"

YESTERDAY EXPIRED,
Deeply regretted by MILLIONS of grateful Americans,
And by *all* GOOD MEN,
The FEDERAL ADMINISTRATION
Of the
GOVERNMENT of the *United States* :
Animated by
A WASHINGTON, an ADAMS ;—a
HAMILTON, KNOX, PICKERING, WOL-
COTT, M'HENRY, MARSHALL,
STODDERT and DEXTER.
Æt. 12 years.

Its death was occasioned by the
Secret Arts, and Open Violence;
Of Foreign and Domestic Demagogues :
Notwithstanding its whole Life
Was devoted to the Performance of every Duty
to promote
The UNION, CREDIT, PEACE, PROSPER-
ITY, HONOR, and
FELICITY OF ITS COUNTRY.

At its birth it found
The Union of the States dissolving like a Rope of snow ;
It hath left it
Stronger than the Threefold cord.

It found the United States
Bankrupts in Estate and Reputation ;
It hath left them
*Unbounded in Credit ; and respected throughout
the World.*

Granger, NYC

Interpret the Evidence

1. Why does the *Columbian Centinel* use a "Monumental Inscription" and various typefaces to represent the Federalist defeat?

2. What do the paper's editors see as the achievements of the Federalists during their twelve years in power and the character of the Democratic-Republican victors?

Put It in Context

What does the tone of this notice suggest about the likelihood of compromise between Federalists and Democratic-Republicans in the new federal administration?

Conclusion: A Young Nation Comes of Age

In the 1780s and 1790s, the United States faced numerous obstacles to securing its place as a nation. Financial hardship, massive debts, hostile Indians, and European diplomacy had to be addressed by a federal government that, under the Articles of Confederation, was relatively weak. By 1787 concerns about national security, fueled by rebellious farmers and frontier conflicts, persuaded some political leaders to advocate a new governmental structure. While it required numerous compromises among groups with competing ideas and interests, the Constitution was drafted and, after a fierce battle in important states, ratified.

With the federal government's power strengthened, George Washington took office as the first American president. His administration sought to enhance U.S. power at home and abroad. Secretary of the treasury Alexander Hamilton proposed a series of measures to stabilize the American economy, pay off Revolutionary War debts, and promote trade and industry. However, these policies also aroused opposition, with leaders like Jefferson and Madison and ordinary farmers and frontiersmen questioning the benefits of Hamilton's economic priorities. Differences over the French Revolution also led to heated debates, while the imposition of an excise tax on whiskey fueled open rebellion on the Pennsylvania frontier. Although a majority of Federalists supported Hamilton and an alliance with Britain, they faced growing opposition from those who advocated agrarian ideals and supported the French Revolution.

While conflicts among Federalists drew many Americans into debates over government programs, large groups remained marginalized or excluded from the political system. Indians, African Americans, and women had little voice in policies that directly affected them. Even white workingmen and farmers found it difficult to influence political priorities and turned to petitions, protests, and even armed uprisings to demonstrate their views.

By 1796, Jefferson and Madison, who led the opposition among Federalists, had formed a separate political party, the Democratic-Republicans. They considered passage of the Alien and Sedition Acts as a direct attack on their supporters, and in 1800 wrested control of Congress and the presidency from the Federalists. Still, this peaceful transition in power boded well for the young United States.

Despite political setbacks, the Federalist legacy remained powerful. Hamilton's policies continued to shape national economic growth, and Federalists retained political power in the Northeast for decades. Meanwhile the benefits that small farmers and frontiersmen like Daniel Shays hoped to gain under Democratic-Republican rule proved largely elusive. Marginalized Americans such as Indians and African Americans also benefited little from the transition to Democratic-Republican leadership. Indeed, the growth of slavery and U.S. westward expansion created new burdens for these groups.

Yet the Democratic-Republican Party would not be seriously challenged for national power until 1824, giving it nearly a quarter century to implement its vision of the United States. Members of this heterogeneous party would now have to learn to compromise with each other if they were going to achieve their goal of limited federal power in an agrarian republic.

CHAPTER 7 REVIEW

TIMELINE OF EVENTS

KEY TERMS

REVIEW & RELATE

1. What challenges did the new nation face in the immediate aftermath of the Revolutionary War?

2. How did farmers, financial leaders, foreign nations, and Indians react to government efforts to address challenges after the Revolution?

3. How did America's experience of the Revolutionary War change the lives of African Americans and women?

4. What do uprisings by farmers and debtors tell us about social and economic divisions in the early Republic?

5. What issues attracted the most intense debate during the drafting and ratification of the Constitution? Why?

6. How did Hamilton's policies stabilize the national economy, and why did they nonetheless arouse opposition?

7. How did events overseas shape domestic American politics and frontier policy in the 1790s?

8. What common concerns underlay the Whiskey Rebellion and Shays's Rebellion? How did the U.S. government deal differently with each?

9. What were the main issues dividing the Federalists and the Democratic-Republicans?

10. What do the Alien and Sedition Acts and the election of 1800 tell us about political partisanship in late-eighteenth-century America?

Debating the Constitution in New York State

Although the Constitution was eventually approved by all thirteen states, the battle over its ratification revealed a deeply divided nation. Antifederalist delegates dominated conventions in Massachusetts, Virginia, and New York, where intense debates erupted. When Massachusetts and Virginia finally ratified the Constitution by close votes, the New York convention was still in session.

As elsewhere, New York delegates debated questions of representation, the increased powers of the federal government, and a bill of rights. Before the convention opened, James Madison, Alexander Hamilton, and John Jay offered fellow New Yorkers pro-Constitution arguments in *The Federalist Papers* (Document 7.5). At the convention, Hamilton emphasized the need for a strong central government in which checks and balances limited the power of any single branch and insisted on accommodating the views of diverse groups, including southern slaveholders (Document 7.7).

A secretary recorded the speeches of Hamilton and other delegates, like Melancton Smith and John Williams. Smith was a large landowner and a New York City merchant, but he led the state's Antifederalists and questioned the expansion of federal power and the limits on representation (Document 7.6). Williams, a farmer from rural Washington County and thus a more typical Antifederalist, criticized the Constitution more adamantly. He distrusted federal power, disliked the system of representation, and worried about America's moral decline (Document 7.8). However, the Federalists eventually prevailed, with Hamilton, Smith, and twenty-eight other delegates voting yes and

Williams one of the twenty-seven no votes. The slim victory elated the Federalist newspaper, the *Massachusetts Centinel*, which followed the debates closely and tracked each state that ratified the Constitution (Document 7.9). The intensity of the ratification debates highlights the competing ideas and interests among Americans. It also shows the willingness of Federalists to compromise on issues like a bill of rights while insisting on the necessity of a new political structure.

Document 7.5

James Madison | *Federalist* 10, The Union as a Safeguard Against Domestic Faction and Insurrection, November 1787

James Madison wrote the most significant of the pro-Constitution essays known collectively as *The Federalist Papers*. In this tenth essay, Madison challenged the widely held belief that republican governments were mostly likely to succeed when they were small and compact. He argued instead that a large and diverse population in which various factions competed for support would keep any one faction from subverting the freedom of other groups.

To the People of the State of New York:

AMONG the numerous advantages promised by a well-constructed Union, none deserves to be more accurately developed than its tendency to break and control the violence of faction. The friend of popular governments never finds himself so much alarmed for their character and fate, as when he contemplates their propensity to this dangerous vice. He will not fail, therefore, to set a due value on any plan which, without violating the principles to which he is attached, provides a proper cure for it. . . .

By a faction, I understand a number of citizens, whether amounting to a majority or a minority of the whole, who are united and actuated by some common impulse of passion, or of interest, adversed to the rights of other citizens, or to the permanent and aggregate interests of the community. . . .

The latent causes of faction are . . . sown in the nature of man; and we see them everywhere brought into different degrees of activity, according to the different circumstances of civil society. . . . But the most common and durable source of factions has been the various and unequal distribution of property. Those who hold and those who are without property have ever formed distinct interests in society. Those who are creditors, and those who are debtors, fall under a like discrimination. A landed interest, a manufacturing interest, a mercantile interest, a moneyed interest, with many lesser interests, grow up of necessity in civilized nations, and divide them into different classes, actuated by different sentiments and views. . . .

[I]t may be concluded that a pure democracy, by which I mean a society consisting of a small number of citizens, who assemble and administer the government in person, can admit of no cure for the mischiefs of faction. A common passion or interest will, in almost every case, be felt by a majority of the whole; a communication and concert result from the form of government itself; and there is nothing to check the inducements to sacrifice the weaker party or an obnoxious individual. . . .

A republic, by which I mean a government in which the scheme of representation takes place, opens a different prospect, and promises the cure for which we are seeking. . . .

[T]he greater number of citizens and extent of territory which may be brought within the compass of republican than of democratic government . . . is th[e] circumstance principally which renders factious combinations less to be dreaded in the former than in the latter. The smaller the society, the fewer probably will be the distinct parties and interests composing it; the fewer the distinct parties and interests, the more frequently will a majority be found of the same party; and the smaller the number of individuals composing a majority, and the smaller the compass within which they are placed, the more easily will they concert and execute their plans of oppression. Extend the sphere, and you take in a greater variety of parties and interests; you make it less probable that a majority of the whole will have a common motive to invade the rights of other citizens; or if such a common motive exists, it will be more difficult for all who feel it to discover their own strength, and to act in unison with each other. . . .

The influence of factious leaders may kindle a flame within their particular States, but will be unable to spread a general conflagration through the other States. A religious sect may degenerate into a political faction in a part of the Confederacy; but the variety of sects dispersed over the entire face of it must secure the national councils against any danger from that source.

Source: *New York Packet*, November 23, 1787, Library of Congress.

Document 7.6

Melancton Smith | Antifederalist Argument at the New York State Convention, June 1788

Melancton Smith was unusually wealthy for an Antifederalist delegate to the New York ratifying convention. Smith also worked alongside Alexander Hamilton in the New York Manumission Society, which encouraged the gradual abolition of slavery. But while Hamilton accepted the three-fifths compromise as necessary, Smith found it odious. He also embraced the traditional view that republics were best governed by smaller governmental bodies.

n the discussion of this question, he [Smith] was disposed to make every reasonable concession, and, indeed, to sacrifice every thing for a union, except the liberties of his country. . . .

The defects of the Old Confederation needed as little proof as the necessity of an Union. But there was no proof in all this that the proposed Constitution was a good one. Defective as the Old Confederation is, . . . no one could deny but it was possible we might have a worse government. . . .

He would agree with the honorable gentlemen [Hamilton] that perfection in any system of government was not to be looked for. . . . But he would observe, that this observation applied with equal force against changing any systems, especially against material and radical changes. Fickleness and inconstancy, he said, were characteristic of a free people; and in framing a Constitution for them, it was, perhaps the most difficult thing to correct this spirit, and guard against the evil effects of it. . . .

He would now proceed to state his objections to the clause just read, (section 2, of article 1, clause 3). . . . In the first place, the rule of apportionment of the representatives is to be according to the whole number of the white inhabitants, with three fifths of all others, that is in plain English, each state is to send Representatives in proportion to the number of freemen, and three fifths of the slaves it contains. He could not see any rule by which slaves were to be included in the ratio of representation. The principle of a representation, being that every free agent should be concerned in governing himself, it was absurd to give that power to a man who could not exercise it. . . . The very operation of it was to give certain privileges to those people who were so wicked as to keep slaves. He knew it would be admitted that this rule of apportionment was founded on unjust principles, but that it was the result of accommodation; which, he supposed, we should be under the necessity of admitting, . . . though utterly repugnant to his feelings. . . .

[And] how was the will of the community to be expressed? . . . [W]e may approach a great way towards perfection by increasing the representation and limiting the powers of Congress. He considered that the great interests and liberties of the people could only be secured by the State Governments. He admitted, that if the new government was only confined to great national objects, it would be less exceptionable; but it extended to every thing dear to human nature. . . . [F]or that power which had both the purse and the sword had the government of the whole country, and might extend its powers to any and to every object.

Source: New York State Ratification Convention, Minutes, June 20, 1788.

Document 7.7

Alexander Hamilton | Federalist Argument at the New York State Convention, June 1788

Alexander Hamilton directly countered Melancton Smith's claims about the three-fifths compromise and the benefits of relying on state governments. Noting that many states failed to provide their share of troops or funds when requisitioned by the confederation government, Hamilton feared that without a stronger central government, the United States would be weakened economically and militarily.

I will not agree with gentlemen who trifle with the weaknesses of our country; and suppose, that they are enumerated to answer a party purpose, and to terrify with ideal dangers. No; I believe these weaknesses to be real, and pregnant with destruction. Yet, however weak our country may be, I hope we never shall sacrifice our liberties. . . .

Sir, it appears to me extraordinary, that, while gentlemen in one breath acknowledge that the old confederation requires many material amendments, they should in the next deny, that its defects have been the cause of our political weakness, and the consequent calamities of our country. . . . [T]he states have almost uniformly weighed the requisitions by their own local interests; and have only executed them so far as answered their particular conveniency or advantage. Hence there have ever been thirteen different bodies to judge of the measures of Congress, and the operations of government have been distracted by their taking different courses. . . .

Shall we take the old Confederation, as the basis of a new system? . . . certainly not. Will any man who entertains a wish for the safety of his country, trust the sword and the purse with a single Assembly organized on principles so defective — so rotten? Though we might give to such a government certain powers with safety, yet to give them the full and unlimited powers of taxation and the national forces would be to establish a despotism; the definition of which is, a government in which all power is concentrated in a single body. . . . These considerations show clearly, that a government totally different must be instituted. . . . [T]he convention . . . therefore formed two branches, and divided the powers, that each might be a check upon the other. . . .

Sir, the natural situation of this country seems to divide its interests into different classes. . . . It became necessary, therefore, to compromise; or the Convention must have dissolved without effecting any thing. . . .

The first thing objected to is that clause which allows a representation for three fifths of the negroes. . . . It is the unfortunate situation of the Southern States to have a great part of their population, as well as property, in blacks. The regulation complained of was one result of the spirit of accommodation, which governed the Convention; and without this indulgence, no union could possibly have been formed. But, Sir, considering some peculiar advantages which we derive from them, it is entirely just that they should be gratified. The Southern States possess certain staples, tobacco, rice, indigo, &c. which must be capital objects in treaties of commerce with foreign nations; and the advantages which they necessarily procure in these treaties, will be felt throughout all the States. . . . [Moreover] representation and taxation go together, and one uniform rule ought to apply to both. Would it be just to compute these slaves in the assessment of taxes; and discard them from the estimate in the apportionment of representatives?

Source: New York State Ratification Convention, Minutes, June 20, 1788.

Document 7.8

John Williams | Antifederalist Argument at the New York State Convention, June 1788

One of four delegates from the northern counties of Washington and Clinton, John Williams represented the interests of rural farmers. An ardent Antifederalist, he preferred that political power be focused at local and state levels. But he also expressed deep concern about the loss of traditional values like thrift and hard work, making the nation vulnerable to mercantile and foreign interests.

I believe that this country has never before seen such a critical period in political affairs. We have felt the feebleness of those ties, by which the States are held together, and the want of that energy which is necessary to manage our general concerns. . . . Indeed, Sir, it appears to me, that many of our present distresses flow from a source very different from the defects in the Confederation. Unhappily for us, immediately after our extrication from a cruel and unnatural war, luxury and dissipation overran the country, banishing all that economy, frugality, and industry, which had been exhibited during the war. . . .

Let us, then, abandon all those foreign commodities which have hitherto deluged our country; which have loaded us with debt, and which, if continued, will forever involve us in difficulties. How many thousands are daily wearing the manufactures of Europe, when by a little industry and frugality, they might wear those of their own country! . . . What dissipation is there from the immoderate use of spirits! Is it not notorious that men cannot be hired, in time of harvest, without giving them, on an average, a pint of rum per day? . . . And, what is worse, the disposition of eight tenths of the commonalty is such, that, if they can get credit, they will purchase unnecessary articles, even to the amount of their crop, before it becomes merchantable. . . . [T]he best government ever devised, without economy and frugality will leave us in a situation no better than the present. . . .

[L]et us examine whether it [the Constitution] be calculated to preserve the invaluable blessings of liberty, and secure the inestimable rights of mankind. . . . [I]f it be found to contain principles that will lead to the subversion of liberty, . . . let us insist upon the necessary alterations and amendments. . . .

In forming a constitution for a free country like this, the greatest care should be taken to define its powers, and guard against an abuse of authority. The Constitution should be so formed as not to swallow up the State governments: the general government ought to be confined to certain national objects; and the States should retain such powers, as concern their own internal police. . . . The number of representatives is, in my opinion, too small to resist corruption. Sir, how guarded is our State Constitution on this head! The number of senate and house of representatives proposed in the Constitution does not surpass those of our State. How great the disparity, when compared with the aggregate number of the United States! . . . Can it be supposed that six men can be a complete representation of the various orders of people of this State?

Source: New York State Ratification Convention, Minutes, June 21, 1788.

Document 7.9

The Eleventh Pillar of the Great National Dome, 1788

Throughout 1788, newspapers like the *Massachusetts Centinel* traced the results of ratifying conventions state by state. A graphic represented each state that ratified the Constitution as a pillar of the new federal superstructure. The importance of New York State is reflected in the flowery verse above and below "the beauteous DOME."

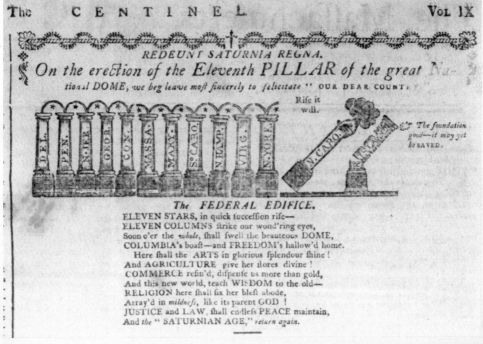

Library of Congress, 3a45782

Interpret the Evidence

1. How do Melancton Smith, Alexander Hamilton, and John Williams each view the problems that exist under the confederation government (Documents 7.6, 7.7, and 7.8)?

2. What does James Madison see as the major source of factions in the United States, and how does he think they can most effectively be contained (Document 7.5)?

3. What are the main arguments for and against the three-fifths compromise in the Constitution (Documents 7.6, 7.7, and 7.8)? What other issues of representation inspired debate?

4. Are there any shared beliefs between the Federalists and Antifederalists in New York (Documents 7.5, 7.6, 7.7, and 7.8)? Do these explain Smith's decision to vote yes on ratification?

5. How does the *Massachusetts Centinel* represent the legacy of New York's ratification of the Constitution (Document 7.9)?

Put It in Context

In what ways does the ratification process in New York State reflect larger debates and divisions in the United States in the 1780s?

The Early Republic

1790–1820

8

WINDOW TO THE PAST

William Clark, Journal, January 28, 1805

William Clark kept a detailed journal of the 1804–1806 expedition he and Meriwether Lewis led to explore the American West. They were aided by many different Indian groups, especially the Mandan Indians along the Missouri River. They camped near the Mandan in the winter of 1804, before heading into the Rocky Mountains.
Here Clark draws a Mandan war hatchet, which was crucial to the tribe's defense.

▸ To discover more about what this primary source can show us, see Document 8.8 on page 272.

American Philosophical Society

After reading this chapter you should be able to:

- Analyze the ways that social and cultural leaders worked to craft an American identity and how that was complicated by racial, ethnic, and class differences.

- Interpret how the Democratic-Republican ideal of limiting federal power was transformed by international events, westward expansion, and Supreme Court rulings between 1800 and 1808.

- Explain the ways that technology reshaped the American economy and the lives of distinct groups of Americans.

AMERICAN HISTORIES

When Parker Cleaveland graduated from Harvard University in 1799, his parents expected him to pursue a career in medicine, law, or the ministry. Instead, he turned to teaching. In 1805 Cleaveland secured a position in Brunswick, Maine, as professor of mathematics and natural philosophy at Bowdoin College. A year later, he married Martha Bush. Over the next twenty years, the Cleavelands raised eight children on the Maine frontier, entertained visiting scholars, corresponded with families at other colleges, and boarded dozens of students. While Parker taught those students math and science, Martha trained them in manners and morals. The Cleavelands also served as a model of new ideals of companionate marriage, in which husbands and wives shared interests and affection.

Professor Cleaveland believed in using scientific research to benefit society. When Brunswick workers asked him to identify local rocks, Parker began studying geology and chemistry. In 1816 he published his *Elementary Treatise on Mineralogy and Geology*, providing a basic text for students and interested adults. He also lectured throughout New England, displaying mineral samples and performing chemical experiments.

The Cleavelands viewed the Bowdoin College community as a laboratory in which distinctly American values and ideas could be developed and sustained. So, too, did the residents of other college towns. Although less than 1 percent of men in the United States attended universities at the time, frontier colleges were considered important vehicles for bringing virtue—especially the desire to act for the public good—to the far reaches of the early republic. Yet several of these colleges were constructed with the aid of slave labor, and all were built on land bought or confiscated from Indians.

The purchase of the Louisiana Territory by President Thomas Jefferson in 1803 marked a new American frontier and ensured further encroachments on native lands. The territory covered 828,000 square miles and stretched from the Mississippi River to the Rocky Mountains and from New Orleans to present-day Montana. The area was home to tens of thousands of Indian inhabitants.

In the late 1780s, a daughter, later named Sacagawea, was born to a family of Shoshone Indians who lived in an area that became part of the Louisiana Purchase. In 1800 she was taken captive by a Hidatsa raiding party. Sacagawea and her fellow captives were marched hundreds of miles to a Hidatsa-Mandan village on the Missouri River. Eventually Sacagawea was sold to a French trader, Toussaint Charbonneau, along with another young Shoshone woman, and both became his wives.

In November 1804, an expedition led by Meriwether Lewis and William Clark set up winter camp near the Hidatsa village where Sacagawea lived. The U.S. government sent Lewis and Clark to document

(*left*) **Parker Cleaveland**. Courtesy the Bowdoin College Library, Brunswick, Maine, USA

(*right*) **Shoshone woman**. (No image of Sacagawea exists.) Joslyn Museum, Omaha, Nebraska, USA/Alecto Historical Editions/Bridgeman Images

flora and fauna in the Louisiana Territory, enhance trade, and explore routes to the Northwest. Charbonneau, who spoke French and Hidatsa, and Sacagawea, who spoke several Indian languages, joined the expedition as interpreters in April 1805.

The only woman in the party, Sacagawea traveled with her infant son strapped to her back. Although no portraits of her exist, her presence was crucial, as Clark noted in his journal: "The Wife of Chabono our interpreter we find reconsiles all the Indians, as to our friendly intentions." Sacagawea did help persuade Indian leaders to assist the expedition, but her extensive knowledge of the terrain and fluency in Indian languages were equally important. ■

The American histories of both Parker Cleaveland and Sacagawea aided the development of the United States. Cleaveland gained fame as part of a generation of intellectuals who symbolized Americans' ingenuity. Although Sacagawea was not considered learned, her understanding of Indian languages and western geography was crucial to Lewis and Clark's success. Like many other Americans, Sacagawea and Cleaveland forged new identities as the young nation developed. Still, racial, class, and gender differences made it impossible to create a single American identity. At the same time, Democratic-Republican leaders sought to shape a new national identity by promising to limit federal power and enhance state authority and individual rights. Instead, western expansion, international crises, and Supreme Court decisions ensured the expansion of federal power.

The Dilemmas of National Identity

In his inaugural address in March 1801, President Thomas Jefferson argued that the vast distance between Europe and the United States was a blessing, allowing Americans to develop their own unique culture and institutions. For many Americans, education offered one means of ensuring a distinctive national identity. Public schools could train American children in republican values, while the wealthiest among them could attend private academies and colleges. Newspapers, sermons, books, magazines, and other printed works could also help forge a common identity among the nation's far-flung citizens. Even the presence of Indians and Africans contributed to art and literature that were uniquely American. In addition, the construction of a new capital city to house the federal government offered a potent symbol of nationhood.

Yet these developments also illuminated political and racial dilemmas in the young nation. The decision to move the U.S. capital south from Philadelphia was prompted by concerns among southern politicians about the power of northern economic and political elites. The very construction of the capital, in which enslaved and free workers labored side by side, highlighted racial and class differences. Educational opportunities differed by race and class as well as by sex. How could a singular notion of American identity be forged in a country where differences of race, class, and sex loomed so large?

Education for a New Nation. The desire to create a specifically American culture began as soon as the Revolution ended. In 1783 Noah Webster, a schoolmaster, declared that "America must be as independent in *literature as in Politics*, as famous for *arts* as for

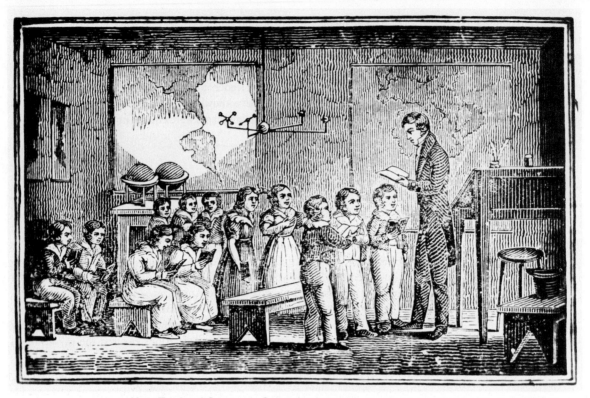

New England Grammar School   In this New England grammar school in the 1790s, boys and girls gather for instruction by their schoolmaster. They likely used one of Noah Webster's spellers or readers. The schoolmaster taught lessons in geography, as can be seen by the wall map and the two globes at the rear of the room. Granger, NYC

arms." To promote his vision, Webster published the *American Spelling Book* (1810) and the *American Dictionary of the English Language* (1828). Webster's books were widely used in the nation's expanding network of schools and academies and led to more standardized spelling and pronunciation of commonly used words.

Before the Revolution, public education for children was widely available in New England and the Middle Atlantic region. In the South, only those who could afford private schooling—perhaps 25 percent of the boys and 10 percent of the girls—received any formal instruction. Few young people enrolled in high school in any part of the colonies. Following the Revolution, state and national leaders proposed ambitious plans for public education, and in 1789 Massachusetts became the first state to demand that each town provide free schools for local children, though attendance policies were decided by the towns.

The American colonies boasted nine colleges that provided higher education for young men, including Harvard, Yale, King's College (Columbia), Queen's College (Rutgers), and the College of William and Mary. After independence, many Americans worried that these institutions were tainted by British and aristocratic influences. New colleges based on republican ideals needed to be founded.

Frontier towns offered opportunities for colleges to enrich the community and bene-fit the nation. The relative isolation of these villages ensured that students would focus on education. And frontier colleges provided opportunities for ethnic and religious groups outside the Anglo-American mainstream—like Scots-Irish Presbyterians—to cement their place in American society. The young nation benefited as well, albeit at the expense of Indians and their lands. For example, the founding of Franklin College in Athens, Georgia, encouraged white settlement in the state's interior, an area still largely populated by the Creek and Cherokee.

Frontier colleges were organized as community institutions composed of extended families, where administrators, faculty, and their wives guided students, hosted social events, and hired local workers, including servants and slaves. Women were viewed as exemplars of virtue in the new nation, and professors' wives served as maternal figures for young adults away from home. Families of modest means could send their sons to these less expensive colleges, depending on faculty couples to expand their intellect and provide moral guidance. In some towns, students at local female academies joined college men at chaperoned events to cultivate proper relations between the sexes.

Literary and Cultural Developments. Older universities also contributed to the development of a national identity. A group known as the Hartford Wits, most of them Yale graduates, gave birth to a new literary tradition. Its members identified mainly as Federalists and published paeans to democracy, satires about Shays's Rebellion, and plays about the proper role of the central government in a republican nation.

A number of novelists emerged in the early republic as well. Advances in printing and the manufacture of paper increased the circulation of novels, a literary genre developed in Britain and continental Europe at the turn of the eighteenth century. Improvements in girls' education then produced a growing audience for novels among women. Authors like Susanna Rowson and Charles Brockden Brown sought to educate readers about virtuous action by placing ordinary women and men in moments of high drama that tested their moral character. Novelists also emphasized new marital ideals, by which husbands and wives became partners and companions in creating a home and family.

Washington Irving became a well-known literary figure in the early republic. He wrote a series of popular folktales, including "The Legend of Sleepy Hollow" and "Rip Van Winkle," that were published in his *Sketchbook* in 1820. They drew on the Dutch culture of the Hudson valley region and often poked fun at more celebratory tales of early American history. In one serious essay, Irving challenged popular accounts of colonial wars that ignored courageous actions by Indians while applauding white atrocities.

Still, books that glorified the nation's past were also enormously popular. Among the most influential were the three-volume *History of the Revolution* (1805) written by Mercy Otis Warren and the *Life of Washington* (1806), a celebratory if fanciful biography by Mason Weems. The influence of American authors increased as residents in both urban and rural areas purchased growing numbers of books.

Artists, too, devoted considerable attention to historical themes. Charles Willson Peale painted Revolutionary generals while serving in the Continental Army and became best known for his portraits of George Washington. Samuel Jennings offered a more radi-cal perspective on the nation's character by incorporating women and African Americans into works like *Liberty Displaying the Arts and Sciences* (1792). Engravings, which were

Explore ▶

See Document 8.1 for one artist's image of republican education.

less expensive than paintings, also circulated widely. Many highlighted national symbols like flags, eagles, and Lady Liberty or uniquely American flora and fauna. William Bartram, the son of a botanist, journeyed through the southeastern United States and Florida, and published beautiful illustrations of plants and animals in his *Travels* (1791).

In 1780, the Massachusetts legislature established the American Academy of Arts and Sciences to promote American literature and science. Six years later, Philadelphia's American Philosophical Society created the first national prize for scientific endeavor. Philadelphia was also home to the nation's first medical college, founded at the University of Pennsylvania. Frontier colleges like Bowdoin also promoted new scientific discoveries. As in the arts, American scientists built on developments in continental Europe and Britain but prided themselves on contributing their own expertise.

The Racial Limits of an American Culture.

American Indians received significant attention from writers and scientists. White Americans in the early republic often wielded native names and symbols as they sought to create a distinct national identity. Some Americans, including whiskey rebels, followed in the tradition of the Boston Tea Party, dressing as Indians to protest economic and political tyranny (see "The Whiskey Rebellion" in Chapter 7). But more affluent whites also embraced Indian names and symbols. Tammany societies, which promoted patriotism and republicanism in the late eighteenth century, were named after a mythical Delaware chief called Tammend. They attracted large numbers of lawyers, merchants, and skilled artisans.

Poets, too, focused on American Indians. In his 1787 poem "Indian Burying Ground," Philip Freneau offered a sentimental portrait that highlighted the lost heritage of a nearly extinct native culture in New England. The theme of lost cultures and heroic (if still savage) Indians became even more pronounced in American poetry in the following decades. Such sentimental portraits of American Indians were less popular along the nation's frontier, where Indians continued to fight for their lands and rights.

Sympathetic depictions of Africans and African Americans by white artists and authors appeared even less frequently. Most were produced in the North and were intended for the rare patrons who opposed slavery. Typical images of blacks and Indians were far more demeaning. When describing Indians in frontier regions, white Americans generally focused on their savagery and their duplicity. Most images of Africans and African Americans exaggerated their perceived physical and intellectual differences from whites, to imply an innate inferiority.

Whether their depictions were realistic, sentimental, or derogatory, Africans, African Americans, and American Indians were almost always presented to the American public through the eyes of whites. Educated blacks like the Reverend Richard Allen of Philadelphia or the Reverend Thomas Paul of Boston wrote mainly for black audiences or corresponded privately with sympathetic whites. Similarly, cultural leaders among American Indians worked mainly within their own nations either to maintain traditional languages and customs or to introduce their people to Anglo-American ideas and beliefs.

The improved educational opportunities available to white Americans generally excluded blacks and Indians. Most southern planters had little desire to teach their slaves to read and write. Even in the North, states did not generally incorporate black children into their plans for public education. African Americans in cities with large free black

Samuel Jennings | Liberty Displaying the Arts and Sciences, 1792

Samuel Jennings was born in Philadelphia and attended the College of Philadelphia before the Revolution. He taught drawing and painted portraits before moving to London to study with Benjamin West in 1787. There his allegorical paintings were exhibited at the Royal Academy. Jennings painted this image for the newly established Library Company of Philadelphia, many of whose directors were Quakers who opposed slavery. The directors requested that he include Lady Liberty with her cap on the end of a pole.

Document 8.1

The Library Company of Philadelphia

| Which arts and sciences are displayed in this painting? | What does the broken chain at the feet of Lady Liberty indicate? | What distinguishes the black people inside and outside the building? |

Put It in Context

What does this painting suggest about how Jennings and the Library Company directors envisioned American identities in the early republic?

populations established the most long-lived schools for their race. The Reverend Allen opened a Sunday school for children in 1795 at his African Methodist Episcopal Church, and other free blacks formed literary and debating societies. Still, only a small percentage of African Americans received an education equivalent to that available to whites in the early republic.

U.S. political leaders were more interested in the education of American Indians, but government officials left their schooling to religious groups. Several denominations sent missionaries to the Seneca, Cherokee, and other tribes, and a few successful students were then sent to American colleges to be trained as ministers or teachers for their own people. This was important since few whites bothered to learn Indian languages.

The divergent approaches that whites took to Indian and African American education demonstrated broader assumptions about the two groups. Most white Americans believed that Indians were untamed and uncivilized, but not innately different from Europeans. Africans and African Americans, on the other hand, were assumed to be inferior, and most whites believed that no amount of education could change that. As U.S. frontiers expanded, white Americans considered ways to "civilize" Indians and incorporate them into the nation. But the requirements of slavery made it much more difficult for whites to imagine African Americans as anything more than lowly laborers, despite free blacks who clearly demonstrated otherwise.

Aware of the limited opportunities available in the United States, some African Americans considered the benefits of moving elsewhere. In the late 1780s, the Newport African Union Society in Rhode Island developed a plan to establish a community for American blacks in Africa. Many whites, too, viewed the settlement of blacks in Africa as the only way to solve the nation's racial dilemma.

Over the next three decades, the idea of emigration (as blacks viewed it) or colonization (as whites saw it) received widespread attention. Those who opposed slavery hoped to persuade slave owners to free or sell their human property on the condition that they be shipped

Benjamin Banneker's *Pennsylvania, Delaware, Maryland, and Virginia Almanac,* **1795** Benjamin Banneker (here spelled Bannaker) was a free black from Baltimore County, Maryland. Largely self-educated, he was a talented astronomer who compiled almanacs that included annual calendars, tide charts, lunar and solar observations, and statistical charts. Almanacs were widely used by farmers, sailors, and the general public. Banneker's almanac included his portrait to highlight his achievements as a black man. Granger, NYC

to Africa. Others assumed that free blacks could find opportunities in Africa that were not available to them in the United States. Still others simply wanted to rid the nation of its race problem by ridding it of blacks. In 1817 a group of southern slave owners and northern merchants formed the **American Colonization Society (ACS)** to establish colonies of freed slaves and free-born American blacks in Africa. Although some African Americans supported this scheme, northern free blacks generally opposed it, viewing colonization as an effort originating "more immediately from prejudice than philanthropy." Ultimately the plans of the ACS proved impractical. Particularly as cotton production expanded from the 1790s on, few slave owners were willing to emancipate their workers.

A New Capital for a New Nation. The construction of Washington City, the new capital, provided an opportunity to highlight the nation's distinctive culture and identity. But here, again, slavery emerged as a crucial part of that identity. The capital was situated along the Potomac River between Virginia and Maryland, an area where more than 300,000 enslaved workers lived. Between 1792 and 1809, hundreds of enslaved men and a few women were hired out by their owners, who were paid $5 per month for each individual's labor. Enslaved men cleared trees and stumps, built roads, dug trenches, baked bricks, and cut and laid sandstone while enslaved women cooked, did laundry, and nursed the

The United States Capitol   This watercolor by William Russell Birch presents a view of the Capitol in Washington, D.C., before it was burned down by the British during the War of 1812. Birch had emigrated from England in 1794 and lived in Philadelphia. As this painting suggests, neither the Capitol nor the city was as yet a vibrant center of republican achievements. Library of Congress, LC-DIG-ppmsca-22593

sick and injured. A small number performed skilled labor as carpenters or assistants to stonemasons and surveyors. Some four hundred slaves worked on the Capitol building alone, more than half the workforce.

Free blacks also participated in the development of Washington. Many worked alongside enslaved laborers, but a few held important positions. Benjamin Banneker, for example, a self-taught clock maker, astronomer, and surveyor, was hired as an assistant to the surveyor Major Andrew Ellicott. In 1791 Banneker helped to plot the 100-square-mile site on which the capital was to be built.

African Americans often worked alongside Irish immigrants, whose wages were kept in check by the availability of slave labor. Most workers, regardless of race, faced poor housing, sparse meals, malarial fevers, and limited medical care. Despite these obstacles, in less than a decade, a system of roads was laid out and cleared, the Executive Mansion was built, and the north wing of the Capitol was completed.

More prosperous immigrants and foreign professionals were also involved in creating the U.S. capital. Irish-born James Hoban designed the Executive Mansion. A French engineer developed the plan for the city's streets. A West Indian physician turned architect drew the blueprints for the Capitol building, the construction of which was directed by Englishman Benjamin Latrobe. Perhaps what was most "American" about the new capital was the diverse nationalities and races of those who designed and built it.

Washington's founders envisioned the city as a beacon to the world, proclaiming the advantages of the nation's republican principles. But its location on a slow-moving river and its clay soil left the area hot, humid, and dusty in the summer and muddy and damp in the winter and spring. When John Adams and his administration moved to Washington in June 1800, they considered themselves on the frontiers of civilization. The tree stumps that remained on the mile-long road from the Capitol to the Executive Mansion made it nearly impossible to navigate in a carriage. On rainy days, when roads proved impassable, officials walked or rode horses to work. Many early residents painted Washington in harsh tones. New Hampshire congressional representative Ebenezer Matroon wrote a friend, "If I wished to punish a culprit, I would send him to do penance in this place . . . this swamp— this lonesome dreary swamp, secluded from every delightful or pleasing thing."

Despite its critics, Washington was the seat of federal power and thus played an important role in the social and political worlds of American elites. From January through March, the height of the social season, the wives of congressmen, judges, and other officials created a lively schedule of teas, parties, and balls in the capital city. When Thomas Jefferson became president, he opened the White House to visitors on a regular basis. Yet for all his republican principles, Jefferson moved into the Executive Mansion with a retinue of slaves.

In decades to come, Washington City would become Washington, D.C., a city with broad boulevards decorated with beautiful monuments to the American political experiment. And the Executive Mansion would become the White House, a proud symbol of republican government. Yet Washington was always characterized by wide disparities in wealth, status, and power, which were especially visible when slaves labored in the Executive Mansion's kitchen, laundry, and yard. President Jefferson's efforts to incorporate new territories into the United States only exacerbated these divisions by providing more economic opportunities for planters, investors, and white farmers while ensuring the expansion of slavery and the decimation of American Indians.

REVIEW & RELATE

- How did developments in education, literature, and the arts contribute to the emergence of a distinctly American identity?

- How did blacks and American Indians both contribute to and challenge the predominantly white view of American identity?

Extending Federal Power

Thomas Jefferson, like other Democratic-Republicans, envisioned the United States as a republic composed of small, independent farmers who had little need and less desire for expansive federal power. Despite Jefferson's early efforts to impose this vision on the government, developments in international affairs soon converged with Supreme Court rulings to expand federal power. But Jefferson, too, contributed to this expansion. Imagining the nation's extensive frontiers as a boon to its development, he purchased the Louisiana Territory from France in 1803. The purchase and development of this vast territory increased federal authority. It also raised new questions about the place of Indians and African Americans in a republican society.

A New Administration Faces Challenges. In 1801 Democratic-Republicans worked quickly to implement their vision of limited federal power. Holding the majority in Congress, they repealed the whiskey tax and let the Alien and Sedition Acts expire. Jefferson significantly reduced government expenditures, and immediately set about slashing the national debt, cutting it nearly in half by the end of his second term. Democratic-Republicans also worked to curb the powers granted to the Bank of the United States and the federal court system.

Soon, however, international upheavals forced Jefferson to make fuller use of his presidential powers. The U.S. government had paid tribute to the Barbary States of North Africa during the 1790s to gain protection for American merchant ships. The new president opposed this practice and in 1801 refused to continue the payments. The Barbary pirates quickly resumed their attacks, and Jefferson was forced to send the U.S. Navy and Marine Corps to retaliate. Although a combined American and Arab force did not achieve their objective of capturing Tripoli, the Ottoman viceroy agreed to negotiate a new agreement with the United States. Seeking to avoid all-out war, Congress accepted a treaty with the Barbary States that reduced the tribute payment.

Jefferson had also followed the developing crisis in the West Indies during the 1790s. In 1791 slaves on the sugar-rich island of Saint Domingue launched a revolt against French rule. The **Haitian Revolution** escalated into a complicated conflict in which free people of color, white slave owners, and slaves formed competing alliances with British and Spanish forces as well as with leaders of the French Revolution. Finally, in December 1799, Toussaint L'Ouverture, a military leader and former slave, claimed the presidency of the new Republic of Haiti. But Napoleon Bonaparte seized power in France that same year and sent thousands of troops to reclaim the island. Toussaint was shipped off to France, where he died in prison, and many Haitians fled to the United States, but other Haitian rebels continued the fight.

Explore ▸

See Documents 8.2 and 8.3 for two views on the revolution in Haiti.

In the United States, reactions to the revolution were mixed, but southern whites feared that it might incite rebellions among their slaves. In 1800 Gabriel,

COMPARATIVE ANALYSIS

White Responses to Black Rebellion

White southerners who feared the effect of the Haitian Revolution were nonetheless shocked when Gabriel, an enslaved blacksmith, plotted a rebellion in Virginia. Upon the plot's discovery, thirty blacks were tried and convicted, and twenty-seven executed for conspiring to rebel. In the first document, President Jefferson expresses concern about slave rebellions but also about the punishment of insurgents. The second document, by Leonore Sansay, the wife of a Saint-Domingue planter, captures the situation in Haiti in 1802 as France fought to reclaim its colony. Sansay, who had earlier met Vice President Aaron Burr, writes to him about conditions on the island.

Document 8.2

Thomas Jefferson | Letter to U.S. Minister to Great Britain Rufus King, July 1802

The course of things in the neighboring islands of the West Indies appears to have given a considerable impulse to the minds of the slaves in different parts of the U.S. A great disposition to insurgency has manifested itself among them, which, in one instance, in the state of Virginia, broke out into actual insurrection. This was easily suppressed; but many of those concerned, (between 20 and 30, I believe) fell victims to the law. So extensive an execution could not but excite sensibility in the public mind, and beget a regret that the laws had not provided, for such cases, some alternative, combining more mildness with equal efficacy. The legislature of the state, at a subsequent meeting, took the subject into consideration, and have communicated to me . . . their wish that some place could be provided, out of the limits of the U.S., to which slaves guilty of insurgency might be transported; and they have particularly looked to Africa as offering the most desirable receptacle. We might for this purpose, enter into negotiations with the natives, on some part of the coast, to obtain a settlement and, by establishing an African company, combine with it commercial operations, which might not only reimburse expenses but procure profit also.

Source: Paul Leicester Ford, ed., *The Writings of Thomas Jefferson* (New York, 1896), 8:161–64.

an enslaved blacksmith in Richmond, Virginia, plotted such a rebellion. Inspired by both the American and Haitian revolutions, supporters rallied around the demand for "Death or Liberty." Gabriel's plan failed when informants betrayed him to authorities. Nonetheless, news of the plot traveled across the South and terrified white residents. Their anxieties were probably heightened when in November 1803, prolonged fighting, yellow fever, and the loss of sixty thousand soldiers forced Napoleon to admit defeat in Haiti. Haiti became the first independent black-led nation in the Americas.

Acquiring the Louisiana Territory. In France's defeat Jefferson saw an opportunity to gain navigation rights on the Mississippi River, which the French controlled. This

Document 8.3

Leonora Sansay | Letter to Aaron Burr, November 1802

The so much desired general Rochambeau is at length here. His arrival was announced . . . by the firing of cannon. . . . Nothing is heard of but the public joy. He is considered as the guardian, as the saviour of the people. Every proprietor feels himself already in his habitation [plantation] and I have even heard some of them disputing about the quality of the coffee they expect soon to gather. . . .

The arrival of General Rochambeau seems to have spread terror among the negroes[.] I wish they were reduced to order so that I might see the so much vaunted habitations where I should repose beneath the shade of orange groves, walk on carpets of rose leaves and Frenchipone; be fanned to sleep by silent slaves. . . .

What a delightful existence! . . .

But the moment of enjoying these pleasures is, I fear, far distant. The negroes have felt during ten years the blessing of liberty, for a blessing it certainly is, however acquired, and then will not easily be deprived of it. They have fought and vanquished French troops, and their strength has increased from a knowledge of the weakness of their opposer, and the climate itself combats for them. . . .

Every evening several old Creoles . . . assemble at our house, and talk of their affairs. One of them . . . now lives in a miserable hut. . . . Yet he still hopes for better days, in which hope they all join him.

Source: Mary Hassal [Leonora Sansay], *Secret History of the Horrors of St. Domingo, in a Series of Letters Written by a Lady at Cape François to Colonel Burr* (Philadelphia: Bradford & Inskelp, 1808), 430–32.

Interpret the Evidence

1. How does Thomas Jefferson view the influence of West Indies rebellions on U.S. slaves, and why is he reluctant to respond to conspiracies by executing large numbers of insurgents?
2. How would you compare Leonora Sansay's response to black rebellion in Saint-Domingue/Haiti with Jefferson's response to conspiracies in Virginia? What accounts for the similarities and differences?

Put It in Context

How might reports of the Haitian Revolution and the Virginia rebellion have contributed to debates over the future of slavery in the early years of the United States?

was a matter of crucial concern to Americans living west of the Appalachian Mountains. Jefferson sent James Monroe to France to offer Napoleon $2 million to ensure Americans the right of navigation and deposit (i.e., offloading cargo from ships) on the Mississippi. To Jefferson's surprise, Napoleon offered instead to sell the entire Louisiana Territory for $15 million.

The president agonized over the constitutionality of this **Louisiana Purchase**. Since the Constitution contained no provisions for buying land from foreign nations, a strict interpretation would prohibit the purchase. In the end, though, the opportunity proved too tempting, and the president finally agreed to buy the Louisiana Territory. Jefferson justified his decision by arguing that the territory would allow for the removal of more Indians from east of the Mississippi River, end European influence in the region, and expand U.S. trade networks. Opponents viewed the purchase as benefiting mainly agrarian interests and suspected Jefferson of trying to offset Federalist power in the Northeast. Neither party seemed especially concerned about the French, Spanish, or native peoples living in the region. They came under U.S. control when the Senate approved the purchase in October 1803. And the acquisition proved popular among ordinary Americans, most of whom focused on the opportunities it offered rather than the expansion of federal power it ensured.

At Jefferson's request, Congress had already appropriated funds for an expedition known as the **Corps of Discovery** to explore territory along the Missouri River. That expedition could now explore much of the Louisiana Territory. The president's personal secretary, Meriwether Lewis, headed the venture and invited fellow Virginian William Clark to serve as co-captain. The two set off with about forty-five men on May 14, 1804. For two years, they traveled thousands of miles up the Missouri River, through the northern plains, over the Rocky Mountains, and beyond the Louisiana Territory to the Pacific coast. Sacagawea and her husband joined them in April 1805 as they headed into the Rocky Mountains. Throughout the expedition, members meticulously recorded observations about local plants and animals as well as Indian residents, providing valuable evidence for young scientists like Parker Cleaveland and fascinating information for ordinary Americans. **See Document Project 8: The Corps of Discovery: Paeans to Peace and Instruments of War, page 270.**

Sacagawea was the only Indian to travel as a permanent member of the expedition, but many other native women and men assisted the Corps when it journeyed near their villages. They provided food and lodging for the Corps, hauled baggage up steep mountain trails, and traded food, horses, and other items. The one African American on the expedition, a slave named York, also helped negotiate trade with local Indians. York, who realized his value as a trader, hunter, and scout, asked Clark for his freedom when the expedition ended in 1806. York did eventually become a free man, but it is not clear whether it was by Clark's choice or York's escape.

Other expeditions followed Lewis and Clark's venture. In 1806 Lieutenant Zebulon Pike led a group to explore the southern portion of the Louisiana Territory (Map 8.1). After traveling from St. Louis to the Rocky Mountains, the expedition entered Mexican territory. In early 1807, Pike and his men were captured by Mexican forces. They were returned to the United States at the Louisiana border that July. Pike had learned a great deal about lands that would eventually become part of the United States and about Mexican desires to overthrow Spanish rule, information that proved valuable over the next two decades.

Early in this series of expeditions, in November 1804, Jefferson easily won reelection as president. His popularity among farmers, already high, increased when Congress reduced the minimum allotment for federal land sales from 320 to 160 acres. This act allowed more farmers to purchase land on their own rather than via speculators. Yet by the time of Jefferson's second inauguration in March 1805, the president's vision of limiting federal power had been shattered by his own actions and those of the Supreme Court.

The Supreme Court Extends Its Reach. In 1801, just before the Federalist-dominated Congress turned over power to the Democratic-Republicans, it passed a new **Judiciary Act**. The act created six additional circuit courts and sixteen new judgeships,

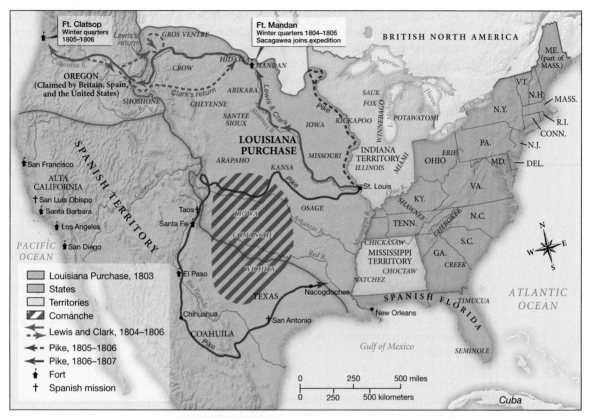

MAP 8.1 Lewis and Clark and Zebulon Pike Expeditions, 1804–1807

The expeditions led by Meriwether Lewis, William Clark, and Zebulon Pike illustrate the vast regions explored in just four years after the U.S. purchase of the Louisiana Territory. Journeying through and beyond the borders of that territory, the explorers gathered information about Indian nations, plants, animals, and the natural terrain even as Comanche and Shoshone nations, with access to horses, transformed the region.

which President Adams filled with Federalist "midnight appointments" before he left office. Jefferson accused the Federalists of having "retired into the judiciary" and worried that "from that battery all the works of Republicanism are to be beaten down and destroyed." Meanwhile John Marshall, chief justice of the United States (1801–1835), insisted that the powers of the Supreme Court must be equal to and balance those of the executive and legislative branches.

One of the first cases to test the Court's authority involved a dispute over President Adams's midnight appointments. Jefferson's secretary of state, James Madison, refused to deliver the appointment papers to several of the appointees, including William Marbury. Marbury and three others sued Madison to receive their commissions. In *Marbury v. Madison* (1803), the Supreme Court ruled that it was not empowered to force the executive branch to give Marbury his commission. But in his decision, Chief Justice Marshall declared that the Supreme Court did have the duty "to say what the law is." He thus asserted a fundamental constitutional power: that the Supreme Court had the authority to decide which federal laws were constitutional. The following year, the Court also claimed the right to rule on the constitutionality of state laws. In doing so, the Court rejected Democratic-Republicans' claim that state legislatures had the power to repudiate federal law.

Over the next dozen years, the Supreme Court continued to assert Federalist principles. In 1810 it insisted that it was the proper and sole arena for determining matters of constitutional interpretation. Then in 1819, the highest court reinforced its loose interpretation of the Constitution's implied powers clause in **McCulloch v. Maryland.** This clause gave the federal government the right to "make all laws which shall be necessary and proper" for carrying out the explicit powers granted to it by the Constitution. Despite Democratic-Republicans' earlier opposition to a national bank, Congress chartered the Second Bank of the United States in 1816, and its branch banks issued notes that circulated widely in local communities. Legislators in Maryland, believing that branch banks had gained excessive power, approved a tax on their operations. Marshall's Court ruled that the establishment of the bank was "necessary and proper" for the functioning of the national government and rejected Maryland's right to tax the branch bank, claiming that "the power to tax involves the power to destroy."

By 1820 the Supreme Court, under the forceful direction of John Marshall, had established the power of judicial review—the authority of the nation's highest court to rule on cases involving states as well as the nation. From the Court's perspective, the judiciary was as important an institution in framing and preserving a national agenda as Congress or the president.

Democratic-Republicans Expand Federal Powers.

Although Democratic-Republicans generally opposed Marshall's rulings, they, too, continued to expand federal power. Once again, international developments drove the Jefferson administration's political agenda. By 1805 the security of the United States was threatened by continued conflicts between France and Great Britain. Both sought alliances with the young nation, and both ignored U.S. claims of neutrality. Indeed, each nation sought to punish Americans for trading with the other. Britain's Royal Navy began stopping American ships carrying sugar and molasses from the French West Indies and, between 1802 and 1811, impressed more than eight thousand sailors from such ships, including many American citizens. France claimed a similar right to stop U.S. ships that continued to trade with Great Britain.

Unable to convince foreign powers to recognize U.S. neutrality, Jefferson and Madison pushed for congressional passage of an embargo that they hoped would, like colonial boycotts, force Great Britain's hand. In 1807 Congress passed the **Embargo Act**, which prohibited U.S. ships from leaving their home ports until Britain and France repealed their restrictions on American trade. Although the act kept the United States out of war, it had a devastating impact on national commerce.

New England merchants immediately voiced their outrage, and some began sending goods to Europe via Canada. In response, Congress passed the Force Act, granting extraordinary powers to customs officials to end such smuggling. The economic pain caused by the rapid decline in trade spread well beyond the merchant class. Parker Cleaveland was forced to sell his home to the Bowdoin trustees and become their tenant. Farmers and urban workers as well as southern planters suffered the embargo's effects more directly.

Opposition to the Embargo Act   Although Congress repealed the Embargo Act in 1809, lawmakers still barred the United States from trading with Great Britain and France, both of which attacked American shipping in violation of U.S. neutrality. This political cartoon by Alexander Anderson criticizes the embargo, which proved costly to merchants, sailors, and dockworkers. Here a merchant carrying a barrel of goods curses the snapping turtle "Ograbme," which is *embargo* spelled backward. Granger, NYC

Exports nearly stopped, and sailors and dockworkers faced escalating unemployment. With the recession deepening, American concerns about the expansion of federal power reemerged. Congress and the president had not simply regulated international trade; they had brought it to a halt.

Still, despite the failure of the Embargo Act, many Americans viewed Jefferson favorably. He had devoted his adult life to the creation of the United States. He had purchased the Louisiana Territory, opening up vast lands to American exploration and development. This geographical boon encouraged inventors and artisans to pursue ideas that would help the early republic take full advantage of its resources and recover from its current economic plight. Some must have wondered, however, how a Democratic-Republican president had so significantly expanded the power of the federal government.

REVIEW & RELATE

- How did the Federalist-dominated courts and the Democratic-Republican president and Congress each contribute to the expansion of the federal government?

- How did the purchase of the Louisiana Territory from France and international conflicts with France and Britain shape domestic issues in the late eighteenth and early nineteenth centuries?

Remaking America's Economic Character

As the United States expanded geographically, techno-logical ingenuity became a highly valued commodity. The spread of U.S. settlements into new territories necessitated improved forms of transportation and communication and increased demands for muskets and other weapons to protect the nation's frontier. The growing population also fueled improvements in agriculture and manufacturing to meet demands for clothing, food, and farm equipment. Continued conflicts with Great Britain and France also highlighted the need to develop the nation's natural resources and technological capabilities. Yet even though American ingenuity was widely praised, the daily lives of most Americans changed slowly. And for some, especially enslaved women and men, technological advances only added to their burdens.

The U.S. Population Grows and Migrates.
Although Democratic-Republi-cans initially hoped to limit the powers of the national government, the rapid growth of the United States pulled in the opposite direction. An increased population, combined with the exhaustion of farmland along the eastern seaboard, fueled migration to the West as well as the growth of cities. These developments heightened conflicts with Indians and over slavery, but they also encouraged innovations in transportation and communication and improvements in agriculture and manufacturing.

As white Americans encroached more deeply on lands long settled by native peoples, Indian tribes were forced ever westward. As early as 1800, groups like the Shoshone, who originally inhabited the Great Plains, had been forced into the Rocky Mountains by Indi-ans moving into the plains from the Mississippi and Ohio valleys (Map 8.2). Sacagawea must have realized that the expedition she accompanied would only increase pressure on the Shoshone and other nations as white migration escalated.

Although the vast majority of Americans continued to live in rural areas, a growing number moved to cities as eastern farmland lost its fertility and young people sought job opportunities in manufacturing, skilled trades, and service work. Cities were defined at the time as places with 8,000 or more inhabitants, but New York City and Philadelphia both counted more than 100,000 residents by 1810. In New York, immigrants, most of them Irish, made up about 10 percent of the population in 1820 and twice that percentage five years later. At the same time, the number of African Americans in New York City increased to more than 10,000. Cities began to emerge along the nation's frontier as well. After the Louisiana Purchase, New Orleans became a key commercial center while west-ern migration fueled cities like Cincinnati. Even smaller frontier towns, like Rock Island, Illinois, served important functions for migrants traveling west. Trading posts appeared across the Mississippi valley, which eased the migration of thousands headed farther west. They served as sites of exchange between Indians and white Americans and created the foundations for later cities (Table 8.1).

Most Americans who headed west hoped to benefit from the increasingly liberal terms for land offered by the federal government. Yeomen farmers sought sufficient acre-age to feed their families and grow some crops for sale. They were eager to settle in west-ern sections of the original thirteen states, in the Ohio River valley, or in newly opened territories along the Missouri and Kansas Rivers. In the South, small farmers had to com-pete with slave-owning planters who headed west in the early nineteenth century. Migrants to the Mississippi valley also had to contend with a sizable population of Spanish and French residents, as well as Chickasaw and Creek Indians in the South and Shawnee, Chippewa, Sauk, and Fox communities farther north.

The development of roads and turnpikes hastened the movement of people and the transportation of goods. Frontier farmers wanted to get their produce to eastern markets quickly and cheaply. Before completion of the Lancaster Turnpike in Pennsylvania, it cost as much to carry wheat overland the sixty-two miles to Philadelphia as it did to ship it by sea from Philadelphia to London. Those who lived farther west faced even greater challenges. With the admission of Kentucky (1792), Tennessee (1796), and Ohio (1803) to the Union,

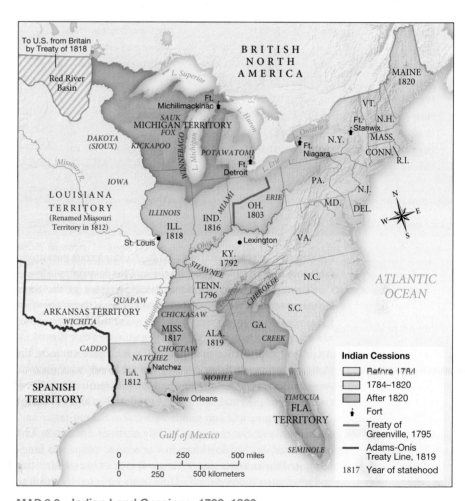

MAP 8.2   Indian Land Cessions, 1790–1820

With the ratification of the Constitution, the federal government gained greater control over Indian relations, including land cessions. At the same time, large numbers of white settlers poured into regions west of the Appalachian Mountains. The U.S. government gained most Indian land by purchase or treaty, but these agreements were often the consequence of military victories by the U.S. Army.

TABLE 8.1   Prices at George Davenport's Trading Post, Rock Island, Illinois, c. 1820

Item	Price	Item	Price
Ax	$6.00	Large copper kettle	$30.00
Beaver trap	$8.00	Lead	$0.20 per pound
Black silk handkerchief	$2.00	Lead shot for guns	$1.00 per 5 pounds
Breechcloth	$3.00	Medium copper kettle	$10.00
Bridles	$2.00–$10.00	Muskrat spear	$2.00
Chain for staking down traps	$0.75 per 6 feet	Muskrat trap	$5.00
Combs	$1.00 per pair	Muslin or calico shirt	$3.00
File (for sharpening axes)	$2.00	Ordinary butcher knife	$0.50
Flannel	$1.00 per yard	Sheet iron kettle	$10.00
Flannel mantle	$3.00	Small copper kettle	$3.00
Gunflints	$1.00 per 15	Spurs	$6.00 per pair
Hand-size mirrors	$0.25	Tin kettle	$14.00
Heavy wool cloth	$10.00 per yard	Tomahawk	$1.50
Hoe	$2.00	Trade gun	$20.00–$25.00
Horn of gunpowder	$1.50	Wool blanket	$4.00
Horses	$35.00–$50.00	Wool mantle (short cloak or shawl)	$4.00

Source: Will Leinicke, Marion Lardner, and Ferrel Anderson, *Two Nations, One Land* (Rock Island, IL: Citizens to Preserve Black Hawk Park, 1981).

demands for congressional support for building transportation routes grew louder. By 1819 five more states had been admitted along the Mississippi River, from Louisiana to Illinois.

During Jefferson's administration, secretary of the treasury Albert Gallatin urged Congress to fund roads and canals to enhance the economic development of the nation. He advocated a "great turnpike road" along the Atlantic seaboard from Maine to Georgia as well as roads to connect the four main rivers that flowed from the Appalachians to the Atlantic Ocean. Although traditionally such projects were funded by the states, in 1815 Congress approved funds for a **National Road** from western Maryland through southwestern Pennsylvania to Wheeling, West Virginia. This so-called Cumberland Road was completed in 1818 and later extended into Ohio and Illinois.

Carrying people and goods by water was even faster and cheaper than transporting them over land, but rivers ran mainly north and south. In addition, although loads could be delivered quickly downstream, the return voyage was long and slow. While politicians advocated the construction of canals along east-west routes to link river systems, inventors and mechanics focused on building boats powered by steam to overcome the problems of sending goods upriver.

In 1804 Oliver Evans, a machinist in Philadelphia, invented a high-pressure steam engine attached to a dredge that cleaned the silt around the docks in Philadelphia harbor. He had insufficient funds, however, to pursue work on a steam-powered boat. Robert Fulton, a New Yorker, improved on Evans's efforts, using the low-pressure steam engine developed in England. In 1807 Fulton launched the first successful steamboat, the *Clermont*, which traveled up the Hudson River from New York City to Albany in only thirty-two hours. The powerful Mississippi River proved a greater challenge, but by combining Evans's high-pressure steam engine with a flat-bottom hull that avoided the river's sandbars, mechanics who worked along the frontier improved Fulton's design and launched the steamboat era in the West.

Technology Reshapes Agriculture and Industry.
Advances in agricultural and industrial technology paralleled the development of roads and steamboats. Here, too, a single invention spurred others, inducing a **multiplier effect** that inspired additional dramatic changes. Two inventions—the cotton gin and the spinning machine—were especially notable in transforming southern agriculture and northern industry, transformations that were deeply intertwined.

American developments were also closely tied to the earlier rise of industry in Great Britain. By the 1770s, British manufacturers had built spinning mills in which steam-powered machines spun raw cotton into yarn. Eager to maintain their monopoly on industrial technology, the British made it illegal for engineers to emigrate. They could not stop

Samuel Slater's Mill, c. 1790   This eighteenth-century painting by an unknown American artist depicts the first cotton mill built in the United States. Constructed by Samuel Slater on the Blackstone River in Pawtucket, Rhode Island, the mill stands next to a waterfall, which supplies the power to run the machinery. While portraying a major industrial innovation, the artist highlights its pastoral setting. Smithsonian Institution, Washington DC, USA/Bridgeman Images

everyone who worked in a cotton mill, however, from leaving. At age fourteen, Samuel Slater was hired as an apprentice in an English mill that used a yarn-spinning machine designed by Richard Arkwright. Slater was promoted to supervisor of the factory, but at age twenty-one he sought greater opportunities in America. While working in New York City, he learned that Moses Brown, a wealthy Rhode Island merchant, was eager to develop a machine like Arkwright's. Funded by Rhode Island investors and assisted by local craftsmen, Slater designed and built a spinning mill in Pawtucket.

The mill opened in December 1790 and began producing yarn, which was then woven into cloth in private shops and homes. By 1815 a series of cotton mills dotted the Pawtucket River. These factories offered workers, most of whom were the wives and children of farmers, a steady income, and they ensured employment for weavers in the countryside. They also increased the demand for cotton in New England just as British manufacturers sought new sources of the crop as well.

Explore ▶

See Document 8.4 for a description of mills in Worcester, Massachusetts.

Ensuring a steady supply of cotton required another technological innovation, this one created by Eli Whitney. After graduating from Yale, Whitney agreed to serve as a private tutor for a planter family in South Carolina. On the ship carrying him south, Whitney met the widow Catherine Greene, who invited him to stay at her Mulberry Plantation near Savannah, Georgia. There local planters complained to him about the difficulty of making a profit on cotton. Long-staple cotton, grown in the Sea Islands, yielded enormous profits, but the soil in most of the South could sustain only the short-staple variety, which required hours of intensive labor to separate its sticky green seeds from the cotton fiber.

In 1793, in as little as ten days, Eli Whitney built a machine that could speed the process of deseeding short-staple cotton. Using mesh screens, rollers, and wire brushes, Whitney's **cotton gin** could clean as much cotton fiber in one hour as several workers could

The Cotton Gin, 1793   This colored lithograph by an anonymous American artist shows Eli Whitney's cotton gin at the center of complex transactions. Enslaved women and men haul and gin cotton. Meanwhile the planter appears to be bargaining with a cotton factor, or agent, who likely wants to purchase his crop for a northern manufacturer. Private Collection/Peter Newark American Pictures/Bridgeman Images

clean in a day. Recognizing the gin's value, Whitney received a U.S. patent, but because the machine was easy to duplicate, he never profited from his invention.

Fortunately, Whitney had other ideas that proved more profitable. In June 1798, amid U.S. fears of a war with France, the U.S. government granted him an extraordinary contract to produce 4,000 rifles in eighteen months. Adapting the plan of Honoré Blanc, a French mechanic who devised a musket with interchangeable parts, Whitney demonstrated the potential for using machines to produce various parts of a musket, which could then be assembled in mass quantities. With Jefferson's enthusiastic support, the federal government extended Whitney's contract, and by 1809 his New Haven factory was turning

SOLO ANALYSIS

Timothy Dwight | Visit to Worcester (Massachusetts) Mills, 1821

American industry began in earnest in New England, and mills there garnered great attention from interested observers at home and abroad. In 1821 Timothy Dwight, the president of Yale College, published his impression of various New England towns in his *Travels*, including the bustling commercial center of Worcester, Massachusetts. After describing the town and the great variety of mills located along the Blackstone River, he notes the ubiquity of such mills throughout New England.

Document 8.4

Few towns in New-England exhibit so uniform an appearance of neatness and taste or contain so great a proportion of good buildings, and so small a proportion of those which are indifferent, as Worcester. There is probably more wealth in it also than in any other, which does not exceed it in dimensions and number of inhabitants. Its trade, considering its inland situation, is believed to be extensive and profitable. . . .

There are in Worcester four grist-mills, four saw-mills, two fulling-mills, and a large paper-mill. The proprietors of the fulling-mills carry on the Clothiers' business to a great extent; and with skill supposed not to be excelled in the State. Scarlet and blue have for some time been dyed here in a superiour manner.

On the subject of *mills* I wish you to observe, once for all, that I shall rarely mention them. There is scarcely a township in New-England which has not a complete set of grist-mills and saw-mills. . . . There is, probably, no country in the world where mill-streams are so numerously and universally dispersed, or grist-mills and saw-mills so universally erected as in New-England. Conveniences of this kind may be said, almost if not quite literally, to be furnished in abundance to every Parish in the Country. To reiterate this fact would be to take very effectual means for wearing out your patience.

Source: Timothy Dwight, *Travels; in New-England and New-York* (New Haven: Timothy Dwight, 1821), 366–67.

Interpret the Evidence

1. How does Dwight characterize Worcester? What role do the mills play in his assessment?
2. Why does Dwight say he is not going to discuss mills elsewhere in his book?

Put It in Context

What does Dwight's report reveal about the industrial innovations occurring in the northeastern United States in the early nineteenth century?

out 7,500 guns annually. Whitney's factory became a model for the **American system of manufacturing**, in which water-powered machinery and the division of production into several small tasks allowed less skilled workers to produce mass quantities of a particular item. Moreover, the factories developed by Whitney and Slater became training grounds for younger mechanics and inventors who devised improvements in machinery or set out to solve new technological puzzles. Their efforts also transformed the lives of generations of workers—enslaved and free—who planted and picked the cotton, spun the yarn, wove the cloth, and sewed the clothes that cotton gins and spinning mills made possible.

Transforming Household Production. Slater and Whitney were among the most influential American inventors, but both required the assistance and collaboration of other inventors, machinists, and artisans to implement their ideas. The achievement of these enterprising individuals was seen by many Americans as part of a larger spirit of inventiveness and technological ingenuity that characterized U.S. identity. Although many Americans built on foreign ideas and models, a cascade of inventions did appear in the United States between 1790 and 1820.

Cotton gins and steam engines, steamboats and interchangeable parts, gristmills and spinning mills—each of these items and processes was improved over time and led to myriad other inventions. For instance, in 1811 Francis Cabot invented a power loom for weaving, a necessary step once spinning mills began producing more yarn than hand weavers could handle.

Despite these rapid technological advances, the changes that occurred in the early nineteenth century were more evolutionary than revolutionary. Most political leaders and social commentators viewed gradual improvement as a blessing. For many Americans, the ideal situation consisted of either small mills scattered through the countryside or household enterprises that could supply neighbors with finer cloth, wool cards, or other items that improved home production.

The importance of domestic manufacturing increased after passage of the Embargo Act as imports of cloth and other items fell dramatically. Small factories, like those along the Pawtucket River, increased their output, and so did ordinary housewives. Blacksmiths, carpenters, and wheelwrights busily repaired and improved the spindles, looms, and other equipment that allowed family members to produce more and better cloth from wool, flax, and cotton. New ideas about companionate marriage, which emphasized mutual obligations, may have encouraged husbands and wives to work more closely in these domestic enterprises. While husbands generally carried out the heavier or more skilled parts of home manufacturing, like weaving, wives spun yarn and sewed together sections of cloth into finished goods.

At the same time, daughters, neighbors, and servants remained critical to the production of household items. In early nineteenth-century Hallowell, Maine, Martha Ballard labored alongside her daughters and a niece, producing cloth and food for domestic consumption, while she supplemented her husband's income as a surveyor by working as a midwife. Yet older forms of mutuality also continued, with neighbors sharing tools and equipment and those with specialized skills assisting neighbors in exchange for items they needed. Perhaps young couples imagined themselves embarking on more egalitarian marriages than those of their parents, but most still needed wider networks of support.

In wealthy households north and south, servants and slaves took on a greater share of domestic labor in the late eighteenth and early nineteenth centuries. Most female servants in the North were young and unmarried. Some arrived with children in tow or became pregnant while on the job, a mark of the rising rate of out-of-wedlock births following the Revolution. Planters' wives in the South had fewer worries in this regard because if household slaves became pregnant, their children added to the owner's labor supply. Moreover, on larger plantations, owners increasingly assigned a few enslaved women to spin, cook, wash clothes, make candles, and wait on table. Plantation mistresses might also hire the wives of small farmers and landless laborers to spin cotton into yarn, weave yarn into cloth, and sew clothing for slaves and children. While mistresses in both regions still engaged in household production, they expanded their roles as domestic managers.

However, most Americans at the turn of the nineteenth century continued to live on family farms, to produce or trade locally to meet their needs, and to use techniques handed down for generations. Yet by 1820, their lives, like those of wealthier Americans, were transformed by the expanding market economy. More and more families sewed clothes with machine-spun thread made from cotton ginned in the American South, worked their fields with newly invented cast-iron plows, and varied their diet by adding items shipped from other regions by steamboat.

Technology, Cotton, and Slaves. Some of the most dramatic technological changes occurred in agriculture, and none was more significant than the cotton gin, which led to the vast expansion of agricultural production and slavery in the South. This in turn fueled regional specialization, ensuring that residents in one area of the nation—the North, South, or West—depended on those in other areas. Southern planters relied on a growing demand for cotton from northern merchants and manufacturers. At the same time, planters, merchants, manufacturers, and factory workers became more dependent on western farmers to produce grain and livestock to feed the nation.

As cotton gins spread across the South, cotton and slavery expanded into the interior of many southern states as well as into the lower Mississippi valley. While rice and sugar were also produced in the South, cotton quickly became the most important crop. In 1790 southern farms and plantations produced about 3,000 bales of cotton, each weighing about 300 pounds. By 1820, with the aid of the cotton gin, the South produced more than 330,000 bales annually (Table 8.2). For southern blacks, increased production meant increased burdens. Because seeds could be separated from raw cotton with much greater efficiency, farmers could plant vastly larger quantities of the crop. Although family members, neighbors, and hired hands performed this work on small farms with only a few or no slaves, wealthy planters, with perhaps a dozen slaves, took advantage of rising cotton prices in the early eighteenth century to purchase more slaves.

The dramatic increase in the amount of cotton planted and harvested each year was paralleled by a jump in the size of the slave population. Thus, even as northern states began to abolish

TABLE 8.2 Growth of Cotton Production in the United States, 1790–1830

Year	Production in Bales
1790	3,135
1795	16,719
1800	73,145
1805	146,290
1810	177,638
1815	208,986
1820	334,378
1825	532,915
1830	731,452

Source: Lewis Cecil Gray, *History of Agriculture in the Southern United States to 1860*, vol. 2 (Gloucester, MA: Peter Smith, 1958).

the institution, southern planters significantly increased the number of slaves they held. In 1790 there were fewer than 700,000 slaves in the United States. By 1820 there were nearly 1.5 million. Despite this population increase, growing competition for field hands drove up the price of slaves, which roughly doubled between 1795 and 1805.

Although the international slave trade was banned in the United States in 1808, some planters smuggled in women and men from Africa and the Caribbean. Most planters, however, depended on enslaved women to bear more children, increasing the size of their labor force through natural reproduction. In addition, planters in the Deep South—from Georgia and the Carolinas west to Louisiana—began buying slaves from farmers in Maryland and Virginia, where cotton and slavery were less profitable. Expanding slave markets in New Orleans and Charleston marked the continued importance of this domestic or internal slave trade as cotton moved west.

In the early nineteenth century, most white southerners believed that there was enough land to go around. And the rising price of cotton allowed small farmers to imagine they would someday be planters. Some southern Indians also placed their hopes in cotton. Cherokee and Creek Indians cultivated the crop, even purchasing black slaves to increase production. Some Indian villages now welcomed ministers to their communities, hoping that embracing white culture might allow them to retain their current lands. Yet other native residents foresaw the increased pressure for land that cotton cultivation produced and organized to defend themselves from whites' invasion. Regardless of the policies adopted by Indians, cotton and slavery expanded rapidly into Cherokee- and Creek-controlled lands in the interior of Georgia and South Carolina. And the admission of the states of Louisiana, Mississippi, and Alabama between 1812 and 1819 marked the rapid spread of southern agriculture farther west.

Enslaved men and women played critical roles in the South's geographical expansion. Without their labor, neither cotton nor sugar could have become mainstays of the South's economy. The heavy work of carving out new plantations led most planters to select young slave men and women to move west, breaking apart families in the process. Some slaves resisted their removal and, if forced to go, used their role in the labor process to limit owners' control. Slaves resisted by working slowly, breaking tools, and feigning illness or injury. Other enslaved women and men hid out temporarily as a respite from brutal work regimes or harsh punishments. Still others ran to areas controlled by Indians, hoping for better treatment, or to regions where slavery was no longer legal.

Yet given the power and resources wielded by whites, most slaves had to find ways to improve their lives within the system of bondage. The end of the international slave trade helped blacks in this regard since planters had to depend more on natural reproduction to increase their labor supply. To ensure that slaves lived longer and healthier lives, planters were forced to provide better food, shelter, and clothing. Some slaves gained leverage to fish, hunt, or maintain small gardens to improve their diet. With the birth of more children, southern blacks also developed more extensive kinship networks, which often allowed other family members to care for children if their parents were compelled to move west. Enslavement was still brutal, but slaves made small gains that improved their chances of survival.

Southern slaves also established their own religious ceremonies, often held in the woods or swamps at night. African Americans were swept up as well in the religious revivals that burned across the southern frontier beginning in the 1790s. Itinerant preachers held camp meetings that tapped into deep emotional wells of spirituality. Baptist and Methodist clergy drew free and enslaved blacks as well as white frontier families to their gatherings and encouraged physical displays of spiritual rebirth, offering poor blacks and whites release from the oppressive burdens of daily life through dancing, shaking, and shouting.

Evangelical religion, combined with revolutionary ideals promoted in the United States and Haiti, proved a potent mix, and planters rarely lost sight of the potential dangers this posed to the system of bondage. Outright rebellions occurred only rarely, yet victory in Haiti and Gabriel's conspiracy in Virginia reminded slaves and owners alike that uprisings were possible. Clearly, the power of new American identities could not be separated from the dangers embedded in the nation's oppressive racial history.

REVIEW & RELATE

- How did new inventions and infrastructure improvements contribute to the development of the American economy?

- Why did slavery expand and become more deeply entrenched in southern society in the early nineteenth century? What fears did this reinforce?

Conclusion: New Identities and New Challenges

The geographical and economic expansion that marked the period from 1790 to 1820 inspired scientific and technological advances as well as literary and artistic tributes to a distinctly American identity. For young ambitious men like Parker Cleaveland, Eli Whitney, Washington Irving, and Meriwether Lewis, the opportunities that opened in education, science, literature, and exploration offered possibilities for fame and financial success. While Whitney, Irving, and Lewis traveled widely, Cleaveland remained a professor of mathematics, mineralogy, and chemistry at Bowdoin, dying in Brunswick, Maine, in 1858.

Lewis's efforts to open up the Louisiana Territory transformed the lives of many Americans. Along with the construction of roads, the invention of steamboats, and the introduction of iron plows, his Corps of Discovery opened up new lands for farming and also fueled the rise of western cities. Many white families sought fertile land, abundant wildlife, or opportunities for trade on the frontier. Yet these families often had to purchase land from speculators or compete with wealthy planters. And those who carved out farms might face Indians angered by the constant encroachment of white Americans on their lands.

New opportunities also appeared in eastern towns and cities as investors, inventors, and skilled artisans established factories and improved transportation. White women of middling or elite status could attend female academies, enter marriages based on ideals of companionship and mutual responsibilities, purchase rather than make cotton thread and cloth, and retain servants to perform the heaviest work. Yet these changes occurred gradually and unevenly. And while poorer white women might more easily find jobs in cotton mills or as servants, the pay was low and the hours long.

Transformations in white society introduced even more difficult challenges for African Americans. Despite the introduction of gradual emancipation in the North and the end of the international slave trade, slavery continued to grow. The invention of the cotton gin ensured the expansion of cotton cultivation into new areas, and many slaves were forced to move west and leave family and friends behind. Enslaved women and men honed means of survival and resistance, but few could imagine a revolution like the one that took place in Haiti.

At the same time, all along the expanding U.S. frontier, American Indians faced continued pressure to leave their lands, embrace white culture, or both. In 1810 Sacagawea, Charbonneau, and their son Baptiste apparently traveled to St. Louis at the invitation of William Clark, who offered to pay for Baptiste's schooling. Sacagawea left Baptiste in Clark's care, and it is not clear whether she ever saw her son again. William Clark wrote "Se car ja we au Dead" on the cover of his cash book for 1825–1828, suggesting that she died during those years. By then, the Shoshone and Hidatsa were facing the onslaught of white settlement. They, along with Indians living in areas like Georgia, the Carolinas, and Tennessee, continued to resist U.S. expansion and struggled to control the embattled frontier.

Indeed, the United States remained embattled throughout the early years of the republic. From 1790 to 1820, Great Britain, France, and the Barbary States of North Africa constantly challenged U.S. sovereignty from abroad while debates over slavery and conflicts over Indian lands multiplied at home. Moreover, as federal power expanded under Democratic-Republic rule, some Americans continued to worry about protecting the rights of states and of individuals. The American identities forged in the early republic would be continually tested as new challenges emerged and older conflicts intensified in the following decades.

TIMELINE OF EVENTS

1789	Massachusetts institutes free public elementary education
1790	Samuel Slater's spinning mill opens
1790–1820	Cotton production in the South increases from 3,000 to 330,000 bales annually
	U.S. slave population rises from 700,000 to 1.5 million
1791–1803	Haitian Revolution
1792–1809	New capital of Washington City constructed
1793	Eli Whitney invents cotton gin
1801	Judiciary Act
	U.S. forces challenge Barbary pirates
1803	Louisiana Purchase
	Marbury v. Madison
1804–1806	Corps of Discovery explores Louisiana Territory and Pacific Northwest
1807	Robert Fulton launches first successful steamboat
	Embargo Act
1810	Population of New York and Philadelphia each exceeds 100,000
1817	American Colonization Society founded
1819	*McCulloch v. Maryland*
1820	Washington Irving publishes *Sketchbook*
1828	Noah Webster publishes *American Dictionary of the English Language*

KEY TERMS

American Colonization Society (ACS), *249*

Haitian Revolution, *251*

Louisiana Purchase, *253*

Corps of Discovery, *254*

Judiciary Act, *254*

Marbury v. Madison , *255*

McCulloch v. Maryland, *256*

Embargo Act, *256*

National Road, *260*

multiplier effect, *261*

cotton gin, *262*

American system of manufacturing, *264*

REVIEW & RELATE

1. How did developments in education, literature, and the arts contribute to the emergence of a distinctly American identity?

2. How did blacks and American Indians both contribute to and challenge the predominantly white view of American identity?

3. How did the Federalist-dominated courts and the Democratic-Republican president and Congress each contribute to the expansion of the federal government?

4. How did the purchase of the Louisiana Territory from France and international conflicts with France and Britain shape domestic issues in the late eighteenth and early nineteenth centuries?

5. How did new inventions and infrastructure improvements contribute to the development of the American economy?

6. Why did slavery expand and become more deeply entrenched in southern society in the early nineteenth century? What fears did this reinforce?

The Corps of Discovery: Paeans to Peace and Instruments of War

From 1804 to 1806, the Corps of Discovery mapped vast regions of the West, documented plants and animals, and initiated trade relations with Indian nations. When the Corps built its winter camp at Fort Mandan in October 1804, its members hoped to develop commercial relations with local Mandan, Hidatsa, and Arikara villages. Most of these tribes had been ravaged by smallpox in the early 1780s and were now subject to raids by more powerful nations in the region. Meriwether Lewis and William Clark hoped to persuade all of these nations that peaceful relations would benefit them politically and economically. To aid negotiations, the Corps offered gifts to the Indian leaders they encountered (Document 8.5). The Mandan, however, expected more gifts than the expedition could offer. Although Lewis and Clark assured Mandan leaders they would benefit from future trade with and protection from the United States, the Indians had heard such promises before and were wary of giving away vital food as winter descended (Document 8.6).

Worried about surviving the winter, Lewis and Clark finally found an unexpected item to trade with the Mandan. When their men finished building a smithy in December 1804, they discovered that Indians would exchange almost any item for metal hatchets, especially those designed for battle (Documents 8.7 and 8.8).

In April the Corps moved west into present-day Idaho and traded with Shoshone leaders for horses. The Shoshone were engaged in a long and lucrative trade in horses with the Comanche, who had split from the Shoshones, moved south, and developed ties with the Spanish. But the Shoshone had a harder time getting guns, a concern they expressed to Lewis (Document 8.9). While Lewis and Clark advocated peace among Indian nations, one of their most desired trade items was weaponry. When their explorations inspired white settlement in this vast western territory, that weaponry would become more important than ever.

Document 8.5

William Clark, Journal | October 12, 1804

As the Corps of Discovery traveled up the Missouri River from St. Louis, they stopped at Indian villages along the way to advocate peace; offer presents from President Jefferson; and learn about local plants, animals, and potential trade items. In his journal entry for October 12, William Clark describes a visit to a Ricara (Arikara) village near where the Corps planned to stay for the winter.

After breakfast, we went on shore to the house of the chief of the second village named Lassel, where we found his chiefs and warriors. They made us a present of about seven bushels of corn, a pair of leggings, a twist of their tobacco, and the seeds of two different species of tobacco. The chief then delivered a speech expressive of his gratitude for the presents and the good counsels which we had given him; his intention of visiting his great father [the president of the United States] but for fear of the Sioux; and requested us to take one of the Ricara chiefs up to the Mandans and negotiate a peace between the two nations. . . . After we had answered and explained the magnitude and power of the United States, the three chiefs came with us to the boat. We gave them some sugar, a little salt, and a sun-glass. Two of them left us, and the chief of the third [village] . . . accompanied us to the Mandans.

[T]he Ricaras . . . were originally colonies of Pawnees, who established themselves on the Missouri. . . . From that situation, a part of the Ricaras emigrated to the neighbourhood of the Mandans, with whom they were then in alliance. The rest of the nation continued near the Chayenne [Cheyenne] till the year 1797, in the course of which, distressed by their wars with the Sioux, they joined their countrymen near the Mandans. Soon after a new war arose between the Ricaras and the Mandans, in consequence of which the former came down the river to their present position. . . .

They [the Ricara] express a disposition to keep at peace with all nations, but they are well armed with fusils [muskets], and being much under the influence of the Sioux, who exchanged the goods which they got from the British for Ricara corn, their minds are sometimes poisoned and they cannot always be depended on.

Source: William Clark Journal, October 12, 1804, *History of the Expeditions of Captains Lewis and Clark, 1804-5-6, Reprinted from the Edition of 1814, with Introduction and Index by James K. Hosmer* (Chicago: A. C. McClurg, 1902), 1:110–11, 114.

Document 8.6

Charles McKenzie | Narrative of a Fur Trader, November 1804

Charles McKenzie was a Scotsman working as a clerk for the Hudson Bay Company. He arrived with six traders at a Hidatsa village in November 1804. Over time, McKenzie adopted Indian dress, married an Indian woman, and became an advocate for Indian concerns. Here he recounts Lewis's frustration in his efforts to gain favor with local Indians as well as Mandan concerns about the Corps' lack of generosity.

Here we also found a party of forty Americans under the command of Captains Lewis and Clark exploring a passage by the Missisour [Missouri] to the Pacific Ocean—they came up the River in a Boat of twenty oars accompanied by two *Peroque*s [open boats or canoes]. Their fortifications for winter Quarters were already complete—they had held a council with the Mandanes, and

distributed many presents; but most of the Chiefs did not accept any thing from them. Some time after Captain Lewis with three Interpreters paid a visit to the *Gros Ventres* [Hidatsa] Village. . . . [N]ext morning he came to the village where I was—and observed to me that he was not very graciously received at the upper Village. . . .

After haranguing the Indians and explaining to them the purport of his [Lewis's] expedition to the Westward, several of them accepted clothing—but notwithstanding they could not be reconciled to like these strangers as they called them:—"Had these Whites come amongst us, Said the Chiefs, with charitable views they would have loaded their Great Boat with necessaries [trade items]. It is true they have ammunition but they prefer throwing it away idly [shooting in the air] than sparing a shot of it to a poor Mandane." . . . "Had I these White warriors in the upper plains, said the *Gros Ventres* Chief, my young men on horseback would soon do for them, as they would do for so many wolves—for, continued he, there are only two sensible men among them— the worker of Iron, and the mender of Guns."

The American Gentlemen gave flags and medals to the Chiefs on condition that they should not go to war unless the enemy attacked them in their Villages. Yet the Chief of the wolves, whose brother had been killed in the fall previous to our arrival, went soon after with a party of fifty men to revenge his death.

Source: W. Raymond Wood and Thomas D. Thiessen, eds., *Early Fur Trade on the Northern Plains: Canadian Traders among the Mandan and Hidatsa Indians, 1738–1818* (Norman: University of Oklahoma Press, 1985), 232–33.

Document 8.7

William Clark | Journal, November 18, 1804

By November 1804, the Corps had built and settled into Fort Mandan, at the convergence of the Missouri and Knife Rivers, for the winter. Lewis and Clark became increasingly aware that their trade with particular groups, like the Mandans, might shift the balance of power in the region. But given the extended journey ahead, they were limited in what goods they could give or trade with local Indians even as they sought to reassure them of U.S. support.

To-day we had a cold windy morning; the Black Cat [a Mandan chief] came to see us, and occupied us for a long time with questions on the usages [customs] of our country. He mentioned that a council had been held yesterday to deliberate on the state of their affairs. It seems that not long ago a party of Sioux fell in with some horses belonging to the Minnetarees and carried them off, but in their flight they were met by some Assiniboins, who killed the Sioux and kept the horses. A Frenchman, too, who had lived many years among the Mandans, was lately killed on his route to the British factory [trading post] on the Assiniboin . . . , all of which being discussed, the council decided that they would not resent the recent insults from the Assiniboins . . . until they had seen whether we had deceived them or not in our promises of furnishing them with arms and ammunition. They had been disappointed in their hopes of receiving them from Mr. Evans, and were afraid that we, too, like him, might tell them what was not true. We advised them to continue at peace, that supplies of every kind would no doubt arrive for them, but that time was necessary to organize the trade. The fact is that the Assiniboins treat the Mandans as the Sioux do the Ricaras; by their vicinity to the British they get all the supplies, which they withhold or give at pleasure to the remoter Indians; the consequence is that, however badly treated, the Mandans and Ricaras are very slow to retaliate lest they should lose their trade altogether.

Source: William Clark Journal, November 18, 1804, *History of the Expeditions of Captains Lewis and Clark, 1804-5-6, Reprinted from the Edition of 1814, with Introduction and Index by James K. Hosmer* (Chicago: A. C. McClurg, 1902), 1:136–37.

Document 8.8

William Clark | Journal, January 28, 1805, and Meriwether Lewis, Journal, February 1, 1805

By early 1805 it was clear to Lewis and Clark that metal goods, especially axes or hatchets, were the most valuable means of obtaining the corn and other items they needed from the Mandans and neighboring Indians. These two short entries, by Clark and then Lewis, describe the value of the trade in hatchets to the Corps and their continued commitment to peace among Indian nations.

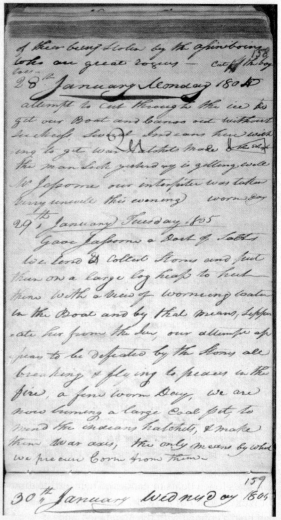

American Philosophical Society

28th January

Attempt to cut through the ice to get our Boat and Canoes out without success. Several Indians here wishing to get war hatchets made [image of one drawn here]. The man sick yesterday is getting well Mr. Jessome [Jessaume], our interpreter was taken very unwell this evening. Warm day.

1st February

A cold, windy day. . . . One of the Minnetaree chiefs . . . came to see us and procure a war hatchet; he also requested that we would suffer him to go to war against the Sioux and Ricaras, who had killed a Mandan some time ago; this we refused for reasons which we explained to him. He acknowledged that we were right, and promised to open his ears to our counsel.

Source: William Clark Journal, January 28, 1805, Codex C: 158 American Philosophical Society, Courtesy of the American Philosophical Society Library; and Meriwether Lewis Journal, February 1, 1805, *History of the Expeditions of Captains Lewis and Clark, 1804-5-6, Reprinted from the Edition of 1814, with Introduction and Index by James K. Hosmer* (Chicago: A. C. McClurg, 1902), 1:168.

Document 8.9

Meriwether Lewis | Journal, August 20, 1805

The Corps was eager to encounter the Shoshone nation in hopes of getting horses and aid in crossing the mountains and the Columbia River. Sacagawea had been raised as a Shoshone, and her brother Cameahwait was now a Shoshone chief. He and Sacagawea were shocked and excited to see each other again, and Lewis was moved by their reunion. But he was more interested in the relations between the Shoshone and tribes to the east as well as Spanish traders to the south.

can discover that these people are by no means friendly to the Spaniards. Their complaint is, that the Spaniards will not let them have fire arms and amunition, that they put them off by telling them that if they suffer them to have guns they will kill each other, thus leaving them defenceless and an easy prey to their bloodthirsty neighbours to the East of them, who being in possession of fire arms hunt them up and murder them without rispect to sex or age and plunder them of their horses on all occasions. They told me that to avoid their enemies who were eternally harrassing them that they were obliged to remain in the interior of these mountains at least two thirds of the year where the[y] suffered as we then saw great heardships for the want of food sometimes living for weeks without meat and only a little fish roots and berries. But this added Câmeahwait, with his ferce eyes and lank jaws grown meager for the want of food, would not be the case if we had guns, we could then live in the country of buffaloe and eat as our enimies do and not be compelled to hide ourselves in these mountains and live on roots and berries as the bear do. We do not fear our enimies when placed on an equal footing with them. I told them that the Minnetares Mandans & Recares of the Missouri had promised us to desist from making war on them & that we would indevour to find the means of making the Minnetares . . . or as they call them Pahkees desist from waging war against them also. That after our finally returning to our homes towards the rising sun whitemen would come to them with an abundance of guns and every other article necessary to their defence and comfort, and that they would be enabled to supply themselves with these articles on reasonable terms in exchange for the skins of the beaver Otter and Ermin so abundant in their country. They expressed great pleasure at this information and said they had been long anxious to see the whitemen that traded guns; and that we might rest assured of their friendship and that they would do whatever we wished them.

Source: Reuben Gold Thwaites, ed., *Original Journals of the Lewis and Clark Expedition, 1804–1808* (New York: Dodd, Mead, 1904), 383–84.

Interpret the Evidence

1. How do European traders and American explorers view the connection between trade with and peaceful relations among Indian nations (Documents 8.5 and 8.6)?

2. After only a month living near the Mandan, how does William Clark describe relations among Indian nations in the region (Document 8.7)?

3. What are the effects of Lewis and Clark's willingness to trade war hatchets for food, and how does this fit with their desire for peace among the Mandan, Arikara, and other Indian nations (Documents 8.8 and 8.9)?

4. What does Lewis's willingness to promise guns to the Shoshone suggest about the Corps' purpose as it encounters Indian nations living in the Spanish commercial sphere (Document 8.9)?

5. Although these sources were written by white men, what can they tell us about Indian attitudes toward European traders and American explorers and their relations with other Indian nations (Documents 8.5 to 8.9)?

Put It in Context

What were the most significant problems faced by Indians as more European and American explorers and traders entered the region explored by the Corps of Discovery?

How did the Corps of Discovery influence relations among Indian nations in the West and with the United States?

Defending and Redefining the Nation

1809–1832

WINDOW TO THE PAST

Crowds Celebrate a Presidential Inauguration

When Andrew Jackson was elected president in 1828, he decided to open the traditional White House reception to ordinary women and men. Some people applauded his democratic inclusion; others were appalled by the "mob scene."

The event drew attention in Great Britain as well as the United States. This 1829 image is from *President's Levee*, drawn by Robert Cruikshank, a British satirical artist. ▸ To discover more about what this primary source can show us, see Document 9.9 on page 309.

Granger, NYC

After reading this chapter you should be able to:

- Analyze the intertwined effects of conflicts with Britain and on the U.S. frontier on federal policies and the lives of white and Indian Americans.

- Explain the role of state and federal governments in the nation's expansion and how expansion affected relations among increasingly distinct regions.

- Evaluate how the panic of 1819 and the Missouri Compromise affected and were affected by the nation's economic expansion and political divisions.

- Discuss how expanded voting rights for white working men, new racial restrictions, and continued debates over federal power led to political realignment.

- Describe the challenges that President Jackson faced in implementing federal policies on the tariff, the national bank, and the removal of the Cherokee.

AMERICAN HISTORIES

Dolley Payne was raised on a Virginia plantation. But her Quaker parents, moved by the Society of Friends' growing antislavery sentiment, decided to free their slaves. In 1783, when Dolley was fifteen, the Paynes moved to Philadelphia. There, Dolley's father suffered heavy economic losses, and Dolley lost her first husband and her younger son to yellow fever. In 1794 the young widow met and married Virginia

(*left*) **Dolley Madison.** Library of Congress, 3b15638

(*right*) **John Ross.** Library of Congress, 3g03156

congressman James Madison. When the newly elected president Thomas Jefferson appointed James secretary of state in 1801, the couple moved to the new capital city of Washington.

Since Jefferson and his vice president, Aaron Burr, were widowers, Dolley Madison served as hostess for White House affairs. When James Madison succeeded Jefferson as president in 1809, he, too, depended on his wife's social skills and networks. Dolley held lively informal receptions to which she invited politicians, diplomats, cabinet officers, and their wives. These social events helped bridge the ideological differences that continued to divide Congress and proved crucial in creating a unified front when Congress declared war on Great Britain in 1812.

During the War of 1812, British forces attacked Washington City and burned the Executive Mansion, now called the White House. With the president away, his wife was left to secure important state papers, emerging as a symbol of national courage at a critical moment in the conflict. When peace came the following year, Dolley Madison quickly reestablished a busy social calendar to help mend conflicts that had erupted during the war.

In 1817, at the end of the president's second term, the Madisons left Washington just as a young trader named John Ross entered the political arena. Born in 1790 in the Cherokee nation, John (also known as Guwisguwi) was the son of a Scottish trader and his wife, who was both Cherokee and Scottish. John Ross was raised in an Anglo-Indian world in eastern Tennessee, where he played with Cherokee children and attended tribal events but was educated by private tutors and in Protestant missionary schools. At age twenty, Ross was appointed as a U.S. Indian agent among the Cherokee and during the War of 1812 served as an adjutant (or administrative assistant) in a Cherokee regiment.

After the war, Ross focused on business ventures in Tennessee, including the establishment of a plantation. He also became increasingly involved in Cherokee political affairs, using his bilingual skills and Protestant training to represent Indian interests to government officials. In 1819 Ross was elected president of the Cherokee legislature. In the 1820s he moved to Georgia, where he served as president of the

Cherokee constitutional convention in 1827. Having overseen the first written constitution produced by an Indian nation, Ross was then elected principal chief in 1828. Over the next decade, he battled to retain the Cherokee homeland against the pressures of white planters and politicians. ■

T he American histories of Dolley Madison and John Ross demonstrate that, while American politics was a white man's game, it was sometimes possible for those on the political margins to influence national developments. Both Madison and Ross sought to defend and expand the democratic ideals that defined the young nation. The First Lady helped to nurture a bipartisan political culture in Washington, which was particularly important following the War of 1812. Dolley Madison also struggled with the issue of slavery, an issue that fueled tensions among Democratic-Republicans when Missouri sought admission to statehood in 1819. Missouri's admission resulted from the nation's rapid geographical expansion. Its economic development proved more volatile, however, with the nation suffering its first major recession in 1819. Working men then demanded the right to vote to protect their economic interests. The Cherokee also asserted their rights. Ross encouraged Cherokees to embrace Anglo-American culture as a path to inclusion. But he could not overcome the power of planters and politicians to wrest valuable territory from his tribe. President Andrew Jackson, elected in 1828, ensured Cherokee removal and supported slavery. Yet he was lauded as a democratic hero for his frontier background and promotion of workingmen's rights. The United States successfully defended itself against British intervention, but still could not agree on which Americans truly belonged in the nation.

Conflicts at Home and Abroad

When Thomas Jefferson completed his second term as president in March 1809, he was succeeded by his friend and ally James Madison. Like Jefferson, Madison sought to end foreign interference in American affairs and to resolve conflicts between Indians and white residents on the nation's frontier. By 1815 the United States had weathered a series of domestic and foreign crises, including another war with Britain, but American sovereignty remained fragile. At the same time, even though Madison (like Jefferson) believed in a national government with limited powers, he, too, found himself expanding federal authority.

Tensions at Sea and on the Frontier. When President Madison took office, Great Britain and France remained embroiled in the Napoleonic Wars in Europe and refused to modify their policies toward American shipping or to recognize U.S. neutrality. American ships were subject to seizure by both nations, and British authorities continued to impress "deserters" into the Royal Navy. Just before Madison's inauguration in March 1809, Congress replaced the Embargo Act with the **Non-Intercourse Act**. The new law restricted trade only with France and Britain and their colonies. Although the continued embargo against Britain encouraged U.S. manufacturing and the act allowed trade with other European nations, many Americans still opposed Congress using its power to deny their right to trade with such important countries.

In the midst of these crises, Madison also faced difficulties in the Northwest Territory. In 1794 General Anthony Wayne had won a decisive victory against a multi-tribe coalition at the **Battle of Fallen Timbers**. But this victory inspired two forceful native leaders to create a pan-Indian alliance in the Ohio River valley. The Shawnee prophet Tenskwatawa and his half-brother Tecumseh, a warrior, encouraged native peoples to resist white encroachments on their territory and to give up all aspects of white society and culture, including liquor and other popular trade goods. They imagined an Indian nation that stretched from the Canadian border to the Gulf of Mexico.

Although powerful Creek and Choctaw nations in the lower Mississippi valley refused to join the alliance, Indians in the upper Midwest rallied around the brothers. In 1808 Tenskwatawa and Tecumseh established Prophet Town along the Tippecanoe River in Indiana Territory. The next year, William Henry Harrison, the territorial governor, tricked several Indian leaders into signing a treaty selling three million acres of land to the United States for only $7,600. An enraged Tecumseh dismissed the treaty, claiming the land belonged to all the Indians together.

Explore ▶

Read part of Tecumseh's response to Harrison in Document 9.1.

In November 1811, fearing the growing power of the Shawnee leaders, President Madison ordered Harrison to attack Prophet Town. With more troops and superior weapons, the U.S. army defeated the allied Indians forces and burned Prophet Town to the ground. The rout damaged Tenskwatawa's stature as a prophet, and he and his supporters fled to Canada, where skirmishes continued along the U.S.-Canadian border.

War Erupts with Britain. Convinced that British officials in Canada fueled Indian resistance, many Democratic-Republicans demanded an end to British intervention on the western frontier. Insisting that the United States also stop British interference in transatlantic trade, some called for the United States to declare war. Yet merchants in the Northeast, who still hoped to renew trade with Great Britain and the British West Indies, feared the commercial disruptions that war entailed. Thus New England Federalists adamantly opposed a declaration of war.

For months, Madison avoided taking a clear stand on the issue. On June 1, 1812, however, with diplomatic efforts exhausted, Madison sent a secret message to Congress outlining U.S. grievances against Great Britain. Within weeks, Congress declared war by sharply divided votes in the House of Representatives and the Senate.

Supporters claimed that a victory over Great Britain would end threats to U.S. sovereignty and raise Americans' stature in Europe, but the nation was ill prepared to launch a major offensive against such an imposing foe. Cuts in federal spending and falling tax revenues over the previous decade had diminished military resources. The U.S. navy, for example, established under President Adams, had been reduced to only six small gunboats by President Jefferson. Democratic-Republicans had also failed to recharter the Bank of the United States when it expired in 1811, so the nation lacked a vital source of credit. Nonetheless, many in Congress believed that Britain would be too engaged by the ongoing conflict with France to attack the United States.

Meanwhile U.S. commanders devised plans to attack Canada, but the U.S. army and navy proved no match for Great Britain and its Indian allies. Instead, Tecumseh, who was appointed a brigadier general in the British army, helped capture Detroit. Joint British and Indian forces also launched successful attacks on Fort Dearborn, Fort Mackinac, and other points along the U.S.-Canadian border.

Even as U.S. forces faced numerous defeats in the summer and fall of 1812, American voters reelected James Madison as president. His narrow victory demonstrated the geographical divisions caused by the war. Madison won most western and southern states, where the war was most popular, and lost in New England and New York, where Federalist opponents held sway.

GUIDED ANALYSIS

Tecumseh | Speech to William Henry Harrison, 1810

In 1809 William Henry Harrison, governor of the Indiana Territory, negotiated a treaty with a coalition of native leaders to cede three million acres to the United States. Unhappy with this treaty, two Shawnee brothers, Tecumseh and Tenskwatawa, united with other Indian nations to resist white settlement of the region. In August 1810 Tecumseh confronted Harrison at Vincennes in the Indiana Territory and urged him to return the land. Harrison refused, and in the fall of 1811 U.S. troops attacked and defeated the Shawnees at Prophet Town.

Document 9.1

Why does Tecumseh consider white Americans untrustworthy?

Brother. Since the peace was made you have kill'd some of the Shawanese, Winebagoes, Delawares, and Miamies and you have taken our lands from us, and I do not see how we can remain at peace with you if you continue to do so. You have given goods to the Kickapoos for the sale of their lands . . . which has been the cause of many deaths among them. You have promised us assistance but I do not see that you have given us any.

You try to force the red people to do some injury. It is you that is pushing them on to do mischief. You endeavor to make distinctions, you wish to prevent the Indians to do as we wish them: to unite and let them consider their land as the common property of the whole.

How does Tecumseh's view of Indian land differ from that negotiated in the treaty?

You take tribes aside and advise them not to come into this measure [coalition] and untill our design is accomplished we do not wish to accept of your invitation to go and visit the President.

How does Tecumseh compare U.S. actions toward Indians with Indian actions toward whites?

The reason I tell you this is you want by your distinctions of Indian tribes in allotting to each a particular track of land to make them to war with each other. You never see an Indian come and endeavour to make the white people do so. You are continually driving the red people when at last you will drive them into the great Lake where they can't eather stand or work.

Source: Logan Esarey, ed., *Messages and Letters of William Henry Harrison* (Indianapolis: Indiana Historical Commission, 1922), 1:465.

Put It in Context

What does Tecumseh reveal about the complex relationships between American Indian nations and the U.S. government in the 1810s?

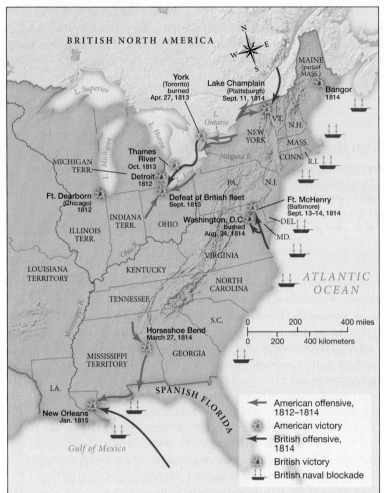

MAP 9.1 The War of 1812

Most conflicts in this war occurred in the Great Lakes region or around Washington, D.C. Yet two crucial victories occurred in the South. At Horseshoe Bend, troops under General Andrew Jackson and aided by Cherokee warriors defeated Creek allies of the British. At New Orleans, Jackson beat British forces shortly after a peace agreement was signed in Europe.

After a year of fighting, U.S. forces finally drove the British back into Canada (Map 9.1). A naval victory on Lake Erie led by Commodore Oliver Perry proved crucial to U.S. success. Soon after, Tecumseh was killed in battle and U.S. forces burned York (present-day Toronto). Yet just as U.S. prospects in the war improved, New England Federalists demanded retreat. The war devastated the New England maritime trade, causing economic distress throughout the region. In the fall of 1813, state legislatures in New England withdrew their support for any invasion of "foreign British soil," and Federalists in Congress sought to block war appropriations and the deployment of local militia units into the U.S. army.

New England Federalists were not powerful enough to change national policy, but they called a meeting at Hartford, Connecticut, in 1814 to "deliberate upon the alarming state of public affairs." Some participants at the **Hartford Convention** called for New England's secession from the United States. Most, however, supported amendments to the U.S. Constitution that would constrain federal power by limiting presidents to a single term and ensuring they were elected from diverse states (ending Virginia's domination of the office). Other amendments would require a two-thirds majority in Congress to declare war or prohibit trade.

The Hartford resolutions gained increased attention as British forces launched new attacks into the United States and British warships blockaded U.S. ports. In August 1814, the British sailed up the Chesapeake. As American troops retreated, Dolley Madison and a family slave, Peter Jennings, gathered up government papers and valuable belongings before fleeing the White House. The redcoats then burned and sacked Washington City. Nonetheless, U.S. troops quickly rallied to defeat the British in Maryland and expel them from Washington and New York.

Meanwhile news arrived in March 1814 that militiamen from Tennessee led by Andrew Jackson had defeated a force of Creek Indians, important British allies. Cherokee warriors (including John Ross), longtime foes of the Creek, joined the fight. At the **Battle of Horseshoe Bend**, in present-day Alabama, the combined U.S.-Cherokee forces slaughtered eight hundred Creek warriors. Although some Americans were appalled at the slaughter, in the resulting treaty the Creek nation lost two-thirds of its tribal domain.

Battle of New Orleans   On January 8, 1815, General Andrew Jackson's troops launched grapeshot and canister bombs against British forces in New Orleans in this final battle of the War of 1812. Jackson's troops included Indian allies, backcountry immigrants, and French-speaking black soldiers. This engraving by Francisco Scacki shows the slain British commander, Major General Sir Edward Pakenham, in the center foreground. Granger, NYC

Despite sporadic victories, the United States was no closer to winning the war when the British ended the war in Europe in June 1814 by defeating Napoleon. Six months later, the British fleet landed thousands of seasoned troops at New Orleans. Still, the British were losing steam as well, and representatives of the two countries met in Ghent, Belgium, to negotiate a peace settlement. On Christmas Eve 1814, the **Treaty of Ghent** was signed, returning to each nation the lands it controlled before the war.

News of the treaty had not yet reached the United States in January 1815, when U.S. troops under General Andrew Jackson attacked and routed the British army at New Orleans. The victory cheered Americans, who, unaware that peace had already been achieved, made Jackson a national hero.

Although the War of 1812 achieved no formal territorial gains, it did represent an important defense of U.S. sovereignty and garnered international prestige for the young nation. In addition, Indians on the western frontier lost a powerful ally when British representatives at Ghent failed to act as advocates for their allies. Thus, in practical terms, the U.S. government gained greater control over vast expanses of land in the Ohio and Mississippi River valleys.

REVIEW & RELATE

| How were conflicts with Indians in the West connected to ongoing tensions between the United States and Great Britain on land and at sea? | What were the long-term consequences of the War of 1812? |

National Expansion and Regional Economies

By further expanding federal powers, the War of 1812 reinforced political changes that had been under way for more than a decade. At the Hartford Convention, Federalists who had once advocated broad national powers called for restrictions on federal authority. By contrast, Democratic-Republicans, who initially demanded restraints on federal power, now applauded its expansion. Indeed, Democratic-Republicans in Congress sought to use federal authority to settle boundary disputes in the West, make investments in transportation, and reestablish a national bank. Some state governments also invested in roads and canals. Federal power was again asserted to settle disputes with Britain and Spain over U.S. borders in the North and the South. At the same time, more secure borders and state and federal investments in transportation fueled overseas trade and the development of increasingly distinct regional economies.

Governments Fuel Economic Growth. In 1800 Thomas Jefferson captured the presidency by advocating a reduction in federal powers and a renewed emphasis on the needs of small farmers and workingmen. Once in power, however, Jefferson and his Democratic-Republican supporters faced a series of economic and political developments that led many of them to embrace a loose interpretation of the U.S. Constitution and support federal efforts to aid economic growth.

Cincinnati Public Landing, 1835   Cities like Cincinnati, Ohio, benefited from western migration and internal improvements. This painting by Jacob Casper Wild, a Swiss artist who moved to the American Midwest in the 1830s, captures the Ohio River waterfront less than twenty years after the city was incorporated. Shops and small factories overlook horse-drawn carriages picking up goods and leaving passengers at waiting steamboats. Cincinnati Museum Center/ Getty Images

Population growth and commercial expansion encouraged these federal efforts. In 1811 the first steamboat traveled down the Mississippi from the Ohio River to New Orleans; over the next decade, steamboat traffic expanded. This development helped western and southern residents but hurt trade on overland routes between northeastern seaports and the Ohio River valley. The federal government began construction of the Cumberland Road in 1811 to reestablish this regional connection by linking Maryland and Ohio. Congress passed additional bills to fund ambitious federal transportation projects, but President Madison vetoed much of this legislation, believing that it overstepped even a loose interpretation of the Constitution.

After the War of 1812, however, Democratic-Republican representative Henry Clay of Kentucky sketched out a coordinated plan to promote U.S. economic growth and advance commercial ties throughout the nation. Called the **American System**, it combined federally funded internal improvements, such as roads and canals, to aid farmers and merchants with federal tariffs to protect U.S. manufacturing. Western expansion fueled demand for these internal improvements. The non-Indian population west of the Appalachian Mountains more than doubled between 1810 and 1820, from 1,080,000 to 2,234,000. Many veterans of the War of 1812 received 160-acre parcels of land in the region as payment for service and settled there. Congress admitted four new states to the Union in just four years: Indiana (1816), Mississippi (1817), Illinois (1818), and Alabama (1819).

Congress also negotiated with Indian nations to secure trade routes farther west. In the 1810s, Americans began trading along an ancient trail from Missouri to Santa Fe, a

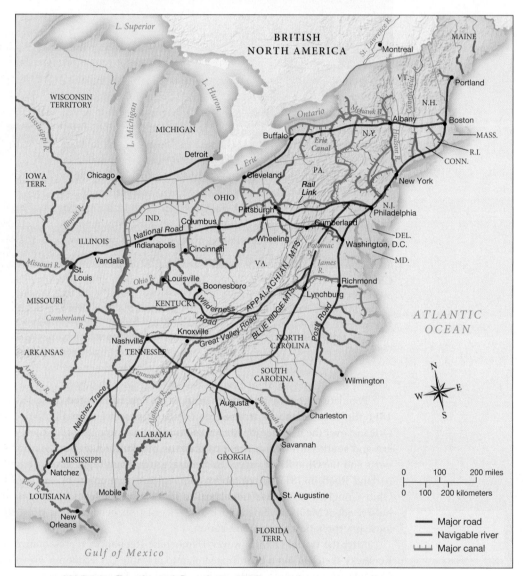

MAP 9.2 Roads and Canals to 1837

During the 1820s and 1830s, state and local governments as well as private companies built roads and canals to foster migration and commercial development. The Erie Canal, completed in 1825, was the most significant of these projects. Many other states, particularly in the Northeast and the old Northwest, sought to duplicate that canal's success over the following decade.

town in northern Mexico. But the trail cut across territory claimed by the Osage Indians. In 1825 Congress approved a treaty with the Osage to guarantee right of way for U.S. merchants. In the following decade, the Santa Fe Trail became a critical route for commerce between the United States and Mexico.

East of the Appalachian Mountains, state governments funded most internal improvement projects. The most significant of these was New York's **Erie Canal**, a 363-mile waterway stretching from the Mohawk River to Buffalo that was completed in 1825. Tolls on the Erie Canal quickly repaid the tremendous cost of its construction. Freight charges and shipping times plunged. And by linking western farmers to the Hudson River, the Erie Canal ensured that New York City became the nation's premier seaport (Map 9.2).

The Erie Canal's success inspired hundreds of similar projects in other states. Canals carried manufactured goods from New England and the Middle Atlantic states to rural households in the Ohio River valley. Western farmers, in turn, shipped agricultural products back east. Canals also linked smaller cities within Pennsylvania and Ohio, facilitating the rise of commercial and manufacturing centers like Harrisburg, Pittsburgh, and Cincinnati. Canals also allowed vast quantities of coal to be transported out of the Allegheny Mountains, fueling industrial development throughout the Northeast.

Americans Expand the Nation's Borders. In 1816, in the midst of the nation's economic resurgence, James Monroe, a Democratic-Republican from Virginia, won an easy victory in the presidential election over Rufus King, a New York Federalist. Monroe hoped to use improved relations with Great Britain to resolve Indian problems on the frontier. With this in mind, he sent John Quincy Adams to London to negotiate treaties that limited U.S. and British naval forces on the Great Lakes, set the U.S.-Canadian border at the forty-ninth parallel, and established joint British-U.S. occupation of the Oregon Territory. In 1817 and 1818, the Senate approved these treaties, which further limited Indian rights and power.

President Monroe harbored grave concerns about the nation's southern boundary as well. He sought to limit Spain's power in North America and stop Seminole Indians in western Florida and Alabama from claiming lands ceded to the United States by the defeated Creeks. Shifting from diplomacy to military force, in 1817 the president sent General Andrew Jackson to force the Seminoles back into Florida. But he ordered Jackson to avoid direct conflict with Spanish forces for fear of igniting another war. However, in spring 1818, Jackson attacked two Spanish forts, hanged two Seminole chiefs, and executed two British citizens.

Jackson's attacks spurred outrage among Spanish and British officials and many members of Congress. The threat of conflict with Britain, Spain, and the Seminole prompted President Monroe to establish the nation's first peacetime army. In the end, the British chose to ignore the execution of citizens engaged in "unauthorized" activities, while Spain decided to sell the Florida Territory to the United States. Indeed, in the **Adams-Onís Treaty** (1819), negotiated by John Quincy Adams, Spain ceded all its lands east of the Mississippi to the United States.

Success in acquiring Florida encouraged the administration to look for other opportunities to limit European influence in the Western Hemisphere. By 1822 Argentina, Chile, Peru, Colombia, and Mexico had all overthrown Spanish rule. In March of that year, President Monroe recognized the independence of these southern neighbors, and Congress quickly established diplomatic relations with the new nations. The following year, President Monroe added a codicil to a treaty with Russia that claimed that the Western Hemisphere was part of the U.S. sphere of influence. Although the United States did not have sufficient power to enforce what later became known as the **Monroe Doctrine**, it had quietly declared its intention to challenge Europeans for authority in the Atlantic world.

By the late 1820s, U.S. residents were moving to and trading with newly independent Mexican territories. Southern whites began settling on Mexican lands in east Texas, while traders traveled the Santa Fe Trail. Meanwhile New England manufacturers and merchants had begun shipping their wares via clipper ships to another Mexican territory, Alta California.

Some Americans looked even farther afield. In the early nineteenth century, U.S. ships carried otter pelts and other merchandise across the Pacific, returning with Chinese porcelains and silks. In the 1810s and 1820s, the Alta California and China trades converged, expanding the reach of U.S. merchants and the demand for U.S. manufactured goods. The desire to expand trade led some Americans to set their sights on Pacific islands, especially Hawaii and Samoa.

Expanded trade routes along with wartime disruptions of European imports fueled the expansion of U.S. manufacturing, which improved opportunities for entrepreneurs and workers. By 1813 the area around Providence, Rhode Island, boasted seventy-six spinning mills. Two years later, Philadelphia claimed pride of place as the nation's top industrial city, turning out glass, chemicals, metalwork, and leather goods.

Regional Economic Development. The roads, rivers, canals, and steamboats that connected a growing nation meant that people in one region could more easily exchange the goods they produced for those they needed. This development fostered the emergence of distinct, regional economies. In the South, for instance, vast Indian land cessions and the acquisition of Florida ensured the expansion of cotton cultivation. Planters extended slavery into new lands to produce cash crops like cotton, sugar, and rice while small farmers planted as much land in cotton as they could manage. They used profits from these staple crops to buy grain and other food items from the West and manufactured shoes and cloth from the North.

When James and Dolley Madison returned to their plantation, Montpelier, in 1817, they experienced the new possibilities and problems of southern agriculture. Plantation homes in long-settled areas like Montpelier in the Virginia piedmont became more fashionable as they incorporated luxury goods imported from China and Europe. But soil exhaustion in the region limited the profits from tobacco and made a shift to cotton impossible. As agricultural production declined in the region, some Virginia planters made money by selling slaves to planters farther south. However, James Madison refused to break up slave families who had worked his plantation for decades and had no desire to move farther west. Thus the Madisons were forced to reduce their standard of living.

Many white Americans, however, benefited from the westward expansion of southern agriculture. Farmers and planters who cultivated cotton made substantial profits in the 1810s. So did western farmers, who shipped vast quantities of agricultural produce to the South. Towns like Cincinnati, located across the Ohio River from Kentucky, sprang up as regional centers of commerce. Americans living in the Northeast increased their commercial connections with the South as well. Northern merchants became more deeply engaged in the southern cotton trade, opening warehouses in cities like Savannah and Charleston and sending agents into the countryside to bargain for cotton to be spun into thread in northern mills.

The southern cotton boom thus fueled northern industrial growth. Indeed, factory owners in New England then shipped growing quantities of yarn, thread, and cloth along with shoes, tools, and leather goods to the South. As merchants in New England and New York focused on the cotton trade, those in Philadelphia and Pittsburgh built ties to western farmers, exchanging manufactured goods for agricultural products. Over time America's regional economies became not only more distinctive but also increasingly interdependent.

REVIEW & RELATE

- What role did government play in early-nineteenth-century economic development?
- How and why did economic development contribute to regional differences and shape regional ties?

Economic and Political Crises

Even as regional economies ensured economic interdependence, they highlighted political differences. For instance, the growth in trade between regions led to an increase in commercial institutions, such as banks, the largest of which were established in the North. When the nation's first severe recession hit in 1819, many southern planters and midwestern farmers blamed it on the banks. In reality, falling prices for cotton and wheat abroad as well as overextension of credit by U.S. banks contributed to the recession. Whatever the cause, the interdependence of regional economies ensured that everyone suffered. At the same time, these economies were built on distinct forms of labor, with the South becoming more dependent on slavery and the North less so. When Missouri, situated between the old Northwest Territory and expanding southern cotton lands, applied for statehood in 1819, these regional differences set off a furious national debate over slavery.

The Panic of 1819. The **panic of 1819** resulted primarily from irresponsible banking practices in the United States and was deepened by the declining overseas demand for American goods, especially cotton. Beginning in 1816, American banks, including the newly chartered Second Bank of the United States, loaned huge sums to settlers seeking land on the frontier and merchants and manufacturers expanding their businesses. Many loans were not backed by sufficient collateral because many banks assumed that continued economic growth would ensure repayment. Then, as agricultural production in Europe revived with the end of the Napoleonic Wars, the demand for American foodstuffs dropped sharply. Farm income plummeted by roughly one-third in the late 1810s.

In 1818 the directors of the Second Bank, fearing a continued expansion of the money supply, tightened the credit they provided to branch banks. This sudden effort to curtail credit led to economic panic. Some branch banks failed immediately. Others survived by calling in loans to companies and individuals, who in turn demanded repayment from those to whom they had extended credit. The chain of indebtedness pushed many people to the brink of economic ruin just as factory owners cut their workforce and merchants

Auction in Chatham Street, New York, 1820 Widespread unemployment between 1819 and 1823 resulted in evictions for thousands of families. Public auctions of the furniture, dishes, and other household goods of evicted families were held regularly in cities across the country. This depiction of an 1820 auction in New York's Chatham Square was painted by E. Didier in 1843, during the next major economic panic. © Museum of the City of New York, USA/Bridgeman Images

decreased orders for new goods. Individuals and businesses faced bankruptcy and foreclosure, and property values fell sharply.

Bankruptcies, foreclosures, unemployment, and poverty spread across the country. Cotton farmers were especially hard hit by declining exports and falling prices. Planters who had gone into debt to purchase land in Alabama and Mississippi were unable to pay their mortgages. Many western residents, who had invested all they had in new farms, lost their land or simply stopped paying their mortgages. This further strained state banks, some of which collapsed, leaving the national bank holding mortgages on vast amounts of western territory.

Many Americans viewed banks as the cause of the panic. Some states defied the Constitution and the Supreme Court by trying to tax Second Bank branches or printing state banknotes with no specie (gold or silver) to back them. Some Americans called for government relief, but there was no system to provide the kinds of assistance needed. When Congress debated how to reignite the nation's economy, regional differences quickly appeared. Northern manufacturers called for even higher tariffs to protect them from foreign competition, but southern planters argued that high tariffs raised the price of manufactured goods while agricultural profits declined. Meanwhile, workingmen and small farmers feared that their economic needs were being ignored by politicians tied to bankers, planters, manufacturers, and merchants.

By 1823 the panic had largely dissipated, but the prolonged economic crisis shook national confidence, and citizens became more skeptical of federal authority and more suspicious of banks. From 1819 until the Civil War, one of the greatest limitations on national growth remained the cycle of economic expansion and contraction.

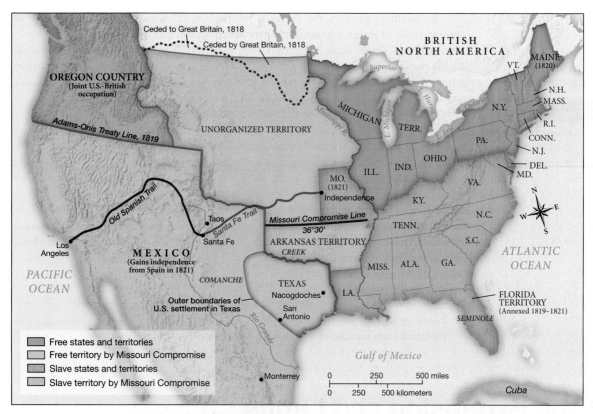

MAP 9.3 The Missouri Compromise and Westward Expansion, 1820s
The debate over the Missouri Compromise occurred as the United States began expanding farther westward. Within a few years of its adoption, the growth of U.S. settlements in eastern Texas and increased trade with a newly independent Mexico suggested the importance of drawing a clear boundary between slave and free states.

Slavery in Missouri. A second national crisis highlighted regional systems of labor. In February 1819 the Missouri Territory applied for statehood. New York congressman James Tallmadge Jr. proposed that Missouri be admitted only if it banned further importation of slaves and passed a gradual emancipation law. Southern congressmen blocked Tallmadge's proposals, but the northern majority in the House of Representatives then rejected Missouri's admission.

Southern politicians were outraged, claiming that since the Missouri Territory allowed slavery, so should the state of Missouri. With cotton production moving ever westward, southern congressmen wanted to ensure the availability of new lands. They also wanted to ensure the South's power in Congress. Because the northern population had grown more rapidly than that in the South, by 1819 northern politicians controlled the House of Representatives. The Senate, however, was evenly divided. If northerners could block the admission of slave states like Missouri while allowing the admission of free states, the balance of power in the Senate would tip in the North's favor.

For southern planters, the decision on Missouri defined the future of slavery. With foreign trade in slaves outlawed, planters relied on natural increase and trading slaves from older to newer areas of cultivation to meet the demand for labor. Moreover, free blacks packed the congressional galleries in Washington to listen to congressmen debate Missouri statehood, leading supporters of slavery to worry that any signs of weakness would fuel resistance to slavery. Recent attacks on Georgia plantations by a coalition of fugitive slaves and Seminole Indians lent power to such fears.

> **Explore ▶**
>
> Compare two critiques of the Missouri Compromise in Documents 9.2 and 9.3.

In 1820 Representative Henry Clay of Kentucky forged a compromise that resolved the immediate issues and promised a long-term solution. Maine was to be admitted as a free state and Missouri as a slave state, thereby maintaining the balance between North and South in the U.S. Senate (Map 9.3). At the same time, Congress agreed that the southern border of Missouri—latitude 36°30'—was to serve as the boundary between slave and free states throughout the Louisiana Territory.

The **Missouri Compromise** ended the crisis for the moment. Still, the debates made clear how quickly a disagreement over slavery could escalate into clashes that threatened the survival of the nation.

REVIEW & RELATE

- How did regional interdependency contribute to the panic of 1819?

- What regional divisions did the conflict over slavery in Missouri reveal?

The **Expansion** and **Limits** of **American Democracy**

With the panic of 1819 and the debates over Missouri shaking many Americans' faith in their economic and political leaders and the frontier moving ever westward, the nation was ripe for change. Workingmen, small farmers, and frontier settlers, who had long been locked out of the electoral system by property qualifications and eastern elites, demanded the right to vote. The resulting political movement ensured voting rights for nearly all white men during the 1820s. Yet African Americans lost political and civil rights in the same period; and Indians fared poorly under the federal administrations brought to power by this expanded electorate. While some white women gained greater political influence as a result of the voting rights gained by fathers and husbands, they did not achieve independent political rights. Finally, as a wave of new voters entered the political fray, ongoing conflicts over slavery, tariffs, and the rights of Indian nations transformed party alignments.

Expanding Voting Rights. Between 1788 and 1820, the U.S. presidency was dominated by Virginia elites and after 1800 by Democratic-Republicans. With little serious political opposition at the national level, few people bothered to vote in presidential elections. Far more people engaged in political activities at the state and local levels. Many towns attracted large audiences to public celebrations on the Fourth of July and election days. Female participants sewed symbols of their partisan loyalties on their clothes and joined in parades and feasts organized by men.

Election Day in Philadelphia, 1815 This engraving, based on a painting by German immigrant John Lewis Krimmel, depicts an election-day celebration in Philadelphia in 1815. The image highlights the widespread popular participation of men, women, and children in political events even before the expansion of voting rights for white men in the 1820s. The Art Archive at Art Resource, NY

The panic of 1819 stimulated even more political activity as laboring men, who were especially vulnerable to economic downturns, demanded the right to vote so they could hold politicians accountable. In New York State, Martin Van Buren, a rising star in the Democratic-Republican Party, led the fight to eliminate property qualifications for voting. At the state constitutional convention of 1821, the committee on suffrage argued that the only qualification for voting should be "the virtue and morality of the people." By the word *people*, Van Buren and the committee meant white men.

Despite opposition from powerful and wealthy men, by 1825 most states along the Atlantic seaboard had lowered or eliminated property qualifications on white male voters. Meanwhile states along the frontier that had joined the Union in the 1810s established universal white male suffrage from the beginning. And by 1824 three-quarters of the states (18 of 24) allowed voters, rather than state legislatures, to elect members of the electoral college.

Yet as white workingmen gained political rights in the 1820s, democracy did not spread to other groups. Indian nations were considered sovereign entities, so Indians voted in their own nations, not in U.S. elections. Women were excluded from voting because of their perceived dependence on men. And African American men faced increasing restrictions on their political rights. No southern legislature had ever granted blacks the right to vote, and northern states began disfranchising them as well in the 1820s. In many cases, expanded voting rights for white men went hand in hand with new restrictions on black men. In New York State, for example, the constitution of 1821, which

Protesting the Missouri Compromise

Missouri's statehood application sparked a crisis over the future of slavery in America, and the resulting Missouri Compromise did little to ease the fears of Americans who wanted to contain its spread. Timothy Claimright and Thomas Jefferson both opposed the Missouri Compromise, but they offered different reasons for doing so. Claimright, of Brunswick, Maine, argues in this poetic broadside that his home state should not join the Union if it means inviting the admission of Missouri as a slave state. Jefferson predicts in a letter that the temporary solution of the compromise will lead only to future tragedy.

Document 9.2

Timothy Claimright | Maine Not to Be Coupled with the Missouri Question, 1820

If the South will not yield, to the West be it known,
That Maine will declare for a *King* of her own;
And *three hundred thousand* of freemen demand
The justice bestow'd on each State in the land.
Free whites of the East are not blacks of the West,
And Republican souls on this principle rest,
That if no respect to their rights can be shown,
They know how to vindicate what are their own. . . .
They are founded on freedom, humanity's right,
Ordained by God against slavery to fight.
And Heaven born liberty sooner than yield,
The whites of Missouri shall dress their own field.
We are hardy and healthy, can till our own soil,
In labour delight; make a pleasure of toil. . . .
They too lazy to work, drive slaves, whom they fear;
We school our own children, and brew our own beer.
We do a day's work and go fearless to bed;
Tho' lock'd up, they dream of slaves, whom they dread. . . .
They may boast of their blacks; we boast of our plenty,
And swear to be free, eighteen hundred and twenty. . . .
A Sister in Union admit her, as free;
To be coupled with slaves, she will never agree.

Source: Timothy Claimright, *Maine Not to Be Coupled with the Missouri Question* (Brunswick, ME, 1820), Library of Congress Ephemera Collection.

eliminated property qualifications for white men, raised property qualifications for African American voters.

When African American men protested their disfranchisement, some whites spoke out on their behalf. They claimed that denying rights to men who had in no way abused the privilege of voting set "an ominous and dangerous precedent." In response, opponents

Document 9.3

Thomas Jefferson | Letter to John Holmes, 1820

Monticello, April 22, 1820

    I thank you, dear Sir, for the copy you have been so kind as to send me of the letter to your constituents on the Missouri question. It is a perfect justification to them. I had for a long time ceased to read newspapers, or pay any attention to public affairs, confident they were in good hands, and content to be a passenger in our bark [ship] to the shore from which I am not distant. But this momentous question, like a fire-bell in the night, awakened and filled me with terror. I considered it at once as the knell of the Union. It is hushed, indeed, for the moment. But this is a reprieve only, not a final sentence. A geographical line, coinciding with a marked principle, moral and political, once conceived and held up to the angry passions of men, will never be obliterated; and every new irritation will mark it deeper and deeper. I can say, with conscious truth, that there is not a man on earth who would sacrifice more than I would to relieve us from this heavy reproach, in any *practicable* way. The cession of that kind of property [slavery], for so it is misnamed, is a bagatelle [an insignificant thing] which would not cost me a second thought, if, in that way, a general emancipation and *expatriation* could be effected; and, gradually, and with due sacrifices, I think it might be. But as it is, we have the wolf by the ears, and we can neither hold him, nor safely let him go. Justice is in one scale, and self-preservation in the other.

Source: Thomas Jefferson Randolph, ed., *Memoirs, Correspondence, and Private Papers of Thomas Jefferson* (London: Henry Colburn and Richard Bentley, 1829), 4:332.

Interpret the Evidence

1. In opposing the Missouri Compromise, how does Claimright differentiate Maine and other northern states from the slave societies of the South?
2. How does Jefferson's opposition to the Missouri Compromise differ from Claimright's and why does Jefferson believe it would exacerbate the conflict over slavery?

Put It in Context

How might supporters of the Missouri Compromise have responded to the concerns of Claimright and Jefferson?

of black suffrage offered explicitly racist justifications. Some argued that black voting would lead to interracial socializing, even marriage. Others feared that black voters might hold the balance of power in close elections, forcing white civic leaders to accede to their demands. Gradually, racist arguments won the day, and by 1840, 93 percent of free blacks in the North were excluded from voting.

Racial Restrictions and Antiblack Violence. Restrictions on voting followed other constraints on African American men and women. As early as 1790, Congress limited naturalization (the process of becoming a citizen) to white aliens, or immigrants. It also excluded blacks from enrolling in federal militias. In 1820 Congress authorized city officials in Washington, D.C., to adopt a separate legal code governing free blacks and slaves. This federal legislation encouraged states, in both the North and the South, to add their own restrictions, including the segregation of public schools, transportation, and accommodations. Some northern legislatures even denied African Americans the right to settle in their state.

In addition, blacks faced mob and state-sanctioned violence across the country. In 1822 officials in Charleston, South Carolina, accused Denmark Vesey, a free black, of following the revolutionary leader Toussaint L'Ouverture's lead and plotting a conspiracy to free the city's slaves. Vesey had helped to organize churches, mutual aid societies, and other black institutions. His accomplishments were considered threatening to the future of slavery by challenging assumptions about black inferiority. Vesey may have organized a plan to free slaves in the city, but it is also possible that white officials concocted the plot to terrorize blacks. Despite scant evidence, Vesey and thirty-four of his alleged co-conspirators were found guilty and hanged. The African Methodist Episcopal Church where they supposedly planned the insurrection was demolished. Northern blacks also suffered from violent attacks by whites. For example, in 1829 white residents of Cincinnati attacked black neighborhoods, and more than half of the city's black residents fled. Many of them resettled in Ontario, Canada. They were soon joined by Philadelphia blacks who had been attacked by groups of white residents in 1832. Such attacks continued in northern cities throughout the 1830s.

CLASS No. 1.

Comprises those prisoners who were found guilty and executed.

Prisoners Names.	Owners' Names.	Time of Commit.	How Disposed of.
Peter	James Poyas	June 18	Hanged on Tuesday the 2d July, 1822, on Blake's lands, near Charleston.
Ned	Gov. T. Bennett,	do.	
Rolla	do.	do	
Batteau	do.	do.	
Denmark Vesey	A free black man	22	
Jessy	Thos. Blackwood	23	
John	Elias Horry	July 5	Do. on the Lines near Ch.; Friday July 12.
Gullah Jack	Paul Pritchard	do.	
Mingo	Wm. Harth	June 21	
Lot	Forrester	27	
Joe	P. L. Jore	July 6	
Julius	Thos. Forrest	8	
Tom	Mrs. Russell	10	
Smart	Robt. Anderson	do.	
John	John Robertson	11	
Robert	do.	do.	
Adam	do.	do.	
Polydore	Mrs. Faber	do.	Hanged on the Lines near Charleston, on Friday, 26th July.
Bacchus	Benj. Hammet	do.	
Dick	Wm. Sims	13	
Pharaoh	— Thompson	do.	
Jemmy	Mrs. Clement	18	
Mauidore	Mordecai Cohen	19	
Dean	— Mitchell	do.	
Jack	Mrs. Purcell	12	
Bellisle	Est. of Jos. Yates	18	
Naphur	do.	do.	
Adam	do.	do.	
Jacob	John S. Glen	16	
Charles	John Billings	18	
Jack	N. McNeill	22	
Caesar	Miss Smith	do.	Do. Tues. July 30.
Jacob Stagg	Jacob Lankester	23	
Tom	Wm. M. Scott	24	
William	Mrs. Garner	Aug. 2	Do. Friday, Aug. 9.

Record of Thirty-five Men Executed for Conspiring to Revolt against Their Masters This official record of executions related to an alleged 1822 slave conspiracy lists the name of Denmark Vesey, the only free black man accused, fifth. The enslaved men are listed next to their owners' names, including the governor of South Carolina, twenty-one other men, and six women. There were no appeals of their convictions, and the hangings took place quickly. Granger, NYC

Political Realignments. Restrictions on black political and civil rights converged with the continued decline of the Federalists. Federalist majorities in New York State had approved the gradual abolition law of 1799. In 1821 New York Federalists advocated equal rights for black and white voters as long as property qualifications limited suffrage to respectable citizens. But Federalists were losing power, and the concerns of African Americans were low on the Democratic-Republican agenda.

Struggles within the Democratic-Republican Party now turned to a large extent on the limits of federal power. Many Democratic-Republicans had come to embrace a more expansive view of federal authority and a looser interpretation of the U.S. Constitution. Others argued forcefully for a return to limited federal power and a strict construction of the Constitution. At the same time, rising young politicians—like Martin Van Buren and Andrew Jackson—and newly enfranchised voters sought to seize control of the party from its longtime leaders.

The election of 1824 brought these conflicts to a head, splitting the Democratic-Republicans into rival factions that by 1828 coalesced into two distinct entities: the **Democrats** and the **National Republicans**. Unable to agree on a single presidential candidate in 1824, the Democratic-Republican congressional caucus fractured into four camps backing separate candidates: John Quincy Adams, Andrew Jackson, Henry Clay, and Secretary of the Treasury William Crawford.

As the race developed, Adams and Jackson emerged as the two strongest candidates. John Quincy Adams's stature rested on his diplomatic achievements and the reputation of his father, former president John Adams. He favored internal improvements and protective tariffs that would bolster northern industry and commerce. Jackson, on the other hand, relied largely on his fame as a war hero and Indian fighter to inspire popular support. He advocated limited federal power.

As a candidate who appealed to ordinary voters, Jackson held a decided edge. Outgoing and boisterous, Jackson took his case to the people. Emphasizing his humble origins, he appealed to small farmers and northern workers. Just as important, Jackson gained the support of Van Buren, who also wanted to expand the political clout of the "common [white] man" and limit the reach of a central government that was becoming too powerful.

The four presidential candidates created a truly competitive race, and turnout at the polls increased significantly. Jackson won the popular vote by carrying Pennsylvania, New Jersey, the Carolinas, and much of the West and led in the electoral college with 99 electors. But with no candidate gaining an absolute majority in the electoral college, the Constitution called for the House of Representatives to choose the president from the three leading contenders—Jackson, Adams, and Crawford. Clay, who came in fourth, asked his supporters to back Adams, ensuring his election. Once in office, President Adams appointed Clay secretary of state. Jackson claimed that the two had engineered a "corrupt bargain," but Adams and Clay, who shared many ideas, formed a logical alliance.

Once in office, President Adams ran into vigorous opposition in Congress led by Van Buren. Calhoun, who had been elected vice president, also opposed his policies. Van Buren argued against federal funding for internal improvements since New York State had financed the Erie Canal with its own monies. Calhoun, meanwhile, joined other southern politicians in opposing any expansion of federal power for fear it would then be used to restrict the spread of slavery.

The most serious battle in Congress, however, involved tariffs. The tariff of 1816 had excluded most cheap English cotton cloth from the United States to aid New England manufacturing. In 1824 the tariff was extended to more expensive cotton and woolen cloth and to iron goods. During the presidential campaign, Adams and Clay appealed to northern voters by advocating even higher duties on these items. When Adams introduced tariff legislation that extended duties to raw materials like wool, hemp, and molasses, he gained support from both Jackson and Van Buren, who considered these tariffs beneficial to farmers on the frontier. Despite the opposition of Vice President Calhoun and congressmen from southeastern states, the tariff of 1828 was approved, raising duties on imports to an average of 62 percent.

The tariff of 1828, however, was Adams's only notable legislative victory. His foreign policy was also stymied by a hostile Congress. Adams thus entered the 1828 election campaign with little to show in the way of domestic or foreign achievements, and Jackson and his supporters took full advantage of the president's political vulnerability.

The Presidential Election of 1828.
The election of 1828 tested the power of the two major factions in the Democratic-Republican Party. President Adams followed the traditional approach of "standing" for office. He told supporters, "If my country wants my services, she must ask for them." Jackson and his supporters chose instead to "run" for office. They took their case directly to the voters, introducing innovative techniques to create enthusiasm among the electorate.

Van Buren managed the first truly national political campaign in U.S. history, seeking to re-create the original Democratic-Republican coalition among farmers, northern artisans, and southern planters while adding a sizable constituency of frontier voters. He was aided in the effort by Calhoun, who again ran for vice president and supported the Tennessee war hero despite their disagreement over tariffs. Jackson's supporters organized state nominating conventions rather than relying on the congressional caucus. They established local Jackson committees in critical states like Virginia and New York. They organized newspaper campaigns and developed a logo, the hickory leaf, based on the candidate's nickname, "Old Hickory."

Jackson traveled the country to build loyalty to himself as well as to his party. His Tennessee background, rise to great wealth, and reputation as an Indian fighter ensured his popularity among southern and western voters. He also reassured southerners that he advocated "judicious" duties on imports, suggesting that he might try to lower the 1828 rates. At the same time, his support of the tariff of 1828 and his military credentials created enthusiasm among northern workingmen and frontier farmers.

President Adams's supporters demeaned the "dissolute" and "rowdy" men who attended Jackson rallies. They also launched personal attacks on the candidate and on his wife, Rachel. They questioned the timing of her divorce from her first husband and remarriage to Jackson. A Cincinnati newspaper headline asked: "Ought a convicted adulteress and her paramour husband be placed in the highest offices of this free and Christian land?" **See Document Project 9: The Election of 1828, page 305.**

Adams distanced himself from his own campaign. He sought to demonstrate his statesmanlike gentility by letting others speak for him. This strategy worked well when only men of wealth and property could vote. But with an enlarged electorate and an astonishing turnout of more than 50 percent of eligible voters, Adams's approach failed and Jackson became president (Figure 9.1).

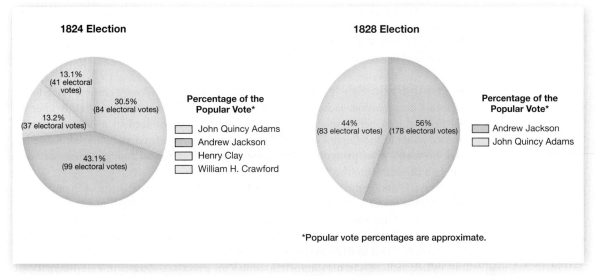

FIGURE 9.1   The Elections of 1824 and 1828

Andrew Jackson lost the 1824 election to John Quincy Adams when the decision was thrown into the House of Representatives. In 1828 Jackson launched the first popular campaign for president, mobilizing working-class white men who were newly enfranchised. Three times as many men—more than one million voters—cast ballots in 1828 than in 1824, ensuring Jackson's election as president.

The election of 1828 formalized a new party alignment. During the campaign Jackson and his supporters referred to themselves as "the Democracy" and forged a new national Democratic Party. In response Adams's supporters called themselves National Republicans. The competition between Democrats and National Republicans heightened interest in national politics among ordinary voters and ensured that the innovative techniques introduced by Jackson would be widely adopted in future campaigns.

REVIEW & RELATE

• How and why did the composition of the electorate change in the 1820s?

• How did Jackson's 1828 campaign represent a significant departure from earlier patterns in American politics?

Jacksonian Politics in Action

Jackson hoped to make government more responsive to the needs of white workers and frontier farmers. But the president's notion of democracy did not extend to Indians or African Americans. During his presidency, Indian nations actively resisted his efforts to take more of their land, and blacks continued to resist their enslavement. Of more immediate importance, once President Jackson had to take clear positions on tariffs and other controversial issues, he could not please all of his constituents. He also confronted experienced adversaries like Henry Clay, Daniel Webster, and John Quincy Adams, who was elected to the House of Representatives from Massachusetts in 1830. The president thus faced considerable difficulty in translating popular support into public policy.

A Democratic Spirit?

On March 4, 1829, crowds of ordinary citizens came to see Jackson's inauguration. Jackson's wife, Rachel, had died of heart failure shortly after his election, leaving her husband devastated. Now Jackson, dressed in a plain black suit, walked alone to the Capitol as vast throngs of supporters waved and cheered. A somber Jackson read a brief inaugural address, took the oath of office, and then rode his horse through the crowds to the White House.

The size and enthusiasm of the crowds soon shattered the decorum of the inauguration. Author Margaret Bayard Smith reported mobs "scrambling, fighting, [and] romping" through the White House reception. Jackson was nearly crushed to death by "rabble" eager to shake his hand. Tubs of punch laced with rum, brandy, and champagne were finally placed on the lawn to draw the crowds outdoors.

While Jackson and his supporters viewed the event as a symbol of a new democratic spirit, others were less optimistic. Bayard Smith and other conservative political leaders saw echoes of the French Revolution in the unruly behavior of the masses. Supreme Court justice Joseph Story, too, feared "the reign of King 'Mob.'"

Tensions between the president and the capital's traditional leaders intensified when Jackson appointed Tennessee senator John Eaton as secretary of war. Eaton had had an affair with a woman thought to be of questionable character and later married her. When Jackson announced his plans to appoint Eaton to his cabinet, congressional leaders urged him to reconsider. When the president appointed Eaton anyway, the wives of Washington's leading politicians snubbed Mrs. Eaton. This time Jackson was outmaneuvered in what became known as the **Petticoat Affair**, and Eaton was eventually forced from office.

In the aftermath of Eaton's resignation, Jackson asked his entire cabinet to resign so he could begin anew. Afterward, however, his legislative agenda stalled in Congress, and National Republicans regained the momentum they had lost with Adams's defeat. The Petticoat Affair reinforced concerns that the president used his authority to reward his friends, as did his reliance on an informal group of advisers, known as the Kitchen Cabinet. While his administration opened up government posts to a wider range of individuals, ensuring more democratic access, Jackson often selected appointees based on personal ties. He believed that "to the victor goes the spoils," and the resulting **spoils system**—continued by future administrations—assigned federal posts as gifts for partisan loyalty rather than as jobs that required experience or expertise.

Confrontations over Tariffs and the Bank.

The Democratic Party that emerged in the late 1820s was built on an unstable foundation. The coalition that formed around Jackson included northern workers who benefited from high tariffs as well as southern farmers and planters who did not. It brought together western voters who sought federal support for internal improvements and strict constructionists who believed such expenditures were unconstitutional. In nearly every legislative battle, then, decisiveness aroused conflict. In 1830 Congress passed four internal improvement bills with strong support from National Republicans. Jackson vetoed each one, which pleased his southern constituency but not his frontier supporters.

Southern congressmen, however, were more interested in his stand on tariffs. The tariff of 1828 still enraged many southern planters and politicians, but most believed that once Jackson reached the White House, he would reverse course and reduce this **Tariff of Abominations**. Instead, he avoided the issue, and southern agriculture continued to suffer. Agricultural productivity in Virginia and other states of the Old South was declining from soil exhaustion, while prices for cotton and rice had not fully recovered after the panic of 1819. At the same time, higher duties on manufactured items raised prices for southerners on many goods.

Even as Calhoun campaigned with Jackson in 1828, the South Carolinian developed a philosophical argument to negate the effects of high tariffs on his state. In *The South Carolina Exposition and Protest*, published anonymously in 1828, Calhoun argued that states should have the ultimate power to determine the constitutionality of laws passed by Congress. When Jackson, after taking office, realized that his vice president advocated **nullification**—the right of individual states to declare individual laws void within their borders—it further damaged their relationship, which was already frayed by the Eaton affair.

When Congress debated the tariff issue in 1830, South Carolina senator Robert Hayne defended nullification. Claiming that the North intended to crush the South economically, he argued that only the right of states to nullify federal legislation could protect southern society. In response, Daniel Webster denounced nullification and the states' rights doctrine on which it was built. Jackson further antagonized southern political leaders by supporting Webster's position.

Matters worsened in 1832 when Congress confirmed the high duties set four years earlier. In response South Carolina held a special convention that approved an Ordinance of Nullification. It stated that duties on imports would not be collected in the state after February 1, 1833, and threatened secession if federal authorities tried to collect them.

The tariff crisis thus escalated in the fall of 1832 just as Jackson faced reelection. The tariff debates had angered many southerners, and Calhoun refused to run again as his vice president. Fortunately for Jackson, opponents in Congress had provided him with another issue that could unite his supporters and highlight his commitment to ordinary citizens: the renewal of the charter of the Bank of the United States.

Clay and Webster persuaded Nicholas Biddle, head of the bank, to request an early recharter of the bank. Jackson's opponents in Congress knew they had the votes to pass a new charter in the summer of 1832, and they hoped Jackson would veto the bill and thereby split the Democratic Party just before the fall elections. The Second Bank was a political quagmire. The bank had stabilized the economy during the 1820s by regularly demanding specie (gold or silver) payments from state-chartered banks. This kept those banks from issuing too much paper money and thereby prevented inflation and higher prices. This tight-money policy also kept banks from expanding too rapidly in the western states. Most financial elites applauded the bank's efforts, but its policies aroused hostility among the wider public. When state-chartered banks closed because of lack of specie, ordinary Americans were often stuck with worthless paper money. Tight-money policies also made it more difficult for individuals to get credit to purchase land, homes, or farm equipment.

As the president's opponents had hoped, Congress approved the new charter, and Jackson vetoed it. Yet rather than dividing the Democrats, Jackson's veto gained enormous support from voters across the country. In justifying his action, the president cast the Second Bank as a "monster" that was "dangerous to the liberties of the people"—particularly farmers, mechanics, and laborers—while promoting "the advancement of the few." Finally,

Explore ▶

For a satirical view of Jackson's attack on the Second Bank, see Document 9.4.

Jackson noted that since wealthy Britons owned substantial shares of the bank's stock, national pride demanded ending the Second Bank's reign over the U.S. economy. Jackson rode the enthusiasm for his bank veto to reelection over National Republican candidate Henry Clay. Within a year, the Second Bank was dead, deprived of government deposits by Jackson.

Soon after his reelection, however, the president faced a grave political crisis related to the tariff issue. Jackson now supported lower tariffs, but he was adamant in his opposition to nullification. In early 1833, he persuaded Congress to pass a Force Bill, which gave him authority to use the military to enforce national laws in South Carolina. At the same time, Jackson made clear that he would work with Congress to reduce tariffs, allowing South Carolina to rescind its nullification ordinance without losing face. Open conflict was averted, but the question of nullification was not resolved.

Contesting Indian Removal. On another long-standing issue—the acquisition of Indian land—Jackson gained the support of white southerners and most frontier settlers. Yet not all Americans agreed with his effort to force Indians off their lands. In the 1820s nations like the Cherokee gained the support of Protestant missionaries who hoped to "civilize" Indians by converting them to Christianity and "American" ways. In 1819 Congress had granted these groups federal funds to advance these goals. Jackson, however, was unsupportive of such efforts and sided with political leaders who sought to force eastern Indians to accept homelands west of the Mississippi River.

In 1825, three years before Jackson was elected president, Creek Indians in Georgia and Alabama were forcibly removed to the Unorganized Territory (previously part of Arkansas Territory and later called Indian Territory) based on a fraudulent treaty. Jackson supported this policy. When he became president, politicians and settlers in Georgia, Florida, the Carolinas, and Illinois demanded federal assistance to force Indian communities out of their states.

The largest Indian nations vehemently protested their removal. The Cherokee, who had fought alongside Jackson at Horseshoe Bend, adopted a republican form of government in 1827 based on the U.S. Constitution. John Ross served as the president of the Cherokee constitutional convention and a year later was elected principal chief. He and the other chiefs then declared themselves a sovereign nation within the borders of the United States. The Georgia legislature rejected Cherokee claims of independence and argued that Indians were simply guests of the state, a position that gained added significance when gold was discovered in Cherokee territory in 1829. Ross appealed to Jackson to recognize Cherokee sovereignty, but the president was affronted by what he saw as a challenge to his authority. He urged Congress to pass the **Indian Removal Act** in 1830, by which the Cherokee and other Indian nations would be forced to exchange their lands in the Southeast for a "clear title forever" on territory west of the Mississippi River. The majority of Cherokees refused to accept these terms.

As the dispute between the Cherokee nation and Georgia unfolded, Jackson made clear his intention to implement the Indian Removal Act. In 1832 he sent federal troops into western Illinois to force Sauk and Fox peoples to move farther west. Instead, whole villages, led by Chief Black Hawk, fled to the Wisconsin Territory. Black Hawk and a thousand warriors confronted U.S. troops at Bad Axe, but the Sauk and Fox warriors were decimated in a brutal daylong battle. The survivors were forced to move west. Meanwhile the

SOLO ANALYSIS

General Jackson Slaying the Many Headed Monster, 1836

Few issues exposed the differences between the Democrats and the National Republicans more clearly than the battle over the national bank. This political cartoon depicts President Andrew Jackson, holding a cane marked "Veto," with his ally Vice President Martin Van Buren and a character named Major Jack Downing. The three attempt to slay "the many headed monster." The American humorist Seba Smith created the fictional Downing to represent a provincial Maine "down-easterner" who used a very broad dialect. He was presented as a close chum of Andrew Jackson to satirize the goings-on in Washington. The hydra features the faces of Nicholas Biddle, the president of the Bank of the United States, and other men who represent the banks of the various states. Biddle wears a hat that says "Penn" and "$35,000,000," which refers to the state of Pennsylvania's effort to recharter the Second Bank in defiance of Jackson's efforts to destroy it.

Document 9.4

Private Collection/Peter Newark American Pictures/Bridgeman Images

Interpret the Evidence

1. How does the artist characterize Jackson, Van Buren, and Downing?
2. Why do you think the artist portrays the national bank as a hydra?

Put It in Context

What does the artist suggest about the feasibility of the Jackson administration's efforts to destroy the bank?

Seminole Indians prepared to go to war to protect their territory, while John Ross pursued legal means to resist removal through state and federal courts. The contest for Indian lands continued well past Jackson's presidency, but the president's desire to force indigenous nations westward would ultimately prevail.

REVIEW & RELATE

- What did President Jackson's response to the Eaton affair and Indian removal reveal about his vision of democracy?
- Which of Jackson's policies benefited or antagonized which groups of southerners?

Conclusion: The **Nation** Faces New Challenges

From the 1810s through the early 1830s, the United States was buffeted by a series of crises. Although early in the period geographical expansion and economic growth led to the federal government to invest in internal improvements, the War of 1812 soon threatened the nation's stability and revealed significant regional divisions. The panic of 1819 then threw the nation into economic turmoil and led to demands for expanded voting rights for white men while African American men experienced increased restrictions on their political participation. Regional differences rooted in distinct regional economies—manufacturing in the North, cotton and rice cultivation in the South, and family agriculture in the Midwest—were increasing in the 1810s. They led to greater economic interdependence across regions, but financial insecurity intensified political debates over issues like tariffs. The admission of Missouri similarly heightened debates over slavery as white southerners saw themselves losing out to the North in population growth and political representation. At the same time, continued western expansion escalated conflicts with a diverse array of Indian nations.

In navigating these difficult issues, some Americans sought to find a middle ground. Dolley Madison worked to overcome partisan divisions through social networking. After the death of her husband, James, in 1836, she returned to Washington and transformed her home into a center of elite social life. Although her son's mismanagement of Montpelier forced her to sell the beloved estate, Dolley secured her old age when Congress purchased President James Madison's papers from her. Similarly, John Ross wielded his biracial heritage to seek rights for Indians within a white-dominated world. He served as both a lobbyist for Cherokee interests in Washington and an advocate of acculturation to Anglo-American ways among the Cherokee. However, congressional passage of the Indian Removal Act challenged Ross's efforts to maintain his tribe's sovereignty and homeland. Henry Clay, too, was widely known for helping to forge key compromises on issues like the admission of Missouri and tariffs. In each case, he brought a deeply divided Congress together and provided time for political leaders to develop more permanent solutions.

Despite the efforts of Madison, Ross, Clay, and others, differences often led to division in the 1820s and 1830s. Indeed, Clay's success in ensuring John Quincy Adams's selection as president in 1824 only furthered partisan divisions, leading to the emergence of two distinct political parties: the Democrats and the National Republicans. Andrew Jackson, who led the new Democratic Party, then transformed the process of political campaigning. He gave voice to white workers and frontier farmers, but he also introduced the spoils system to government, smashed the Second Bank of the United States, and forced thousands of Indians off their lands. Indian removal, in turn, fostered the expansion of white settlement southward and westward, contributing to the growth of slavery.

Dolley Madison, who lived into the late 1840s, and John Ross, who survived the Civil War, observed the continuing conflicts created by geographical expansion and partisan agendas. Ross, however, faced much more difficult circumstances as the Cherokee nation divided over whether to accept removal and continued to face internal dissent and pressure from the federal government for years.

Despite the dramatically different backgrounds and careers of Madison and Ross, both worked to bridge differences in the young nation, and both defended it against attack. Ultimately, however, neither had the power to overcome the partisan rivalries and economic crises that shaped the young nation or to halt the rising tensions over Indian lands and slave labor that would continue to plague Americans in the decades to come.

CHAPTER 9 REVIEW

TIMELINE OF EVENTS

1809	Non-Intercourse Act
1811	First steamboat travels down the Mississippi
	William Henry Harrison defeats Shawnees at Prophet Town
June 1812	War of 1812 begins
1814	Hartford Convention
March 1814	Battle of Horseshoe Bend
August 1814	British burn Washington City
December 1814	Treaty of Ghent
1815	Battle of New Orleans
1817–1818	Andrew Jackson fights Spanish and Seminole forces in Florida
1818	Great Britain and United States agree to joint occupation of Oregon Territory
1819	Adams-Onís Treaty
1819–1823	Panic of 1819
1820	Missouri Compromise
1821	White traders begin using Santa Fe Trail
1822	Denmark Vesey accused of organizing a slave uprising
1823	Monroe Doctrine articulated
1825	Erie Canal completed
1828	Tariff of 1828 (Tariff of Abominations)
	John Ross elected principal chief of the Cherokee nation
1829	Petticoat Affair
1830	Indian Removal Act
1832	South Carolina passes Ordinance of Nullification
1833	Force Bill

KEY TERMS

Non-Intercourse Act, *277*

Battle of Fallen Timbers, *278*

Hartford Convention, *280*

Battle of Horseshoe Bend, *281*

Treaty of Ghent, *282*

American System, *283*

Erie Canal, *285*

Adams-Onís Treaty, *285*

Monroe Doctrine, *286*

panic of 1819, *287*

Missouri Compromise, *290*

Democrats and National Republicans, *295*

Petticoat Affair, *298*

spoils system, *298*

Tariff of Abominations, *299*

nullification, *299*

Indian Removal Act, *300*

REVIEW & RELATE

1. How were conflicts with Indians in the West connected to ongoing tensions between the United States and Great Britain on land and at sea?

2. What were the long-term consequences of the War of 1812?

3. What role did government play in early-nineteenth-century economic development?

4. How and why did economic development contribute to regional differences and shape regional ties?

5. How did regional interdependency contribute to the panic of 1819?

6. What regional divisions did the conflict over slavery in Missouri reveal?

7. How and why did the composition of the electorate change in the 1820s?

8. How did Jackson's 1828 campaign represent a significant departure from earlier patterns in American politics?

9. What did President Jackson's response to the Eaton affair and Indian removal reveal about his vision of democracy?

10. Which of Jackson's policies benefited or antagonized which groups of southerners?

The Election of 1828

Following the bargain that brought John Quincy Adams to power in 1824, followers of Andrew Jackson had four years to plan for the next election. In the interim Adams did little to distinguish himself in office. During the campaign season of 1828, supporters of Jackson and Adams debated political programs and ideas, but they spent even more energy discussing the personal character of the candidates. Adams did not campaign directly. But his supporters held conventions and wrote editorials in which they smeared Jackson in a number of ways (Documents 9.5 and 9.6). They even accused him of adultery and bigamy for marrying Rachel Donelson, whose divorce from a previous husband was never officially finalized. They also ridiculed Jackson's supporters as rowdy and unrefined—charges many of those supporters likely embraced (Document 9.9).

Jackson's campaign took an even more active approach. Spearheaded by vice presidential candidate Martin Van Buren, "Jackson men" fanned out across the country, organizing rallies and drumming up grassroots support. They portrayed Jackson as "Old Hickory," a patriotic war hero who understood the importance of expanding American democracy and winning popular support (Document 9.7). They also assailed Adams for his elite upbringing, inherited career, and undemocratic vision and charged his supporters with slandering Jackson (Documents 9.7 and 9.8). In the end, the Jackson prevailed. He easily won the popular election and the electoral college vote, the latter by a count of 178 to 83. Jackson did particularly well in the South and West, where he benefited from voter rolls significantly expanded by the elimination or decrease in property requirements.

While some earlier campaigns had featured attacks on candidates' qualifications, the campaign of 1828 set a new standard for future contests. The following documents reveal how the character of candidates came to dominate political discourse as partisan differences sharpened. While Jackson supporters reveled in his military victories, for instance, opponents were often appalled. Consider how each campaign attempted to appeal to people's passions rather than national priorities and policies.

Document 9.5

Proceedings of the Anti-Jackson Convention in Richmond, 1828

Across the country, voters held rallies and conventions to declare their support for candidates. At an "Anti-Jackson" convention in Richmond, Virginia, participants listed a litany of reasons why Jackson was not fit to hold the nation's highest office. The following document is an excerpt from the official publication of the convention's proceedings.

It is not in wantonness, that we speak.—but in the sadness of our hearts, we are compelled to declare,—that while we yield our confidence to the present Chief Magistrate in very different degrees, we are unanimous, and unhesitating in the opinion, that Andrew Jackson is altogether unfit for the Presidency, and that his election would be eminently dangerous,—that while we cheerfully accord to him his full share of the glory, which renders the anniversary of the 8th of January a day of joy and triumph to our land,—we must, in the most solemn manner, protest against a claim to civil rule, founded exclusively upon military renown,—and avow, that nothing has occurred in the history of our country, so much calculated to shake our confidence in the capacity of the people for self-government, as the efforts, which have been made, and are yet making, to elevate to the first office in the nation, the man, who, disobeying the orders of his superiors, trampling on the laws and constitution of his country, sacrificing the liberties and lives of men, has made his own arbitrary will, the rule of his conduct. . . .

Gen. Jackson has lived beyond the age of 60 years, and was bred to the profession best calculated to improve and display the faculties, which civil employment requires;—yet the history of his public life, in these employments, is told in a few brief lines, on a single page of his biography. He filled successively, for very short periods,—the office of member of the Tennessee Convention, which formed their State constitution,—representative and senator in Congress,—judge of the supreme court of Tennessee,—and again senator, in the Congress of the United States. Here was ample opportunity for distinction, if he had possessed the talent, taste and application suited for civil eminence. But he resigned three, and passed through all these stations, acknowledging his unfitness in two instances,—manifestly feeling it in all,—and leaving no single act, no trace behind, which stamps his qualification above mediocrity.

For civil government,—and in no station more emphatically, than in that of President of the United States,—a well governed temper is of admitted importance; Gen. Jackson's friends lament the impetuosity of his, and all the work has evidence of its fiery misrule.

To maintain peace and harmony, in the delicate relations existing between the government of the Union and the various State governments, in our confederacy, requires a courtesy and forbearance in their intercourse, which no passions should disturb. . . .

[Our claims] in accusing General Jackson of being unmindful of their [law and constitution] voice . . . will be acknowledged by impartial posterity, when they review the history of his Indian campaigns—and especially when they read the stories, of the cold blooded massacre, at the Horse-shoe [Bend]—and of the decoyed and slaughtered [Seminole] Indians at St. Mark's [Florida]. . . .

[W]e regard Gen. Jackson, as wholly disqualified for the Presidency, and look to the prospect of his election with forebodings.

Source: *Proceedings of the Anti-Jackson Convention, Held at the Capitol in the City of Richmond, with Their Address to the People of Virginia* (Richmond: Franklin Press, 1828), 17–19.

Document 9.6

John Binns | Monumental Inscriptions, 1828

The 1828 election was fought with words and images. Adams supporters seized on the controversy surrounding Jackson's ordering of six executions during the War of 1812. The men who were eventually executed were tried and convicted of leaving their unit at Mobile, Alabama, in summer 1814. John Binns, a Philadelphia journalist, created the following "coffin handbill" to dramatize this story. Numerous versions of the anti-Jackson handbill appeared throughout the campaign season. The headline and the text from two of the coffins are transcribed below.

Paragraph Below the Headline

These Inscriptions, compiled from authentic sources, but principally from OFFICIAL DOCUMENTS, communicated by the Department of War to *Congress*, on the 25th of January, 1828, are, in this form, submitted to the serious consideration of the AMERICAN PEOPLE, under the firm conviction, that the facts embodied in them, ought to, and will, produce a cool and deliberate examination of the qualifications, from Nature and Education, of General ANDREW JACKSON, for the high Civil Station to which he aspires, and to attain which he electioneers with a boldness and pertinacity, unexampled in this Republic. If he shall be found guilty of having ILLEGALLY AND WANTONLY SHED THE BLOOD OF HIS COUNTRYMEN AND FELLOW SOLDIERS, ENTRUST NOT THE LIBERTY AND HAPPINESS OF THIS MOST FREE AND MOST HAPPY COUNTRY TO HIS KEEPING.

Library of Congress, 3a44143r

21st of February, 1815, Having only Four Days Notice of his fate, During which time, He buried himself in writing to his AFFLICTED WIFE, Consoling her, and urging her to bring up his *Nine* Children in the love and foot (?) of THE LORD. An outraged country erects this Monument July 4, 1828.

Coffin from bottom row, right

THIS MARBLE CELL CONTAINS THE MOULDERING REMAINS OF THE GALLANT DAVID HUNT, *He was the Son of a Soldier of the Revolution.* A Volunteer in the Creek War, He faithfully served his country until his Tour of Duty had expired, When he left the Camp, And returned to the home of his Brave Parent; Where learning that his tour of duty had possibly not expired He returned to the Camp and to his Duty, The Veteran Father saying, "Go my Son, I am sure no harm can come to you; I too have been a soldier, and under WASHINGTON A soldier returning to duty which he had left in error always found mercy." *But the Son never more saw the face of his Venerable Father!* He was Arrested, Tried, and SHOT TO DEATH BY ORDER OF GEN. ANDREW JACKSON *On the 21st February, 1815.* The Militia of his Native State erected this simple slab to his Memory on the 4th of July, 1828.

Coffin from bottom row, center

SACRED TO THE MEMORY OF JOHN HARRIS. *He was a Preacher of the Gospel of Christ to the Heathen in the Wilderness.* His temporal substance was destroyed by Fire. TO EARN BREAD For a Wife and Nine Children, he entered as a SUBSTITUTE In the Militia during the Creek War. *He sought information from his Colonel as to his legal Tour of Duty.* IT WAS WITHHELD FROM HIM. He was instructed by his Officers that his Tour of duty would Expire on the 20th September; On that day he surrendered his musket to his Captain, took from him a receipt for it, Departed from Camp, and Returned to the wretched hovel which contained his family. Fearing that he might have erred, he VOLUNTARILY RETURNED TO CAMP, And offered to do duty, if he had mistaken his rights. FOR THESE ACTS HE WAS Arrested, Tried, and by the Orders of GEN. ANDREW JACKSON, SHOT TO DEATH On the

---

Document 9.7

New Jersey Pro-Jackson Convention, 1828

Jackson's supporters organized a greater number of rallies and conventions than Adams's supporters did and campaigned from the western frontier to the East Coast. The following excerpt comes from the proceedings of a pro-Jackson convention in Trenton, New Jersey.

I t is true, no titled honors cluster around his brow. He received not his education in the colleges of foreign potentates, nor was it ever his lot to mingle with princes and imbibe the corruption of their Courts. *He is an American, and nothing but an American.* Without the aid of family or patronage, his intrinsic merit alone, has placed him before the

American people, as worthy of the highest honours of the country. And notwithstanding the unprincipled attacks of hireling presses, aided by all the efforts of a sinking administration, his talents and services are daily better appreciated. His entire devotion to his country's welfare; his stern integrity; his unbending republican simplicity; his enlarged and national views, commend themselves to the intelligence and affections of a free and generous people.

Andrew Jackson was rocked in the cradle of the Revolution. His mind is deeply imbued with the spirit and principles, which, at that day, pervaded the community, and gave a tone to public feeling. While yet a boy, he stood forth in defense of his country's rights, and gave earnest of that lofty spirit of independence, which has ever since characterized the man, whether in the field, the senate chamber, or the retirement of domestic life. . . .

But, Fellow-Citizens, notwithstanding General Jackson has long been known to the American people, as a firm and incorruptible patriot; an honest and able politician, and a virtuous man, yet, a system of warfare has been opened upon him, at which candour and decency must blush and be ashamed. It can find no apology, save in that phrenzy of desperation which excites pity rather than contempt. He has been openly accused of adultery, cruelty, murder; and, last of all, of such gross ignorance as scarcely to be able to read or write! Yes, the man whom you have delighted to honor; and who in 1824, received a much larger proportion of the votes for President, than any other candidate, is now discovered to be the most base, infamous and ignorant of men!! "'Tis strange—'tis passing strange!" . . .

Slanders like these, so gross, so palpable, carry their own refutation with them. They can have no weight with sensible and reflecting men, and on such they were not intended to operate. But they are oft repeated, and reiterated by every press in the interest of the administration. And we grieve to say, that even our members of Congress, our Senators, and the heads of the departments, aid in their circulation.

And why is it that such desperate efforts are made to tarnish the fame of General Jackson? It is because he is sustained by the people, and is advancing with sure and rapid strides in their affections. It is that ill-gotten power may be retained, until the line of safe precedents shall be better established. Those who are now in power, are aware, that they have been weighed and found wanting. Fear hath taken hold of them, and their hour is at hand. Hence it is that every means is resorted to, and truth and honesty sacrificed, to accomplish their unhallowed purpose.

Source: *Proceedings and Address of the New-Jersey State Convention, Assembled at Trenton, on the Eighth Day of January, 1828* (Trenton: Joseph Justice, 1828), 15, 18–19.

Document 9.8

Resolution of the Albany County Republican Convention, 1828

Adams's family connections had certainly benefited his political career, but they also left him vulnerable to criticism. Many of Jackson's supporters linked the younger Adams, a former Federalist, with the unpopular, one-term administration of his father. A pro-Jackson convention in Albany, New York, claims that Adams's background makes him an ineffective president. It also focuses on the War of 1812, in which then–Secretary of State John Quincy Adams served as a peace negotiator.

Resolved, That we oppose the re-election of John Quincy Adams—

Because we believe him to be now, as in all his early hostility to Jefferson and the democracy, imbued with the principles and wedded to the distinctions of the aristocracy—

Because he came to the democratic party, with tales of treason against his former political associates, but with unchanged principles and with personal views—

Because, his ends being selfish, he was willing to prey upon any party that chanced to be predominant—. . .

Because, in that eventful period, when his patriot competitor devoted his whole energies to his country, and, instead of accusing his government of feebleness and penury and holding out the disgraceful language of fear and submission, raising the banner of his country, and inviting to its defence, by the most elevated examples of constancy, devotion and courage, the brave volunteers and militia of the west, freely pledging his private fortune for a people whom he loved, and for hearths that were assailed, showing himself at every point of danger, exciting all to the noble discharge of their duty, animating them by his presence and relieving them by his sacrifices, passing days of fatigue and sleepless nights in preparing for the gallant resistance which the invader afterwards met with at his hands and the hands of his undaunted compatriots, and appearing in that hour of peril in the midst of the conflict, holding to all the inspired and encouraging language, *"Remember that our watch-word is victory or death: our country must*

and shall be defended: we will enjoy our liberty or perish in the last ditch,"—John Quincy Adams predicted our overthrow without raising a finger to avert it, and declared that it could not be expected that "we should resist the mass of force which the gigantic power of Britain had collected to crush us at a blow!"—. . .

Because, bred amongst the aristocracy and educated in foreign courts, his habits and principles are not congenial with the spirit of our institutions and the notions of a democratic people.

Source: *The Striking Similitude between the Reign of Terror of the Elder Adams, and the Reign of Corruption of the Younger Adams: An Address Adopted by the Albany Republican County Convention* (Albany, NY: D. M'Glashan, 1828), 1.

President Andrew Jackson's First Inauguration, 1829

This illustration by the British satirical artist Robert Cruikshank, entitled *President's Levee, or All Creation Going to the White House*, depicts crowds attending Andrew Jackson's White House inaugural reception in 1829. As Margaret Bayard Smith, a well-connected Washington insider, described the scene, "The *Majesty of the People* had disappeared, and a rabble, a mob, of boys, negros, women, children, scrambling, fighting, romping. What a pity! what a pity!"

Granger, NYC

Interpret the Evidence

1. Why, according to the Anti-Jackson convention in Richmond, was Andrew Jackson unfit for president (Document 9.5)? How do the delegates characterize Jackson's political and military career?
2. What was the purpose of the coffin handbill (Document 9.6)? How do the descriptions of the men executed contrast with Jackson's supposed support for ordinary workingmen?
3. How does the Trenton Convention description of Jackson differ from that offered by the Richmond convention (Documents 9.5 and 9.7)? How does it distinguish between Jackson and Adams?
4. How would you compare the Trenton and Albany Conventions' critiques of Adams (Document 9.7 and 9.8)?
5. Why does Cruikshank focus on the outside of the White House in his image of the inauguration (Document 9.9)? How might the various convention delegates and John Binns respond to this illustration?

Put It in Context

Supporters of President Andrew Jackson viewed him as an advocate for ordinary Americans. In what ways does the election of 1828 confirm or contest this claim?

How do these sources reflect the popular campaign style that Jackson introduced into presidential elections?

10

Slavery Expands South and West

1830–1850

War News from Mexico

The Mexican-American War of 1846–1848 was the first U.S. war that Americans could follow through detailed newspaper coverage. People often shared newspapers with family, friends, and neighbors. Newspapers were also sometimes posted on the buildings where they were printed, and individuals read articles aloud to gatherings of interested men and women. This painting highlights the eagerness with which people awaited the latest reports from Mexico. ▶ To discover more about what this primary source can show us, see Document 10.4 on page 338.

Richard Caton Woodville, *War News from Mexico*, 1858. Oil on canvas, 27 × 25 in (68.6 × 63.5 cm). Crystal Bridges Museum of American Art, Bentonville, Arkansas. Photography by The Walters Art Museum, Susan Tobin

After reading this chapter you should be able to:

- Explain the development of a plantation society and the impact on planters and their families as well as slaves and their families.

- Describe the importance of slave labor and the development of a distinctive slave culture, including forms of slave resistance.

- Analyze the differences among southern whites as slavery expanded and compare the techniques used by planters to control blacks and non-slaveholding whites.

- Evaluate the challenges that Indians, the panic of 1837, Texas independence, and the Whig Party posed for the Democratic Party.

- Discuss the ways that the idea of manifest destiny shaped national elections and intensified debates over slavery.

AMERICAN HISTORIES

Although James Henry Hammond became a wealthy plantation owner, he initially planned to pursue the law. Born in 1807 near Newberry, South Carolina, Hammond opened a law practice in Columbia, the state capital, in 1828. Two years later, bored by his profession, he established a newspaper, the *Southern Times*. Writing bold editorials that supported nullification of the "Tariff of Abominations,"

(*left*) **James Henry Hammond** Documenting the American South, University Library, The University of North Carolina at Chapel Hill, http://docsouth.unc.edu/fpn/clay/ill18.html

(*right*) **Solomon Northrup** Documenting the American South, University Library, The University of North Carolina at Chapel Hill, http://docsouth.unc.edu/fpn/northup/frontis.html

Hammond quickly gained attention. He soon married Catherine Fitzsimmons, the daughter of a wealthy, politically connected family. The marriage made Hammond the master of Silver Bluff, a 7,500-acre plantation worked by 147 slaves. A successful planter and agricultural reformer, Hammond was elected to the U.S. House of Representatives in 1834.

In 1836 Hammond campaigned successfully for congressional passage of the so-called gag rule, ensuring that antislavery petitions would be tabled rather than read on the floor of the House. Soon afterward, he took ill and resigned from Congress but returned to politics in 1842 as South Carolina's governor. His ambitions were stymied again, however, when Catherine discovered that her husband had made sexual advances on his four nieces, aged thirteen to sixteen. Fearing public exposure, Hammond withdrew from politics, but then joined southern intellectuals in arguing that slavery was a positive good rather than a necessary evil.

Solomon Northrup was an African American who endured the ravages of slavery and held a distinctly different view of the institution than James Henry Hammond. His father, Mintus, was born into slavery but freed by his owner's will. He moved to Minerva, New York, married and had a son, Solomon, in 1808. At the age of twenty-one, the free-born Northrup married Anne Hampton and worked transporting goods on the region's waterways. He was also hired as a fiddle player, while Anne worked as a cook. In 1834 the couple moved to Saratoga Springs, where they raised their three children until tragedy struck.

In March 1841 Northrup met two white circus performers who hired him to play the fiddle for them on tour. They paid his wages up front and told him to obtain documents proving his free status. After reaching Washington, D.C., however, Northrup was drugged, chained, and sold to James Birch, a notorious slave trader. Northrup was resold in New Orleans to William Ford, who changed his name to Platt. Ford put him to work as a raftsman while Northrup tried unsuccessfully to get word to his wife.

In 1842 Ford sold "Platt" to a neighbor, John Tibeats, who, unlike Ford, whipped and abused his workers. When Tibeats attacked Northrup with an ax, he fought back and fled to Ford's house. His former owner shielded him from Tibeats's wrath and arranged his sale to the planter Edwin Epps. For the next ten years, Northrup worked the cotton fields and played the fiddle at local dances.

Finally, in 1852 Samuel Bass, a Canadian carpenter who openly acknowledged his antislavery views, came to work on Epps's house. Northrup persuaded Bass to send a letter to his wife in Saratoga Springs. Anne Northrup, astonished to hear that her husband was still alive, took the letter to lawyer Henry Northrup, the son of Mintus's former owner. After months of legal efforts, a local judge freed Solomon Northrup in January 1853. ■

The American histories of James Henry Hammond and Solomon Northrup were both intertwined with the struggle over slavery. By 1850 slave labor had become central to the South's and the nation's economic success, even as slave ownership became concentrated in the hands of a small proportion of wealthy white families. These powerful planter families gained increased authority over free blacks and non-slaveowning whites as well as slaves. The concentration of more slaves on each plantation did strengthen African American communities, although it did not negate the brutality they faced. At the same time, the volatility of the cotton market fueled economic instability, contributing to an economic panic in 1837. Planters insisted that only expanding into new lands to cultivate more cotton could ensure economic growth. In response, Democratic administrations forcibly removed Indians from the Southeast, supported independence for Texas, and proclaimed war on Mexico. But these policies led to growing conflicts with western Indian nations, heightened political conflicts over slavery, and inspired the emergence of the Whig Party.

Planters Expand the **Slave System**

The cotton gin, developed in the 1790s, ensured the growth of southern agriculture into the 1840s. As the cotton kingdom spread west, **planters**, those who owned the largest plantations, forged a distinctive culture around the institution of slavery. But this slave-based agricultural economy limited the development of cities, technology, and educational institutions, leaving the South increasingly dependent on the North and West for many of its needs. In addition, westward expansion extended the trade in slaves within the South, shattering black families. Still, southern planters viewed themselves as national leaders, both the repository of traditional American values and the engine of economic progress.

A Plantation Society Develops in the South. Plantation slavery existed throughout the Americas in the early nineteenth century. Extensive plantations worked by large numbers of slaves existed in the West Indies and South America. In the U.S. South, however, the volatile cotton market and a scarcity of fertile land kept most plantations relatively small before 1830. But over the next two decades, territorial expansion and the profits from cotton, rice, and sugar fueled a period of conspicuous consumption. Successful southern planters now built grand houses and purchased a variety of luxury goods.

As plantations grew, especially in states like South Carolina and Mississippi, where slaves outnumbered whites, a wealthy aristocracy sought to ensure productivity by employing harsh methods of discipline. Although James Henry Hammond imagined himself a progressive master, he used the whip liberally, hoping thereby to ensure that his estate generated sufficient profits to support a lavish lifestyle.

Increased attention to comfort and luxury helped make the heavy workload of plantation mistresses tolerable. Mistresses were expected to manage their own families and the domestic slaves as well as the feeding, clothing, and medical care of the entire labor force. They were also expected to organize social events, host relatives and friends for extended stays, and sometimes direct the plantation in their husband's absence.

Still, plantation mistresses were relieved of the most arduous labor by enslaved women, who cooked, cleaned, and washed for the family, cared for the children, and even nursed the babies. Wealthy white women benefited from the best education, the greatest access to music and literature, and the finest clothes and furnishings. Yet the pedestal on which plantation mistresses stood was shaky, built on a patriarchal system in which husbands and fathers held substantial power. For example, most wives tried to ignore the sexual relations that husbands initiated with female slaves. Catherine Hammond did not. She moved to Charleston with her two youngest daughters when she discovered James's sexual abuse of an enslaved mother and daughter. Others, however, took out their anger and frustration on slave women already victimized by their husbands. Moreover, some mistresses owned slaves themselves, gave them as gifts or bequests to family members and friends, and traded them on the open market.

Not all slaveholders were wealthy planters like the Hammonds, with fifty or more slaves and extensive landholdings. Far more planters in the 1830s and 1840s owned between twenty and fifty slaves, and an even larger number of farmers owned just three to six slaves. These small planters and farmers could not afford to emulate the lives of the largest slave owners. Still, as Hammond wrote a friend in 1847, "The planters here are essentially what the nobility are in other countries. They stand at the head of society & politics."

Urban Life in the Slave South. The insistence on the supremacy of slave owners had broad repercussions. The richest men in the South invested in slaves, land, and household goods, with little left to develop industry, technology, or urban institutions. The largest factory in the South, the Tredegar Iron Works in Richmond, Virginia, employed several hundred free and enslaved African Americans by 1850. Most southern industrialists, however, like South Carolina textile manufacturer William Gregg, employed poor white women and children. But neither Tredegar nor a scattering of textile mills fundamentally reshaped the region's economy.

The South also fell behind in urban development. The main exception was port cities. Yet even in Baltimore, Charleston, and Savannah, commerce was often directed by northern agents, especially cotton brokers. In addition, nearly one-third of southern whites had no access to cash and instead bartered goods and services, further restricting the urban economy.

Southern cities did attract many free blacks. The growing demand for cheap domestic labor in urban areas and planters' greater willingness to emancipate less valuable single female slaves meant that free black women generally outnumbered men in southern cities. These women worked mainly as washerwomen, cooks, and general domestics, while free black men labored as skilled artisans, dockworkers, or sailors. Free blacks competed for these jobs with slaves and growing numbers of European immigrants who flocked to

New Orleans, 1841 New Orleans was one of the few major urban areas in the South and, like Baltimore and Charleston, prospered through its seaport. The port of New Orleans attracted sailing ships engaged in foreign commerce, steamships carrying goods along the Mississippi River, and slave traders from across the eastern United States. Eileen Tweedy/The Art Archive at Art Resource, NY

southern cities in the 1840s and 1850s. The presence of immigrants and free blacks and the reputation of ports as escape hatches for runaway slaves ensured that cities remained suspect in the South.

The scarcity of cities and industry also curtailed the development of transportation. State governments invested little in roads, canals, and railroads. Most small farmers traded goods locally, and most planters used the South's extensive river system to ship goods to commercial hubs. Only Virginia and Maryland, with their proximity to the nation's capital, developed extensive road and rail networks.

The Consequences of Slavery's Expansion.

Outside the South, industry and agriculture increasingly benefited from technological innovation. Planters, however, continued to rely on intensive manual labor. Even reform-minded planters focused on fertilizer and crop rotation rather than machines to enhance productivity. The limited use of new technologies—such as iron plows or seed drills—resulted from a lack of investment capital and planters' refusal to purchase expensive equipment that they feared might be broken or purposely sabotaged by slaves. Instead, they relied on continually expanding the acreage under cultivation.

One result of these practices was that a declining percentage of white Southerners came to control vast estates with large numbers of enslaved laborers. Between 1830 and

1850, the absolute number of both slaves and owners grew. But slave owners became a smaller proportion of all white Southerners because the white population grew faster than the number of slave owners. At the same time, distinctions among wealthy planters, small slaveholders, and whites who owned no slaves also increased.

The concern with productivity and profits and the concentration of more slaves on large plantations did have some benefits for black women and men. The end of the

Slave Population, 1820
• One dot equals 200 slaves

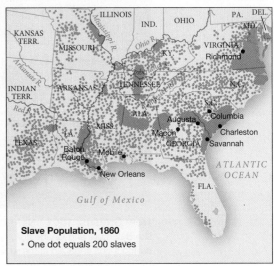

Slave Population, 1860
• One dot equals 200 slaves

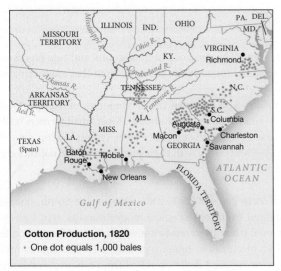

Cotton Production, 1820
• One dot equals 1,000 bales

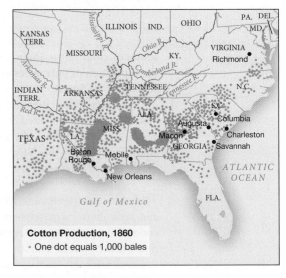

Cotton Production, 1860
• One dot equals 1,000 bales

MAP 10.1   The Spread of Slavery and Cotton, 1820–1860

While tobacco, rice, and sugar remained important crops in a few states, cotton became the South's and the nation's major export. The need to find more fertile fields led planters to migrate to Alabama, Mississippi, and Louisiana. As a result of cotton's success, the number of enslaved people increased dramatically, the internal slave trade expanded, and labor demands intensified.

international slave trade in 1808 forced planters to rely more heavily on natural reproduction to increase their labor force. Thus many planters thought more carefully about how they treated their slaves, who were increasingly viewed as "valuable property." It was no longer good business to work slaves to death or cripple them by severe punishments.

Nonetheless, owners continued to whip slaves and made paltry investments in their diet and health care. Most slaves lived in small houses with dirt floors and little furniture and clothing. They ate a diet high in calories, especially fats and carbohydrates, but with little meat, fish, fresh vegetables, or fruits. The high mortality rate among slave infants and children—more than twice that of white children to age five—reflected the limits of planters' care.

The spread of slavery into Mississippi, Louisiana, Alabama, Missouri, and eventually Texas affected both white and black families, though again not equally. The younger sons of wealthy planters were often forced to move to the frontier, and their families generally lived in rough quarters on isolated plantations. Such moves were far more difficult for slaves, however. Between 1830 and 1850, more than 440,000 slaves were forced to move from the Upper South to the Lower South (Map 10.1), often tearing them away from their families through sales to new masters. On the southern frontier, they endured especially harsh conditions as they cleared and cultivated new lands.

Explore ▶

See Document 10.1 for one visitor's description of a slave pen in Washington, D.C.

By the 1830s, slave markets blossomed in key cities across the South. Solomon Northrup was held in one in Washington, D.C., where a woman named Eliza watched as her son Randall was "won" by a planter from Baton Rouge. She promised "to be the most faithful slave that ever lived" if he would also buy her and her daughter. The slave trader threatened the desperate mother with a hundred lashes, but neither his threats nor her tears could change the outcome. As slavery spread westward, such scenes were repeated thousands of times.

REVIEW & RELATE

- What role did the planter elite play in southern society and politics?

- What were the consequences of the dominant position of slave-based plantation agriculture for the southern economy?

Slave Society and Culture

Because slave labor formed the backbone of the southern economy, enslaved workers gained some leverage against owners and overseers. But these women and men did not simply define themselves in relation to whites. They also developed relationships, identities, and cultural practices within the slave quarters. Many also found small ways to resist their enslavement on an everyday basis. Others resisted more openly, and a small number organized rebellions against their masters.

Slaves Fuel the Southern Economy. The labor of enslaved blacks drove the nation's economy as well as the South's. In 1820 the South produced some 500,000 bales of cotton, much of it exported to England. By 1850 the region produced nearly 3 million bales, feeding textile mills in New England and abroad. A decade later, cotton accounted for nearly two-thirds of the U.S. export trade and added nearly $200 million a year to the American economy.

Edward Strutt Abdy | Description of Washington, D.C., Slave Pen, 1833

Slavery and the slave trade had always been legal in Washington, D.C., and enslaved laborers cleared land and constructed buildings. As the debate over slavery increased in the nineteenth century, abolitionists often highlighted the incongruence of slavery in the capital city of American democracy. Visitors wrote with disgust about slave auctions held within sight of the Capitol steps. In the 1830s the English writer Edward Strutt Abdy toured the United States and described the scene at a slave pen.

Document 10.1

How does Abdy describe the construction of the slave pen and its relation to the U.S. Capitol?

How are whites and blacks described?

How might northern and southern audiences have reacted to this description of a slave pen? How might readers in Great Britain, where slavery had just been abolished, have responded?

One day I went to see the "slaves' pen"—a wretched hovel, "right against" the Capitol, from which it is distant about half a mile, with no house intervening. The outside alone is accessible to the eye of a visitor; what passes within being reserved for the exclusive observation of its owner (a man of the name of Robey) and his unfortunate victims. It is surrounded by a wooden paling fourteen or fifteen feet in height, with the posts outside to prevent escape, and separated from the building by a space too narrow to admit of a free circulation of air. At a small window above, which was unglazed and exposed alike to the heat of summer and the cold of winter, so trying to the constitution, two or three sable faces appeared, looking out wistfully to while away the time and catch a refreshing breeze; the weather being extremely hot. In this wretched hovel, all colors, except white—the only guilty one—both sexes, and all ages, are confined, exposed indiscriminately to all the contamination which may be expected in such society and under such seclusion. The inmates of the gaol, of this class I mean, are even worse treated; some of them, if my informants are to be believed, having been actually frozen to death, during the inclement winters which often prevail in the country. While I was in the city, Robey had got possession of a woman, whose term of slavery was limited to six years. It was expected that she would be sold before the expiration of that period, and sent away to a distance, where the assertion of her claim would subject her to ill-usage. Cases of this kind are very common.

Source: Edward Strutt Abdy, *Journal of a Residence and Tour in the United States of North America, from April, 1833, to October, 1834* (London: John Murray, 1835), 2:96–97.

Put It in Context

How did the spread of cotton, south and west fuel the development of slave traders and slave pens?

Plantation Slaves at Work   Slaves performed a wide variety of labor, such as planting and harvesting crops, domestic work, and blacksmithing. This panel painted by William Henry Brown in about 1842 shows slaves, perhaps an enslaved family, behind a wagon hauling cotton. Although most tasks were physically demanding, workers who carried goods to market at least had the chance to briefly leave the plantation. The Historic New Orleans Collection/Bridgeman Images

Enslaved laborers, of course, saw little of this wealth. Carpenters, blacksmiths, and other skilled slaves were sometimes hired out and allowed to keep a small amount of the money they earned. They traveled to nearby households, compared their circumstances to those on other plantations, and sometimes made contact with free blacks. Some skilled slaves also learned to read and write and had access to tools and knowledge denied to field hands. Still, they were constantly hounded by whites who demanded travel passes and deference, and they were often suspected of involvement in rebellions.

Household slaves sometimes received old clothes and bedding or leftover food from their owners. Yet they were under the constant surveillance of whites, and women especially were vulnerable to sexual abuse. Moreover, the work they performed was physically demanding. Fugitive slave James Curry recalled that his mother, a cook in North Carolina, rose early each morning to milk cows, bake bread, and churn butter. She was responsible for meals for her owners and the slaves. In summer, she cooked her last meal around eight o'clock, after which she milked the cows again. Then she returned to her quarters, put her children to bed, and often fell asleep while mending clothes.

Once slaves reached the age of ten to twelve, they were put to work full-time, usually in the fields. Although field labor was defined by its relentless pace and drudgery, it also brought together large numbers of slaves for the entire day and thus helped forge bonds among laborers on the same plantation. Songs provided a rhythm for their work and offered slaves the chance to communicate their frustrations or hopes.

Field labor was generally organized by task or by gang. Under the task system, typical on rice plantations, slaves could return to their quarters once the day's task was completed. This left time for slaves to cultivate gardens, fish, or mend clothes. In the gang system, widely used on cotton plantations, men and women worked in groups under the supervision of a driver. Often working from sunup to sundown, they swept across fields hoeing, planting, or picking. **See Document Project 10: Lives in Slavery, page 342.**

Developing an African American Culture.
Amid hard work and harsh treatment, slaves created social bonds and a rich culture of their own. Thus African Americans continued for generations to employ African names, like Cuffee and Binah. Even if masters gave them English names, they might use African names in the slave quarters to sustain family memories and community networks. Elements of West African and Caribbean languages, agricultural techniques, medical practices, forms of dress, folktales, songs and musical instruments, dances, and courtship rituals—all demonstrated the continued importance of these cultures to African Americans. This hybrid culture was disseminated as slaves hauled cotton to market, forged families across plantation boundaries, or were sold farther south. It was also handed down across generations through storytelling, music, rituals, and religious services.

Religious practices offer an important example of this blended slave culture. Africans from Muslim communities often continued to pray to Allah even if they were also required to attend Protestant churches, while black Protestant preachers developed rituals that combined African and American elements. In the early nineteenth century, many slaves eagerly embraced the evangelical teachings offered by Baptist and Methodist preachers, which echoed some of the expressive spiritual forms in West Africa. On Sundays, slaves who listened in the morning to white ministers proclaim slavery as God's will might gather in the evening to hear their own preachers declare God's love and the possibilities of liberation, at least in the hereafter. Slaves often incorporated drums, dancing, or other West African elements into these worship services.

Although most black preachers were men, a few enslaved women also gained a spiritual following. Many female slaves embraced religion enthusiastically, hoping that Christian baptism might substitute for West African rituals that protected newborn babies. Enslaved women sometimes called on church authorities to intervene when white owners, overseers, or even enslaved men abused them. They also considered the church one means of sanctifying slave marriages that were not recognized legally.

Slaves also generally provided health care for their community. Most slave births were attended by black midwives, and African American healers often turned to herbal medicines, having discovered southern equivalents to cures used in West Africa.

Resistance and Rebellion.
Many slave owners worried that black preachers and West African folktales inspired blacks to resist enslavement. Fearing defiance, planters went to incredible lengths to control their slaves. Although they were largely successful in quelling open revolts, they were unable to eliminate more subtle forms of opposition, like slowing the pace of work, feigning illness, and damaging equipment. More overt forms of resistance—such as truancy and running away, which disrupted work and lowered profits—also proved impossible to stamp out.

HORRID MASSACRE IN VIRGINIA·

Nat Turner's Rebellion   This woodcut depicts the rebellion in the top panel and the capture of rebels below. It was published in 1831 by Samuel Warner, a New York publisher who based his lurid account on eyewitness testimony and the supposed confessions of participants. He linked the Turner rebellion to the Haitian Revolution and to suspected (though unproven) conspiracies else-where in the South. Library of Congress, 3a33960

The forms of everyday resistance slaves employed varied in part on their location and resources. Skilled artisans, mostly men, could do more substantial damage because they used more expensive tools, but they were less able to protect themselves through pleas of ignorance. Field laborers could often damage only hoes, but they could do so regularly without exciting suspicion. House slaves could burn dinners, scorch shirts, break china, and even poison owners. Often considered the most loyal slaves, they were also among the most feared because of their intimate contact with white families. Single male slaves were the most likely to run away, planning their escape to get as far away as possible before their absence was noticed. Women who fled plantations were more likely to hide out for short periods in the local area. Eventually, isolation, hunger, or concern for children led most of these truants to return if slave patrols did not find them first.

Despite their rarity, efforts to organize slave uprisings, such as the one supposedly hatched by Denmark Vesey in 1822, continued to haunt southern whites. Rebellions in the West Indies, especially the one in Saint Domingue (Haiti), also echoed through the early nineteenth century. Then in 1831 a seemingly obedient slave named Nat Turner organized a revolt in rural Virginia that stunned whites across the South. Turner was a religious visionary who believed that God had given him a mission. On the night of August 21, he and his followers killed his owners, the Travis family, and then headed to nearby planta-tions in Southampton County. The insurrection led to the deaths of 57 white men, women, and children and liberated more than 50 slaves. But on August 22, outraged white militia-men burst on the scene and eventually captured the black rebels. Turner managed to hide out for two months but was eventually caught, tried, and hung. Virginia executed 55 other African Americans suspected of assisting Turner.

Nat Turner's rebellion instilled panic among white Virginians, who beat and killed some 200 blacks with no connection to the uprising. White Southerners worried they might be killed in their sleep by seemingly submissive slaves. News of the rebellion traveled through slave communities as well, inspiring both pride and anxiety. The execution of Turner and his followers reminded African Americans how far whites would go to protect the institution of slavery.

A mutiny on the Spanish slave ship *Amistad* in 1839 reinforced white Southerners' fears of rebellion. When Africans being transported for sale in the West Indies seized control of the ship near Cuba, the U.S. navy captured the vessel and imprisoned the enslaved rebels. But international treaties outlawing the Atlantic slave trade and pressure applied by abolitionists led to a court case in which former president John Quincy Adams defended the right of the Africans to their freedom. The widely publicized case reached the U.S. Supreme Court in 1841, and the Court freed the rebels. While the ruling was cheered by abolitionists, white Southerners were shocked that the justices would liberate enslaved men.

REVIEW & RELATE

- How did enslaved African Americans create ties of family, community, and culture?

- How did enslaved African Americans resist efforts to control and exploit their labor?

Planters Tighten Control

Fears of rebellion led to stricter regulations of black life, and actual uprisings temporarily reinforced white solidarity. Yet yeomen farmers, poor whites, and middle-class professionals all voiced some doubts about the ways in which slavery affected southern society. To ensure white unity, planters wielded their economic and political authority, highlighted bonds of kinship and religious fellowship, and promoted an ideology of white supremacy. Their efforts intensified as northern states and other nations began eradicating slavery.

Harsher Treatment for Southern Blacks.

Slave revolts led many southern states to impose harsher controls; however, Nat Turner's rebellion led some white Virginians to question slavery itself. In December 1831, the state assembly established a special committee to consider the crisis. Representatives from western counties, where slavery was never profitable, argued for gradual abolition laws and the colonization of the state's black population in Africa. Hundreds of women in the region sent petitions to the Virginia legislature supporting these positions.

While advocates of colonization gained significant support, eastern planters vehemently opposed abolition or colonization, and leading intellectuals argued for the benefits of slavery. Professor Thomas Dew, president of the College of William and Mary, insisted that slaveholders performed godly work in raising Africans from the status of brute beast to civilized Christian. "Every one acquainted with southern slaves," he claimed, "knows that the slave rejoices in the elevation and prosperity of his master." In the fall of 1832 the Virginia legislature embraced Dew's proslavery argument, rejected gradual emancipation, and imposed new restrictions on slaves and free blacks.

From the 1820s to the 1840s, more stringent codes were passed across the South. Most southern legislatures prohibited owners from manumitting their slaves, made it illegal for whites to teach slaves to read or write, placed new limits on independent black churches, abolished slaves' limited access to courts, outlawed slave marriage, banned antislavery literature, defined rape as a crime only against white women, and outlawed assemblies of more than three blacks without a white person present.

States also regulated the lives of free blacks. Some prohibited free blacks from residing within their borders, others required large bonds to ensure good behavior, and most forbade free blacks who left the state from returning. The homes of free blacks could be raided at any time, and the children of free black women were subject to stringent apprenticeship laws that kept many in virtual slavery.

Such measures proved largely successful in controlling slaves, but there was a price to pay. Restricting education and mobility for blacks often hindered schooling and transportation for poor whites as well. Moreover, characterizing the region's primary labor force as savage and lazy discouraged investment in industry and other forms of economic development. And the regulations increased tensions between poorer whites, who were often responsible for enforcement, and wealthy whites, who benefited most clearly from their imposition.

White Southerners without Slaves.
Yeomen farmers, independent owners of small plots who owned few or no slaves, had a complex relationship with the South's plantation economy. Many were related to slave owners, and they often depended on planters to ship their crops to market. Some made extra money by hiring themselves out to planters. Yet yeomen farmers also recognized that their economic interests often diverged from those of planters. As growing numbers gained the right to vote in the 1820s and 1830s, they voiced their concerns in county and state legislatures.

Most yeomen farmers believed in slavery, but they sometimes challenged planters' authority and assumptions. In the Virginia slavery debates, for example, small farmers from western districts advocated gradual abolition. In other states, they advocated more liberal policies toward debtors. Yeomen farmers also questioned certain ideals embraced by elites. Although plantation mistresses considered manual labor beneath them, the wives and daughters of many small farmers worked in the fields, hauled water, and chopped wood. Still, yeomen farmers' ability to diminish planter control was limited by the continued importance of cotton to the southern economy.

In their daily lives, however, many small farmers depended more on friends and neighbors than on the planter class. Barn raisings, corn shuckings, quilting bees, and other collective endeavors offered them the chance to combine labor with sociability. Church services and church socials also brought communities together.

An even larger number of white Southerners owned no property at all. These poor whites depended on hunting and fishing in frontier areas, performing day labor on farms and plantations, or working on docks or as servants in southern cities. Poor whites competed with free blacks and slaves for employment and often harbored resentments as a result. Yet some, including poor immigrants from Ireland, Wales, and Scotland, built alliances with blacks based on their shared economic plight.

Some poor whites remained in the same community for decades, establishing themselves on the margins of society. They attended church regularly, performed day labor for

North Carolina Emigrants, 1845   James Henry Beard, who later gained fame for his portraits of political leaders and of dogs, captures in this painting a family of poor whites hoping to find better opportunities farther west. The family was fortunate to own a cow, but the children are barefoot and the mother cradles her infant on a horse that carries all their worldly possessions. Cincinnati Art Museum, Ohio, USA / Gift of the Procter & Gamble Company/Bridgeman Images

affluent families, and taught their children to defer to those higher on the social ladder. Other poor whites moved frequently and survived by combining legal and illegal ventures. They might perform day labor while also stealing food from local farmers. These men and women often had few ties to local communities and little religious training or education. Although poor whites unnerved southern elites by flouting the law and sometimes befriending poor blacks, they could not mount any significant challenge to planter control.

The South's small but growing middle class distanced themselves from poorer whites in pursuit of stability and respectability. They worked as doctors, lawyers, teachers, and shopkeepers and often looked to the North for models to emulate. Many were educated in northern schools and developed ties with their commercial or professional counterparts in that region. They were avid readers of newspapers, religious tracts, and literary periodicals published in the North. And like middle-class Northerners, southern businessmen often depended on their wives' social and financial skills to succeed.

Nonetheless, middle-class southern men shared many of the social attitudes and political priorities of slave owners. They participated alongside planters in benevolent, literary, and temperance (anti-alcohol) societies and agricultural reform organizations. Most middle-class Southerners also adamantly supported slavery. In fact, some suggested that bound labor might be useful to industry. Despite the emergence of a small middle class, however, the gap between rich and poor continued to expand in the South.

Planters Seek to Unify Southern Whites.

Planters faced another challenge as nations in Europe and South America began to abolish slavery. Antislavery views, first widely expressed by Quakers, gained growing support among evangelical Protestants in Great Britain and the United States and among political radicals in Europe. Slave rebellions in Saint Domingue and the British West Indies in the early nineteenth century intensified these efforts. In 1807 the British Parliament forbade the sale of slaves within its empire and in 1834 emancipated all those who remained enslaved. France followed suit in 1848. As Spanish colonies such as Mexico and Nicaragua gained their independence in the 1820s and 1830s, they, too, eradicated the institution. Meanwhile gradual abolition laws in the northern United States slowly eliminated slavery there. Although slavery continued in Brazil and in Spanish colonies such as Cuba, and serfdom remained in Russia, international attitudes toward human bondage were shifting.

In response, planters wielded their political and economic power to forge tighter bonds among white Southerners. According to the three-fifths compromise in the U.S. Constitution, areas with large slave populations gained more representatives in Congress than those without. The policy also applied to state elections, giving such areas disproportionate power in state politics. In addition, planters used their resources to provide credit for those in need, offer seasonal employment for poorer whites, transport crops to market for yeomen farmers, and help out in times of crisis. Few whites could afford to antagonize these affluent benefactors.

Wealthy planters also emphasized ties of family and faith. James Henry Hammond, for example, regularly assisted his siblings and other family members financially. Many slave owners worshipped alongside their less well-to-do neighbors, and both the pastor and the congregation benefited from maintaining good relations with the wealthiest congregants. Most church members, like many relatives and neighbors, genuinely admired and respected planter elites who looked out for them.

Still, planters did not take white solidarity for granted. From the 1830s on, they relied on the ideology of **white supremacy** to cement the belief that all whites, regardless of class or education, were superior to all blacks. Following on Thomas Dew, southern elites argued with growing vehemence that the moral and intellectual failings of blacks meant that slavery was not just a necessary evil but a positive good. At the same time, they insisted that blacks harbored deep animosity toward whites, which could be controlled only by regulating every aspect of their lives. Combining racial fear and racial pride, planters forged bonds with poor and middling whites to guarantee their continued dominance. They continued to seek support from state and national legislators as well.

REVIEW & RELATE

- What groups made up white southern society? How did their interests overlap or diverge?

- How and why did the planter elite seek to reinforce white solidarity?

Democrats Face Political and Economic Crises

Southern planters depended on federal power to expand and sustain the system of slavery. Despite differences on tariffs, both President Andrew Jackson and his successor, Martin Van Buren, stood with southern planters in support of Indian removal and independence for Texas from Mexico. But Van Buren faced a more well-organized opposition in the **Whig Party**, which formed in the 1830s, while U.S. rebels in Texas faced powerful resistance from Mexican and Comanche forces. Then in 1837 a prolonged and severe economic panic gripped the nation, creating an opportunity for the Whigs to end Democratic control of the federal government.

The Battle for Texas. As southern agriculture expanded westward, some whites looked toward Texas for fresh land. White Southerners had begun moving into eastern Texas in the early nineteenth century, but the Adams-Onís Treaty of 1819 guaranteed Spanish control of the territory. Then in 1821 Mexicans overthrew Spanish rule and claimed Texas as part of the new Republic of Mexico. But Mexicans faced serious competition from Comanche Indians, who controlled vast areas in northern Mexico and launched frequent raids into Texas.

Eager to increase settlement in the area and to create a buffer against the Comanches, the Mexican government granted U.S. migrants some of the best land in eastern Texas. It hoped these settlers would eventually spread into the interior, where Comanche raids had devastated Mexican communities. To entice more Southerners, the Mexican government negotiated a special exemption for U.S. planters when it outlawed slavery in 1829. But rather than spreading into the interior, American migrants stayed east of the Colorado River, out of reach of Comanche raids and close to U.S. markets in Louisiana.

Moreover, U.S. settlers resisted assimilation into Mexican society. Instead, they continued to worship as Protestants, speak English, send their children to separate schools, and trade mainly with the United States. By 1835 the 27,000 white Southerners and their 3,000 slaves far outnumbered the 3,000 Mexicans living in eastern Texas.

Forming a majority of the east Texas population and eager to expand their plantations and trade networks, growing numbers of U.S. settlers demanded independence. Then in 1836 Mexicans elected a strong nationalist leader, General Antonio López de Santa Anna, as president. He sought to calm **Tejanos** (Mexican Texans) angered by their vulnerability to Comanche attacks and to curb U.S. settlers seeking further concessions. However, when Santa Anna appointed a military commander to rule Texas, U.S. migrants organized a rebellion and, on March 2, declared their independence. Some elite Tejanos, long neglected by authorities in Mexico City, sided with the rebels. But the rebellion appeared to be short-lived. On March 6, 1836, General Santa Anna crushed settlers defending the **Alamo** in San Antonio. Soon thereafter, he captured the U.S. settlement at Goliad.

At this point, Santa Anna was convinced that the uprising was over. But the U.S. government, despite its claims of neutrality, aided the rebels with funds and army officers. American newspapers picked up the story of the Alamo and published accounts of the battle, describing the Mexican fighters as brutal butchers bent on saving Texas for the pope. These stories, though more fable than fact, increased popular support for the war at a time when many Americans were increasingly hostile to Catholic immigrants in the United States.

As hundreds of armed volunteers headed to Texas, General Sam Houston led rebel forces in a critical victory at San Jacinto in April 1836. While the Mexican government refused to recognize rebel claims, it did not try to regain the lost territory. Few of the U.S. volunteers arrived in time to participate in the fighting, but some settled in the newly liberated region. The Comanche nation quickly recognized the Republic of Texas and developed trade relations with residents to gain access to the vast U.S. market. Still, Santa Anna's failure to recognize Texas independence kept the U.S. government from granting the territory statehood for fear it would lead to war with Mexico.

Explore ▸

See Documents 10.2 and 10.3 for opposing views on Texas independence and annexation.

President Jackson also worried that admitting a new slave state might split the national Democratic Party before the fall elections. To limit debate on the issue, Congress passed a **gag rule** in March 1836 that tabled all antislavery petitions without being read. Nevertheless, thousands of antislavery activists still flooded the House of Representatives with petitions opposing the annexation of Texas.

Indians Resist Removal. At the same time as the United States and Mexico battled over Texas, the United States also faced continued challenges from Indian nations. After passage of the Indian Removal Act in 1830, Congress hoped to settle the most powerful eastern Indian tribes on land west of the Mississippi River. But some Indian peoples resisted. While federal authorities forcibly removed the majority of Florida Seminoles to Indian Territory between 1832 and 1835, a minority fought back. Jackson and his military commanders expected that this **Second Seminole War** would be short-lived. However, they misjudged the Seminoles' strength; the power of their charismatic leader, Osceola; and the resistance of black fugitives living among the Seminoles.

The conflict continued long after Jackson left the presidency. During the seven-year guerrilla war, 1,600 U.S. troops died. U.S. military forces defeated the Seminoles in 1842 only by luring Osceola into an army camp with false promises of a peace settlement. Instead, officers took him captive, finally breaking the back of the resistance. Still, to end the conflict, the U.S. government had to allow fugitive slaves living among the Seminoles to accompany the tribe to Indian Territory.

Unlike the Seminole, members of the Cherokee nation challenged removal by peaceful means, believing that their prolonged efforts to coexist with white society would ensure their success. Indian leaders like John Ross had urged Cherokees to embrace Christianity, white gender roles, and a republican form of government as the best means to ensure control of their communities. Large numbers had done so, but in 1829 and 1830, Georgia officials sought to impose new regulations on the Cherokee living within the state's borders. Tribal leaders took them to court, demanding recognition as a separate nation and using evidence of their Americanization to claim their rights. In 1831 *Cherokee Nation v. Georgia* reached the Supreme Court, which denied a central part of the Cherokee claim. It ruled that all Indians were "domestic dependent nations" rather than fully sovereign governments. Yet the following year, in *Worcester v. Georgia*, the Court declared that the state of Georgia could not impose *state* laws on the Cherokee, for they had "territorial boundaries, within which their authority is exclusive," and that both their land and their rights were protected by the federal government.

COMPARATIVE ANALYSIS

Two Views on Texas Independence

In March 1836, U.S.-born Texans declared an independent republic. Under attack by Mexican forces at the Alamo, twenty-six–year-old Colonel William Travis and others appealed for reinforcements (Document 10.2). While all the men were killed, their appeals inspired hundreds of U.S. volunteers to join military efforts in Texas. They contributed to winning Texas independence, but that victory fueled intense debates over the question of annexation. Abolitionist and Quaker editor Benjamin Lundy was among those who argued that annexation would benefit the "Slaveholding Interest" (Document 10.3). These men offer competing perspectives on the relationship between Texas independence and national honor.

Document 10.2

Colonel William Travis | Appeal for Reinforcements, March 3, 1836

I hope your honorable body will hasten on reinforcements, ammunition, and provisions to our aid. . . . At least five hundred pounds of cannon powder, and two hundred rounds of six, nine, twelve, and eighteen pound balls—ten kegs of rifle powder, and a supply of lead, should be sent to this place without delay, under a sufficient guard.

If these things are promptly sent and large reinforcements are hastened to this frontier, this neighborhood will be the great and decisive battle ground. The power of Santa Ana is to be met here, or in the colonies; we had better meet them here, than to suffer a war of desolation to rage in our settlements. A blood-red banner waves from the church of Bejar, and in the camp above us, in token that the war is one of vengeance against rebels; they have declared us such, and demanded that we should surrender at discretion, or that this garrison should be put to the sword. Their threats have had no influence on me, or my men, but to make all fight with desperation, and that high souled courage which characterizes the patriot, who is willing to die in defence of his country's liberty and his own honor.

The citizens of this municipality are all our enemies except those who have joined us heretofore; . . . those who have not joined us in this extremity, should be declared public enemies, and their property should aid in paying the expenses of the war.

The bearer of this will give your honorable body a statement more in detail should he escape through the enemies lines.

God and Texas—Victory or Death!!
Your obedient ser't

W. Barrett Travis, Lieut. Col. Comm.

Source: *Telegraph and Texas Register*, March 12, 1836, 3.

President Jackson, who sought Cherokee removal, argued that only the tribe's removal west of the Mississippi River could ensure its "physical comfort," "political advancement," and "moral improvement." Most southern whites, seeking to mine gold and expand cotton production in Cherokee territory, agreed. But Protestant women and men in the North launched a massive petition campaign in 1830 supporting the Cherokees' right to their land. The Cherokee themselves forestalled action through Jackson's second term.

Document 10.3

Benjamin Lundy | The War in Texas, 1836

It is generally admitted that the war in Texas has assumed a character which must seriously affect both the interests and honor of this nation. It implicates the conduct of a large number of our citizens, and even the policy and measures of the government are deeply involved in it. . . . The great fundamental principles of universal liberty—the perpetuity of our free republican institutions—the prosperity, the welfare, and the happiness of future generations—are measurably connected with the prospective issue of this fierce and bloody conflict.

But the prime cause and the real objects of this war are not distinctly understood by a large portion of the honest, disinterested, and well-meaning citizens of the United States. . . . [M]any of them have been deceived and misled by the misrepresentations of those concerned in it, and especially by hireling writers for the newspaper press. They have been induced to believe that the inhabitants of Texas were engaged in a legitimate contest for the maintenance of the sacred principles of Liberty, and the natural, inalienable

Rights of Man: whereas . . . . the immediate cause and the leading object of this contest originated in a settled design, among the slaveholders of this country (with land speculators and slave-traders), to wrest the large and valuable territory of Texas from the Mexican Republic, in order to re-establish the SYSTEM OF SLAVERY; to open a vast and profitable SLAVE-MARKET therein; and, ultimately, to annex it to the United States. . . . The Slaveholding Interest is now paramount in the Executive branch of our national government; and its influence operates, indirectly, yet powerfully, through that medium, in favor of this Grand Scheme of Oppression and Tyrannical Usurpation. Whether the national Legislature will join hands with the Executive, and lend its aid to this most unwarrantable, aggressive attempt, will depend on the VOICE OF THE PEOPLE, expressed in their primary assemblies, by their petitions, and through the ballot-boxes.

Source: Benjamin Lundy, *The War in Texas* (Philadelphia: Merrihew and Gunn, 1836), 3.

Interpret the Evidence

1. According to William Travis, why was it crucial for the United States to defend the Alamo and Texas independence?
2. How would you compare Travis's appeal for aid with Benjamin Lundy's claims about the rationale for the war and the interests supporting independence? How does each define U.S. national interests?

Put It in Context

What do the battle for Texas independence and debates over Texas annexation reveal about sectional divisions in the United States in the 1830s and 1840s?

In December 1835, however, U.S. officials convinced a small group of Cherokee men—without tribal sanction—to sign the **Treaty of New Echota**. It proposed the exchange of 100 million acres of Cherokee land in the Southeast for $68 million and 32 million acres in Indian Territory. Outraged Cherokee leaders like John Ross lobbied Congress to reject the treaty. But in May 1836, Congress approved the treaty by a single vote and set the date for final removal two years later (Map 10.2).

In 1838, the U.S. army forcibly removed Cherokees who had not yet resettled in Indian Territory. That June, General Winfield Scott, assisted by 7,000 U.S. soldiers, forced some 15,000 Cherokees into forts and military camps. Indian families spent the next several months without sufficient food, water, sanitation, or medicine. In October, when the Cherokees finally began the march west, torrential rains were followed by snow. Although the U.S. army planned for a trip of less than three months, the journey actually took five months. As supplies ran short, many Indians died. The remaining Cherokees completed this **Trail of Tears**, as it became known, in March 1839. But thousands remained near starvation a year later.

Following the Trail of Tears, Seneca Indians petitioned the federal government to stop their removal from western New York. Federal agents had negotiated the Treaty of Buffalo

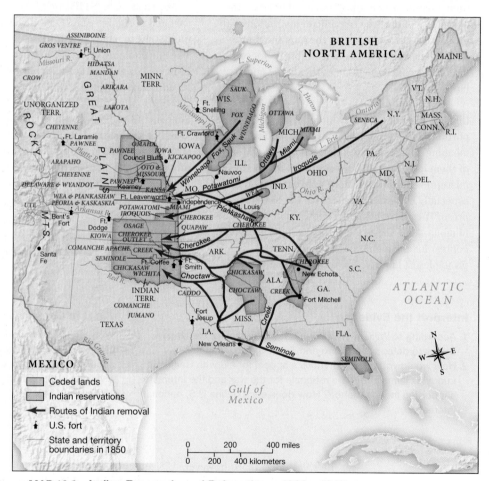

MAP 10.2   Indian Removals and Relocations, 1820s–1840s

In the 1820s and 1830s, the federal government used a variety of tactics, including military force, to expel Indian nations residing east of the Mississippi River. As these tribes resettled in the West, white migration along the Oregon and other trails began to increase. The result, by 1850, was the forced relocation of many western Indian nations as well.

Cherokee Removal, 1838   This woodcut appeared in a U.S. geography textbook about 1850. The title "Indian Emigrants" and the image of Cherokee disembarking from a steamboat falsely suggest that the emigration was voluntary and the means of travel relatively easy. The U.S. fort on the hill symbolizes the role of the federal government in forcing the Cherokee to move west of the Mississippi. Granger, NYC

Creek with several Iroquois leaders in 1838. But some Seneca chiefs claimed the negotiation was marred by bribery and fraud. With the aid of Quaker allies, the Seneca petitioned Congress and the president for redress. Perhaps reluctant to repeat the Cherokee and Seminole debacles, Congress approved a new treaty in 1842 that allowed the Seneca to retain two of their four reservations in western New York.

Van Buren and the Panic of 1837. Although Jackson proposed the Indian Removal Act, it was President Martin Van Buren who confronted ongoing challenges from Indian nations. When Van Buren ran for president in 1836, the Whigs hoped to defeat him by bringing together diverse supporters: evangelical Protestants who objected to Jackson's Indian policy, financiers and commercial farmers who advocated internal improvements and protective tariffs, merchants and manufacturers who favored a national bank, and Southerners who were antagonized by the president's heavy-handed use of federal authority. But the Whigs could not agree on a single candidate, and this lack of unity allowed Democrats to prevail. Although Van Buren won the popular vote by only a small margin (50.9 percent), he secured an easy majority in the electoral college.

Inaugurated on March 4, 1837, President Van Buren soon faced a major financial crisis. The **panic of 1837** started in the South and was rooted in the changing fortunes of American cotton in Great Britain. During the 1830s, the British invested heavily in cotton plantations and brokerage firms, and southern planters used the funds to expand production and improve shipping facilities. British banks also lent large sums to states such as New York to fund internal improvements, which fueled inflation.

In late 1836, the Bank of England, faced with bad harvests and declining demand for textiles, tightened credit to limit the flow of money out of the country. This forced British investors to call in their loans and drove up interest rates in the United States just as cotton prices started to fall. Some large American cotton merchants were forced to declare bankruptcy. The banks where they held accounts then failed—ninety-eight of them in March and April 1837 alone.

The economic crisis hit the South hard. Cotton prices fell by nearly half in less than a year. Land values declined dramatically, port cities came to a standstill, and cotton communities on the southern frontier collapsed. The damage soon radiated throughout the United States. Northern brokers, shippers, and merchants were devastated by losses in the cotton trade, and northern banks were hit by unpaid debts incurred for canals and other internal improvements. Entrepreneurs who borrowed money to expand their businesses defaulted in large numbers. Shopkeepers, artisans, and farmers in the North and Midwest suffered unemployment and foreclosures.

In the North and West, many Americans blamed Jackson's war against the Bank of the United States for precipitating the panic and were outraged at Van Buren's refusal to intervene in the crisis. While it is unlikely that any federal policy could have resolved the nation's economic problems, the president's apparent disinterest in the plight of the people inspired harsh criticisms from ordinary citizens as well as political opponents. Worse, despite brief signs of recovery in 1838, the depression deepened in 1839 and continued for four more years.

The Whigs Win the White House.

Eager to exploit the weakness of Van Buren and the Democrats, the Whig Party organized its first national convention in fall 1840 and united behind military hero William Henry Harrison. Harrison was born to a wealthy planter family in Virginia, but he was portrayed as a self-made man who lived in a simple log cabin in Indiana. His running mate, John Tyler, another Virginia gentleman and a onetime Democrat, joined the Whigs because of his opposition to Jackson's stand on nullification. Whig leaders hoped he would attract southern votes. Taking their cue from the Democrats, the Whigs organized rallies, barbecues, parades, and mass meetings. They turned the tables on their foe by portraying Van Buren as an aristocrat and Harrison as a war hero and friend of the common man. Reminding voters that Harrison had defeated Tenskwatawa at the Battle of Tippecanoe, the Whigs adopted the slogan "Tippecanoe and Tyler Too."

The Whigs also welcomed women into the campaign. By 1840 thousands of women had circulated petitions against Cherokee removal, organized temperance societies, promoted religious revivals, and joined charitable associations. They embodied the kind of moral force that the Whig Party claimed to represent. In October 1840, Whig senator Daniel Webster spoke to a gathering of 1,200 women, calling on them to encourage their brothers and husbands to vote for Harrison.

The Whig strategy paid off handsomely on election day. Harrison won easily, and the Whigs gained a majority in Congress. Yet the election's promise was shattered when Harrison died of pneumonia a month after his inauguration. Whigs in Congress now had to deal with John Tyler, whose sentiments were largely southern and Democratic. Vetoing many Whig efforts at reform, Tyler allowed the Democratic Party to regroup and set the stage for close elections in 1844 and 1848.

William Henry Harrison Campaign Poster, 1840 In posters announcing rallies in support of Harrison, the candidate was portrayed as man of humble origins although his father was a wealthy Virginia planter. He was also represented as a frontier farmer, although his most important role on the frontier was as a military leader who defeated Tenskwatawa at the Battle of Tippecanoe. Library of Congress, rbpe 01601000

REVIEW & RELATE

How did westward expansion affect white Southerners, white Northerners, enslaved blacks, and American Indians in the 1830s and 1840s?

What economic and political developments led to a Whig victory in the election of 1840?

The **National Government Looks** to the **West**

Despite the Whig victory in 1840, planters wielded considerable clout in Washington, D.C., because of the importance of cotton to the U.S. economy. In turn, Southerners needed federal support to expand into more fertile areas. The presidential election of 1844 turned on this issue, with Democratic candidate James K. Polk demanding continued expansion into Oregon and Mexico. Once Polk was in office, his claims were contested not only by Britain and Mexico but also by the Comanche. After the United States won vast Mexican territories in 1848, conflicts with Indians and debates over slavery only intensified.

Expanding to Oregon and Texas. Southerners eager to expand the plantation economy were at the forefront of the push for territorial expansion. Yet expansion was not merely a southern strategy. Northerners demanded that the United States reject British claims to the Oregon Territory, and some northern politicians and businessmen advocated acquiring Hawaii and Samoa to benefit U.S. trade. In 1844 the Democratic Party built on these expansionist dreams to recapture the White House.

The Democrats nominated a Tennessee congressman and governor, James K. Polk. The Whigs, unwilling to nominate Tyler for president, chose Kentucky senator Henry Clay. Polk declared himself in favor of the annexation of Texas. Clay, meanwhile, waffled on the issue. This proved his undoing when the Liberty Party, a small antislavery party founded in 1840, denounced annexation. Liberty Party candidate James G. Birney captured just enough votes in New York State to throw the state and the election to Polk.

In February 1845, a month before Polk took office, Congress passed a joint resolution annexing the Republic of Texas. That summer, John L. O'Sullivan, editor of the *Democratic Review*, captured the American mood by declaring that nothing must interfere with "the

Astoria, Oregon, 1848 In 1845 the British army sent Lieutenant Henry Warre to the Oregon Country to gather intelligence on American settlements in case of war with the United States. Warre sketched Astoria, which lies at the mouth of the Columbia River. The first permanent settlement in the Oregon Country, it was established by John Jacob Astor's Pacific Fur Company in 1811. Granger, NYC

fulfillment of our manifest destiny to overspread the continent allotted by Providence." This vision of **manifest destiny**—of the nation's God-given right to expand its borders— defined Polk's presidency.

With the Texas question seemingly resolved, President Polk turned his attention to Oregon, which stretched from the forty-second parallel to latitude 54°40' and was jointly occupied by Great Britain and the United States.

In 1842, three years before Polk took office, glowing reports of the mild climate and fertile soil around Puget Sound had inspired thousands of farmers and traders to flood into Oregon's Willamette Valley. Alarmed by this "Oregon fever," the British tried to confine Americans to areas south of the Columbia River. But U.S. settlers demanded access to the entire territory. President Polk encouraged migration into Oregon but was unwilling to risk war with Great Britain. Instead, diplomats negotiated a treaty in 1846 that extended the border with British Canada (the forty-ninth parallel) to the Pacific Ocean. Over the next two years, Congress admitted Iowa and Wisconsin to statehood, reassuring northern residents that expansion benefited all regions of the nation.

Many of the lands newly claimed by the U.S. government were home to vast numbers of Indians. Indeed, the West had become more crowded as the U.S. government forced eastern tribes to move west of the Mississippi (see Map 10.2). When the Cherokee and other southeastern tribes were removed to Indian Territory, for example, they confronted tribes such as the Osage. Pushed into the Southwest, the Osage came into conflict with the Comanche, who had earlier fought the Apache for control of the southern plains. Other Indian nations were pushed onto the northern plains from the Old Northwest. When tribes like the Mandan were decimated by smallpox in the 1830s, the Sioux dominated the region.

The flood of U.S. migrants into Texas and the southern plains transformed relations among Indian nations as well as with Mexico. In the face of Spanish and then Mexican claims on their lands, for example, the Comanche forged alliances with former foes like the Wichita and the Osage. The Comanche also developed commercial ties with tribes in Indian Territory and with both Mexican and Anglo-American traders. They thereby hoped to benefit from the imperial ambitions of the United States and Mexico while strengthening bonds among Indians in the region.

Comanche expansion was especially problematic for Mexico. The young nation did not have sufficient resources to sustain the level of gift giving that Spanish authorities had used to maintain peace. As a result, Comanche warriors launched continual raids against Tejano settlements in Texas. But the Comanche also developed commercial relations with residents of New Mexico, who flaunted trade regulations promulgated in Mexico City. By 1846 Comanche trade and diplomatic relations with New Mexican settlements had seriously weakened the hold of Mexican authorities on their northern provinces.

Pursuing War with Mexico. At the same time, with Texas now a state, Mexico faced growing tensions with the United States. Conflicts centered on Texas's western border. Mexico insisted on the Nueces River as the boundary line, while Americans claimed all the land to the Rio Grande. In January 1846, Polk secretly sent emissary John Slidell to negotiate a border treaty with Mexico. But Polk also sent U.S. troops under General Zachary Taylor across the Nueces River. Mexican officials refused to see Slidell and instead sent their own troops across the Rio Grande. Meanwhile U.S. naval commanders prepared to seize San Francisco Bay from the Mexicans if war was declared. The Mexican government responded by sending more troops into the disputed Texas territory.

When fighting erupted near the Rio Grande in May 1846 (Map 10.3), Polk claimed that "American blood had been shed on American soil" and declared a state of war. Many Whigs in Congress opposed the declaration, arguing that the president had provoked the conflict. However, antiwar Whigs failed to convince the Democratic majority, and

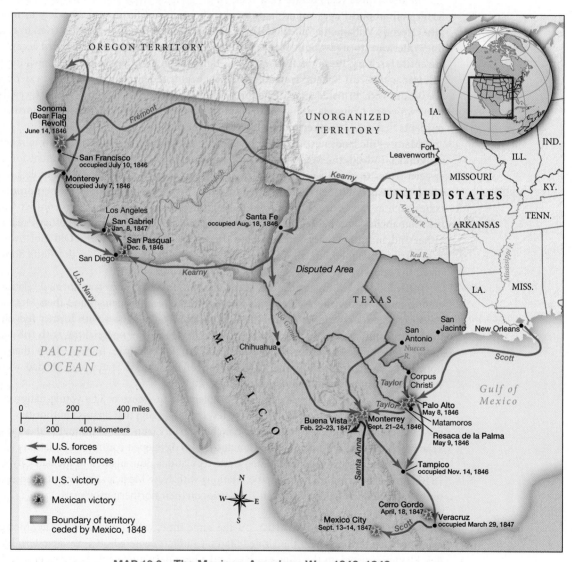

MAP 10.3   The Mexican-American War, 1846–1848

Although a dispute over territory between the Nueces River and the Rio Grande initiated the Mexican-American War, most of the fighting occurred between the Rio Grande and Mexico City. In addition, U.S. forces in California launched battles to claim independence for that region even before gold was discovered there.

Congress voted to finance the war. Although northern opponents of slavery protested the war, most Americans—North and South—considered westward expansion a boon.

Once the war began, battles erupted in a variety of locations. In May 1846, U.S. troops defeated Mexican forces in Palo Alto and Resaca de la Palma. A month later, the U.S. army captured Sonoma, California, with the aid of local settlers. John Frémont then led U.S. forces to Monterey, where the navy launched a successful attack and declared the California territory part of the United States. That fall, U.S. troops gained important victories at Monterrey, Mexico, just west of the Rio Grande, and Tampico, along the Gulf coast.

Explore ▸

For one artist's view of Americans' interest in the Mexican War, see Document 10.4.

Despite major U.S. victories, Santa Anna, who reclaimed the presidency of Mexico during the war, refused to give up. In February 1847, his troops attacked U.S. forces at Buena Vista and nearly secured a victory. Polk then agreed to send General Winfield Scott to Veracruz with 14,000 soldiers. Capturing the port in March, Scott's army marched on to Mexico City. After a crushing defeat of Santa Anna at Cerro Gordo, the president-general was removed from power and the new Mexican government sought peace.

With victory ensured, U.S. officials faced a difficult decision: How much Mexican territory should they claim? The U.S. army in central Mexico faced continued guerrilla attacks. Meanwhile Whigs and some northern Democrats denounced the war as a southern conspiracy to expand slavery. In this context, Polk agreed to limit U.S. claims to the northern regions of Mexico. The president signed the **Treaty of Guadalupe Hidalgo** in February 1848, committing the United States to pay Mexico $15 million in return for control over Texas north and east of the Rio Grande plus California and the New Mexico territory.

Debates over Slavery Intensify. News of the U.S. victory traveled quickly across the United States. In the South, planters imagined slavery spreading into the lands acquired from Mexico. Northerners, too, applauded the expansion of U.S. territory but focused on California as a center for agriculture and commerce. Yet the acquisition of new territory only heightened sectional conflicts. Debates over slavery had erupted during the war, with a few northern Democrats joining Whigs in denouncing "the power of SLAVERY" to "govern the country, its Constitutions and laws." In August 1846, Democratic congressman David Wilmot of Pennsylvania proposed outlawing slavery in all territory acquired from Mexico so that the South could not profit from the war. While the **Wilmot Proviso** passed in the House, southern and proslavery northern Democrats in the Senate killed it.

The presidential election of 1848 opened with the unresolved question of whether to allow slavery in the territories acquired from Mexico. With Polk declining to run for a second term, Democrats nominated Lewis Cass, a Michigan senator and ardent expansionist. Hoping to keep northern antislavery Democrats in the party, Cass argued that residents in each territory should decide whether to make the region free or slave. This strategy put the slavery question on hold but satisfied almost no one.

The Whigs, too, hoped to avoid the slavery issue for fear of losing southern votes. They nominated Mexican-American War hero General Zachary Taylor, a Louisiana slaveholder who had no declared position on slavery in the western territories. But they sought to reassure their northern wing by nominating Millard Fillmore of Buffalo, New York, for vice president. As a member of Congress in the 1830s, Fillmore had opposed the annexation of Texas.

The Liberty Party, disappointed in the Whig ticket, decided to run its own candidate for president. But leaders who hoped to expand their support reconstituted themselves as

SOLO ANALYSIS

Richard Caton Woodville | *War News from Mexico*, 1848

Richard Caton Woodville was born in Baltimore in 1825 but spent most of his adult life in Europe. Still, he painted mainly American scenes, and his paintings were often turned into inexpensive prints for popular consumption. In this image, he highlights the importance of newspapers in reporting the Mexican-American War. Reports were often read aloud to groups of people eager to hear the latest news.

Document 10.4

Richard Caton Woodville, *War News from Mexico*, 1858. Oil on canvas, 27 x 25 in (68.6 x 63.5 cm). Crystal Bridges Museum of American Art, Bentonville, Arkansas. Photography by The Walters Art Museum, Susan Tobin

Interpret the Evidence

1. What does the name of the hotel—American Hotel—and the diversity of characters portrayed here indicate about Woodville's understanding of the Mexican-American War?
2. What does the placement of the lone woman, the two African Americans, and the white men suggest about the investment of different groups of Americans in the ongoing war?

Put It in Context

Why was the news of the Mexican-American War so important to diverse groups of Americans?

the Free-Soil Party. Its leaders focused more on excluding slaves from the western territories than on the moral injustice of slavery. The party nominated former president Martin Van Buren and appealed to small farmers and urban workers who hoped to benefit from western expansion.

Once again, the presence of a third party affected the outcome of the election. While Whigs and Democrats tried to avoid the slavery issue, Free-Soilers demanded attention to it. By focusing on the exclusion of slavery in western territories rather than its abolition, the Free-Soil Party won more adherents in northern states. Indeed, Van Buren won enough northern Democrats so that Cass lost New York State and the 1848 election. Zachary Taylor and the Whigs won, but only by placing a southern slaveholder in the White House.

REVIEW & RELATE

How did the battle over Texas affect relations among Indian nations, among white Americans, and between Indians and whites?

How did the Mexican-American War reshape national politics and intensify debates over slavery?

Conclusion: Geographical Expansion and Political Division

By the mid-nineteenth century, the United States stood at a crossroads. Most Americans considered expansion advantageous and critical to revitalizing the economy. Planters believed it was vital to slavery's success. Yet as the number of slaves and the size of plantations grew, planters also sought to impose stricter controls over blacks, enslaved and free, and to bind non-slaveowning whites more firmly to their interests. Enslaved blacks, meanwhile, developed an increasingly rich culture by combining traditions and rituals from Africa and the Caribbean with U.S. customs and beliefs. This African American culture served as one form of resistance against slavery's brutality. Many enslaved laborers resisted in other ways as well: sabotaging tools, feigning illness, running away, or committing arson or theft. Smaller numbers engaged in outright rebellions.

While most white Northerners were willing to leave slavery alone where it already existed, many hoped to keep it out of newly acquired territories. In this sense, the removal of the Cherokee did not disturb Northerners since it was largely yeoman farmers who would benefit from access to their land. Instead, many northern whites opposed removal on moral grounds. When it came to the Mexican-American War, however, more Northerners—black and white—feared victory would mainly benefit southern planters. The vast lands gained from Mexico in 1848 intensified the debates over slavery and led small but growing numbers of white Northerners to join African Americans, American Indians, and Mexicans in protesting U.S. expansion. Even some yeomen farmers and middle-class professionals in the South questioned whether extending slavery benefited the region economically and politically.

It was the panic of 1837, however, that opened the way for a new political alignment. The extended depression allowed the newly formed Whig Party to gain support for its economic and reform agenda. In 1840 Whigs captured the White House and Congress, and a new antislavery force, the Liberty Party, emerged as well. But just four years later, James K. Polk's support of westward expansion and manifest destiny returned Democrats to power. The political volatility continued when the U.S. victory in the war with Mexico intensified debates over slavery in the territories, fracturing the Democratic Party and inspiring the founding of the Free-Soil Party.

Political realignments continued over the next decade, fueled by growing antislavery sentiment in the North and proslavery beliefs in the South. In 1853 Solomon Northrup horrified thousands of antislavery readers with his book *Twelve Years a Slave*, which vividly described his life in bondage. Such writings alarmed planters like James Henry Hammond, who continued to believe that slavery was a divine blessing. Yet in insisting on the benefits of slave labor, the planter elite inspired further conflict with Northerners, whose lives were increasingly shaped by commercial and industrial developments and the expansion of free labor.

TIMELINE OF EVENTS

1830	Indian Removal Act
1830–1850	440,000 slaves from Upper South sold to owners in Lower South
1831	*Cherokee Nation v. Georgia*
	Nat Turner leads slave uprising in Virginia
	Virginia's Assembly establishes special committee on slavery
1832	*Worcester v. Georgia*
1834	Britain abolishes slavery
1835–1842	Second Seminole War
1836	Treaty of New Echota
March 2, 1836	U.S. settlers declare eastern Texas an independent republic
March 6, 1836	General Santa Anna crushes U.S. rebels at the Alamo
March 1836	Congress passes gag rule
1837–1843	Panic of 1837 triggers extended depression
1838–1839	Cherokee driven west on Trail of Tears
1840	Whigs win the presidency and gain control of Congress
1841	Solomon Northrup kidnapped and sold into slavery
1842	Seneca Indians win treaty to remain in New York
1845	U.S. annexes Texas
1846	U.S. settles dispute with Great Britain over Oregon
May 1846– February 1848	Mexican-American War
August 1846	David Wilmot proposes Wilmot Proviso
March 1848	Treaty of Guadalupe Hidalgo

KEY TERMS

planters, *313*

Nat Turner's rebellion, *321*

yeomen farmers, *323*

white supremacy, *325*

Whig Party, *326*

Tejanos, *326*

Alamo, *326*

gag rule, *327*

Second Seminole War, *327*

Treaty of New Echota, *329*

Trail of Tears, *330*

panic of 1837, *331*

manifest destiny, *335*

Treaty of Guadalupe Hidalgo, *337*

Wilmot Proviso, *337*

REVIEW & RELATE

1. What role did the planter elite play in southern society and politics?

2. What were the consequences of the dominant position of slave-based plantation agriculture for the southern economy?

3. How did enslaved African Americans create ties of family, community, and culture?

4. How did enslaved African Americans resist efforts to control and exploit their labor?

5. What groups made up white southern society? How did their interests overlap or diverge?

6. How and why did the planter elite seek to reinforce white solidarity?

7. How did westward expansion affect white Southerners, white Northerners, enslaved blacks, and American Indians in the 1830s and 1840s?

8. What economic and political developments led to a Whig victory in the election of 1840?

9. How did the battle over Texas affect relations among Indian nations, among white Americans, and between Indians and whites?

10. How did the Mexican-American War reshape national politics and intensify debates over slavery?

Lives in Slavery

Slaves lived under a system of severe subjugation and routinely suffered brutal working conditions, violence, and the devastating separation of families (Documents 10.5, 10.6, 10.7, and 10.8). Yet many slaves found ways to resist their bondage and carve out autonomous spaces. They feigned illness, ran away or hid for a few days, and developed a distinctive African American culture (Document 10.9).

A rich body of slave narratives has helped historians understand slave life. During the nineteenth century a few escaped slaves published books about their lives. Often sponsored by white abolitionists, these books highlighted the humanity of blacks and the horrors of slavery. Frederick Douglass, William Wells Brown, Solomon Northup, and Harriet Jacobs all published narratives that revealed hidden aspects of slaves' experience (Documents 10.5, 10.6, and 10.7). In the twentieth century the Works Progress Administration, a federal program to provide work during the Great Depression of the 1930s, hired mostly white writers to conduct interviews with ex-slaves. Of course, those interviewed were old at the time but had been relatively young while enslaved. Still, the interviews with people such as Mary Reynolds (Document 10.9) offer valuable insight into the lives of slaves who had no way to record their stories during the slave era.

Whites also documented the lives of the enslaved in the nineteenth century. Both abolitionists and planters wrote extensively about slavery, though from opposing perspectives. Many Europeans were fascinated by American slavery, and some captured the institution in books and paintings (Document 10.8). These white-produced sources can be valuable when analyzed in the context of slaves' stories about their own lives.

Document 10.5

William Wells Brown | Memories of Childhood

William Wells Brown was born into slavery in 1814 on a Missouri farm and later worked on Mississippi riverboats. He escaped in 1834, fleeing first to Cleveland and then to western New York and Boston. He became a popular antislavery lecturer and published his narrative in 1847. While he focuses here on his time as a household slave, he also recalls the cries of his mother being whipped in the fields.

[T]he field hands . . . were summoned to their unrequited toil every morning at four o'clock, by the ringing of a bell. . . . They were allowed half an hour to eat their breakfast, and get to the field. At half past four, a horn was blown by the overseer, which was the signal to commence work; and every one that was not on the spot at the time, had to receive ten lashes from the negro-whip, . . . The handle was about three feet long, with the butt-end filled with lead, and the lash six or seven feet in length, made of cowhide, with platted wire on the end of it. This whip was put in requisition very frequently and freely, and a small offence on the part of a slave furnished an occasion for its use. . . . I was a house servant—a situation preferable to that of a field hand, as I was better fed, better clothed, and not obliged to rise at the ringing of the bell, but about half an hour after. I have often laid and heard the crack of the whip, and the screams of the slave. My mother was a field hand, and one morning was ten or fifteen minutes behind the others in getting into the field. As soon as she reached the spot where they were at work, the overseer commenced whipping her. She cried, "Oh! pray—Oh! pray—Oh! pray"— . . . . I heard her voice, and knew it, and jumped out of my bunk, and went to the door. Though the field was some distance from the house, I could hear every crack of the whip, and every groan and cry of my poor mother. . . . The cold chills ran over me, and I wept aloud. After giving her ten lashes, the sound of the whip ceased, and I returned to my bed, and found no consolation but in my tears. It was not yet daylight.

Source: William Wells Brown, *Narrative of William W. Brown, A Fugitive Slave, Written by Himself* (Boston: Anti-Slavery Office, 1847), 14–16.

Document 10.6

Harriet Jacobs | A Girl Threatened by Sexual Exploitation

Harriet Jacobs was born into slavery in 1813 in Edenton, North Carolina. She made a daring escape in 1835 but remained hidden for seven years in a crawlspace in the house of her grandmother, a free black woman. She finally reached the North in 1842 and became active in abolitionist circles. In her 1861 autobiography, published under the pseudonym Linda Brent, Jacobs describes in harrowing detail her master's attempted sexual exploitation.

But I now entered on my fifteenth year—a sad epoch in the life of a slave girl. My master began to whisper foul words in my ear. Young as I was, I could not remain ignorant of their import. I tried to treat them with indifference or contempt. The master's age, my extreme youth, and the fear that his conduct would be reported to my grandmother, made him bear this treatment for many months. He was a crafty man, and resorted to many means to accomplish his purposes. Sometimes he had stormy, terrific ways, that made his victims tremble; sometimes he assumed a gentleness that he thought must surely subdue. Of the two, I preferred his stormy moods, although they left me trembling. He tried his utmost to corrupt the pure principles my grandmother had instilled. He peopled my young mind with unclean images. . . . I turned from him with disgust and hatred. But he was my master. I was compelled to live under the same roof with him—where I saw a man forty years my senior daily violating the most sacred commandments of nature. He told me I was his property; that I must be subject to his will in all things. My soul revolted against the mean tyranny. But where

could I turn for protection? No matter whether the slave girl be as black as ebony or as fair as her mistress. In either case, there is no shadow of law to protect her from insult, from violence, or even from death; all these are inflicted by fiends who bear the shape of men. The mistress, who ought to protect the helpless victim, has no other feelings towards her but those of jealousy and rage. . . .

Even the little child, who is accustomed to wait on her mistress and her children, will learn, before she is twelve years old, why it is that her mistress hates such and such a one among the slaves. Perhaps the child's own mother is among those hated ones. . . . She will become prematurely knowing in evil things. Soon she will learn to tremble when she hears her master's footfall. She will be compelled to realize that she is no longer a child. If God has bestowed beauty upon her, it will prove her greatest curse. That which commands admiration in the white woman only hastens the degradation of the female slave.

Source: Linda Brent [Harriet Jacobs], *Incidents in the Life of a Slave Girl* (Boston: Published for the Author, 1861), 44–46.

Document 10.7

Solomon Northup | Endless Labor and Constant Fear

Solomon Northup, who was born free in New York State in 1808, was kidnapped and sold into slavery in 1841. After he regained his freedom in 1853, he wrote an autobiography, *Twelve Years a Slave*, about his experiences under slavery. In this excerpt, he describes the labor regimen of his owner, Edwin Epps, a planter in southern Louisiana.

The hands are required to be in the cotton field as soon as it is light in the morning, and, with the exception of ten or fifteen minutes, which is given them at noon to swallow their allowance of cold bacon, they are not permitted to be a moment idle until it is too dark to see, and when the moon is full, they often times labor till the middle of the night. They do not dare to stop even at dinner time, nor return to the quarters, however late it be, until the order to halt is given by the driver.

The day's work over in the field, the baskets are . . . carried to the gin-house, where the cotton is weighed. No matter how fatigued and weary he may be—no matter how much he longs for sleep and rest—a slave never approaches the gin-house with his basket of cotton but with fear. If it falls short in weight—if he has not performed the full task appointed him, he knows that he must suffer. And if he has exceeded it by ten or twenty pounds, in all probability his master will measure the next day's task accordingly. . . . Most frequently they have too little, and therefore it is they are not anxious to leave the field. After weighing, follow the whippings; and then the baskets are carried to the cotton house, and their contents stored away like hay, all hands being sent in to tramp it down. . . .

This done, the labor of the day is not yet ended, by any means. Each one must then attend to his respective chores. One feeds the mules, another the swine—another cuts the wood, and so forth; besides, the packing is all done by candle light. Finally, at a late hour, they reach the quarters, sleepy and overcome with the long day's toil. Then a fire must be kindled in the cabin, the corn ground in the small hand-mill, and supper, and dinner for the next day in the field, prepared. All that is allowed them is corn and bacon, which is given out at the corncrib and smoke-house every Sunday morning. . . . That is all—no tea, coffee, sugar, and with the exception of a very scanty sprinkling now and then, no salt. . . .

The softest couches in the world are not to be found in the log mansion of the slave. The one whereon I reclined year after year, was a plank twelve inches wide and ten feet long. My pillow was a stick of wood. The bedding was a coarse blanket, and not a rag or shred beside. Moss might be used, were it not that it directly breeds a swarm of fleas. . . .

An hour before day light the horn is blown. . . . Then the fears and labors of another day begin.

Source: Solomon Northrup, *Twelve Years a Slave* (Auburn, NY: Derby and Miller, 1853), 167–69, 171.

Document 10.8

Friedrich Shulz, *The Slave Market*

American slave markets regularly appeared in etchings, engravings, and paintings in the nineteenth century. Several images were produced by European artists traveling through the South. The German artist Friedrich Shulz (1825–1875) visited the United States in the 1840s or 1850s and painted this image of a slave auction. The beautiful colors and rich tones belie the tragic scenes taking place in this southern market.

Hirshhorn Museum & Sculpture Garden, Washington D.C., USA/Bridgeman Images

Mary Reynolds | Recalling Work, Punishment, and Faith c. 1850s

Ex-slaves interviewed in the 1930s offered a wealth of information. Mary Reynolds claimed to be more than a hundred years old when interviewed in 1937, but her memories were vivid. She was one of the older interviewees and thus had experienced slavery longer than many who told their stories in this period. Here she recalls life with her parents and sisters on the Kilpatrick family plantation in Black River, Louisiana.

Massa Kilpatrick wasn't no piddlin' man. He was a man of plenty. He had a big house. . . . He was a medicine doctor and they was rooms in the second story for sick folks what come to lay in. It would take two days to go all over the land he owned. He had cattle and stock and sheep and more'n a hundred slaves and more besides. He bought the bes' of niggers near every time the spec'lators come that way. He'd make a swap of the old ones and give money for young ones what could work. . . .

He raised corn and cotton and cane and 'taters and goobers [potatoes and peanuts], 'sides the peas and other feedin' for the niggers. I 'member I helt a hoe handle mighty onsteady when they put a old women to larn me and some other chillun to scrape the fields. . . . She say, "For the love of Gawd, you better larn it right, or Solomon will beat the breath out you body." Old man Solomon was the nigger driver. . . .

The times I hated most was pickin' cotton when the frost was on the bolls. My hands git sore and crack open and bleed. We'd have a li'l fire in the fields and iffen the ones with tender hands couldn't stand it no longer, we'd run and warm our hands a li'l bit. . . .

Sometimes massa let niggers have a li'l patch. They'd raise 'taters or goobers . . . to help fill out on the victuals. . . .

Once in a while they's give us a li'l piece of Sat'day evenin' to wash out clothes. . . . When they'd git through with the clothes on Sat'day evenin's the niggers . . . brung fiddles and guitars and come out and play. The others clap they hands and stomp they feet and we young'uns cut a step round. I was plenty biggity and like to cut a step.

We was scart of Solomon and his whip, though, and he didn't like frolickin'. He didn't like for us niggers to pray, either. We never heared of no church, but us have prayin' in the cabins. . . . I know that Solomon is burnin' in hell today, and it pleasures me to know it.

Once my maw and paw taken me and Katherine after night to slip to 'nother place to a prayin' and singin'. A nigger man with white beard told us a day am comin' when niggers only be slaves of Gawd. We prays for the end of Trib'lation and the end of beatin's and for shoes that fit our feet. We prayed that us niggers could have all we wanted to eat and special for fresh meat. . . .

When we's comin' back from that prayin', I thunk I heared the nigger [tracking] dogs and somebody on horseback. . . . Maw listens and say, "Sho 'nough, them dogs am runnin' and Gawd help us!" Then she and paw . . . take us to a fence corner and stands us up 'gainst the rails and say don't move. . . . They went to the woods, so the hounds chase them and not git us. Me and Katherine stand there, holdin' hands, shakin' so we can hardly stand. We hears the hounds come nearer, but we don't move. They goes after paw and maw, but they circles round to the cabins and gits in. Maw say its the power of Gawd.

Source: Ex-Slave Stories: Mary Reynolds, in "Born in Slavery: Slave Narratives from the Federal Writers' Project, 1936–1938," American Memory, Library of Congress, Texas, vol. 16, pt. 3, pp. 238–41.

Interpret the Evidence

1. What do these documents tell us about the working lives of slaves? What differences and similarities do they reveal across age, sex, and region (Documents 10.5, 10.7, and 10.9)?

2. How do these documents illuminate the family experiences of slaves and the distinct challenges faced by enslaved parents (Documents 10.5, 10.6, 10.8, and 10.9)?

3. What were the greatest threats or fears confronted by enslaved women and men? What do they suggest about enslaved peoples' view of their owners and other whites (Documents 10.5, 10.6, 10.7, 10.8, 10.9)?

4. How did enslaved women and men seek to create a sense of community and culture (Documents 10.7 and 10.9)?

5. Most of these documents offer a snapshot of one moment in a slave's life, but in reading across documents, how does the experience of slavery change over the course of a person's lifetime (Documents 10.5, 10.6, 10.7, 10.8, and 10.9)?

Put It in Context

How would proslavery Southerners respond to the experiences revealed in these documents?

What do these sources suggest about slave resistance and white efforts to control slaves' behavior?

Social and Cultural Ferment in the North

1820–1850

11

WINDOW TO THE PAST

What, to the American Slave, Is Your 4th of July?

Tensions over the expansion and brutalities of slavery intensified following the U.S. military victory over Mexico in 1848. Former slaves like Frederick Douglass became important advocates for abolition in this period. Douglass gave an impassioned and provocative speech on July 5, 1852, to a mixed-race audience in his hometown of Rochester, New York, in which he challenged white Americans to consider the meaning of their national holiday. ▶ To discover more about what this primary source can show us, see Document 11.4 on page 372.

What, to the American slave, is your 4th of July? I answer; a day that reveals to him, more than all other days in the year, the gross injustice and cruelty to which he is the constant victim. To him, your celebration is a sham; your boasted liberty, an unholy license; your national greatness, swelling vanity; your sounds of rejoicing are empty and heartless; your denunciations of tyrants, brass fronted impudence; your shouts of liberty and equality, hollow mockery; your prayers and hymns, your sermons and thanksgivings, with all your religious parade, and solemnity, are, to him, mere bombast, fraud, deception, impiety, and hypocrisy—a thin veil to cover up crimes which would disgrace a nation of savages. There is not a nation on the earth guilty of practices, more shocking and bloody, than are the people of these United States, at this very hour.

Courtesy of the Department of Rare Books, Special Collections and Preservation, University of Rochester River Campus Libraries

After reading this chapter you should be able to:

- Explain the growth of and changes in northern cities, including issues of immigration, class stratification, and gender roles.

- Analyze how industrialization transformed workers' lives, was affected by the boom and bust economic cycle, and contributed to class and ethnic tensions.

- Describe the range and appeal of religious movements that emerged in the 1830s and 1840s

- Evaluate the emergence of reform movements and the strategies they embraced.

- Explain the various forms of antislavery activism and their impact on other social and political changes.

AMERICAN HISTORIES

The great revival preacher Charles Grandison Finney was born in 1792 and raised in rural New York State. As a young man, Finney studied the law. But in 1821, like many others of his generation, he experienced a powerful religious conversion. No longer interested in a legal career, he turned to the ministry instead.

After being ordained in the Presbyterian Church, Finney joined "New School" ministers who rejected the more conservative traditions of the Presbyterian Church and embraced a vigorous evangelicalism. In the early 1830s the Reverend Finney traveled throughout New York State preaching about Christ's

(left) **Charles Grandison Finney** Oberlin College Archives
(right) **Amy Kirby Post** Courtesy of the Department of Rare Books and Special Collections, University of Rochester River Campus Libraries

place in a changing America. He held massive revivals in cities along the Erie Canal, most notably in Rochester, New York. He achieved his greatest success in places experiencing rapid economic development and an influx of migrants and immigrants, where the clash of cultures and classes fueled fears of moral decay.

Finney urged Christians to actively seek salvation. Once individuals reformed themselves, he said, they should work to abolish poverty, intemperance, prostitution, and slavery. He expected women to participate in revivals and good works but advised them to balance these efforts with their domestic responsibilities.

In many ways, Amy Kirby Post fit Finney's ideal. Born into a farm family in Jericho, New York, she found solace in spirituality and social reform. Like many other people in this period, Amy experienced the loss of loved ones. In 1825, at age twenty-three, Amy's fiancé died, and two years later she lost the sister to whom she was closest. The next year, Amy married a widower, Isaac Post. She mothered his two young children and bore five children of her own, two of whom died young. Yet Amy Post did not embrace evangelical revivals, but focused instead on the quiet piety preferred by her Quaker community.

Still, the personal upheavals Amy experienced in her twenties occurred amid heated controversies within the Society of Friends (Quakers). Elias Hicks claimed that the Society had abandoned its spiritual roots and become too much like a traditional church. His followers, called Hicksites, insisted that Quakers should reduce their dependence on disciplinary rules, elders, and preachers and rely instead on the "Inner Light"—the spirit of God dwelling within each individual. When the Society of Friends divided into Hicksite and Orthodox branches in 1827, Amy Kirby and Isaac Post joined the Hicksites.

In 1836 Amy Post moved with her husband and children to Rochester, New York. In a city marked by the spirit of Finney's revivals, Quakers emphasized quiet contemplation rather than emotional conversions, but the Society of Friends allowed members, including women, to preach when moved by the spirit. Quaker women also held separate meetings to discipline female congregants, evaluate marriage proposals, and write testimonies on important religious and social issues.

Amy Post's spiritual journey was increasingly shaped by the rising tide of abolition. Committed to ending slavery, she joined hundreds of local evangelical women in signing an 1837 antislavery petition. Five years later, she helped found the Western New York Anti-Slavery Society, which included Quakers and evangelicals, women and men, and blacks and whites. Post's growing commitment to abolition caused tensions in the Hicksite meeting since some members opposed working in "worldly" organizations alongside non-Quakers. In 1848 Post and other radical Friends formed a new, more activist-oriented Quaker meeting and embraced women's rights as well as abolition. ■

The American histories of Charles Finney and Amy Post were shaped by the dynamic religious, social, and economic developments in the early-nineteenth-century United States. Finney changed the face of American religion, aided by masses of evangelical Protestants. The rise of cities and the expansion of industry in the northern United States made problems like poverty, unemployment, alcohol abuse, crime, and prostitution more visible, drawing people to Finney's message. Other Americans brought their own religious traditions to bear on the problems of the day. Some, like Post, were so outraged by the moral stain of slavery that they burst traditional religious bonds and reconsidered what it meant to do God's work. For both Finney and Post, Rochester—the fastest-growing city in the nation between 1825 and 1835—exemplified the problems and the possibilities created by urban expansion and social change.

The Growth of Northern Cities

Commercial and industrial development, immigration from Europe, and migration from rural areas led to the rapid growth of cities in the northern United States from 1820 on. Urbanization fueled economic growth but also created social upheaval. Cultural divisions intensified in urban areas where Catholics and Protestants, workers and the well-to-do, immigrants, African Americans, and native-born whites lived side by side. Class dynamics also changed with the development of a clear middle class of shopkeepers, professionals, and clerks. Self-conscious about their status as an emerging class, many middle-class Northerners highlighted their distinctiveness from the classes above and below them.

The Lure of Urban Life.
Across the North, urban populations boomed. As commercial centers, seaports like New York and Philadelphia were the most populous cities in the early nineteenth century. Between 1820 and 1850, the number of cities with 100,000 inhabitants increased from two to six; five were seaports. The sixth was the river port of Cincinnati, Ohio. Smaller boomtowns, like Rochester, New York, also emerged along inland waterways. Rochester grew rapidly once the Erie Canal was completed in 1825.

Cities increased not only in size but also in diversity. During the 1820s, some 150,000 European immigrants entered the United States; during the 1830s, nearly 600,000; and during the 1840s, more than 1,700,000. This surge of immigrants included more Irish and German settlers than ever before as well as large numbers of Scandinavians. Many settled along the eastern seaboard, but others added to the growth of frontier cities such as Cincinnati, St. Louis, and Chicago.

While many Scots-Irish Presbyterian families had settled in North America in the colonial era, Irish Catholics migrated in much larger numbers in the 1830s and 1840s. The Irish countryside was plagued by bad weather, a potato blight, and harsh economic policies imposed by the English government. In 1845 to 1846 a full-blown famine forced thousands more Irish Catholic families to emigrate. Young Irish women, who could easily find work as domestics or seamstresses, emigrated in especially large numbers. Poor harvests, droughts, failed revolutions, and repressive landlords convinced large numbers of Germans, including Catholics, Lutherans, and Jews, and Scandinavians to flee their homelands as well. By 1850 the Irish made up about 40 percent of immigrants to the United States, and Germans nearly a quarter (Figure 11.1).

These immigrants provided an expanding pool of cheap labor as well as skilled artisans who further fueled northern commerce and industry. Banks, mercantile houses, and dry-goods stores multiplied. Urban industrial enterprises included both traditional workshops and mechanized factories. Credit and insurance agencies emerged to aid entrepreneurs in their ventures. The increase in business also drove the demand for ships, commercial newspapers, warehouses, and other commercial necessities, which created a surge in jobs for many urban residents.

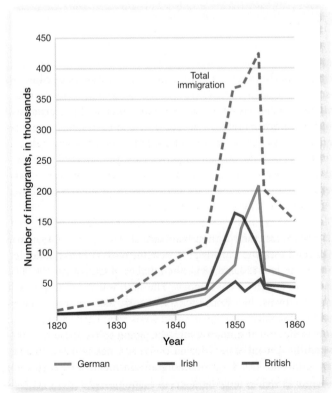

FIGURE 11.1 Immigration to the United States, 1820–1860

Famine, economic upheaval, and political persecution led masses of people from Ireland, Germany, and Britain to migrate to the United States from the 1820s through the 1850s. The vast majority settled in cities and factory towns in the North or on farms in the Midwest. An economic recession in the late 1850s finally slowed immigration, though only temporarily.

Jenny Lind at Castle Garden, 1850   American showman P. T. Barnum convinced Swedish opera star Jenny Lind to tour the United States in 1850. Huge crowds greeted her arrival in New York harbor and packed her concerts, leading reporters to describe the phenomenon as "Lind mania." In this lithograph, Nathaniel Currier captures the crowd at her first appearance at Castle Garden in New York. Granger, NYC

Businesses focused on leisure also flourished. In the 1830s theater became affordable to working-class families, who attended comedies, musical revues, and morality plays. They also joined middle- and upper-class audiences at productions of Shakespeare and contemporary dramas. Minstrel shows mocked self-important capitalists but also portrayed African Americans in crude caricatures. One of the most popular characters was Jim Crow, who appeared originally in an African American song. In the 1820s he was incorporated into a song-and-dance routine by Thomas Rice, a white performer who blacked his face with burnt cork.

The lures of urban life were especially attractive to the young. Single men and women and newly married couples flocked to cities. By 1850 half the residents of New York, Philadelphia, and other seaport cities were under sixteen years old. Young men sought work in manufactories, construction, and the maritime trades or in banks and commercial houses, while young women competed for jobs as seamstresses and domestic servants.

The Roots of Urban Disorder.

While immigrant labor stimulated northern economic growth, immigrant families transformed the urban landscape. They crowded into houses and apartments and built ethnic institutions, including synagogues and convents—visible indicators of the growing diversity of northern cities. While most native-born Protestants applauded economic growth, cultural diversity aroused anxieties. Anti-Catholicism and anti-Semitism flourished in the 1830s and 1840s. Crude stereotypes portrayed Jews as manipulative moneylenders and Catholic nuns and priests as sexually depraved. Ethnic groups also battled stereotypes. Irishmen, for example, were often pictured as habitual drunkards.

Still, rising immigration did not deter rural Americans from seeking economic opportunities in the city. Native-born white men often set out on their own, but most white women settled in cities under the supervision of a husband, landlady, or employer. African Americans, too, sought greater opportunities in urban areas. In the 1830s, more blacks joined Philadelphia's vibrant African American community, attracted by its churches, schools, and mutual aid societies. New Bedford, Massachusetts, a thriving whaling center, recruited black workers and thus attracted fugitive slaves as well.

Yet even as cities welcomed many migrants and immigrants, newcomers also faced dangers. Racial and ethnic minorities regularly faced discrimination and hostility. Physical battles erupted between immigrant and native-born residents, Protestant and Catholic gangs, and white and black workers. Criminal activity flourished as well, and disease spread quickly through densely populated neighborhoods. When innovations in transportation made it possible for more affluent residents to distance themselves from crowded inner cities, they moved to less congested neighborhoods on the urban periphery. Horse-drawn streetcar lines, first built in New York City in 1832, hastened this development.

By the 1840s, economic competition intensified, fueling violence among those driven to the margins. Native-born white employers and workers pushed Irish immigrants to the bottom of the economic ladder, where they competed with African Americans. Yet Irish workers insisted that their whiteness gave them a higher status than even the most skilled blacks. When black temperance reformers organized a parade in Philadelphia in August 1842, white onlookers—mostly Irish laborers—attacked the marchers, and the conflict escalated into a riot.

Americans who lived in small towns and rural areas regularly read news of urban violence and vice. Improvements in printing created vastly more and cheaper newspapers while the construction of the first telegraph in 1844 ensured that news could travel more quickly from town to town. Tabloids wooed readers with sensational stories of crime, sex, and scandal. Even more respectable newspapers reported on urban mayhem, and religious periodicals warned parishioners against urban immorality. In response to both a real and a perceived increase in crime, cities replaced voluntary night watchmen with paid police forces.

The New Middle Class. Members of the emerging middle class, which developed mainly in the North, included ambitious businessmen, successful shopkeepers, doctors, and lawyers as well as teachers, journalists, ministers, and other salaried employees. At the top rungs, successful entrepreneurs and professionals adopted affluent lifestyles. At the lower rungs, a growing cohort of salaried clerks and managers hoped that their hard work, honesty, and thrift would be rewarded with upward mobility.

Education, religious affiliation, and sobriety were important indicators of middle-class status. A well-read man who attended a well-established church and drank in strict moderation was marked as belonging to this new rank. He was also expected to own a comfortable home, marry a pious woman, and raise well-behaved children. Entrance to the middle class required the efforts of wives as well as husbands, with many couples adopting new marital ideals of affection and companionship. In most middle-class households, husbands provided financial security while wives managed the domestic realm. Yet

Shoe Shopping from *Godey's Lady's Book*   In the 1830s and 1840s, women's magazines appeared to promote new ideals of middle-class womanhood and to guide them as consumers. This 1848 image of women shopping for shoes from *Godey's Lady's Book* encouraged female outings to elegant emporiums. The lavish engravings created by *Godey's* quickly made it the best-selling "ladies" magazine in the United States. Archive Photos/Getty Images

this ideal of separate spheres for men and women was flexible, with many wives involved in church work and civic activities and many husbands presiding over the family dinner. Moreover, the ideal had little relevance to the lives of the millions of women toiling on farms, in factories, or as domestic servants.

The rise of the middle class inspired a flood of advice books, ladies' magazines, religious periodicals, and novels advocating new ideals of womanhood. These publications emphasized the centrality of child rearing and homemaking to women's identities. This **cult of domesticity** ideally restricted wives to home and hearth, where they provided their husbands with respite from the cares and corruptions of the world. But women were also expected to cement social and economic bonds by entertaining the wives of business associates, serving in charitable societies, and organizing Sabbath schools. In carrying out these duties, the ideal woman bolstered her family's status by performing public as well as private roles.

Middle-class families also played a crucial role in the growing market economy. Wives and daughters were responsible for much of the family's consumption. They purchased cloth, rugs and housewares, and, if wealthy enough, European crystal and Chinese porcelain figures. Middling housewives bought goods once made at home, such as butter and candles, and arranged music lessons and other educational opportunities for their children.

Although increasingly recognized for their ability to consume wisely, middle-class women still performed significant domestic labor. Only upper-middle-class women could afford servants. Most middle-class women cut and sewed garments, cultivated gardens, canned fruits and vegetables, plucked chickens, cooked meals, and washed and ironed clothes. As houses expanded in size and clothes became fancier, these chores remained laborious and time-consuming. But they were also increasingly invisible, focused inwardly on the family rather than outwardly as part of the market economy.

Middle-class men contributed to the consumer economy as well by creating and investing in industrial and commercial ventures. Moreover, in carrying out business and professional obligations, many enjoyed restaurants, the theater, or sporting events. Men attended plays and lectures with their wives and visited museums and circuses with their children. They also purchased hats, suits, mustache wax, and other accouterments of middle-class masculinity.

REVIEW & RELATE

- As northern cities became larger and more diverse in the first half of the nineteenth century, what changes and challenges did urban residents face?

- What values and beliefs did the emerging American middle class embrace?

The **Rise** of **Industry**

In the mid-nineteenth century, industrial enterprises in the Northeast transformed the nation's economy even though they employed less than 10 percent of the U.S. labor force. In the 1830s and 1840s, factories grew considerably in size, and some investors, especially in textiles, constructed factory towns. New England textile mills relied increasingly on the labor of girls and young women, while urban workshops hired children, young women and men, and older adults. However, as industrial jobs expanded, employment for skilled male artisans declined. An economic panic in 1837 exacerbated this trend and increased tensions that made it more difficult for workers to organize across differences of skill, ethnicity, race, and sex.

Factory Towns and Women Workers. In the late 1820s investors and manufacturers joined forces to create factory towns in the New England countryside. The most famous mill town, Lowell, Massachusetts, was based on an earlier experiment in nearby Waltham. In the Waltham system, every step of the production process was mechanized, and planned communities included factories, boardinghouses, government offices, and churches. Agents for the Waltham system recruited the daughters of New England farm families as workers, assuring parents that they would be watched over by managers and foremen as well as landladies. The young women were required to attend church and observe curfews, and their labor was regulated by clocks and bells to ensure discipline and productivity.

Farm families needed more cash because of the growing market economy, and daughters in the mills could contribute to family finances and save money for the clothes and linens required for married life. Factory jobs also provided an alternative to marriage as young

New England men moved west and left a surplus of women behind. Boardinghouses provided a relatively safe, all-female environment for the young mill workers, and sisters and neighbors often lived together. Despite nearly constant supervision, many rural women viewed factory work as an adventure. They could set aside a bit of money for themselves, attend lectures and concerts, meet new people, and acquire a wider view of the world.

During the 1830s, however, working conditions began to deteriorate. Factory owners cut wages, lengthened hours, and sped up machines. Boardinghouses became overcrowded, and company officials regulated both rents and expenses so that higher prices for lodging did not necessarily mean better food or furnishings. Factory workers launched numerous strikes in the 1830s against longer hours, wage cuts, and speedups in factory production. The solidarity required to sustain these strikes was forged in boardinghouses and at church socials as well as on the factory floor.

Explore ▶

See Document 11.1 for a firsthand account of a mill strike.

Despite mill workers' solidarity, it was difficult to overcome the economic power wielded by manufacturers. Working women's efforts at collective action were generally short-lived, lasting only until a strike was settled. Then employees returned to their jobs until the next crisis hit. And as competition increasingly cut into profits, owners resisted mill workers' demands more vehemently. When the panic of 1837 intensified fears of job loss, women's organizing activities were doomed until the economy recovered.

The Decline of Craft Work and Workingmen's Responses.

While the construction of factory towns expanded economic opportunities for young women, the gradual decline of time-honored crafts narrowed the prospects for workingmen. Craft workshops gradually increased in size and hired fewer skilled workers and more men who performed single tasks, like attaching soles to shoes. Many tasks also became mechanized during the nineteenth century. The final product was less distinctive than an entire item crafted by a skilled artisan, but it was less expensive and available in mass quantities.

The shift from craft work to factory work threatened to undermine workingmen's skills, pay, and labor conditions. Masters began hiring foremen to regulate the workforce and installing bells and clocks to regulate the workday. As this process of **deskilling** transformed shoemaking, printing, tailoring, and other trades, laboring men fought to maintain their status.

Some workers formed mutual aid societies to provide assistance in times of illness, injury, or unemployment. Others participated in religious revivals or joined fraternal orders to find the camaraderie they once enjoyed at work. The expansion of voting rights in the 1820s offered another avenue for action. The first workingmen's political party was founded in Philadelphia in 1827, and working-class men in the North joined forces to support politicians sympathetic to their needs. Most workingmen's parties focused on practical proposals: government distribution of free land in the West, abolishing compulsory militia service and imprisonment for debt, public funding for education, and regulations on banks and corporations. Although the electoral success of these parties was modest, in the 1830s Democrats and Whigs adopted many of their proposals.

Workingmen also formed unions to demand better wages and working conditions. In the 1820s and 1830s, skilled journeymen held mass meetings to protest employers' efforts to lengthen the workday, merge smaller workshops into larger factories, and cut wages. In New York City in 1834, labor activists formed a citywide federation, the General Trades

Union, which provided support for striking workers. The National Trades Union was established later that year, with delegates representing more than twenty-five thousand workers across the North. These organizations aided skilled workers but refused admission to women and unskilled men.

GUIDED ANALYSIS

Harriet Robinson | Reflections on the 1836 Lowell Mills Strike, 1898

In the 1830s, a faltering economy led to reduced wages, long hours, and demands for increased productivity at New England textile mills. The women workers in Lowell, Massachusetts, organized to protest these changes and went on strike several times. The following selection was written by Harriet Robinson, who entered the mills at age ten in 1834. She published a memoir in 1898 in which she recalls her critical role in a strike in 1836.

Document 11.1

My own recollection of this first strike (or "turn out" as it was called) is very vivid. I worked in a lower room, where I had heard the proposed strike fully, if not vehemently, discussed; I had been an ardent listener to what was said against this attempt at "oppression" on the part of the corporation, and naturally I took sides with the strikers. When the day came on which the girls were to turn out, those in the upper rooms started first, and so many of them left that our mill was at once shut down. Then, when the girls in my room stood irresolute, uncertain what to do, asking each other, "Would you?" or "Shall we turn out?" . . . [I]

Why does Robinson take the lead on her floor in joining the strike?

became impatient, and started on ahead, saying, with childish bravado, "I don't care what you do, I am going to turn out, whether any one else does or not"; and I marched out, and was followed by the others.

As I looked back at the long line that followed me, I was more proud than I have ever been since at any success I may have achieved, and more proud than I shall ever be again until my own beloved State gives to its women citizens the right of suffrage.

How does Robinson link the strike at Lowell to women's rights more generally?

The agent of the corporation where I then worked took some small revenges on the supposed ringleaders. . . .

It is hardly necessary to say that so far as results were concerned this strike did no good. The dissatisfaction of the operatives subsided, or burned itself out, and though the authorities did not accede to their demands, the majority returned to their work, and the corporation went on cutting down the wages.

What were the effects of the 1836 strike according to Robinson?

Source: Harriet H. Robinson, *Loom and Spindle; or, Life among the Early Mill Girls* (New York: Thomas Y. Crowell, 1898), 84–86.

Put It in Context

What difficulties did female and male workers face in organizing to improve their wages and working conditions in this period?

It proved difficult to establish broader labor organizations, however. Most skilled workers considered unskilled workers as competitors, not allies. Many workingmen feared women workers would undercut their wages and so refused to organize alongside them. And anti-immigrant and racist beliefs among many native-born Protestant workers interfered with organizing across racial and ethnic lines. With the onset of the panic of 1837, the common plight of workers became clearer. But the economic crisis made unified action nearly impossible as individuals sought to hold on to what little they had.

The Panic of 1837 in the North. The panic of 1837 began in the South but hit northern cotton merchants hard (see "Van Buren and the Panic of 1837" in chapter 10). With cotton shipments sharply curtailed, textile factories drastically cut production, unemployment rose, and merchants and investors went broke. Those still employed saw their wages cut in half. In Rochester the Posts moved in with family members to save their small business from foreclosure. Petty crime, prostitution, and violence also rose as men and women struggled to make ends meet.

In Lowell, hours increased and wages fell. Just as important, the process of deskilling intensified. Factory owners considered mechanization one way to improve their economic situation. A cascade of inventions, including power looms, steam boilers, and the steam press, transformed industrial occupations and led factory owners to invest more of their

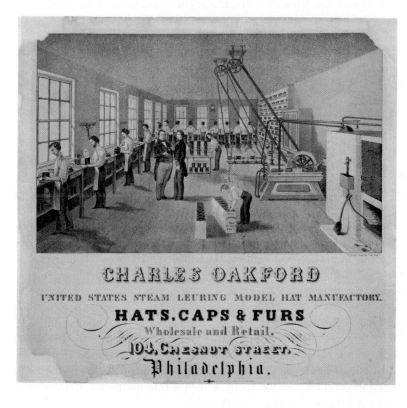

Hat Manufacturing, 1850   This 1850 lithograph advertises Charles Oakford's hat factory in Philadelphia. Like many industries, hat making became increasingly mechanized in the 1840s. Here Oakford talks with a client in the center of the room, across from his steam-powered lathe, while workers stand at stations shaping and stacking hats. A boy packs the merchandise into a box ready for shipping. © Philadelphia History Museum at the Atwater Kent/The Bridgeman Art Library

limited resources in machines. At the same time, the rising tide of immigrants provided a ready supply of relatively cheap labor. Artisans tried to maintain their traditional skills and status, but in many trades they were fighting a losing battle.

By the early 1840s, when the panic subsided, new technologies did spur new jobs. Factories demanded more workers to handle machines that ran at a faster pace. In printing, the steam press allowed publication of more newspapers and magazines, creating positions for editors, publishers, printers, engravers, reporters, and sales agents. Similarly, mechanical reapers sped the harvest of wheat and inspired changes in flour milling that required engineers to design machines and mechanics to build and repair them.

These changing circumstances fueled new labor organizations as well. Many of these unions comprised a particular trade or ethnic group, and almost all continued to address primarily the needs of skilled male workers. Textile operatives remained the one important group of organized female workers. In the 1840s, workingwomen joined with workingmen in New England to fight for a ten-hour day. Slowly, however, farmers' daughters left the mills as desperate Irish immigrants flooded in and accepted lower wages.

For most women in need, charitable organizations offered more support than unions. Organizations like Philadelphia's Female Association for the Relief of Women and Children in Reduced Circumstances provided a critical safety net for many poor families since public monies for such purposes were limited. Although most northern towns and cities now provided some form of public assistance, they never had sufficient resources to meet local needs in good times, much less the extraordinary demands posed by the panic.

REVIEW & RELATE

How and why did American manufacturing change during the first half of the nineteenth century?

How did new technologies, immigration, and the panic of 1837 change the economic opportunities and organizing strategies for northern workers?

Saving the Nation from Sin

In the first half of the nineteenth century, men and women of all classes and races embraced the Protestant religious revival known as the **Second Great Awakening** to express deeply held beliefs and reclaim a sense of the nation's godly mission. Yet evangelical Protestantism was not the only religious tradition to thrive in this period. Catholic churches and Jewish synagogues multiplied with immigration, and in the North Quaker meetings and Unitarian congregations flourished as well. New religious groups also attracted thousands of followers while transcendentalists sought deeper engagements with nature as another path to spiritual renewal.

The Second Great Awakening. Although diverse religious traditions flourished in the United States, evangelical Protestantism proved the most powerful in the 1820s and 1830s. Evangelical churches hosted revivals, celebrated conversions, and organized prayer and missionary societies. This second wave of religious revivals began in Cane Ridge, Kentucky, in 1801, and took root across the South. It then spread northward, transforming Protestant churches and the social fabric of northern life.

Ministers like Charles Grandison Finney adopted techniques first wielded by southern Methodists and Baptists: plain speaking, powerful images, and mass meetings. But Finney molded these techniques for a more affluent audience and held his "camp meetings" in established churches. By the late 1820s, boomtown growth along the Erie Canal aroused deep concerns among religious leaders about the rising tide of sin. In response, the Reverend Finney arrived in Rochester in September 1830. He began preaching in local Presbyterian churches, leading crowded prayer meetings that lasted late into the night. Individual supplicants walked to special benches designated for anxious sinners, who were prayed over in public. Female parishioners played crucial roles, encouraging their husbands, sons, friends, and neighbors to submit to God.

Thousands of Rochester residents joined in the evangelical experience as Finney's powerful message engulfed other denominations (Map 11.1). The significance of these revivals went far beyond an increase in church membership. Finney converted "the great mass of the most influential people" in the city: merchants, lawyers, doctors, master craftsmen, and shopkeepers. Equally important, he proclaimed that if Christians were "united all over the world the Millennium [Christ's Second Coming] might be brought about in three months." Preachers in Rochester and the surrounding towns took up his call, and converts committed themselves to preparing the world for Christ's arrival.

Developments in Rochester were replicated in cities across the North. Presbyterian, Congregational, and Episcopalian churches overflowed with middle-class and wealthy Americans, while Baptists and Methodists ministered to more laboring women and men. Black Baptists and Methodists evangelized in their own communities, combining powerful preaching with rousing spirituals. In Philadelphia, African Americans built fifteen churches between 1799 and 1830. A few black women joined men in evangelizing to their fellow African Americans.

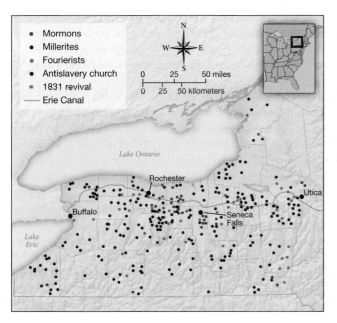

MAP 11.1 Religious Movements in the Burned-Over District, 1831–1848

Western and central New York State was burned over by the fires of religious revivalism in the 1830s and 1840s. But numerous other religious groups also formed or flourished in the region In these decades, including Quakers, Mormons, and Millerites. In the 1840s, Fourierist phalanxes, the Oneida community, and other utopian experiments were also established here.

Source: Whitney R. Cross, *The Burned-Over District: The Social and Intellectual History of Enthusiastic Religion in Western New York, 1800–1850* (Ithaca, NY: Cornell University Press, 1950).

Tens of thousands of black and white converts embraced evangelicals' message of moral outreach. No reform movement gained greater impetus from the revivals than **temperance**, whose advocates sought to moderate and then ban the sale and consumption of alcohol. In the 1820s Americans fifteen years and older consumed six to seven gallons of distilled alcohol per person per year (about double the amount consumed today). Middle-class evangelicals, who once accepted moderate drinking as healthful, now insisted on eliminating alcohol consumption altogether.

New Visions of Faith and Reform.

Although enthusiasm for temperance and other reforms waned during the panic of 1837 and many churches lost members, the Second Great Awakening continued in its aftermath. But now evangelical ministers competed for souls with a variety of other religious groups, many of which supported good works and social reform. The Society of Friends, the first religious group to refuse fellowship to slaveholders, expanded throughout the early nineteenth century, but largely in the North and Midwest. Having divided in 1827 and again in 1848, the Society of Friends continued to grow. So, too, did its influence in reform movements as activists like Amy Post carried Quaker testimonies against alcohol, war, and slavery into the wider society. Unitarians also combined religious worship with social reform. They differed from other Christians by believing in a single unified higher spirit rather than the Trinity of the Father, the Son, and the Holy Spirit. Emerging mainly in New England in the early nineteenth century, Unitarian societies slowly spread west and south in the 1830s. Opposed to evangelical revivalism and dedicated to a rational approach to understanding the divine, Unitarians attracted prominent literary figures such as James Russell Lowell and Harvard luminaries like William Ellery Channing.

Other churches grew as a result of immigration. Dozens of Catholic churches were established to meet the needs of Irish and some German immigrants. With the rapid increase in Catholic churches, Irish priests multiplied in the 1840s and 1850s, and women's religious orders became increasingly Irish as well. At the same time, synagogues, Hebrew schools, and Hebrew aid societies signaled the growing presence of Jewish immigrants, chiefly from Germany, in the United States. These religious groups were less active in social reform and more focused on assisting their own congregants in securing a foothold in their new home

Entirely new religious groups also flourished in the 1840s. One of the most important was the Church of Jesus Christ of Latter-Day Saints, or Mormons, founded by Joseph Smith. Smith began to receive visions from God at age fifteen and was directed to dig up gold plates inscribed with instructions for redeeming the Lost Tribes of Israel. *The Book of Mormon* (1830), supposedly based on these inscriptions, served, along with the Bible, as the scriptural foundation of the Church of Jesus Christ of Latter-Day Saints, which Smith led as the Prophet.

Smith founded not only a church but a theocracy (a community governed by religious leaders). In the mid-1830s Mormons established a settlement at Nauvoo, Illinois, and recruited followers—black and white—from the eastern United States and England. When Smith voiced antislavery views, some local residents expressed outrage. But it was his claim to revelations sanctioning polygamy that led local authorities to arrest him and his brother. When a mob then lynched the Smith brothers, Brigham Young, a successful missionary, took over as Prophet. In 1846 he led 12,000 followers west, 5,000 of whom settled

Mormons Head West, 1846   Brigham Young's leadership of the Latter-Day Saints did not lessen anti-Mormon sentiments in Illinois, so in 1846 he led thousands of followers west to Nebraska and then Utah. This wood engraving, published in Paris in 1853, shows Mormons migrating across the Great Plains that winter. The clothing of several makes clear that they are more affluent than many other western pioneers. Universal History Archive/UIG/Bridgeman Images

near the Great Salt Lake, in what would soon become the Utah Territory. Isolated from anti-Mormon mobs, Young established a thriving theocracy. In this settlement, leaders practiced polygamy and denied black members the right to become priests.

New religious groups also formed by separating from established denominations. William Miller, a prosperous farmer and Baptist preacher, claimed that the Bible proved that the Second Coming of Jesus Christ would occur in 1843. Thousands of Americans joined the Millerites. When various dates for Christ's Second Coming passed without incident, however, Millerites developed competing interpretations for the failure and divided into distinct groups. The most influential group formed the Seventh-Day Adventist Church in the 1840s.

Transcendentalism.   Another important movement for spiritual renewal was rooted in the transcendent power of nature. The founder of this transcendentalist school of thought was Ralph Waldo Emerson. Raised a Unitarian, Emerson began challenging the church's ideas. His 1836 essay entitled "Nature" expounded his newfound belief in a Universal Being. This Being existed as an ideal reality beyond the material world and was accessible through nature. Emerson's natural world was distinctly American and suggested that moral perfection could be achieved in the United States. Emerson expressed his ideas in widely read essays and books and in popular lectures.

Emerson's hometown of Concord, Massachusetts, served as a haven for writers, poets, intellectuals, and reformers who were drawn to **transcendentalism**. In 1840 Margaret Fuller, a close friend of Emerson, became the first editor of *The Dial*, a journal dedicated to transcendental thought. In 1844 she moved to New York City, where Horace Greeley hired her as a critic at the *New York Tribune*. She soon published a book, *Woman in the Nineteenth Century* (1845), which combined transcendental ideas with arguments for women's rights.

Henry David Thoreau also followed the transcendentalist path. He grew up in Concord and read "Nature" while a student at Harvard in the mid-1830s. In July 1845 Thoreau moved to a cabin near Walden Pond and launched an experiment in simple living. A year later he was imprisoned overnight for refusing to pay his taxes as a protest against slavery and the Mexican-American War. In the anonymous *Civil Disobedience* (1846), Thoreau argued that individuals of conscience had the right to resist government policies they believed to be immoral. Five years later, he published *Walden*, which highlighted the interplay among a simple lifestyle, natural harmony, and social justice.

Like Emerson, many American artists embraced the power of nature. Led by Thomas Cole, members of the Hudson River School painted romanticized landscapes from New York's Catskill and Adirondack Mountains. Some northern artists also traveled to the West, painting the region's grand vistas. Pennsylvanian George Catlin portrayed the dramatic scenery of western mountains, gorges, and waterfalls and also painted moving portraits of Plains Indians.

REVIEW & RELATE

- What impact did the Second Great Awakening have in the North?

- What new religious organizations and viewpoints emerged in the first half of the nineteenth century, *outside* of Protestant evangelical denominations?

Organizing for Change

Both religious commitments and secular problems spurred social activism in the 1830s and 1840s. In cities, small towns, and rural communities, Northerners founded organizations, launched campaigns, and established institutions to better the world around them. Yet even Americans who agreed that society needed to be reformed still often disagreed over priorities and solutions. Moreover, while some activists employed moral arguments to persuade Americans to follow their lead, others insisted that laws that imposed reform were the only effective means of change.

Varieties of Reform.
Middle-class Protestants formed the core of many reform movements in the mid-nineteenth-century North. They had more time and money to devote to social reform than did their working-class counterparts and were less tied to traditional ways than their wealthy neighbors. Nonetheless, workers and farmers, African Americans and immigrants, Catholics and Jews also participated in efforts to improve society.

Reformers used different techniques to pursue their goals. Since women could not vote, for example, they were excluded from direct political participation. Instead, they established charitable associations, distributed food and medicine, constructed asylums, circulated petitions, organized boycotts, arranged meetings and lectures, and published newspapers and pamphlets. Other groups with limited political rights—African Americans and immigrants, for instance—embraced similar modes of action and also formed mutual aid societies. Native-born white men wielded these forms of activism and, in addition, organized political campaigns and lobbied legislators. The reform techniques chosen were also affected by the goals of a particular movement. Moral suasion worked best with families, churches, and local communities, while legislation was more likely to succeed if the goal involved transforming people's behavior across a whole state or region.

Reformers often used a variety of tactics to support a single cause, and many changed their approach over time. For instance, reformers who sought to eradicate prostitution in the 1830s prayed in front of urban brothels and attempted to rescue "fallen" women. They soon launched *The Advocate of Moral Reform*, a monthly journal filled with morality tales, advice to mothers, and lists of men who visited brothels. In small towns, moral reformers sought to alert young women and men to the dangers of city life. By the 1840s, urban reformers opened Homes for Virtuous and Friendless Females to provide safe havens for vulnerable women. And across the country, moral reformers began petitioning state legislators to make punishments for men who hired prostitutes as harsh as those for prostitutes themselves.

The Problem of Poverty. Poverty had existed since the colonial era, but the panic of 1837 aroused greater public concern. Leaders of both government and private charitable endeavors increasingly linked relief to the moral character of those in need. Affluent Americans had long debated whether the poor would learn habits of industry and thrift if they were simply given aid without working for it. The debate was deeply gendered. Women and children were considered the worthiest recipients of aid, and middle- and upper-class women the appropriate dispensers of charity. Successful men, meanwhile, often linked poverty to weakness and considered giving pennies to a beggar an unmanly act that indulged the worst traits of the poor.

While towns and cities had long relegated the poorest residents to almshouses or workhouses, charitable societies in the early nineteenth century sought to change the conditions that produced poverty. As the poor increased with urban growth, northern charitable ladies began visiting poor neighborhoods, offering blankets, clothing, food, and medicine to needy residents. But the problem seemed intractable, and many charitable organizations began building orphan asylums, hospitals, and homes for working women to provide deserving but vulnerable individuals with resources to improve their life chances.

Explore ▶

See Documents 11.2 and 11.3 for the views of two reformers on ways to uplift the poor.

The "undeserving" poor faced grimmer choices. They generally received assistance only through the workhouse or the local jail. By the 1830s images of rowdy men who drank or gambled away what little they earned, prostitutes who tempted respectable men into vice, and immigrants who preferred idle poverty to virtuous labor became stock figures in debates over the causes of and responses to poverty.

At the same time, young poor women—at least if they were white and Protestant—were increasingly portrayed as the victims of immoral men or unfortunate circumstance.

How Can We Help the Poor?

Americans who sought to uplift the poor offered various solutions. Some supported workhouses; others provided clothes and medicine to the "deserving" poor; and still others established employment agencies for single women and widows. The sources below capture the views of two affluent northern reformers. Matthew Carey, a prominent publisher and civic leader in Philadelphia, challenged reformers to address the dire plight of working women. Emily G. Kempshall, a longtime officer of the Rochester Female Charitable Society, lost faith in the ability of female benevolence to improve the situation of impoverished families and resigned in 1838.

Document 11.2

Matthew Carey | *Appeal to the Wealthy of the Land*, 1833

Let us now turn to the appalling case of seamstresses, . . . [who are] Beset . . . by poverty and wretchedness, with scanty and poor fare, miserable lodgings, clothing inferior in quality . . . , without the most distant hope of amelioration of condition, by a course of unrelenting and unremitting industry. . . .

IT is frequently asked—what remedy can be found for the enormous and cruel oppression experienced by females employed as seamstresses . . . ? . . . [A] complete remedy for the evil is . . . impracticable. I venture, to suggest a few palliatives.

1. Public opinion, a powerful instrument, ought to be brought to bear on the subject. All honourable members of society, male and female, ought to unite in denouncing those who "grind the faces of the poor." . . .

2. Let the employments of females be multiplied as much as possible . . . especially in shop-keeping in retail stores. . . .

4. Let the Provident Societies, intended to furnish employment for women in winter, be munificently supported; and let those Societies give fair and liberal wages. . . .

6. Let schools be opened for instructing poor women in cooking. Good cooks are always scarce. . . .

8. Ladies who can afford it, ought to give out their sewing and washing, and pay fair prices. . . .

9. In the towns in the interior of the state, and in those in western states, there is generally a want of females as domestics, seamstresses, etc. . . . [The rich should] provide for sending some of the superabundant poor females of our cities to those places.

Source: Matthew Carey, *Appeal to the Wealthy of the Land, Ladies as well as Gentlemen* (Philadelphia: L. Johnson, 1833), 13, 15, 33–34.

In fictional tales, naive girls were seduced and abandoned by manipulative men. One of the first mass-produced books in the United States, Nathaniel Hawthorne's *The Scarlet Letter* (1850), was set in Puritan New England but addressed contemporary concerns about the seduction of innocents. It illustrated the social ostracism and poverty suffered by a woman who bore a child out of wedlock.

Document 11.3

Emily G. Kempshall | Letter to the Rochester Female Charitable Society, 1838

[T]he Board . . . have asked my reasons for withdrawing my . . . members[hip]. . . . I reply . . . that I look upon the <u>funds</u> of your society, however judiciously distributed, among the destitute sick of our city, as being wholly inadequate to meet their necessities. . . . I dare not draw a single Dollar, to relieve one poor family, lest in doing this I rob another <u>poorer</u> family, perhaps of what they must have. . . . I know [also] . . . that whole Districts are appointed to females as visitors of the S[ociety] where no decent female should go, to look after and try to assist, their vile and degraded inhabitants. . . .

And now were I addressing the . . . Common Council of this City I would say, "Give the ladies power to point, in their visits of mercy, to a work House, where idle drunken fathers and mothers <u>must</u> go and <u>work</u>." . . . [T]his being granted, the idle Drunken inhabitants . . . Being safely . . . out of the way of the sick members of their own families . . . the objection to becoming a visitor . . . will be lessened at once. . . .

[H]as not the day gone by, when your Flag of Charity may wave over its Lake, River, Canal, and Rail Road, inviting the outcasts of every city in the Union, . . . to seek . . . their subsistence from your bounty. . . . And so while your Banner, whose merciful insignia on the one side is Relief for the destitute sick, has been held up as a beacon of hope, it is painful to tell them to read the other side where want of funds has written Despair of further Relief.

Source: Emily G. Kempshall to President of the Female Charitable Society of Rochester, January 30, 1838, Rochester Female Charitable Society Papers, Rare Books and Special Collections, University of Rochester, Rochester, New York.

Interpret the Evidence

1. How are poor women and families portrayed by Matthew Carey and Emily Kempshall, both leaders in benevolent reform in their cities? Who would Kempshall send to a workhouse if one existed in Rochester?

2. How might Carey and Kempshall respond to each other's assessments of aiding the poor?

Put It in Context

What do these documents suggest about class tensions and conflicts in northern cities? How might the panic of 1837 have affected such conflicts?

Other fictional tales placed the blame for fallen women on foreigners, especially Catholics. Such works drew vivid portraits of young nuns ravished by priests and then thrown out pregnant and penniless. These stories heightened anti-Catholic sentiment, which periodically boiled over into attacks on Catholic homes, schools, churches, and convents.

At the same time, economic competition intensified conflicts between immigrants and native-born Americans. By the 1840s Americans who opposed immigration took the name **nativists** and launched public political campaigns that blamed foreigners for poverty and crime. Samuel F. B. Morse, the inventor of the telegraph, was among the most popular anti-immigrant spokesmen. Irish Catholics were often targeted in attacks against immigrants. In May 1844 working-class nativists clashed with Irishmen in Philadelphia after shots were fired from a firehouse. A dozen nativists and one Irishman were killed the first day. The next night, nativists looted and burned Irish businesses and Catholic churches.

Many nativists blamed poverty among immigrants on their drinking habits. Others considered alcohol abuse, whether by native-born or immigrant Americans, the root cause not only of poverty but of many social evils.

The Temperance Movement. Temperance advocates first organized officially in 1826 with the founding of the American Temperance Society. This all-male organization was led by clergy and businessmen but focused on alcohol abuse among working-class men. Religious revivals inspired the establishment of some 5,000 local chapters, and black and white men founded other temperance organizations as well. Over time, the temperance movement changed its goal from moderation to total abstinence, targeted middle-class and

Drunkard's Home, 1850 Temperance societies undertook a variety of activities to publicize the dangers of alcohol. This engraved illustration is from *The National Temperance Offering*, published by the Sons of Temperance, one of the oldest temperance organizations in the United States. It suggests the harm men's alcohol abuse creates for working-class women and children. From *The National Temperance Offering, and Sons and Daughters of Temperance Gift*, Clifton Waller Barrett Library of American Literature, Albert and Shirley Small Special Collections Library, University of Virginia

elite as well as working-class men, and welcomed women's support. Wives and mothers were expected to persuade male kin to stop drinking and sign a temperance pledge. Women founded dozens of temperance societies in the 1830s, which funded the circulation of didactic tales, woodcuts, and etchings about the dangers of "demon rum."

Some workingmen viewed temperance as a way to gain dignity and respect. For Protestants, in particular, embracing temperance distinguished them from Irish Catholic workers. A few working-class temperance advocates criticized liquor dealers, whom they claimed directed "the vilest, meanest, most earth-cursing and hell-filling business ever followed." More turned to self-improvement. In the 1840s small groups of laboring men formed Washingtonian societies—named in honor of the nation's founder—to help each other stop excessive drinking. Martha Washington societies appeared shortly thereafter, composed of the wives, mothers, and sisters of male alcoholics.

Despite the rapid growth of temperance organizations, moral suasion failed to reduce alcohol consumption significantly. As a result, many temperance advocates turned to legal reform. In 1851 Maine was the first state to legally prohibit the sale of alcoholic beverages. By 1855 twelve more states had restricted the manufacture or sale of alcohol. Yet these stringent measures inspired a backlash. Hostile to the imposition of middle-class Protestant standards on the population at large, Irish workers in Maine organized the Portland Rum Riot in 1855. It led to the Maine law's repeal the next year. Still, the diverse strategies used by temperance advocates gradually reduced, but did not eliminate, the consumption of beer, wine, and spirits across the United States.

Utopian Communities.

While most reformers reached out to the wider society to implement change, some activists established self-contained communities to serve as models for others. The architects of these **utopian societies**, most formed in the North and Midwest, gained inspiration from European intellectuals and reformers as well as American religious and republican ideals.

In the 1820s Scottish and Welsh labor radicals such as Frances Wright, Robert Owen, and his son Robert Dale Owen established several utopian communities in the United States. They perceived the young republic as open to experiments in communal labor, gender equality, and (in Wright's case) racial justice. Their efforts ultimately failed, but they did arouse impassioned debate.

Then in 1841, former Unitarian minister George Ripley established a transcendentalist community at Brook Farm in Massachusetts. Four years later, Brook Farm was reorganized according to the principles of the French socialist Charles Fourier. Fourier believed that cooperation across classes was necessary to temper the conflicts inherent in capitalist society. He developed a plan for communities, called phalanxes, where residents chose jobs based on individual interest but were paid according to the contribution of each job to the community's well-being. Fourier also advocated equality for women. More than forty Fourierist phalanxes were founded in the northern United States during the 1840s.

A more uniquely American experiment, the Oneida community, was established in central New York by John Humphrey Noyes in 1848. He and his followers believed that Christ's Second Coming had already occurred and embraced the communalism of the early Christian church. Noyes required members to relinquish their private property to the community and to embrace the notion of "complex marriage," in which women and men were free to have sexual intercourse with any consenting adult. He also introduced a form

"Children's Hour" at the Oneida Community This etching, created in the 1850s, depicts the communal character of the Oneida community. Children dance in the sitting room of the Mansion House, which also included sleeping quarters, meeting rooms, and dining halls. Adults observing the dance considered themselves guardians of all children in the community. The images were first published in *Frank Leslie's Illustrated Weekly* in 1870. ©Corbis

of birth control that sought to ensure women's freedom from constant childbearing and instituted communal child-rearing practices. Divorce and remarriage were also permitted. Despite the public outrage provoked by Oneida's economic and sexual practices, the community recruited several hundred residents and thrived for more than three decades.

REVIEW & RELATE

• How did efforts to alleviate poverty and temper alcohol consumption reflect the range of reform tactics and participants during the 1830s and 1840s?

• What connections can you identify between utopian communities and mainstream reform movements in the first half of the nineteenth century?

Abolitionism Expands and **Divides**

For a small percentage of Northerners, slavery was the ultimate injustice. While most Northerners considered it sufficient to rid their own region of human bondage, antislavery advocates argued that the North remained complicit in the institution. After all, slaves labored under brutal conditions to provide cotton for New England factories, sugar and molasses for northern tables, and profits for urban traders. Free blacks were the earliest advocates of abolition, but their role in the movement generated conflict as more whites joined in the 1830s. The place of the church, of women, and of politics in antislavery efforts also stirred controversy. By the 1840s abolitionists disagreed over whether to focus on abolishing slavery in the South or simply preventing its extension into western territories. These debates often weakened individual organizations but expanded the range of antislavery associations and campaigns.

The Beginnings of the Antislavery Movement.
In the 1820s African Americans and a few white Quakers led the fight to abolish slavery. They published pamphlets, lectured to small audiences, and helped runaway slaves reach freedom. In 1829 David Walker wrote the most militant antislavery statement, ***Appeal . . . to the Colored Citizens of the World***. The free son of an enslaved father, Walker left his North Carolina home for Boston in the 1820s and became a writer for *Freedom's Journal*, the country's first newspaper published by African Americans. In his *Appeal*, Walker warned that slaves would claim their freedom by force if whites did not agree to emancipate them. Some northern blacks feared Walker's radical *Appeal* would unleash a white backlash, while Quaker abolitionists like Benjamin Lundy, editor of the *Genius of Universal Emancipation*, admired Walker's courage but rejected his call for violence. Nonetheless the *Appeal* circulated widely among free and enslaved blacks, with copies spreading from northern cities to Charleston, Savannah, New Orleans, and Norfolk.

William Lloyd Garrison, a white Bostonian who worked on Lundy's newspaper, was inspired by Walker's radical stance. In 1831 he launched his own abolitionist newspaper, the ***Liberator***. He urged white antislavery activists to embrace the goal of immediate emancipation without compensation to slave owners, a position first advocated by the English Quaker Elizabeth Heyrick.

The *Liberator* demanded that whites take an absolute stand against slavery but use moral persuasion rather than armed force to halt its spread. With like-minded black and white activists in Boston, Philadelphia, and New York City, Garrison organized the **American Anti-Slavery Society (AASS)** in 1833. By the end of the decade, the AASS boasted branches in dozens of towns and cities across the North. Members supported lecturers and petition drives, criticized churches that refused to denounce slavery, and proclaimed the U.S. Constitution a proslavery document. Some Garrisonians also participated in the work of the **underground railroad**, a secret network of activists who assisted fugitives fleeing enslavement.

The Underground Railroad in Action   Once Frederick Douglass moved to Rochester, New York, he became central to efforts to assist fugitive slaves. He relied on networks of black and white abolitionists to hide fugitives until they could be sent to Canada. Since hiding fugitives was illegal, notes like this one to Amy Post are rare. Most were destroyed once fugitives reached freedom.   Courtesy of the Department of Rare Books and Special Collections, University of Rochester River Campus Libraries

In 1835 Sarah and Angelina Grimké joined the AASS and soon began lecturing for the organization. Daughters of a prominent South Carolina planter, they had moved to Philadelphia and converted to Quakerism. As white Southerners, their denunciations of slavery carried particular weight. Yet as women, their public presence aroused fierce opposition. In 1837 Congregationalist ministers in Massachusetts decried their presence in front of "promiscuous" audiences of men and women, but 1,500 female millworkers still turned out to hear them at Lowell's city hall.

Maria Stewart, a free black widow in Boston, spoke out against slavery even earlier. In 1831 to 1832, she lectured to mixed-sex and interracial audiences, demanding that northern blacks take more responsibility for ending slavery and fighting racial discrimination. In 1833 free black and white Quaker women formed an interracial organization, the Philadelphia Female Anti-Slavery Society, which advocated the boycott of cotton, sugar, and other slave-produced goods.

The abolitionist movement quickly expanded to the frontier, where debates over slave and free territory were especially intense. In 1836 Ohio claimed more antislavery groups than any other state, and Ohio women initiated a petition drive to abolish slavery in the District of Columbia. The petition campaign, which spread across the North, inspired the first national meeting of women abolitionists in 1837. Other antislavery organizations, like the AASS, recruited male and female abolitionists, black and white. And still others remained all-white, all-black, and single-sex.

Abolition Gains Ground and Enemies.

The growth of the abolitionist movement shocked many Northerners, and in the late 1830s violence often erupted in response to antislavery agitation. Northern manufacturers and merchants were generally hostile, fearing abolitionists' effect on the profitable trade in cotton, sugar, cloth, and rum. And white workingmen feared increased competition for jobs. In the 1830s mobs routinely attacked antislavery meetings, lecturers, and presses. At the 1838 Antislavery Convention of American Women at Philadelphia's Pennsylvania Hall, mobs forced black and white women to flee and then burned the hall to the ground.

Massive antislavery petition campaigns in 1836 and 1837 generated opposition in and between the North and South. Thousands of abolitionists, including Amy Post and her husband, Isaac, signed petitions to ban slavery in the District of Columbia, end the internal slave trade, and oppose the annexation of Texas. Some evangelical women considered such efforts part of their Christian duty, but most ministers (including Finney) condemned antislavery work as outside women's sphere. Most female evangelicals retreated in the face of clerical disapproval, but others continued their efforts alongside their non-evangelical sisters. **See Document Project 11: Religious Faith and Women's Activism, page 376.** Meanwhile Southern politicians, incensed by antislavery petitions, persuaded Congress to pass the gag rule in 1836.

But gag rules did not silence abolitionists. Indeed new groups of activists, especially fugitive slaves, offered potent personal tales of the horrors of bondage. The most famous fugitive abolitionist was Frederick Douglass, a Maryland-born slave who in 1838 fled to New Bedford, Massachusetts. He met Garrison in 1841, joined the AASS, and four years later published his life story, *Narrative of the Life of Frederick Douglass, as Told by Himself.* Having revealed his identity as a former slave, Douglass sailed for England, where he launched a successful two-year lecture tour. While he was abroad, British abolitionists

Explore ▶

See Document 11.4 for a
black abolitionist's
challenge to celebrating the
Fourth of July.

purchased Douglass's freedom from his owner, and Douglass returned to the United States a free man. In 1847 he decided to launch his own antislavery newspaper, the *North Star*, a decision that Garrison and other white AASS leaders opposed. Douglass moved to Rochester, where he had earlier found free black and white Quaker allies, including Amy Post.

While eager to have fugitive slaves tell their dramatic stories, many white abolitionists did not match Post's vigorous support of African Americans who asserted an independent voice. Some abolitionists opposed slavery but still believed that blacks were racially inferior; others supported racial equality but assumed that black abolitionists would defer to white leaders. Thus several affiliates of the AASS refused to accept black members. Ultimately, the independent efforts of Douglass and other black activists expanded the antislavery movement even as they made clear the limits of white abolitionist ideals.

Conflicts also arose over the responsibility of churches to challenge slavery. The major Protestant denominations included southern as well as northern churches. If mainstream churches—Presbyterians, Baptists, Methodists—refused communion to slave owners, their southern branches would secede. Still, from the 1830s on, abolitionists pressured churches to take Christian obligations seriously and denounce human bondage. Individual congregations responded, but aside from the Society of Friends, larger denominations failed to follow suit.

In response, abolitionists urged parishioners to break with churches that admitted slaveholders as members. Antislavery preachers pushed the issue, and some worshippers "came out" from mainstream churches to form antislavery congregations. White Wesleyan Methodists and Free Will Baptists joined African American Methodists and Baptists in insisting that their members oppose slavery. Although these churches remained small, they served as a living challenge to mainstream denominations.

Abolitionism and Women's Rights. Women were increasingly active in the AASS and the "come outer" movement, but their growing participation aroused opposition even among abolitionists. By 1836 to 1837, female societies formed the backbone of many antislavery petition campaigns. More women also joined the lecture circuit, including Abby Kelley, a fiery orator who demanded that women be granted an equal role in the movement. But when Garrison and his supporters appointed Kelley to the AASS business committee in May 1839, angry debates erupted over the propriety of women participating "in closed meetings with men." Of the 1,000 abolitionists in attendance, some 300 walked out in protest. The dissidents, including many evangelical men, soon formed a new organization, the American and Foreign Anti-Slavery Society, which excluded women from public lecturing and office holding but encouraged them to support men's efforts.

Those who remained in the AASS then continued to expand the roles of women. In 1840 local chapters appointed a handful of female delegates, including Lucretia Mott of Philadelphia, to the World Anti-Slavery Convention in London. The majority of men at the meeting, however, rejected the female delegates' credentials. Women were then forced to watch the proceedings from a separate section of the hall, confirming for some that women could be effective in campaigns against slavery only if they gained more rights for themselves.

Finally, in July 1848, a small circle of women, including Lucretia Mott and a young American she met in London, Elizabeth Cady Stanton, organized the first convention focused explicitly on women's rights. Held in Stanton's hometown of Seneca Falls, New York, the convention attracted three hundred women and men. James Mott, husband of Lucretia, presided over the convention, and Frederick Douglass spoke, but women dominated the proceedings. One hundred participants, including Amy Post, signed the **Declaration of Sentiments**, which called for women's equality in everything from education and

SOLO ANALYSIS

Frederick Douglass | What, to the American Slave, Is Your 4th of July?

With antislavery issues arousing growing conflict, the Rochester Ladies Anti-Slavery Society invited Frederick Douglass to speak at the city's grand Corinthian Hall on Independence Day, 1852. Douglass agreed only if he could speak on the following day, July 5. His black and white supporters packed the hall and cheered his powerful and provocative speech, but many whites found his criticisms of the United States deeply disturbing.

Document 11.4

Fellow-citizens, pardon me, allow me to ask, why am I called upon to speak here to-day? What have I, or those I represent, to do with your national independence? Are the great principles of political freedom and of natural justice, embodied in that Declaration of Independence, extended to us? . . .

Fellow citizens; above your national, tumultuous joy, I hear the mournful wail of millions! whose chains, heavy and grievous yesterday, are, to-day, rendered more intolerable by the jubilee shouts that reach them. . . .

What, to the American slave, is your 4th of July? I answer; a day that reveals to him, more than all other days in the year, the gross injustice and cruelty to which he is the constant victim. To him, your celebration is a sham; your boasted liberty, an unholy license; your national greatness, swelling vanity; your sounds of rejoicing are empty and heartless; your denunciations of tyrants, brass fronted impudence; your shouts of liberty and equality,

hollow mockery; your prayers and hymns, your sermons and thanksgivings, with all your religious parade, and solemnity, are, to him, mere bombast, fraud, deception, impiety, and hypocrisy—a thin veil to cover up crimes which would disgrace a nation of savages. There is not a nation on the earth guilty of practices, more shocking and bloody, than are the people of these United States, at this very hour.

Go where you may, search where you will, roam through all the monarchies and despotisms of the old world, travel through South America, search out every abuse, and when you have found the last, lay your facts by the side of the every day practices of this nation, and you will say with me, that, for revolting barbarity and shameless hypocrisy, America reigns without a rival.

Source: Frederick Douglass, *Oration, Delivered in Corinthian Hall, Rochester, July 5, 1852* (Rochester, NY: Lee, Mann, 1852), 14–15, 20–21.

Interpret the Evidence

1. Why did Douglass choose to give his speech on July 5 rather than July 4?
2. How does Douglass explain the meaning of the Fourth of July for African Americans?

Put It in Context

How might Whigs, Democrats, white Southerners and anti-abolitionist Northerners have responded to Douglass's speech?

employment to legal rights and voting. Two weeks later, Post helped organize a second convention in Rochester, where participants took the radical action of electing a woman, Abigail Bush, to preside. Here, too, Douglass spoke alongside other black abolitionists and local working women.

Although abolitionism provided much of the impetus for the women's rights movement, other movements also contributed. Strikes by seamstresses and mill workers in the 1830s and 1840s highlighted women's economic needs. Utopian communities experimented with gender equality, and temperance reformers focused attention on domestic violence and sought changes in divorce laws. A diverse coalition also advocated for married women's property rights in the mid-1840s. Women's rights were debated among New York's Seneca Indians as well. Like the Cherokee, Seneca women had lost traditional rights over land and tribal policy as their nation adopted Anglo-American ways. In the summer of 1848, the creation of a written constitution threatened to enshrine these losses in writing. The Seneca constitution did strip women of their dominant role in selecting chiefs but protected their right to vote on the sale of tribal lands. Earlier in 1848, revolutions had erupted against repressive regimes in France and elsewhere in Europe. Antislavery newspapers like the *North Star* covered developments in detail, including European women's demands for political and civil recognition. The meetings in Seneca Falls and Rochester drew on these ideas and influences even as they focused primarily on the rights of white American women.

The Rise of Antislavery Parties.
As women's rights advocates demanded female suffrage, debates over the role of partisan politics in the antislavery campaign intensified. Keeping slavery out of western territories depended on the actions of Congress, as did abolishing slavery in the nation's capital and ending the internal slave trade. Moral suasion had seemingly done little to change minds in Congress or in the South. To force abolition onto the national political agenda, the **Liberty Party** was formed in 1840. Many Garrisonians were appalled at the idea of participating in national elections when the federal government supported slavery in numerous ways, from the three-fifths compromise to allowing slavery in newly acquired territories. Still, the Liberty Party gained significant support among abolitionists in New York, the Middle Atlantic states, and the Midwest.

The Whigs and Democrats generally avoided the antislavery issue to keep their southern and northern wings intact, but that strategy became more difficult once the Liberty Party entered campaigns. In 1840 the party won less than 1 percent of the popular vote but organized rallies that attracted large crowds. In 1844 the party more than doubled its votes, which was sufficient to deny Henry Clay a victory in New York State and thus ensure the election of James K. Polk (see "Expanding to Oregon and Texas" in chapter 10).

When President Polk led the United States into war with Mexico, interest in an antislavery political party surged. In 1848 the Liberty Party gained the support of antislavery Whigs, also called Conscience Whigs; northern Democrats who opposed the extension of slavery into the territories; and African American leaders like Frederick Douglass, who broke with Garrison on the utility of electoral politics. Seeing a political opportunity, more practically minded political abolitionists founded the **Free-Soil Party**, which quickly subsumed the Liberty Party. Free-Soilers focused less on the moral wrongs of slavery than on the benefits of keeping western territories free for northern whites seeking economic opportunity. The Free-Soil Party nominated Martin Van Buren, a former Democrat, for president in 1848 and won 10 percent of the popular vote. But once again, the result was to send a slaveholder to the White House—Zachary Taylor, a Mexican War hero. Nonetheless, the Free-Soil Party had expanded beyond the Liberty Party, raising fears in the South and in the two major parties that the battle over slavery could no longer be contained.

REVIEW & RELATE

How did the American Anti-Slavery Society differ from earlier abolitionist organizations?

How did conflicts over gender, race, and tactics shape the development of the abolitionist movement in the 1830s and 1840s?

Conclusion: From the North to the Nation

Charles Grandison Finney followed these political developments from Oberlin College, where he served as president in the 1840s. Skeptical that electoral politics could transform society, he continued to view individual conversions as the wellspring of change. As the nation expanded westward, he trained ministers to travel the frontier converting American Indians to Christianity and reminding pioneering families of their religious obligations. Amy Post took a more militant stand, rejecting any participation in a government that accepted slavery and fomented war. She disagreed with Frederick Douglass's decision to support the Liberty Party, but he argued that moral persuasion alone would never convince planters to end slavery.

The efforts of the tens of thousands of Northerners inspired by religious and reform movements between 1820 and 1850 had a greater impact because of the growth of cities and improvements in transportation and communication. It was far easier by the 1830s for evangelicals, Quakers, Mormons, transcendentalists, utopian communalists, and other activists to spread their ideas through sermons, lectures, newspapers, pamphlets, and conventions.

Urban development was driven by the migration of native-born Americans from rural areas and small towns as well as the increase in immigration from Ireland, Germany, and other European nations. While the panic of 1837 fueled an economic crisis that lasted several years, it also inspired many Americans to organize against poverty, intemperance, prostitution, and other urban problems. At the same time, the concentration of workers, immigrants, and free blacks in cities allowed them to unite and claim rights for themselves. For workers, the need to organize was heightened by the growth of factories and factory towns even as the increasing diversity of the labor force aroused tensions among distinct racial and ethnic groups. Thus numerous attacks occurred against free blacks who competed for jobs with immigrants and poor whites even as the antislavery movement expanded across the North.

Of the numerous reform movements that emerged in this period, abolitionism carried the most powerful national implications by 1850. The addition of vast new territories at the end of the Mexican-American War in 1848 ensured that those concerns would become even more pressing in the decade ahead.

TIMELINE OF EVENTS

1820–1850	Northern cities grow; immigration surges
1823	Lowell mills built
1826	American Temperance Society founded
1827	First workingmen's political party founded
1829	David Walker publishes *Appeal . . . to the Colored Citizens of the World*
1830	Joseph Smith publishes *The Book of Mormon*
1830–1831	Second Great Awakening in Rochester, New York
1833	William Lloyd Garrison founds American Anti-Slavery Society (AASS)
1834	National Trades Union founded
1837–1842	Panic of 1837
1839	American Anti-Slavery Society splits over the role of women
1840	Liberty Party formed
	World Anti-Slavery Convention, London
1844	Congress funds construction of the first telegraph line
May 1844	Anti-immigrant violence in Philadelphia
1845	Frederick Douglass publishes *Narrative of the Life of Frederick Douglass*
	Margaret Fuller publishes *Woman in the Nineteenth Century*
1845–1846	Irish potato famine
1846	Henry David Thoreau publishes *Civil Disobedience*
1848	Free-Soil Party formed
July 1848	Seneca Falls Woman's Rights Convention
1851	Maine prohibits the sale of alcoholic beverages

KEY TERMS

cult of domesticity, *353*
deskilling, *355*
Second Great Awakening, *358*
temperance, *360*
transcendentalism, *362*
nativists, *366*
utopian societies, *367*
Appeal . . . to the Colored Citizens of the World, *369*
Liberator, *369*
American Anti-Slavery Society (AASS), *369*
underground railroad, *369*
Declaration of Sentiments, *372*
Liberty Party, *373*
Free-Soil Party, *373*

REVIEW & RELATE

1. As northern cities became larger and more diverse in the first half of the nineteenth century, what changes and challenges did urban residents face?

2. What values and beliefs did the emerging American middle class embrace?

3. How and why did American manufacturing change during the first half of the nineteenth century?

4. How did new technologies, immigration, and the panic of 1837 change the economic opportunities and organizing strategies for northern workers?

5. What impact did the Second Great Awakening have in the North?

6. What new religious organizations and viewpoints emerged in the first half of the nineteenth century, *outside* of Protestant evangelical denominations?

7. How did efforts to alleviate poverty and temper alcohol consumption reflect the range of reform tactics and participants during the 1830s and 1840s?

8. What connections can you identify between utopian communities and mainstream reform movements in the first half of the nineteenth century?

9. How did the American Anti-Slavery Society differ from earlier abolitionist organizations?

10. How did conflicts over gender, race, and tactics shape the development of the abolitionist movement in the 1830s and 1840s?

Religious Faith and Women's Activism

During the 1830s, religious revivals and growing religious diversity raised new questions about women's place in public life. In many white evangelical churches, women played prominent roles during revivals, leading prayer circles and persuading others to seek salvation. Still, male ministers retained sole authority and often emphasized women's subjection during the conversion process (Document 11.5). While accepting their subordinate role, many evangelical women nevertheless labored on behalf of temperance, moral reform, and even abolition (Document 11.6).

Male ministers also dominated black churches, but a few black women were recognized as itinerant evangelicals by the 1830s. It was Maria Stewart, however, a free black widow and evangelical convert, who spoke out most publicly about slavery, racial prejudice, and the challenges facing northern African American communities (Document 11.7).

Quaker, Unitarian, Catholic, and Jewish women also combined faith and social activism. They, too, advocated temperance, expanded charitable efforts, and promoted moral uplift. Quaker women also took on prominent roles in the antislavery movement, promoting abolition alongside white men and African Americans. These efforts generated heated debates over women's sphere. When Sarah and Angelina Grimké, daughters of a South Carolina slave owner, moved to Philadelphia and converted to Quakerism, the American Anti-Slavery Society invited them to lecture on behalf of abolition. Their 1837 lecture tour attracted large audiences of men and women, leading Congregational ministers in New England to denounce their unwomanly conduct (Document 11.8). While many white evangelical women then retreated from antislavery activities, Quaker and black evangelical women continued their activities and Sarah Grimké published a spirited defense of women's antislavery activism (Document 11.9). Like Stewart, Grimké linked female efforts on behalf of racial advancement to women's need for more rights for themselves.

Document 11.5

Charles G. Finney | An Influential Woman Converts, 1830

Women were among the earliest converts in the Reverend Charles Finney's revivals in Rochester, New York. Many then persuaded friends and relatives to seek salvation. In describing the conversion of Mrs. Selah Mathews, Finney reinforces conventional ideas about female subordination while recognizing Mrs. Mathews's influence among local elites. Mrs. Mathews later joined a short-lived female antislavery society and worked on behalf of moral reform.

The wife of a prominent lawyer . . . was one of the first converts. She was a woman of high standing, a lady of culture and extensive influence. . . .

Mrs. M[athews] had been a gay, worldly woman, and very fond of society. She afterward told me that when I first came there, she greatly regretted it, and feared [that] . . . a revival would greatly interfere with the pleasures and amusements that she had promised herself that winter. On conversing with her I found that the Spirit of the Lord was indeed dealing with her. . . . She was bowed down with great conviction of sin. . . . I pressed her earnestly to renounce sin, and the world, and self, and everything for Christ. . . . [W]e knelt down to pray; and my mind being full of the subject of the pride of her heart . . . I very soon introduced the text: "Except ye be converted and become as little children, ye shall in no wise enter into the kingdom of heaven." . . . [A]lmost immediately I heard Mrs M[athews] . . . repeating that text:

"Except ye be converted and become as little children—as little children—Except ye be converted and become as little children." I observed that her mind was taken with that, and the Spirit of God was pressing it upon her heart. I therefore continued to pray, holding that subject before her mind. . . .

. . . Her heart broke down, her sensibility gushed forth, and before we rose . . . , she was indeed a little child. . . . From that moment she was out-spoken in her religious convictions, and zealous for the conversion of her friends.

Source: Charles G. Finney, *The Memoirs of Rev. Charles G. Finney, Written by Himself* (New York: F. H. Revell, 1876), 287–88.

Document 11.6

Elizabeth Emery and Mary P. Abbott | Founding a Female Anti-Slavery Society, 1836

Many women who converted during the Second Great Awakening engaged in social activism. Some believed they were called to rid America of the sin of slavery. Women in Andover, Massachusetts, organized a Female Anti-Slavery Society. Elizabeth Emery and Mary Abbott, two leaders in the society, wrote a letter to the *Liberator*, expressing their belief in Christian women's moral responsibility to end slavery.

Mr. Editor:

In these days of women's doings, it may not be amiss to report the proceedings of some ladies in Andover. . . .

The call of our female friends across the waters—the energetic appeal of those untiring sisters in the work of emancipation in Boston—above all, the sighs, the groans, the deathlike struggles of scourged sisters in the South—these have moved our hearts, our hands. We feel that woman has a place in this Godlike work, for woman's woes, and woman's

wrongs, are borne to us on every breeze that flows from the South; woman has a place, for she forms a part in God's created intelligent instrumentality to reform the world. . . . When man proves recreant [remiss] to his duty and faithless to his Maker, woman, with her feeling heart, should rouse him— should start his sympathies—should cry in his ear, and raise such a storm of generous sentiment, as shall never let him sleep again. We believe God gave woman a heart to feel—an eye to weep—a hand to work—a tongue to speak. Now let her use that tongue to speak on slavery. Is it not a curse—a heaven-daring abomination? Let her employ that hand, to labor for the slave. Does not her sister in bonds, labor night and day without reward? Let her heart grieve, and her eye fill with tears, in view of a female's body dishonored—a female's mind debased—a female's soul forever ruined! Woman nothing to do with slavery! Abhorred the thought!! We will pray to abhor it more and more. Is not woman abused—woman trampled upon—woman spoiled of her virtue, her probity, her influence, her joy! And this, not in India—not in China—not in Turkey—not in Africa but in America—in the United States of America. . . .

As Christian women, we will do a Christian woman's duty. . . .

Our preamble gives our creed:

"We believe American Slavery is a sin against God—at war with the dictates of humanity, and subversive of the principles of freedom, because it regards rational beings as goods and chattel; robs them of compensation for their toil—denies to them the protection of law—disregards the relation of husband and wife, brother and sister, parent and child; shuts out from the intellect the light of knowledge; overwhelms hope in despair and ruins the soul—thus sinking to the level of brutes, more than one million of American females, who are created in God's image, a little lower than the angels', and consigns them over to degradation, physical, social, intellectual, and moral.

Source: Elizabeth Emery and Mary P. Abbott, "Letter to *The Liberator*," *Liberator*, August 27, 1836, 138.

Maria Stewart | On Religion and the Pure Principles of Morality, 1831

Maria Stewart was orphaned in 1808 at age five. She then worked as a servant for fifteen years, gaining an education by attending Sunday school. Married at twenty-three and widowed at twenty-six, she experienced a religious conversion the next year and began speaking publicly in 1831 to mixed-sex and interracial audiences. She urged black women to claim their God-given rights and improve themselves and their community. When some black Bostonians criticized her views, Stewart moved to New York City and later Washington, D.C.

O ye daughters of Africa, awake! awake! arise! no longer sleep nor slumber, but distinguish yourselves. Show forth to the world that ye are endowed with noble and exalted faculties. . . .

I am of a strong opinion, that the day on which we unite, heart and soul, and turn our attention to knowledge and improvement, that day the hissing and reproach among the nations of the earth against us will cease. . . .

. . . Why cannot we do something to distinguish ourselves, and contribute some of our hard earnings that would reflect honor upon our memories, and cause our children to arise and call us blessed? Shall it any longer be said of the daughters of Africa, they have no ambition . . . ? By no means. Let every female heart become united; and let us raise a fund ourselves; and at the end of one year and a half, we might be able to lay the corner-stone for the building of a High School . . . and God would raise us up, and enough to aid us in our laudable designs. . . .

How long shall the fair daughters of Africa be compelled to bury their minds and talents beneath a load of iron pots and kettles? . . . How long shall a mean set of men flatter us with their smiles, and enrich themselves with our hard earnings; their wives' fingers sparkling with rings, and they themselves laughing at our folly? Until we begin to promote and patronize each other. . . . We have never had an opportunity of displaying our talents; therefore the world thinks we know nothing. . . . Do you ask the disposition I would have you possess?

Possess the spirit of independence. The Americans do, and why should not you? Possess the spirit of men, bold and enterprising, fearless and undaunted. Sue for your rights and privileges. . . . That day we, as a people, harken unto the voice of the Lord our God, . . . and we shall begin to flourish.

Source: Maria Stewart, "Religion and the Pure Principles of Morality," in *Meditations from the Pen of Mrs. Maria W. Stewart . . . . First Published by W. Lloyd Garrison & Knapp* (Washington, DC: Enterprise, 1879), 25, 31–32.

Congregational Pastoral Letter, 1837

White women's increased involvement in abolitionism generated considerable controversy. In August 1837 Congregational Church leaders circulated a letter to ministers throughout New England. They were outraged by Angelina and Sarah Grimké's lecturing on antislavery to mixed-sex audiences and condemned both them and women's public activism generally.

W e invite your attention to the dangers which at present seem to threaten the female character with wide-spread and permanent injury. The appropriate duties and influence of woman are clearly stated in the New Testament. Those duties and that influence are unobtrusive and private, but the source of mighty power. When the mild, dependent, softening influence of woman upon the sternness of man's opinions is fully exercised, society feels the effects of it in a thousand ways. The power of woman is in her dependence, flowing from the consciousness of that weakness which God has given her for her protection. . . . There are social influences which females use in promoting piety and the great objects of Christian benevolence which we cannot too highly commend. We appreciate the unostentatious prayers and efforts of woman in advancing the cause of religion at home and abroad; in Sabbath-schools; . . . and in all such associated effort as becomes the modesty of her sex. . . .

But when she assumes the place and tone of man as a public reformer, our care and protection of her seem unnecessary; . . . and her character becomes unnatural. If the vine, whose strength and beauty is to lean upon the trellis-work and half conceal its clusters, thinks to assume the independence and the overshadowing nature of the elm, it will not only cease to bear fruit, but fall in shame and dishonor into the dust. We cannot, therefore, but regret the mistaken conduct of those who encourage females to bear an obtrusive and ostentatious part in measures of reform, and countenance any of that sex who so far forget themselves as to incinerate in the character of public lecturers and teachers. . . . We especially deplore the intimate acquaintance and promiscuous conversation of females with regard to things "which ought not to be named"; by which that modesty and delicacy . . . which constitutes the true influence of woman in society, is consumed, and the way opened . . . for degeneracy and ruin.

Source: "Pastoral Letter of the General Association of Massachusetts to the Congregational Churches under Their Care," *Liberator*, August 11, 1837.

Document 11.9

Sarah Grimké | Response to the Pastoral Letter, 1837

In response to the ministers' criticism, Sarah Grimké wrote a letter to the *Liberator* that she later published in a book of essays. Having converted to Quakerism, she and her sister felt obligated to speak out against the evils of slavery, which they had witnessed firsthand on their father's South Carolina plantation. The criticisms leveled at them inspired Sarah to develop arguments in support of women's rights as well as abolition.

Dear Friend,

. . . I am persuaded that when the minds of men and women become emancipated from the thraldom [bondage] of superstition and "traditions of men," the sentiments contained in the Pastoral Letter will be recurred to with as much astonishment as the opinions of Cotton Mather and other distinguished men of his day, on the subject of witchcraft. . . .

But to the letter. It says, "We invite your attention to the dangers which at present seem to threaten the female character with wide-spread and permanent injury." I rejoice that they have called the attention of my sex to this subject, because I believe if woman investigates it, she will soon discover that danger is impending, though from a totally different source . . . —danger from those who, having long held the reins of *usurped* authority, are unwilling to permit us to fill that sphere which God created us to move in, and who have entered into league to crush the immortal mind of woman. I rejoice, because I am persuaded that the rights of woman, like the rights of slaves, need only be examined to be understood and asserted. . . .

"The appropriate duties and influence of women are clearly stated in the New Testament. Those duties are unobtrusive and private, but the sources of *mighty power*. . . ." No one can desire more earnestly than I do, that woman may move exactly in the sphere which her Creator has assigned her; and I believe her having been displaced from that sphere has introduced confusion into the world. It is, therefore, of vast importance to herself and to all the rational creation, that she should ascertain what are her duties and her privileges as a responsible and immortal being. . . .

But . . . her light is not to shine before man like that of her brethren; but she is passively to let the lords of the creation, as they call themselves, put the bushel over it, lest peradventure [perhaps] it might appear that the world has been benefitted by the rays of *her* candle. So that her quenched light, according to their judgment, will be of more use than if it were set on the candlestick. "Her influence is the source of mighty power." This has ever been the flattering language of man since he laid aside the whip as a means to keep woman in subjection. He spares her body; but the war he has waged against her mind, her heart, and her soul, has been no less destructive to her as a moral being. . . . She has surrendered her dearest RIGHTS, and been satisfied with the privileges which man has assumed to grant her. . . . He has adorned the creature whom God gave him as a companion, with baubles and gewgaws [showy things], turned her attention to personal attractions, offered incense to her vanity, and made her the instrument of his selfish gratification. . . .

We are told, "the power of woman is in her dependence, flowing from a consciousness of that weakness which God has given her for her protection." If physical weakness is alluded to, I cheerfully concede the superiority . . . but if they mean to intimate, that mental or moral weakness belongs to woman, more than to man, I utterly disclaim the charge. . . . [N]o where does God say that he made any distinction between us, as moral and intelligent beings. . . .

As to the pretty simile . . . , "If the vine whose strength and beauty is to lean upon the trellis work, and half conceal its clusters. . . ." etc. I shall only remark that it might well suit the poet's fancy . . . ; but it seems to me utterly inconsistent with the dignity of a Christian body, to endeavor to draw such an anti-scriptural distinction between men and women. Ah! how many of my sex feel . . . , under the gentle appellation of protection, that what they have leaned upon has proved a broken reed at best, and oft a spear.

Source: Sarah Grimké, *Letters on the Equality of the Sexes and the Condition of Woman* (Boston: Isaac Knapp, 1838), 14–18, 21.

Interpret the Evidence

1. What does Charles Finney's account of Mrs. Mathews's conversion indicate about the subordination and influence of evangelical women (Document 11.5)?

2. Why do Elizabeth Emery and Mary Abbott describe enslaved women as their sisters (Document 11.6)? Would Maria Stewart agree with their view (Document 11.7)?

3. Why does Stewart highlight the actions and character of free black women (Document 11.7)?

4. How do the criticisms of female activism in the Pastoral Letter (Document 11.8) compare with Finney's understanding of female influence (Document 11.5)?

5. How do white and black women activists justify women's roles in the abolitionist movement (Documents 11.6, 11.7, and 11.9)?

Put It in Context

How do the arguments of Emery, Abbott, Stewart, and Grimké challenge mid-nineteenth-century beliefs about men's and women's proper spheres? Why did evangelical ministers denounce the Grimkés' speeches before mixed-sex audiences but not Stewart's?

What roles did religion and antislavery activism play in expanding or limiting women's spheres?

12

Imperial Ambitions and Sectional Crises

1842–1861

WINDOW TO THE PAST

Republican Party Presidential Ticket, 1860

The Republican Party needed to attract votes from northern farmers, workers, and businessmen to win the 1860 presidential election. It thus produced an image to appeal to voters on the frontier and in cities as well as both workers and elites. The banner shows two men dressed as workers, one holding an ax, with smoke stacks and a ship in the background and a motto promoting higher tariffs. ▶ To discover more about what this primary source can show us, see Document 12.4 on page 403.

Library of Congress, 3a09182

After reading this chapter you should be able to:

- Compare the experiences of different groups living in and migrating to the West.

- Explain how geographical expansion heightened sectional conflicts and how those conflicts shaped and were shaped by federal policies like the Compromise of 1850 and the Fugitive Slave Act.

- Analyze the ways that the spread of antislavery sentiments, partisan politics, and federal court decisions intensified sectional divisions.

- Evaluate the importance of John Brown's raid and the election of Abraham Lincoln to the presidency in convincing southern states to secede from the Union.

AMERICAN HISTORIES

John C. Frémont, a noted explorer and military leader, rose from humble beginnings. He was born out of wedlock to Anne Beverley Whiting Pryor of Savannah, Georgia, who abandoned her wealthy husband and ran off with a French immigrant. Frémont attended the College of Charleston, where he excelled at mathematics, but was eventually expelled for neglecting his studies. At age twenty, in 1833, he was hired to teach aboard a navy ship through the help of an influential South Carolina politician. He then obtained a surveying position to map new railroad lines and Cherokee lands in Georgia and was finally

appointed a second lieutenant in the Corps of Topographical Engineers.

In 1840 Lieutenant Frémont moved to Washington, D.C., where he worked on maps and reports based on his surveys. The following year, he eloped with Jessie Benton, the daughter of Missouri senator Thomas Hart Benton. Despite the scandal, Senator Benton supported his son-in-law's selection for a federally funded expedition to the West. In 1842 Frémont and his guide, Kit Carson, led twenty-three men along the emerging Oregon Trail. Two years later, John returned to Washington, where Jessie helped him turn his notes into a vivid report on the Oregon Territory and California. Congress published the report, which inspired a wave of hopeful migrants to head west.

Frémont's success was tainted, however, by a quest for personal glory. On a federal mapping expedition in 1845, he left his post and headed to Sacramento, California. In the winter of 1846, he stirred support among U.S. settlers there for war with Mexico. His brash behavior nearly provoked a bloody battle. Frémont then fled to the Oregon Territory, where he and Kit Carson initiated conflicts with local Indians. As the United States moved closer to war with Mexico, Frémont returned to California to support Anglo-American settlers' efforts to declare the region an independent republic. After the war, Frémont worked tirelessly for California's admission to the Union and served as one of the state's first senators. With his wife's encouragement, he embraced abolition and in 1856 was nominated for president by the new Republican Party.

Dred Scott also traveled the frontier in the 1830s and 1840s, but not of his own free will. Born a slave in Southampton, Virginia, around 1800, he and his master, Peter Blow, moved west to Alabama in 1818 and then to St. Louis, Missouri, in 1830. Three years later, Blow sold Scott to Dr. John Emerson, an assistant surgeon in the U.S. army. In 1836 Emerson took Scott to Fort Snelling in the Wisconsin Territory, a free territory. There Scott met Harriet Robinson, a young African American slave. Her master, an Indian agent, allowed the couple to marry in 1837 and transferred ownership of Harriet to Dr. Emerson. When Emerson moved back to St. Louis, the Scotts

(*left*) **John C. Frémont** Library of Congress
(*right*) **Dred Scott** LC-DIG-ppmsca-03210 and Library of Congress, 3a0841

returned with him. After the doctor's death in 1843, the couple was hired out to local residents by Emerson's widow.

In April 1846, the Scotts initiated lawsuits to gain their freedom. The Missouri Supreme Court had ruled in earlier cases that slaves who resided for any time in free territory must be freed, and the Scotts had lived and married in Wisconsin. In 1850 the Missouri Circuit Court ruled in the Scotts' favor. However, the Emerson family appealed the decision to the state supreme court, with Harriet's case to follow the outcome of her husband's. Two years later, that court ruled against all precedent and overturned the lower court's decision. Dred Scott then appealed to the U.S. Supreme Court, but it, too, ultimately ruled against the Scotts, leaving them enslaved. ■

The American histories of John Frémont and Dred Scott were shaped by the explosive combination of westward expansion and growing regional divisions over the issue of slavery. Whereas Frémont joined expeditions to map and conquer the West, Scott followed the migrations of slave owners and soldiers. Both Frémont and Scott were supported by strong women, and both men advocated government action to end slavery. Only Frémont, however, had the right to vote, run for office, and join the Republican Party. From their different positions, these two men reflected the dramatic changes that occurred as westward expansion pushed the issues of empire and slavery to the center of national debate.

Claiming the West

During the 1830s and 1840s, national debates over slavery intensified. The most important battles now centered on western territories gained through victory in the war with Mexico. Before 1848, government-sponsored expeditions had opened up vast new lands for American pioneers seeking opportunity, and migrants moved west in growing numbers. Then, following the Mexican-American War and the discovery of gold in California, tens of thousands of men rushed to the Pacific coast seeking riches. But the West was already home to a diverse population that included Indians, Mexicans, Mormons, and missionaries. Pioneers converged, and often clashed, with these groups.

Traveling the Overland Trail. In the 1830s a growing number of migrants followed overland trails to the far West. In 1836 Narcissa Whitman and Eliza Spaulding joined a group traveling to the Oregon Territory, the first white women to make the trip. They accompanied their husbands, both Presbyterian ministers, who hoped to convert the region's Indians. Their letters to friends and co-worshippers back east described the rich lands and needy souls in the Walla Walla valley. Such missives were widely shared and encouraged further migration.

The panic of 1837 also prompted families to head west. Thousands of U.S. migrants and European immigrants sought better economic prospects in Oregon, the Rocky Mountain region, and the eastern plains, while Mormons continued to settle in Salt Lake City. Some pioneers opened trading posts where Indians exchanged goods with Anglo-American settlers or with merchants back east. Small settlements developed around these posts and near the expanding system of U.S. forts that dotted the region.

For many pioneers, the journey on the **Oregon Trail** began at St. Louis. From there, they traveled by wagon train across the Great Plains and the Rocky Mountains to the Pacific coast. By 1860 some 350,000 Americans had made the journey, claimed land from the Mississippi River to the Pacific, and transformed the United States into an expanding empire.

Because the journey west required funds for wagons and supplies, most pioneers were of middling status. The majority of pioneers made the three- to six-month journey with family members, to help share the labor. Men, mainly farmers, comprised some 60 percent of these western migrants, but women and children traveled in significant numbers, often alongside relatives or neighbors from back east. Some courageous families headed west alone, but most traveled in wagon trains— from a few wagons to a few dozen—that provided support and security.

Explore ▶

See Document 12.1 for one account of the journey west.

Traditional gender roles often broke down on the trail, and even conventional domestic tasks posed novel problems. Women had to cook unfamiliar food over open fires in all kinds of weather and with only a few pots and utensils. They washed laundry in rivers or streams and on the plains hauled water from great distances. Wood, too, was scarce on the plains, and women and children gathered buffalo dung (called "chips") for fuel. Men frequently had to gather food rather than hunt and fish, or they had to learn to catch strange (and sometimes dangerous) animals, such as jack rabbits and rattlesnakes. Few men were prepared for the dangerous work of floating wagons across rivers. Nor were many of them expert in shoeing horses or fixing wagon wheels, tasks that were performed by skilled artisans at home.

Emigrant Party Headed to California, 1850   This hand-colored engraving of a wagon train heading through a mountain pass shows the presence of many family groups and the need for many adults and children to walk and carry goods for parts of the journey. Presenting a wide rolling trail on a clear day, it does not capture the many obstacles faced by pioneers crossing the Rocky Mountains. Library of Congress, LC-DIG-ppmsca-02887

Expectations changed dramatically when men took ill or died. Then wives often drove the wagon, gathered or hunted for food, and learned to repair axles and other wagon parts. When large numbers of men were injured or ill, women might serve as scouts and guides or pick up guns to defend wagons under attack by Indians or wild animals. Yet despite their growing burdens, pioneer women gained little power over decision making. Moreover, the addition of men's jobs to women's responsibilities was rarely reciprocated. Few men cooked, did laundry, or cared for children on the trail.

GUIDED ANALYSIS

Elizabeth Smith Geer | Oregon Trail Diary, 1847

Like thousands of other families, Elizabeth and Cornelius Smith and their seven children set out for the Oregon Territory in the spring of 1847. They fared well through the summer, but in the fall heavy rains made things difficult. In November Cornelius became sick, but the Smiths arrived in Portland, Oregon, by Thanksgiving. However, Cornelius died two months later, and in 1849 Elizabeth married Joseph Geer, the father of ten children whose wife also died after journeying across the Oregon Trail.

Document 12.1

November 18.

It rains and snows. We start around the falls this morning with our wagons. We have five miles to go. I carry my babe and lead, or rather carry another, through snow, mud, and water almost to my knees. It is the worst road a team could possibly travel. I went ahead with my children and I was afraid to look behind me for fear of seeing the wagons overturn into the mud and water with everything in them. My children gave out with cold and fatigue and could not travel, and the boys had to unhitch the oxen and bring them and carry the children on to camp. I was so cold and numb that I could not tell by the feeling that I had any feet. We started this morning at sunrise and did not camp until after dark, and there was not one dry thread on one of us—not even on the babe. I had carried my babe and I was so fatigued that I could scarcely speak or step. When I got here I found my husband lying in Welch's wagon very sick. He had brought Mrs. Polk down the day before and was taken sick. We had to stay up all night for our wagons were left halfway back. I have not told half we suffered. I am not adequate to the task.

How did weather affect the ability of families to travel on the Oregon Trail?

How did children both assist and create problems for their parents?

How did the roles of husbands and wives change during the journey?

Source: Theodore Thurston Geer, *Fifty Years in Oregon* (New York: Neale, 1912), 146.

Put It in Context

Despite widespread fear of Indian attacks on the trail, what were the most serious dangers that men and women pioneers faced on the journey west?

In one area, however, relative equality reigned. Men and women were equally susceptible to disease, injury, and death during the journey. Accidents, gunshot wounds, drownings, broken bones, and infections affected people on every wagon train. Some groups were struck as well by deadly epidemics of measles or cholera. In addition, about 20 percent of women on the overland trail became pregnant, which posed even greater dangers than usual given the lack of medical services and sanitation. About the same percentage of women lost children or spouses on the trip west. Overall, about one in ten to fifteen migrants died on the western journey.

The Gold Rush. Despite the hazards, more and more Americans traveled overland to the Pacific coast, although only a few thousand Americans initially settled in California. Some were agents sent there by eastern merchants to purchase fine leather made from the hides of Spanish cattle. Several agents married into families of elite Mexican ranchers, known as Californios, and adopted their culture, even converting to Catholicism.

However, the Anglo-American presence in California changed dramatically after 1848 when gold was discovered at Sutter's Mill in northeastern California. Beginning in 1849 news of the discovery brought tens of thousands of settlers from the eastern United States, South America, Europe, and Asia. In the **gold rush**, "forty-niners" raced to claim riches in California, and men vastly outnumbered women.

The rapid influx of gold seekers heightened tensions between newly arrived whites, local Indians, and Californios. Forty-niners confiscated land owned by Californios, shattered

Gold Rush Miner, 1849
This prospector was one of some 80,000 who arrived in northeast California in 1849 after gold was discovered at Sutter's Mill. Photographed fully equipped with the tools of his trade—pickax, hoe, and pan—he, like other miners, was capable of digging out only surface gold. The prospector's two pistols suggest the dangers miners faced. Private Collection/Peter Newark American Pictures/ Bridgeman Images

the fragile ecosystem in the California mountains, and forced Mexican and Indian men to labor for low wages or a promised share in uncertain profits. New conflicts erupted when migrants from Asia and South America joined the search for wealth. Forty-niners from the United States regularly stole from and assaulted these foreign-born competitors.

The gold rush also led to the increased exploitation of women as thousands of male migrants demanded food, shelter, laundry, and medical care. While some California women earned a good living by renting rooms, cooking meals, washing clothes, or working as prostitutes, many faced exploitation and abuse. Indian and Mexican women were especially vulnerable to sexual harassment and rape, while Chinese women were imported specifically to provide sexual services for male miners.

Chinese men were also victims of abuse by whites, who ran them off their claims. Yet some Chinese men used the skills traditionally assigned them in their homeland—cooking and washing clothes—to earn a far steadier income than prospecting for gold could provide. Other men also took advantage of the demand for goods and services. Levi Strauss, a German Jewish immigrant, moved from New York to San Francisco to open a dry-goods store in 1853. He soon made his fortune producing canvas and then denim pants that could withstand harsh weather and long wear.

A Crowded Land.
While U.S. promoters of migration continued to depict the West as open territory, it was in fact the site of competing national ambitions in the late 1840s. Despite granting statehood to Texas in 1845 and winning the war against Mexico in 1848, the United States had to battle for control of the Great Plains with powerful Indian nations, like the Sioux and Cheyenne (Map 12.1).

Although attacks on wagon trains were rare, Indians did threaten frontier settlements throughout the 1840s and 1850s. Settlers often retaliated, and U.S. army troops joined them in efforts to push Indians back from areas newly claimed by whites. Yet in many parts of the West, Indians were as powerful as whites, and they did not cede territory without a fight. The Reverend Marcus Whitman and his wife, Narcissa, became victims of their success in promoting western settlement when pioneers brought a deadly measles epidemic to the region, killing thousands of Cayuse and Nez Percé Indians. In 1847, convinced that whites brought disease but no useful medicine, a group of Cayuse Indians killed the Whitmans and ten other white settlers.

Yet violence against whites could not stop the flood of migrants into the Oregon Territory. Indeed, attacks by one Indian tribe were often used to justify assaults on any Indian tribe. Thus John Frémont and Kit Carson, whose party was attacked by Modoc Indians in Oregon in 1846, retaliated by destroying a Klamath Indian village and killing its inhabitants. The defeat of Mexico and the discovery of gold in California only intensified such conflicts.

Although Indians and white Americans were the main players in many battles, Indian nations also competed with each other. In the southern plains, drought and disease exacerbated those conflicts in the late 1840s and dramatically changed the balance of power there. In 1845 the southern plains were struck by a dry spell, which lasted on and off until the mid-1860s. In 1848, smallpox ravaged Comanche villages, and a virulent strain of cholera was introduced into the region the next year by forty-niners traveling to California. In the late 1840s, the Comanche nation was the largest Indian group, with about twenty thousand members; by the mid-1850s, less than half that number remained.

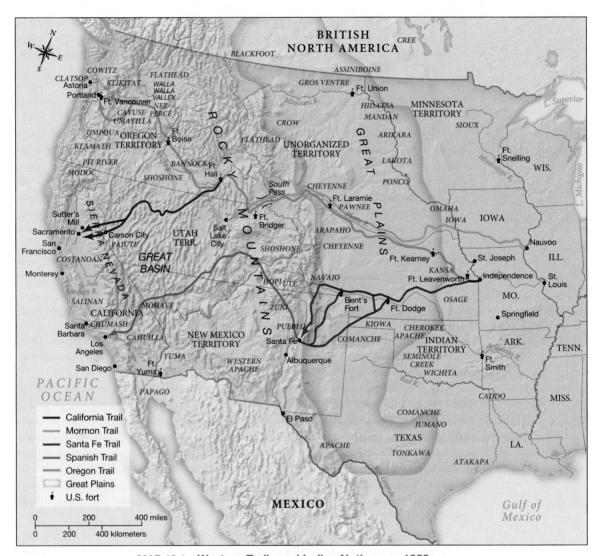

MAP 12.1 Western Trails and Indian Nations, c. 1850

As wagon trains and traders journeyed west in rapidly growing numbers during the 1830s and 1840s, the United States established forts along the most well-traveled routes. At the same time, Indians claimed or were forced into new areas through the pressure of Indian removals, white settlement, and the demands of hunting, trade, and agriculture.

Yet the collapse of the Comanche empire was not simply the result of outside forces. As the Comanche expanded their trade networks and incorporated smaller Indian nations into their orbit, they overextended their reach. Most important, they allowed too many bison to be killed to meet the needs of their Indian allies and the demand of Anglo-American and European traders. The Comanche also herded growing numbers of horses, which required expansive grazing lands and winter havens in the river valleys and forced the bison onto more marginal lands. Opening the Santa Fe Trail to commerce multiplied the problems by destroying vegetation and polluting springs, thereby diminishing resources in more of the region. The prolonged drought completed the depopulation of the bison on the southern plains. Without bison, the Comanche lost a trade item critical to sustaining their commercial and political control. As the Comanche empire collapsed, former Indian allies sought to advance their own interests. These developments reignited Indian wars on the southern plains as tens of thousands of pioneers poured through the region.

African Americans also participated in these western struggles. Many were held as slaves by southeastern tribes forced into Indian Territory, while others were freed and married Seminole or Cherokee spouses. The Creeks proved harsh masters, prompting some slaves to escape north to free states or south to Mexican or Comanche territory. Yet as southern officers in the U.S. army moved to frontier outposts, they carried more slaves into the region. Many, including Dr. John Emerson, changed posts frequently, taking slaves like Dred Scott into both slave and free territories. Still, it was white planters who brought the greatest numbers of African Americans into Texas, Missouri, and Kansas, pushing the frontier of slavery ever westward. At the same time, some free blacks joined the migration voluntarily in hopes of finding better economic opportunities and less overt racism in the West.

REVIEW & RELATE

- Why did Americans go west in the 1830s and 1840s, and what was the journey like?

- What groups competed for land and resources in the West? How did disease, drought, and violence shape this competition?

Expansion and the Politics of Slavery

The place of slavery in the West aroused intense political debates as territories in the region began to seek statehood. Debates over the eradication of slavery and limits on its expansion had shaped the highly contested presidential election of 1848. After the Mexican-American War, the debate intensified and focused more specifically on slavery's westward expansion. Each time a territory achieved the requirements for statehood, a new crisis erupted. To resolve these crises required strong political leadership, judicial moderation, and a spirit of compromise among the American people. None of these conditions prevailed. Instead, passage of the Fugitive Slave Act in 1850 aroused deeper hostilities, and President Franklin Pierce (1853–1857) encouraged further expansion but failed to address the crises that ensued.

California and the Compromise of 1850. In the winter of 1849, just before President Zachary Taylor's March inauguration, California applied for admission to the Union as a free state. Some California political leaders opposed slavery on principle. Others wanted to "save" the state for whites by outlawing slavery, discouraging free black migration, and restricting the rights of Mexican, Indian, and Chinese residents. Yet the internal debates among Californians were not uppermost in the minds of politicians. Southerners were concerned about the impact of California's free-state status on the sectional balance in Congress, while northern Whigs were shocked when President Taylor suggested that slavery should be allowed anywhere in the West.

The United States Senate, A.D. 1850   This print captures seventy-three-year-old Henry Clay presenting his Compromise of 1850 to colleagues in the Old Senate Chamber. An aged John C. Calhoun, seated to the left of the Speaker's chair, denounced the compromise, as did antislavery Whigs and Free-Soilers. Daniel Webster, sitting to the left of Clay, offered a passionate defense but failed to gain the compromise's passage. Library of Congress, 3g01724

Other debates percolated in Congress at the same time. Many Northerners were horrified by the spectacle of slavery and slave trading in the nation's capital and argued that it damaged America's international reputation. Southerners, meanwhile, complained that the Fugitive Slave Act of 1793 was being widely ignored in the North. A boundary dispute between Texas and New Mexico irritated western legislators, and Texas continued to claim that debts it accrued while an independent republic and during the Mexican-American War should be assumed by the federal government.

Senator Henry Clay of Kentucky, the Whig leader who had hammered out the Missouri Compromise in 1819 and 1820, again tried to resolve the many conflicts that stalled congressional action. He offered a compromise by which California would be admitted as a free state; the remaining land acquired from Mexico would be divided into two territories—New Mexico and Utah—and slavery there would be decided by popular sovereignty; the border dispute between New Mexico and Texas would be decided in favor of New Mexico, but the federal government would assume Texas's war debts; the slave trade (but not slavery) would be abolished in the District of Columbia; and a new and more effective fugitive slave law would be approved. Although Clay's compromise offered something to everyone, his colleagues did not immediately embrace it.

By March 1850, after months of passionate debate, the sides remained sharply divided, as did their most esteemed leaders. John C. Calhoun, a proslavery senator from South Carolina, refused to support any compromise that allowed Congress to decide the fate of slavery in the western territories. William H. Seward, an antislavery Whig senator from New York, proclaimed he could not support a compromise that forced Northerners to help hunt down fugitives from slavery. While Daniel Webster, a Massachusetts Whig, urged fellow senators to support the compromise to preserve the Union, Congress adjourned with the fate of California undecided.

Before the Senate reconvened in September 1850, however, the political landscape changed in unexpected ways. Henry Clay retired the previous spring, leaving the Capitol with his last great legislative effort unfinished. On March 31, 1850, Calhoun died; his absence from the Senate made compromise more likely. Then in July, President Taylor died unexpectedly, and his vice president, Millard Fillmore, became president. Fillmore then appointed Webster as secretary of state, removing him from the Senate as well.

In fall 1850, with President Fillmore's support, a younger cohort of senators and representatives steered the **Compromise of 1850** through Congress, one clause at a time. This tactic allowed legislators to support only those parts of the compromise they found palatable. In the end, all the provisions passed, and Fillmore quickly signed the bills into law.

The Compromise of 1850, like the Missouri Compromise thirty years earlier, fended off a sectional crisis but signaled future problems. Would popular sovereignty prevail when later territories sought admission to the Union, and would Northerners abide by a fugitive slave law that called on them to aid directly in the capture of runaway slaves?

The Fugitive Slave Act Inspires Northern Protest.

The fugitive slave laws of 1793 and 1824 mandated that all states aid in apprehending and returning runaway slaves to their owners. The **Fugitive Slave Act of 1850** was different in two important respects. First, it eliminated jury trials for alleged fugitives. Second, the law required individual citizens, not just state officials, to help return runaways. The act angered many Northerners who believed that the federal government had gone too far in protecting the rights of slaveholders and thereby aroused sympathy for the abolitionist cause.

Before 1850, the most well-known individuals aiding fugitives were free blacks such as David Ruggles in New York City; Jermaine Loguen in Syracuse, New York; and, after his own successful escape, Frederick Douglass. Their main allies in this work were white Quakers such as Amy and Isaac Post in Rochester; Thomas Garrett in Chester County, Pennsylvania; and Levi and Catherine Coffin in Newport, Indiana.

Following passage of the Fugitive Slave Act, the number of slave owners and hired slave catchers pursuing fugitives increased dramatically. But so, too, did the number of northern abolitionists helping blacks escape. Once escaped slaves crossed into free territory, most contacted free blacks or sought out Quaker, Baptist, or Methodist meetinghouses whose members might be sympathetic to their cause. They then began the often slow journey along the underground railroad, from house to house or barn to barn, until they found safe haven. A small number of fortunate slaves were led north by fugitives like Harriet Tubman, who returned south repeatedly to free dozens of family members and other enslaved men and women. Fugitives followed disparate paths through the Midwest, Pennsylvania, New York, and New England, and there was little coordination among the "conductors" from one region to another. But the underground railroad was nonetheless

The Resurrection of Henry "Box" Brown at Philadelphia Henry Brown escaped enslavement in Virginia in March 1849 by having himself shipped to Philadelphia in a crate. One of the most innovative means of gaining freedom, it required substantial assistance from supporters in Richmond and Philadelphia. This 1850 lithograph popularized Brown's escape, furthering his career as a lecturer but making it difficult for other slaves to replicate his strategy. Library of Congress, LC-DIG-pga-04518

an important resource for fugitives, some of whom sought refuge in Canada while others hoped to blend into free black communities in the United States.

Free blacks were endangered by the claim that slaves hid themselves in their midst. In Chester County, Pennsylvania, on the Maryland border, newspapers reported on at least a dozen free blacks who were kidnapped or arrested as runaways in the first three months of 1851. One provision of the Fugitive Slave Act encouraged such arrests: Commissioners were paid $10 for each slave sent back but only $5 if a slave was not returned. Without the right to a trial, a free black could easily be sent south as a fugitive.

At the same time, a growing number of Northerners challenged the federal government's right to enforce the law. Blacks and whites organized protest meetings throughout the free states. At a meeting in Boston in 1851, William Lloyd Garrison denounced the law: "We execrate it, we spit upon it, we trample it under our feet." Abolitionists also joined forces to rescue fugitives who had been arrested. In Syracuse in October 1851, Jermaine Loguen, Samuel Ward, and the Reverend Samuel J. May led a well-organized crowd that broke into a Syracuse courthouse and rescued a fugitive known as Jerry. They successfully hid him from authorities before spiriting him to Canada.

Explore ▶

See Documents 11.2 and
11.3 for two responses to
the Fugitive Slave Act.

Meanwhile Americans continued to debate the law's effects. John Frémont, one of the first two senators from California, helped defeat a federal bill
that would have imposed harsher penalties on those who assisted runaways.
And Congress felt growing pressure to calm the situation, including from
foreign officials who were horrified by the violence required to sustain slavery
in the United States. Frederick Douglass and other black abolitionists
denounced the Fugitive Slave Act across Canada, Ireland, and England, intensifying foreign concern over the law. Great Britain and France had abolished slavery in their West
Indian colonies and could not support what they saw as extreme policies to keep the
institution alive in the United States. Yet southern slaveholders refused to compromise
further, as did northern abolitionists.

Pierce Encourages U.S. Expansion.

In the presidential election of 1852, the
Whigs and the Democrats tried once again to appeal to voters across the North-South
divide by running candidates who either skirted the slavery issue or voiced ambiguous
views. The Democrats nominated Franklin Pierce of New Hampshire. A northern opponent of abolition, Pierce had served in Congress from 1833 to 1842 and in the U.S. army
during the Mexican-American War. The Whigs rejected President Millard Fillmore, who
had angered many by supporting popular sovereignty and vigorous enforcement of the
Fugitive Slave Act. They turned instead to General Winfield Scott of Virginia. General
Scott had never expressed any proslavery views and had served with distinction in the war
against Mexico. The Whigs thus hoped to gain southern support while maintaining their
northern base. The Free-Soil Party, too, hoped to expand its appeal by nominating John
Hale, a New Hampshire Democrat.

Franklin Pierce's eventual victory left the Whigs and the Free-Soilers in disarray.
Seeking a truly proslavery party, a third of southern Whigs threw their support to the
Democrats in the election. Many Democrats who had supported Free-Soilers in 1848 were
driven to vote for Pierce by their enthusiasm over the admission of California as a free
state. But despite the Democratic triumph, that party also remained fragile. The nation
now faced some of its gravest challenges under a president with limited political experience and no firm base of support and a cabinet that included men of widely differing
views. When confronted with difficult decisions, Pierce received contradictory advice and
generally pursued his own expansionist vision.

Early in his administration, Pierce focused on expanding U.S. trade and extending the
"civilizing" power of the nation to other parts of the world. Trade with China had declined
in the 1840s, but the United States had begun commercial negotiations with Japan in 1846.
These came to fruition in 1854, when U.S. emissary Commodore Matthew C. Perry, a
renowned naval officer and founder of the Naval Engineer Corps, obtained the first formal
mutual trade agreement with Japan. Within four years, the United States had expanded
commercial ties and enhanced diplomatic relations with Japan, in large part by supporting
the island nation against its traditional enemies in China, Russia, and Europe.

Pierce had rejected Commodore Perry's offer to take military possession of Formosa
and other territories near Japan, but he was willing to consider conquests in the Caribbean
and Central America. For decades, U.S. politicians, particularly Southerners, had looked
to gain control of Cuba, Mexico, and Nicaragua. A "Young America" movement within the
Democratic Party imagined manifest destiny reaching southward as well as westward. In

COMPARATIVE ANALYSIS

The Fugitive Slave Law Contested

The Fugitive Slave Law was enacted on September 18, 1850, and soon after African Americans in Boston called a meeting to discuss their response (Document 12.2). Having heard rumors of arrests elsewhere, participants demanded the right to defend themselves. On February 15, 1851, local abolitionists, led by Lewis Hayden, rescued fugitive Shadrach Minkins from the Boston federal courthouse and spirited him to Canada. Three days later, President Millard Fillmore issued a proclamation demanding that citizens obey the law or be prosecuted (Document 12.3). Seven black men and two whites were arrested in Boston, but all were acquitted by juries.

Document 12.2

William C. Nell | Meeting of Colored Citizens of Boston, September 30, 1850

The Chairman [Lewis Hayden] announced, as a prominent feature in calling the present meeting—Congress having passed the infamous Fugitive Slave Bill—the adoption of ways and means for the protection of those in Boston liable to be seized by the prowling man-thief. He said that safety was to be obtained only by an united and persevering resistance of this ungodly, anti-republican law. . . .

The following resolutions were submitted, as a platform for vigilant action in the trial hour:—

Resolved, That the Fugitive Slave Bill, recently adopted by the United States Congress, puts in imminent jeopardy the lives and liberties of ourselves and our children; it deprives us of trial by jury, when seized by the infernal slave-catcher, and by high penalties forbids the assistance of those who would otherwise obey their heart-promptings in our behalf; in making it obligatory upon marshals to become bloodhounds in pursuit of human prey; leaving us no alternative . . . but to be prepared in the emergency for self-defense; therefore, assured that God has no attribute which can take sides with oppressors, we have counted the cost, and as we prefer *liberty* to *life*, we mutually pledge to defend ourselves and each other in resisting this God-defying and inhuman law, at any and every sacrifice, invoking Heaven's defense of the right.

Resolved, That . . . eternal vigilance is the price of liberty, and that they who would be free, themselves must strike the first blow.

Source: "Meeting of the Colored Citizens of Boston," *Liberator*, October 4, 1850.

hopes of stirring up rebellious Cubans against Spanish rule, some Democrats joined with private adventurers to send three unauthorized expeditions, known as **filibusters**, to invade Cuba. In 1854 the capture of one of the filibustering ships led to an international incident. Spanish officials confiscated the ship, and southern Democrats urged Pierce to seek an apology and redress from Spain. But many northern Democrats rejected any effort to obtain another slave state, and Pierce was forced to renounce the filibusters.

Other politicians still pressured Spain to sell Cuba to the United States. These included Pierce's secretary of state, William Marcy, and the U.S. ambassador to Great Britain, James Buchanan, as well as the ministers to France and Spain. In October 1854 these

Document 12.3

President Millard Fillmore | Proclamation 56 Calling on Citizens to Assist in the Recapture of a Fugitive Slave, February 18, 1851

Whereas information has been received that sundry lawless persons, principally persons of color, combined and confederated together for the purpose of opposing by force the execution of the laws of the United States, did, at Boston, in Massachusetts, on the 15th of this month, make a violent assault on the marshal or deputy marshals of the United States for the district of Massachusetts, in the court-house, and did overcome the said officers, and did by force rescue from their custody a person arrested as a fugitive slave, and then and there a prisoner lawfully holden by the said marshal or deputy marshals of the United States, and other scandalous outrages did commit in violation of law:

Now, therefore, to the end that the authority of the laws may be maintained and those concerned in violating them brought to immediate and condign punishment, I have issued this my proclamation, calling on all well-disposed citizens to rally to the support of the laws of their country, and requiring and commanding all officers, civil and military, and all other persons, civil or military, who shall be found within the vicinity of this outrage, to be aiding and assisting by all means in their power in quelling this and other such combinations and assisting the marshal and his deputies in recapturing the above-mentioned prisoner; and I do especially direct that prosecutions be commenced against all persons who shall have made themselves aiders or abettors in or to this flagitious offense.

Source: *The Messages and Papers of the Presidents, 1789–1913* (Washington, DC: U.S. Government Printing Office, 1913), 988.

Interpret the Evidence

1. How did African Americans in Boston justify their right to defend themselves in defiance of the Fugitive Slave Law and how would they have responded to Fillmore's Proclamation 56?
2. How does President Fillmore characterize the Boston abolitionists who sought to free fugitives like Shadrach Minkins, and what consequences does he propose for flouting the law?

Put It in Context

What do the conflicts over implementation of the Fugitive Slave Law in Boston suggest about the long-term impact of the law?

ministers met in Ostend, Belgium, and sent a letter to Pierce urging the conquest of Cuba. When the **Ostend Manifesto** was leaked to the press, Northerners were outraged. They viewed the episode as "a dirty plot" to gain more slave territory and forced Pierce to give up plans to obtain Cuba. In 1855 a private adventurer named William Walker, who had organized four filibusters to Nicaragua, invaded that country and set himself up as ruler. He then invited southern planters to come to Nicaragua and establish plantations. Pierce and many Democrats endorsed his plan, but neighboring Hondurans forced Walker from power in 1857 and executed him three years later. Although Pierce's expansionist dreams failed, his efforts heightened sectional tensions.

REVIEW & RELATE

What steps did legislators take in the 1840s and early 1850s to resolve the issue of the expansion of slavery? Were they successful?

How were slavery and American imperialist ambitions intertwined in the 1840s and 1850s?

Sectional Crises Intensify

The political crises of the early 1850s created a lively trade in antislavery literature. This cultural turmoil, combined with the weakness and fragmentation of the existing political parties, helped give rise to the Republican Party in 1854. The Republican Party soon absorbed enough Free-Soilers, Whigs, and northern Democrats to become a major political force. The events that drove these cultural and political developments included the publication of *Uncle Tom's Cabin*, continued challenges to the Fugitive Slave Act, a battle over the admission of Kansas to the Union, and a Supreme Court ruling in the *Dred Scott* case.

Popularizing Antislavery Sentiment. The Fugitive Slave Act forced Northerners to reconsider their role in sustaining the institution of slavery. In 1852, just months before Franklin Pierce was elected president, their concerns were heightened by the publication of the novel ***Uncle Tom's Cabin*** by Harriet Beecher Stowe. Stowe's father, Lyman Beecher, and brother Henry were among the nation's leading evangelical clergy, and her sister Catharine had opposed Cherokee removal and promoted women's education. Stowe was inspired to write *Uncle Tom's Cabin* by passage of the Fugitive Slave Act in 1850. Published in both serial and book forms, the novel created a national sensation.

Uncle Tom's Cabin built on accounts by former slaves as well as tales gathered by abolitionist lecturers and writers, which gained growing attention in the North. The autobiographies of Frederick Douglass (1845), Josiah Henson (1849), and Henry Bibb (1849) set the stage for Stowe's novel. So, too, did the expansion of the antislavery press, which by the 1850s included dozens of newspapers. Antislavery poems and songs also circulated widely and were performed at abolitionist conventions and fund-raising fairs.

Still, nothing captured the public's attention as did *Uncle Tom's Cabin*. Read by millions in the United States and England and translated into French and German, the book reached a mass audience. Its sentimental portrait of saintly slaves and its vivid depiction of cruel masters and overseers offered white Northerners a way to identify with enslaved blacks. Although some African Americans expressed frustration that a white woman's fictional account gained far more readers than their factual narratives, most recognized the book's important contribution to the antislavery cause.

Yet the real-life stories of fugitive slaves could often surpass their fictional counterparts for drama. In May 1854 abolitionists sought to free fugitive slave Anthony Burns from a Boston courthouse, where his master was attempting to reclaim him. They failed to secure his release, and Burns was soon marched to the docks to be shipped south. Twenty-two companies of state militia held back tens of thousands of angry Bostonians who lined the streets. A year later, supporters purchased Burns's freedom from his master, but the incident raised anguished questions among local residents. In a city that was home to so many intellectual, religious, and antislavery leaders, Bostonians wondered how they had come so far in aiding and abetting slavery.

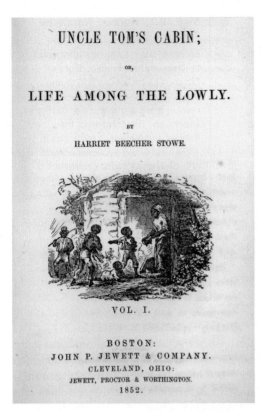

UNCLE TOM'S CABIN;

OR,

LIFE AMONG THE LOWLY.

BY

HARRIET BEECHER STOWE.

VOL. I.

BOSTON:
JOHN P. JEWETT & COMPANY.
CLEVELAND, OHIO:
JEWETT, PROCTOR & WORTHINGTON.
1852.

Original Cover of *Uncle Tom's Cabin*　Harriet Beecher Stowe's novel increased sympathy for slaves among northern whites. Ex-slave William Wells Brown proclaimed that the book "has come down upon the dark abodes of slavery like a morning sunlight, unfolding to view its enormities in a manner which has fastened all eyes upon the 'peculiar situation,' and awakening sympathy in hearts that never before felt for the slave."　Newberry Library, Chicago, Illinois, USA/Bridgeman Images

The Kansas-Nebraska Act Stirs Dissent. Kansas provided the first test of the effects of *Uncle Tom's Cabin* on northern sentiments toward slavery's expansion. As white Americans displaced Indian nations from their homelands, diverse groups of Indians settled in the northern half of the Louisiana Territory. This unorganized region had once been considered beyond the reach of white settlement, but Democratic senator Stephen Douglas of Illinois was eager to have a transcontinental railroad run through his home state. He needed the federal government to gain control of land along the route he proposed and thus argued for the establishment of a vast Nebraska Territory. But to support his plan, Douglas also needed to convince southern congressmen, who sought a route through their own region. According to the Missouri Compromise, states lying above the southern border of Missouri were automatically free. To gain southern support, Douglas sought to reopen the question of slavery in the territories.

In January 1854 Douglas introduced the **Kansas-Nebraska Act** to Congress. The act extinguished Indians' long-held treaty rights in the region and repealed the Missouri Compromise. Two new territories—Kansas and Nebraska—would be carved out of the unorganized lands, and voters in each would determine whether to enter the nation as a slave or a free state (Map 12.2). The act spurred intense opposition from most Whigs and some northern Democrats who wanted to retain the Missouri Compromise line. Months of fierce debate followed, but the bill was ultimately voted into law.

Passage of the Kansas-Nebraska Act enraged many Northerners who considered the dismantling of the Missouri Compromise a sign of the rising power of the South. They were infuriated that the South—or what some now called the "Slave Power"—had again benefited from northern politicians' willingness to compromise. Although few of these opponents considered the impact of the law on Indians, the act also shattered treaty provisions that had protected the Arapaho, Cheyenne, Ponco, Pawnee, and Sioux nations. These Plains Indians lost half the land they had held by treaty as thousands of settlers swarmed into the newly organized territories. In the fall of 1855, conflicts between white settlers and Indians erupted across the Great Plains. The U.S. army then sent six hundred troops to retaliate against a Sioux village, killing eighty-five residents of Blue Water in the Nebraska Territory and triggering continued violence throughout the region.

As tensions escalated across the nation, Americans faced the 1854 congressional elections. The Democrats, increasingly viewed as supporting the priorities of slaveholders, lost badly in the North. But the Whig Party also proved weak, having failed to stop the Slave

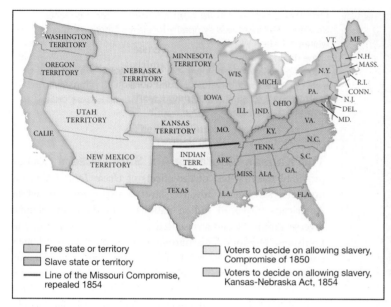

MAP 12.2   Kansas-Nebraska Territory

From 1820 on, Congress attempted to limit sectional conflict. But the Missouri Compromise (1820) and the Compromise of 1850 failed to resolve disagreements over slavery's expansion. The creation of the Kansas and Nebraska territories in 1854 heightened sectional conflict and ensured increased hostilities with Indians in the region.

Power from extending its leverage over federal policies. A third party, the American Party, was founded in the early 1850s and attracted native-born workers and Protestant farmers who were drawn to its anti-immigrant and anti-Catholic message. Responding to these political realignments, another new party, led by antislavery Whigs and Free-Soilers—the **Republican Party**—was founded in the spring of 1854. Among its early members was a Whig politician from Illinois, Abraham Lincoln.

Although established only months before the fall 1854 elections, the Republican Party gained significant support in the Midwest, particularly in state and local campaigns. Meanwhile the American Party gained control of the Massachusetts legislature and nearly captured New York. These victories marked the demise of the Whigs. The Republicans replaced the Whig Party—built initially on a national constituency—with a party rooted solely in the North. Like Free-Soilers, the Republicans argued that slavery should not be extended into new territories. But the Republicans also advocated a program of commercial and industrial development and internal improvements to attract a broader base than earlier antislavery parties. The Republican Party attracted both ardent abolitionists and men whose main concern was keeping western territories open to free white men. This latter group was more than willing to accept slavery where it already existed.

Bleeding Kansas and the Election of 1856. The 1854 congressional elections exacerbated sectional tensions by bringing representatives from a strictly northern party—the Republicans—into Congress. But the conflicts over slavery reached far beyond the nation's capital. After passage of the Kansas-Nebraska Act, advocates and opponents of slavery poured into Kansas in anticipation of a vote on whether the state would enter the Union slave or free.

As Kansas prepared to hold its referendum, settlers continued to arrive daily, making it difficult to determine who was eligible to vote. In 1855 Southerners installed a proslavery

Clarina Howard Nichols   An abolitionist, journalist, and women's rights advocate in Vermont, Clarina Howard Nichols joined the New England Emigrant Aid Society in 1854. The next year, she moved with her family to the Kansas Territory, where this photograph was taken. Nichols advocated women's legal rights through lectures and editorials and was the only woman to participate in the Kansas constitutional convention of 1859. Kansas State Historical Society

government at Shawnee Mission, while abolitionists established a stronghold in Lawrence. Violence erupted when proslavery settlers invaded Lawrence, killing one resident, demolishing newspaper offices, and plundering shops and homes. Fearing that southern settlers in Kansas were better armed than anti-slavery Northerners in the territory, eastern abolitionists raised funds to ship rifles to Kansas.

In 1856 longtime abolitionist John Brown carried his own rifles to Kansas. Four of his sons already lived in the territory. To retaliate for proslavery attacks on Lawrence, the Browns and two friends kidnapped five proslavery advocates from their homes along Pottawatomie Creek and hacked them to death. The so-called Pottawatomie Massacre infuriated southern settlers, who then drew up the Lecompton Constitution, which declared Kansas a slave state. President Pierce made his support of the proslavery government clear, but Congress remained divided. While Congress deliberated, armed battles continued. In the first six months of 1856, another two hundred settlers—on both sides of the conflict—were killed in what became known as **Bleeding Kansas.**

Fighting also broke out on the floor of Congress. Republican senator Charles Sumner of Massachusetts delivered an impassioned speech against the continued expansion of the Slave Power. He launched scathing attacks on planter politicians like South Carolina senator Andrew Butler. Butler's nephew, Preston Brooks, a Democratic member of the House of Representatives, rushed to defend his family's honor. He assaulted Sumner in the Senate chamber, beating him senseless with a cane. Sumner, who never fully recovered from his injuries, was considered a martyr in the North. Meanwhile Brooks was celebrated throughout South Carolina.

The presidential election of 1856 began amid an atmosphere poisoned by violence and recrimination. The Democratic Party nominated James Buchanan of Pennsylvania, a proslavery advocate. Western hero John C. Frémont headed the Republican Party ticket. The American Party, in its final presidential contest, selected former president Millard Fillmore as its candidate. The strength of nativism in politics was waning, however, and Fillmore won only the state of Maryland. Meanwhile Frémont attracted cheering throngs as he traveled across the nation. Large numbers of women turned out to see Jessie Frémont, the first presidential candidate's wife to play a significant role in a campaign.

Frémont carried most of the North and the West. Buchanan captured the South along with Pennsylvania, Indiana, and Illinois. Although Buchanan won only 45.2 percent of the popular vote, he received a comfortable majority in the electoral college, securing his victory. The nation was becoming increasingly divided along sectional lines, and President Buchanan would do little to resolve these differences.

The *Dred Scott* Decision. Just two days after Buchanan's inauguration, the Supreme Court finally announced its decision in the *Dred Scott* case (see "American Histories" on page 382). Led by Chief Justice Roger Taney, a proslavery Southerner, the majority ruled that a slave was not a citizen and therefore could not sue in court. Indeed, Taney claimed that black men had no rights that a white man was bound to respect. The ruling annulled Scott's suit and meant that he and his wife remained enslaved. But the ruling went further. The **Dred Scott decision** declared that Congress had no constitutional authority to exclude slavery from any territory, thereby nullifying the Missouri Compromise and any future effort to restrict slavery's expansion. The ruling outraged many Northerners, who were now convinced that a Slave Power conspiracy had taken hold of the federal government, including the judiciary.

In 1858, when Stephen Douglas faced reelection to the U.S. Senate, the Republican Party nominated Abraham Lincoln, a successful lawyer from Springfield, Illinois, to oppose him. The candidates participated in seven debates in which they explained their positions on slavery in the wake of the *Dred Scott* decision. Pointing to the landmark ruling, Lincoln asked Douglas how he could favor popular sovereignty, which allowed residents to keep slavery out of a territory, and yet support the *Dred Scott* decision, which protected slavery in all territories. Douglas claimed that if residents did not adopt local legislation to protect slaveholders' property, they could thereby exclude slavery for all practical purposes. At the same time, he accused Lincoln of advocating "negro equality," a position that went well beyond Lincoln's views. Lincoln did support economic opportunity for free blacks, but not political or social equality. Still, the Republican candidate did declare that "this government cannot endure permanently half slave and half free. . . . It will become all one thing or all the other."

The Lincoln-Douglas debates attracted national attention, but the Illinois legislature selected the state's senator. Narrowly controlled by Democrats, it returned Douglas to Washington. Although the senator retained his seat, he was concerned by how far the Democratic Party had tilted toward the South. So when President Buchanan tried to push the Lecompton Constitution through Congress, legitimating the proslavery government in Kansas, Douglas opposed him. The two struggled over control of the party, with Douglas winning a symbolic victory in January 1861 when Kansas was admitted as a free state. By then, however, the Democratic Party had split into southern and northern wings, and the nation was on the verge of civil war.

REVIEW & RELATE

- What factors contributed to the spread of antislavery sentiment in the North beyond committed abolitionists?

- How did the violence in Kansas and the *Dred Scott* decision reflect and intensify the growing sectional divide within the nation?

From **Sectional Crisis** to **Southern Secession**

During the 1850s, a profusion of abolitionist lectures, conventions, and literature swelled anti-slavery sentiment in the North. Mainstream newspapers regularly covered rescues of fugitives, the *Dred Scott* case, and the bloody crisis in Kansas. Republican candidates in state and local elections also kept concerns about slavery's expansion and southern power alive. Nothing, however, riveted the nation's attention as much as John Brown's raid on the federal arsenal at Harpers Ferry, Virginia, in 1859. Less than a year later, Republican Abraham Lincoln captured the White House. In the wake of his election, South Carolina seceded from the Union.

John Brown's Raid. John Brown was committed not only to the abolition of slavery but also to complete equality between whites and blacks. A militant abolitionist and deeply religious man, Brown held views quite similar to those of David Walker, whose 1829 *Appeal* warned that slaves would eventually rise up and claim their freedom by force. Following the bloody battles in Kansas, Brown was convinced that direct action was the only answer. After the Pottawatomie killings, he went into hiding and reappeared back east, where he hoped to initiate an uprising to overthrow slavery.

Brown focused his efforts on the federal arsenal in **Harpers Ferry, Virginia.** With eighteen followers—five African Americans and thirteen whites, including three of his sons—Brown planned to capture the arsenal and distribute arms to slaves in the surrounding area. He hoped this action would ignite a rebellion that would destroy the plantation system. He tried to convince Frederick Douglass to join the venture, but Douglass considered it a foolhardy plan. However, Brown did manage to persuade a small circle of white abolitionists to bankroll the effort.

On the night of October 16, 1859, Brown and his men successfully kidnapped some leading townsmen and seized the arsenal. Local residents were stunned but managed to alert authorities, and state militia swarmed into Harpers Ferry. The next day, federal troops arrived, led by Colonel Robert E. Lee. With troops flooding into the town, Brown and his men were soon under siege, trapped in the arsenal. Fourteen rebels were killed, including two of Brown's sons. On October 18, Brown and three others were captured.

As word of the daring raid spread, Brown was hailed as a hero by many devoted abolitionists and depicted as a madman by southern planters. Southern whites were sure the raid was part of a widespread conspiracy led by power-hungry abolitionists. Federal authorities moved quickly to quell slaveholders' fears and end the episode. Brown rejected his lawyer's advice to plead insanity, and a local jury found him guilty of murder, criminal conspiracy, and treason. He was hanged on December 2, 1859.

John Brown's execution unleashed a massive outpouring of grief, anger, and uncertainty across the North. Abolitionists organized parades, demonstrations, bonfires, and tributes to the newest abolitionist martyr. Even many Quakers and other pacifists viewed John Brown as a hero for giving his life in the cause of emancipation. But most northern politicians and editors condemned the raid as a rash act that could only intensify sectional tensions. **See Document Project 12: Visions of John Brown, page 408.**

Among southern whites, fear and panic greeted the raid on Harpers Ferry, and the execution of John Brown did little to quiet their outrage. By this time, southern intellectuals had developed a sophisticated proslavery argument that, to them, demonstrated the benefits of bondage for African Americans and its superiority to the northern system of wage labor. They argued that slave owners provided care and guidance for blacks from birth to death. Considering blacks too childlike to fend for themselves, proslavery advocates saw no problem with the enslaved providing labor and obedience in return for their care. Such arguments failed to convince abolitionists, who highlighted the brutality, sexual abuse, and shattered families that marked the system of bondage. In this context, Americans on both sides of the sectional divide considered the 1860 presidential election critical to the nation's future.

The Election of 1860. Brown's hanging set the tone for the 1860 presidential campaign. The Republicans met in Chicago five months after Brown's execution and distanced themselves from the more radical wing of the abolitionist movement. The party platform condemned both John Brown and southern "Border Ruffians," who initiated the violence in Kansas. The platform accepted slavery where it already existed, but continued to advocate its exclusion from western territories. Finally, the platform insisted on the need for federally funded internal improvements and protective tariffs. The Republicans nominated Abraham Lincoln as their candidate for president. Recognizing the impossibility of gaining significant votes in the South, the party focused instead on winning large majorities in the Northeast and Midwest.

Explore ▶

See Document 12.4 for the Republican Party's vision of America in 1860.

The Democrats met in Charleston, South Carolina. Although Stephen Douglas was the leading candidate, southern delegates were still angry with him over Kansas being admitted as a free state. When Mississippi senator Jefferson Davis introduced a resolution to protect slavery in the territories, Douglas's northern supporters rejected it. President Buchanan also came out against Douglas, and the Democratic convention ended without choosing a candidate. Instead, various factions met separately. A group of largely northern Democrats met in Baltimore and nominated Douglas. Southern Democrats selected John Breckinridge, the vice president, a slaveholder, and an advocate of annexing Cuba. The Constitutional Union Party, comprised mainly of former southern Whigs, advocated "no political principle other than the Constitution of the country, the union of the states, and the enforcement of the laws." Its members nominated Senator John Bell of Tennessee.

Although Lincoln won barely 40 percent of the popular vote, he carried a clear majority in the electoral college. With the admission of Minnesota and Oregon to the Union in 1858 and 1859, free states outnumbered slave states eighteen to fifteen, and Lincoln won all but one of them. Moreover, free states were more populous than slave states and therefore controlled a large number of electoral votes. Douglas ran second to Lincoln in the popular vote, but Bell and Breckinridge captured more electoral votes than Douglas did. Despite a deeply divided electorate, Lincoln became president (Map 12.3).

Although many abolitionists were wary of the Republicans, who were willing to leave slavery alone where it existed, most were nonetheless relieved at Lincoln's victory and hoped he would become more sympathetic to their views once in office. Meanwhile, southern whites, especially those in the deep South, were furious that a Republican had won the White House without carrying a single southern state.

SOLO ANALYSIS

Republican Party Presidential Ticket, 1860

The Republican Party had no hope of gaining significant votes in the South, so this campaign banner for Abraham Lincoln and Hannibal Hamlin sought to appeal to voters in the North and West. Crowded with imagery to attract the various interests that made up the new party, the banner was displayed at campaign rallies and party offices.

Document 12.4

THE UNION MUST AND SHALL BE PRESERVED

FREE SPEECH, FREE HOMES, FREE TERRITORY

PROTECTION TO AMERICAN INDUSTRY

FOR PRESIDENT
ABRAHAM LINCOLN
OF ILLINOIS

FOR VICE PRESIDENT
HANNIBAL HAMLIN
OF MAINE

Library of Congress, 3a09182

Interpret the Evidence

1. What aspects of this banner highlight Lincoln's and Hamlin's backwoods origins?
2. How does the banner seek to appeal to both manufacturers and workingmen?

Put It in Context

What would the motto "Free Speech, Free Homes, Free Territory" indicate to voters, given developments surrounding slavery and western expansion in the 1850s?

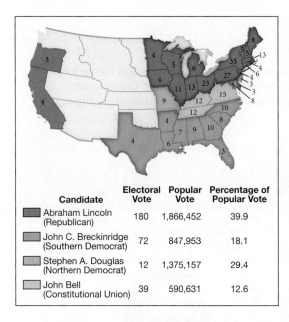

MAP 12.3 The Election of 1860

Four candidates vied for the presidency in 1860, and the voters split along clearly sectional lines. Although Stephen Douglas ran a vigorous campaign and gained votes in all regions of the country, he won a majority only in Missouri. Lincoln triumphed in the North and far West, and Breckinridge in most of the South.

Candidate	Electoral Vote	Popular Vote	Percentage of Popular Vote
Abraham Lincoln (Republican)	180	1,866,452	39.9
John C. Breckinridge (Southern Democrat)	72	847,953	18.1
Stephen A. Douglas (Northern Democrat)	12	1,375,157	29.4
John Bell (Constitutional Union)	39	590,631	12.6

The Lower South Secedes. On December 20, 1860, six weeks after Lincoln's election, the legislature of South Carolina announced that because "a sectional party" had engineered "the election of a man to the high office of President of the United States whose opinions and purposes are hostile to slavery," the people of South Carolina dissolve their union with "the other states of North America." In early 1861, Mississippi, Florida, Alabama, Georgia, Louisiana, and Texas followed suit. Representatives from these states met on February 8 in Montgomery, Alabama, where they adopted a provisional constitution, elected Jefferson Davis as their president, and established the **Confederate States of America** (Map 12.4).

President Buchanan did nothing to stop the secession movement. His cabinet included three secessionists and two unionists, one of whom resigned in frustration over Buchanan's failure to act. But Washington, D.C., was filled with southern sympathizers, who urged caution on an already timid president. Although some Northerners were shocked by the decision of South Carolina and its allies, many others supported their right to leave or believed they would return to the Union when they realized they could not survive economically on their own. Moreover, with Virginia, Maryland, and other Upper South slave states still part of the nation, the secession movement seemed unlikely to succeed.

In the midst of the crisis, Kentucky senator John Crittenden proposed a compromise that gained significant support. Indeed, Congress approved the first part of his plan, which called for a constitutional amendment to protect slavery from federal interference in any state where it already existed. But the second part of the **Crittenden plan** failed to win Republican votes. It would have extended the Missouri Compromise line (latitude 36°30') to the California border and barred slavery north of that line. South of that line, however, slavery would be protected, including in any territories "acquired hereafter." Fearing that

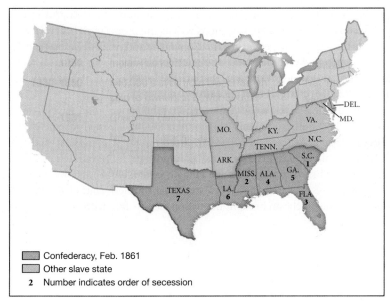

MAP 12.4 The Original Confederacy

Seven states in the Lower South seceded from the United States and formed the Confederate States of America in February 1861. While the original Confederacy was too limited in population and resources to defend itself against the U.S. government, its leaders hoped that other slave states would soon join them.

passage would encourage southern planters to again seek territory in Cuba, Mexico, or Central America, Republicans in Congress rejected the proposal. Despite the hopes of the Buchanan administration, it was becoming apparent that compromise was impossible.

REVIEW & RELATE

● How and why did John Brown's raid on Harpers Ferry move the country closer to civil war?

● Why did many in the South believe that the election of Abraham Lincoln was cause for secession?

Conclusion: A Nation Divided

Dred Scott did not live to see Abraham Lincoln take the oath of office in March 1861. Following the Supreme Court's 1857 ruling, Scott was returned to Irene Emerson, who had married abolitionist Calvin Chaffee. Unwilling to be the owner of the most well-known slave in America, Chaffee quickly returned Dred Scott and his family to his original owners, the Blow family. The Blows then freed the Scotts. For the next year and a half, before dying of tuberculosis, Dred Scott lived as a free man. Although Harriet and their daughters lived to see slavery abolished, in the spring of 1861 they could not imagine how that goal would be reached.

In 1860 John C. Frémont believed the nation was headed to war; and he was willing, once again, to serve a country he had helped expand. His work as a surveyor and soldier opened new territories to white settlement, and the gold rush then ensured California's admission to the Union. Yet what Frémont and other advocates of manifest destiny saw as U.S. victories had decimated many Indian nations as well as the property rights and livelihoods of many Mexicans. Despite the efforts of the Comanche and other tribes to fend off white encroachment, the U.S. government and white settlers claimed more and more territory. It was these western territories, moreover, that heightened conflicts over slavery and led the nation to the situation it faced in spring 1861.

While some Confederate planters imagined expanding the nation—and slavery—into Cuba, Nicaragua, and other southern regions, Northerners fought any such schemes. Outraged by the Fugitive Slave Act and appalled by Bleeding Kansas, militant activists applauded John Brown's raid at Harpers Ferry. Just as important, more moderate Northerners increasingly opposed slavery and voted for Lincoln in the fall of 1860. By the time Abraham Lincoln took office in March 1861, however, seven southern states had seceded, and the ever-widening political chasm brought the nation face-to-face with civil war.

TIMELINE OF EVENTS

KEY TERMS

REVIEW & RELATE

1. Why did Americans go west in the 1830s and 1840s, and what was the journey like?

2. What groups competed for land and resources in the West? How did disease, drought, and violence shape this competition?

3. What steps did legislators take in the 1840s and early 1850s to resolve the issue of the expansion of slavery? Were they successful?

4. How were slavery and American imperialist ambitions intertwined in the 1840s and 1850s?

5. What factors contributed to the spread of antislavery sentiment in the North beyond committed abolitionists?

6. How did the violence in Kansas and the *Dred Scott* decision reflect and intensify the growing sectional divide within the nation?

7. How and why did John Brown's raid on Harpers Ferry move the country closer to civil war?

8. Why did many in the South believe that the election of Abraham Lincoln was cause for secession?

Visions of John Brown

On October 16, 1859, John Brown led a group of eighteen men on a raid on the federal arsenal at Harpers Ferry, Virginia. The plan failed, and Brown and his surviving accomplices were captured and put on trial. On December 2, a mere seven weeks after the raid began, Brown was executed by hanging.

The raid shocked the nation, not least because John Brown was a white man leading an uprising to free enslaved blacks. Brown's quick trial and execution were designed to calm southern fears and minimize northern support for his actions. Neither goal was accomplished. The northern press and political establishment denounced the raid, but also condemned the brutalities of slavery that inspired it. Although most abolitionists were appalled by Brown's violent methods, they wrote tributes to Brown and organized a "Day of Mourning" for his execution (Documents 12.6 and 12.7). White Southerners and some northern Democrats labeled Brown a terrorist, believing he was part of a vast abolitionist conspiracy to violently overthrow slavery (Documents 12.5 and 12.8). The raid on Harpers Ferry thus intensified sectional conflicts and gave both sides a new focal point for their anger. The following sources highlight the competing images of John Brown—painting him as a hero, a saint, a brute, and a fanatic. The 1863 painting suggests the continued importance of his legacy to racial progressives (Documents 12.9). As you examine them, consider what these documents reveal about America on the eve of the Civil War.

Document 12.5

State Register (Springfield, Illinois) | The Irrepressible Conflict, 1859

While many Northerners shared Brown's antislavery beliefs, most opposed his use of violence. The following editorial in the State Register (Springfield, Illinois), a Democratic Party paper, reflects the outrage felt throughout the nation. The State Register blamed Republicans for the Harpers Ferry raid, condemning William Seward and Abraham Lincoln for speeches they claimed had fueled the actions of John Brown.

The telegraphic dispatches yesterday morning startled the public with an account of one of the most monstrous villainies ever attempted in this country. It was no less than an effort on the part of a party of abolitionists and negroes to take possession of one of the national arsenals, at Harpers Ferry, with the military stores and the public money there deposited. Under the lead of the most infamous of the Kansas crew of black republican marauders, Ossawatomie Brown, the insurgents, to the number of five or six hundred, attacked and took possession of the whole town of Harpers Ferry, including the government buildings and stores, stopped the mails, imprisoned peaceable citizens, and, before they were dislodged, numbers were killed and wounded on both sides.

It was scarcely credible, when the first dispatch was received yesterday, that the object of the ruffians could be other than plunder, but late dispatches . . . show, conclusively, that the movement was a most extensive one, having for its object the uprising of the negroes throughout the south, a servile war, and its consequences—murder, rapine, and robbery.

The leader chosen was just the man to initiate the work. Bankrupt in fortune and character, an outlaw and an outcast, he was just the man to commence the work which ultra Abolitionism, through its diligent Parkers and Garrisons, hope to reach the millennium of their traitorous designs. Their open-mouthed treason . . . is but the logical sequence of the teachings of Wm. H. Seward and Abraham Lincoln—the one boldly proclaiming an "irrepressible conflict" between certain states of the Union . . . and the other declaring . . . that the Union cannot continue as the fathers made it—part slave and part free states. When such men, by specious demagogism [promoting factionalism], in the name of freedom and liberty, daily labor to weaken the bonds of our glorious governmental fabric, the work of sages and patriots, themselves the holders of black men as slaves, is it to be wondered at that ignorant, unprincipled, and reckless camp followers of the party for which these leaders speak, attempt, practically, to illustrate the doctrines which they preach. . . .

Brown, though a blood-stained ruffian, is a bold man. As a black republican he practices what his leaders preach. As it is urged by statesmen (save the mark!) of his party that there is an "irrepressible conflict," he wants it in tangible, material shape. He believes in blows, not words, and the Harpers Ferry villainy is the first in his line of performance.

Source: "The 'Irrepressible Conflict' Fruits of the Lincoln-Seward Doctrine," *State Register* (Springfield, Illinois), October 20, 1859.

Document 12.6

Henry David Thoreau | A Plea for Captain John Brown, 1859

Most abolitionists were quick to condemn John Brown's use of armed force, but Henry David Thoreau rushed to his defense. The transcendentalist author had been introduced to Brown years earlier by Franklin Sanborn, who helped finance the Harpers Ferry raid. On the day Brown was to be hung, Thoreau delivered a speech, "A Plea for Captain John Brown," in front of a public gathering in Concord, Massachusetts. The widely circulated speech helped establish Brown as a martyr for the abolitionist cause.

Little as I know of Captain Brown, I would fain [willingly] do my part to correct the tone and the statements of the newspapers, and of my countrymen generally, respecting his character and actions. It costs us nothing to be just. We can at least express our sympathy with, and admiration of, him and his companions, and that is what I now propose to do. . . .

. . . He was a superior man. He did not value his bodily life in comparison with ideal things. He did not recognize unjust human laws, but resisted them as he was bid. For once we are lifted out of the trivialness and dust of politics into the region of truth and manhood. No man in America has ever stood up so persistently and effectively for the dignity of human nature, knowing himself for a man, and the equal of any and all governments. In that sense he was the most American of us all. . . . He was more than a match for all the judges that American voters, or office-holders of whatever grade, can create. He could not have been tried by a jury of his peers, because his peers did not exist. When a man stands up serenely against the condemnation and vengeance of mankind, rising above them literally *by a whole body*—even though he were of late the vilest murderer, who has settled that matter with himself—the spectacle is a sublime one . . . and we become criminal in comparison. Do yourselves the honor to recognize him. . . .

It was his peculiar doctrine that a man has a perfect right to interfere by force with the slaveholder, in order to rescue the slave. I agree with him. They who are continually shocked by slavery have some right to be shocked by the violent death of the slaveholder, but no others. Such will be more shocked by his life than by his death. I shall not be forward to think him mistaken in his method who quickest succeeds to liberate the slave. I speak for the slave when I say, that I prefer the philanthropy of Captain Brown to that philanthropy which neither shoots me nor liberates me. . . . I do not wish to kill nor to be killed, but I can foresee circumstances in which both these things would be by me unavoidable. We preserve the so-called peace of our community by deeds of petty violence every day. Look at the policeman's billy and handcuffs! Look at the jail! Look at the gallows! Look at the chaplain of the regiment! . . . I know that the mass of my countrymen think that the only righteous use that can be made of Sharpe's rifles and revolvers is to fight duels with them, when we are insulted by other nations, or to hunt Indians, or shoot fugitive slaves with them, or the like. I think that for once the Sharpe's rifles and revolvers were employed in a righteous cause. . . .

The question is not about the weapon, but the spirit in which you use it. No man has appeared in America, as yet, who loved his fellow-man so well, and treated him so tenderly. He [Brown] lived for him. He took up his life and he laid it down for him. . . .

I am here to plead his cause with you. I plead not for his life, but for his character—his immortal life; and so it becomes your cause wholly, and is not his in the least. Some eighteen hundred years ago Christ was crucified; this morning, perchance, Captain Brown was hung. These are the two ends of a chain which is not without its links. He is not Old Brown any longer; he is an angel of light.

Source: James Redpath, *Echoes of Harper's Ferry* (Boston: Thayer and Eldridge, 1860), 2, 30, 37–38, 41–42.

Document 12.7

Reverend J. Sella Martin | Day of Mourning Speech, December 2, 1859

On the day of John Brown's execution, black and white abolitionists around the country held a "Day of Mourning" in his honor. In Boston four thousand people gathered at the Tremont Temple to celebrate Brown's life. There Reverend J. Sella Martin, a former slave and the pastor of the Joy Street Baptist Church, proclaimed his support for Brown and his methods.

I know that John Brown, in thus rebuking our public sin, in thus facing the monarch, has had to bear just what John the Baptist bore. His head today, by Virginia—that guilty maid of a more guilty mother, the American Government—has been cut off, and it has been presented to the ferocious and insatiable hunger, the terrible and inhuman appetite, of this corrupt government. Today, by the telegraph, we have received the intelligence that John Brown has forfeited his life—all this honesty, all this straight-forwardness, all this self-sacrifice has been manifested in Harper's Ferry. . . .

I know that there is some quibbling, some querulousness, some fear, in reference to an out-and-out endorsement of his course. Men of peace principles object to it, in consequence of their religious conviction; politicians in the North object to it, because they are afraid that it will injure their party; pro-slavery men in the South object to it, because it has touched their dearest idol; but I am prepared, my friends . . . in the light of all human history, to approve of the *means*; in the light of all Christian principle, to approve of the *end*. (Applause.) I say this is not the language of rage, because I remember that our Fourth-of-July orators sanction the same thing; because I remember that Concord, and Bunker Hill, and every historic battlefield in this country, and the celebration of those events, all go to approve the means that John Brown has used; the only difference being, that in our battles, in America, means have been used for *white* men and that John Brown has used his means for *black* men. (Applause.) And I say, that so far as principle is concerned, so far as the sanctions of the Gospel are concerned, I am prepared to endorse his end; and I endorse it because God Almighty has told us that we should feel with them that are in bonds as being bound with them. I endorse his end, because every single instinct of our nature rises and tells us that it is right. I find an endorsement of John Brown's course in the large assembly gathered here this evening. . . .

Now, I bring this question down to the simple test of the Gospel. . . . I look at this question as a peace man. I say, in accordance with the principles of peace, that I do not believe the sword should be unsheathed . . . until there is in the system to be assailed such terrible evidences of corruption, that it becomes the *dernier* [last] *resort*. And my friends, we are not to blame the application of the instrument, we are to blame the disease itself. When a physician cuts out a cancer from my face, I am not to blame the physician for the use of the knife; but the impure blood, the obstructed veins, the disordered system, that have caused the cancer, and rendered the use of the instrument necessary.

Source: *Liberator*, December 9, 1859, in *Blacks on John Brown*, ed. Benjamin Quarles (Urbana: University of Illinois Press, 1972), 26–27.

vast quantities of breast pins, lockets, and bracelets, containing bits of the "rope which hung Old Brown" for sale. [P. T.] Barnum is already in the market for Old Brown's old clothes, and hopes and expects to make [a good] speculation out of them.

Source: "Execution of John Brown," *Register* (Raleigh, North Carolina), December 3, 1859.

Document 12.8

A Southern Paper Reacts to Brown's Execution, December 3, 1859

The following article appeared in a North Carolina newspaper the day after Brown's execution. It predicts that the North will make Brown a martyr and ridicules the Day of Mourning held in his honor. The article singles out the celebration in Boston (Document 12.7) for particular condemnation and labels its participants treasonous.

t is to be hoped, with Brown's exit from the world, the excitement at the North will subside. But we must confess that this hope is but of the faintest character. Fanaticism at the North is rampant, and overrides every thing. On yesterday, the godly city of Boston, built up and sustained by the products of negro slave labor, went into mourning, fasting, and prayer, over the condign [deserved] punishment of a negro stealer, murderer, and traitor, and from fifty pulpits the Praise-God-Bare-bones belched forth volumes of blasphemy and treason.

In all the Noo England towns and villages, we may expect to hear that mock funerals have been celebrated, and all kinds of nonsensically lugubrious displays made. (It is a pity that they haven't a witch or two to drown or burn, by way of variety.) We hope that Gov. Wise [of Virginia] will have the gallows on which Brown was hung burned, and give notice of the fact. Our reasons for this wish is this: The Yankees have no objection to mingling money making with their grief, and they will, unless Brown's gallows is known to have been burned, set to work and make all kinds of jimcracks and notions out of what they will call parts of Old John Brown's gallows and sell them. Let the rope which choked him, too, be burned and the fact advertised, or we shall see

Document 12.9

Currier and Ives | John Brown on His Way to Execution, 1863

In the weeks after Brown's death, newspapers were filled with accounts of his final days and execution. The *New York Tribune* published a story claiming that Brown had kissed a slave child he encountered on his way to the gallows. Although this story was false, it was widely repeated and became the subject of a painting by Louis Ransom. This 1863 Currier and Ives lithograph based on Ransom's painting further cemented the legend.

Library of Congress, 3a06486

Interpret the Evidence

1. How do these different sources describe Brown? What language and imagery do they use? How is religious imagery employed in the various documents?

2. In what ways do Brown's admirers, such as Henry David Thoreau (Document 12.6) and J. Sella Martin (Document 12.7), support Brown and his use of violence?

3. Critics of Brown used his raid to condemn abolitionism. On what basis did they make more generalized claims of northern guilt (Documents 12.5 and 12.8)?

4. In what ways do these sources characterize Brown before his execution (Documents 12.5 and 12.6) and after (Documents 12.7, 12.8, and 12.9)?

5. What images and messages are used in the Currier and Ives illustration (Document 12.9) to portray Brown as a martyr?

Put It in Context

How do the reactions to John Brown's raid on Harpers Ferry illuminate the conflicts that led to Abraham Lincoln's election in 1860 and South Carolina's secession shortly after?

What are the connections between northern political opposition to slavery, Garrisonian moral persuasion, and Brown's armed raid?

Civil War

1861–1865

13

WINDOW TO THE PAST

Union Soldiers in Camp c. 1863

The Civil War was the first military conflict in U.S. history to be photographically documented. Many photographers took formal portraits of soldiers, individually or in groups, while others captured the bloody aftermath of battles. This picture offers a rare informal glimpse of soldiers in camp. Their range of poses and expressions suggests the various ways that soldiers responded to a lull in the conflict. ▶ To discover more about what this primary source can show us, see Document 13.2 on page 426.

Library of Congress, LC-DIG-ppmsca-34191

After reading this chapter you should be able to:

- Explain why southern states seceded and describe the advantages and disadvantages that marked the Confederacy and the Union at the beginning of the Civil War.

- Describe the changing roles of African Americans, free and enslaved, in the war and the growing sentiment for emancipation in the North.

- Evaluate how the war changed northern and southern political priorities and the lives of soldiers and civilians.

- Identify turning points in the Civil War, including key battles in the eastern and western theaters of war, and explain the factors that led to Union victory and the abolition of slavery.

AMERICAN HISTORIES

Born into slavery in 1818, Frederick Douglass became a celebrated orator, editor, and abolitionist in the 1840s. In 1845 Douglass published his autobiography, *Narrative of the Life of Frederick Douglass*, which described his enslavement in Maryland, his defiance against his masters, and his eventual escape to New York in 1838 with the help of Anna Murray, a free black servant.

After marrying in New York, Frederick and Anna moved to New Bedford, Massachusetts, and changed

(left) **Frederick Douglass** Beinecke Rare Book and Manuscript Library, Yale University

(right) **Rose O'Neal Greenhow** Documenting the American South, University Library, The University of North Carolina at Chapel Hill, http://docsouth.unc.edu/fpn/greenhow/frontis.html

their last name to Douglass to avoid capture. In 1841 the American Anti-Slavery Society hired Frederick to present his vivid tale of slave life in public. Four years later, Douglass launched a British lecture tour that attracted enthusiastic audiences. Supporters in Britain purchased his freedom, and Douglass returned to Massachusetts a free man in 1847.

Late that year, Frederick moved to Rochester, New York, with Anna and their children to launch his abolitionist paper, the *North Star*. Soon after, he broke with the Garrisonians and embraced the Liberty Party and eventually the Republicans. When war erupted in April 1861, Douglass lobbied President Lincoln relentlessly to make emancipation a war aim.

Initially Douglass feared that Lincoln was more committed to reconstituting the Union than abolishing slavery. But when the president issued the Emancipation Proclamation in January 1863, Douglass spoke enthusiastically on its behalf. He also argued that it was essential for black men to serve in the Union army. When African Americans were finally allowed to join in 1862 to 1863, Douglass helped recruit volunteers but also protested discrimination against black troops and the denial of black civil rights.

Like Douglass, Rose O'Neal was born on a Maryland plantation, but she was white and free. Her father was John O'Neal, a planter who was killed in 1817 when Rose was about four. In her teens, she and her sister moved to Washington, D.C., where their aunt ran a fashionable boardinghouse. Her boarders included John C. Calhoun, whose states' rights views Rose eagerly embraced. Rose was welcomed into elite social circles and in 1835 married Virginian Robert Greenhow, who worked for the State Department.

Rose O'Neal Greenhow quickly became a favorite Washington hostess, entertaining congressmen, cabinet ministers, and foreign diplomats. Ardent proslavery expansionists, the Greenhows supported efforts to acquire Cuba and expand slavery into western territories. When Robert died in 1854, Rose and their four children remained in D.C. and continued to entertain powerful political leaders.

In May 1861, as the Civil War commenced, a U.S. army captain about to join the Confederate cause recruited Greenhow to head an espionage ring in

Washington, D.C. With her close ties to southern sympathizers in the capital, Greenhow gathered intelligence on Union plans. Although she initially avoided suspicion, by August 1861 Greenhow was investigated and placed under house arrest. After continuing to smuggle out letters, she was sent to the Old Capitol Prison in January 1862. When Greenhow again managed to transmit information, she was exiled to Richmond, where Confederate president Jefferson Davis hailed her as a hero. ■

The American histories of Frederick Douglass and Rose O'Neal Greenhow were shaped by the conflict over slavery, which culminated in secession and war. They were among hundreds of thousands of Americans who saw the war as a means to achieve their goals: a free nation, a haven for slavery, or a reunited country. Once conflict erupted at Fort Sumter in April 1861, more southern states seceded although four slave states, reluctantly, remained in the Union. Even with the addition of more states, the Confederacy lagged behind the Union in population, industrial and agricultural production, and railroad lines. These differences became more important as the war unfolded. Initially, however, skilled officers and knowledge of the southern terrain benefited the Confederate army. On the home front, hundreds of thousands of Americans labored on farms and in factories, burgeoning government offices, and hospitals to support the Union or the Confederacy. After 1862, tens of thousands of African Americans joined the Union army, both free blacks and enslaved men freed by Union forces. The next year, the Emancipation Proclamation ensured that a Union victory would eradicate slavery. As the war dragged on, antiwar protests erupted North and South, fueled by inflation, conscription acts, and mounting casualties. Finally in 1865, the greater resources of the North, complemented by General Ulysses S. Grant's hard war strategy, led to Union victory and the final abolition of slavery.

The **Nation Goes** to **War, 1861**

When Abraham Lincoln took office, seven states in the Lower South had already formed the Confederate States of America, and more states threatened to secede. Lincoln had promised not to interfere with slavery where it existed, but many southern whites doubted such assurances. By seceding, southern slaveholders also proclaimed their unwillingness to become a permanent minority in the nation. Still, not all slave states were yet willing to cut their ties to the nation. Northerners, too, disagreed about the appropriate response to secession. Once fighting erupted, however, preparations for war became the primary focus in both the Union and the Confederacy.

The South Embraces Secession. Confederate president Jefferson Davis joined other planters in arguing that Lincoln's victory jeopardized the future of slavery and that secession was therefore a necessity. Advocates of secession contended that the federal government had failed to implement fully the Fugitive Slave Act and the *Dred Scott* decision. They were convinced that a Republican administration would do even less to support southern interests. White Southerners also feared that Republicans might inspire a massive uprising of slaves, and secession allowed whites to maintain control over the South's black population.

Still, when Lincoln was inaugurated, some legislators in the Upper South hoped a compromise could be reached, and the president hoped to bring the Confederates back into the Union without using military force. Most northern merchants, manufacturers, and bankers approved, wanting to maintain their economic ties to southern planters. Yet Lincoln also realized he must demonstrate Union strength to curtail further secessions. He focused on **Fort Sumter** in South Carolina's Charleston harbor, where a small Union garrison was running low on food and medicine. On April 8, 1861, Lincoln dispatched ships to the fort but promised to use force only if the Confederates blocked his peaceful effort to send supplies.

The Confederate government would now have to choose. It could attack the Union vessels and bear responsibility for starting a war or permit a "foreign power" to maintain a fort in its territory. President Davis and his advisers chose the aggressive course, demanding Fort Sumter's immediate and unconditional surrender. The commanding officer refused, and on April 12 Confederate guns opened fire. Two days later, Fort Sumter surrendered. On April 15, Lincoln called for 75,000 volunteers to put down the southern insurrection.

The declaration of war led whites in the Upper South to reconsider secession. Some small farmers and landless whites were drawn to Republican promises of free labor and free soil and remained suspicious of the goals and power of secessionist planters. Yet the vast majority of southern whites, rich and poor, defined their liberty in relation to black bondage. They feared that Republicans would free the slaves and introduce racial amalgamation, the mixing of whites and blacks, in the South.

Explore ▸

See Document 13.1 for a Georgia congressman's views on secession.

Fearing more secessions, Lincoln used the powers of his office to keep the border states that allowed slavery—Maryland, Delaware, Missouri, and Kentucky—in the Union. He waived the right of habeas corpus (which protects citizens against arbitrary arrest and detention), jailed secessionists, arrested state legislators, and limited freedom of the press. However, four other slave states—North Carolina, Virginia, Tennessee, and Arkansas—seceded. Virginia, with its strategic location near the nation's capital, was by far the most significant. Richmond, which would soon become the capital of the Confederacy, was also home to the South's largest iron manufacturer, which could produce weapons and munitions.

While Northerners differed over how to respond when the first seven states seceded, the firing on Fort Sumter prompted most to line up behind Lincoln's call for war. Manufacturers and merchants, once intent on maintaining commercial links with the South, now rushed to support the president, while northern workers, including immigrants, responded to Lincoln's call for volunteers. They assumed that the Union, with its greater resources and manpower, could quickly set the nation right. New York editor Horace Greeley proclaimed, "Jeff Davis and Co. will be swingin' from the battlements at Washington at least by the 4th of July."

Both Sides Prepare for War. At the onset of the war, the Union certainly held a decided advantage in resources and population. The Union states held more than 60 percent of the U.S. population; and the Confederate population included several million slaves who would not be armed for combat. The Union also far outstripped the Confederacy in manufacturing and even led the South in agricultural production. The North's many miles of railroad track ensured greater ease in moving troops and supplies. And the Union could launch far more ships to blockade southern ports (Figure 13.1).

GUIDED ANALYSIS

Robert Toombs | Supporting Secession in Georgia, 1860

Immediately after Abraham Lincoln's election, several southern states began to discuss secession. Georgia called a special convention to debate the issue on November 13–14, 1860, immediately following the presidential election. One of the principal speakers was Robert Toombs, a U.S. congressman. In the following selection, Toombs argues in favor of secession, and Georgia became the fifth state to secede, two months before Lincoln took office.

Document 13.1

	The stern, steady march of events has brought us in conflict with our non-slaveholding confederates upon the fundamental principles of our compact of Union. We have not sought this conflict; we have sought too long to avoid it. . . . The door of conciliation and compromise is finally
Who in Toombs's view forced the issue of secession?	closed by our adversaries, and it remains only to us to meet the conflict with the dignity and firmness of men worthy of freedom. . . .
	. . . The South at all times demanded nothing but equality in the common territories, equal enjoyment of them with their property, to that extended to Northern citizens and their property—nothing more. . . . In
How does Toombs seek to demonstrate the humane character of slavery?	1790 we had less than eight hundred thousand slaves. Under our mild and humane administration of the system they have increased above four millions. The country has expanded to meet this growing want, and Florida, Alabama, Mississippi, Louisiana, Texas, Arkansas, Kentucky, Tennessee, and Missouri have received this increasing tide of African labor; before the end of this century, at precisely the same rate of increase, the Africans among us in a subordinate condition will amount to eleven millions of persons. What shall be done with them? We must
What actions of the North threatened the security of the South and slavery?	expand or perish. . . . The North understand it better—they have told us for twenty years that their object was to pen up slavery within its present limits—surround it with a border of free States, and like the scorpion surrounded with fire, they will make it sting itself to death.

Source: Frank Moore, ed., *The Rebellion Record: A Diary of American Events* (New York: G. P. Putnam and Henry Holt, 1864), 1:362–63, 365.

Put It in Context

Explain the importance of the issue of slavery and expansion to Toombs' arguments regarding secession.

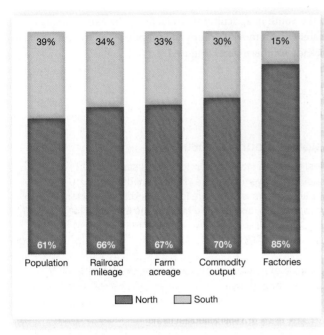

39%	34%	33%	30%	15%
61%	66%	67%	70%	85%
Population	Railroad mileage	Farm acreage	Commodity output	Factories

■ North   □ South

FIGURE 13.1   Economies of the North and South, 1860

This figure provides graphic testimony to the enormous advantages in resources the North held on the eve of the Civil War. The North led the South in farm acreage as well as factories and commodity output. Over four years of war, the North's significantly larger population would also prove crucial.

Source: Data from Stanley Engerman, "The Economic Impact of the Civil War," in *The Reinterpretation of American Economic History*, ed. Robert W. Fogel and Stanley Engerman (New York: Harper and Row, 1971).

Yet Union forces were less prepared for war than the Confederates, who had been organizing troops and gathering munitions for months. To match their efforts, Winfield Scott, general in chief of the U.S. army, told Lincoln he would need at least 300,000 men committed to serve for two or three years. Scott believed that massing such huge numbers of soldiers would force the Confederacy to negotiate a peace. But fearing to unnerve Northerners, the president asked for only 75,000 volunteers for three months. Moreover, rather than forming a powerful national army led by seasoned officers, Lincoln left recruitment, organization, and training largely to the states. The result was disorganization and the appointment of officers based more on political connections than military expertise.

Confederate leaders also initially relied on state militia units and volunteers, but they prepared for a prolonged war from the start. Before the firing on Fort Sumter, President Davis signed up 100,000 volunteers for a year's service. The labor provided by slaves allowed a large proportion of white working-age men to volunteer for military service. And Southerners knew they were likely to be fighting mainly on home territory, where they had expert knowledge of the terrain. When the final four states joined the Confederacy, the southern army also gained important military leadership. It ultimately recruited 280 West Point graduates, including Robert E. Lee, Thomas "Stonewall" Jackson, James Longstreet, and others who had proved their mettle in the Mexican-American War.

The South's advantages were apparent in the first major battle of the war. But Confederate troops were also aided by information on Union plans sent by Rose Greenhow. Confederate forces were thus well prepared when 30,000 Union troops marched on northern Virginia on July 21, 1861. At the **Battle of Bull Run** (or **Manassas**), later known as the First Battle of Bull Run, 22,000 Confederates repelled the Union attack. Civilians from Washington who traveled to the battle site to view the combat had to flee for their lives to escape Confederate artillery.

Battle of Wilson's Creek   This illustration depicts the First Iowa Regiment, led by General Nathaniel Lyon, charging Confederate forces at the Battle of Wilson's Creek, near Springfield, Missouri, on August 10, 1861. Lyon was shot in the head and killed, becoming the first Union general to die in the war. The Confederates won the battle, marking their second victory. Library of Congress, LC-USZ62-121404

Despite Union defeats at Bull Run and then at Wilson's Creek, Missouri, in August 1861, the Confederate army did not launch major strikes against Union forces. Meanwhile the Union navy began blockading the South's deepwater ports. By the time the armies settled into winter camps in 1861–1862, both sides had come to realize that the war was likely to be a long and costly struggle.

REVIEW & RELATE

What led four more states to join the Confederacy in 1861 and four other slave states to remain in the Union?

What advantages and disadvantages did each side have at the onset of the war?

Military Conflict and Political Strife, 1861–1862

The Union and the Confederacy faced very different tasks in the war. The South had to defend its territory and force the federal government to halt military action. The North had a more complicated challenge. Initially, northern political leaders believed that secession was driven mainly by slave owners and that high death rates and destruction of property would only alienate southern whites who favored reconciliation. But a policy of conciliation depended on early Union victories. With early defeats, it was clear the North would have to invade the South and isolate it from potential allies abroad. At the same time, most northern politicians believed that the nation could be reunited without abolishing slavery while abolitionists argued that only emancipation could resolve the problems that led to war. Meanwhile, enslaved Southerners immediately looked for ways to loosen their bonds.

The Wartime Roles of African Americans and Indians. The outbreak of war intensified debates over abolition. Some 225,000 African Americans lived in the free states, and many offered their services in an effort to end slavery. African American leaders in Cleveland proclaimed, "Today, as in the times of '76, we are ready to go forth and do battle in the common cause of our country." But Secretary of War Simon Cameron had no intention of calling up black soldiers.

Northern optimism about a quick victory contributed to the rejection of African American volunteers. Union leaders feared that whites would not enlist if they had to serve alongside blacks. In addition, Lincoln and his advisers were initially wary of letting a war to preserve the Union become a war against slavery, and they feared that any further threat to slavery might drive the four slave states that remained in the Union into the Confederacy. This political strategy, however, depended on quick and overwhelming victories; and with U.S. soldiers posted mainly on the western frontier and a third of officers joining the Confederacy, victories were few. Nonetheless a rush of volunteers allowed Union troops to push into Virginia while the Union navy captured crucial islands along the Confederate coast.

Wherever Union forces appeared, southern slaves began considering freedom as a possibility. Enslaved workers living near battle sites circulated information on Union troop movements. Then, as planters in Virginia began sending male slaves to more distant plantations for fear of losing them, some managed to flee and headed to Union camps. Many slave owners tracked fugitives behind Union lines and demanded their return. Some Union commanders denied slaves entrance or returned them to their masters. However, a few Union officers recognized these fugitives' value: They knew the local geography well, could dig trenches and provide other services, and drained the Confederate labor supply. At the Union outpost at Fort Monroe, Virginia, in May 1861, General Benjamin Butler offered fugitive slaves military protection. He claimed them as **contraband** of war: property forfeited by the act of rebellion.

Lincoln endorsed Butler's policy because it allowed the Union to strike at the institution of slavery without proclaiming a general emancipation that might prompt border states where slavery remained legal to secede. Congress expanded Butler's policy in August 1861 by passing a confiscation act. It proclaimed that any owner whose slaves were used by the Confederate army would lose all claim to those slaves. Although it was far from a clear-cut declaration of freedom, the act spurred the hopes of northern abolitionists and many southern slaves.

While Northerners continued to debate African Americans' role in the war effort, the Union army recruited a wide array of other ethnic and racial groups, including American Indians. Unlike blacks, however, Indians did not necessarily all support the Union. The Comanche negotiated with both Union and Confederate agents while raiding the Texas frontier for horses and cattle. The Confederacy gained significant support from slaveholding Indians who had earlier been removed from the Southeast. The Cherokee split over the

Portrait of Loots-Tow-Oots and Wife   This 1868 portrait of Pawnee warrior Loots-Tow-Oots, also known as Rattlesnake and George Esaw, reflects the dual identities carried by American Indians who served in the Civil War. While both he and his wife wear combinations of native and white clothing, Loots-Tow-Oots's Indian feather and leggings offer an especially stark contrast to his Union uniform and cavalry sword.   National Anthropological Archives, Smithsonian Institution [GN 01260]

war as they had over removal. General Stand Watie led a pan-Indian force into battle for the Confederates. Initially John Ross joined the Confederates as well, but later he led a group of Cherokee into Union army ranks alongside the Osage, Delaware, Seneca, and other Indian nations. Ely Parker, a Seneca sachem and engineer, became a lieutenant colonel in the Union army, serving with General Ulysses S. Grant.

Indians played crucial roles in a number of important early battles, particularly on the Confederate side. Cherokee and Seminole warriors fought valiantly with Confederates at the Battle of Pea Ridge in Tennessee in March 1862, but were defeated by a smaller but better supplied Union force. In August 1862 Indians contributed to the Confederate victory at the Second Battle of Bull Run and the following month participated in the bloodiest single day of battle in U.S. history at Antietam (Sharpsburg). The Confederate army recruited Mexican-American soldiers as well, hoping to gain control of the West's gold and silver mines. But a Union victory gained by a troop of Colorado miners at Glorieta Pass near Sante Fe, New Mexico, ended that Confederate dream.

While both Union and Confederate armies recruited Indian regiments, African Americans were barred from enlisting as soldiers on either side. However, a series of Union military defeats helped transform the attitudes of northern whites. In the spring of 1862, Confederate general Stonewall Jackson won a series of stunning victories against three Union armies in Virginia's Shenandoah Valley. That June and July, General Robert E. Lee fought Union forces under General George B. McClellan to a standstill in the Seven Days Battle near Richmond. Then in August, Lee, Jackson, and General James Longstreet joined together to defeat Union troops at the Second Battle of Bull Run (Map 13.1).

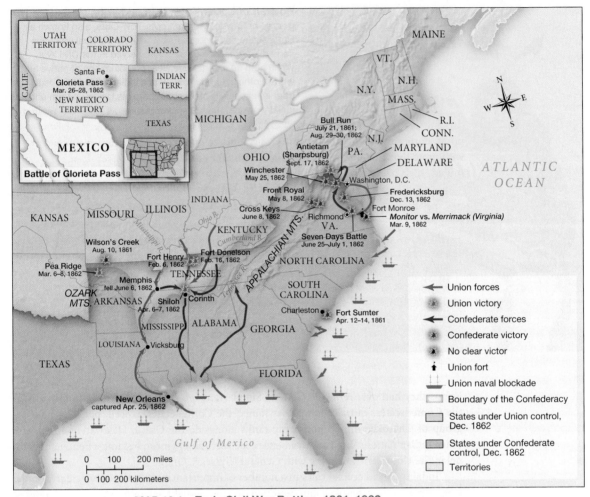

MAP 13.1   Early Civil War Battles, 1861–1862

In 1861 and 1862, the Confederate army stunned Union forces with a series of dramatic victories in Virginia and Missouri. However, the Union army won a crucial victory at Antietam (Sharpsburg); gained control of Confederate territory in Tennessee, Arkansas, and Mississippi; fended off Confederate efforts to gain New Mexico Territory; and established a successful naval blockade of Confederate ports.

As the war turned against the North, the North turned against slavery. In April 1862 Congress had approved a measure to abolish slavery in the District of Columbia, symbolizing a significant shift in Union sentiment. During that bloody summer, Congress passed a second confiscation act, declaring that the slaves of anyone who supported the Confederacy should be "forever free of their servitude, and not again held as slaves." In July Congress also approved a militia act that allowed African Americans to serve in "any military or naval service for which they may be found competent."

Support for the 1862 militia act built on Union victories as well as defeats. In April 1862 a Union blockade led to the capture of New Orleans, while the **Battle of Shiloh** in

Tennessee provided the army entrée to the Mississippi valley. There Union troops came face-to-face with slavery. Few of these soldiers were abolitionists, but many were shocked by what they saw, including instruments used to torture slaves. One Union soldier reported he had seen "enough of the horror of slavery to make one an Abolitionist forever." Southern blacks also provided important intelligence to northern officers, making clear their value to the Union war effort.

Whether in victory of defeat, rising death tolls increased support for African American enlistment. The Battle of Shiloh was the bloodiest battle in American history to that point. Earlier battles had resulted in a few hundred or even a few thousand casualties, but with more than 23,000 casualties, Shiloh raised the carnage to a new level. As the war continued, such brutal battles became routine. The Union army would need every available man—white, black, and Indian—to sustain its effort against the Confederates.

Indian regiments had already proven themselves in battle, and African Americans soon followed suit. In October 1862 a group of black soldiers in the First Kansas Colored Volunteers repulsed Confederates at a battle in Missouri. In the South, white abolitionists serving as Union officers organized former slaves into units like the First South Carolina Volunteers in January 1863. A few months later, another black regiment—the Massachusetts Fifty-fourth—attracted recruits from across the North, including Frederick Douglass's three sons. For the next two years, tens of thousands of African American soldiers fought valiantly in dozens of battles.

Union Politicians Consider Emancipation.

By the fall of 1862, African Americans and abolitionists had gained widespread support for emancipation as a necessary goal of the war. Lincoln and his cabinet realized that embracing abolition as a war aim would likely prevent international recognition of southern independence. As Massachusetts senator Charles Sumner proclaimed, "You will observe that I propose no crusade for abolition. [Emancipation] is to be presented strictly as a measure of military necessity." Still, some Union politicians feared that emancipation might arouse deep animosity in the slaveholding border states and drive them from the Union.

From the Confederate perspective, international recognition was critical. Support from European nations might persuade the North to accept southern independence. More immediately, recognition would ensure markets for southern agriculture and access to manufactured goods and war materiel. Confederate officials were especially focused on Britain, the leading market for cotton and a leading producer of industrial products. President Davis considered sending Rose Greenhow to England to promote the Confederate cause.

Fearing that the British might capitulate to Confederate pressure, abolitionist lecturers toured Britain, reminding residents of their early leadership in the antislavery cause. The Union's formal commitment to emancipation would certainly increase British support for its position and prevent diplomatic recognition of the Confederacy. By the summer of 1862, Lincoln was convinced, but he wanted to wait for a military victory before making a formal announcement regarding emancipation.

Instead, the Union suffered a series of defeats that summer, and Lee marched his army into Union territory in Maryland. On September 17, Longstreet joined Lee in a fierce battle along Antietam Creek as Union troops brought the Confederate advance to a standstill near the town of Sharpsburg. Union forces suffered more than 12,000 casualties and the Confederates more than 10,000, the bloodiest single day of battle in U.S. history. Yet

President Lincoln Presenting the Emancipation Proclamation to His Cabinet
In this engraving, Lincoln reads the draft of his Emancipation Proclamation to his cabinet in
September 1862. On the left are Secretary of War Edwin Stanton (seated) and Secretary of the
Treasury Salmon P. Chase, the two strongest supporters of the proclamation. Postmaster
General Montgomery Blair and Attorney General Edward Bates (seated), who opposed the plan,
are on the right. Library of Congress, LC-DIG-pga-02502

because Lee and his army were forced to retreat, Lincoln claimed the **Battle of Antietam**
as a great victory. Five days later, the president announced his preliminary **Emancipation
Proclamation** to the assembled cabinet, promising to free slaves in all seceding states.

On January 1, 1863, Lincoln signed the final edict, proclaiming that slaves in areas
still in rebellion were "forever free" and inviting them to enlist in the Union army. In many
ways, the proclamation was a moderate document. Its provisions exempted from emancipation the 450,000 slaves in the loyal border states, as well as more than 300,000 slaves in
Union-occupied areas of Tennessee, Louisiana, and Virginia. The proclamation also justified the abolition of southern slavery on military, not moral, grounds. Despite its limits,
the Emancipation Proclamation inspired joyous celebrations among free blacks and white
abolitionists, who viewed it as the first step toward slavery's final eradication. It also
ensured the Union army's full use of black soldiers in the difficult battles ahead.

REVIEW & RELATE

How and why did the Union and the
Confederacy treat American Indian and
African American participation in the war
differently?

What events occurred to make the Civil War
become a war to end slavery?

War Transforms the North and the South

For soldiers and civilians seeking to survive the upheaval of war, political pronouncements rarely alleviated the dangers they faced. The war's extraordinary death tolls shocked Americans on both sides. On the home front, the prolonged conflict created labor shortages and severe inflation in both North and South. The war initially disrupted industrial and agricultural production as men were called to service, but the North recovered quickly by building on its prewar industrial base and technological know-how. In the South, manufacturing increased, with enslaved laborers pressed into service as industrial workers, but this created shortages on plantations. The changed circumstances of the war required women to take on new responsibilities as well. Yet these dramatic transformations also inspired dissent and protest as rising death tolls and rising prices made the costs of war ever clearer.

Life and Death on the Battlefield. Few soldiers entered the conflict knowing what to expect. A young private wrote that his idea of combat had been that the soldiers "would all be in line, all standing in a nice level field fighting, a number of ladies taking care of the wounded, etc., etc., but it isn't so." **See Document Project 13: Civil War Letters and Journals, page 442.** Improved weaponry turned battles into scenes of bloody carnage. The shift from smoothbore muskets to rifles, which had grooves that spun the bullet, made weapons far more effective at longer distances. The use of minié balls—small bullets with a deep cavity that expanded upon firing—increased fatalities as well. By 1863 Union army sharpshooters acquired new repeating rifles with metal cartridges. With more accurate rifles and deadlier bullets, the rival armies increasingly relied on heavy fortifications, elaborate trenches, and distant mortar and artillery fire when they could. Still, casualties continued to rise, especially since the trenches served as breeding grounds for disease.

Explore ▸

For two images of soldiers in wartime, see Documents 13.2 and 13.3.

The hardships and discomforts of war extended beyond combat itself. As General Lee complained before Antietam, many soldiers fought in ragged uniforms and without shoes. Rations, too, ran short. Food was dispensed sporadically and was often spoiled. Many Union troops survived primarily on an unleavened biscuit called hardtack as well as small amounts of meat and beans and enormous quantities of coffee. Their diet improved over the course of the war, however, as the Union supply system grew more efficient while Confederate troops subsisted increasingly on cornmeal and fatty meat. As early as 1862, Confederate soldiers began gathering food from the haversacks of Union dead.

For every soldier who died as a result of combat, three died of disease. Measles, dysentery, typhoid, and malaria killed thousands who drank contaminated water, ate tainted food, and were exposed to the elements. And infected soldiers on both sides carried yellow fever and malaria into towns where they built fortifications. Prisoner-of-war camps were especially deadly locales. Debilitating fevers in a camp near Danville, Virginia, spread to the town, killing civilians as well as soldiers.

The sufferings of African American troops were particularly severe. The death rate from disease for black Union soldiers was nearly three times greater than that for white Union soldiers, reflecting their poorer health upon enlistment, the hard labor they performed, and the minimal medical care they received in the field. Southern blacks who began their army careers in contraband camps fared even worse, with a camp near Nashville losing a quarter of its residents to death in just three months in 1864.

COMPARATIVE ANALYSIS

Photographers Bring the War Home

The development of battlefield photography in the 1860s offered civilians new perspectives on warfare. Photographs were exhibited in photographers' studios and reproduced as engravings in newspapers across the country. The photographs here offer stark contrasts between soldiers on and off the battlefield. In the first, Union soldiers rest at a camp with sturdy wooden cabins. For this picture, some men stopped in the midst of work while others caroused for the camera. In the second, Union dead lie in front of the Dunker Church on the Antietam battlefield, where more than 3,600 were killed in a single day.

Document 13.2

Union Soldiers in Camp, c. 1863

Library of Congress, LC-DIG-ppmsca-34191

For all soldiers, medical assistance was primitive. Antibiotics did not exist, antiseptics were still unknown, and anesthetics were scarce. Union medical care improved with the **U.S. Sanitary Commission**, which was established by the federal government in June 1861 to promote and coordinate better medical treatment for soldiers. Nonetheless, a commentator accurately described most field hospitals as "dirty dens of butchery and horror," where amputations often occurred with whiskey as the only anesthetic.

As the horrors of war sank in, large numbers of soldiers deserted or refused to reenlist. As volunteers declined and deserters increased, both the Confederate and the Union governments were forced to institute conscription laws to draft men into service.

Document 13.3

Battlefield Dead at Antietam, 1862

Library of Congress, LC-DIG-ppmsca-32887

Interpret the Evidence

1. How do the soldiers present themselves in the Union camp photo? How would this photograph have affected viewers on the home front?
2. How might the photograph of the Antietam battlefield affect civilians and influence soldiers like those shown in the Union camp photo?

Put It in Context

How might images like these affect attitudes toward the war among politicians, military leaders, and the public, North and South?

The Northern Economy Expands. As the war dragged on, the North's economic advantages became more apparent. Initially, the effects of the war on northern industry had been little short of disastrous. Raw cotton for textiles disappeared, southern planters stopped ordering shoes, and trade fell off precipitously. By 1863, however, the northern economy was in high gear and could provide more arms, food, shoes, and clothing to its troops as well as for those back home. As cotton production declined, woolen manufacturing doubled; and northern iron and coal production increased 25 to 30 percent during the war. Northern factories turned out weapons and ammunition while shipyards built the fleets that blockaded southern ports.

These economic improvements were linked to a vast expansion in the federal government's activities. War Department orders fueled the industrial surge. It also created the U.S. Military Railroads unit to construct tracks in newly occupied southern territories and granted large contracts to northern railroads to carry troops and supplies. With southern Democrats out of federal office, Congress also raised tariffs on imported goods to protect northern industries. In addition, the government hired thousands of "sewing women," who were contracted to make uniforms for Union soldiers. Other women joined the federal labor force as clerical workers to sustain the expanding bureaucracy and the voluminous amounts of government-generated paperwork.

That paperwork multiplied exponentially when the federal government created a national currency and a national banking system. Before the Civil War, private banks (chartered by the states) issued their own banknotes, which were used in most economic transactions. During the war, Congress revolutionized this system, giving the federal government the power to create currency, issue federal charters to banks, and take on national debt. The government then flooded the nation with treasury bills, commonly called greenbacks. The federal budget mushroomed as well—from $63 million in 1860 to nearly $1.3 billion in 1865. By the end of the war, the federal bureaucracy had become the nation's largest single employer.

Northern manufacturers faced one daunting problem: a shortage of labor. Over half a million workers left their jobs to serve in the Union army, and others were hired by the expanding federal bureaucracy. Manufacturers dealt with the problem primarily by mechanizing more tasks and by hiring more women and children, native-born and immigrant. Combining the lower wages paid to these workers with production speedups, manufacturers improved their profits while advancing the Union cause.

Urbanization and Industrialization in the South.
Although Southerners had gone to war to protect an essentially rural lifestyle, the war encouraged the growth of cities and industry. The creation of a large governmental and military bureaucracy brought thousands of Southerners to the Confederate capital of Richmond. As the war expanded, refugees also flooded into Atlanta, Savannah, Columbia, and Mobile.

Industrialization contributed to urban growth as well. With the South unable to buy industrial goods from the North and limited in its trade with Europe, military necessity spurred southern industry. Clothing and shoe factories had "sprung up almost like magic" in Natchez and Jackson, Mississippi. The Tredegar Iron Works in Richmond expanded significantly as well, employing more than 2,500 men, black and white. More than 10,000 people labored in war industries in Selma, Alabama, where one factory produced cannons. With labor in short supply, widows and orphans, enslaved blacks, and white men too old or injured to fight were recruited for industrial work in many cities.

Women Aid the War Effort.
Women of all classes contributed to the war effort, North and South. Thousands filled jobs in agriculture, industry, and the government that were traditionally held by men while others assisted the military effort more directly. Most Union and Confederate officials initially opposed women's direct engagement in the war. Yet it was women's voluntary organization of relief efforts that inspired the federal government to establish the U.S. Sanitary Commission. By 1862 tens of thousands of women volunteered funds and assistance through hundreds of local chapters across the North. They

Dr. Mary E. Walker   Dr. Mary E. Walker received her medical degree from Syracuse Medical College and became the first female army surgeon. Wearing bloomers (pants under a skirt), she assisted soldiers and civilians in numerous battlefield areas. Captured by Confederate troops in 1864, Walker soon returned to Union ranks. She was the first woman awarded the Medal of Honor for military service.   Library of Congress, LC-DIG-ppmsca-19911

hosted fund-raising fairs, coordinated sewing and knitting circles, rolled bandages, and sent supplies to the front lines. With critical shortages of medical staff, some female nurses and doctors eventually gained acceptance in northern hospitals and field camps. Led by such memorable figures as Clara Barton, Mary Ann "Mother" Bickerdyke, and Dr. Mary Walker, northern women almost entirely replaced men as military nurses by the end of the war.

In the South, too, much of the medical care was performed by women. But without government support, nursing was never recognized as a legitimate profession for women, and most nurses worked out of their own homes. As a result, a Confederate soldier's chances of dying from wounds or disease were greater than those of his Union counterpart. Southern women also worked tirelessly to supply soldiers with clothes, blankets, munitions, and food. But this work, too, was often performed locally and by individuals rather than as part of a coordinated Confederate effort.

Some Union and Confederate women played more unusual roles in the war. A few dozen women joined Rose Greenhow in gathering information for military and political leaders. One of the most effective spies on the Union side was the former fugitive Harriet Tubman, who gathered intelligence in South Carolina, including from many slaves, between 1862 and 1864. Even more women served as couriers, carrying messages across battle lines to alert officers of critical changes in military orders or in the opponent's position. In addition, at least four hundred women disguised themselves as men and fought as soldiers.

Union women also sought to influence wartime policies. Following the Emancipation Proclamation, Elizabeth Cady Stanton, Susan B. Anthony, and Lucy Stone founded the **Women's National Loyal League** and launched a massive petition drive to broaden Lincoln's policy. Collecting 260,000 signatures, two-thirds of them from women, the League demanded a congressional act "emancipating all persons of African descent" everywhere in the nation.

Dissent and Protest in the Midst of War.   Dissent roiled some border states from the start of the war. In 1863 and 1864, frustration spread across the North and the South generally with increasing casualties, declining numbers of volunteers, and rising inflation. As the war dragged on, many white Northerners began to wonder whether defeating the Confederacy was worth the cost, and many white Southerners whether saving it was.

From 1861 on, battles raged among residents in the border state of Missouri, with Confederate sympathizers refusing to accept living in a Union state. Pro-southern residents formed militias and staged guerrilla attacks on Union supporters. The militias, with the tacit support of Confederate officials, claimed thousands of lives during the war and forced the Union army to station troops in the area.

By 1863, dissent broadened to include Northerners who earlier embraced the Union cause. Some white Northerners had always opposed emancipation, based on racial prejudice or fear that a flood of black migrants would increase competition for jobs. Then, just two months after the Emancipation Proclamation went into effect, a new law deepened concerns among many working-class Northerners. The **Enrollment Act**, passed by Congress in March 1863, established a draft system to ensure sufficient soldiers for the Union army. While draftees were to be selected by an impartial lottery, the law allowed a person with $300 to pay the government in place of serving or to hire another man as a substitute. Many workers deeply resented the draft's profound inequality.

Dissent turned to violence in July 1863 when the new law went into effect. Riots broke out in cities across the North. In New York City, where inflation caused tremendous suffering and a large immigrant population solidly supported the Democratic Party, implementation of the draft triggered four days of the worst rioting Americans had ever seen. Women and men—including many Irish and German immigrants—attacked Republican draft officials, wealthy businessmen, and the free black community. Between July 13 and 16, rioters lynched at least a dozen African Americans and looted and burned the city's

New York City Draft Riots, July 1863   On July 13 the draft riots in New York City began with an attack on the Colored Orphan Asylum on Fifth Avenue. As the matron led 233 African American children to safety, mobs of white men and women looted the building and set it ablaze. This wood engraving appeared in illustrated weeklies from New York to London. Granger, NYC

Colored Orphan Asylum. The violence ended only when Union troops put down the riots by force. By then, more than one hundred New Yorkers, most of them black, lay dead.

By 1864 inflation also fueled protests in the North as it eroded the earnings of rural and urban residents. Women, children, and old men took over much of the field labor in the Midwest, trying to feed their families and the army while struggling to pay their bills. Factory workers, servants, and day laborers felt the pinch as well. With federal greenbacks flooding the market and military production a priority, the price of consumer goods climbed about 20 percent faster than wages. Although industrialists garnered huge profits, workers suffered. A group of Cincinnati seamstresses complained to President Lincoln in 1864 about employers "who fatten on their contracts by grinding immense profits out of the labor of their operatives." At the same time, employers persuaded some state legislatures to prohibit strikes in wartime. The federal government, too, supported business over labor. When workers at the Parrott arms factory in Cold Spring, New York, struck for higher wages in 1864, the government declared martial law and arrested the strike leaders.

Northern Democrats saw the widening unrest as a political opportunity. Although some Democratic leaders supported the war effort, many others—whom opponents called **Copperheads**, after the poisonous snake—rallied behind Ohio politician Clement L. Vallandigham in opposing the war. Presenting themselves as the "peace party," these Democrats enjoyed considerable success in eastern cities where inflation was rampant and immigrant workers were caught between low wages and military service. The party was also strong in parts of the Midwest, like Missouri, where sympathy for the southern cause and antipathy to African Americans ran deep.

In the South, too, some whites expressed growing dissatisfaction with the war. In April 1862 Jefferson Davis had signed the first conscription act in U.S. history, inciting widespread opposition. Here, too, men could hire a substitute if they had enough money, and an October 1862 law exempted men owning twenty or more slaves from military service. Thus, large planters, many of whom served in the Confederate legislature, had effectively exempted themselves from fighting. As one Alabama farmer fumed, "All they want is to get you pumpt up and go to fight for their infernal negroes, and after you do their fighting you may kiss their hine parts for all they care."

Small farmers were also hard hit by policies that allowed the Confederate army to take whatever supplies it needed. The army's forced acquisition of farm produce intensified food shortages that had been building since early in the war. Moreover, the lack of an extensive railroad or canal system in the South limited the distribution of what food was available.

Food shortages drove up prices on basic items like bread and corn, while the Union blockade and the focus on military needs dramatically increased prices on other consumer goods. As the Confederate government issued ever more treasury notes to finance the war, inflation soared 2,600 percent in less than three years. In spring 1863 food riots led by working-class women erupted in cities across the South, including the Confederate capital of Richmond.

Some state legislatures then tried to control food prices, but Richmond workers continued to voice their resentment. In fall 1863 a group proclaimed, "From the fact that he consumes all and produces nothing, we know that without [our] labor and production the man with money could not exist."

The devastation of the war added to all these grievances. Since most battles were fought in the Upper South or along the Confederacy's western frontier, small farmers in these regions saw their crops, animals, and fields devastated. A phrase that had seemed cynical in 1862—"A rich man's war and a poor man's fight"—became the rallying cry of the southern peace movement in 1864. Secret peace societies flourished mainly among small farmers and in regions, like the western mountains, where plantation slavery did not develop. A secret organization centered in North Carolina provided Union forces with information on southern troop movements and encouraged desertion by Confederates. In mountainous areas, draft evaders and deserters formed guerrilla groups that attacked draft officials and actively impeded the war effort. Women joined these efforts, hiding deserters, raiding grain depots, and burning the property of Confederate officials.

When slaveholders led the South out of the Union in 1861, they had assumed the loyalty of yeomen farmers, the deference of southern ladies, and the privileges of the southern way of life. Far from preserving social harmony and social order, however, the war undermined ties between elite and poor Southerners, between planters and small farmers, and between women and men. Although most white Southerners still supported the Confederacy in 1864 and internal dissent alone did not lead to defeat, it did weaken the ties that bound soldiers to their posts in the final two years of the war.

REVIEW & RELATE

- What were the economic effects of the war on the North and the South?

- How did social conflicts created or heightened by the war fuel dissent and protest in the North and the South?

The **Tide** of **War** Turns, **1863–1865**

In spring 1863, amid turmoil on the home front, General Robert E. Lee's army defeated a Union force twice its size at Chancellorsville, Virginia. The victory set the stage for a Confederate thrust into Pennsylvania, but Lee's decision to go on the offensive proved the Confederacy's undoing. In July 1863 the Union won two decisive military victories: at Gettysburg, Pennsylvania, and Vicksburg, Mississippi. At the same time, the flood of African Americans, including former slaves, into the Union army transformed the very meaning of the war. By 1864, with the momentum favoring the Union, General Ulysses S. Grant implemented policies of hard war that forced the Confederacy to consider surrender.

Key Victories for the Union. In mid-1863 Confederate commanders believed the tide was turning in their favor. Following victories at Fredericksburg and Chancellorsville, General Lee launched an invasion of northern territory. While the Union army maneuvered to protect Washington, D.C., General Joseph Hooker resigned as its head. When Lincoln appointed George A. Meade as the new Union commander, the general immediately faced a major engagement at the **Battle of Gettysburg** in Pennsylvania. If Confederates won a victory there, European countries might finally recognize the southern nation and force the North to accept peace.

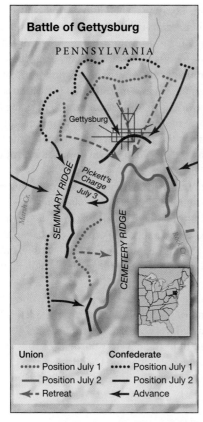

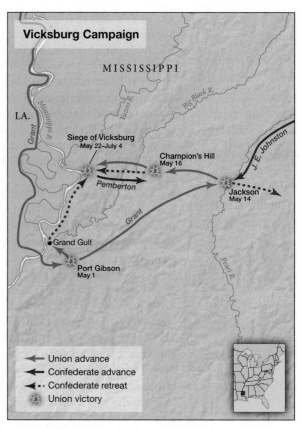

MAP 13.2   Battles of Gettysburg and Vicksburg, 1863

The three-day Battle of Gettysburg and the six-week siege of Vicksburg led to critical victories for the Union. Together, these victories forced General Lee's troops back into Confederate territory and gave the Union control of the Mississippi River. Still, the war was far from over. Confederate troops controlled the southern heartland, and Northerners wearied of the ever-increasing casualties.

Neither Lee nor Meade set out to launch a battle in this small Pennsylvania town. But Lee was afraid of outrunning his supply lines, and Meade wanted to keep Confederates from gaining control of the roads that crossed at Gettysburg. So between July 1 and July 3, the opposing armies fought a desperate battle with Union troops occupying the high ground and Confederate forces launching deadly assaults from below (Map 13.2). Ultimately, Gettysburg proved a disaster for the South: More than 4,700 Confederates were killed, including a large number of officers; another 18,000 were wounded, captured, or missing. Although the Union suffered similar casualties, it had more men to lose, and it could claim victory.

As Lee retreated to Virginia, the South suffered another devastating defeat. Troops under General Grant had been pounding Vicksburg, Mississippi, since May 1863. The **siege of Vicksburg** ended with the surrender of Confederate forces on July 4. This victory was even more important strategically than Gettysburg (Map 13.2). Combined with a victory five days later at Port Hudson, Louisiana, the Union army controlled the entire Mississippi valley, the richest plantation region in the South. This series of victories also effectively cut Louisiana, Arkansas, and Texas off from the rest of the Confederacy, ensuring Union control of the West. In November 1863 Grant's troops achieved another major victory at Chattanooga, opening up much of the South's remaining territory to invasion. Thousands of slaves deserted their plantations, and many joined the Union war effort.

As 1864 dawned, the Union had twice as many forces in the field as the Confederacy, whose soldiers were suffering from low morale, high mortality, and dwindling supplies. Although some difficult battles lay ahead, the war of attrition (in which the larger, better-supplied Union forces slowly wore down their Confederate opponents) had begun to pay dividends.

The changing Union fortunes increased support for Lincoln and his congressional allies. Union victories and the Emancipation Proclamation also convinced Great Britain not to recognize the Confederacy as an independent nation. And the heroics of African American soldiers, who engaged in direct and often brutal combat against southern troops, expanded support for emancipation. Republicans, who now fully embraced abolition as a war aim, were nearly assured the presidency and a congressional majority in the 1864 elections.

Northern Democrats still campaigned for peace and the readmission of Confederate states with slavery intact. They nominated George B. McClellan, the onetime Union commander, for president. McClellan attracted working-class and immigrant voters who traditionally supported the Democrats and bore the heaviest burdens of the war. But Democratic hopes for victory in November were crushed when Union general William Tecumseh Sherman captured Atlanta, Georgia, just two months before the election. Lincoln and the Republicans won easily, giving the party a clear mandate to continue the war to its conclusion.

African Americans Contribute to Victory.

African Americans Contribute to Victory. Lincoln's election secured the eventual downfall of slavery. Yet the president and Congress did not eradicate human bondage on their own. From the fall of 1862 on, African Americans enlisted in the Union army and helped ensure that nothing short of universal emancipation would be the outcome of the war. As Private Thomas Long, a former slave serving with the First South Carolina Volunteers, explained: "If we hadn't become sojers, all might have gone back as it was before. . . . But now tings can neber go back, because we have showed our energy and our courage and our naturally manhood."

In the border states, which were exempt from the Emancipation Proclamation, enslaved men were adamant about enlisting since those who served in the Union army were granted their freedom. Because of this provision, slaveholders in these states did everything in their power to prevent their slaves from joining the army. Despite these efforts, between 25 and 60 percent of military-age enslaved men in the four border states stole away and joined the Union army. By the end of the war, nearly 200,000 black men had served officially in the army and navy, and some 37,000 blacks had given their lives for the Union.

Yet despite their courage and commitment, black soldiers felt the sting of racism. They were segregated in camps, given the most menial jobs, and often treated as inferiors by white soldiers and officers. Particularly galling was the Union policy of paying black soldiers less

The 107th U.S. Colored Infantry Band   The 107th U.S. Colored Infantry Band was photographed at Fort Corcoran in Arlington, Virginia. These 20 African American soldiers with their musical instruments were among the nearly 200,000 black men who volunteered for military service. They served as soldiers and sailors to prove their manhood and their worthiness for full citizenship. Some 37,000 black soldiers died during the Civil War.   Library of Congress, LC-DIG-cwpb-04279

than whites. African American soldiers openly protested this discrimination even after a black sergeant who voiced his views was charged with mutiny and executed by firing squad in February 1864. The War Department finally equalized wages four months later.

One primary concern of African American soldiers was to liberate slaves as Union armies moved deeper into the South. At the same time, thousands of southern slaves headed for Union lines. Even those forced to remain on plantations learned when Union troops were nearby and talked openly of emancipation. "Now they gradually threw off the mask," a slave remembered, "and were not afraid to let it be known that the 'freedom' in their songs meant freedom of the body in this world."

The Final Battles of a Hard War. In the spring of 1864, the war in the East entered its final stage. That March, Lincoln placed General Grant in charge of all Union forces. Grant embarked on a strategy of **hard war**, in which soldiers not only attacked military targets but also destroyed civilian crops, livestock, fields, and property to undermine morale and supply chains. Grant was also willing to accept huge casualties to achieve victory. Over the next year, he led his troops overland through western Virginia in an effort to take Richmond. Meanwhile, General Philip Sheridan devastated "The Breadbasket of the Confederacy" in Virginia's Shenandoah Valley, and General Sherman laid waste to the remnants of the plantation system in Georgia and the Carolinas.

Grant's troops headed toward Richmond, where Lee's army controlled strong defensive positions. The Confederates won a series of narrow, bloody victories, but Grant continued to push forward. Although Lee lost fewer men, they were losses he could not afford given the Confederacy's much smaller population. Combining high casualties with desert-ers, Lee's army was melting away with each engagement. Although soldiers and civilians—North and South—called Grant "the butcher" for his seeming lack of regard for human life, the Union general was not deterred.

In the fall of 1864, implementing hard war tactics, Sheridan rendered the Shenandoah Valley a "barren waste." Called "the burning" by local residents, Sheridan's soldiers torched fields, barns, and homes and destroyed thousands of bushels of grain along with livestock, shops, and mills. His campaign demoralized civilians in the region and denied Confeder-ate troops crucial supplies.

In the preceding months, Sherman had laid siege to Atlanta, but on September 2 his forces swept around the city and destroyed the roads and rails that connected it to the rest of the Confederacy. When General John B. Hood and his Confederate troops abandoned their posts, Sherman telegraphed Lincoln: "Atlanta is ours, and fairly won." That victory cut the South in two, but Sherman continued on. **Sherman's March to the Sea** introduced hard war tactics to Southerners along the three-hundred-mile route from the Atlantic coast north through the Carolinas. His troops cut a path of destruction fifty to sixty miles wide. They confiscated or destroyed millions of pounds of cotton, corn, wheat, and other agricultural items; tore up thousands of miles of railroad tracks; and burned Columbia, the South Carolina capital. Despite later claims that Sherman's men ravaged white women, instances of such behavior were rare. Union soldiers did ransack homes and confiscate food and clothing, and many exhausted white women reacted with fear and anxiety. But other women remained defiant, offering Union sol-diers vitriolic tongue-lashings.

Explore ▶

See Document 13.4 for an account of Sherman's destruction of Columbia, South Carolina.

Enslaved blacks hoped that Sherman's arrival marked their emancipation. During his victorious march, nearly 18,000 enslaved men, women, and children fled ruined planta-tions and sought to join the victorious troops. To their dismay, soldiers refused to take them along. Union soldiers realized that they could not care for this vast number of people and carry out their military operations. But some Union soldiers also abused African American men, raped black women, or stole their few possessions. Angry Confederates captured many blacks who were turned away, killing some and reenslaving others.

These actions caused a scandal in Washington. In January 1865, Lincoln dispatched Secretary of War Edwin Stanton to Georgia to investigate the charges. At an extraordinary meeting in Savannah, Stanton and Sherman met with black ministers to hear their com-plaints and hopes. The ministers spoke movingly of the war lifting "the yoke of bondage." Freed blacks, they argued, "could reap the fruit of their own labor" and, if given land, "take care of ourselves, and assist the Government in maintaining our freedom." In response, Sherman issued **Field Order Number 15**, setting aside more than 400,000 acres of cap-tured Confederate land to be divided into small plots for former slaves. The order proved highly controversial, but it offered blacks some hope of significant change.

If many African Americans were disappointed by the actions of Union soldiers in the East, American Indians were even more devastated by developments in the West. Despite Indian nations' substantial aid to Union armies, any hope of being rewarded for their efforts vanished by 1864. Tens of thousands of whites migrated west of the Mississippi during the Civil War, and congressional passage of the Homestead Act in 1864 increased the numbers. At the same time, the U.S. army grew exponentially during the war, using its increased power to assault western Indian nations.

Eleanor Cohen Seixas | Journal Entry, February 1865

In February 1865 General Sherman and his men reached Columbia, South Carolina, intent on destroying as much property as possible. Thousands of residents fled the Columbia fires, including Philip and Cordelia Cohen and their daughter Eleanor. Philip was a pharmacist, slave owner, and part of the state's small Jewish population, who had moved his family to Columbia seeking safety. Eleanor recorded the trials of wartime and her hopes for southern victory in her journal. In this selection, she describes the arrival of Sherman's troops.

Document 13.4

The fire raged fearfully all night, but on Saturday perfect quiet reigned. The vile Yankees took from us clothing, food, jewels, all our cows, horses, carriages, etc., and left us in a deplorable condition after stealing from us. Sherman, with great generosity, presented the citizens with 500 cattle, so poor they could hardly stand up. No words of mine can give any idea of the brutality of the ruffians. They swore, they cussed, plundered, and committed every excess. No age or sex was safe from them. Sometimes, after saving some valueless token, it was ruthlessly snatched from our hands by some of their horde. Our noble women were insulted by words, and some, I have heard of, in deeds, but none came under my knowledge, for I myself, God be praised, I received no rude word from any of them. I did not speak . . . to them at all. The fire burned eighty-four squares, and nothing can tell the quantity of plunder they carried off as on Monday they left us, and though we feared starvation, yet we were glad to be rid of them.

Source: Jacob R. Marcus, ed., *Memoirs of American Jews, 1775–1885* (Philadelphia: Jewish Publication Society of America, 1955), 3:363.

Interpret the Evidence

1. What does this journal entry suggest about how Southerners viewed the Union army?
2. How does Seixas's description of the actions of Sherman's troops compare with rumors about their actions?

Put It in Context

How does this journal entry illuminate the impact of the Union army's hard war strategy?

Attacks on Indians were not an extension of hard war policies, but rather a government-sanctioned effort to terrorize native communities. Beginning in 1862, Dakota Sioux went to war with the United States over broken treaties. After being defeated, four hundred warriors were arrested by military officials and thirty-eight executed. In 1863 California Volunteers slaughtered more than two hundred men, women, and children in a Shoshone-Bannock village in Idaho. Meanwhile thousands of white settlers had been flooding into Colorado after gold was discovered in 1858, forcing Cheyenne and Arapaho Indians off their land. In 1864 these Indians were promised refuge at Sand Creek by officers at nearby Fort Lyon. Instead, Colonel John M. Chivington led his Third Colorado Calvary in a rampage that left 125 to 160 Indian men, women, and children dead. The Sand Creek Massacre ensured that white migrants traveling in the region would be subject to Indian attacks for years to come. At the same time, in the Southwest, the Navajo were defeated by U.S. troops and their Ute allies and forced into a four-hundred-mile trek to a reservation in New Mexico.

U.S. army officers considered "winning the West" one way to restore national unity once the Civil War ended. For Indian nations, the increased migration, expanded military presence, and sheer brutality they experienced in 1863 to 1864 boded ill for their future, whichever side won the Civil War.

The War Comes to an End. As the defeat of the Confederacy loomed, the U.S. Congress finally considered abolishing slavery throughout the nation. With intense lobbying by abolitionists, petitioning by the Women's National Loyal League, and the support of President Lincoln, Congress passed the **Thirteenth Amendment** to the U.S. Constitution on January 31, 1865. It prohibited slavery and involuntary servitude anywhere in the United States. Some northern and western states had already enacted laws to ease racial inequities. Ohio, California, and Illinois repealed statutes barring blacks from testifying in court and serving on juries. Then, in May 1865, Massachusetts passed the first comprehensive public-accommodations law in U.S. history, ensuring equal treatment in stores, schools, theaters, and other social spaces. Cities from San Francisco to Cincinnati and New York also desegregated their streetcars.

Richmond in Ruins, April 1865   This photograph shows the Richmond and Petersburg Railroad Depot following the capture of the Confederate capital by General Grant and his troops in April 1865. The black man sitting amid the devastation no doubt realized that Richmond's fall marked the defeat of the South. Library of Congress, LC-DIG-cwpb-02709

Still hoping to stave off defeat, southern leaders also began rethinking their racial policies. The Confederate House passed a law to recruit slaves into the army in February 1865, but the Senate defeated the measure. It was too late to make a difference anyway.

In early April 1865, with Sherman heading toward Raleigh, North Carolina, Grant captured Petersburg, Virginia, and then drove Lee and his forces out of Richmond. Seasoned African American troops led the final assault on the city and were among the first Union soldiers to enter the Confederate capital. On April 9, after a brief engagement at Appomattox Court House, Virginia, Lee surrendered to Grant. Within hours, Lee's troops began heading home. While sporadic fighting continued—Cherokee Stand Watie was the last Confederate general to surrender in June 1865—the back of the Confederate army had been broken.

With Lee's surrender, many Northerners hoped that the reunited nation would be stronger and more just. Jubilation in the North was short-lived, however. On April 14, Abraham Lincoln was shot at Ford's Theatre by a Confederate fanatic named John Wilkes Booth. The president died the next day, leading to great uncertainty about how peace and national unity would be achieved.

REVIEW & RELATE

What role did African Americans play in the defeat of the South? How did attitudes toward African Americans change in the final year of the war?	How did the Union win the war against the Confederacy while defeating Indians in the West?

Conclusion: An Uncertain Future

The Civil War devastated and transformed the nation. The deadliest conflict in American history—some 600,000 to 750,000 Americans died—the Civil War freed nearly 4 million Americans who had been enslaved. Soldiers who survived brought new experiences and knowledge back to their families and communities, but many were also marked—like former slaves—by deep physical and emotional wounds. The war transformed the home front as well. Northern and southern women entered the labor force and the public arena in numbers never before imagined. The northern economy flourished and the South became more urbanized, but the Confederacy was left economically ruined. Meanwhile the federal government significantly expanded during the war. It also initiated programs, like the Homestead Act, that fueled migration, intensifying conflicts in the West and devastating numerous Indian nations. Altogether, the Civil War dramatically accelerated the pace of economic, political, and social change, transforming American society both during the war and for decades afterward.

Still, the legacies of the war were far from certain in 1865. Protests during the war reflected a growing sense of class inequalities while the abolition of slavery highlighted ongoing racial disparities. Moreover, even in defeat, white Southerners honored Lee and other "heroes" of the "Lost Cause" with portraits, parades, and statues. Confederate women also worked tirelessly to preserve the memory of ordinary Confederate soldiers and of heroines like Rose O'Neal Greenhow, who had drowned in 1864 while returning from a mission to gain support in Europe.

Victorious Northerners celebrated wartime heroes as well but recognized that much still needed to be done. Frederick Douglass joined other former abolitionists in seeking to enfranchise African American men to secure their rights as freedpeople. He and his colleagues had no illusions about the lengths to which many whites would go to protect their traditional privileges. Yet many northern whites, exhausted by four years of war, hoped to leave the problems of slavery and secession behind. Others sought to rebuild the South quickly to ensure the nation's economic stability. These competing visions—between Northerners and Southerners and within each group—would shape the uncertainties of peace in ways few could imagine at the end of the war.

TIMELINE OF EVENTS

1861
- Fort Sumter attacked
- Slaves declared "contraband"
- U.S. Sanitary Commission established
- Battle of Bull Run (Manassas)
- Confiscation Act passed

1862
- Battle of Shiloh
- Conscription act signed in South
- Battle of Antietam

1863
- Emancipation Proclamation signed
- Enrollment Act passed in North
- New York City draft riots
- Battle of Gettysburg
- Siege of Vicksburg

1864
- Atlanta falls
- Sand Creek Massacre
- Sherman's "March to the Sea"

1865
- More than 200,000 African Americans serve in the Union army and navy
- Field Order Number 15
- Thirteenth Amendment passed
- Lee surrenders to Grant
- Lincoln assassinated

KEY TERMS

Fort Sumter, *416*

Battle of Bull Run (Manassas), *418*

contraband, *420*

Battle of Shiloh, *422*

Battle of Antietam, *424*

Emancipation Proclamation, *424*

U.S. Sanitary Commission, *426*

Women's National Loyal League, *429*

Enrollment Act, *430*

Copperheads, *431*

Battle of Gettysburg, *432*

siege of Vicksburg, *433*

hard war, *435*

Sherman's March to the Sea, *436*

Field Order Number 15, *436*

Thirteenth Amendment, *438*

REVIEW & RELATE

1. What led four more states to join the Confederacy in 1861 and four other slave states to remain in the Union?

2. What advantages and disadvantages did each side have at the onset of the war?

3. How and why did the Union and the Confederacy treat American Indian and African American participation in the war differently?

4. What events occurred to make the Civil War become a war to end slavery?

5. What were the economic effects of the war on the North and the South?

6. How did social conflicts created or heightened by the war fuel dissent and protest in the North and the South?

7. What role did African Americans play in the defeat of the South? How did attitudes toward African Americans change in the final year of the war?

8. How did the Union win the war against the Confederacy while defeating Indians in the West?

Civil War Letters and Journals

Throughout the Civil War, soldiers and their families kept in close touch by writing letters. The volume of wartime correspondence was immense, with ninety thousand letters a day processed in the Union alone. Other men and women kept journals to record their experiences, which some used as the basis for published reminiscences years later. Soldiers' letters were especially important in capturing the daily experiences of war, from the boredom of encampments to the excitement or horrors of battle to concerns about their families back home (Document 13.6). Soldiers' letters also expressed their views on the causes of the war and their changing understandings of its meaning (Documents 13.5). For black soldiers this often meant coming to terms with discrimination by the very government for which they were fighting (Document 13.8). Female volunteers provide another dramatic perspective on the war. Suzy King Taylor, who ran away from a Georgia plantation to work for the Union army, is the only former slave who published her memoirs of the war (Document 13.7). Far more women experienced the war from the home front, but for many Confederate women this often meant living near army outposts and even prisoner-of-war camps (Document 13.9).

The letters and journals reprinted here, from both Northerners and Southerners, represent an array of experiences, including those of soldiers and civilians, women and men, blacks and whites. Covering nearly the whole expanse of the war, they help us trace transformations among soldiers, female volunteers, and civilians.

Document 13.5

Frederick Spooner | Letter to His Brother Henry, April 30, 1861

At the start of the war, many Northerners expected a quick victory, as evidenced in this letter written by seventeen-year old Frederick Spooner to his older brother Henry. A native of Providence, Rhode Island, Frederick believed the South was weakened by its reliance on slavery. Perhaps inspired by these same beliefs, Henry enlisted in the Union army in 1862 and later practiced law in Rhode Island and served in the U.S. House of Representatives.

Dear Henry,

Your letter was received, and I now sit down in my shirt sleeves (as it is warm) to write in return.

For the last few weeks there has been great excitement here, and nothing has been thought of scarcely except that one subject which now received the undivided attention of the whole loyal North—war.

And well may war, so hideous and disgusting in itself receive such attention when carried on for such noble and just principles as in the present case.

Traitors have begun the conflict, let us continue and end it. Let us settle it now, once and for all.

Let us settle it, even if the whole South has to be made one common graveyard, and their cotton soaked in blood. Let us do it *now* while the whole North is aroused from the inactivity and apparent laziness in which it has been so long.

There are plenty of men, an abundance of money, and a military enthusiasm never before known in the annals of history, all of which combined will do the work nice and clean, and if need be will wipe out that palmetto, pelican, rattlesnake region entirely. The holy cause in which our volunteers are enlisted will urge them on to almost superhuman exertions. The South *may* be courageous but I doubt it, they can *gas* and *hag* [complain and bluster] first rate; they can lie and steal to perfection, but I really do believe that they cannot fight. . . .

But granting them to be brave (which I don't believe can be proven) they have no chance to overturn this government. They haven't the resources, the "almighty dollar," that powerful ally, or formidable enemy—is against them. They have no money—their property has legs and will be continually disappearing.

They have prospered dealing in human flesh— let them now take the results of it.

They have had what *they* consider the *blessings* of slavery—let them now receive the *curses* of it.

They must be put down, conquered, and thoroughly subdued if need be. . . . The fifteen weak states of the South can stand no chance against the nineteen powerful states of the North. . . .

When I began I did not intend to give a lecture or write a composition on the "crisis," . . . but unconsciously I got on the all-absorbing topic at the very commencement, and it was hard work to let go of it.

There hasn't been much studying lately, and it is very hard work to think or write concerning any other subject than that on which I've paused so long.

So therefore excuse my "crisis" beginning.

Source: Nina Silber and Mary Beth Sievens, eds., *Yankee Correspondence: Civil War Letters between New England Soldiers and the Home Front* (Charlottesville: University Press of Virginia, 1996), 55–56.

Document 13.6

John Hines | Letter to His Parents, April 22, 1862

Confederate soldier John Hines describes the Battle of Shiloh in southwestern Tennessee in this letter written to his parents back home in Kentucky. The bloodiest battle up to that point in the war, Shiloh was also Hines's first combat experience. As was common for soldiers on both sides of the conflict, Hines's early enthusiasm for the war and his opinion of the enemy changed with his first taste of battle.

Dear Ma and G. Pa

. . . I was in the battle of Shiloh from beginning to end. It is said to have been the hardest fought battle ever fought on this continent. Persons who were in the battles of Manassas [Bull Run] and Ft. Donelson say they were skirmishes in comparison. . . .

Our squadron was ordered close to the federal [Union] lines on Saturday evening. We stopped close enough to hear their drums beating. We were very tired and hungry. Some of the men not having et [eaten] for 36 hours. I gave a teamster 50 cents for a biscuit. Tied my horse close to me and laid down without taking off boots or pistols and slept soundly until just at dawn the loud peal of some half dozen cannons aroused us. In a few moments we were in our saddles, overcoats and extra equipment lashed to our saddles. In our shirt sleeves, we sat on our horses examining our arms, ready for the coming fray, for we knew we would give the enemy battle if they would stand.

The increased roaring of artillery and an occasional ambulance bearing off wounded soldiers told that, as we say in camp, the ball was open. Before the sun was up we were marching to the scene of action, which was perhaps a mile off. We had not marched very far before we came upon our line of infantry. For three miles in one unbroken line stood our troops, their fixed bayonets glistening in the new sunbeams, for the sun was just coming over the top of a small elevation.

Almost every hill now on both sides looked like a volcano, for the deep mouthed cannon were roaring on every side. Soon the rattle of musketry announced that our vanguard had found the foe. The dark line of men now moved quickly in. After minutes more the volleys of musketry announced that they too had entered the bloody arena. It was really a grand scene now: you could not distinguish a musket shot now, it was one continual roar like the rushing of a storm. . . . . A shell or cannonball would tear some of your comrades to pieces and a person could not tell whose turn it might be next.

Being mounted and ordered to different places during the day, I had an opportunity to see everything that happened almost and I can assure you that a battlefield is far from being a pleasant place, laying aside the dangers of being hurt, because you can't get out of hearing the groans of the dying or out of sight of the dead. It seemed to me like my acquaintances were always lying in the most auspicious places. Turn what way we might I could find some ghastly looking face that perhaps an hour ago I had seen rushing to the contest with a smile on his face. . . .

We have again returned to camp which is now outside of the former federal lines and are resting quietly. I've a good slice of cheese and a can of oysters which I took out of a federal tent before setting fire to it. I have nothing to do but think over what has happened in the last few days. . . .

Your affectionate son,
J. H. Hines

Source: Rod Gragg, ed., *The Illustrated Confederate Reader* (New York: HarperCollins, 1989), 99–100.

Suzy King Taylor | Caring for the Thirty-third U.S. Colored Troops, 1863

In 1862 Suzy King Taylor escaped with other family members to a contraband camp on the Sea Islands. There she married Edward King, a black noncommissioned officer with the Thirty-third U.S. Colored Troops. Since black soldiers did not get their full pay for more than a year, many wives worked for the army as well. Suzy King was hired as a laundress but also served as a teacher, nurse, and cook. This selection is from a memoir of her experiences published in 1902.

Fort Wagner being only a mile from our camp, I went there two or three times a week, and would go up on the ramparts to watch the gunners send their shells into Charleston. . . . Outside of the fort were many skulls lying about. . . . The comrades and I would have quite a debate as to which side the men fought on. . . . They were a gruesome sight, those fleshless heads and grinning jaws, but by this time I had become accustomed to worse things. . . .

It seems strange how our aversion to seeing suffering is overcome in time of war,—how we are able to see the most sickening sights, such as men with their limbs blown off and mangled by the deadly shells without a shudder; and instead of turning away, how we hurry to assist in alleviating their pain, bind up their wounds, and press cool water to their parched lips. . . .

Finally orders were received to prepare to take Fort Gregg. . . .

About four o'clock, July 2, the charge was made. The firing could be plainly heard in camp. . . . When the wounded arrived, or rather began to arrive, the first one brought was Samuel Anderson of our company. He was badly wounded. Then others of our boys, some with their legs off, arm gone, foot off, and wounds of all kinds imaginable. . . .

My work now began. I gave my assistance to alleviate their sufferings. I asked the doctor of the hospital what I could get for them to eat. . . . I had a few cans of condensed milk and some turtle eggs, so I thought I would try to make some custard. . . . This I carried to the men, who enjoyed it very much. My services were given at all times for the comfort of these men. . . . I was enrolled as company laundress, but I did very little of it, because . . . I was employed all the time doing something for the officers and comrades.

Source: Suzy King Taylor, *Reminiscences of my Life in Camp with the 33rd United States Colored Troops, Late 1st S.C. Volunteers* (Boston: By the Author, 1902).

Thomas Freeman | Letter to His Brother-in-Law, March 26, 1864

The Massachusetts Fifty-fourth Colored Infantry, one of the Union's first black units, was recognized for its valor and heroism. The unit was also known for protesting the mistreatment of black soldiers, including a regiment-wide pay boycott to demand equal salaries for black and white soldiers. In this letter to his brother-in-law, Thomas Freeman of Worcester, Massachusetts, echoes black soldiers' discontent with discrimination and poor treatment.

Jacksonville, Florida
March 26, 1864

Dear William

I will devote some spare moments I have in writing you a few lines which I hope may find you and all your family the same, also all of my many Friends in Worcester. Since the Regiment Departure from Morris Island I have enjoyed the best of health. . . . The Regiment in general are in Good Health but in Low Spirits and no reason why for they have all to a man done there duty as a soldier. It is 1 year the 1st Day of April since I enlisted and there is men here in the regiment that have been in Enlisted 13 Months and have never received one cent But there bounty and they more or less have family, and 2 thirds have never received any State Aid, and how do you think men can feel to do there duty as Soldiers, but let me say we are not Soldiers but Labourers working for Uncle Sam for nothing but our board and clothes. . . . We never can be Elevated in this country while such rascality is Performed. Slavery with all its horrorrs can not Equalise this for it is nothing but work from morning till night Building Batteries, Hauling Guns, Cleaning Bricks, clearing up land for other Regiments to settle on and if a Man Says he is sick it is the Doctors Priveledge to say yes or no. If you cannot work then you are sent to the Guard House Bucked Gagged and stay so till they see fit to relieve You and if you dont like that some white man will Give you a crack over the Head with his sword. Now do you call this Equality? If so God help such

Equality. . . . I want You to consult some counsel in Relation to the Matter and see if a man could not sue for his Discharge . . . and let me know immiedeitely for I am tired of such treatment. Please answer as soon as you can and Oblidge Yours

T. D. Freeman

Source: Nina Silber and Mary Beth Sievens, eds., *Yankee Correspondence: Civil War Letters between New England Soldiers and the Home Front* (Charlottesville: University Press of Virginia, 1996), 47–48.

Eliza Frances Andrews | On Union Prisoners of War, 1865

Eliza Frances Andrews was the daughter of a Georgia planter and a staunch Confederate. In her early twenties when the Civil War began, she kept a journal that included reports on her visits to various army camps. In January 1865 she and a friend visited Captain Bonham at a local fort and met a Yankee prisoner, Peter Louis, who had been transferred from Andersonville Prison because of his skills as a shoemaker. Some 13,000 Union soldiers died at Andersonville.

expect the poor Yank [Peter Louis] is glad to get away from Anderson on any terms. Although matters have improved somewhat with the cool weather, the tales that are told of the condition of things there last summer are appalling. Mrs. Brisbane heard all about it from Father Hamilton, a Roman Catholic priest from Macon, who has been working like a good Samaritan in those dens of filth and misery. It is a shame to us Protestants that we have let a Roman Catholic get so far ahead of us in this work of charity and mercy. Mrs. Brisbane says Father Hamilton told her that during the summer the wretched prisoners burrowed in the ground like moles to protect themselves from the sun. It was not safe to give them material to build shanties as they might use it for clubs to overcome the guards. These underground huts, he said, were alive with vermin and stank like charnel [burial] houses. Many of the prisoners were stark naked, having not so much as a shirt to their backs. . . . Father Hamilton said that at one time the prisoners died at a rate of 150 a day. . . . Dysentery was the most fatal disease. . . . My heart aches for the poor wretches, Yankees though they are, and I am afraid God will suffer some terrible retribution to fall upon us for letting such things happen. . . . And yet, what can we do? The Yankees are really more to blame than we, for they won't exchange these prisoners, and our poor, hard-pressed Confederacy had not the means to provide for them when our own soldiers are starving in the field. Oh, what a horrible thing war is when stripped of all its pomp and circumstance!

Source: Eliza Frances Andrews, *The War-Time Journal of a Georgia Girl, 1864–1865* (New York: D. Appleton, 1908), 76–79.

Interpret the Evidence

1. According to these sources, what accounts for the early popular support for the war and changes in sentiment over the course of the war?
2. Compare the letters from Fred Spooner (Document 13.5) and John Hines (Document 13.6). How did each view the enemy and the causes of the war?
3. In what ways do Suzy King Taylor (Document 13.7) and Eliza Frances Andrews (Document 13.9) defy or confirm contemporary gender roles? How does their race and their status shape these roles?
4. How do the experiences of Suzy King Taylor and Thomas Freeman (Documents 13.7 and 13.8) compare to those of the white writers (Documents 13.5, 13.6, and 13.9)?
5. What was life like for soldiers at the front (Documents 13.5, 13.6, and 13.8)? How would you compare the different war experiences revealed in these letters?

Put It in Context

In what ways do these personal sources complement or challenge the more well-known political and military history of the Civil War?

14

Emancipation and Reconstruction

1863–1877

WINDOW TO THE PAST

Sharecropping Agreement, 1870

After the end of slavery, plantation owners needed to find new ways to work their land and former slaves needed to find employment. As a result, freedpeople sought to enter into sharecropping agreements, such as the one shown here, to farm on behalf of landowners because they lacked money and tools and wanted to farm their own land. However, despite their best efforts, they usually found themselves in debt to the white planter-merchants who controlled the accounts and sold them supplies. ▶ To discover more about what this primary source can show us, see Document 14.4 on page 467.

Alabama Department of Archives and History, Montgomery, Alabama

After reading this chapter you should be able to:

- Discuss the challenges newly freed African Americans faced and how they responded to them.

- Analyze the influence of the president and Congress on Reconstruction policy and evaluate the successes and shortcomings of the policies they enacted.

- Evaluate the changes that took place in the society and economy of the South during Reconstruction.

- Explain how and why Reconstruction came to an end by the mid-1870s.

AMERICAN HISTORIES

Jefferson Franklin Long spent his life improving himself and the lives of others of his race. Born a slave in Alabama in 1836, Long showed great resourcefulness in profiting from the limited opportunities available to him under slavery. His master, a tailor who moved his family to Georgia, taught him the trade, but Long taught himself to read and write. When the Civil War ended, he opened a tailor shop in Macon, Georgia. His business success allowed him to venture into Republican Party politics. Elected as Georgia's first black congressman in 1870, Long fought for the political rights of freed slaves. In his first appearance on the House floor, he opposed a bill that would allow former Confederate officials to return to Congress, noting that many belonged to secret societies, such as the Ku Klux Klan, that

(left) **Jefferson Franklin Long** Library of Congress, LC-DIG-cwpbh-556
(right) **Andrew Johnson** Library of Congress, 3a53290

intimidated black citizens. Despite his pleas, the measure passed, and Long decided not to run for reelection.

By the mid-1880s, Long had become disillusioned with the ability of black Georgians to achieve their objectives via electoral politics. Instead, he counseled African Americans to turn to institution building as the best hope for social and economic advancement. Long helped found the Union Brotherhood Lodge, a black mutual aid society with branches throughout central Georgia, which provided social and economic services for its members. He died in 1901, as political disfranchisement and racial segregation swept through Georgia and the rest of the South.

Jefferson Long and Andrew Johnson shared many characteristics, but their views on race could not have been more different. Whereas Long fought for the right of self-determination for African Americans, Johnson believed that whites alone should govern. Born in 1808 in Raleigh, North Carolina, Johnson grew up in poverty. At the age of thirteen or fourteen, he became a tailor's apprentice and, after moving to Tennessee in 1826, like Long, opened a tailor shop. The following year, Johnson married and began to prosper, purchasing a farm and a small number of slaves.

As he made his mark in Greenville, Tennessee, Johnson became active in Democratic Party politics. A social and political outsider, Johnson gained support by championing the rights of workers and small farmers against the power of the southern aristocracy. Political success followed, and by the time the Civil War broke out, he was a U.S. senator.

When the Civil War erupted, Johnson remained loyal to the Union even after Tennessee seceded in 1861. President Abraham Lincoln rewarded Johnson by appointing him as military governor of Tennessee. In 1864 the Republican Lincoln chose the Democrat Johnson to run with him as vice president. Less than six weeks after their inauguration in March 1865, Johnson became president upon Lincoln's assassination.

Fate placed Reconstruction in the hands of Andrew Johnson. After four years, the brutal Civil War had come to a close. Yet the hard work of reunion remained. Toward this end, President Johnson oversaw the reestablishment of state governments in the former Confederate states. He considered the southern states as having fulfilled their obligations for rejoining the Union, even as they passed measures that restricted black civil and political rights. Most Northerners reached a different conclusion. Having won the bloody war, they feared losing the peace to Johnson and the defeated South. ∎

The American histories of Andrew Johnson and Jefferson Long intersected in Reconstruction, amid hard-fought battles to determine the fate of the postwar South and the meaning of freedom for newly emancipated African Americans. Former slaves sought to reunite their families, obtain land, and seek an education. President Johnson rejected their pleas for assistance to fulfill these aims. However, Congress passed laws to ensure civil rights and extend the vote to African American men, although African American women, like white women, remained disenfranchised. In the South, whites attempted to restore their economic and political power over African Americans by resorting to intimidation and violence. By 1877, they succeeded in bringing Reconstruction to an end with the consent of the federal government.

Emancipation

Even before the war came to a close, Reconstruction had begun on a small scale. During the Civil War, blacks remaining in Union-occupied areas, such as the South Carolina Sea Islands, gained some experience with freedom. When Union troops arrived, most southern whites fled, but enslaved workers chose to stay on the land. Some farmed for themselves, but most worked for northern whites who moved south to demonstrate the profitability of free black labor. After the war, however, former plantation owners returned. Rather than work for these whites, freedpeople preferred to establish their own farms. If forced to hire themselves out, they insisted on negotiating the terms of their employment. Wives and mothers often refused to labor for whites at all in favor of caring for their own families. These conflicts reflected the priorities that would shape the actions of freedpeople across the South in the immediate aftermath of the war. For freedom to be meaningful, it had to include economic independence, the power to make family decisions, and the right to control some community decisions.

African Americans Embrace Freedom. When U.S. troops arrived in Richmond, Virginia, in April 1865, the city's enslaved population knew that freedom was, finally, theirs. Four days after Union troops arrived, 1,500 African Americans, including a large number of soldiers, packed First African Baptist, the largest of the city's black churches. During the singing of the hymn "Jesus My All to Heaven Is Gone," they raised their voices at the line "This is the way I long have sought." As news of the Confederacy's defeat spread, newly freed African Americans across the South experienced similar emotions. Many years later, Houston H. Holloway, a Georgia slave who had been sold three times before he was twenty years old, recalled the day of emancipation: "I felt like a bird out a cage. Amen. Amen, Amen. I could hardly ask to feel any better than I did that day."

For southern whites, however, the end of the war brought fear, humiliation, and uncertainty. From their perspective, the jubilation of former slaves poured salt in their wounds. In many areas, blacks celebrated their freedom under the protection of Union soldiers. When the army moved out, freedpeople suffered deeply for their enthusiasm. Whites beat, whipped, raped, and shot blacks who they felt had been too joyous in their celebration or too helpful to the Yankee invaders. As one North Carolina freedman testified, the Yankees "tol' us we were free," but once the army left, the planters "would get cruel to the slaves if they acted like they were free."

Newly freed blacks also faced less visible dangers. During the 1860s, disease swept through the South and through the contraband camps that housed many former slaves; widespread malnutrition and poor housing heightened the problem. A smallpox epidemic that spread south from Washington, D.C., killed more than sixty thousand freedpeople.

Despite the dangers, southern blacks eagerly pursued emancipation. They moved; they married; they attended school; they demanded wages; they refused to work for whites; they gathered together their families; they created black churches and civic associations; they held political meetings. Sometimes, black women and men acted on their own, pooling their resources to advance their freedom. At other times, they received help from private organizations—particularly northern missionary and educational associations—staffed mostly by former abolitionists, free blacks, and evangelical Christians.

Emancipated slaves also called on federal agencies for assistance and support. The most important of these agencies was the newly formed Bureau of Refugees, Freedmen, and Abandoned Lands, popularly known as the **Freedmen's Bureau**. Created by Congress in 1865 and signed into law by President Lincoln, the bureau provided ex-slaves with economic and legal resources. The Freedmen's Bureau also aided many former slaves in achieving one of their primary goals: obtaining land. A South Carolina freedman summed up the feeling of the newly emancipated. "Give us our own land and we take care of ourselves," he remarked. "But without land, the old masters can hire or starve us, as they

> **Explore ▶**
>
> See Document 14.1 for freedpeople's views about ownership of land.

please." During the last years of the war, the federal government had distributed to the freedpeople around 400,000 acres of abandoned land from the South Carolina Sea Islands to Florida. Immediately after hostilities ceased, the Freedmen's Bureau made available hundreds of thousands of additional acres to recently emancipated slaves.

Reuniting Families Torn Apart by Slavery.

The first priority for many newly freed blacks was to reunite families torn apart by slavery. Men and women traveled across the South to find family members. Well into the 1870s and 1880s, parents ran advertisements in newly established black newspapers, providing what information they knew about their children's whereabouts and asking for assistance in finding them. Milly Johnson wrote to the Freedmen's Bureau in March 1867, after failing to locate the five children she had lost under slavery. She finally located three of them, but any chance of discovering the whereabouts of the other two disappeared because the records of the slave trader who purchased them burned during the war. Despite such obstacles, thousands of slave children were reunited with their parents in the 1870s.

Husbands and wives, or those who considered themselves as such despite the absence of legal marriage under slavery, also searched for each other. Those who lived on nearby plantations could now live together for the first time. Those whose spouse had been sold to distant plantations had a more difficult time. They wrote (or had letters written on their behalf) to relatives and friends who had been sold with their mate; sought assistance from

Freedpeople Petition for Land, 1865

A committee of former slaves in Edisto Island, South Carolina, wrote President Johnson requesting that they be allowed to purchase land promised them by the government during the Civil War. The president intended to restore the properties to the former rebel landholders. The spelling and punctuation is in the original.

Document 14.1

Edisto Island S.C. Oct 28th 1865.

... Here is where secession was born and Nurtured Here is were we have toiled nearly all Our lives as slaves and were treated like dumb Driven cattle, This is our home, we have made These lands what they are. we were the only true and Loyal people that were found in posession of these Lands. we have been always ready to strike for Liberty and humanity yea to fight if needs be To preserve this glorious union. Shall not we who Are freedman and have been always true to this Union have the same rights as are enjoyed by Others? Have we broken any Law of these United States? Have we forfieted our rights of property In Land?– If not then! are not our rights as A free people and good citizens of these United States To be considered before the rights of those who were Found in rebellion against this good and just Government.

We have been encouraged by government to take up these lands in small tracts, receiving Certificates of the same– we have thus far Taken Sixteen thousand (16000) acres of Land here on This Island. We are ready to pay for this land When Government calls for it and now after What has been done will the good and just government take from us all this right and make us Subject to the will of those who have cheated and Oppressed us for many years God Forbid! We the freedmen of this Island and of the State of South Carolina–Do therefore petition to you as the President of these United States, that some provisions be made by which Every colored man can purchase land. and Hold it as his own. ...

In behalf of the Freedmen Committee
Henry Bram. Ishmael. Moultrie. yates. Sampson.

Source: Henry Bram et al. to the President of these United States, 28 Oct. 1865, filed as P-27 1865, Letters Received, series 15, Washington Headquarters, Bureau of Refugees, Freedmen, & Abandoned Lands, Record Group 105, National Archives.

Why do the freedpeople believe their request justified?

Why do they think the former landowners do not deserve the land?

How does this show the importance of land-ownership to them?

Put It in Context

Why was landownership so important to the freed slaves?

Wedding Ceremony in the Cabin Newly freed from slavery, African Americans hold a wedding ceremony in a cabin surrounded by friends and family. This engraving appeared in the widely read *Frank Leslie's Illustrated Newspaper* on August 19, 1871. Northern periodicals published such illustrations to depict the respectability of emancipated slaves. Mansell/Mansell/The LIFE Picture Collection/ Getty Images

government officials, churches, and even their former masters; and traveled to areas where they thought their spouse might reside.

These searches were complicated by long years of separation and the lack of any legal standing for slave marriages. In 1866 Philip Grey, a Virginia freedman, located his wife, Willie Ann, and their daughter Maria, who had been sold away to Kentucky years before. Willie Ann was eager to reunite with her husband, but in the years since being sold, she had remarried and borne three children. Her second husband had joined the Union army and was killed in battle. When Willie Ann wrote to Philip in April 1866, she explained her new circumstances, concluding: "If you love me you will love my children and you will have to promise me that you will provide for them all as well as if they were your own. . . . I know that I have lived with you and loved you then and love you still."

Most black spouses who found each other sought to legalize their relationship. A superintendent for marriages for the Freedmen's Bureau in northern Virginia reported that he gave out seventy-nine marriage certificates on a single day in May 1866. In another case, four couples went right from the fields to a local schoolhouse, still dressed in their work clothes, where the parson married them.

Of course, some former slaves hoped that freedom would allow them to leave unhappy relationships. Having never been married under the law, couples could simply separate and move on. Complications arose, however, if they had children. In Lake City, Florida, in 1866, a Freedmen's Bureau agent asked his superiors for advice on how to deal with Madison Day and Maria Richards. They refused to legalize the relationship forced on them under slavery, but both sought custody of their three children. As with white couples in the mid-nineteenth century, the father was granted custody on the assumption that he had the best chance of providing for the children financially.

Freedom to Learn.

Seeking land and reuniting families were only two of the many ways that southern blacks proclaimed their freedom. Learning to read and write was another. The desire to learn was all but universal. Slaves had been forbidden to read and write, and with emancipation they pursued what had been denied them. A newly liberated father in Mississippi proclaimed, "If I nebber does nothing more while I live, I shall give my children a chance to go to school, for I considers education [the] next best ting to liberty."

A variety of organizations opened schools for former slaves during the 1860s and 1870s. By 1870 nearly a quarter million blacks were attending one of the 4,300 schools established by the Freedmen's Bureau. Black and white churches and missionary societies sent hundreds of teachers, black and white, into the South to establish schools in former plantation areas. Their attitudes were often paternalistic and the schools were segregated, but the institutions they founded offered important educational resources for African Americans.

Freedmen's Bureau School   This photograph of a one-room Freedmen's Bureau school in North Carolina in the late 1860s shows the large number and diverse ages of students who sought to obtain an education following emancipation. The teachers included white and black northern women sent by missionary and reform organizations as well as southern black women who had already received some education. Granger, NYC

Parents worked hard to keep their children in school during the day. As children gained the rudiments of education, they passed on their knowledge to parents and older siblings whose jobs prevented them from attending school. Still, many adult freedpeople insisted on getting a bit of education for themselves. In New Bern, North Carolina, where many blacks labored until eight o'clock at night, a teacher reported that they then spent at least an hour "in earnest application to study."

Freedmen and freedwomen sought education for a variety of reasons. Some viewed it as a sign of liberation. Others knew that they must be able to read the labor contracts they signed if they were ever to challenge exploitation by whites. Some freedpeople were eager to correspond with relatives, others to read the Bible. Growing numbers hoped to participate in politics, particularly the public meetings organized by blacks in cities across the South. When such gatherings set priorities for the future, the establishment of public schools was high on the list.

Despite the enthusiasm of blacks and the efforts of the federal government and private agencies, schooling remained severely limited throughout the South. A shortage of teachers and of funding kept enrollments low among blacks and whites alike. The isolation of black farm families and the difficulties in eking out a living limited the resources available for education. By 1880, only about a quarter of African Americans were literate.

Freedom to Worship and the Leadership Role of Black Churches.   One of the constant concerns freedpeople expressed was the desire to read the Bible and interpret it for themselves. A few black congregations had existed under slavery, but most slaves were forced to listen to white preachers who claimed that God created slavery.

From the moment of emancipation, freedpeople gathered at churches to celebrate community events. Black Methodist and Baptist congregations spread rapidly across the South following the Civil War. In these churches, African Americans were no longer forced to sit in the back benches or punished for moral infractions defined by white masters. Now blacks invested community resources in their own religious institutions where they filled the pews, hired the preachers, and selected boards of deacons and elders. Churches were the largest structures available to freedpeople in many communities and thus were used by a variety of community organizations. They often served as schools and hosted picnics, dances, weddings, funerals, festivals, and other events that brought blacks together. Church leaders also often served as arbiters of community standards of morality.

In the early years of emancipation black churches also served as important sites for political organizing. Some black ministers worried that political concerns would overwhelm spiritual devotions. Others agreed with the Reverend Charles H. Pearce of Florida, who declared, "A man in this State cannot do his whole duty as a minister except he looks out for the political interests of his people." Whatever the views of ministers, black churches were among the few places where African Americans could express their political views free from white interference.

REVIEW & RELATE

What were freedpeople's highest priorities in the years immediately following the Civil War? Why?

How did freedpeople define freedom? What steps did they take to make freedom real for themselves and their children?

National Reconstruction

Presidents Abraham Lincoln and Andrew Johnson viewed Reconstruction as a process of national reconciliation. They sketched out terms by which the former Confederate states could reclaim their political representation in the nation without serious penalties. Congressional Republicans, however, had a more thoroughgoing reconstruction in mind. Like many African Americans, Republican congressional leaders expected the South to extend constitutional rights to the freedmen and to provide them with the political and economic resources to sustain their freedom. Over the next decade, these competing visions of Reconstruction played out in a hard-fought and tumultuous battle over the meaning of the South's defeat and the emancipation of blacks.

Abraham Lincoln Plans for Reunification. In December 1863, President Lincoln issued the **Proclamation of Amnesty and Reconstruction**, which asked relatively little of the southern states. Lincoln declared that defeated states would have to accept the abolition of slavery, but then new governments could be formed when 10 percent of those eligible to vote in 1860 (which in practice meant white southern men but not blacks) swore an oath of allegiance to the United States. Lincoln's plan granted amnesty to all but the highest-ranking Confederate officials, and the restored voters in each state would elect members to a constitutional convention and representatives to take their seats in Congress. In the next year and a half, Arkansas, Louisiana, and Tennessee reestablished their governments under Lincoln's "Ten Percent Plan."

Republicans in Congress had other ideas. Radical Republicans argued that the Confederate states should be treated as "conquered provinces" subject to congressional supervision. In 1864 Congress passed the Wade-Davis bill, which established much higher barriers for readmission to the Union than did Lincoln's plan. For instance, the Wade-Davis bill substituted 50 percent of voters for the president's 10 percent requirement. Lincoln put a stop to this harsher proposal by using a pocket veto—refusing to sign it within ten days of Congress's adjournment.

Although Lincoln and congressional Republicans disagreed about many aspects of postwar policy, Lincoln was flexible, and his actions mirrored his desire both to heal the Union and to help southern blacks. For example, the president supported the Thirteenth Amendment, abolishing slavery, which passed Congress in January 1865 and was sent to the states for ratification. In March 1865, Lincoln signed the law to create the Freedmen's Bureau. That same month, the president expressed his sincere wish for reconciliation between the North and the South. "With malice toward none, with charity for all," Lincoln declared in his second inaugural address, "let us strive on to finish the work . . . to bind up the nation's wounds." Lincoln would not, however, have the opportunity to implement his balanced approach to Reconstruction. When he was assassinated in April 1865, it fell to Andrew Johnson, a very different sort of politician, to lead the country through the process of reintegration.

Andrew Johnson and Presidential Reconstruction. The nation needed a president who could transmit northern desires to the South with clarity and conviction and ensure that they were carried out. Instead, the nation got a president who substituted his own aims for those of the North, refused to engage in meaningful compromise, and misled the South into believing that he could achieve restoration quickly. In the 1864 election, Lincoln chose Johnson, a southern Democrat, as his running mate in a thinly veiled effort to attract border-state voters. The vice presidency was normally an inconsequential role, so it mattered little to Lincoln that Johnson was out of step with many Republican Party positions.

As president, however, Johnson's views took on profound importance. Born into rural poverty, Johnson had no sympathy for the southern aristocracy. Yet he had been a slave owner, so his political opposition to slavery was not rooted in moral convictions. Instead, it sprang from the belief that slavery gave plantation owners inordinate power and wealth, which came at the expense of the majority of white Southerners, who owned no slaves. Johnson saw emancipation as a means to "break down an odious and dangerous [planter] aristocracy," not to empower blacks. Consequently, he was unconcerned with the fate of African Americans in the postwar South. Six months after taking office, President Johnson rescinded the wartime order to distribute confiscated land to freedpeople in the Sea Islands. He saw no reason to punish the Confederacy's leaders, because he believed that the end of slavery would doom the southern aristocracy. He hoped to bring the South back into the Union as quickly as possible and then let Southerners take care of their own affairs.

Johnson's views, combined with a lack of political savvy and skill, ensured his inability to work constructively with congressional Republicans, even the moderates who constituted the majority. Moderate Republicans shared the prevalent belief of their time that blacks were inferior to whites, but they argued that the federal government needed to protect newly emancipated slaves. Senator Lyman Trumbull of Illinois, for example, warned that without national legislation, ex-slaves would "be tyrannized over, abused, and virtually reenslaved." The moderates expected southern states, where 90 percent of African Americans lived, to extend basic civil rights to the freedpeople, including equal protection, due process of law, and the right to work and hold property.

Nearly all Republicans shared these positions, but the Radical wing of the party wanted to go further. Led by Senator Charles Sumner of Massachusetts and Congressman Thaddeus Stevens of Pennsylvania, this small but influential group advocated suffrage, or voting rights, for African American men as well as the redistribution of southern plantation lands to freed slaves. Stevens called on the federal government to provide freedpeople "a homestead of forty acres of land," which would give them some measure of autonomy. These efforts failed, and the Republican Party proved unable to pass a comprehensive land distribution program that enabled freed blacks to gain economic independence. Nonetheless, whatever disagreements between Radicals and moderates, all Republicans believed that Congress should have a strong voice in determining the fate of the former Confederate states. From May to December 1865, with Congress out of session, they waited to see what Johnson's restoration plan would produce, ready to assert themselves if his policies deviated too much from their own.

At first, it seemed as if Johnson would proceed as they hoped. He appointed provisional governors to convene new state constitutional conventions and urged these conventions to ratify the Thirteenth Amendment, abolishing slavery, and revoke the states' ordinances of secession. He also allowed the majority of white Southerners to obtain amnesty and a pardon by swearing their loyalty to the U.S. Constitution, but he required those who had held more than $20,000 of taxable property—the members of the southern aristocracy—to petition him for a special pardon to restore their rights. Republicans

Mourning at Stonewall Jackson's Gravesite,1866
Many Northerners were concerned that the defeat of the Confederacy did not lessen white Southerners' devotion to the "Lost Cause" or the heroism of soldiers who fought to maintain a society based on the domination of African Americans. Women, who led the efforts to memorialize Confederate soldiers, are shown at the gravesite of General Stonewall Jackson in Lexington, Virginia. Virginia Military Institute Archives

expected him to be harsh in dealing with his former political foes. Instead, Johnson relished the reversal of roles that put members of the southern elite at his mercy. As the once prominent petitioners paraded before him, the president granted almost all of their requests for pardons.

By the time Congress convened in December 1865, Johnson was satisfied that the southern states had fulfilled his requirements for restoration. Moderate and Radical Republicans disagreed, seeing few signs of change or contrition in the South. Mississippi, for example, rejected ratification of the Thirteenth Amendment. As a result of Johnson's liberal pardon policy, many former leaders of the Confederacy won election to state constitutional conventions and to Congress. Indeed, Georgians elected Confederate vice president Alexander H. Stephens to the U.S. Senate.

Far from providing freedpeople with basic civil rights, the southern states passed a variety of **black codes** intended to reduce African Americans to a condition as close to slavery as possible. Some laws prohibited blacks from bearing arms; others outlawed intermarriage and excluded blacks from serving on juries. The codes also made it difficult for blacks to leave plantations unless they proved they could support themselves. Laws like this were designed to ensure that white landowners had a supply of cheap black labor despite slavery's abolition.

Northerners viewed this situation with alarm. In their eyes, the postwar South looked very similar to the Old South, with a few cosmetic adjustments. If the black codes prevailed, one Republican proclaimed, "then I demand to know of what practical value is the amendment abolishing slavery?" Others wondered what their wartime sacrifices meant if the South admitted no mistakes, was led by the same people, and continued to oppress its black inhabitants. **See Document Project 14: Testing and Contesting Freedom, page 476.**

Johnson and Congressional Resistance.

Faced with growing opposition in the North, Johnson stubbornly held his ground. He insisted that the southern states had followed his plan and were entitled to resume their representation in Congress. Republicans objected, and in December 1865 they barred the admission of southern lawmakers. But Johnson refused to compromise. In January 1866, the president rejected a bill passed by Congress to extend the life of the Freedmen's Bureau for two years. A few months later, he vetoed the Civil Rights Act, which Congress had passed to protect freedpeople from the restrictions placed on them by the black codes. These bills represented a consensus among moderate and Radical Republicans on the federal government's responsibility toward former slaves.

Johnson justified his vetoes on both constitutional and personal grounds. He and other Democrats contended that so long as Congress refused to admit southern representatives, it could not legally pass laws affecting the South. The president also condemned the Freedmen's Bureau bill because it infringed on the right of states to handle internal affairs such as education and economic policies. Johnson's vetoes exposed his racism and his lifelong belief that the evil of slavery lay in the harm it did to poor whites, not to enslaved blacks. Johnson argued that the bills he vetoed discriminated against whites, who would receive no benefits under them, and thus put whites at a disadvantage with blacks who received government assistance. Johnson's private secretary reported in his diary, "The president has at times exhibited a morbid distress and feeling against the Negroes."

Johnson's actions united moderates and Radicals against him. In April 1866, Congress repassed both the Freedmen's Bureau extension and Civil Rights Act over the president's vetoes. In June, lawmakers adopted the **Fourteenth Amendment**, which incorporated many of the provisions of the Civil Rights Act, and submitted it to the states for ratification (see Appendix). Reflecting its confrontational dealings with the president, Congress wanted to ensure more permanent protection for African Americans than simple legislation could provide. Lawmakers also wanted to act quickly, as the situation in the South seemed to be deteriorating rapidly. In May 1866, a race riot had broken out in Memphis, Tennessee. For a day and a half, white mobs, egged on by local police, went on a rampage, during which they terrorized blacks and burned their homes and churches. "The late riots in our city," the white editor of a Memphis newspaper asserted, "have satisfied all of one thing, that the *southern man* will not be ruled by the *negro*."

> **Explore ▶**
>
> See Documents 14.2 and 14.3 for two perspectives on the Freedmen's Bureau.

The Fourteenth Amendment defined citizenship to include African Americans, thereby nullifying the ruling in the *Dred Scott* case of 1857, which declared that blacks were not citizens. It extended equal protection and due process of law to all persons, not only citizens. The amendment repudiated Confederate debts, which some state governments had refused to do, and it barred Confederate officeholders from holding elective office unless Congress removed this provision by a two-thirds vote. Although most Republicans were upset with Johnson's behavior, at this point they were not willing to embrace the Radical position entirely. Rather than granting the right to vote to black males at least twenty-one years of age, the Fourteenth Amendment gave the states the option of excluding blacks and accepting a reduction in congressional representation if they did so.

Johnson remained inflexible. Instead of counseling the southern states to accept the Fourteenth Amendment, which would have sped up their readmission to the Union, he encouraged them to reject it. In the fall of 1866, Johnson decided to take his case directly to northern voters before the midterm congressional elections. Campaigning for

Memphis Race Riot   A skirmish between white policemen and black Union veterans on May 1, 1866, resulted in three days of rioting by white mobs that attacked the black community of Memphis, Tennessee. Before federal troops restored peace, numerous women had been raped, and forty-six African Americans and two whites had been killed. This illustration from *Harper's Weekly* depicts the carnage.   Granger, NYC

candidates who shared his views, he embarked on a swing through the Midwest. Out of touch with northern opinion, Johnson attacked Republican lawmakers and engaged in shouting matches with audiences. On election day, Republicans increased their majorities in Congress and now controlled two-thirds of the seats, providing them with greater power to override presidential vetoes.

Congressional Reconstruction.

When the Fortieth Congress convened in 1867, Republican lawmakers charted a new course for Reconstruction. With moderates and Radicals united against the president, Congress intended to force the former Confederate states not only to protect the basic civil rights of African Americans but also to grant them the vote. Moderates now agreed with Radicals that unless blacks had access to the ballot, they would not be able to sustain their freedom. Extending the suffrage to African Americans also aided the fortunes of the Republican Party in the South by adding significant numbers of new voters. By the end of March, Congress enacted three Military Reconstruction Acts. Together they divided ten southern states into five military districts, each under the supervision of a Union general (Map 14.1). The male voters of each state, regardless of race, were to elect delegates to a constitutional convention; only former Confederate officials were disfranchised. The conventions were required to draft constitutions that guaranteed black suffrage and ratified the Fourteenth Amendment. Within a year, North Carolina, South Carolina, Florida, Alabama, Louisiana, and Arkansas had fulfilled these obligations and reentered the Union.

Debating the Freedmen's Bureau

From the start, the Freedmen's Bureau generated controversy. To its Republican supporters, it helped southern blacks make the transition from slavery to freedom. For most white Southerners and many northern Democrats, however, the bureau was little more than an expensive social welfare program that rewarded idleness in blacks. Both points of view are represented in the following documents. In a report written to the Congressional Joint Committee on Reconstruction, Colonel Eliphalet Whittlesey, the assistant head of the Freedmen's Bureau in North Carolina, outlined the bureau's initial accomplishments. The anti-bureau cartoon reprinted here was created during the height of the conflict over Reconstruction between the Republican Congress and President Andrew Johnson; it was intended to support the election of a Democratic candidate for governor of Pennsylvania, an ally of Johnson.

Document 14.2

Colonel Eliphalet Whittlesey | Report on the Freedmen's Bureau, 1865

All officers of the bureau are instructed—

To aid the destitute, yet in such a way as not to encourage dependence.

To protect freedmen from injustice.

To assist freedmen in obtaining employment and fair wages for their labor.

To encourage education, intellectual and moral. . . .

. . . [W]e have in our camps at Roanoke Island and Newbern, many women and children, families of soldiers who have died in the service, and refugees from the interior during the war, for whom permanent provision must be made. . . . The reports prepared by Surgeon Hogan will show the condition of freedmen hospitals. In the early part of the summer much suffering and mortality occurred for want of medical attendance and supplies. This evil is now being remedied by the employment of surgeons by contract. . . .

Contrary to the fears and predictions of many, the great mass of colored people have remained quietly at work upon the plantations of their former masters during the entire summer. The crowds seen about the towns in the early part of the season had followed in the wake of the Union army, to escape from slavery. After hostilities ceased these refugees returned to their homes, so that but few vagrants can now be found. In truth, a much larger amount of vagrancy exists among the whites than among the blacks. It is the almost uniform report of officers of the bureau that freedmen are industrious.

The report is confirmed by the fact that out of a colored population of nearly 350,000 in the State, only about 5,000 are now receiving support from the government. Probably some others are receiving aid from kind-hearted men who have enjoyed the benefit of their services from childhood. To the general quiet and industry of this people there can be no doubt that the efforts of the bureau have contributed greatly.

Source: *The Reports of the Committees of the House of Representatives Made during the First Session, Thirty-ninth Congress, 1865–1866* (Washington, DC: Government Printing Office, 1866), 186–87, 189.

Document 14.3

Democratic Flier Opposing the Freedmen's Bureau Bill, 1866

Library of Congress, 3a41094

Interpret the Evidence

1. According to Colonel Whittlesey, what needs does the Freedmen's Bureau address? How does he measure the bureau's success?

2. Why might this portrayal of the Freedmen's Bureau have appealed to some whites. North and South? How would Whittlesey and other bureau supporters have responded?

Put It in Context

How did prevailing racial assumptions shape both the cartoon and the report?

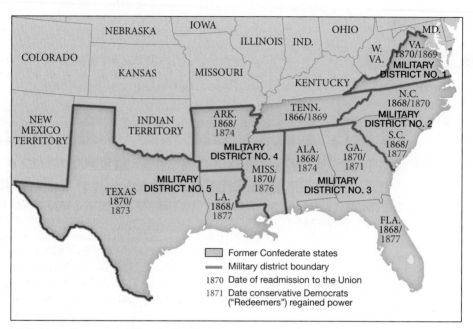

MAP 14.1 Reconstruction in the South

In 1867 Congress enacted legislation dividing the former Confederate states into five military districts. All the states were readmitted to the Union by 1870, and white conservative Democrats (Redeemers) had replaced Republicans in most states by 1875. Only in Florida, Louisiana, and South Carolina did federal troops remain until 1877.

Having ensured congressional Reconstruction in the South, Republican lawmakers turned their attention to disciplining the president. Johnson continued to resist their policies and used his power as commander in chief to order generals in the military districts to soften the intent of congressional Reconstruction. In response, Congress passed the Command of the Army Act in 1867, which required the president to issue all orders to army commanders in the field through the General of the Army in Washington, D.C., Ulysses S. Grant. The Radicals knew they could count on Grant to carry out their policies. Even more threatening to presidential power, Congress passed the **Tenure of Office Act**, which prevented Johnson from firing cabinet officers sympathetic to congressional Reconstruction. This measure barred the chief executive from removing from office any appointee that the Senate had ratified previously without returning to the Senate for approval.

Convinced that the new law was unconstitutional and outraged at the effort to limit his power, the quick-tempered Johnson chose to confront the Radical Republicans directly rather than seek a way around a congressional showdown. In February 1868, Johnson fired Secretary of War Edwin Stanton, a Lincoln appointee and a Radical sympathizer, without Senate approval. In response, congressional Radicals prepared articles of impeachment.

In late February, the House voted 126 to 47 to impeach Johnson, the first president ever to be impeached, or charged with unlawful activity. The case then went to trial in the Senate, where the chief justice of the United States presided and a two-thirds vote was necessary for conviction and removal from office. After a six-week hearing, the Senate fell one vote short of convicting Johnson. Most crucial for Johnson's fate were the votes of seven moderate Republicans who refused to find the president guilty of violating his oath to uphold the Constitution. They were convinced that Johnson's actions were insufficient to merit the enormous step of removing a president from office. Although Johnson remained in office, Congress effectively ended his power to shape Reconstruction policy.

The Republicans had restrained Johnson, and in 1868 they won back the presidency. Ulysses S. Grant, the popular Civil War general, ran against Horatio Seymour, the Democratic governor of New York. Although an ally of the Radical Republicans, Grant called for reconciliation with the South. He easily defeated Seymour, winning nearly 53 percent of the popular vote and 73 percent of the electoral vote.

The Struggle for Universal Suffrage.

In February 1869, Congress passed the **Fifteenth Amendment** to protect black male suffrage, which had initially been guaranteed by the Military Reconstruction Acts. A compromise between moderate and Radical Republicans, the amendment prohibited voting discrimination based on race, but it did not deny states the power to impose qualifications based on literacy, payment of taxes, moral character, or any other standard that did not directly relate to race. Subsequently, the wording of the amendment provided loopholes for white leaders to disfranchise African Americans. The amendment did, however, cover the entire nation, including the North, where states like Connecticut, Kansas, Michigan, New York, Ohio, and Wisconsin still excluded blacks from voting.

The Fifteenth Amendment sparked serious conflicts not only within the South but also among old abolitionist allies. The American Anti-Slavery Society disbanded with emancipation, but many members believed that important work remained to be done to guarantee the rights of freedpeople. They formed the **American Equal Rights Association** immediately following the war, but members divided over the Fifteenth Amendment.

Frances Ellen Watkins Harper Born a free person of color in Baltimore, Frances Ellen Watkins Harper distinguished herself as a poet, a teacher, and an abolitionist. After the Civil War, she became a staunch advocate of women's suffrage and a supporter of the Fifteenth Amendment, which set her at odds with the suffragists Susan B. Anthony and Elizabeth Cady Stanton. Documenting the American South, The University of North Carolina at Chapel Hill http://docsouth.unc.edu/neh/brownhal/ill22.html

Some women's rights advocates, including Elizabeth Cady Stanton and Susan B. Anthony, had earlier objected to the Fourteenth Amendment because it inserted the word *male* into the Constitution for the first time when describing citizens. Although they had supported abolition before the war, Stanton and Anthony worried that postwar policies intended to enhance the rights of southern black men would further limit the rights of women. Some African American activists also voiced concern. At a meeting of the Equal Rights Association in 1867, Sojourner Truth noted, "There is quite a stir about colored men getting their rights, but not a word about colored women."

The Fifteenth Amendment ignored women. At the 1869 meeting of the Equal Rights Association, differences over the measure erupted into open conflict. Stanton and Anthony denounced suffrage for black men only, and Stanton now supported her position on racial grounds. She claimed that the "dregs of China, Germany, England, Ireland, and Africa" were degrading the U.S. polity and argued that white, educated women should certainly have the same rights as immigrant and African American men. Black and white supporters of the Fifteenth Amendment, including Frances Ellen Watkins Harper, Wendell Phillips, Abby Kelley, and Frederick Douglass, denounced Stanton's bigotry. Believing that southern black men urgently needed suffrage to protect their newly won freedom, they argued that ratification of the Fifteenth Amendment would speed progress toward the enfranchisement of black and white women.

This conflict led to the formation of competing organizations committed to women's suffrage. The National Woman Suffrage Association, established by Stanton and Anthony, allowed only women as members and opposed ratification of the Fifteenth Amendment. The American Woman Suffrage Association, which attracted the support of women and men, white and black, supported ratification. Less than a year later, in the spring of 1870, the Fifteenth Amendment was ratified and went into effect.

Since the amendment did not grant the vote to either white or black women, women suffragists attempted to use the Fourteenth Amendment to achieve their goal. In 1875 Virginia Minor, who had been denied the ballot in Missouri, argued that the right to vote was one of the "privileges and immunities" granted to all citizens under the Fourteenth Amendment. In *Minor v. Happersatt*, the Supreme Court ruled against her, and women were denied national suffrage for decades thereafter.

REVIEW & RELATE

- What was President Johnson's plan for reconstruction? How were his views out of step with those of most Republicans?

- What characterized congressional Reconstruction? What priorities were reflected in congressional Reconstruction legislation?

Remaking the **South**

With President Johnson's power effectively curtailed, reconstruction of the South moved quickly. New state legislatures, ruled by a coalition of southern whites and blacks and white northern migrants, enacted political, economic, and social reforms that improved the overall quality of life in the South. Despite these changes, many black and white Southerners barely eked out a living under the planter-dominated share-cropping system. Moreover, the biracial Reconstruction governments lasted a relatively short time, as conservative whites used a variety of tactics, including terror and race baiting, to defeat their opponents at the polls.

Whites Reconstruct the South.

During the first years of congressional Reconstruction, two groups of whites occupied the majority of elective offices in the South. A significant number of native-born Southerners joined Republicans in forging postwar constitutions and governments. Before the war, some had belonged to the Whig Party and opposed secession from the Union. Western sections of Alabama, Georgia, North Carolina, and Tennessee had demonstrated a fiercely independent strain, and many residents had remained loyal to the Union. Small merchants and farmers who detested large plantation owners also threw in their lot with the Republicans. Even a few ex-Confederates, such as General James A. Longstreet, decided that the South must change and allied with the Republicans. The majority of whites who continued to support the Democratic Party viewed these whites as traitors. They showed their distaste by calling them **scalawags**, an unflattering term meaning "scoundrels."

At the same time, Northerners came south to support Republican Reconstruction. They had varied reasons for making the journey, but most considered the South a new frontier to be conquered culturally, politically, and economically. Some—white and black—had served in the Union army during the war, liked what they saw of the region, and decided to settle there. Some of both races came to provide education and assist the freedpeople in adjusting to their new lives. As a relatively underdeveloped area, the South also beckoned fortune seekers and adventurers who saw opportunities to get rich. Southern Democrats denounced such northern interlopers, particularly whites, as **carpetbaggers**, suggesting that they invaded the region with all their possessions in a satchel, seeking to plunder it and then leave. This characterization applied to some, but it did not accurately describe the motivations of most transplanted Northerners.

While Northerners did seek economic opportunity, they were acting as Americans always had in settling new frontiers and pursuing dreams of success. In dismissing them as carpetbaggers, their political enemies employed a double standard because they did not apply this demeaning label to those who traveled west in search of economic opportunity at the expense of Indians and Mexicans settled there. Much of the negative feelings directed toward white carpetbaggers resulted primarily from their attempts to ally with African Americans in reshaping the South.

Black Political Participation and Economic Opportunities.

Still, the primary targets of southern white hostility were African Americans who attempted to exercise their hard-won freedom. Blacks constituted a majority of voters in five states—Alabama, Florida, South Carolina, Mississippi, and Louisiana—while in Georgia, North Carolina, Texas, and Virginia they fell short of a majority. They did not use their ballots to impose black rule on the South, as many white Southerners feared. Only in South Carolina did African Americans control the state legislature, and in no state did they manage to elect a governor. Nevertheless, for the first time in American history, blacks won a wide variety of elected positions. More than six hundred blacks served in state legislatures; another sixteen, including Jefferson Long, held seats in the U.S. House of Representatives; and two from Mississippi were chosen to serve in the U.S. Senate.

Former slaves showed enthusiasm for politics in other ways, too. African Americans considered politics a community responsibility, and in addition to casting ballots, they held rallies and mass meetings to discuss issues and choose candidates. Although they could not vote, women attended these gatherings and helped influence their outcome. Covering a Republican convention in Richmond in October 1867, held in the First African Baptist Church, the *New York Times* reported that "the entire colored population of Richmond" attended. In addition, freedpeople formed mutual aid associations to promote education, economic advancement, and social welfare programs, all of which they saw as deeply intertwined with politics.

Southern blacks also bolstered their freedom by building alliances with sympathetic whites. These interracial political coalitions produced considerable reform in the South. They created the first public school systems; provided funds for social services, such as poor relief and state hospitals; upgraded prisons; and rebuilt the South's transportation system. Moreover, the state constitutions that the Republicans wrote brought a greater measure of political democracy and equality to the South by extending suffrage to poor white men as well as black men. Some states allowed married women greater control over their property and liberalized the criminal justice system. In effect, these Reconstruction governments brought the South into the nineteenth century.

Obtaining political representation was one way in which African Americans defined freedom. Economic independence constituted a second. Without government-sponsored land redistribution, however, the options for southern blacks remained limited. Lacking capital to purchase farms, most entered into various forms of tenant contracts with large landowners. **Sharecropping** proved the most common arrangement. Blacks and poor whites became sharecroppers for much the same reasons. They received tools and supplies from landowners and farmed their own plots of land on the plantation. In exchange, sharecroppers turned over a portion of their harvest to the owner and kept the rest for themselves.

Explore ▶

See Document 14.4 for an example of a sharecropping agreement.

The benefits of sharecropping proved more valuable to black farmers in theory than in practice. To tide them over during the growing season, croppers had to purchase household provisions on credit from a local merchant, who was often also their landlord. At the mercy of store owners who kept the books and charged high interest rates, tenants usually found themselves in considerable debt at the end of the year. To satisfy the debt, merchants devised a crop lien system in which tenants pledged a portion of their yearly crop to satisfy what they owed. Falling prices for agricultural crops in this period ensured that most indebted tenants did not receive sufficient return on their produce to get out of debt and thus remained bound to their landlords. For many African Americans, sharecropping turned into a form of virtual slavery.

The picture for black farmers was not all bleak, however. About 20 percent of black farmers managed to buy their own land. Through careful management and extremely hard work, black families planted gardens for household consumption and raised chickens for eggs and food. Despite its pitfalls, sharecropping provided a limited measure of labor independence and allowed some blacks to accumulate small amounts of cash.

Following the war's devastation, many of the South's white small farmers, known as yeomen, also fell into sharecropping. Meanwhile, many planters' sons abandoned farming and became lawyers, bankers, and merchants. Despite these changes, one thing remained

SOLO ANALYSIS

Sharecropping Agreement, 1870

Because Congress did not generally provide freedpeople with land, African Americans lacked the capital to start their own farms. At the same time, plantation owners needed labor to plant and harvest their crops for market. Out of mutual necessity, white plantation owners entered into sharecropping contracts with blacks to work their farms in exchange for a portion of the crop, such as the following contract between Willis P. Bocock and several of his former slaves. Bocock owned Waldwick Plantation in Marengo County, Alabama.

Document 14.4

Contract made the 3rd day of January in the year 1870 between us the free people who have signed this paper of one part, and our employer, Willis P. Bocock, of the other part. . . . We are to furnish the necessary labor . . . and are to have all proper work done, ditching, fencing, repairing, etc., as well as cultivating and saving the crops of all kinds, so as to put and keep the land we occupy and tend in good order for cropping, and to make a good crop ourselves; and to do our fair share of job work about the place. . . . We are to be responsible for the good conduct of ourselves, our hands, and families, and agree that all shall be respectful to employer, owners, and manager, honest, industrious, and careful about every thing . . . and then our employer agrees that he and his manager shall treat us kindly, and help us to study our interest and do our duty. If any hand or family proves to be of bad character, or dishonest, or lazy, or disobedient, or any way unsuitable our employer or manager has the right, and we have the right, to have such turned off. . . .

For the labor and services of ourselves and hands rendered as above stated, we are to have one third part of all the crops, or their net-proceeds, made and secured, or prepared for market by our force. . . .

We are to be furnished by our employer through his manager with provisions if we call for them . . . to be charged to us at fair market prices.

And whatever may be due by us, or our hands to our employer for provisions or any thing else, during the year, is to be a lien on our share of the crops, and is to be retained by him out of the same before we receive our part.

Source: Waldwick Plantation Records, 1834–1971, LPR174, box 1, folder 9, Alabama Department of Archives and History.

Interpret the Evidence

1. What did Bocock seek to gain from his workforce?
2. How might putting a lien on crops for debts owed create difficulties for the black farmer?

Put It in Context

Why would free blacks and poor whites be willing to enter into such a contract?

the same: White elites ruled over blacks and poor whites, and they kept these two economically exploited groups from uniting by fanning the flames of racial prejudice.

Economic hardship and racial bigotry drove many blacks to leave the South. In 1879 former slaves, known as **Exodusters**, pooled their resources to create land companies and purchase property in Kansas on which to settle. They encouraged an exodus of some 25,000 African Americans from the South. Kansas was ruled by the Republican Party and

Exodusters This photograph of two black couples standing on their homestead was taken around 1880 in Nicodemus, Kansas. These settlers, known as Exodusters, had migrated to north-west Kansas following the end of Reconstruction. They sought economic opportunity free from the racial repression sweeping the South. Library of Congress, HABS KANS, 33-NICO, 1-6

had been home to the great antislavery martyr John Brown. As one hopeful freedman from Louisiana wrote to the Kansas governor in 1879, "I am anxious to reach your state . . . because of the sacredness of her soil washed in the blood of humanitarians for the cause of black freedom." Poor-quality land and unpredictable weather often made farming on the Great Plains hard and unrewarding. Nevertheless, for many black migrants, the chance to own their own land and escape the oppression of the South was worth the hardships. In 1880 the census counted 40,000 blacks living in Kansas.

White Resistance to Congressional Reconstruction.

Despite the Republican record of accomplishment during Reconstruction, white Southerners did not accept its legitimacy. They accused interracial governments of conducting a spending spree that raised taxes and encouraged corruption. Indeed, taxes did rise significantly, but mainly because legislatures funded much-needed educational and social services. Corruption on building projects and railroad construction was common during this time. Still, it is unfair to single out Reconstruction governments and especially black legislators as inherently depraved, as their Democratic opponents acted the same way when given the opportunity. Economic scandals were part of American life after the Civil War. As enormous business opportunities arose in the postwar years, many economic and political leaders made unlawful deals to enrich themselves. Furthermore, southern opponents of Reconstruction exaggerated its harshness. In contrast to revolutions and civil wars in other countries, only one rebel was executed for war crimes (the commandant of Andersonville Prison in Georgia); only one high-ranking official went to prison (Jefferson Davis); no official was forced into exile, though some fled voluntarily; and most rebels regained voting rights and the ability to hold office within seven years after the end of the rebellion.

Most important, these Reconstruction governments had only limited opportunities to transform the South. By the end of 1870, civilian rule had returned to all of the former Confederate states, and they had reentered the Union. Republican rule did not continue past 1870 in Virginia, North Carolina, and Tennessee and did not extend beyond 1871 in Georgia and 1873 in Texas. In 1874 Democrats deposed Republicans in Arkansas and Alabama; two years later, Democrats triumphed in Mississippi. In only three states—Louisiana, Florida, and South Carolina—did Reconstruction last until 1877.

The Democrats who replaced Republicans trumpeted their victories as bringing "redemption" to the South. Of course, these so-called **Redeemers** were referring to the white South. For black Republicans and their white allies, redemption meant defeat. Democratic victories came at the ballot boxes, but violence, intimidation, and fraud paved the way. In 1865 in Pulaski, Tennessee, General Nathan Bedford Forrest organized Confederate veterans into a social club called the **Knights of the Ku Klux Klan (KKK)**. Spreading

Visit of the Ku Klux Klan   This 1872 wood engraving by the noted magazine illustrator Frank Bellew appeared at the height of Ku Klux Klan violence against freed blacks in the South. This image depicts a black family seemingly secure in their home in the evening while masked Klansmen stand in their doorway ready to attack with rifles. Library of Congress, 3c27756

throughout the South, its followers donned robes and masks to hide their identities and terrify their victims. Gun-wielding Ku Kluxers rode on horseback to the homes and churches of black and white Republicans to keep them from voting. When threats did not work, they beat and murdered their victims. In 1871, for example, 150 African Americans were killed in Jackson County in the Florida Panhandle. A black clergyman lamented, "That is where Satan has his seat." There and elsewhere, many of the individuals targeted had managed to buy property, gain political leadership, or in other ways defy white stereotypes of African American inferiority. Other white supremacist organizations joined the Klan in waging a reign of terror. During the 1875 election in Mississippi, which toppled the Republican government, armed terrorists killed hundreds of Republicans and scared many more away from the polls.

To combat the terror unleashed by the Klan and its allies, Congress passed three **Force Acts** in 1870 and 1871. These measures empowered the president to dispatch officials into the South to supervise elections and prevent voting interference. Directed specifically at the KKK, one law barred secret organizations from using force to violate equal protection of the laws. In 1872 Congress established a joint committee to probe Klan tactics, and its investigations produced thirteen volumes of gripping testimony about the horrors perpetrated by the Klan. Elias Hill, a freedman from South Carolina who had become a Baptist preacher and teacher, was one of those who appeared before Congress. He and his brother lived next door to each other. The Klansmen went first to his brother's house, where, as Hill testified, they "broke open the door and attacked his wife, and I heard her screaming and mourning [moaning]. . . . At last I heard them have [rape] her in the yard." When the Klansmen discovered Elias Hill, they dragged him out of his house and beat, whipped, and threatened to kill him. On the basis of such testimony, the federal government prosecuted some 3,000 Klansmen. Only 600 were convicted, however. As the Klan disbanded in the wake of federal prosecutions, other vigilante organizations arose to take its place.

REVIEW & RELATE

What role did black people play in remaking southern society during Reconstruction?	How did southern whites fight back against Reconstruction? What role did terrorism and political violence play in this effort?

The **Unraveling** of **Reconstruction**

The violence, intimidation, and fraud perpetrated by Redeemers does not fully explain the unraveling of Reconstruction. By the early 1870s most white Northerners had come to believe that they had done more than enough for black Southerners, and it was time to focus on other issues. Growing economic problems intensified this feeling. Many northern whites came to believe that any debt owed to black people for northern complicity in the sin of slavery had been wiped out by the blood shed during the Civil War. Burying and memorializing the Civil War dead emerged as a common concern among white Americans, north and south. White America was once again united, if only in the shared belief that it was time to move on, consigning the issues of slavery and civil rights to history.

The Republican Retreat. Most northern whites shared the racial prejudices of their counterparts in the South. Although they had supported protection of black civil rights and suffrage, they still believed that African Americans were inferior to whites and were horrified by the idea of social integration. They began to sympathize with Southern whites' racist complaints that blacks were not capable of governing honestly and effectively.

In 1872 a group calling themselves Liberal Republicans challenged the reelection of President Grant. Financial scandals had racked the Grant administration. This high-level corruption reflected other get-rich-quick schemes connected to economic speculation and development following the Civil War. Outraged by the rising level of immoral behavior in government and business, Liberal Republicans nominated Horace Greeley, editor of the *New York Tribune*, to run against Grant. They linked government corruption to the expansion of federal power that accompanied Reconstruction and called for the removal of troops from the South and amnesty for all former Confederates. They also campaigned for civil service reform, which would base government employment on a merit system and abolish the "spoils system"—in which the party in power rewarded loyal supporters with political appointments—that had been introduced by Andrew Jackson in the 1820s.

The Democratic Party believed that Liberal Republicans offered the best chance to defeat Grant, and it endorsed Greeley. Despite the scandals that surrounded him, Grant remained popular. Moreover, the main body of Republicans "waved the bloody shirt," reminding northern voters that a ballot cast for the opposition tarnished the memory of brave Union soldiers killed during the war. The president won reelection with an even greater margin than he had four years earlier. Nevertheless, the attacks against Grant foreshadowed the Republican retreat on Reconstruction. Among the Democrats sniping at Grant was Andrew Johnson. Johnson had returned to Tennessee, and in 1874 the state legislature chose the former president to serve in the U.S. Senate. He continued to speak out against the presence of federal troops in the South until his death in 1875.

Congressional and Judicial Retreat. By the time Grant began his second term, Congress was already considering bills to restore officeholding rights to former Confederates who had not yet sworn allegiance to the Union. Black representatives, including Georgia congressman Jefferson Long, as well as some white lawmakers, remained opposed to such measures, but in 1872 Congress removed the penalties placed on former Confederates by the Fourteenth Amendment and permitted nearly all rebel leaders the right to vote and hold office. Two years later, for the first time since the start of the Civil War, the Democrats gained a majority in the House of Representatives and prepared to remove the remaining troops from the South.

Republican leaders also rethought their top priority with economic concerns increasingly replacing racial considerations. In 1873 a financial panic resulting from the collapse of the Northern Pacific Railroad triggered a severe economic depression lasting late into the decade. Tens of thousands of unemployed workers across the country worried more about finding jobs than they did about black civil rights. Businessmen, too, were plagued with widespread bankruptcy. When strikes erupted across the country in 1877, most notably the Great Railway Strike, in which more than half a million workers walked off the job, employers asked the U.S. government to remove troops from the South and dispatch them against strikers in the North and West.

While white Northerners sought ways to extricate themselves from Reconstruction, the Supreme Court weakened enforcement of the civil rights acts. In 1873 the *Slaughterhouse* cases defined the rights that African Americans were entitled to under the Fourteenth Amendment very narrowly. Reflecting the shift from moral to economic concerns, the justices interpreted the amendment as extending greater protection to corporations in conducting business than to blacks. As a result, blacks had to depend on southern state governments to protect their civil rights, the same state authorities that had deprived them of their rights in the first place. In *United States v. Cruikshank* (1876), the high court narrowed the Fourteenth Amendment further, ruling that it protected blacks against abuses only by state officials and agencies, not by private groups such as the Ku Klux Klan. Seven years later, the Court struck down the Civil Rights Act of 1875, which had extended "full and equal treatment" in public accommodations for persons of all races.

The Presidential Compromise of 1876. The presidential election of 1876 set in motion events that officially brought Reconstruction to an end. The Republicans nominated the governor of Ohio, Rutherford B. Hayes, who was chosen partly because he was untainted by the corruption that plagued the Grant administration. The Democrats selected their own anticorruption crusader, Governor Samuel J. Tilden of New York.

The outcome of the election depended on twenty disputed electoral votes, nineteen from the South and one from Oregon. Tilden won 51 percent of the popular vote, but Reconstruction political battles in Florida, Louisiana, and South Carolina put the election up for grabs. In each of these states, the outgoing Republican administration certified Hayes as the winner, while the incoming Democratic regime declared for Tilden.

MAP 14.2   The Election of 1876

The presidential election of 1876 got swept up in Reconstruction politics. Democrats defeated Republicans in Florida, Louisiana, and South Carolina, but both parties claimed the electoral votes for their candidates. A federal electoral commission set up to investigate the twenty disputed votes, including one from Oregon, awarded the votes and the election to the Republican, Rutherford B. Hayes.

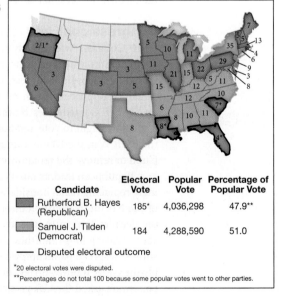

Candidate	Electoral Vote	Popular Vote	Percentage of Popular Vote
Rutherford B. Hayes (Republican)	185*	4,036,298	47.9**
Samuel J. Tilden (Democrat)	184	4,288,590	51.0
—— Disputed electoral outcome			

*20 electoral votes were disputed.
**Percentages do not total 100 because some popular votes went to other parties.

The Constitution assigns Congress the task of counting and certifying the electoral votes submitted by the states. Normally, this is a mere formality, but 1876 was different. Democrats controlled the House, Republicans controlled the Senate, and neither branch would budge on which votes to count. Hayes needed all twenty for victory; Tilden needed only one. To break the logjam, Congress created a fifteen-member Joint Electoral Commission, composed of seven Democrats, seven Republicans, and one independent. Ultimately, a majority voted to count all twenty votes for the Republican Hayes, making him president (Map 14.2).

Still, Congress had to ratify this count, and disgruntled southern Democrats in the Senate threatened a filibuster—unlimited debate—to block certification of Hayes. With the March 4, 1877, date for the presidential inauguration creeping perilously close and no winner officially declared, behind-the-scenes negotiations finally settled the controversy. A series of meetings between Hayes supporters and southern Democrats led to a bargain. According to the agreement, Democrats would support Hayes in exchange for the president appointing a Southerner to his cabinet, withdrawing the last federal troops from the South, and endorsing construction of a transcontinental railroad through the South. This **compromise of 1877** averted a crisis over presidential succession, underscored increased southern Democratic influence within Congress, and marked the end of strong federal protections for African Americans in the South.

REVIEW & RELATE

- Why did northern interest in Reconstruction wane in the 1870s?

- What common values and beliefs among white Americans were reflected in the compromise of 1877?

Conclusion: The **Legacies** of Reconstruction

Reconstruction was, in many ways, profoundly limited. Notwithstanding the efforts of the Freedmen's Bureau, African Americans did not receive the landownership that would have provided them with economic independence and bolstered their freedom from the racist assaults of white Southerners. The civil and political rights that the federal government conferred did not withstand the efforts of former Confederates to disfranchise and deprive the freedpeople of equal rights. The Republican Party shifted its priorities, and Democrats gained enough political power nationally to short-circuit federal intervention, even as numerous problems remained unresolved in the South. Northern support for racial equality did not run very deep, so white Northerners, who shared many of the prejudices of white Southerners, were happy to extricate themselves from further intervention in southern racial matters. Nor was there sufficient support to give women, white or black, the right to vote. Finally, federal courts, with growing concerns over economic rather than social issues, sanctioned Northerners' retreat by providing constitutional legitimacy for abandoning black Southerners and rejecting women's suffrage in court decisions that narrowed the interpretation of the Fourteenth and Fifteenth Amendments.

Despite all of this, Reconstruction did transform the country. As a result of Reconstruction, slavery was abolished and the legal basis for freedom was enshrined in the Constitution. Indeed, blacks exercised a measure of political and economic freedom during Reconstruction that never entirely disappeared over the decades to come. In many areas, freedpeople, exemplified by Congressman Jefferson Franklin Long and many others, asserted what they never could have during slavery—control over their lives, their churches, their labor, their education, and their families. What they could not practice during their own time, their descendants would one day revive through the promises codified in the Fourteenth and Fifteenth Amendments.

African Americans transformed not only themselves; they transformed the nation. The Constitution became much more democratic and egalitarian through inclusion of the Reconstruction amendments. Reconstruction lawmakers took an important step toward making the United States the "more perfect union" that the nation's Founders had pledged to create. Reconstruction established a model for expanding the power of the federal government to resolve domestic crises that lay beyond the abilities of states and ordinary citizens. It remained a powerful legacy for elected officials who dared to invoke it. And Reconstruction transformed the South to its everlasting benefit. It modernized state constitutions, expanded educational and social welfare systems, and unleashed the repressed potential for industrialization and economic development that the preservation of slavery had restrained. Ironically, Reconstruction did as much for white Southerners as it did for black Southerners in liberating them from the past.

TIMELINE OF EVENTS

1863 Lincoln issues Proclamation of Amnesty and Reconstruction

1865 Ku Klux Klan formed

Freedmen's Bureau established

Thirteenth Amendment passed

Lincoln assassinated; Andrew Johnson becomes president

1866 Freedmen's Bureau and Civil Rights Act extended over Johnson's presidential veto

Fourteenth Amendment passed

1867 Military Reconstruction Acts

Command of the Army and Tenure of Office Acts passed

1868 Andrew Johnson impeached

1869 Fifteenth Amendment passed

Women's suffrage movement splits over support of Fifteenth Amendment

1870 250,000 blacks attend schools established by the Freedmen's Bureau

Civilian rule returns to the South

1870–1872 Congress takes steps to curb Ku Klux Klan violence in the South

1873 Financial panic sparks depression

1873–1883 Supreme Court limits rights of African Americans

1875 Civil Rights Act passed

1877 Rutherford B. Hayes becomes president

Reconstruction ends

1879 Black Exodusters migrate from South to Kansas

KEY TERMS

Freedmen's Bureau, *450*

Proclamation of Amnesty and Reconstruction, *455*

black codes, *457*

Fourteenth Amendment, *458*

Tenure of Office Act, *462*

Fifteenth Amendment, *463*

American Equal Rights Association, *463*

scalawags, *465*

carpetbaggers, *465*

sharecropping, *466*

Exodusters, *467*

Redeemers, *469*

Knights of the Ku Klux Klan, *469*

Force Acts, *470*

compromise of 1877, *473*

REVIEW & RELATE

1. What were freedpeople's highest priorities in the years immediately following the Civil War? Why?

2. How did freedpeople define freedom? What steps did they take to make freedom real for themselves and their children?

3. What was President Johnson's plan for reconstruction? How were his views out of step with those of most Republicans?

4. What characterized congressional Reconstruction? What priorities were reflected in congressional Reconstruction legislation?

5. What role did black people play in remaking southern society during Reconstruction?

6. How did southern whites fight back against Reconstruction? What role did terrorism and political violence play in this effort?

7. Why did northern interest in Reconstruction wane in the 1870s?

8. What common values and beliefs among white Americans were reflected in the compromise of 1877?

Testing and Contesting Freedom

Nine months after the Civil War ended in April 1865, twenty-seven states ratified the Thirteenth Amendment, abolishing slavery throughout the United States. Freedom, however, did not guarantee equal rights or the absence of racial discrimination. Immediately following the North's victory, white southern leaders enacted black codes, which aimed to prevent freedpeople from improving their social and economic status (Document 14.5). Although Lincoln's successor, Andrew Johnson, did not support the codes, he did nothing to overturn them. A southern advocate of limited government, Johnson clashed repeatedly with Congress over Reconstruction, vetoing renewal of the Freedmen's Bureau bill and opposing ratification of the Fourteenth Amendment. In 1867 the Republican majority in Congress passed the Military Reconstruction Acts, placing the South under military rule and forcing whites to extend equal political and civil rights to African Americans.

Then in 1870, the ratification of the Fifteenth Amendment extended suffrage to black men. In alliance with white Republicans, blacks won election to a variety of public offices, including seats in local and state governments. These interracial legislatures improved conditions for blacks and whites, providing funds for public education, hospitals, and other social services (Document 14.6). But their opponents succeeded in tarring them with claims of fraud, corruption, wasteful spending, and "Black Rule" (Document 14.8). By the mid-1870s, many white Northerners sought reconciliation rather than continued conflict while southern whites created vigilante groups like the Ku Klux Klan that used violence to intimidate black and white Republicans (Documents 14.9 and 14.7). By 1877, these attacks on black political access crushed southern Republicanism, leaving African Americans struggling to retain the freedoms they had gained during Reconstruction.

As you read the following documents, consider these general questions: How did blacks and whites view freedom? How essential was it for the federal government to supervise the movement from slavery to freedom? Why didn't southern whites accept the extension of civil rights for blacks, if only in a limited way? How did views about Reconstruction change over time?

Document 14.5

Mississippi Black Code, 1865

Southern legislatures created black codes primarily to limit the rights of free blacks after emancipation and return them to a condition as close as possible to slavery. Mississippi was one of the first states to enact a black code. Although its laws did legalize marriage for blacks and allowed them to own property and testify in court, its primary intent was to limit freedpeople's mobility and economic opportunities.

An Act to Confer Civil Rights on Freedmen, and for other Purposes

. . . SECTION 2. All freedmen, free negroes and mulattoes may intermarry with each other, in the same manner and under the same regulations that are provided by law for white persons: Provided, that the clerk of probate shall keep separate records of the same.

SECTION 3. All freedmen, free negroes or mulattoes who do now and have herebefore lived and cohabited together as husband and wife shall be taken and held in law as legally married, and the issue shall be taken and held as legitimate for all purposes; and it shall not be lawful for any freedman, free negro or mulatto to intermarry with any white person; nor for any person to intermarry with any freedman, free negro or mulatto; and any person who shall so intermarry shall be deemed guilty of felony, and on conviction thereof shall be confined in the State penitentiary for life; and those shall be deemed freedmen, free negroes and mulattoes who are of pure negro blood, and those descended from a negro to the third generation, inclusive, though one ancestor in each generation may have been a white person.

SECTION 4. In addition to cases in which freedmen, free negroes and mulattoes are now by law competent witnesses, freedmen, free negroes or mulattoes shall be competent in civil cases, when a party or parties to the suit, either plaintiff or plaintiffs, defendant or defendants; also in cases where freedmen, free negroes and mulattoes is or are either plaintiff or plaintiffs, defendant or defendants. They shall also be competent witnesses in all criminal prosecutions where the crime charged is alleged to have been committed by a white person upon or against the person or property of a freedman, free negro or mulatto. . . .

An Act to Amend the Vagrant Laws of the State . . .

SECTION 2. All freedmen, free negroes and mulattoes in this State, over the age of eighteen years, found on the second Monday in January, 1866, or thereafter, with no lawful employment or business, or found unlawful[ly] assembling themselves together, either in the day or night time, and all white persons assembling themselves with freedmen, free negroes or mulattoes, or usually associating with freedmen, free negroes or mulattoes, on terms of equality, or living in adultery or fornication with a freed woman, freed negro or mulatto, shall be deemed vagrants, and on conviction thereof shall be fined in a sum not exceeding, in the case of a freedman, free negro or mulatto, fifty dollars, and a white man two hundred dollars, and imprisonment at the discretion of the court, the free negro not exceeding ten days, and the white man not exceeding six months. . . .

SECTION 6. The same duties and liabilities existing among white persons of this State shall attach to freedmen, free negroes or mulattoes, to support their indigent families and all colored paupers; and that in order to secure a support for such indigent freedmen, free negroes, or mulattoes, it shall be lawful, and is hereby made the duty of the county police of each county in this State, to levy a poll or capitation tax on each and every freedman, free negro, or mulatto, between the ages of eighteen and sixty years, not to exceed the sum of one dollar annually to each person so taxed, which tax, when collected, shall be paid into the county treasurer's hands, and constitute a fund to be called the Freedman's Pauper Fund, . . . for the maintenance of the poor of the freedmen, free negroes and mulattoes of this State.

Source: *Laws of the State of Mississippi, Passed at a Regular Session of the Mississippi Legislature, Held in the City of Jackson, October, November, and December, 1865* (Jackson, MS, 1866), 82–86, 165–67.

Document 14.6

Richard H. Cain | Federal Aid for Land Purchase, 1868

Richard H. Cain, a free black minister raised in Ohio, went to South Carolina after the war and served as a Republican member of the U.S. House of Representatives for two terms in the 1870s. The following excerpt comes from a speech Cain made in 1868 as a representative to the South Carolina constitutional convention. Cain proposed that the convention petition Congress for a $1 million loan to purchase land that could be resold to freedmen at a reasonable price.

believe the best measure to be adopted is to bring capital to the State, and instead of causing revenge and unpleasantness, I am for even-handed justice. I am for allowing the parties who own lands to bring them into the market and sell them upon such terms as will be satisfactory to both sides. I believe a measure of this kind has a double effect: first, it brings capital, what the people want; second, it puts the people to work; it gives homesteads, what we need; it relieves the Government and takes away

477

its responsibility of feeding the people; it inspires every man with a noble manfulness, and by the thought that he is the possessor of something in the State; it adds also to the revenue of the country. By these means men become interested in the country as they never were before. . . . I will also guarantee that after one year's time, the Freedman's Bureau will not have to give any man having one acre of land anything to eat.

Source: *Proceedings of the South Carolina Constitutional Convention of 1868* (Charleston, SC, 1868), 420–21.

Ellen Parton | Testimony on Klan Violence, 1871

In March 1871, white mobs killed some thirty African Americans in Meridian, Mississippi. Later that month, a joint committee of the United States Congress held hearings on the violence, which included the following testimony by Ellen Parton of Mississippi, a former slave and domestic worker. The Klan suspected that Parton's husband was involved in the Union League, a southern affiliate of the Republican Party. Congress also conducted hearings on the vigilante violence against blacks throughout the South.

Ellen Parton, being sworn, states:

I reside in Meridian; have resided here nine years; occupation, washing and ironing and scouring; Wednesday night was the last night they came to my house; by "they" I mean bodies or companies of men; they came on Monday, Tuesday, and Wednesday. On Monday night they said that they came to do us no harm. On Tuesday night they said they came for the arms; I told them there was none, and they said they would take my word for it. On Wednesday night they came and broke open the wardrobe and trunks, and committed rape upon me; there were eight of them in the house; I do not know how many there were outside; they were white men; there was a light in the house; I was living in Marshal Ware's house; there were three lights burning. Mr. Ware has been one of the policemen of this town. He was concealed at the time they came; they took the claw hammer and broke open the pantry where he was lying; he was concealed in the pantry under some plunder, covered up well; I guess he covered himself up. A man said "here is Marshal's hat, where is Marshal?" I told him "I did not know"; they went then into everything in the house, and broke open the wardrobe; I called upon Mr. Mike Slamon, who was one of the crowd, for protection; I said to him "please protect me tonight, you have known me for a long time." This man covered up his head then; he had a hold of me at this time; Mr. Slamon had an oil-cloth and put it before his face, trying to conceal himself, and the man that had hold of me told me not to call Mr. Slamon's name any more. He then took me in the dining room, and told me that I had to do just what he said: I told him I could do nothing of that sort; that was not my way, and he replied "by God, you have got to," and then threw me down. This man had a black eye, where some one had beaten him; he had a black velvet cap on. After he got through with me he came through the house, and said that he was after the Union Leagues; I yielded to him because he had a pistol drawn; when he took me down he hurt me of course; I yielded to him on that account.

Source: *Report of the Joint Select Committee [of Congress] to Inquire into the Condition of Affairs in the Late Insurrectionary States, Mississippi* (Washington, DC: Government Printing Office, 1872), 1:38–39.

Document 14.8

Thomas Nast | *Colored Rule in a Reconstructed (?) State*, 1874

Thomas Nast began drawing for the popular magazine *Harper's Weekly* in 1859. Nast initially used his illustrations to rouse northern public sentiment for the plight of blacks in the South after the Civil War. By 1874, however, many Northerners had become disillusioned with federal efforts to enforce Reconstruction. Like them, Nash accepted the white southern point of view that "Black Reconstruction" was a recipe for corruption and immorality. Note the figure of Columbia (at the top right), who represents the nation, chastising black lawmakers with a switch. Nast highlights Columbia's message in the caption: "You are Aping the lowest Whites. If you disgrace your Race in this way you had better take Back Seats."

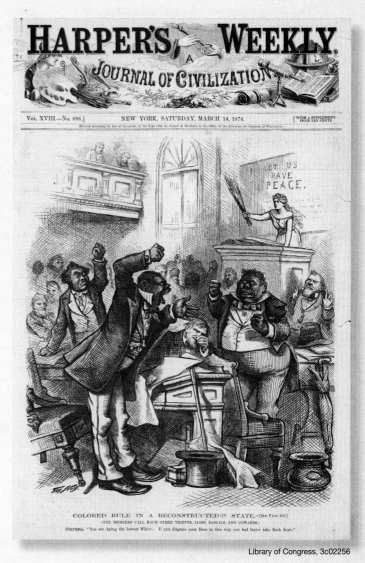

Library of Congress, 3c02256

Document 14.9

What the Centennial Ought to Accomplish, 1875

The following editorial appeared in the northern periodical *Scribner's Journal*. A year before the celebration of the nation's centennial, Northerners as well as Southerners were calling for national unity and reconciliation, and thus a true end to Reconstruction. Rather than dwelling on the "Lost Cause," the magazine's editors remind southern readers of the glories of the old nation.

We are to have grand doings next year. There is to be an Exposition. There are to be speeches, and songs, and processions, and elaborate ceremonies and general rejoicings. Cannon are to be fired, flags are to be floated, and the eagle is expected to scream while he dips the tip of either pinion in the Atlantic and the Pacific, and sprinkles the land with a new baptism of freedom. . . .

. . . Before we begin our celebration of this event, would it not be well for us to inquire whether we have a nation? In a large number of the States of this country there exists not only a belief that the United States do not constitute a nation, but a theory of State rights which forbids that they ever shall become one. We hear about the perturbed condition of the Southern mind. We hear it said that multitudes there are just as disloyal as they were during the civil war. This, we believe, we are justified in denying. . . . They are not actively in rebellion, and they do not propose to be. They do not hope for the re-establishment of slavery. They fought bravely and well to establish their theory, but the majority was against them; and if the result of the war emphasized any fact, it was that *en masse* the people of the United States constitute a nation—indivisible in constituents, in interest, in destiny. . . . Unless this fact is fully recognized throughout the Union, our Centennial will be but a hollow mockery. If we are to celebrate anything worth celebrating, it is the birth of a nation. If we are to celebrate anything worth celebrating, it should be by the whole heart and united voice of the nation. If we can make the Centennial an occasion for emphasizing the great lesson of the war, and universally assenting to the results of the war, it will, indeed, be worth all the money expended upon and the time devoted to it. . . .

A few weeks ago, Mr. Jefferson Davis, the ex-President of the Confederacy, was reported to have exhorted an audience to which he was speaking to be as loyal to the old flag of the Union now as they were during the Mexican War. If the South could know what music there was in these words to Northern ears—how grateful we were to their old chief for them—it would appreciate the strength of our longing for a complete restoration of the national feeling that existed when Northern and Southern blood mingled in common sacrifice on Mexican soil. This national feeling, this national pride, this brotherly sympathy *must be restored*; and accursed be any Northern or Southern man, whether in power or out of power, whether politician, theorizer, carpet-bagger, president-maker, or plunderer, who puts obstacles in the way of such a restoration. Men of the South, we want you. Men of the South, we long for the restoration of your peace and your prosperity. We would see your cities thriving, your homes happy, your plantations teeming with plenteous harvests, your schools overflowing, your wisest statesmen leading you, and all causes and all memories of discord wiped out forever.

Source: "What the Centennial Ought to Accomplish," *Scribner's Monthly*, August 1875, 509–10.

Interpret the Evidence

1. How did the black codes (Document 14.5) attempt to reimpose bondage on former slaves?
2. Why did African Americans consider property holding a fundamental right (Document 14.6)?
3. Contrast the image of South Carolina's black politicians as presented in Richard Cain's speech (Document 14.6) and Thomas Nast's cartoon (Document 14.8).
4. Despite Ku Klux Klan intimidation and the fear it produced in African Americans, what does the testimony of Ellen Parton (Document 14.7) reveal about black attempts to resist it?
5. What sources of unity existed between the North and the South that would bring Reconstruction to an end (Document 14.9)? Compare northern attitudes about protecting freedpeople in the South in 1876 to that in 1865.

Put It in Context

How much did Reconstruction transform the South and the nation?

What were the greatest limitations of federal Reconstruction policies and the greatest challenges to implementing them?

THE **DECLARATION** OF **INDEPENDENCE**

In Congress, July 4, 1776.

The unanimous Declaration of the thirteen United States of America

When in the course of human events, it becomes necessary for one people to dissolve the political bands which have connected them with another, and to assume, among the powers of the earth, the separate and equal station to which the laws of nature and of nature's God entitle them, a decent respect to the opinions of mankind requires that they should declare the causes which impel them to the separation.

We hold these truths to be self-evident, that all men are created equal; that they are endowed by their Creator with certain unalienable rights; that among these, are life, liberty, and the pursuit of happiness. That, to secure these rights, governments are instituted among men, deriving their just powers from the consent of the governed; that, whenever any form of government becomes destructive of these ends, it is the right of the people to alter or to abolish it, and to institute a new government, laying its foundation on such principles, and organizing its powers in such form, as to them shall seem most likely to effect their safety and happiness. Prudence, indeed, will dictate that governments long established, should not be changed for light and transient causes; and, accordingly, all experience hath shown, that mankind are more disposed to suffer, while evils are sufferable, than to right themselves by abolishing the forms to which they are accustomed. But, when a long train of abuses and usurpations, pursuing invariably the same object, evinces a design to reduce them under absolute despotism, it is their right, it is their duty, to throw off such government and to provide new guards for their future security. Such has been the patient sufferance of these colonies, and such is now the necessity which constrains them to alter their former systems of government. The history of the present King of Great Britain is a history of repeated injuries and usurpations, all having, in direct object, the establishment of an absolute tyranny over these States. To prove this, let facts be submitted to a candid world: He has refused his assent to laws the most wholesome and necessary for the public good.

He has forbidden his governors to pass laws of immediate and pressing importance, unless suspended in their operation till his assent should be obtained; and, when so suspended, he has utterly neglected to attend to them.

He has refused to pass other laws for the accommodation of large districts of people, unless those people would relinquish the right of representation in the legislature; a right inestimable to them, and formidable to tyrants only.

He has called together legislative bodies at places unusual, uncomfortable, and distant from the depository of their public records, for the sole purpose of fatiguing them into compliance with his measures.

He has dissolved representative houses repeatedly for opposing, with manly firmness, his invasions on the rights of the people.

He has refused, for a long time after such dissolutions, to cause others to be elected; whereby the legislative powers, incapable of annihilation, have returned to the people at large for their exercise; the state remaining in the mean-time exposed to all the danger of invasion from without, and convulsions within.

He has endeavoured to prevent the population of these States; for that purpose, obstructing the laws for naturalization of foreigners, refusing to pass others to encourage their migration hither, and raising the conditions of new appropriations of lands.

He has obstructed the administration of justice, by refusing his assent to laws for establishing judiciary powers.

He has made judges dependent on his will alone, for the tenure of their offices, and the amount and payment of their salaries.

He has erected a multitude of new offices, and sent hither swarms of officers to harass our people, and eat out their substance.

He has kept among us, in times of peace, standing armies, without the consent of our legislature.

He has affected to render the military independent of, and superior to, the civil power.

He has combined, with others, to subject us to a jurisdiction foreign to our Constitution, and unacknowledged by our laws; giving his assent to their acts of pretended legislation:

For quartering large bodies of armed troops among us:

For protecting them by a mock trial, from punishment, for any murders which they should commit on the inhabitants of these States:

For cutting off our trade with all parts of the world:

For imposing taxes on us without our consent:

For depriving us, in many cases, of the benefit of trial by jury:

For transporting us beyond seas to be tried for pretended offences:

For abolishing the free system of English laws in a neighboring province, establishing therein an arbitrary government, and enlarging its boundaries, so as to render it at once an example and fit instrument for introducing the same absolute rule into these colonies:

For taking away our charters, abolishing our most valuable laws, and altering, fundamentally, the powers of our governments:

For suspending our own legislatures, and declaring themselves invested with power to legislate for us in all cases whatsoever.

He has abdicated government here, by declaring us out of his protection, and waging war against us.

He has plundered our seas, ravaged our coasts, burnt our towns, and destroyed the lives of our people.

He is, at this time, transporting large armies of foreign mercenaries to complete the works of death, desolation, and tyranny, already begun, with circumstances of cruelty and perfidy scarcely paralleled in the most barbarous ages, and totally unworthy the head of a civilized nation.

He has constrained our fellow citizens, taken captive on the high seas, to bear arms against their country, to become the executioners of their friends, and brethren, or to fall themselves by their hands.

He has excited domestic insurrections amongst us, and has endeavored to bring on the inhabitants of our frontiers, the merciless Indian savages, whose known rule of warfare is an undistinguished destruction of all ages, sexes, and conditions.

In every stage of these oppressions, we have petitioned for redress; in the most humble terms; our repeated petitions have been answered only by repeated injury. A prince, whose character is thus marked by every act which may define a tyrant, is unfit to be the ruler of a free people.

Nor have we been wanting in attention to our British brethren. We have warned them, from time to time, of attempts made by their legislature to extend an unwarrantable jurisdiction over us. We have reminded them of the circumstances of our emigration and settlement here. We have appealed to their native justice and magnanimity, and we have conjured them, by the ties of our common kindred, to disavow these usurpations, which would inevitably interrupt our connections and correspondence. They, too, have been deaf to the voice of justice and consanguinity. We must, therefore, acquiesce in the necessity which denounces our separation, and hold them as we hold the rest of mankind, enemies in war, in peace, friends.

We, therefore, the representatives of the United States of America, in general Congress assembled, appealing to the Supreme Judge of the world for the rectitude of our intentions, do, in the name, and by authority of the good people of these colonies, solemnly publish and declare, that these united colonies are, and of right ought to be, free and independent states: that they are absolved from all allegiance to the British Crown, and that all political connection between them and the state of Great Britain is, and ought to be, totally dissolved; and that, as free and independent states, they have full power to levy war, conclude peace, contract alliances, establish commerce, and to do all other acts and things which independent states may of right do. And, for the support of this declaration, with a firm reliance on the protection of Divine Providence, we mutually pledge to each other our lives, our fortunes, and our sacred honor.

The foregoing Declaration was, by order of Congress, engrossed, and signed by the following members:

JOHN HANCOCK

New Hampshire
Josiah Bartlett
William Whipple
Matthew Thornton

Massachusetts Bay
Samuel Adams
John Adams
Robert Treat Paine
Elbridge Gerry

Rhode Island
Stephen Hopkins
William Ellery

Connecticut
Roger Sherman
Samuel Huntington
William Williams
Oliver Wolcott

New York
William Floyd
Phillip Livingston
Francis Lewis
Lewis Morris

New Jersey
Richard Stockton
John Witherspoon
Francis Hopkinson
John Hart
Abraham Clark

Pennsylvania
Robert Morris
Benjamin Rush
Benjamin Franklin
John Morton
George Clymer

James Smith
George Taylor
James Wilson
George Ross
Caesar Rodney
George Read
Thomas M'Kean

Maryland
Samuel Chase
William Paca
Thomas Stone
Charles Carroll, of Carrollton

North Carolina
William Hooper
Joseph Hewes
John Penn

South Carolina
Edward Rutledge
Thomas Heyward, Jr.
Thomas Lynch, Jr.
Arthur Middleton

Virginia
George Wythe
Richard Henry Lee
Thomas Jefferson
Benjamin Harrison
Thomas Nelson, Jr.
Francis Lightfoot Lee
Carter Braxton

Georgia
Button Gwinnett
Lyman Hall
George Walton

Resolved, That copies of the Declaration be sent to the several assemblies, conventions, and committees, or councils of safety, and to the several commanding officers of the continental troops; that it be proclaimed in each of the United States, at the head of the army.

THE **ARTICLES** OF **CONFEDERATION** AND **PERPETUAL UNION**

Agreed to in Congress, November 15, 1777.
Ratified March 1781.

Between the states of New Hampshire, Massachusetts Bay, Rhode Island and Providence Plantations, Connecticut, New York, New Jersey, Pennsylvania, Delaware, Maryland, Virginia, North Carolina, South Carolina, Georgia.*

Article 1
The stile of this confederacy shall be "The United States of America."

Article 2
Each State retains its sovereignty, freedom and independence, and every power, jurisdiction, and right, which is not by this confederation expressly delegated to the United States, in Congress assembled.

Article 3
The said states hereby severally enter into a firm league of friendship with each other for their common defence, the security of their liberties and their mutual and general welfare; binding themselves to assist each other against all force offered to, or attacks made upon them, or any of them, on account of religion, sovereignty, trade, or any other pretence whatever.

Article 4
The better to secure and perpetuate mutual friendship and intercourse among the people of the different states in this union, the free inhabitants of each of these states, paupers, vagabonds, and fugitives from justice excepted, shall be entitled to all privileges and immunities of free citizens in the several states; and the people of each State shall have free ingress and regress to and from any other State, and shall enjoy therein all the privileges of trade and commerce, subject to the same duties, impositions, and restrictions, as the inhabitants thereof respectively; provided, that such restrictions shall not extend so far as to prevent the removal of property, imported into any State, to any other State of which the owner is an inhabitant; provided also, that no imposition, duties, or restriction, shall be laid by any State on the property of the United States, or either of them. If any person guilty of, or charged with treason, felony, or other high misdemeanor in any State, shall flee from justice and be found in any of the United States, he shall, upon demand of the governor or executive power of the State from which he fled, be delivered up and removed to the State having jurisdiction of his offence. Full faith and credit shall be given in each of these states to the records, acts, and judicial proceedings of the courts and magistrates of every other State.

Article 5
For the more convenient management of the general interests of the United States, delegates shall be annually appointed, in such manner as the legislature of each State shall direct, to meet in Congress, on the 1st Monday in November in every year, with a power reserved to each State to recall its delegates, or any of them, at any time within the year, and to send others in their stead for the remainder of the year.

*This copy of the final draft of the Articles of Confederation to taken from the Journals, 9:907–925, November 15, 1777.

No State shall be represented in Congress by less than two, nor by more than seven members; and no person shall be capable of being a delegate for more than three years in any term of six years; nor shall any person, being a delegate, be capable of holding any office under the United States, for which he, or any other for his benefit, receives any salary, fees, or emolument of any kind.

Each State shall maintain its own delegates in a meeting of the states, and while they act as members of the committee of the states.

In determining questions in the United States, in Congress assembled, each State shall have one vote.

Freedom of speech and debate in Congress shall not be impeached or questioned in any court or place out of Congress: and the members of Congress shall be protected in their persons from arrests and imprisonments, during the time of their going to and from, and attendance on Congress, except for treason, felony, or breach of the peace.

Article 6

No State, without the consent of the United States, in Congress assembled, shall send any embassy to, or receive any embassy from, or enter into any conference, agreement, alliance, or treaty with any king, prince, or state; nor shall any person, holding any office of profit or trust under the United States, or any of them, accept of any present, emolument, office or title, of any kind whatever, from any king, prince, or foreign state; nor shall the United States, in Congress assembled, or any of them, grant any title of nobility.

No two or more states shall enter into any treaty, confederation, or alliance, whatever, between them, without the consent of the United States, in Congress assembled, specifying accurately the purposes for which the same is to be entered into, and how long it shall continue.

No state shall lay any imposts or duties which may interfere with any stipulations in treaties entered into by the United States, in Congress assembled, with any king, prince, or state, in pursuance of any treaties already proposed by Congress to the courts of France and Spain.

No vessels of war shall be kept up in time of peace by any State, except such number only as shall be deemed necessary by the United States, in Congress assembled, for the defence of such State or its trade; nor shall any body of forces be kept up by any State, in time of peace, except such number only as, in the judgment of the United States, in Congress assembled, shall be deemed requisite to garrison the forts necessary for the defence of such State; but every State shall always keep up a well regulated and disciplined militia, sufficiently armed and accoutred, and shall provide, and constantly have ready for use, in public stores, a due number of field pieces and tents, and a proper quantity of arms, ammunition and camp equipage.

No State shall engage in any war without the consent of the United States, in Congress assembled, unless such State be actually invaded by enemies, or shall have received certain advice of a resolution being formed by some nation of Indians to invade such State, and the danger is so imminent as not to admit of a delay till the United States, in Congress assembled, can be consulted; nor shall any State grant commissions to any ships or vessels of war, nor letters of marque or reprisal, except it be after a declaration of war by the United States, in Congress assembled, and then only against the kingdom or state, and the subjects thereof, against which war has been so declared, and under such regulations as shall be established by the United States, in Congress assembled, unless such State be infested by pirates, in which case vessels of war may be fitted out for that occasion, and kept so long as the danger shall continue, or until the United States, in Congress assembled, shall determine otherwise.

Article 7

When land forces are raised by any State for the common defence, all officers of or under the rank of colonel, shall be appointed by the legislature of each State respectively, by whom such forces shall be raised, or in such manner as such State shall direct; and all vacancies shall be filled up by the State which first made the appointment.

Article 8

All charges of war and all other expences, that shall be incurred for the common defence or general welfare, and allowed by the United States, in Congress assembled, shall be defrayed out of a common treasury, which shall be supplied by the several states, in proportion to the value of all land within each State, granted to or surveyed for any person, as such land and the buildings and improvements thereon shall be estimated according to such mode as the United States, in Congress assembled, shall, from time to time, direct and appoint.

The taxes for paying that proportion shall be laid and levied by the authority and direction of the legislatures of the several states, within the time agreed upon by the United States, in Congress assembled.

Article 9

The United States, in Congress assembled, shall have the sole and exclusive right and power of determining on peace and war, except in the cases mentioned in the 6th article; of sending and receiving ambassadors; entering into treaties and alliances, provided that no treaty of commerce shall be made, whereby the legislative power of the respective states shall be restrained from imposing such imposts and duties on foreigners as their own people are subjected to, or from prohibiting the exportation or importation of any species of goods or commodities whatsoever; of establishing rules for deciding, in all cases, what captures on land or water shall be legal, and in what manner prizes, taken by land or naval forces in the service of the United States, shall be divided or appropriated; of granting letters of marque and reprisal in times of peace; appointing courts for the trial of piracies and felonies committed on the high seas, and establishing courts for receiving and determining, finally, appeals in all cases of captures; provided, that no member of Congress shall be appointed a judge of any of the said courts.

The United States, in Congress assembled, shall also be the last resort on appeal in all disputes and differences now subsisting, or that hereafter may arise between two or more states concerning boundary, jurisdiction or any other cause whatever; which authority shall always be exercised in the manner following: whenever the legislative or executive authority, or lawful agent of any State, in controversy with another, shall present a petition to Congress, stating the matter in question, and praying for a hearing, notice thereof shall be given, by order of Congress, to the legislative or executive authority of the other State in controversy, and a day assigned for the appearance of the parties by their lawful agents, who shall then be directed to appoint, by joint consent, commissioners or judges to constitute a court for hearing and determining the matter in question; but, if they cannot agree, Congress shall name three persons out of each of the United States, and from the list of such persons each party shall alternately strike out one, the petitioners beginning, until the number shall be reduced to thirteen; and from that number not less than seven, nor more than nine names, as Congress shall direct, shall, in the presence of Congress, be drawn out by lot; and the persons whose names shall be so drawn, or any five of them, shall be commissioners or judges to hear and finally determine the controversy, so always as a major part of the judges who shall hear the cause shall agree in the determination; and if either party shall neglect to attend at the day appointed, without shewing reasons which Congress shall judge sufficient, or, being present, shall refuse to strike, the Congress shall proceed to nominate three persons out of each State, and the secretary of Congress shall strike in behalf of such party absent or refusing; and the judgment and sentence of the court to be appointed, in the manner before prescribed, shall be final and conclusive; and if any of the parties shall refuse to submit to the authority of such court, or to appear or defend their claim or cause, the court shall nevertheless proceed to pronounce sentence or judgment, which shall, in like manner, be final and decisive, the judgment or sentence and other proceedings begin, in either case, transmitted to Congress, and lodged among the acts of Congress for the security of the parties concerned: provided, that every commissioner, before he sits in judgment, shall take an oath, to be administered by one of the judges of the supreme or superior court of the State where the cause shall be tried, "well and truly to hear and determine the matter in question, according to the best of his judgment, without favour, affection, or hope of reward:" provided, also, that no State shall be deprived of territory for the benefit of the United States.

All controversies concerning the private right of soil, claimed under different grants of two or more states, whose jurisdictions, as they may respect such lands and the states which passed such grants, are adjusted, the said grants, or either of them, being at the same time claimed to have originated antecedent to such settlement of jurisdiction, shall, on the petition of either party to the Congress of the United States, be finally determined, as near as may be, in the same manner as is before prescribed for deciding disputes respecting territorial jurisdiction between different states.

The United States, in Congress assembled, shall also have the sole and exclusive right and power of regulating the alloy and value of coin struck by their own authority, or by that of the respective states; fixing the standard of weights and measures throughout the United States; regulating the trade and managing all affairs with the Indians not members of any of the states; provided that the legislative right of any State within its own limits be not infringed or violated; establishing and regulating post offices from one State to another throughout all the United States, and exacting such postage on the papers passing through the same as may be requisite to defray the expences of the said office; appointing all officers of the land forces in the service of the United States, excepting regimental officers; appointing all the officers of the naval forces, and commissioning all officers whatever in the service of the United States; making rules for the government and regulation of the said land and naval forces, and directing their operations.

The United States, in Congress assembled, shall have authority to appoint a committee to sit in the recess of Congress, to be denominated "a Committee of the States," and to consist of one delegate from each State, and to appoint such other committees and civil officers as may be necessary for managing the general affairs of the United States, under their direction; to appoint one of their number to preside; provided that no person be allowed to serve in the office of president more than one year in any term of three years; to ascertain the necessary sums of money to be raised for the service of the United States, and to appropriate and apply the same for defraying the public expences; to borrow money or emit bills on the credit of the United States, transmitting, every half year, to the respective states, an account of the sums of money so borrowed or emitted; to build and equip a navy; to agree upon the number of land forces, and to make requisitions from each State for its quota, in proportion to the number of white inhabitants in such State; which requisitions shall be binding; and thereupon, the legislature of each State shall appoint the regimental officers, raise the men, and cloathe, arm, and equip them in a soldier-like manner, at the expence of the United States; and the officers and men so cloathed, armed, and equipped, shall march to the place appointed and within the time agreed on by the United States, in Congress assembled; but if the United States, in Congress assembled, shall, on consideration of circumstances, judge proper that any State should not raise men, or should raise a smaller number than its quota, and that any other State should raise a greater number of men than the quota thereof, such extra number shall be raised, officered, cloathed, armed, and equipped in the same manner as the quota of such State, unless the legislature of such State shall judge that such extra number cannot be safely spared out of the same, in which case they shall raise, officer, cloathe, arm, and equip as many of such extra number as they judge can be safely spared. And the officers and men so cloathed, armed, and equipped, shall march to the place appointed and within the time agreed on by the United States, in Congress assembled.

The United States, in Congress assembled, shall never engage in a war, nor grant letters of marque and reprisal in time of peace, nor enter into any treaties or alliances, nor coin money, nor regulate the value thereof, nor ascertain the sums and expences necessary for the defence and welfare of the United States, or any of them: nor emit bills, nor borrow money on the credit of the United States, nor appropriate money, nor agree upon the number of vessels of war to be built or purchased, or the number of land or sea forces to be raised, nor appoint a commander in chief of the army or navy, unless nine states assent to the same; nor shall a question on any other point, except for adjourning from day to day, be determined, unless by the votes of a majority of the United States, in Congress assembled.

The Congress of the United States shall have power to adjourn to any time within the year, and to any place within the United States, so that no period of adjournment be for a longer duration than the space of six months, and shall publish the journal of their proceedings monthly, except such parts thereof, relating to treaties, alliances or military operations, as, in their judgment, require secrecy; and the yeas and nays of the delegates of each State on any question shall be entered on the journal, when it is desired by any delegate; and the delegates of a State, or any of them, at his, or their request, shall be furnished with a transcript of the said journal, except such parts as are above excepted, to lay before the legislatures of the several states.

Article 10

The committee of the states, or any nine of them, shall be authorized to execute, in the recess of Congress, such of the powers of Congress as the United States, in Congress assembled, by the consent of nine states, shall, from time to time, think expedient to vest them with; provided, that no power be delegated to the said committee, for the exercise of which, by the articles of confederation, the voice of nine states, in the Congress of the United States assembled, is requisite.

Article 11

Canada acceding to this confederation, and joining in the measures of the United States, shall be admitted into and entitled to all the advantages of this union; but no other colony shall be admitted into the same, unless such admission be agreed to by nine states.

Article 12

All bills of credit emitted, monies borrowed and debts contracted by, or under the authority of Congress before the assembling of the United States, in pursuance of the present confederation, shall be deemed and considered as a charge against the United States, for payment and satisfaction whereof the said United States and the public faith are hereby solemnly pledged.

Article 13

Every State shall abide by the determinations of the United States, in Congress assembled, on all questions which, by this confederation, are submitted to them. And the articles of this confederation shall be inviolably observed by every State, and the union shall be perpetual; nor shall any alteration at any time hereafter be made in any of them, unless such alteration be agreed to in a Congress of the United States, and be afterwards confirmed by the legislatures of every State.

These articles shall be proposed to the legislatures of all the United States, to be considered, and if approved of by them, they are advised to authorize their delegates to ratify the same in the Congress of the United States; which being done, the same shall become conclusive.

THE CONSTITUTION OF THE UNITED STATES*

Agreed to by Philadelphia Convention, September 17, 1787. Implemented March 4, 1789.

Preamble

We the people of the United States, in order to form a more perfect union, establish justice, insure domestic tranquility, provide for the common defense, promote the general welfare, and secure the blessings of liberty to ourselves and our posterity, do ordain and establish this Constitution for the United States of America.

Article I

Section 1. All legislative powers herein granted shall be vested in a Congress of the United States, which shall consist of a Senate and a House of Representatives.

Section 2. The House of Representatives shall be composed of members chosen every second year by the people of the several States, and the electors in each State shall have the qualifications requisite for electors of the most numerous branch of the State Legislature.

No person shall be a Representative who shall not have attained to the age of twenty-five years, and been seven years a citizen of the United States, and who shall not, when elected, be an inhabitant of that State in which he shall be chosen.

Representatives and direct taxes shall be apportioned among the several States which may be included within this Union, according to their respective numbers, *which shall be determined by adding to the whole number of free persons, including those bound to service for a term of years and excluding Indians not taxed, three-fifths of all other persons.* The actual enumeration shall be made within three years after the first meeting of the Congress of the United States, and within every subsequent term of ten years, in such manner as they shall by law direct. The number of Representatives shall not exceed one for every thirty thousand, but each State shall have at least one Representative; and until such enumeration shall be made, *the State of New Hampshire shall be entitled to choose three, Massachusetts eight, Rhode Island and Providence Plantations one, Connecticut five, New York six, New Jersey four, Pennsylvania eight, Delaware one, Maryland six, Virginia ten, North Carolina five, South Carolina five, and Georgia three.*

*Passages no longer in effect are in italic type.

When vacancies happen in the representation from any State, the Executive authority thereof shall issue writs of election to fill such vacancies.

The House of Representatives shall choose their Speaker and other officers; and shall have the sole power of impeachment.

Section 3. The Senate of the United States shall be composed of two Senators from each State, *chosen by the legislature thereof,* for six years; and each Senator shall have one vote.

Immediately after they shall be assembled in consequence of the first election, they shall be divided as equally as may be into three classes. The seats of the Senators of the first class shall be vacated at the expiration of the second year, of the second class at the expiration of the fourth year, and of the third class at the expiration of the sixth year, so that one-third may be chosen every second year; and if vacancies happen by resignation or otherwise, during the recess of the legislature of any State, the Executive thereof may make temporary appointments until the next meeting of the legislature, which shall then fill such vacancies.

No person shall be a Senator who shall not have attained to the age of thirty years, and been nine years a citizen of the United States, and who shall not, when elected, be an inhabitant of that State for which he shall be chosen.

The Vice-President of the United States shall be President of the Senate, but shall have no vote, unless they be equally divided.

The Senate shall choose their other officers, and also a President pro tempore, in the absence of the Vice-President, or when he shall exercise the office of President of the United States.

The Senate shall have the sole power to try all impeachments. When sitting for that purpose, they shall be on oath or affirmation. When the President of the United States is tried, the Chief Justice shall preside: and no person shall be convicted without the concurrence of two-thirds of the members present.

Judgment in cases of impeachment shall not extend further than to removal from the office, and disqualification to hold and enjoy any office of honor, trust or profit under the United States: but the party convicted shall nevertheless be liable and subject to indictment, trial, judgment and punishment, according to law.

Section 4. The times, places and manner of holding elections for Senators and Representatives shall be prescribed in each State by the legislature thereof; but the Congress may at any time by law make or alter such regulations, except as to the places of choosing Senators.

The Congress shall assemble at least once in every year, and such meeting *shall be on the first Monday in December, unless they shall by law appoint a different day.*

Section 5. Each house shall be the judge of the elections, returns and qualifications of its own members, and a majority of each shall constitute a quorum to do business; but a smaller number may adjourn from day to day, and may be authorized to compel the attendance of absent members, in such manner, and under such penalties, as each house may provide.

Each house may determine the rules of its proceedings, punish its members for disorderly behavior, and with the concurrence of two-thirds, expel a member.

Each house shall keep a journal of its proceedings, and from time to time publish the same, excepting such parts as may in their judgment require secrecy; and the yeas and nays of the members of either house on any question shall, at the desire of one fifth of those present, be entered on the journal.

Neither house, during the session of Congress, shall, without the consent of the other, adjourn for more than three days, nor to any other place than that in which the two houses shall be sitting.

Section 6. The Senators and Representatives shall receive a compensation for their services, to be ascertained by law and paid out of the treasury of the United States. They shall in all cases except treason, felony and breach of the peace, be privileged from arrest during their attendance at the session of their respective houses, and in going to and returning from the same; and for any speech or debate in either house, they shall not be questioned in any other place.

No Senator or Representative shall, during the time for which he was elected, be appointed to any civil office under the authority of the United States, which shall have been created, or the emoluments whereof shall have been increased, during such time; and no person holding any office under the United States shall be a member of either house during his continuance in office.

Section 7. All bills for raising revenue shall originate in the House of Representatives; but the Senate may propose or concur with amendments as on other bills.

Every bill which shall have passed the House of Representatives and the Senate, shall, before it become a law, be presented to the President of the United States; if he approve he shall sign it, but if not he shall return it with objections to that house in which it shall have originated, who shall enter the objections at large on their journal, and proceed to reconsider it. If after such reconsideration two-thirds of that house shall agree to pass the bill, it shall be sent, together with the objections, to the other house, by which it shall likewise be reconsidered, and, if approved by two-thirds of that house, it shall become a law. But in all such cases the votes of both houses shall be determined by yeas and nays, and the names of the persons voting for and against the bill shall be entered on the journal of each house respectively. If any bill shall not be returned by the President within ten days (Sundays excepted) after it shall have been presented to him, the same shall be a law, in like manner as if he had signed it, unless the Congress by their adjournment prevent its return, in which case it shall not be a law.

Every order, resolution, or vote to which the concurrence of the Senate and House of Representatives may be necessary (except on a question of adjournment) shall be presented to the President of the United States; and before the same shall take effect, shall be approved by him, or being disapproved by him, shall be repassed by two-thirds of the Senate and House of Representatives, according to the rules and limitations prescribed in the case of a bill.

Section 8. The Congress shall have power

To lay and collect taxes, duties, imposts, and excises, to pay the debts and provide for the common defense and general welfare of the United States; but all duties, imposts and excises shall be uniform throughout the United States;

To borrow money on the credit of the United States;

To regulate commerce with foreign nations, and among the several States, and with the Indian tribes;

To establish an uniform rule of naturalization, and uniform laws on the subject of bankruptcies throughout the United States;

To coin money, regulate the value thereof, and of foreign coin, and fix the standard of weights and measures;

To provide for the punishment of counterfeiting the securities and current coin of the United States;

To establish post offices and post roads;

To promote the progress of science and useful arts by securing for limited times to authors and inventors the exclusive right to their respective writings and discoveries;

To constitute tribunals inferior to the Supreme Court;

To define and punish piracies and felonies committed on the high seas and offences against the law of nations;

To declare war, grant letters of marque and reprisal, and make rules concerning captures on land and water;

To raise and support armies, but no appropriation of money to that use shall be for a longer term than two years;

To provide and maintain a navy;

To make rules for the government and regulation of the land and naval forces;

To provide for calling forth the militia to execute the laws of the Union, suppress insurrections and repel invasions;

To provide for organizing, arming, and disciplining the militia, and for governing such part of them as may be employed in the service of the United States, reserving to the States respectively the appointment of the officers, and the authority of training the militia according to the discipline prescribed by Congress;

To exercise exclusive legislation in all cases whatsoever, over such district (not exceeding ten miles square) as may, by cession of particular States, and the acceptance of Congress, become the seat of the government of the United States, and to exercise like authority over all places purchased by the consent of the legislature of the State, in which the same shall be, for erection of forts, magazines, arsenals, dock-yards, and other needful buildings;—and

To make all laws which shall be necessary and proper for carrying into execution the foregoing powers, and all other powers vested by this Constitution in the government of the United States, or in any department or officer thereof.

Section 9. *The migration or importation of such persons as any of the States now existing shall think proper to admit shall not be prohibited by the Congress prior to the year one thousand eight hundred and eight; but a tax or duty may be imposed on such importation, not exceeding ten dollars for each person.*

The privilege of the writ of habeas corpus shall not be suspended, unless when in cases of rebellion or invasion the public safety may require it.

No bill of attainder or ex post facto law shall be passed.

No capitation, or other direct, tax shall be laid, unless in proportion to the census or enumeration herein before directed to be taken.

No tax or duty shall be laid on articles exported from any State.

No preference shall be given by any regulation of commerce or revenue to the ports of one State over those of another; nor shall vessels bound to, or from, one State be obliged to enter, clear, or pay duties in another.

No money shall be drawn from the treasury, but in consequence of appropriations made by law; and a regular statement and account of the receipts and expenditures of all public money shall be published from time to time.

No title of nobility shall be granted by the United States: and no person holding any office of profit or trust under them, shall, without the consent of the Congress, accept of any present, emolument, office, or title, of any kind whatever, from any king, prince, or foreign state.

Section 10. No State shall enter into any treaty, alliance, or confederation; grant letters of marque and reprisal; coin money; emit bills of credit; make anything but gold and silver coin a tender in payment of debts; pass any bill of attainder, ex post facto law, or law impairing the obligation of contracts, or grant any title of nobility.

No State shall, without the consent of Congress, lay any imposts or duties on imports or exports, except what may be absolutely necessary for executing its inspection laws: and the net produce of all duties and imposts, laid by any State on imports or exports, shall be for the use of the treasury of the United States; and all such laws shall be subject to the revision and control of the Congress.

No State shall, without the consent of Congress, lay any duty of tonnage, keep troops, or ships of war in time of peace, enter into any agreement or compact with another State, or with a foreign power, or engage in war, unless actually invaded, or in such imminent danger as will not admit of delay.

Article II

Section 1. The executive power shall be vested in a President of the United States of America. He shall hold his office during the term of four years, and, together with the Vice-President, chosen for the same term, be elected as follows:

Each State shall appoint, in such manner as the legislature thereof may direct, a number of electors, equal to the whole number of Senators and Representatives to which the State may be entitled in the Congress; but no Senator or Representative, or person holding an office of trust or profit under the United States, shall be appointed an elector.

The electors shall meet in their respective States, and vote by ballot for two persons, of whom one at least shall not be an inhabitant of the same State with themselves. And they shall make a list of all the persons voted for, and of the number of votes for each; which list they shall sign and certify, and transmit sealed to the seat of government of the United States, directed to the President of the Senate. The President of the Senate shall, in the presence of the Senate and House of Representatives, open all the certificates, and the votes shall then be counted. The person having the greatest number of votes shall be the President, if such number be a majority of the whole number of electors appointed; and if there be more than one who have such majority, and have an equal number of votes, then the House of Representatives shall immediately choose by ballot one of them for President; and if no person have a majority, then from the five highest on the list said house shall in like manner choose the President. But in choosing the President the votes shall be taken by States, the representation from each State having one vote; a quorum for this purpose shall consist of a member or members from two-thirds of the States, and a majority of all the States shall be necessary to a choice. In every case, after the choice of the President, the person having the greatest number of votes of the electors shall be the Vice-President. But if there should remain two or more who have equal votes, the Senate shall choose from them by ballot the Vice-President.

The Congress may determine the time of choosing the electors, and the day on which they shall give their votes; which day shall be the same throughout the United States.

No person except a natural-born citizen, *or a citizen of the United States at the time of the adoption of this Constitution*, shall be eligible to the office of President; neither shall any person be eligible to that office who shall not have attained to the age of thirty-five years, and been fourteen years a resident within the United States.

In cases of the removal of the President from office or of his death, resignation, or inability to discharge the powers and duties of the said office, the same shall devolve on the Vice-President, and the Congress may by law provide for the case of removal, death, resignation, or inability, both of the President and Vice-President, declaring what officer shall then act as President, and such officer shall act accordingly, until the disability be removed, or a President shall be elected.

The President shall, at stated times, receive for his services a compensation, which shall neither be increased nor diminished during the period for which he shall have been elected, and he shall not receive within that period any other emolument from the United States, or any of them.

Before he enter on the execution of his office, he shall take the following oath or affirmation:—"I do solemnly swear (or affirm) that I will faithfully execute the office of the President of the United States, and will to the best of my ability preserve, protect and defend the Constitution of the United States."

Section 2. The President shall be commander in chief of the army and navy of the United States, and of the militia of the several States, when called into the actual service of the United States; he may require the opinion, in writing, of the principal officer in each of the executive departments, upon any subject relating to the duties of their respective offices, and he shall have power to grant reprieves and pardons for offenses against the United States, except in cases of impeachment.

He shall have power, by and with the advice and consent of the Senate, to make treaties, provided two-thirds of the Senators present concur; and he shall nominate, and by and with the advice and consent of the Senate, shall appoint ambassadors, other public ministers and consuls, judges of the Supreme Court, and all other officers of the United States, whose appointments are not herein otherwise provided for, and which shall be established by law: but Congress may by law vest the appointment of such inferior officers, as they think proper, in the President alone, in the courts of law, or in the heads of departments.

The President shall have power to fill up all vacancies that may happen during the recess of the Senate, by granting commissions which shall expire at the end of their next session.

Section 3. He shall from time to time give to the Congress information of the state of the Union, and recommend to their consideration such measures as he shall judge necessary and expedient; he may, on extraordinary occasions, convene both houses, or either of them, and in case of disagreement between them, with respect to the time of adjournment, he may adjourn them to such time as he shall think proper; he shall receive ambassadors and other public ministers; he shall take care that the laws be faithfully executed, and shall commission all the officers of the United States.

Section 4. The President, Vice-President and all civil officers of the United States shall be removed from office on impeachment for, and on conviction of, treason, bribery, or other high crimes and misdemeanors.

Article III

Section 1. The judicial power of the United States shall be vested in one Supreme Court, and in such inferior courts as the Congress may from time to time ordain and establish. The judges, both of the Supreme and inferior courts, shall hold their offices during good behavior, and shall, at stated times, receive for their services a compensation which shall not be diminished during their continuance in office.

Section 2. The judicial power shall extend to all cases, in law and equity, arising under this Constitution, the laws of the United States, and treaties made, or which shall be made, under their authority;—to all cases affecting ambassadors, other public ministers and consuls;—to all cases of admiralty and maritime jurisdiction;—to controversies to which the United States shall be a party;—to controversies between two or more States;—between a State and citizens of another State;—between citizens of different States;—between citizens of the same State claiming lands under grants of different States, and between a State, or the citizens thereof, and foreign states, citizens or subjects.

In all cases affecting ambassadors, other public ministers and consuls, and those in which a State shall be party, the Supreme Court shall have original jurisdiction. In all the other cases before mentioned, the Supreme Court shall have appellate jurisdiction, both as to law and fact, with such exceptions, and under such regulations, as the Congress shall make.

The trial of all crimes, except in cases of impeachment, shall be by jury; and such trial shall be held in the State where said crimes shall have been committed; but when not committed within any State, the trial shall be at such place or places as the Congress may by Law have directed.

Section 3. Treason against the United States shall consist only in levying war against them, or in adhering to their enemies, giving them aid and comfort. No person shall be convicted of treason unless on the testimony of two witnesses to the same overt act, or on confession in open court.

The Congress shall have power to declare the punishment of treason, but no attainder of treason shall work corruption of blood, or forfeiture except during the life of the person attainted.

Article IV

Section 1. Full faith and credit shall be given in each State to the public acts, records, and judicial proceedings of every other State. And the Congress may by general laws prescribe the manner in which such acts, records, and proceedings shall be proved, and the effect thereof.

Section 2. The citizens of each State shall be entitled to all privileges and immunities of citizens in the several States.

A person charged in any State with treason, felony, or other crime, who shall flee from justice, and be found in another State, shall on demand of the executive authority of the State from which he fled, be delivered up, to be removed to the State having jurisdiction of the crime.

No Person held to service or labor in one State, under the laws thereof, escaping into another, shall, in consequence of any law or regulation therein, be discharged from such service or labor, but shall be delivered up on claim of the party to whom such service or labor may be due.

Section 3. New States may be admitted by the Congress into this Union; but no new State shall be formed or erected within the jurisdiction of any other State; nor any State be formed by the junction of two or more States, or parts of States, without the consent of the legislatures of the States concerned as well as of the Congress.

The Congress shall have power to dispose of and make all needful rules and regulations respecting the territory or other property belonging to the United States; and nothing in this Constitution shall be so construed as to prejudice any claims of the United States, or of any particular State.

Section 4. The United States shall guarantee to every State in this Union a republican form of government, and shall protect each of them against invasion; and on application of the legislature, or of the executive (when the legislature cannot be convened), against domestic violence.

Article V

The Congress, whenever two-thirds of both houses shall deem it necessary, shall propose amendments to this Constitution, or, on the application of the legislatures of two-thirds of the several States, shall call a convention for proposing amendments, which, in either case, shall be valid to all intents and purposes, as part of this Constitution, when ratified by the legislatures of three-fourths of the several States, or by conventions in three-fourths thereof, as the one or the other mode of ratification may be proposed by the Congress; *provided that no amendments which may be made prior to the year one thousand eight hundred and eight shall in any manner affect the first and fourth clauses in the ninth section of the first article;* and that no State, without its consent, shall be deprived of its equal suffrage in the Senate.

Article VI

All debts contracted and engagements entered into, before the adoption of this Constitution, shall be as valid against the United States under this Constitution, as under the Confederation.

This Constitution, and the laws of the United States which shall be made in pursuance thereof; and all treaties made, or which shall be made, under the authority of the United States, shall be the supreme law of the land; and the judges in every State shall be bound thereby, anything in the Constitution or laws of any State to the contrary notwithstanding.

The Senators and Representatives before mentioned, and the members of the several State legislatures, and all executive and judicial officers, both of the United States and of the several States, shall be bound by oath or affirmation to support this Constitution; but no religious test shall ever be required as a qualification to any office or public trust under the United States.

Article VII

The ratification of the conventions of nine States shall be sufficient for the establishment of this Constitution between the States so ratifying the same.

Done in convention by the unanimous consent of the States present, the seventeenth day of September in the year of our Lord one thousand seven hundred and eighty-seven and of the Independence of the United States of America the twelfth. In witness whereof we have hereunto subscribed our names.

GEORGE WASHINGTON, President and Deputy from Virginia

New Hampshire
John Langdon
Nicholas Gilman

Massachusetts
Nathaniel Gorham
Rufus King

Connecticut
William Samuel
  Johnson
Roger Sherman

New York
Alexander Hamilton

New Jersey
William Livingston
David Brearley
William Paterson
Jonathan Dayton

Pennsylvania
Benjamin Franklin
Thomas Mifflin
Robert Morris
George Clymer
Thomas FitzSimons
Jared Ingersoll
James Wilson
Gouverneur Morris

Delaware
George Read
Gunning Bedford, Jr.
John Dickinson
Richard Bassett
Jacob Broom

Maryland
James McHenry
Daniel of St. Thomas Jenifer
Daniel Carroll

Virginia
John Blair
James Madison, Jr.

North Carolina
William Blount
Richard Dobbs
  Spaight
Hugh Williamson

South Carolina
John Rutledge
Charles Cotesworth
  Pinckney
Charles Pinckney
Pierce Butler

Georgia
William Few
Abraham Baldwin

AMENDMENTS TO THE CONSTITUTION

(including six unratified amendments)

Amendment I   [Ratified 1791]

Congress shall make no law respecting an establishment of religion, or prohibiting the free exercise thereof; or abridging the freedom of speech, or of the press; or the right of the people peaceably to assemble, and to petition the government for a redress of grievances.

Amendment II   [Ratified 1791]

A well-regulated militia being necessary to the security of a free State, the right of the people to keep and bear arms shall not be infringed.

Amendment III   [Ratified 1791]

No soldier shall, in time of peace, be quartered in any house without the consent of the owner, nor in time of war, but in a manner to be prescribed by law.

Amendment IV   [Ratified 1791]

The right of the people to be secure in their persons, houses, papers, and effects, against unreasonable searches and seizures, shall not be violated, and no warrants shall issue but upon probable cause, supported by oath or affirmation, and particularly describing the place to be searched, and the persons or things to be seized.

Amendment V   [Ratified 1791]

No person shall be held to answer for a capital, or otherwise infamous crime, unless on a presentment or indictment of a grand jury, except in cases arising in the land or naval forces, or in the militia, when in actual service in time of war or public danger; nor shall any person be subject for the same offence to be twice put in jeopardy of life or limb; nor shall be compelled in any criminal case to be a witness against himself, nor be deprived of life, liberty, or property, without due process of law; nor shall private property be taken for public use without just compensation.

Amendment VI   [Ratified 1791]

In all criminal prosecutions, the accused shall enjoy the right to a speedy and public trial, by an impartial jury of the State and district wherein the crime shall have been committed, which district shall have been previously ascertained by law, and to be informed of the nature and cause of the accusation; to be confronted with the witnesses against him; to have compulsory process for obtaining witnesses in his favor, and to have the assistance of counsel for his defence.

Amendment VII   [Ratified 1791]

In suits at common law, where the value in controversy shall exceed twenty dollars, the right of trial by jury shall be preserved, and no fact tried by a jury shall be otherwise reexamined in any court of the United States, than according to the rules of the common law.

Amendment VIII   [Ratified 1791]

Excessive bail shall not be required, nor excessive fines imposed, nor cruel and unusual punishments inflicted.

Amendment IX [Ratified 1791]

The enumeration in the Constitution, of certain rights, shall not be construed to deny or disparage others retained by the people.

Amendment X [Ratified 1791]

The powers not delegated to the United States by the Constitution, nor prohibited by it to the States, are reserved to the States respectively, or to the people.

Unratified Amendment

[Reapportionment Amendment (proposed by Congress September 25, 1789, along with the Bill of Rights)]

After the first enumeration required by the first article of the Constitution, there shall be one Representative for every thirty thousand, until the number shall amount to one hundred, after which the proportion shall be so regulated by Congress, that there shall be not less than one hundred Representatives, nor less than one Representative for every forty thousand persons, until the number of Representatives shall amount to two hundred; after which the proportion shall be so regulated by Congress, that there shall not be less than two hundred Representatives, nor more than one Representative for every fifty thousand persons.

Amendment XI [Ratified 1798]

The judicial power of the United States shall not be construed to extend to any suit in law or equity, commenced or prosecuted against one of the United States by citizens of another State, or by citizens or subjects of any foreign state.

Amendment XII [Ratified 1804]

The electors shall meet in their respective States, and vote by ballot for President and Vice-President, one of whom, at least, shall not be an inhabitant of the same State with themselves; they shall name in their ballots the person voted for as President, and in distinct ballots the person voted for as Vice-President, and they shall make distinct lists of all persons voted for as President, and of all persons voted for as Vice-President, and of the number of votes for each, which lists they shall sign and certify, and transmit sealed to the seat of government of the United States, directed to the President of the Senate;—the President of the Senate shall, in the presence of the Senate and House of Representatives, open all the certificates and the votes shall then be counted;—the person having the greatest number of votes for President shall be the President, if such number be a majority of the whole number of electors appointed; and if no person have such majority, then from the persons having the highest numbers not exceeding three on the list of those voted for as President, the House of Representatives shall choose immediately, by ballot, the President. But in choosing the President, the votes shall be taken by States, the representation from each State having one vote; a quorum for this purpose shall consist of a member or members from two-thirds of the States, and a majority of all the States shall be necessary to a choice. And if the House of Representatives shall not choose a President whenever the right of choice shall devolve upon them, before *the fourth day of March* next following, then the Vice-President shall act as President, as in the case of the death or other constitutional disability of the President.

The person having the greatest number of votes as Vice-President shall be the Vice-President, if such number be a majority of the whole number of electors appointed; and if no person have a majority, then from the two highest numbers on the list the Senate shall choose the Vice-President; a quorum for the purpose shall consist of two-thirds of the whole number of Senators, and a majority of the whole number shall be necessary to a choice. But no person constitutionally ineligible to the office of President shall be eligible to that of Vice-President of the United States.

Unratified Amendment

[Titles of Nobility Amendment (proposed by Congress May 1, 1810)]

If any citizen of the United States shall accept, claim, receive or retain any title of nobility or honor or shall, without the consent of Congress, accept and retain any present, pension, office or emolument of any kind whatever, from any emperor, king, prince or foreign power, such person shall cease to be a citizen of the United States, and shall be incapable of holding any office of trust or profit under them or either of them.

Unratified Amendment

[Corwin Amendment (proposed by Congress March 2, 1861)]

No amendment shall be made to the Constitution which will authorize or give to Congress the power to abolish or interfere, within any State, with the domestic institutions thereof, including that of persons held to labor or service by the laws of said State.

Amendment XIII   [Ratified 1865]

Section 1. Neither slavery nor involuntary servitude, except as a punishment for crime whereof the party shall have been duly convicted, shall exist within the United States, or any place subject to their jurisdiction.

Section 2. Congress shall have power to enforce this article by appropriate legislation.

Amendment XIV   [Ratified 1868]

Section 1. All persons born or naturalized in the United States, and subject to the jurisdiction thereof, are citizens of the United States and of the State wherein they reside. No State shall make or enforce any law which shall abridge the privileges or immunities of citizens of the United States; nor shall any State deprive any person of life, liberty, or property, without due process of law; nor deny to any person within its jurisdiction the equal protection of the laws.

Section 2. Representatives shall be appointed among the several States according to their respective numbers, counting the whole number of persons in each State, excluding Indians not taxed. But when the right to vote at any election for the choice of Electors for President and Vice-President of the United States, Representatives in Congress, the executive and judicial officers of a State, or the members of the legislature thereof, is denied to any of the *male* inhabitants of such State, being *twenty-one* years of age and citizens of the United States, or in any way abridged, except for participation in rebellion, or other crime, the basis of representation therein shall be reduced in the proportion which the number of such male citizens shall bear to the whole number of *male* citizens *twenty-one* years of age in such State.

Section 3. No person shall be a Senator or Representative in Congress, or Elector of President and Vice-President, or hold any office, civil or military, under the United States, or under any State, who, having previously taken an oath, as a member of Congress, or as an officer of the

United States, or as a member of any State legislature, or as an executive or judicial officer of any State, to support the Constitution of the United States, shall have engaged in insurrection or rebellion against the same, or given aid or comfort to the enemies thereof. Congress may, by a vote of two-thirds of each house, remove such disability.

Section 4. The validity of the public debt of the United States, authorized by law, including debts incurred for payment of pensions and bounties for services in suppressing insurrection or rebellion, shall not be questioned. But neither the United States nor any State shall assume or pay any debt or obligation incurred in aid of insurrection or rebellion against the United States, or any claim for the loss or emancipation of any slave; but all such debts, obligations, and claims shall be held illegal and void.

Section 5. The Congress shall have power to enforce, by appropriate legislation, the provisions of this article.

Amendment XV [Ratified 1870]

Section 1. The right of citizens of the United States to vote shall not be denied or abridged by the United States or by any State on account of race, color, or previous condition of servitude.

Section 2. The Congress shall have power to enforce this article by appropriate legislation.

Amendment XVI [Ratified 1913]

The Congress shall have power to lay and collect taxes on incomes, from whatever source derived, without apportionment among the several States, and without regard to any census or enumeration.

Amendment XVII [Ratified 1913]

Section 1. The Senate of the United States shall be composed of two Senators from each State, elected by the people thereof, for six years; and each Senator shall have one vote. The electors in each State shall have the qualifications requisite for electors of [voters for] the most numerous branch of the State legislatures.

Section 2. When vacancies happen in the representation of any State in the Senate, the executive authority of such State shall issue writs of election to fill such vacancies: Provided, that the Legislature of any State may empower the executive thereof to make temporary appointments until the people fill the vacancies by election as the Legislature may direct.

Section 3. *This amendment shall not be so construed as to affect the election or term of any Senator chosen before it becomes valid as part of the Constitution.*

Amendment XVIII

[Ratified 1919; repealed 1933 by Amendment XXI]

Section 1. *After one year from the ratification of this article the manufacture, sale, or transportation of intoxicating liquors within, the importation thereof into, or the exportation thereof from the United States and all territory subject to the jurisdiction thereof, for beverage purposes, is hereby prohibited.*

Section 2. *The Congress and the several States shall have concurrent power to enforce this article by appropriate legislation.*

Section 3. *This article shall be inoperative unless it shall have been ratified as an amendment to the Constitution by the legislatures of the several States, as provided by the Constitution, within seven years from the date of the submission thereof to the States by the Congress.*

Amendment XIX   [Ratified 1920]

Section 1. The right of citizens of the United States to vote shall not be denied or abridged by the United States or by any State on account of sex.

Section 2. Congress shall have the power to enforce this article by appropriate legislation.

Unratified Amendment

[Child Labor Amendment (proposed by Congress June 2, 1924)]

Section 1. *The Congress shall have power to limit, regulate, and prohibit the labor of persons under eighteen years of age.*

Section 2. *The power of the several States is unimpaired by this article except that the operation of State laws shall be suspended to the extent necessary to give effect to legislation enacted by Congress.*

Amendment XX   [Ratified 1933]

Section 1. The terms of the President and Vice-President shall end at noon on the 20th day of January, and the terms of Senators and Representatives at noon on the 3rd day of January, of the years in which such terms would have ended if this article had not been ratified; and the terms of their successors shall then begin.

Section 2. The Congress shall assemble at least once in every year, and such meeting shall begin at noon on the 3rd day of January, unless they shall by law appoint a different day.

Section 3. If, at the time fixed for the beginning of the term of the President, the President-elect shall have died, the Vice-President-elect shall become President. If a President shall not have been chosen before the time fixed for the beginning of his term, or if the President-elect shall have failed to qualify, then the Vice-President-elect shall act as President until a President shall have qualified; and the Congress may by law provide for the case wherein neither a President-elect nor a Vice-President-elect shall have qualified, declaring who shall then act as President, or the manner in which one who is to act shall be selected, and such person shall act accordingly until a President or Vice-President shall have qualified.

Section 4. The Congress may by law provide for the case of the death of any of the persons from whom the House of Representatives may choose a President whenever the right of choice shall have devolved upon them, and for the case of the death of any of the persons from whom the Senate may choose a Vice-President whenever the right of choice shall have devolved upon them.

Section 5. Sections 1 and 2 shall take effect on the 15th day of October following the ratification of this article.

Section 6. This article shall be inoperative unless it shall have been ratified as an amendment to the Constitution by the Legislatures of three-fourths of the several States within seven years from the date of its submission.

Amendment XXI   [Ratified 1933]

Section 1. The eighteenth article of amendment to the Constitution of the United States is hereby repealed.

Section 2. The transportation or importation into any State, Territory, or Possession of the United States for delivery or use therein of intoxicating liquors, in violation of the laws thereof, is hereby prohibited.

Section 3. This article shall be inoperative unless it shall have been ratified as an amendment to the Constitution by conventions in the several States, as provided in the Constitution, within seven years from the date of the submission thereof to the States by the Congress.

Amendment XXII   [Ratified 1951]

Section 1. No person shall be elected to the office of the President more than twice, and no person who has held the office of President, or acted as President, for more than two years of a term to which some other person was elected President shall be elected to the office of President more than once. But this article shall not apply to any person holding the office of President when this Article was proposed by the Congress, and shall not prevent any person who may be holding the office of President, or acting as President, during the term within which this Article becomes operative from holding the office of President or acting as President during the remainder of such term.

Section 2. This article shall be inoperative unless it shall have been ratified as an amendment to the Constitution by the legislatures of three-fourths of the several States within seven years from the date of its submission to the States by the Congress.

Amendment XXIII   [Ratified 1961]

Section 1. The District constituting the seat of Government of the United States shall appoint in such manner as the Congress may direct: A number of electors of President and Vice-President equal to the whole number of Senators and Representatives in Congress to which the District would be entitled if it were a State, but in no event more than the least populous State; they shall be in addition to those appointed by the States, but they shall be considered for the purposes of the election of President and Vice-President, to be electors appointed by a State; and they shall meet in the District and perform such duties as provided by the twelfth article of amendment.

Section 2. The Congress shall have the power to enforce this article by appropriate legislation.

Amendment XXIV   [Ratified 1964]

Section 1. The right of citizens of the United States to vote in any primary or other election for President or Vice-President, for electors for President or Vice-President, or for Senator or Representative in Congress, shall not be denied or abridged by the United States or any State by reason of failure to pay any poll tax or other tax.

Section 2. The Congress shall have the power to enforce this article by appropriate legislation.

Amendment XXV   [Ratified 1967]

Section 1. In case of the removal of the President from office or of his death or resignation, the Vice-President shall become President.

Section 2. Whenever there is a vacancy in the office of the Vice-President, the President shall nominate a Vice-President who shall take office upon confirmation by a majority vote of both Houses of Congress.

Section 3. Whenever the President transmits to the President pro tempore of the Senate and the Speaker of the House of Representatives his written declaration that he is unable to discharge the powers and duties of his office, and until he transmits to them a written declaration to the contrary, such powers and duties shall be discharged by the Vice-President as Acting President.

Section 4. Whenever the Vice-President and a majority of either the principal officers of the executive departments or of such other body as Congress may by law provide, transmit to the President pro tempore of the Senate and the Speaker of the House of Representatives their written declaration that the President is unable to discharge the powers and duties of his office, the Vice-President shall immediately assume the powers and duties of the office as Acting President.

Thereafter, when the President transmits to the President pro tempore of the Senate and the Speaker of the House of Representatives his written declaration that no inability exists, he shall resume the powers and duties of his office unless the Vice-President and a majority of either the principal officers of the executive department[s] or of such other body as Congress may by law provide, transmit within four days to the President pro tempore of the Senate and the Speaker of the House of Representatives their written declaration that the President is unable to discharge the powers and duties of his office. Thereupon Congress shall decide the issue, assembling within forty-eight hours for that purpose if not in session. If the Congress, within twenty-one days after receipt of the latter written declaration, or, if Congress is not in session, within twenty-one days after Congress is required to assemble, determines by two-thirds vote of both Houses that the President is unable to discharge the powers and duties of his office, the Vice-President shall continue to discharge the same as Acting President; otherwise, the President shall resume the powers and duties of his office.

Amendment XXVI   [Ratified 1971]

Section 1. The right of citizens of the United States, who are eighteen years of age or older, to vote shall not be denied or abridged by the United States or by any State on account of age.

Section 2. The Congress shall have power to enforce this article by appropriate legislation.

Unratified Amendment

[Equal Rights Amendment (proposed by Congress March 22, 1972; seven-year deadline for ratification extended to June 30, 1982)]

Section 1. *Equality of rights under the law shall not be denied or abridged by the United States or by any State on account of sex.*

Section 2. *The Congress shall have the power to enforce, by appropriate legislation, the provisions of this article.*

Section 3. *This amendment shall take effect two years after the date of ratification.*

Unratified Amendment

[D.C. Statehood Amendment (proposed by Congress August 22, 1978)]

Section 1. *For purposes of representation in the Congress, election of the President and Vice-President, and article V of this Constitution, the District constituting the seat of government of the United States shall be treated as though it were a State.*

Section 2. *The exercise of the rights and powers conferred under this article shall be by the people of the District constituting the seat of government, and as shall be provided by Congress.*

Section 3. *The twenty-third article of amendment to the Constitution of the United States is hereby repealed.*

Section 4. *This article shall be inoperative, unless it shall have been ratified as an amendment to the Constitution by the legislatures of three-fourths of the several states within seven years from the date of its submission.*

Amendment XXVII   [Ratified 1992]

No law, varying the compensation for the services of the Senators and Representatives, shall take effect, until an election of Representatives shall have intervened.

Admission of States to the Union

State	Year of Admission	State	Year of Admission
Delaware	1787	Michigan	1837
Pennsylvania	1787	Florida	1845
New Jersey	1787	Texas	1845
Georgia	1788	Iowa	1846
Connecticut	1788	Wisconsin	1848
Massachusetts	1788	California	1850
Maryland	1788	Minnesota	1858
South Carolina	1788	Oregon	1859
New Hampshire	1788	Kansas	1861
Virginia	1788	West Virginia	1863
New York	1788	Nevada	1864
North Carolina	1789	Nebraska	1867
Rhode Island	1790	Colorado	1876
Vermont	1791	North Dakota	1889
Kentucky	1792	South Dakota	1889
Tennessee	1796	Montana	1889
Ohio	1803	Washington	1889
Louisiana	1812	Idaho	1890
Indiana	1816	Wyoming	1890
Mississippi	1817	Utah	1896
Illinois	1818	Oklahoma	1907
Alabama	1819	New Mexico	1912
Maine	1820	Arizona	1912
Missouri	1821	Alaska	1959
Arkansas	1836	Hawaii	1959

Presidents of the United States

President	Term	President	Term
George Washington	1789–1797	Benjamin Harrison	1889–1893
John Adams	1797–1801	Grover Cleveland	1893–1897
Thomas Jefferson	1801–1809	William McKinley	1897–1901
James Madison	1809–1817	Theodore Roosevelt	1901–1909
James Monroe	1817–1825	William H. Taft	1909–1913
John Quincy Adams	1825–1829	Woodrow Wilson	1913–1921
Andrew Jackson	1829–1837	Warren G. Harding	1921–1923
Martin Van Buren	1837–1841	Calvin Coolidge	1923–1929
William H. Harrison	1841	Herbert Hoover	1929–1933
John Tyler	1841–1845	Franklin D. Roosevelt	1933–1945
James K. Polk	1845–1849	Harry S. Truman	1945–1953
Zachary Taylor	1849–1850	Dwight D. Eisenhower	1953–1961
Millard Fillmore	1850–1853	John F. Kennedy	1961–1963
Franklin Pierce	1853–1857	Lyndon B. Johnson	1963–1969
James Buchanan	1857–1861	Richard M. Nixon	1969–1974
Abraham Lincoln	1861–1865	Gerald R. Ford	1974–1977
Andrew Johnson	1865–1869	Jimmy Carter	1977–1981
Ulysses S. Grant	1869–1877	Ronald Reagan	1981–1989
Rutherford B. Hayes	1877–1881	George H. W. Bush	1989–1993
James A. Garfield	1881	Bill Clinton	1993–2001
Chester A. Arthur	1881–1885	George W. Bush	2001–2009
Grover Cleveland	1885–1889	Barack Obama	2009–2017

GLOSSARY OF KEY TERMS

Adams-Onís Treaty Treaty negotiated by John Quincy Adams and signed in 1819 by which Spain ceded all of its lands east of the Mississippi River to the United States. (p. 285)

Alamo Texas fort captured by General Santa Anna on March 6, 1836, from rebel defenders. Sensationalist accounts of the siege of the Alamo increased popular support in the United States for Texas independence. (p. 326)

Albany Congress June 1754 meeting in Albany, New York, of Iroquois and colonial representatives meant to facilitate better relations between Britain and the Iroquois Confederacy. Benjamin Franklin also put forward a plan for colonial union that was never implemented. (p. 140)

Alien and Sedition Acts 1798 security acts passed by the Federalist-controlled Congress. The Alien Act allowed the president to imprison or deport noncitizens; the Sedition Act placed significant restrictions on political speech. (p. 230)

American Anti-Slavery Society (AASS) Abolitionist society founded by William Lloyd Garrison in 1833 that became the most important northern abolitionist organization of the period. (p. 369)

American Colonization Society (ACS) Organization formed in 1817 to establish colonies of freed slaves and freeborn blacks in Africa. The ACS was led by a group of white elites whose primary goal was to rid the nation of African Americans. (p. 249)

American Equal Rights Association Group of black and white women and men formed in 1866 to promote gender and racial equality. The organization split in 1869 over support for the Fifteenth Amendment. (p. 463)

American System Plan proposed by Henry Clay to promote the U.S. economy by combining federally funded internal improvements to aid farmers with federal tariffs to protect U.S. manufacturing and a national bank to oversee economic development. (p. 283)

American system of manufacturing Production system focused on water-powered machinery, division of labor, and the use of interchangeable parts. The introduction of the American system in the early nineteenth century greatly increased the productivity of American manufacturing. (p. 264)

Antifederalists Opponents of ratification of the Constitution. Antifederalists were generally more rural and less wealthy than the Federalists. (p. 221)

Appeal . . . to the Colored Citizens of the World Radical abolitionist pamphlet published by David Walker in 1829. Walker's work inspired some white abolitionists to take a more radical stance on slavery. (p. 369)

Articles of Confederation Plan for national government proposed by the Continental Congress in 1777 and ratified in March 1781. The Articles of Confederation gave the national government limited powers, reflecting widespread fear of centralized authority. (p. 187)

Aztecs Spanish term for the Mexica, an indigenous people who built an empire in present-day Mexico in the centuries before the arrival of the Spaniards. The Aztecs built their empire through conquest. (p. 5)

Bacon's Rebellion 1676 uprising in Virginia led by Nathaniel Bacon. Bacon and his followers, many of whom were former servants, were upset by the Virginia governor's unwillingness to send troops to intervene in conflicts between settlers and Indians and by the lack of representation of western settlers in the House of Burgesses. (p. 51)

Battle of Antietam Fought in September 1862, this Civil War battle was the bloodiest single day in U.S. military history, but it gave Abraham Lincoln the victory he sought before announcing the Emancipation Proclamation. (p. 424)

Battle of Bull Run (Manassas) First major battle of the Civil War at which Confederate troops routed Union forces in July 1861. (p. 418)

Battle of Bunker Hill Early Revolutionary War battle in which British troops narrowly defeated patriot militias, emboldening patriot forces. (p. 175)

Battle of Fallen Timbers Battle at which U.S. General Anthony Wayne won a major victory over a multi-tribe coalition of American Indians in the Northwest Territory in 1794. (p. 278)

Battle of Gettysburg Key July 1863 battle that helped turn the tide for the Union. Union victory at Gettysburg, combined with a victory at Vicksburg that same month, positioned the Union to push farther into the South. (p. 432)

Battle of Horseshoe Bend In 1814, Tennessee militia led by Andrew Jackson fought alongside Cherokee warriors to defeat Creek forces allied with Britain during the War of 1812. (p. 281)

Battle of Oriskany In one of the bloodiest Revolutionary War battles, a force of German-American farmers and Oneida Indians deterred British troops and their Indian allies in central New York State, leaving British forces further east vulnerable to attack by the Continental Army. (p. 184)

Battle of Saratoga Key Revolutionary War battle fought at Saratoga, New York. The patriot victory there in October 1777 provided hope that the colonists could prevail and increased the chances that the French would formally join the patriot side. (p. 186)

Battle of Shiloh April 1862 battle in Tennessee that provided the Union entrance to the Mississippi valley. Shiloh was the bloodiest battle in American history to that point. (p. 422)

Battle of Yorktown Decisive battle in which the surrender of British forces on October 19, 1781, at Yorktown, Virginia, effectively sealed the patriot victory in the Revolutionary War. (p. 195)

benign neglect British colonial policy from about 1700 to 1760 that relaxed supervision of internal colonial affairs as long as the North American colonies produced sufficient raw materials and revenue; also known as *salutary neglect*. (p. 150)

Beringia Land bridge that linked Siberia and Alaska during the Wisconsin period. Migrants from northeast Asia used this bridge to travel to North America. (p. 3)

Bill of Rights The first ten amendments to the Constitution. These ten amendments helped reassure Americans who feared that the federal government established under the Constitution would infringe on the rights of individuals and states. (p. 222)

black codes Racial laws passed in the immediate aftermath of the Civil War by southern legislatures. The black codes were intended to reduce free African Americans to a condition as close to slavery as possible. (p. 457)

Black Death The epidemic of bubonic plague that swept through Europe beginning in the mid-fourteenth century and wiped out roughly half of Europe's population. (p. 11)

Bleeding Kansas The Kansas Territory during a period of violent conflicts over the fate of slavery in the mid-1850s. The violence in Kansas intensified the sectional division over slavery. (p. 399)

Boston Massacre 1770 clash between colonial protesters and British soldiers in Boston that led to the death of five colonists. The bloody conflict was used to promote the patriot cause. (p. 158)

carpetbaggers Derogatory term for white Northerners who moved to the South in the years following the Civil War. Many white Southerners believed that such migrants were intent on exploiting their suffering. (p. 465)

Church of England National church established by Henry VIII after he split with the Catholic Church. (p. 40)

Coercive Acts (Intolerable Acts) 1774 act of Parliament passed in response to the Boston Tea Party. The Coercive Acts were meant to force the colonists into submission, but they only resulted in increased resistance. Colonial patriots called them the Intolerable Acts. (p. 161)

Columbian exchange The biological exchange between the Americas and the rest of the world. Although the initial impact of the Columbian exchange was strongest in the Americas and Europe, it was soon felt all over the world. (p. 21)

committee of correspondence Type of committee first established in Massachusetts to circulate concerns and reports of protests and other events to leaders in other colonies in the aftermath of the Sugar Act. (p. 151)

Common Sense Pamphlet arguing in favor of independence written by Thomas Paine and published in 1776. *Common Sense* was widely read and had an important impact on the debate over declaring independence from Britain. (p. 176)

Compromise of 1850 Series of acts following California's application for admission as a free state. Meant to quell sectional tensions over slavery, the act was intended to provide something for all sides but ended up fueling more conflicts. (p. 391)

Compromise of 1877 Compromise between Republicans and southern Democrats that resulted in the election of Rutherford B. Hayes. Southern

Democrats agreed to support Hayes in the disputed presidential election in exchange for his promise to end Reconstruction. (p. 473)

Confederate States of America Nation established in 1861 by the eleven slave states that seceded between December 1860 and April 1861. (p. 404)

conquistadors Spanish soldiers who were central to the conquest of the civilizations of the Americas. Once conquest was complete, conquistadors often extracted wealth from the people and lands they now ruled. (p. 23)

Continental Congress Congress convened in Philadelphia in 1774 in response to the Coercive Acts. The delegates hoped to reestablish the freedoms colonists had enjoyed in earlier times. (p. 161)

contraband Designation assigned to escaped slaves by Union general Benjamin Butler in May 1861. By designating slaves as property forfeited by the act of rebellion, the Union was able to strike at slavery without proclaiming a general emancipation. (p. 420)

Copperheads Northern Democrats who did not support the Union war effort. Such Democrats enjoyed considerable support in eastern cities and parts of the Midwest. (p. 431)

Corps of Discovery Expedition organized by the U.S. government to explore the Louisiana Territory. Led by Meriwether Lewis and William Clark, the expedition set out in May 1804 and journeyed to the Pacific coast and back by 1806 with the aid of interpreters like Sacagawea. (p. 254)

cotton gin Machine invented by Eli Whitney in 1793 to deseed short-staple cotton. The cotton gin dramatically reduced the time and labor involved in deseeding, facilitating the expansion of cotton production in the South and West. (p. 262)

Crittenden plan A political compromise over slavery which failed after seven southern states seceded from the Union in early 1861. It would have protected slavery from federal interference where it already existed and extended the Missouri Compromise line to California. (p. 404)

Crusades Eleventh- and twelfth-century campaigns to reclaim the Holy Land for the Roman Catholic Church. The Crusades were, on the whole, a military failure, but they did stimulate trade and inspire Europeans to seek better connections with the larger world. (p. 10)

cult of domesticity New ideals of womanhood that emerged alongside the middle class in the 1830s and 1840s that advocated women's relegation to the domestic sphere where they could devote themselves to the care of children, the home, and hard-working husbands. (p. 353)

Declaration of Independence Document declaring the independence of the colonies from Great Britain. Drafted by Thomas Jefferson and then debated and revised by the Continental Congress, the Declaration was made public on July 4, 1776. (p. 178)

Declaration of Sentiments Call for women's rights in marriage, family, religion, politics, and law issued at the 1848 Seneca Falls convention. It was signed by 100 of the 300 participants. (p. 372)

Democratic-Republicans Political party that emerged out of opposition to Federalist policies in the 1790s. The Democratic-Republicans chose Thomas Jefferson as their presidential candidate in 1796, 1800, and 1804. (p. 229)

Democrats and National Republicans Two parties that resulted from the split of the Democratic-Republicans in the early 1820s. Andrew Jackson emerged as the leader of the Democrats. (p. 295)

deskilling The replacement of skilled labor with unskilled labor and machines. (p. 355)

***Dred Scott* decision** 1857 Supreme Court case centered on the status of Dred Scott and his family. In its ruling, the Court denied the claim that black men had any rights and blocked Congress from excluding slavery from any territory. (p. 400)

Dunmore's Proclamation 1775 proclamation issued by the British commander Lord Dunmore that offered freedom to all enslaved African Americans who joined the British army. The proclamation heightened concerns among some patriots about the consequences of independence. (p. 176)

Emancipation Proclamation January 1, 1863, proclamation that declared all slaves in areas still in rebellion "forever free." While stopping short of abolishing slavery, the Emancipation Proclamation was, nonetheless, seen by blacks and abolitionists as a great victory. (p. 424)

Embargo Act 1807 act that prohibited American ships from leaving their home ports until Britain and France repealed restrictions on U.S. trade. The act had a devastating impact on American commerce. (p. 256)

encomienda System first established by Christopher Columbus by which Spanish leaders in the Americas received land and the labor of all Indians residing on it. From the Indian point of view, the encomienda system amounted to little more than enslavement. (p. 16)

Enlightenment European cultural movement that emphasized rational and scientific thinking over traditional religion and superstition. Enlightenment thought appealed to many colonial elites. (p. 122)

Enrollment Act March 1863 Union draft law that provided for draftees to be selected by an impartial lottery. A loophole in the law that allowed wealthy Americans to escape service by paying $300 or hiring a substitute created widespread resentment. (p. 430)

Enterprise of the Indies Christopher Columbus's proposal to sail west across the Atlantic to Japan and China. In 1492 Columbus gained support for the venture from Ferdinand and Isabella of Spain. (p. 16)

Erie Canal Canal built in the early 1820s that made water transport from the Great Lakes to New York City possible. The success of the Erie Canal inspired many similar projects and ensured New York City's place as the premier international port in the United States. (p. 285)

Federalists Supporters of ratification of the Constitution, many of whom came from urban and commercial backgrounds. (p. 221)

Field Order Number 15 Order issued by General William Sherman in January 1865 setting aside more than 400,000 acres of Confederate land to be divided into plots for former slaves. Sherman's order came in response to pressure from African American leaders. (p. 436)

Fifteenth Amendment Amendment to the Constitution prohibiting the abridgment of a citizen's right to vote on the basis of "race, color, or previous condition of servitude." From the 1870s on, southern states devised numerous strategies for circumventing the Fifteenth Amendment. (p. 463)

filibusters Unauthorized military expeditions launched by U.S. adventurers to gain control of Cuba, Nicaragua, and other Spanish territories in the 1850s. (p. 394)

Force Acts Three acts passed by the U.S. Congress in 1870 and 1871 in response to vigilante attacks on southern blacks. The acts were designed to protect black political rights and end violence by the Ku Klux Klan and similar organizations. (p. 470)

Fort Sumter Union fort that guarded the harbor in Charleston, South Carolina. The Confederacy's decision to fire on the fort and block resupply in April 1861 marked the beginning of the Civil War. (p. 416)

Fourteenth Amendment Amendment to the Constitution defining citizenship and protecting individual civil and political rights from abridgment by the states. Adopted during Reconstruction, the Fourteenth Amendment overturned the *Dred Scott* decision. (p. 463)

Freedmen's Bureau Federal agency created in 1865 to provide ex-slaves with economic and legal resources. The Freedmen's Bureau played an active role in shaping black life in the postwar South. (p. 450)

Free-Soil Party Party founded by political abolitionists in 1848 to expand the appeal of the Liberty Party by focusing less on the moral wrongs of slavery and more on the benefits of providing economic opportunities for northern whites in western territories. (p. 373)

Fugitive Slave Act of 1850 Act strengthening earlier fugitive slave laws, passed as part of the Compromise of 1850. The Fugitive Slave Act provoked widespread anger in the North and intensified sectional tensions. (p. 391)

gag rule Rule passed by the House of Representatives in 1836 to table, or postpone action on, all antislavery petitions without hearing them read to stifle debate over slavery. It was renewed annually until it was rescinded in 1844. (p. 327)

Glorious Revolution 1688 rebellion that forced James II from the English throne and replaced him with William and Mary. The Glorious Revolution led to greater political and commercial autonomy for the British colonies. (p. 72)

gold rush The rapid influx of migrants into California after the discovery of gold in 1848. Migrants came from all over the world seeking riches. (p. 386)

Great Awakening Series of religious revivals in colonial America that began in 1720 and lasted to about 1750. (p. 123)

Haitian Revolution Revolt against French rule by free and enslaved blacks in the 1790s on the island of Saint Domingue. The revolution led in 1803 to the establishment of Haiti, the first independent black-led nation in the Americas. (p. 251)

hard war The strategy promoted by General Ulysses S. Grant in which Union forces destroyed civilian crops, livestock, fields, and property to undermine Confederate morale and supply chains. (p. 435)

Harpers Ferry, Virginia Site of the federal arsenal that was the target of John Brown's 1859 raid. Brown hoped to rouse the region's slave population to a violent uprising. (p. 401)

Hartford Convention 1814 convention of Federalists opposed to the War of 1812. Delegates to the convention considered a number of constitutional amendments, as well as the possibility of secession. (p. 280)

Hopewell people Indian people who established a thriving culture near the Mississippi River in the early centuries C.E. (p. 8)

horticulture A form of agriculture in which people work small plots of land with simple tools. (p. 5)

House of Burgesses Local governing body in Virginia established by the English crown in 1619. (p. 48)

import duty Tax imposed on goods imported into the colonies, paid by the importer rather than directly by the consumer; also known as a *tariff*. (p. 151)

impressment The forced enlistment of civilians into the army or navy. The impressment of residents of colonial seaports into the British navy was a major source of complaint in the eighteenth century. (p. 127)

Incas Andean people who built an empire in the centuries before the arrival of the Spaniards. At the height of their power in the fifteenth century, the Incas controlled some sixteen million people. (p. 6)

indentured servants Servants contracted to work for a set period of time without pay. Many early migrants to the English colonies indentured themselves in exchange for the price of passage to North America. (p. 48)

Indian Removal Act 1830 act by which Indian peoples in the East were forced to exchange their lands for territory west of the Mississippi River. Andrew Jackson was an ardent supporter of Indian removal. (p. 300)

Intolerable Acts *See* Coercive Acts.

Jamestown The first successful English colony in North America. Settled in 1607, Jamestown was founded by soldiers and adventurers under the leadership of Captain John Smith. (p. 46)

Jay Treaty 1796 treaty that required British forces to withdraw from U.S. soil, required American repayment of debts to British firms, and limited U.S. trade with the British West Indies. (p. 226)

Judiciary Act Act passed in 1801 by the Federalist-controlled Congress to expand the federal court system by creating sixteen circuit (regional) courts, with new judges appointed for each, just before Democratic-Republicans took control of the presidency and Congress. (p. 254)

Kansas-Nebraska Act 1854 act creating the territories of Kansas and Nebraska out of what was then Indian land. The act stipulated that the issue of slavery would be settled by a popular referendum in each territory. (p. 397)

King Philip's War 1675–1676 conflict between New England settlers and the region's Indians. The settlers were the eventual victors, but fighting was fierce and casualties on both sides were high. (p. 60)

King William's War 1689–1697 war that began as a conflict over competing French and English interests on the European continent but soon spread to the American frontier. Both sides pulled Indian allies into the war. (p. 76)

Knights of the Ku Klux Klan (KKK) Organization formed in 1865 by General Nathan Bedford Forrest to enforce prewar racial norms. Members of the KKK used threats and violence to intimidate blacks and white Republicans. (p. 469)

Liberator Radical abolitionist newspaper launched by William Lloyd Garrison in 1831. Through the *Liberator*, Garrison called for immediate, uncompensated emancipation of slaves. (p. 369)

Liberty Party Antislavery political party formed in 1840. The Liberty Party, along with the Free-Soil Party, helped place slavery at the center of national political debates. (p. 373)

Louisiana Purchase U.S. government's 1803 purchase from France of the vast territory stretching from the Mississippi River to the Rocky Mountains and from New Orleans to present-day Montana, doubling the size of the nation. (p. 253)

loyalist A colonial supporter of the British during the Revolutionary War. Loyalists came from all economic backgrounds and had a variety of motives for siding with the British. (p. 179)

manifest destiny Term coined by John L. O'Sullivan in 1845 to describe what he saw as the nation's God-given right to expand its borders. Throughout the nineteenth century, the concept of manifest destiny was used to justify U.S. expansion. (p. 335)

Marbury v. Madison 1803 Supreme Court decision that established the authority of the Supreme Court to rule on the constitutionality of federal laws. (p. 255)

Maya People who established large cities in the Yucatán peninsula. Mayan civilization was strongest between 300 and 800 C.E. (p. 6)

Mayflower Compact Written constitution created by the Pilgrims upon their arrival in Plymouth. The Mayflower Compact was the first written constitution adopted in North America. (p. 55)

McCulloch v. Maryland 1819 Supreme Court decision that reinforced the federal government's ability to employ an expansive understanding of the implied powers clause of the Constitution. (p. 256)

mercantilism Economic system centered on the maintenance of a favorable balance of trade for the home country, with more gold and silver flowing into that country than flowed out. Seventeenth- and eighteenth-century British colonial policy was heavily shaped by mercantilism. (p. 81)

Middle Passage The brutal voyage of slave ships laden with human cargo from Africa to the Americas. The voyage was the middle segment in a triangular journey that began in Europe, went first to Africa, then to the Americas, and finally back to Europe. (p. 85)

Missouri Compromise 1820 act that allowed Missouri to enter the Union as a slave state and Maine to enter as a free state and established the southern border of Missouri as the boundary between slave and free states throughout the Louisiana Territory. (p. 290)

Monroe Doctrine Assertion by President James Monroe in 1823 that the Western Hemisphere was part of the U.S. sphere of influence. Although the United States lacked the power to back up this claim, it signaled an intention to challenge Europeans for authority in the Atlantic world. (p. 286)

multiplier effect The diverse changes spurred by a single invention, including other inventions it spawns and the broader economic, social, and political transformations it fuels. (p. 261)

Nat Turner's rebellion 1831 slave uprising in Virginia led by Nat Turner. Turner's rebellion instilled panic among white Southerners, leading to tighter control of African Americans and reconsideration of the institution of slavery. (p. 321)

National Republicans *See* Democrats and National Republicans.

National Road Road constructed using federal funds that ran from western Maryland through southwestern Pennsylvania to Wheeling, West Virginia; also called the Cumberland Road. Completed in 1818, the road was part of a larger push to improve the nation's infrastructure. (p. 260)

nativists Anti-immigrant Americans who launched public campaigns against foreigners in the 1840s. Nativism emerged as a response to increased immigration to the United States in the 1830s and 1840s, particularly the large influx of Catholic immigrants. (p. 366)

Navigation Acts Acts passed by Parliament in the 1650s and 1660s that prohibited smuggling, established guidelines for legal commerce, and set duties on trade items. In the 1760s, British authorities sought to fully enforce these laws, leading to resistance by colonists. (p. 141)

New Jersey Plan A proposal to the 1787 Constitutional Convention that highlighted the needs of small states by creating one legislative house in the federal government and granting each state equal representation in it. (p. 219)

New Light clergy Colonial clergy who called for religious revivals and emphasized the emotional aspects of spiritual commitment. The New Lights were leaders in the Great Awakening. (p. 121)

Non-Intercourse Act Act passed by Congress in 1809 allowing Americans to trade with every nation except France and Britain. The act failed to stop the seizure of American ships or improve the economy. (p. 277)

Northwest Ordinance Act of the confederation congress that provided for the survey, sale, and eventual division into states of the Northwest Territory. The 1787 act clarified the process by which territories could become states. (p. 209)

nullification The doctrine that individual states have the right to declare federal laws unconstitutional and, therefore, void within their borders. South Carolina attempted to invoke the doctrine of nullification in response to the tariff of 1832. (p. 299)

Old Light clergy Colonial clergy from established churches who supported the religious status quo in the early eighteenth century. (p. 121)

Oregon Trail The route west from the Missouri River to the Oregon Territory. By 1860, some 350,000 Americans had made the three- to six-month journey along the trail. (p. 384)

Ostend Manifesto This 1854 letter from U.S. ambassadors and the Secretary of State to President Franklin Pierce urged him to conquer Cuba. When it was leaked to the press, Northerners voiced outrage at what they saw as a plot to expand slave territories. (p. 395)

panic of 1819 The nation's first severe recession. The panic of 1819 lasted four years and resulted from irresponsible banking practices and the declining demand abroad for American goods, including cotton. (p. 287)

panic of 1837 Severe economic recession that began shortly after Martin Van Buren's presidential inauguration. The panic of 1837 started in the South and was rooted in the changing fortunes of American cotton in Great Britain. (p. 287, 331)

patriarchal family Model of the family in which fathers have absolute authority over wives, children, and servants. Most colonial Americans accepted the patriarchal model of the family, at least as an ideal. (p. 109)

Peace of Paris 1763 peace treaty that brought the Seven Years' War to a close. Under the terms of the treaty, Britain gained control of North America east of the Mississippi River and of present-day Canada. (p. 143)

Pequot War 1636–1637 conflict between New England settlers, their Narragansett allies, and the Pequots. The English saw the Pequots as both a threat and an obstacle to further English expansion. (p. 58)

Petticoat Affair 1829 political conflict over Andrew Jackson's appointment of John Eaton as secretary of war. Eaton was married to a woman of allegedly questionable character, and the wives of many prominent Washington politicians organized a campaign to snub her. (p. 298)

Pietists German Protestants who decried the power of established churches and urged individuals to follow their hearts rather than their heads in spiritual matters. Pietism had a profound influence on the leaders of the Great Awakening. (p. 122)

Pilgrims Group of English religious dissenters who established a settlement at Plymouth, Massachusetts, in 1620. Unlike more mainstream Protestants, the Pilgrims were separatists who aimed to sever all connections with the Church of England. (p. 55)

Pinckney Treaty 1796 treaty that defined the boundary between U.S. and Spanish territory in the South and opened the Mississippi River and New Orleans to U.S. shipping. (p. 229)

Planters Southern whites who owned the largest plantations and forged a distinct culture and economy around the institution of slavery. (p. 313)

Powhatan Confederacy Large and powerful Indian confederation in Virginia. The Jamestown settlers had a complicated and contentious relationship with the leaders of the Powhatan Confederacy. (p. 47)

Proclamation Line of 1763 Act of Parliament that restricted colonial settlement west of the Appalachian Mountains. The Proclamation Line sparked protests from rich and poor colonists alike. (p. 145)

Proclamation of Amnesty and Reconstruction 1863 proclamation that established the basic parameters of President Abraham Lincoln's approach to Reconstruction. Lincoln's plan would have readmitted the South to the Union on relatively lenient terms. (p. 455)

proprietary colonies Colonies granted to individuals, rather than held directly by the crown or given to chartered companies. Proprietors of such colonies, such as William Penn of Pennsylvania, had considerable leeway to distribute land and govern as they pleased. (p. 72)

Protestantism Religious movement initiated in the early sixteenth century that resulted in a permanent division within European Christianity. Protestants differed with Catholics over the nature of salvation, the role of priests, and the organization of the church. (p. 39)

Pueblo revolt 1680 uprising of Pueblo Indians against Spanish forces in New Mexico that led to the Spaniards' temporary retreat from the area. The uprising was sparked by mistreatment and the suppression of Indian culture and religion. (p. 75)

Puritans Radical English Protestants who hoped to reform the Church of England. The first Puritan settlers in the Americas arrived in Massachusetts in 1630. (p. 56)

Redeemers White, conservative Democrats who challenged and overthrew Republican rule in the South during Reconstruction. (p. 469)

redemptioners Immigrants who borrowed money from shipping agents to cover the costs of transport to America, loans that were repaid, or "redeemed," by colonial employers. Redemptioners worked for their "redeemers" for a set number of years. (p. 90)

Regulators Local organizations formed in North and South Carolina to protest and resist unpopular policies. After first seeking redress through official institutions, Regulators went on to establish militias and other institutions of self-governance. (p. 146)

Renaissance The cultural and intellectual flowering that began in Italy in the fifteenth century and then spread north. The Renaissance occurred at the same time that European rulers were pushing for greater political unification of their states. (p. 11)

Republican Party Party formed in 1854 that was committed to stopping the expansion of slavery and advocated economic development and internal improvements. Although their appeal was limited to the North, the Republicans quickly became a major political force. (p. 398)

scalawags Derisive term for white Southerners who supported Reconstruction. (p. 465)

Second Continental Congress Assembly of colonial representatives that served as a national government during the Revolutionary War. Despite limited formal powers, the Continental Congress coordinated the war effort and conducted negotiations with outside powers. (p. 175)

Second Great Awakening Evangelical revival movement that began in the South in the early nineteenth century and then spread to the North. The social and economic changes of the first half of the nineteenth century were a major spur to religious revivals, which in turn spurred social reform movements. (p. 358)

Second Seminole War 1835–1842 war between the Seminoles, including fugitive slaves who had joined the tribe, and the U.S. government over whether the Seminoles would be forced to leave Florida and settle west of the Mississippi River. Despite substantial investments of men, money, and resources, it took seven years for the United States to achieve victory. (p. 327)

sharecropping A system that emerged as the dominant mode of agricultural production in the South in the years after the Civil War. Under the sharecropping system, sharecroppers received tools and supplies from landowners in exchange for a share of the eventual harvest. (p. 466)

Shays's Rebellion 1786 rebellion by western Massachusetts farmers caused primarily by economic turmoil in the aftermath of the Revolutionary War. (p. 217)

Sherman's March to the Sea Hard war tactics employed by General William Tecumseh Sherman to capture Atlanta and huge swaths of Georgia and the Carolinas, devastating this crucial region of the Confederacy in 1864. (p. 436)

siege of Vicksburg After a prolonged siege, Union troops forced Confederate forces to surrender at Vicksburg, Mississippi, leading to Union control of the rich Mississippi River valley. (p. 433)

slave laws A series of laws that defined slavery as a distinct status based on racial identity and which passed that status on through future generations. (p. 94)

Solidarity Polish trade union movement led by Lech Walesa. During the 1980s, Solidarity played a central role in ending Communist rule in Poland. (p. 946)

Sons of Liberty Boston organization first formed to protest the Stamp Act. The Sons of Liberty spread to other colonies and played an important role in the unrest leading to the American Revolution. (p. 152)

spectral evidence Evidence given by spirits acting through possessed individuals. A number of the accused in the 1692 Salem witch trials were convicted on the basis of spectral evidence. (p. 106)

spoils system Patronage system introduced by Andrew Jackson in which federal offices were awarded on the basis of political loyalty. The system remained in place until the late nineteenth century. (p. 298)

Stamp Act 1765 act of Parliament that imposed a duty on all transactions involving paper items. The Stamp Act prompted widespread, coordinated protests and was eventually repealed. (p. 152)

Stono rebellion 1739 uprising by African and African American slaves in South Carolina. In the aftermath of the uprising, white fear of slave revolts intensified. (p. 96)

Sugar Act 1764 act of Parliament that imposed an import tax on sugar, coffee, wines, and other luxury items. The Sugar Act sparked colonial protests that would escalate over time as new revenue measures were enacted. (p. 151)

Tariff of Abominations White Southerners' name for the 1828 Congressional tariff act that benefited northern manufacturers and merchants at the expense of agriculture, especially southern plantations. (p. 299)

Tejanos Mexican residents of Texas. Although some Tejano elites allied themselves with American settlers, most American settlers resisted the adoption of Tejano culture. (p. 326)

temperance The movement to moderate and then ban the sale and consumption of alcohol. The American temperance movement emerged in the early nineteenth century as part of the larger push for improving society from the 1820s to the 1850s. (p. 360)

Tenure of Office Act Law passed by Congress in 1867 to prevent President Andrew Johnson from removing cabinet members sympathetic to the Republican Party's approach to congressional Reconstruction without Senate approval. Johnson was impeached, but not convicted, for violating the act. (p. 462)

Thirteenth Amendment Amendment to the Constitution abolishing slavery. The Thirteenth Amendment was passed in January 1865 and sent to the states for ratification. (p. 438)

three-fifths compromise Compromise between northern and southern delegates to the 1787 Constitutional Convention to count enslaved persons as three-fifths of a free person in apportioning representation in the House of Representatives and taxation by the federal government. (p. 220)

Townshend Act 1767 act of Parliament that instituted an import tax on a range of items including glass, lead, paint, paper, and tea. The Townshend Act prompted a boycott of British goods and contributed to violence between British soldiers and colonists. (p. 154)

Trail of Tears The forced march of some 15,000 Cherokees from Georgia to Indian Territory. Inadequate planning, food, water, sanitation, and medicine led to the deaths of thousands of Cherokees. (p. 330)

transcendentalism A movement founded by Ralph Waldo Emerson in the 1830s that proposed that individuals look inside themselves and to nature for spiritual and moral guidance rather than to the dogmas of formal religion. Transcendentalism attracted a number of important American writers and artists to its vision. (p. 362)

Treaty of Fort Stanwix 1784 treaty in which U.S. commissioners coerced Iroquois delegates into ceding vast tracts of land in western New York and the Ohio River Valley to the United States. (p. 209)

Treaty of Ghent Accord signed in December 1814 ending the War of 1812 and returning to U.S. and Britain the lands each controlled before the war. (p. 282)

Treaty of Greenville 1795 treaty signed following the Battle of Fallen Timbers through which Indians in the Northwest Territory were forced to ceded vast tracts of land to the United States. (p. 227)

Treaty of Guadalupe Hidalgo 1848 treaty ending the Mexican-American War. By the terms of the treaty, the United States acquired control over Texas north and east of the Rio Grande plus the New Mexico territory, which included present-day Arizona and New Mexico and parts of Utah, Nevada, and Colorado. The treaty also ceded Alta California, which had declared itself an independent republic during the war, to the United States. (p. 337)

Treaty of New Echota 1836 treaty in which a group of Cherokee men agreed to exchange their land in the Southeast for money and land in Indian Territory. Despite the fact that the treaty was obtained without tribal sanction, it was approved by the U.S. Congress. (p. 329)

Treaty (Peace) of Paris 1783 treaty that formally ended the conflict between Britain and its North American colonies. The newly established United States gained benefits from the treaty. (p. 196)

Tuscarora War War launched by Tuscarora Indians from 1711 to 1715 against European settlers in North Carolina and their allies from the Yamasee, Catawba, and Cherokee nations. The Tuscaroras forfeited their lands when they signed the peace treaty and many then joined the Iroquois Confederacy to the north. (p. 78)

U.S. Sanitary Commission Federal organization established in June 1861 to improve and coordinate the medical care of Union soldiers. Northern women played a key role in the work of the commission. (p. 426)

Uncle Tom's Cabin Novel published in 1852 by Harriet Beecher Stowe. Meant to publicize the evils of slavery, the novel struck an emotional chord in the North and was an international best seller. (p. 396)

underground railroad A series of routes from southern plantation areas to northern free states and Canada along which abolitionist supporters, known as conductors, provided hiding places and transportation for runaway slaves seeking freedom. (p. 369)

utopian societies Communities formed in the first half of the nineteenth century to embody alternative social and economic visions and to create models for society at large to follow. (p. 367)

Valley Forge Site of Continental Army winter encampment in 1777–1778. Despite the harsh conditions, the Continental Army emerged from its encampment at Valley Forge as a more effective fighting force. (p. 186)

Virginia and Kentucky Resolutions Resolutions passed by legislatures in Virginia and Kentucky that declared the Alien and Sedition Acts (1798) "void and of no force" in their states. (p. 230)

Virginia Plan Plan put forth at the beginning of the 1787 Constitutional Convention that introduced the ideas of a strong central government, a bicameral legislature, and a system of representation based on population. (p. 219)

Walking Purchase 1737 treaty that allowed Pennsylvania to expand its boundaries at the expense of the Delaware Indians. The treaty, quite possibly a forgery, allowed the British to add territory that could be walked off in a day and a half. (p. 119)

War of the Spanish Succession 1702–1713 war over control of Spain and its colonies; also called Queen Anne's War. Although the Treaty of Utrecht that ended the war in 1713 was intended to bring peace through the establishment of a balance of power, imperial conflict continued to escalate. (p. 76)

Whig Party Political party formed in the 1830s to challenge the power of the Democratic Party. The Whigs attempted to forge a diverse coalition from around the country by promoting commercial interests and moral reforms. (p. 326)

Whiskey Rebellion Uprising by western Pennsylvania farmers who led protests against the excise tax on whiskey in the early 1790s. (p. 227)

white supremacy An ideology promoted by southern planters and intellectuals that maintained that all whites, regardless of class or education, were superior to all blacks. (p. 325)

Wilmot Proviso 1846 proposal by Democratic congressman David Wilmot of Pennsylvania to outlaw slavery in all territory acquired from Mexico. The proposal was defeated, but the fight over its adoption foreshadowed the sectional conflicts of the 1850s. (p. 337)

Women's National Loyal League Organization founded by abolitionist women during the Civil War to press Lincoln and Congress to enact universal emancipation. (p. 429)

Works Progress Administration (WPA) New Deal agency established in 1935 to put unemployed Americans to work on public projects ranging from construction to the arts. (p. 737)

XYZ affair 1798 incident in which French agents demanded bribes before meeting with American diplomatic representatives. (p. 230)

Yamasee War A pan-Indian war from 1715 to 1717 led by the Yamasee who intended, but failed, to oust the British from South Carolina. (p. 78)

yeomen farmers Southern independent landowners who did not own slaves. Although yeomen farmers had connections to the South's plantation economy, many realized that their interests were not always identical to those of the planter elite. (p. 323)

INDEX

*Letters in parentheses following page numbers refer to documents *(d)*, figures *(f)*, illustrations *(i)*, maps *(m)*, and tables *(t)*.